The Mystical Sources of Existentialist Thought

At the time when existentialism was a dominant intellectual and cultural force, a number of commentators observed that some of the language of existential philosophy, not least its interpretation of human existence in terms of nothingness, evoked the language of so-called mystical writers. This book takes on this observation and explores the evidence for the influence of mysticism on the philosophy of existentialism.

It begins by delving into definitions of mysticism and existentialism and then traces the elements of mysticism present in German and French thought during the late nineteenth and early twentieth centuries. The book goes on to make original contributions to the study of figures including Kierkegaard, Buber, Heidegger, Beauvoir, Sartre, Marcel, Camus, Weil, Bataille, Berdyaev, and Tillich, linking their existentialist philosophy back to some of the key concerns of the mystical tradition.

Providing a unique insight into how these two areas have overlapped and interacted, this study is vital reading for any academic with an interest in twentieth-century philosophy, theology, and religious studies.

George Pattison is 1640 Professor of Divinity at the University of Glasgow, UK, and formerly Lady Margaret Professor of Divinity at the University of Oxford. He has published widely in the areas of modern theology and philosophy of religion, including *Anxious Angels: A Retrospective View of Religious Existentialism* (1999), *The Routledge Philosophy Guidebook to the Later Heidegger* (2000), and *Kierkegaard and the Quest for Unambiguous Life* (2012) and is co-editor of the *Oxford Handbook of Theology and Modern European Thought* (2013).

Kate Kirkpatrick is Lecturer in Religion, Philosophy, and Culture at King's College London, UK. She is the author of *Sartre and Theology* (2017), *Sartre on Sin: Between Being and Nothingness* (2017), and *Becoming Beauvoir: A Life* (2019).

Contemporary Theological Explorations in Mysticism

Series Editors: Patricia Z. Beckman, Oliver Davies, and George Pattison

This series facilitates new points of synergy and fresh theological engagements with Christian mystical traditions. Reflecting the plurality of theological approaches to Christian mystical theology, books in the series cover historical, literary, practical, and systematic perspectives as well as philosophical, psychological, and phenomenological methods.

Although the primary focus of the series is the Christian tradition, exploration of texts from other traditions also highlights the theological, psychological, and philosophical questions that Christian mysticism brings to the fore.

Mystical Anthropology
Authors from the Low Countries
Edited by John Arblaster and Rob Faesen

Mystical Theology and Continental Philosophy
Interchange in the Wake of God
Edited by David Lewin, Simon D. Podmore, and Duane Williams

Mystical Theology and Contemporary Spiritual Practice
Renewing the Contemplative Tradition
Edited by Christopher C. H. Cook, Julienne McLean, and Peter Tyler

Art and Mysticism
Interfaces in the Medieval and Modern Periods
Edited by Helen Appleton and Louise Nelstrop

Mystical Doctrines of Deification
Case Studies in the Christian Tradition
Edited by John Arblaster and Rob Faesen

The Mystical Sources of Existentialist Thought
Being, Nothingness, Love
George Pattison and Kate Kirkpatrick

For more information about this series, please visit: www.routledge.com/Contemporary-Theological-Explorations-in-Mysticism/book-series/ACONTHEOMYS

The Mystical Sources of Existentialist Thought

Being, Nothingness, Love

George Pattison and Kate Kirkpatrick

Routledge
Taylor & Francis Group
LONDON AND NEW YORK

First published 2019
by Routledge
2 Park Square, Milton Park, Abingdon, Oxon OX14 4RN

and by Routledge
52 Vanderbilt Avenue, New York, NY 10017

First issued in paperback 2020

Routledge is an imprint of the Taylor & Francis Group, an informa business

British Library Cataloguing-in-Publication Data
A catalogue record for this book is available from the British Library

Library of Congress Cataloging-in-Publication Data
A catalog record for this book has been requested

ISBN 13: 978-0-367-58231-9 (pbk)
ISBN 13: 978-1-138-09237-2 (hbk)

Typeset in Sabon
by Apex CoVantage, LLC

MIX
Paper from responsible sources
FSC™ C013985

Printed in the United Kingdom
by Henry Ling Limited

Contents

Acknowledgements

This is a book I have long wanted to write. However, I was also aware that to do so would require a more extensive study of French existentialism than I was able to undertake. When I realized that Kate Kirkpatrick was working on just those sources that were missing from my own studies it was obvious what needed to happen and I am therefore grateful to Kate for this collaboration, from which I have learned much. Glasgow University provided the opportunity to give undergraduate teaching on mysticism, and this has been a great help in focusing my thinking in this area. Frances O'Donnell and Jessica Suarez facilitated my use of the Paul Tillich Archive at Harvard Divinity School, and I am grateful to them and to the Divinity School for access to this resource. Kevin Smith gave important assistance with references. Chapter 2 includes material published in my article 'The role of mysticism in the formation of Heidegger's phenomenology' in David Lewin, Simon D. Podmore, and Duane Williams (eds.), *Mystical Theology and Continental Philosophy: Interchange in the Wake of God* (London: Routledge, 2017), and I am grateful for permission to represent it here. Hilary has lived with existentialism and mysticism for a long time now, and I am appreciative of her interest, her questioning, and her patience. Perhaps there are some good ideas in here!

George Pattison

This is a book I am very glad to have written. So my first thanks are to George Pattison for the invitation to write it, for this collaboration, and for the ongoing conversation of which it is a part. I have learned a great deal through this joint project. I am grateful to the University of Hertfordshire for the opportunity to teach Nietzsche, which helped clarify my thoughts on mysticism, negation, and affirmation in the French reception of Nietzsche, and to the Mystical Theology Network for opportunities to present aspects of this work in progress at their conferences over recent years – especially passages on Beauvoir, Sartre, Weil, and Bataille. I am also grateful to Pamela Sue Anderson for her much-missed conversations about Beauvoir, Joan of Arc, and the mysticism of action. Finally, I am grateful to Matt for all of the ways he says yes to life together, not least for his conversations and his patience.

Kate Kirkpatrick

Introduction

This is primarily a book about existentialism. In particular it is about the role that tropes, themes, and texts from authors and traditions that are often referred to as 'mystical' played in the work of key representatives of existentialist philosophy and theology, notably Kierkegaard, Buber, Heidegger, Beauvoir, Sartre, Marcel, Camus, Weil, Bataille, Berdyaev, and Tillich.

That being said, it is immediately necessary to say what this book is not about. It is not an argument aimed at showing that existentialism really was a species of mysticism. This was a claim made in the heyday of existentialism by both supporters and detractors. For the latter, this amounted to saying that existentialism was a case of philosophical obscurantism, but whilst we reject this inference, we are happy to affirm real, genuine, and significant connections between existentialism and mystical traditions. Jean Wahl, who played an important role in introducing both Kierkegaard and Heidegger to a French academic readership, clearly saw Kierkegaard as some kind of mystic.[1] In a semipopular survey of existentialist thinkers, Frederick Patka says of Kierkegaard, Bergson, Jaspers, and Marcel that 'They believe that the Absolute Being is present and He reveals Himself to the philosopher in his mystical experiences'.[2] Another commentator, Helmut Kuhn, sees the connection differently, as a negative version of Christian contemplation.[3] Colin Wilson, who did much to popularize existentialism in Britain (despite having a poor grasp of its philosophical basis), links the existentialists to visionaries such as George Fox and William Blake.[4] We might also mention Iris Murdoch as someone whose work makes intuitive connections between existentialism and mysticism.[5]

But our point is not that the existentialists 'really were' mystics dressed up in modern secular guise. It is simply that what became known as existentialism drew on and was at least in part shaped by its relation to what we might call its mystical sources, using the word 'sources' in a very broad and open sense. In virtually every case, however, these sources were radically transformed when they were taken up by existentialist thinkers – deliberately, spontaneously, or unconsciously.

Nor is the book about what existentialist writers or those more or less loosely connected with existentialism wrote explicitly about mysticism. In most cases, it will certainly involve attending to those more or less extensive passages in which mysticism is mentioned or discussed, but our interpretation will be focused on what this can tell us about the central philosophical and theological concerns of the thinker in question. Kierkegaard, for example, says very little explicitly about mysticism, and when he does use the term, it is usually in a sense rather different from how we shall be using it. Nevertheless, it is possible to show not only that he was deeply read in mystical literature but that this reading fed into some of his key insights about the meaning of human existence. Buber, on the other hand, is as well known for his retelling of Hasidic tales and legends as he is for his contribution to existential philosophy. However, the nature of our focus means that we shall not be dwelling on Buber as a mediator of the Hasidic tradition but will focus instead on how mystical elements became worked into his basic philosophical thought, even after the point at which he declared himself to have renounced mysticism. Each case is, of course, distinctive. Tillich gave a number of university courses on mysticism in ways that both reflected and fed into his own original thinking, and we shall therefore need to attend to both aspects if we are fully to grasp the thrust of Tillichian mysticism.

What, then, is the positive point of this study?

Essentially, it is a modest but nevertheless (we think) worthwhile attempt to fill in an aspect of the genesis and development of a major movement in modern European thought that has been neglected by both philosophical and theological scholarship. It is not intended as a complete re-reading or re-envisioning of existentialism, but it is intended to help us read existentialism better by reading it more fully.

However, it is immediately obvious that everything here depends on what we mean by existentialism and what we mean by mysticism. Both are deeply and sometimes ferociously contested terms. In both cases many of those designated 'existentialists' or 'mystics' did or quite probably would have refused the label, and in any event, many of their commentators have often refused it on their behalves.[6] In both cases, especially that of mysticism, there are also arguments as to whether there really is any such thing or whether it is merely an academic construct. It will therefore be prudent to begin with some preliminary observations about our basic terms and about the kinds of connections we see between them. We shall do this in two main steps. Firstly, we shall set out how we are understanding our basic terms 'existentialism' and 'mysticism'. At the very least, this will make clear our presuppositions, whether or not all readers are able to share them. Secondly, we shall draw attention to what we see as the decisive role of German Idealism and those influenced by it in developing a complex of ideas that not only gave a formative impulse to the modern study of mysticism but also served as a constant point of reference in the development of existentialism, from Kierkegaard, to Freiburg, to the Left Bank – where, as we shall see, it was joined with elements from French religious and intellectual traditions. However, German Idealism itself involved an explicit affiliation to the entire history of Western philosophy, and, as Kierkegaard's sarcastic comments on the Danish Hegelians made clear, this involved a particular emphasis on the importance of Descartes, who is an abiding if often shadowy presence in this history.

Existentialism

It is beyond doubt that the term 'existentialism' achieved international renown as a result of Jean-Paul Sartre's *Being and Nothingness* and the explanatory 1945 lecture known in English as 'Existentialism Is a Humanism'. In the years that followed, it was often perceived as much in terms of a thoroughly modern lifestyle (embracing jazz, Gauloise cigarettes, roll-neck jumpers, and sexual experimentation) or social attitudes (the outsider or rebel spoken of by Camus and Wilson) as for its philosophical claims. Nevertheless, there were a number of philosophical commitments that were essential to Sartre's own existentialism. These included an emphasis on the radical freedom of the human individual, the primacy of action over theory (summed up in such dicta as 'existence precedes essence' and 'human beings are nothing more than the sum of their actions'), the irrelevance of God in human affairs (though he acknowledged that there were also Christian versions of existentialism), and the view that an honest account of the circumstances of human existence revealed the ineluctability of anxiety, despair, and mutual antagonism.

Sartre himself soon moved, perhaps implausibly, toward combining this with an idiosyncratic version of Marxism. In any case, when we speak of existentialism, we are not just talking about the existentialism of Sartre, Simone de Beauvoir, and other habitués of what Sarah Bakewell has called 'the existentialist café' on the Parisian Left Bank in the years following World War II.[7] Existentialism may have acquired a paradigmatic form in that place and time, but it did not appear out of nowhere. Weil and Bataille – whose classification as 'existentialist' might be disputed – have been included in order to show the way that several factors in early twentieth-century France contributed to the thought of the period: namely (i) the resurgence of interest in mysticism as a topic of philosophical study; (ii) questions about the relationship between Hellenism, Christianity, and modernity; and (iii) a revaluation of values in the absence of God.

An especially important part of the background to the philosophical fireworks of 1945 was what, in the 1920s, had become known as the philosophy of Existenz, especially associated with the work of Karl Jaspers and Martin Heidegger. The title of Sartre's own breakthrough work, *Being and Nothingness*, clearly references Heidegger's own *Being and Time* (but also, as we shall see, Descartes's fourth meditation as well as the language of key seventeenth-century theological figures). Nor is the link merely verbal since Heidegger's analysis hinged on understanding time as being decisively revealed in human beings' thrownness toward death and annihilation. Understanding this situation and embracing it (or, in Heidegger's phrase, 'running towards' it) constitutes what it is to exist authentically, and, as would be the case for Sartre, this involved both radical individuation and radical freedom. For both, understanding the human being as the radically free subject of his or her own existence was something essentially different from the kind of knowledge pursued in any other field of science – natural, social, or humanistic. And, like Sartre, Heidegger also judged anxiety to be that basic mood in which the truth of the human condition became most clearly manifest.

Yet there were also important differences between the two thinkers, and not only in their politics. Even if Heidegger's view of the human condition seems almost as bleak as Sartre's, he doesn't specifically insist on despair or the necessity of mutual antagonism. (Sometimes, he even hints that love is a basic existential possibility.) Furthermore, even as we find ourselves thrown toward annihilation in death, we have, he thinks, at least the possibility of what he calls the question of being. What Heidegger meant by being is, unsurprisingly, deeply contested, but he does seem to be thinking of some kind of ground for meaningful human life that is more than the arbitrary will of the individual. Indeed, by the time of Sartre's *Being and Nothingness*, Heidegger himself has moved toward writing quasi-poetical and, many thought, mystical meditations on what he called 'the history of being'.

A further important aspect of the connection between Sartre and Heidegger is that both directly drew on the philosophical method of phenomenology, as developed by Edmund Husserl. Heidegger had been Husserl's '*Assistent*' and, following the publication of *Being and Time* (dedicated to Husserl), succeeded to the older thinker's chair at Freiburg University. To attempt to explicate phenomenology in any detail would take us on an overlong diversion (and, in any case, many excellent introductions are available), but a couple of brief points may be helpful for what follows. The first is that, as the name implies, phenomenology does not attempt to explain its subject matter in the way that, for example, psychology tries to explain human behaviour. Instead, it limits itself to *describing* the phenomena as they actually appear to us. However, and this is our second point, the actual appearing of phenomena is not the same as the kind of view arrived at in popular empiricism. The late French poet Yves Bonnefoy, himself a student of philosophy in the era of existentialism, wrote that poetry shows us the tree before we know it is a tree and, in a sense, phenomenology is trying to do something similar: to train us to see the world and, in the case of existential phenomenology, our life in the world as it is before we frame it in terms of our cultural, intellectual, and other assumptions. The world as revealed by phenomenology is no more like the world of common-sense realism than the world shown by a Cézanne or a Picasso is like the world shown in a photograph.

Indeed, art and literature are entwined in the entire history of existential phenomenology and Proust, Flaubert, Dostoevsky, Baudelaire, Mallarmé, and even older literary sources such as Racine were arguably no less important to the development of French existentialism than were Heidegger or Husserl. Apart from the novels and plays of Sartre, Beauvoir, Camus, and Marcel, writers such as Bernanos, Genet, Beckett, James Joyce, Graham Greene, and their contemporaries are also significant presences in the history of existentialism. Something similar holds in the case of Heidegger, for whom the German poet Hölderlin became a decisive point of reference in his later work.

This mix of art, literature, and philosophy also characterizes what has sometimes been called the proto-existentialism that sprang up in the first decade of the twentieth century in Austro-Hungary. Representatives of this innovative movement in ideas included Buber, Kafka, Lukacs, and others, and this new thinking was also reflected in the radical Tyrolean journal *Der Brenner* of which Heidegger (amongst many others) was a regular reader. Not only was this a milieu welcoming to a range of mystical sources, it was also shaped by such key nineteenth-century figures as Kierkegaard, Nietzsche, and Dostoevsky, each of whom would be regularly referenced by later existentialist thinkers.[8]

How far back can we take the story of existentialism? Some genealogies cite remoter sources such as Pascal, Meister Eckhart, and Augustine, and anticipations of existentialism are sometimes said to go all the way back to the Bible. We shall consider some of these further in the conclusion to this chapter, but at this point we focus more specifically on the modern antecedents of existentialism and, in particular, on the influence of Kierkegaard on Heidegger and Sartre. Whether or not Kierkegaard was an 'existentialist' in a narrower sense, it is clear that he did provide existentialist philosophy with an account of the human condition that Heidegger described as 'philosophically essential' for his own philosophical work, which, in turn, was an element (but not an exclusive one) in the formation of Sartrean existentialism.

We have touched on the importance of anxiety in both Heidegger and Sartre and both acknowledge Kierkegaard as an important source for this idea. For Kierkegaard, anxiety arises out of our awareness of 'being able'. A prime example, which Sartre also cites, is the sense of vertigo that comes from the realization not that we might fall from some great height but that we are actually free to throw ourselves off. But it is not just in extreme situations that anxiety discloses the situation that we are free and responsible for how we live out the possibilities with which life (or, for Kierkegaard, God) has endowed us. Such anxiety accompanies us every step of the way.

Anxiety reveals another key Kierkegaardian idea: that truth is subjectivity. In other words, truth is not just a matter of what is or isn't the case (as in: it is true that the apple is red and false that the apple is green).

Kierkegaard doesn't deny the fact of such objective truths, but more important, he claims, are the truths in which my own life is at issue, truths for which I am prepared to live or die. Whether human beings have an immortal soul or whether Jesus of Nazareth thought he was the Messiah are, if true, objective truths. Subjectively, however, the issue is about what is going to happen to me or what I am going to do: Will I find eternal happiness? Am I prepared to forsake all and follow Him?

Like Heidegger and Sartre, Kierkegaard thought that the burden of freedom in the face of such questions was probably too much for most people. On the whole we prefer to go along with the crowd, to think what everyone else thinks, and to do what everyone else does. Sometimes he talked about his mission as being to detach the individual from the crowd. But this is not easy. In fact the way in which we have been shaped by culture and history is so pervasive that really to stand on our own seems to mean letting everything else go, which, seen from another angle, is (as Kierkegaard says) to become nothing, to adopt a position that our friends and neighbours are likely to think merely absurd. Such radical singularity can have no supporting rationale, it seems. As Kierkegaard says of Abraham, if God does not exist, then Abraham is lost.

There is, of course, more to Kierkegaard than this and, for that matter, more to Kierkegaard's contribution to the history of existentialism than this.[9] Here, however, we have a complex of ideas that would come to be central to later existentialist thought: (1) the primacy of subjectivity; (2) the freedom of the human subject; (3) the anxiety generated by this freedom as typically leading human beings to fall into what Sartre would call 'bad faith' and Heidegger inauthenticity; (4) authentic existence, understood as readiness to bear the burden of the ultimate non-being of the projects through which we give meaning to our lives; (5) acceptance of the radical singularity in which we take up our responsibility for ourselves; and (6) readiness to endure the reproaches of absurdity and irrationality that will come our way if we do so.

All this is effectively summed up in two assertions from Sartre and from Paul Tillich, an atheistic and a Christian existentialist respectively. For Sartre 'existence precedes essence', meaning that human beings are defined by what they live through in their actual existence and not by any pre-existing essence, metaphysical or biological. For Tillich, the etymology of the term 'existence' itself points to a situation in which human beings 'stand out' into nothingness, never just 'being' a certain way but always having to choose and take responsibility for who they are. If, in the one case, this means that human beings are without God in the world whilst, in the other, the encounter with nothingness becomes the place of our encounter with God, then we are alerted to the fact that we shall in each case need to attend not only to the keywords and catchphrases that helped popularize existentialism in the mid–twentieth century but also to the fine detail of what is actually being said.

We shall return to these themes at many points in what follows but turn next to consider what we understand by 'mysticism'.

Mysticism

It almost goes without saying that if existentialism is a debated and seemingly elusive term, the same is true – perhaps even more emphatically true – in the case of mysticism.

For much of the early twentieth century, mysticism was a key term in the study of religion and often provided the conceptual basis for comparative studies of the different world religions. William James's *Varieties of Religious Experience* provided a defining point of reference for twentieth-century usage.[10] Although mysticism was not the only form of religious experience James considered, it played a central role in his overall account of religion. Mystical experience, he suggested, was very possibly the basis on which the whole of religion rested, at least in relation to psychology. James described mystical experience as ineffable: that is, as beyond words, and yet as having what he called a 'noetic' quality, meaning that it involved the perception of a certain definite reality. Mystical experiences are, however, transient, brief moments in time like flashes of inspiration. And, lastly, mystic states are passive: where the ethical personality acts or the scientist investigates, the mystic is acted upon. He or she is therefore incapable of conjuring up the mystic experience: either it happens or it doesn't; it comes upon us from beyond and sometimes contrary to our conscious intentions, or, as religious believers are likely to say, it is a matter of grace.

James's *Varieties* is the text of Gifford lectures given in 1901 and 1902 at the University of Edinburgh, and it both reflected a rising tide of interest in religion as a sui generis phenomenon of human consciousness and gave added impetus to studies of 'the mystical', whether in the service of Christian theology (Dean Inge,[11] Evelyn Underhill,[12] Baron von Hügel[13]) or of comparative studies (Rudolf Otto,[14] Friedrich Heiler[15]) or the emerging phenomenology of religion developed by figures such as Max Scheler[16] and Gerhard van der Leeuw.[17]

In various ways, then, early twentieth-century scholars seemed able to agree that there was a certain kind of experience that was distinctive to religion, that this experience was appropriately identified as 'mystical', and that it was crucial to claims concerning the meaning and significance – even the truth – of religious life. At its maximum, the claim was that 'mystical experience' was the unifying element behind the manifold of world religions and that despite all the differences of culture and creed, Meister Eckhart and the Zen Masters, Teresa of Avila and the Sufi poet Rumi, *The Cloud of Unknowing* and Advaita Hinduism were all giving expression to the 'same' experience. Sometimes these parallels were qualified by subdividing mystical experience into personal and impersonal types, the former being usually more typical of the West and the latter more typical of the East.

Nevertheless, these were still largely treated as if they were two species of the same essential genus.[18]

In the late twentieth century this view was widely rejected, with particular emphasis now coming to be placed on the role of linguistic and cultural construction.[19] The parallels to be found between Eastern and Western mystics were in this perspective not so much examples of a universal mystical experience underlying the diversity of religious expression as a means of constructing a lingua franca between newly convergent civilizations. In this view, there is in reality no such thing as mysticism, and the whole picture presented by early twentieth-century writers simply reflects the humanistic, psychologizing prejudices of that age.

The continuing debate as to what mysticism is or even as to whether there is such a thing at all continues to run its course. In the present context, however, the following point is crucial: namely, that in the period when existentialism took shape as a coherent intellectual and cultural movement, there was a widely agreed set of assumptions as to what mysticism was or, at least, as to the kinds of claims that went along with appeals to mystical experience. These assumptions were shared both by those who wrote as advocates of one or other form of mysticism and by those who saw it as epitomizing all the errors of religion. So what were these assumptions? For our present purposes, they included such elements as the supposition of an immediate intuition of absolute being, a suspension or transcendence of logic and dialectic in favour of a direct apprehension of truth, a privileging of feeling and passion at the expense of intellect and ethics, and a preference for the immediacy of personal experience in opposition to institutional authority. These themes inevitably allow for considerable variation: for example, whether being is conceived personally (theistically) or impersonally (as, it was claimed, in Buddhist nirvana). At the same time, whilst 'the mystic' is pictured as seeking the immediacy of the divine presence, this search is also seen as being so radical as simultaneously to heighten the sense of alienation or separation from God – the dark night of the soul through which those wanting a more-than-conventional God-relationship must pass. Because of its tendency to go beyond the limits of reason, mysticism could be seen as having an affinity to some kinds of madness, although defenders of mysticism were likely to see it as serving the essential interests of reason itself.[20]

This last point indicates the way in which the awakening of interest in mysticism coincided with reflection on a set of problems bequeathed by Kant and brought back into the spotlight in the neo-Kantianism of the early twentieth century, a movement that was influential in Anglophone and Francophone circles as much as in Germany itself. And it is also here that we can see how mysticism (as it was conceived in this period) came into contact with the philosophical agenda of existentialism. For existentialism, too, involved an ongoing struggle with assumptions about the nature of subjectivity going back to Descartes and sharpened by the Kantian supposition that we do not have direct access to reality other than as mediated by the categorical structure of the human mind. And if existentialism introduced its own dualisms, it shared with mysticism (as that was understood in the early twentieth century) the ambition of reconnecting human thinking to reality and the privileging of direct self-experience as the point of ontological revelation.

Existentialism, mysticism, and German Idealism

The link between the Kantian problematization of the relationship between mind and reality and mysticism is clearly made by Evelyn Underhill in the opening chapter of her study *Mysticism*, amongst the most influential of all the early twentieth-century works. Underhill takes her point of departure in the human quest for truth, suggesting that this receives basically only three answers in the history of ideas: empiricism, idealism, and scepticism. Mysticism, however, offers a fourth way, and Underhill claims that 'mysticism alone postulates, and in the persons of its great initiates proves . . . the existence of a discoverable "real", a spark of true being, within the seeking subject, which can, on that ineffable experience which they call the "act of union", fuse itself with and thus apprehend the reality of the sought Object'.[21]

What Underhill sought (and believed she had found) in mysticism was what the generation of German Idealist philosophers after Kant sought by more philosophical means: namely, an explication of how, despite Kant, we can be confident that our representations really do show us the world as it is 'in itself'. Each did this in a distinctive way.[22]

A useful point of orientation in relation to the extensive relevant literature on the subject is a dissertation that the young theologian Paul Tillich wrote in 1911 for his theology licentiate entitled *Mysticism and Guilt-Consciousness in Schelling*. As will be discussed further in Chapter 8, the dissertation established a template for Tillich's subsequent intellectual development, but the title also nicely epitomizes the way in which German Idealism provides us with a framework for thinking about the relationship between mysticism and existentialism. By 'mysticism' here Tillich means much the same as Underhill: namely, the subject's direct experience of identity with absolute being. Yet for Tillich (interpreting Schelling), such an experience was only ever encountered in dialectical relation to what he calls 'guilt-consciousness': that is, consciousness of being separated or alienated from this absolute ground and thrown out into the realm of historical relativity. In this situation, the life of the subject is shaped as a struggle to return to the primal unity of the mystical consciousness, a struggle that, Schelling thinks, cannot be completed by intellectual means alone but involves an act of will or self-choice. This act of will must at the same time embrace and synthesize all the disparate elements of our estranged life in the world, including anxiety and suffering. For Schelling, as for Tillich, this is a pattern that plays itself out at metaphysical, cultural-historical, and individual levels. Precisely because later existentialism would take its bearings from this separated, alienated, temporal, and individualized 'guilty' subject, Tillich's formulation neatly specifies not only the opposition but also the necessary interdependence of mysticism and existential thinking that was already present in German Idealism. Let us look more closely at what is going on here in relation to three key figures: Schelling, Hegel, and Schopenhauer.

In his early thought, Schelling had thought to solve the problem of the mind's access to ultimate reality by appealing to a kind of incorrigible intuition that he variously described as intellectual or aesthetic. In intellectual intuition the mind has a direct vision of the reality of its own activity, whilst in aesthetic intuition we see the unity of mind and world: an artistic image doesn't offer arguments or hypotheses about the world but shows us the world precisely as it appears. True art is not just invention but revelation, and the artist is elevated to the rank of seer or prophet. Hegel soon dismissed such claims as being entirely vacuous – the night in which all cows are black, as he put it. Instead, Hegel argued that the dialectic that could be seen at work in the laws of logic and in the unfolding of human history and culture was capable of explaining all possible phenomena, from the laws of physics through to the achievements of fine art. Yet Hegel, too, turns to mysticism as corroborating his philosophical claims, affirming the validity of Meister Eckhart's saying that the eye with which I see God is the same eye as the eye with which God sees me.[23]

Although Hegel had little direct knowledge of the primary sources of Eckhart's thought (still at that time very limited), he did have a good knowledge of the Protestant mystic Jacob Boehme, to whom he dedicated a section of his lectures on the history of philosophy and whom (despite what he called the barbarity of Boehme's style) he called 'the first German philosopher'. Especially, Hegel seems to have taken from Boehme the speculative idea of a self-diremption within the life of God but also seems to have been influenced by Boehme's visionary account of how God is progressively manifested through all levels of material as well as spiritual creation. This dynamic and progressive revelation proceeds from an initial state of nothingness (the Boehmian 'Ungrund') that, in an undefined sense, precedes the self-conscious life of God. This develops through an at-first blind impulse of will that is the originating power of God Himself but that further manifests through the Fall and materialization, before returning to the joy of divine life. This dynamic pattern of repeated self-othering, of difference-in-unity, and the role of will offered Hegel a kind of blueprint that he then worked out in a systematic and rigorous way in his dialectics.[24]

Boehme also reappears as a major presence in the later thought of Schelling. However, his treatment of the 'cobbler of Goerlitz' (as Boehme was often referred to) is significantly different from that of Hegel. In later works, such as his *Treatise on Human Freedom*, Schelling asserts the precedence of will over reason in a way that is, arguably, truer to Boehme's own writings, where wilfulness applies both to the wrath that introduces difference into the divine life and the patient good will of the devout heart set on God, a motif developed from medieval spiritual writers such as Eckhart and Tauler. Not systematic reason, but a kind of lightning flash in which will and intuition are fused provides the point of contact between the estranged life of human beings in their material and individuated fallenness and the self-fulfilling eternal bliss of God.

The role of the will is also prominent in a third philosophical variation on post-Kantian metaphysics, namely that of Arthur Schopenhauer. Schopenhauer conceded that whilst our representation does indeed fail to mirror reality as it is, we have direct access to reality through the underlying presence in each of us (as in every living thing) of the essentially blind and purposeless will to exist that is the generative source of all that is. Although Schopenhauer's system can be read as materialist rather than mystical, since there is no God for the self to be united with, he nevertheless identified a number of points in common with mystical writers, in particular with those promoting a negative or apophatic theological position. They, too, he claimed, shared his insight that we can never reach reality in itself through knowledge and must therefore abandon all concepts and images if we are to know ourselves as being at one with the universal will. And although he especially saw analogies between his position and Buddhism, he also regarded Christian writers such as Eckhart and Madame Guyon and the evidence of Christian asceticism as pointing in the same direction.[25]

German Idealist philosophy, then, provided a number of ways of legitimating a purely philosophical interest in mysticism which, at the same time, also defined and propagated a particular way of understanding what, exactly, mysticism is: namely, a kind of consciousness in which the mind or self has incorrigible and immediate certainty of its identity with reality itself.

Alongside the philosophers, other representatives of German Idealism took a more avowedly religious or theological approach, and here the approval of mystical sources seems even more apparent. Although Franz von Baader (who seems to have been the source for Hegel's knowledge of Eckhart) would play little role in the history of existentialism, he did much to promote interest in and study of mysticism amongst the German Idealists. The Danish Hegelian theologian H. L. Martensen wrote one of the earliest monographs on Eckhart, arguing for the medieval thinker having anticipated the central aims of idealist epistemology, especially with regard to the possibility of a direct intuition of absolute being. At the same time, editors such as Franz Pfeiffer drove forward with the work of identifying and publishing primary sources of medieval mysticism, Eckhart, and others.[26]

Schleiermacher's 1799 *Speeches on Religion*, often regarded as the founding document of modern theology, described a momentary feeling of identity between the finite self and the infinite universe as the 'natal hour of everything living in religion', and this could easily be seen as a 'mystical' experience.[27] Although not cited by James (who probably only knew Schleiermacher's work indirectly, if at all),[28] Schleiermacher's poetically coloured description of this 'natal hour' would seem to fit well with James's account of mystical experience as being ineffable, transient, and passive and as also having a certain noetic quality: it is an experience of reality and not a merely subjective affective or imaginary event. And whilst Schleiermacher did not draw the conclusion that this removed religion from the sphere of rational enquiry, it did mean that the Schleiermacherian account of the history of religion would never be as neatly ordered as that of Hegel since, necessarily, the development of doctrine and forms of association would be dependent on the primacy of experience. The study of religion was not the application of a dialectical logic but the study of a living organic movement constantly manifesting itself in a rich diversity of forms. Already in the *Speeches*, then, we see the beginnings of what would blossom into a thoroughgoing comparativist approach to religion by the end of the nineteenth century.

Intriguingly, Heidegger was especially attentive to Schleiermacher when preparing the outline for a series of lectures on mysticism that he never in fact delivered. Schleiermacher, Heidegger seems to argue, offers the best modern version of what medieval mysticism was attempting to articulate – although, in the end, the outline suggests that such a re-appropriation was not directly possible in, with, and under the conditions of modernity.

Another important development in the 'Early Romantic' circles to which Schleiermacher belonged was the beginning of an interest in the mystical character of Eastern religion. Schopenhauer, too, would embrace an orientalist perspective on mysticism, identifying Buddhist nirvana with the self-annihilation of which Christian mystics spoke. Again, this would become a prominent feature of the study of religion in the late nineteenth and early twentieth centuries, and 'the mystical East' remains a trope of popular religious culture.

As well as looking East, Romantic idealism also looked back to the Middle Ages, to a time in which (as the Romantics pictured it) human beings still lived in a kind of immediate unity with society and nature. This unity, the story went, had been broken by the individualism of Renaissance culture and the rationalism of the modern world, often epitomized in the person of Descartes but also exacerbated and given social power through the expansion of science and technology.

This had several consequences in relation to the interpretation of mysticism. Firstly, it gave impetus to the historical retrieval of mystical texts from the Middle Ages. Eckhart has already been mentioned as a case in point, but although he was doubtless the most important, he was also only one of many. Secondly, and at the same time, it meant that there was a bias toward reading medieval texts as 'mystical' in a sense congruent with the idealists' own agendas. Whether or not this led to significant misreading lies outside the scope of this study, but it is important to us to note that not only the concept of mysticism but also the history of mysticism is in many ways a construct of German Idealism.

But what has any of this to do with existentialism?

The answer to this question has already been anticipated in our comments about Tillich's licentiate dissertation: existentialism is the negative corollary of mysticism in the specific sense that these represent the Scylla and Charybdis between which idealism attempts to steer but that repeatedly, albeit in opposite ways, bring about the ruin of idealist ambitions.

However, the relation of existentialism to idealism is not solely negative. This can be seen by the way in which the reception of, for example, Hegel by each of Heidegger, Sartre, and even Kierkegaard is marked by positive as well as negative elements. If, from an existentialist point of view, Hegel was too optimistic with regard to the prospect of providing an exhaustive systematic account of the genesis of human knowledge of reality, his very commitment to totality obliged him to draw, for example, passion, negation, and the confrontation with death into the orbit of philosophy. In this sense, Hegel provided critics from Kierkegaard onward with the materials for demolishing his own system. A purely ideal idealism might have its own problems, but once idealism starts to make claims about the concrete situation of human beings living in the world, it faces a different and infinitely more demanding set of challenges. Thus Kierkegaard insists he has no objection to systems of pure logic or mathematics, nor does he deny that the world is a unitary and harmonious whole when seen from the viewpoint of God. What he cannot believe is that concretely existing human beings can ever be in a position to share that viewpoint.

Alexandre Kojève's lectures on Hegel's *Phenomenology*, which electrified his Parisian audiences and provided a major impetus to the development of French existentialism, doubtless read Hegel too much through the lens of Kierkegaard and Heidegger, but they illustrate just how an 'existential' Hegel could be rescued from the deadening hand of the pedantic Teutonic didact lampooned in Heinrich Heine's satire on the 'German Professor'.[29] And, of course, although Husserl and Heidegger were the more immediate sources of the phenomenological orientation of existentialism, Hegel remained unavoidable as, in his own way, an originating figure in the development of phenomenological method. Specific topics of existentialist thought, such as the dialectic of master and slave or the characterization of consciousness in terms of negation, are directly indebted to Hegel, however much they may have been adapted or developed in new ways. If 'Hegel', man and work, is often used as shorthand for everything to which existentialism was opposed, it is nevertheless clear that it was this same Hegel who provided existentialism with the tools with which to demolish his own system.

Let us sum up. Working on a set of philosophical problems bequeathed by Kant's critical philosophy, the German Idealists and their early twentieth-century inheritors proposed a kind of immediate consciousness of reality that they saw as having significant continuity with the testimony of mystics from within and beyond Christianity. In support of this view, their work also gave impetus to the study of the history of mysticism and the development of a canon of mystical literature that would be widely accepted in the later nineteenth and early twentieth centuries. At the same time they brought philosophy face to face with the actual alienation of human beings existing in historically specific and finite circumstances. Mysticism and existentialism thus emerge as the dissimilar twins of German Idealism, and to the extent that this is so, their subsequent relationship has involved repeated attraction and repulsion. Buber would give up what he called mysticism for the sake of life in the world, but Tillich would see mysticism as an abiding element in the religious response to modern alienation. And, as we shall see, the history of existentialism and mysticism displays manifold variations on the themes of either/or and both/and – and neither formula is alone sufficient to capture the complexity of the relationships involved.

Existential antecedents

If German Idealism provides us with the most important context for thinking together the conceptual and historical interdependence of existentialism and mysticism, the literature of existentialism has also pointed to a somewhat eclectic range of other figures and movements that seem to anticipate existentialism in the narrower modern sense. In the light of what we have seen thus far, several of these can also be seen as in some sense 'mystical' – bearing in mind, however, that such conjectural historical readings have themselves borne the marks of the idealist historiography of mysticism that was discussed in the previous section. Nevertheless, it will be helpful for the further development of our argument to briefly survey some of these points of shared historical reference, returning to them in more detail in the body of our work.

In the first instance we might mention the Bible, often seen as offering a point of common reference for both existentialism and mysticism. It was the Bible that provided Kierkegaard with some of the most enduring tropes of existentialist literature, such as Abraham's absurd faith or Job's protest against God's injustice. And although Abraham's trial and Job's despair do not in the first instance seem 'mystical', suggesting as they do the hiddenness and inscrutability of God, they do at the same time seem to insist that the individual has the possibility of a direct and unmediated God relationship. The Biblical story of Creation suggests the possibility of such a relationship, but it also suggests this was quickly jeopardized by the Fall, to the extent that even Christ on the cross felt alienated from the Creator, crying out, 'My God, my God, why have you forsaken me?' But in addition to the hiddenness of God in the *Akedah* or Job's despair, in Adam's Eden or Christ's experiences of abandonment at Gethsemane and Golgotha, existentialists drew on mystical interpretations of biblical texts that emphasized love and action, such as Jesus's command 'to love your neighbour as yourself'.

Another point of reference that is no less important for having played a major role in so many other currents of European thought and literature is the life and work of Augustine of Hippo, often referred to as 'the first modern man' on the basis of the direct expression of subjectivity and inwardness found in his *Confessions*. Augustine develops a view of the self that both focuses on subjective self-experience and defines this experience through its relation to a God who is the constant and abiding condition of its existence (who is present to it, even when it turns away from Him) yet constantly eludes the grasp and ambition of the self. Consequently, it is a self in a state of constant anxiety, searching, and longing, marked by fallenness and guilt.

Inevitably, a thinker of the scope and stature of Augustine has been called into the service of the most diverse intellectual traditions, informing both the Protestant Reformation and its Catholic opponents. That Augustine has been a source both for Christian mysticism (Dom Cuthbert Butler referred to him as a 'Prince of Mystics'[30]) and for existentialism (as in Heidegger's early lectures on the *Confessions*[31]) does not mean that mystics and existentialists are reading Augustine in the same way.

In seventeenth-century France, for example, we find each of Descartes, Pascal, and Fénelon claiming an Augustinian inheritance – but although each can be seen as following the so-called 'Father of Grace' with regard to the intensification of human subjectivity, they did so with varying methodological efforts and to varying effects.

The early seventeenth-century renaissance of Augustinian thought – and, indeed, mysticism – has been traced to the writings of Pierre de Bérulle, one of the so-called 'masters of the masters' of French mysticism and founder of the Oratory of France, who introduced Spanish mystics such as John of the Cross and Theresa of Avila into contemporary discussion. Bérulle's mystical theology led to a renewed emphasis on creaturely nothingness and the negating effects of sin, and this emphasis would permeate what Henri Brémond called '*l'école française de spiritualité*' (which he also referred to as the 'mystical invasion' and eventual 'mystical conquest' of France).[32] Bérulle's Augustinian anthropology viewed the human being as between being and nothingness, continuously (re-)created by God at each instant. It was not only among mystics and Oratorians, however, that Bérulle's influence was felt. Bérulle's young pupil René Descartes was to consider the effects of nothingness in epistemological terms in the fourth of his *Meditations*.

However, if Descartes was satisfied that consciousness could provide assurance as to its own grounding in being and testify to the necessity of divine being, his contemporary Blaise Pascal offered a bleaker view. The seventeenth century has been seen as marked by a 'quarrel of Augustinianisms', and Pascal's Augustinianism was of the more sombre kind associated with the schools of Port-Royal, almost as akin to Calvinism as to mainstream Catholic thinking. Reflecting on the new cosmology, Pascal saw human existence as cast adrift in a limitless space of nothingness and, as he wrote, 'the eternal silence of these infinite spaces terrifies me'.[33] The human being was but a 'thinking reed', and so far from thought providing us with access to the world and to God, it was itself as weak and vulnerable as a blade of grass.[34] Yet, as his so-called 'memorial' showed, Pascal did seem to find relief from the anguish of this situation in what is plausibly read as a mystical revelation. Here is an extract, including, in its opening lines, a distinction between the God of the philosophers and the God of faith that would become a leitmotif in much existential literature:

Fire

God of Abraham, God of Isaac, God of Jacob,
not of the philosophers and scientists.
Certainty, certainty. Feeling. Joy. Peace.
God of Jesus Christ.
Deum meum et Deum vestrum.
Thy God shall be my God.
Forgetfulness of the world and of all, except God.
He is to be found only by the ways taught in the Gospel.
Greatness of the human soul.
O righteous Father, the world hath not known Thee, but I have
Known Thee.
Joy, joy, joy, tears of joy.
I separated myself from Him.
Dereliquerunt me fontem aquæ vivæ.
My God, wilt Thou forsake me?
May I never be separated from Him eternally.[35]

Fénelon's argument for 'The Existence of God and His Attributes drawn from purely intellectual Proofs and the Idea of Infinity itself' evokes both Cartesian and Pascalian themes. The early parts of this argument read almost like a paraphrase of Descartes's own method of doubt, as when Fénelon writes that 'It seems to me that the only way of avoiding error entirely is to doubt without exception all the things in which I do not find clear evidence . . . I am willing to acquiesce only when I am forced to do so by evidence and the entire certitude of [the] things [I am considering]'.[36] But the outcome of such systematic doubt is more Pascalian than Cartesian. Even the thought that 'it is impossible to doubt that I am' because 'to doubt and to deceive oneself is to think' and one could not think if one was nothing (*rien*) offers only temporary respite. 'What I have just said is a kind of glimmer that presents itself to me in this abyss of shadows in which I am plunged', he immediately adds.[37] Afflicted by new doubts, he considers that the view that it is impossible to doubt any idea that is truly clear and distinct is itself just an unfounded presupposition or an illusion. What if reason is a 'false measure?'[38] 'Perhaps what [my] spirit represents as clear is actually an utter absurdity. Perhaps nothing [*néant*] is capable of thinking and, in thinking, I am nothing [*rien*]. Perhaps the same thing can altogether exist and not exist'.[39]

Such reflections lead him to a proof for the existence of God 'drawn from the imperfection of human being':

> I search within myself. I study myself. I indeed see that I am but I do not know how I am nor if I ever began to be, nor by what I am able to exist. What a prodigy, I am certain only of myself and this I in which I enclose myself astonishes me, surpasses me, confounds me and escapes me as soon as I think I have a hold on it. Did I make myself? No, since to do so I would have had to be. Nothing [*néant*] makes nothing [*rien*].[40]

Yet I do find within myself an idea of the infinite 'that is in me, that is more than me; it seems to be everything and I nothing. . . . Behold the prodigy that I always carry within me. I myself am a prodigy. Being nothing . . . I am a nothing that knows the infinite'.[41] Caught midway between the infinite being of God and our own nothingness, Fénelon's conclusion is that 'There are only two truths in the world, that concerning God being all and that concerning the creature being nothing [*rien*]; for humility to be genuine, it is necessary for us . . . to remain in our place, which is to love and to be nothing'.[42]

This is a position that is neither neatly existential nor mystical, yet it is fed by mystical sources (such as John of the Cross) and anticipates existential themes of the human being as poised between being and nothingness. Fénelon himself especially emphasized the importance of François de Sales, and whilst much of de Sales's own imagery and rhetoric veers toward the sweet and sentimental, he, too, offers figurations of the human condition that even anticipate twentieth-century notions of the absurd, as in his parable of the deaf musician. Imagine, he says, that there was once a supremely gifted lutenist and singer, so renowned that he is summoned by his prince to play and sing for the royal pleasure. As a true subject, nothing gives him greater joy than to dedicate the service of his gift to the prince. However, as time goes on he becomes so completely deaf that he himself can no longer hear the music he performs. Nevertheless, he continues to rejoice in the fact that by singing and playing he is able to give pleasure to his prince. But now the prince decides to amuse himself hunting. Still, as he sets out, he commands the musician to continue singing and playing, even in his absence. Now the musician can no longer hear the music he makes, nor is the one for whom he is playing there to hear it. And yet his joy is undiminished since, even though no one hears, he is doing all that he has ever wished to do: namely, to be faithful to his Lord's will.[43]

Such images indicate that neither de Sales nor Fénelon affirmed a direct experience of God in this life, although they did affirm the possibility of an unconditional and 'pure' love of God in which God is loved for God's sake alone and not for any rewards he might bestow or punishments he might inflict – a position that would, at the end of the century, be condemned by the Church. Nevertheless, the nature and possibility of love would emerge as major themes in mystical aspects of existentialist thought.

The divergence between Descartes on the one side and Pascal and Fénelon on the other – a divergence that is at one and the same time religious and philosophical – is emblematic of a tension that has run through French philosophy ever since, although in the English-speaking world it is not commonly noted by either philosophers or theologians. One anthology of mysticism from 1941 comments that since the *siècle des lumières*, it has become axiomatic that France does not have a mystical soul – *l'âme mystique* – but rather a philosophical one.[44] But Pascal and Fénelon are, in their way, as representative of the French intellectual tradition as Descartes and Voltaire. And for philosophers trained in the generation of Simone de Beauvoir, Jean-Paul Sartre, and Simone Weil, the *agrégation* included many thinkers who would fit the English label 'mystic' better than 'philosopher'. Indeed, Sartre himself was engaged in debates over this particular word – accusing Georges Bataille of being a mystic and disputing that he himself was one.[45]

It might seem odd to mention Nietzsche in reflecting on the common sources of mysticism and existentialism (and to do so is, of course, to make a considerable leap from the spirituality of seventeenth-century France), not least in the light of Nietzsche's belligerent insistence on the death of God and his thoroughgoing affirmation of this-worldly immanence. Yet even with regard to the death of God, there seem to be echoes of a theme anticipated in Christian piety, and the sense of divine abandonment has been as much a theme of some mystical writings as of modern existentialism. More positively, the intuition and affirmation of eternal recurrence, not least as that is articulated in the poetic and parabolic discourses of Zarathustra, seem to echo a mystical account of union filtered through Nietzsche's insistence on the limitlessness of temporality and the primacy of living will over intellectual contemplation. Strikingly, Nietzsche was often read (even if also misread) in the late nineteenth- and early twentieth-century milieu of Russian religious philosophy as offering a 'mystical' teaching. This may be a mysticism of radical immanence, but (at least this is how some of the God-seekers read Nietzsche) this need not of itself strip it of all religious significance. After all, if the unity of all dimensions of being is an ultimate given of the mystical (as many in the late nineteenth century believed to be the case), then the division between immanence and transcendence is itself redundant. Immanence itself can just be transcendence. The eternal as it recurs in time might then be just as valid an object of religious longing as an eternal being that was represented as located in a transcendent metaphysical space. And, negatively, Nietzsche (like Kierkegaard) suggested to modernists at the turn of the century that the key to understanding human life was not theory, not intellect, logic, or systematic thought, but ecstatic participation in the flow of life itself and the consequent abandonment of the individualized rational ego – a negative goal certainly shared with proponents of the mystical. Understanding Nietzsche in light of certain mystics may illuminate his claim that 'Pascal's blood flows in my veins'.[46]

Conclusion

In this introduction we have not aimed to identify mystical sources of existentialist positions in detail. That will be the matter of the chapters that follow. All that we hope to have shown here is that the sources for the emerging modern understanding of mysticism and for the development of existential philosophy overlap and interact in manifold and significant ways that cumulatively construct a broad horizon or atmosphere that is relevant to the interpretation of both mysticism and existentialism. However, this should not be understood to imply that there is a single horizon or single atmosphere that adequately accounts for all the convergences between mystics and existentialists. We are dealing with a wide range of sources, each subject to variable interpretations and contextualizations with the result that their roles will play out very differently in different cases. We have, for example, mentioned that Nietzsche was read in a 'religious' sense by a number of Russian religious thinkers in a way that was much rarer in the West whilst, conversely, Augustine figures only remotely in relation to Russian religious thought. There are also individual variables that play into each thinker's relation to the mystical: Kierkegaard's Pietist background (not entirely remote from that of Schleiermacher) seems to have predisposed him toward a certain kind of passionate inwardness, whilst Heidegger's lecture notes on Eckhart, Marcel's doctoral work on Schelling, and Camus's master's thesis on Augustine suggest specific as well as more general affiliations. Each case is distinctive, and it will be the work of the following chapters to explore both variations and commonalities. But what we are persuaded of is that the theme identified by the terms 'existentialism' and 'mysticism' identifies a coherent theme within the history of ideas and within the modern experience and understanding of what it means to be religious.

Every enquiry has its limits, and one of the limits of this enquiry is that we focus only on European sources. However, it is clear that both existentialism and mysticism provided means of articulating ways in which Asian thought might fruitfully engage with and be engaged by the West, as in, for example, Japan's Kyoto School of philosophy. However, that is work for the appropriate specialists.[47]

With regard to the particular selection of 'existential' figures through whom we aim to develop our theme, we believe that this is appropriate to the topic. Whether or not anyone apart from Sartre ever really was an existentialist and whether Sartre himself was an existentialist after 1945 are the sorts of questions it is always possible to argue ad nauseam. As was stated at the start of this introduction, all significant movements in the history of ideas come in a variety of forms and often edge off into what will ultimately be classifiable as something different again. In this regard 'existentialism' is no worse off than idealism, empiricism, psychoanalysis, impressionism, socialism, or for that matter Christianity. Rather than justifying our choices by reference to a definition of existentialism that will, in any case, be inevitably contestable, we believe that the figures through whom we will develop our argument are readily justifiable as entries in the catalogue of modern existentialist thought. That each of them was 'existentialist' in a different way is not denied; indeed, it is of the essence. Naturally, it also follows that the ways in which each of them was also in some sense nourished by mystical sources will be similarly variable.

Notes

1 See, for example, 'La catégorie de ce qui est au-dessus des catégories' in Jean Wahl, *Études Kierkegaardiennes* (Paris: Vrin, 1974), pp. 404–15.
2 Frederick Patka, *Existentialist Thinkers and Thought* (New York: Citadel Press, 1962), p. 70. Patka gives special emphasis to this point in discussing Marcel.
3 See Helmut Kuhn, *Encounter with Nothingness: An Essay on Existentialism* (London: Methuen, 1951), esp. pp. 69ff.
4 See Chapter 8, 'The Outsider as Visionary' in Colin Wilson, *The Outsider* (London: Picador, 1978).
5 The title of Iris Murdoch's *Existentialists and Mystics: Writings on Philosophy and Literature* is telling. See Iris Murdoch, *Existentialists and Mystics: Writings on Philosophy and Literature* (London: Chatto and Windus, 1997) – though only published in 1997 it contains essays going back many years and reflecting her long-term engagement with each of mysticism, existentialism, and literature.
6 Likewise, many scholars are very unhappy about associating Kierkegaard in any way with existentialism, even though he is regularly seen as some kind of ancestor figure for twentieth-century existentialism, and Heidegger spoke of him in the 1920s as being 'philosophically essential' for his own investigation of the question of being.
7 See Sarah Bakewell, *At the Existentialist Café: Freedom, Being, and Apricot Cocktails* (London: Chatto and Windus, 2016).
8 For further discussion see Chapter 2.
9 Not least Kierkegaard's emphasis on action in *Works of Love*, in which he emphasizes (like many French mystics) that love is 'sheer action'. See Søren Kierkegaard, *Works of Love*, trans. Howard Hong and Edna Hong (Princeton: Princeton University Press, 1998), pp. 98–100.
10 See William James, 'Lectures XVI and XVII' in *The Varieties of Religious Experience* (London: Collins, 1962).
11 William R. Inge, *Christian Mysticism: Considered in Eight Lectures Delivered before the University of Oxford* (London: Methuen, 1899).
12 See Evelyn Underhill, *Mysticism: A Study in the Nature and Development of Man's Spiritual Consciousness* (London: Methuen, 1911).
13 See Baron Friedrich von Hügel, *The Mystical Element of Religion* (London: James Clarke, 1962 [1909]).
14 Rudolf Otto, *The Idea of the Holy: An Inquiry into the Non-Rational Factor in the Idea of the Divine and Its Relation to the Rational*, trans. John W. Harvey (Oxford: Oxford University Press, 1923); Rudolf Otto, *Mysticism East*

and West: A Comparative Analysis of the Nature of Mysticism, trans. Bertha L. Bracey and Richenda C. Payne (London: Palgrave Macmillan, 1932).

15 Friedrich Heiler, *Prayer: A Study in the History and Psychology of Religion*, ed. and trans. Samuel McComb (London: Oxford University Press, 1932).

16 Max Scheler, *On the Eternal in Man* (London: SCM Press, 1960 [German edition 1921]).

17 Gerhard van der Leeuw, *Religion in Essence & Manifestation: A Study in Phenomenology*, trans. J. E. Turner (London: George Allen & Unwin, 1938).

18 Many of the authors alluded to in the preceding notes nuanced this idea in often significant ways yet probably did not succeed in breaking the essentialist paradigm.

19 See Steven T. Katz, 'Language, Epistemology, and Mysticism' in Steven T. Katz (ed.), *Mysticism and Philosophical Analysis* (London: Sheldon Press, 1978), pp. 22–74; Robert Sharf, 'The Rhetoric of Experience and the Study of Religion' *Journal of Consciousness Studies* 7(11–12) (2000): 267–87; Leigh Eric Schmidt, 'The Making of "Mysticism" in the Anglo-American World: From Henry Coventry to William James' in Julian Lamm (ed.), *The Wiley-Blackwell Companion to Christian Mysticism* (Oxford: Blackwell, 2012), pp. 452–72.

20 Having indicated that there is scope for considerable variation on this point, it should also be pointed out that it will often be the case that this variation will relate to the particular mystics in question, as we shall see in, for example, the special role played by Meister Eckhart in Heidegger, Jacob Boehme in Berdyaev and Tillich, and Plotinus in Camus.

21 Underhill, *Mysticism*, pp. 23–4.

22 The connection between German Idealism and mysticism was already being made in the nineteenth century. Ernst Benz cites the nineteenth-century writer Friedrich Theodor Fischer as remarking, 'Have you forgotten that the new philosophy came forth from the school of the old mystics, especially from Jacob Boehme?' See Ernst Benz, *The Mystical Sources of German Romantic Philosophy* (Allison Park, PA: Pickwick, 1983), p. 2.

23 Georg Wilhelm Friedrich Hegel, 'Vorlesungen über die Philosophie der Religion' in *Werke*, vol. 16 (Frankfurt am Main: Suhrkamp, 1969), p. 209.

24 See Georg Wilhelm Friedrich Hegel, 'Vorlesungen über die Geschichte der Philosophie' in *Werke*, vol. 20 (Frankfurt am Main: Suhrkamp, 1971), pp. 91–119.

25 We note that although Schopenhauer was largely ignored by philosophers in the nineteenth century he had, by the end of that century, become a significant influence on literary and artistic culture, not least in France and, especially, in the kinds of movements to which the expression 'fin de siècle' is often applied.

26 See Cyril O'Regan, 'Eckhart Reception in the Nineteenth Century', in Jeremiah M. Hackett (ed.), *A Companion to Meister Eckhart* (Leiden: Brill, 2013). For further discussion see Chapter 1.

27 Friedrich Daniel Ernst Schleiermacher, *On Religion: Speeches to Its Cultured Despisers*, trans. R. Crouter (Cambridge: Cambridge University Press, 1988), p. 113.

28 See, for example, Stephen S. Bush, *Visions of Religion: Experience, Meaning and Power* (Oxford: Oxford University Press, 2014), pp. 26–7.

29 See Alexandre Kojève, *Introduction to the Reading of Hegel: Lectures on the Phenomenology of Spirit*, ed. Allan Bloom and trans. J. H. Nicholas, Jr. (New York: Basic Books, 1969).

30 See Dom Cuthbert Butler, *Western Mysticism* (London: Constable, 1922), p. 80.

31 See Martin Heidegger, 'Augustinus und der Neuplatonismus' in Martin Heidegger, *Phänomenologie des religiösen Lebens* (Frankfurt am Main: Vittorio Klostermann, 1995), pp. 160–331.

32 Henri Brémond, *Histoire littéraire du sentiment religieux*, tome 3 (Paris: Librarie Bloud et Gay, 1923).

33 Blaise Pascal, *Pensées*, ed. Léon Brunschvicg (Paris: Flammarion, 1976 [1897]), p. 110.
34 Pascal, *Pensées*, p. 149. Pascal did, however, immediately add that although human beings are as easily destroyed as a reed they have the advantage over the universe that crushes them that they are aware of their predicament and their fate.
35 Pascal, *Pensées*, p. 43. Quoted in the translation given in Denzil G. Miller Patrick, *Pascal and Kierkegaard: A Study in the Strategy of Evangelism* (London: Lutterworth Press, 1947), pp. 76–7.
36 François de Salignac de la Mothe Fénelon, *Œuvres*, ed. J. Le Brun, vol. 2 (Paris: Gallimard, 1983), p. 596.
37 Fénelon, *Œuvres*, vol. 2, p. 602.
38 Fénelon, *Œeuvres*, vol. 2, p. 602.
39 Fénelon, *Œeuvres*, vol. 2, p. 602.
40 Fénelon, *Œeuvres*, vol. 2, p. 611.
41 Fénelon, *Œeuvres*, vol. 2, p. 618.
42 Fénelon, *Œeuvres*, vol. 1, p. 690.
43 For further discussion see George Pattison, *A Phenomenology of the Devout Life* (Oxford: Oxford University Press, 2018).
44 Henri Daniel-Rops, *Les mystiques de France* (Paris: Corea, 1941).
45 See Chapter 6. When contemporary critic Emile Bouvier applied the word 'mystic' to him, Sartre was astonished, writing in his *War Diaries*: 'I'd never have believed that anyone would consign me to mysticism.' (Jean-Paul Sartre, *The War Diaries: November 1939–March 1940*, trans. Quintin Hoare (New York: Pantheon, 1984), p. 158).
46 Cited in Sarah Melzer, *Discourses of the Fall* (Berkeley: University of California Press, 1986), p. 1.
47 See, however, Keiji Nishitani, *Religion and Nothingness*, trans. Jan van Bragt (Berkeley: University of California Press, 1983).

Works cited

Benz, Ernst, *The Mystical Sources of German Romantic Philosophy* (Allison Park, PA: Pickwick, 1983).

Brémond, Henri, *Histoire littéraire du sentiment religieux*, tome III (Paris: Librarie Bloud et Gay, 1923).

Bush, Stephen S., *Visions of Religion: Experience, Meaning and Power* (Oxford: Oxford University Press, 2014).

Butler, Dom Cuthbert, *Western Mysticism* (London: Constable, 1922).

Daniel-Rops, Henri, *Les mystiques de France* (Paris: Corea, 1941).

Fénelon, François de Salignac de la Mothe, *Oeuvres*, ed. J. Le Brun, vol. 2 (Paris: Gallimard, 1983).

Hegel, Georg Wilhelm Friedrich, *Vorlesungen über die Philosophie der Religion* in *Werke*, vol. 16 (Frankfurt: Suhrkamp, 1969).

———, *Vorlesungen über die Geschichte der Philosophie* in *Werke*, vol. 20 (Frankfurt: Suhrkamp, 1971).

Heidegger, Martin, 'Augustinus und der Neuplatonismus', in idem. (ed.), *Phänomenologie des religiösen Lebens* (Frankfurt: Klostermann, 1995), pp. 160–331.

Heiler, Friedrich, *Prayer: A Study in the History and Psychology of Religion*, trans. and ed. Samuel McComb (London: Oxford University Press, 1932).

Hügel, Baron Friedrich von, *The Mystical Element of Religion* (London: James Clarke, 1962 [1909]).

Inge, William R. *Christian Mysticism: Considered in Eight Lectures Delivered before the University of Oxford* (London: Methuen, 1899).
James, William, 'Lectures XVI and XVII', in *The Varieties of Religious Experience* (London: Collins, 1962).
Katz, Steven T., 'Language, Epistemology, and Mysticism', in idem. (ed.), *Mysticism and Philosophical Analysis* (London: Sheldon Press, 1978), pp. 22–74.
Kierkegaard, Søren, *Works of Love*, trans. Howard Hong and Edna Hong (Princeton: Princeton University Press, 1998).
Kojève, Alexandre, *Introduction to the Reading of Hegel: Lectures on the Phenomenology of Spirit*, ed. Allan Bloom, trans. J. H. Nicholas, Jr. (New York: Basic Books, 1969).
Kuhn, Helmut, *Encounter with Nothingness: An Essay on Existentialism* (London: Methuen, 1951).
Leeuw, Gerhard van der, *Religion in Essence & Manifestation: A Study in Phenomenology*, trans. J. E. Turner (London: George Allen & Unwin, 1938).
Melzer, Sarah, *Discourses of the Fall* (Berkeley: University of California Press, 1986).
Murdoch, Iris, *Existentialists and Mystics: Writings on Philosophy and Literature* (London: Chatto and Windus, 1997).
Nishitani, Keiji, *Religion and Nothingness*, trans. Jan van Bragt (Berkeley: University of California Press, 1983).
O'Regan, Cyril, 'Eckhart Reception in the Nineteenth Century', in Jeremiah M. Hackett (ed.), *A Companion to Meister Eckhart* (Leiden: Brill, 2013).
Otto, Rudolf, *The Idea of the Holy: An Inquiry into the Non-Rational Factor in the Idea of the Divine and Its Relation to the Rational*, trans. John W. Harvey (Oxford: Oxford University Press, 1923).
———, *Mysticism East and West: A Comparative Analysis of the Nature of Mysticism*, trans. Bertha L. Bracey and Richenda C. Payne (London: Macmillan, 1932).
Pascal, Blaise, *Pensées*, ed. L. Brunschvicg (Paris: Flammarion, 1976 [1897]).
Patka, Frederick, *Existentialist Thinkers and Thought* (New York: Citadel, 1962).
Patrick, Denzil G. M., *Pascal and Kierkegaard: A Study in the Strategy of Evangelism* (London: Lutterworth Press, 1947).
Pattison, George, *A Phenomenology of the Devout Life* (Oxford: Oxford University Press, 2018).
Sartre, Jean-Paul, *The War Diaries: November 1939–March 1940*, trans. Quintin Hoare (New York: Pantheon, 1984).
Schleiermacher, Friedrich Daniel Ernst, *On Religion: Speeches to Its Cultured Despisers*, trans. R. Crouter (Cambridge: Cambridge University Press, 1988).
Schmidt, Leigh Eric, 'The Making of "Mysticism" in the Anglo-American World: From Henry Coventry to William James', in Julian Lamm (ed.), *The Wiley-Blackwell Companion to Christian Mysticism* (Oxford: Blackwell, 2012), pp. 452–72.
Scheler, Max, *On the Eternal in Man* (London: SCM Press, 1960 [German edition 1921]).
Sharf, Robert, 'The Rhetoric of Experience and the Study of Religion', *Journal of Consciousness Studies* 7(11–12) (2000): 267–87.
Underhill, Evelyn, *Mysticism: A Study in the Nature and Development of Man's Spiritual Consciousness* (London: Methuen, 1911).
Wahl, Jean, 'La catégorie de ce qui est au-dessus des catégories', in *Études Kierkegaardiennes* (Paris: Vrin, 1974), pp. 404–15.
Wilson, Colin, *The Outsider* (London: Picador, 1978).

1 Kierkegaard

Annihilation in love

Kierkegaard's knowledge of mysticism

We have seen that the development and dissemination of the modern idea of mysticism is intimately bound up with the history of German Idealism in both its Romantic and philosophical forms. Of course, for Kierkegaard, as for other existentialist thinkers, the relation to German Idealism was not a straightforward relation of affiliation but one involving significant contestation. If there is a relationship between Hegelian or Schellingian mysticism and Kierkegaardian mysticism, we can reasonably assume that the differences will be as striking as the similarities. Here, as often, we should not despise the obvious, and we might also reasonably assume that these differences will have to do with Kierkegaard's promotion of an individual, passionate kind of subjectivity that dispenses with the need to seek anything like the assured objective knowledge sought by the philosophers as well as with the religious rather than scholarly atmosphere of Kierkegaardian thought.

Kierkegaard's own knowledge of sources that could typically be regarded as 'mystical' was quite extensive. His family regularly attended the Pietist meetinghouse in Copenhagen, and Pietism played an important role in sustaining a continuing mystical tradition within Protestantism. For example, Kierkegaard's fiancée, Regine Olsen (whose family also attended the Pietist meetings), declared Thomas à Kempis's *The Imitation of Christ* to be her favourite reading. Kierkegaard himself tells us that Johann Arndt's *True Christianity* was his daily reading, along with the sermons of J. P. Mynster. This is important because Arndt himself recycled a significant amount of material from older mystical sources, including Eckhart and Tauler.

In 1843 Kierkegaard's sometime tutor and lifelong rival H. L. Martensen published a study of Meister Eckhart, including a selection of primary materials that Kierkegaard is likely to have read.[1] But we know that Kierkegaard also had first-hand knowledge of a range of mystical writers, including Tauler and the Protestant Tersteegen, as well as Catholic writers such as François de Sales, Fénelon, and Pascal, whilst Danish figures such as the eighteenth-century Bishop H. A. Brorson, whose hymns emphasized the suffering imitation of Christ, can also be credited as offering mystical perspectives.[2] Kierkegaard also had some knowledge of figures such as Bernard of Clairvaux and, despite his aversion to anything having to do with Martensen, Eckhart and Boehme as well.[3]

Kierkegaard as critic of mysticism

Kierkegaard is often seen as an essentially anti-mystical writer. In *Either/Or* the fictional Assessor Vilhelm offers a strong criticism of a mystical approach to life, which, as he makes clear, refers specifically to Christian mysticism. Although he speaks of the mystic's life as 'profound' and says that the mystic has 'chosen himself absolutely' and has 'chosen God', 'his action is internal action'. The mystic 'chooses himself in his perfect isolation; for him the whole world is dead and exterminated, and the wearied soul chooses God or himself'.[4] Developing the point further, he adds that 'For the mystic the whole world is dead; he has fallen in love with God. Now the development of his life is the unfolding of this love. . . . [T]he mystic is absorbed in contemplation of the divine, whose image is reflected more and more in his loving soul, and thus the mystic renews and revives the lost image of God in humankind. The more he contemplates, the more this image is reflected in him, the more he himself comes to resemble this image'.[5] Going on, the Assessor comments that the expression of this love is essentially prayer: prayer 'is the only language in which he can address the deity, with whom he has fallen in love'.[6] And 'Just as . . . lovers feel most blissful in [their] whispering when they actually have nothing at all to talk about, so for the mystic his prayer is all the more blessed, his love all the happier, the less content his prayer had, the more he in his sighing almost vanishes from himself'.[7]

All this could be read as positive and is in some respects not a travesty of what is said in many mystical writings. However, the Assessor's own favoured life-view is what he calls the ethical life-view, which, in his terms, means choosing oneself in the concrete circumstances of one's life in the world and fulfilling one's duty to God by taking up the work and social roles in which one has been placed by divine providence. The mystic may acquire 'religious or contemplative virtues', but he does not acquire 'personal virtues'.[8] His life is a life of withdrawal from the world rather than acting within it. The Assessor adds some further, arguably harsher criticisms: 'the mystic cannot be absolved of a certain obtrusiveness in his relationship with God',[9] nor can he be absolved of a certain 'softness and weakness',[10] and, finally, his attitude is 'a deception of the world in which he lives, a deception of the persons to whom he is bound or with whom he could establish a relationship if it had not pleased him to become a mystic'.[11] The mystic, in other words, becomes alienated from and indifferent to others, but that is not what Christianity means by the love of God since this love also implies love of others. The Assessor drives home his point with an anecdote about one Ludvig Blackfeldt.

Had Blackfeldt lived in the Middle Ages, he says, he would almost certainly have become a monk but because this was not an option in the present age, he ended by killing himself. Citing a letter from Blackfeldt himself, he takes it as evidence that mysticism and suicide are, essentially, twin versions of what he calls the 'negative form' of 'infinite freedom'.[12]

The Assessor's views cannot, of course, be taken as definitive of Kierkegaard's own – he is, after all, only a fictional character in a pseudonymous work, and many commentators view him as merely a transitional figure toward a more radical kind of religiosity. Certainly his comments flag up a concern that we do meet elsewhere in other pseudonymous works and in works published under Kierkegaard's own name. In a similar vein the pseudonym Johannes Climacus warns that the flight to the monastery cannot be a decisive expression of Christian discipleship, whilst a later pseudonym, Anti-Climacus (said by Kierkegaard himself to represent a radically Christian position) insists that the point of Christian discipleship is that it is carried out on weekdays, on the streets, even (he says) in Copenhagen's bustling Amager Square. But the concern that the mystic might be seen as exemplifying only a negative freedom or be engaged in a flight from the world does not exclude the possibility of a positive reception of mystical texts, sources, and themes in Kierkegaard's own version of Christianity, and this is, indeed, what the texts themselves suggest. So what exactly are the mystical elements in Kierkegaard's thought?

Mysticism in Kierkegaard's religious writings

The passages that have the most clearly pronounced mystical features are probably not amongst the best-known Kierkegaard proof texts, not least because they are largely from the upbuilding discourses that have for such a long time been the poor relations of Kierkegaard commentary. But they are there, and they are of a kind that would certainly merit the epithet 'mystical' in any standard use of the term.

A common theme of mystical writing is, for example, the annihilation of the ego or self as a condition of union with God, often focused in particular on the annihilation of the will. So, in the discourse entitled 'Human beings' greatest perfection is to know their need of God', Kierkegaard describes how a person who is aroused to concern about their own existence will discover that they are in fact unable to complete the project of self-mastery. Instead, they will find themselves in a situation in which the better self is pitted against another self, the lower self, but, as Kierkegaard notes, no one is stronger than himself, and neither side will be able to prevail over the other. Those who engage in this struggle for self-overcoming therefore find themselves 'capable of nothing' but 'He who is himself altogether capable of nothing, cannot undertake even the smallest thing without God's help, that is to say, without being aware that there is a God'.[13] And 'he who, on the contrary, knows from himself [his own experience] that he can do nothing at all, has every day and in very moment the wished-for and incontrovertible opportunity of experiencing that God lives'.[14] Annihilation of the self is thus the negative aspect of a positive experience of God.

This positive experience is more fully emphasized in the closing discourse from the same collection, 'The person who prays aright strives in prayer and triumphs by allowing God to triumph'. Here Kierkegaard asks 'Who should the one who thus struggles [in prayer] wish to be like if not God?' To which he replies that

> if he himself is anything [in his own eyes] or wants to be anything, then this something is enough to prevent the likeness [from appearing]. Only when he himself becomes utterly nothing, only then can God shine through him, so that he becomes like God. Whatever he may otherwise amount to, he cannot express God's likeness but God can only impress his likeness in him when he has become nothing. When the sea exerts all its might, then it is precisely impossible for it to reflect the image of the heavens, and even the smallest movement means that the reflection is not quite pure; but when it becomes still and deep, then heaven's image sinks down into its nothingness.[15]

This same image recurs in more or less identical form at the end of the discourse 'On the Occasion of Confession':

> And so we liken the heart to the sea, because its purity and constancy are in its depth and transparency. . . . As when the sea lies still and transparent to its depths, so does the heart become pure when it desires the good. As the sea reflects heaven's loftiness in its depths, just so, when it is stilly and deeply transparent, does the heart reflect heaven's sublime loftiness in its pure depths.[16]

Light, reflection, and transparency are recurrent themes in mystical literature. Strikingly, both the text and many of the illustrations in older editions of Johann Arndt's *True Christianity* play on just such images: in one, for example, we see light shining through a glass window and being reflected off a mirror laid out on a table, providing the same combination of reflection and transparency that we find in Kierkegaard's text. A similar image is provided by Meister Eckhart, cited by Martensen, only this time it is the image of a mirror placed in the bottom of a bucket of water, reflecting the sun that shines down through the water – again combining both reflection and transparency.

In a later discourse ('Joy' from 1849), Kierkegaard deploys another key figure of mystical discourse in speaking of the presence of the eternal in the moment of time:

> What is joy or what is being joyful? In truth, it is to be present to oneself. But to be present to oneself in truth, that is this 'today': it is this – to *be*

> today, in truth to *be today*. And to the same degree that it is true that you *are* today, and in the same degree that you are entirely present to yourself in being today, in that same degree will misfortune's 'next day' not exist for you. Joy is the present time, where the entire stress lies on *the present time*. That is why God is blessed, for in all eternity He says, 'Today' – He who is eternally and infinitely present to Himself in being today. And that is why the lily and the bird are joy, because silently and obediently they are entirely present to themselves in being today.[17]

Indeed, Kierkegaard seems here to be as close to Zen mindfulness as to prototypes drawn from the history of Christian mysticism (though these are not lacking).

Such passages, and there are more, offer a strong textual basis for seeing Kierkegaard as in some respects a mystical writer. Nevertheless, it might be objected that he is not simply a mystical writer. Especially, it might seem (1) that his emphasis on the difference between divine and human seriously qualifies any mystical tendencies there might be in his thought; (2) that his religious thought is radically Christocentric and therefore essentially different from a mysticism that speaks only of the immediacy of the divine-human relationship (in other words, Christian faith is never without the specific mediation offered by Christ); (3) that, connected with this, one of Kierkegaard's major contributions to the history of philosophy is precisely to have valorized the experience of temporality and the concreteness of life in such a way as to conflict with the mystical devaluation of time; and (4) that the idea of mystical immediacy obfuscates the 'demand' character of Kierkegaardian ethics with its almost Levinasian insistence on the 'command' as the basis of our obligation to love.

However, while these are all valid points – and are importantly interconnected – they can be read as qualifying rather than negating the 'mystical' element of Kierkegaardian thought. Indeed, rather than counting against a mystical reading, they open a way to a deeper and more expansive view of Kierkegaard's mystical element that coheres with major currents of Christian mysticism as well as throwing a bridge from Christian experience to existential accounts of the human condition.

We begin with the objection that a mystical reading ignores the characteristically Kierkegaardian emphasis on the infinite absolute difference between divine and human. A key text here is a passage from the 1847 discourses on the lilies and the birds in which Kierkegaard offers a distinctive and original account of what it means for human beings to be made in the image of God. In this passage he is drawing a distinction between the lilies and the birds, which witness to God's creative rule, and human beings, unique in being made in the image of God. Of course, what it means for human beings to be made in the image of God has been subject to a range of interpretations in Christian history, amongst the most prominent of which have been (a) the identification of the image with reason and (b) human beings' dominion over other creatures. As we shall see, the Kierkegaardian account of the 'image' contests both these interpretations, the latter explicitly, the former implicitly.

Again, we find Kierkegaard taking his cue from the image of something being reflected in the sea. He writes: 'When a person sees his image in the mirror of the sea, then he indeed sees his image but the sea itself is not that person's image and when he goes away the image goes too: the sea is not the image and cannot retain the image'.[18] Kierkegaard's point here is that in the external world, no one thing can actually *be* the image of another and, since the lilies and the birds belong to the external world and lack inwardness, they cannot *be* the image of God. In the world of spirit, however, things are different:

> But God is Spirit, [He] is invisible and the image of the Invisible is also Invisible: thus does the invisible Creator reflect himself in that invisibility that is an attribute of Spirit, and God's image is precisely the invisible glory. If God were visible, then there could be nothing that could be like him or be His image; for there can be no image of anything that is visible and in the whole realm of visible things there is nothing, not a single blade of grass, that is the likeness of any other or is its image: if that were to happen then the image would be the object itself.[19]

There are some extraordinary claims here that ride fairly roughshod over vast areas of philosophically disputable territory, but Kierkegaard's main point is in what follows: namely, that since human beings' essential identity is their spiritual and not their external or visible identity, then they, uniquely amongst creatures, can be 'like' God. 'To be Spirit: this is humanity's invisible glory'.[20] Consequently, it is a mistake to see human beings' God-likeness in what makes them externally and visibly distinct from the rest of creation, as in their upright carriage, their commanding gaze, or their dominion over other creatures. Instead, as Kierkegaard says

> [I]t is glorious to stand erect and have dominion, but most glorious of all is to be nothing in the act of adoration. To adore is not to exercise dominion, and yet adoration is precisely that wherein humanity is like God, and, in truth, to be able to adore [God] is what gives the invisible glory pre-eminence over the rest of creation. . . . Humanity and God are not to be likened in any direct way, but inversely: it is only when God has infinitely become the eternally omnipresent object of adoration, and humanity remains forever the one who adores that they are 'alike'. If humanity would seek to be like God by exercising dominion, then it has forgotten God, God has departed and humanity is playing at being Lord in His absence.[21]

Each of the distinguishing external features (such as the upright carriage, etc.) may witness to God in the same way as any other work of creation (such as the beauty of the lily or the bird's lack of care for the morrow) by inviting reflection on the divine power and wisdom – but that is something different from the direct relationship between the image and what it is an image of. The external witness is a sign pointing us toward God, but the image of God shows us what God is like. However, Kierkegaard's account gives a significant twist in that this showing, though direct, is also inverse, since it is only in the relationship of worship and adoration that we truly and fully exemplify our original created being as the image of God. We are not the image of God when we are, as it were, God-like through the exercise of reason or in our dominion over other creatures but only when we are entirely given over to self-annihilation in worship and adoration.

Does this emphasis on the difference and distance between God and human beings implied by the categories of worship and annihilation negate the immediacy of the mystical relation of the individual to God? We suggest not, since, on Kierkegaard's account, when we are annihilated in adoration we are immediately present to God, and conversely, God is immediately present to us in the moment of adoring annihilation. In other words, what we see here is the same basic pattern of annihilation of self and immediacy of presence to God that we have encountered in other Kierkegaardian discourses, and that is itself a salient element in mystical literature. Here, however, it is not just a question of a possible experience that each individual (or some individuals) may have. As in any Christian account of what it is to be made in the image of God, it is a matter of the essential structure of what it is to be human. In this way, Kierkegaard's theology of the image makes it possible to see the mystical moment of annihilation/ presence as offering the fulfilment of a basic human possibility. An important point to note, however, is that since this basic possibility is essentially relational, Kierkegaardian mysticism is not a matter of simple ontological identity (as when it is claimed that human being is directly participant in divine being) but of an identity that subsists solely in and through love, the adoring love of creature for creator. But this is far from rendering Kierkegaard's account as non-mystical since it reflects a taxonomic division that falls within the literature on mysticism itself: namely, the distinction between mystical doctrines of non-duality and of the entire fusion or identity of the self with God (or the Absolute) and those who see the immediacy of the God-relationship as the immediacy of love.[22]

It has been mentioned that this also has significance in relation to Kierkegaard's criticism of Hegel, although we might note that the discourse comes from a time (1847) when Kierkegaard seems to be leaving his earlier, somewhat obsessive interest in Hegel behind. The point here is this. If mysticism involves affirming the immediacy of the divine-human relation, then this is something that Hegel, too, would seem well placed to go along with (and we have noted his own positive comments on both Boehmean and Eckhartian mysticism). For Hegel, it is precisely because the God-relationship is immediately given in human self-consciousness that it is possible to develop this consciousness through the manifold of historical and conceptual mediations into the idea of absolute Spirit. From Kierkegaard's point of view, however, this exposes the fact that, in reality, Hegelianism systematically commits itself to understanding God from within the immanent horizons of human consciousness. In other words, what Hegel offers is a view based on the assumption of ultimate ontological identity, therefore excluding the element of difference that is presupposed by any relationship describable as one of love.[23]

And there is a further point. Kierkegaard's attack on Hegel in *Concluding Unscientific Postscript* focuses on the claim that the system begins with the pure immediacy of thought. But, Kierkegaard claims, what Hegel seems to have ignored is that this immediacy is only brought about by a willed act of abstraction from all the given contents of actual thought. In other words, it is so far from being a pure immediacy as to be a willed immediacy: a reflex, as it were, of a more basic intentional act. But the negation or annihilation of the historically concrete content of our lives in the world for the sake of recovering the original immediacy of being may actually have vastly differing outcomes. In the Hegelian account, we are left with a pure, indeterminate immediacy of undifferentiated being. In the Kierkegaardian account, however, there is never a pure, indeterminate immediacy but only an immediacy of relationship. On the other hand, since it excludes a relationship of adoration, the neutrality of Hegel's pure immediacy or pure Being is so far from being truly neutral as to be a veiled form of self-assertion. Not the abstraction from existential content but only the annihilation of the self in loving adoration can therefore restore us to a true 'second immediacy'.[24]

And here we make a further qualification or deepening of Kierkegaardian mysticism. If it is objected that everything said thus far ignores the decisively Christological character of Kierkegaardian theology, it is striking that, especially in the discourses from 1848 onward, the now-familiar tropes of annihilation, image, and adoration are given a specifically Christological focus. This is especially true in the discourses relating to Luke 7 and the gospel story of the sinful woman. The woman, Kierkegaard tells us, is, amongst other things, characterized by the fact that she understood 'that, with regard to finding forgiveness she herself was able to do absolutely nothing'. He continues:

> If we consider her behaviour from first to last, we have to say that she did absolutely nothing. She did not wait to go to that house where she would find the Saviour and salvation: she did not wait until she felt herself worthy. No, for then she would have long remained absent and perhaps never come there or gone in. She resolved to go straightaway, unworthy as she was: the mere feeling of unworthiness drove her in such a way that the decision to go was instantaneous. Thus she herself did nothing or understood that there was nothing she could do, and can this be expressed more strongly than by saying that it was precisely the

> feeling of unworthiness that determined what she should do? . . . She enters in. She is entirely aware that she herself can do nothing. Therefore she doesn't give herself up to the passion of self-accusation by her cries, as if that might have brought salvation closer or might make her more well-pleasing. She does not exaggerate and, in truth, no one is able to indict her on that account. No, she does nothing. She is silent. She weeps. She weeps. Perhaps someone will say that she did, then, do something. But, no, she couldn't hold her tears back – and if it had struck her that these tears might be regarded as doing something, then she would even have been able to hold them back.[25]

But she has not simply forgotten herself: she has allowed herself to become nothing, to be annihilated in love, and in this annihilation, she becomes the image of divine love, according to the 'inverse' logic of the definition of the image in the 1847 discourse.

> She says nothing, so she is in no way what she says. Rather, she is what she does not say, or what she does not say is what she is, she *is* a sign, like an image: she has forgotten speech and language and the restlessness of thoughts and, what is even more restless, forgotten this self, forgotten herself, she, the lost one who is now lost in her Saviour, lost in resting at his feet, like an image. And it is almost as if the Saviour himself saw her and saw the matter like this, as if she was not an actual person but an image. It was certainly in order to heighten the impact of the application of his words on those who were there that he does not talk to her: he does not say, 'Your many sins are forgiven, because you loved much', but he talks *about* her, he says, 'her many sins are forgiven her, because she loved much'. Even though she is present it is almost as if she is absent, it is almost as if he turned her into a picture, a parable.[26]

If the 1844 discourses could have suggested that Kierkegaard was thinking of a purely theocentric mysticism, the encounter with God is here more specifically characterized as a Christ-centred mysticism. This, of course, is by no means novel in the history of Christian mysticism. On the contrary, from Augustine, through Bernard, and through Pietist spirituality, the immediate relation of the loving soul to God is typically a relation to God in Christ. But what can this mean? Is it really just a question of dressing up an essentially abstract God-relationship in figurative guise, as in the Hegelian view of positive religious language as 'picture-thinking'? Is devotion to Christ perhaps just a means of bringing the distracted worldly soul via visualization and emotional focus to a point of transition to a more purely spiritual or non-dual kind of mysticism, the simple ontological immediacy of 'Thou art that'? And how, in any case, does such an 'inward' Christ-relationship relate to the historical testimony of the gospels or to the concrete demands of discipleship in the world? Is the contemporaneity with Christ that Kierkegaard counsels in *Philosophical Fragments* reducible to a purely imaginative, dehistoricized 'inward' relation to a visualization of the gospels? And if that is so, isn't the radical demand of the gospel then being subordinated to a purely inward and ultimately fictive relationship?[27]

These questions can be addressed and in some measure answered by turning to the third of the objections listed at the start of this chapter: namely, that to read Kierkegaard as a mystical writer is to neglect everything that he contributed to the interpretation of human existence in terms of its concrete temporality. Recall the insistence in the 1849 discourse on the 'Now' of the self's immediate apprehension of God. Of course, the existence of the text cannot be denied, but how does it square, how can it possibly square, with, for example, the earlier discourses in which patience was highlighted as the condition for appropriating a God-relationship that was temporally extended?

> Behold this day, eternity's day, it never ends. Therefore hold with unconditional firmness to the fact that His is the Kingdom, the power, and the glory forever and ever, eternally, in order that 'today' might be for you the day that never ends, a today in which you can become eternally present to yourself. So let the heavens fall and the stars change their places and all things be overthrown, let the bird die and the lily wither – the joy you have in worship and you in your joy will nevertheless *today* survive the end of all things. Consider, that even if it is not true for you that just by virtue of being human it is nevertheless true for you as a Christian that, Christianly speaking, the peril of death is so meaningless that it is a matter of 'even today you will be with me in paradise'. So rapid, then, is the transition from time to eternity – the greatest possible distance – that even if it were to involve the end of all things it would still be so rapid that even *today* you are in paradise if, Christianly, you *remain in God*.[28]

This 'now' in which the self is present to God seems not to be simply the 'now' of 'the eternal now' or T. S. Eliot's intersection of the timeless moment with time. Rather, it is the presence in the 'Now' of the eschatological moment, the moment from beyond the death of the individual and the transformation of the cosmos, and, as such, it means that the self that knows itself through such a 'Now' is also a self-characterized by the kind of future relation that Heidegger would call 'care'. Consequently, knowing oneself through a Now of this kind, an eschatological Now as we might call it, is not an escape from the concrete demands of life in time but a kind of hinge that enables the self to relate to these demands in a freedom that is not constrained by the accumulation of past causality. An example of this is already given in earlier discourses such as 'Patience in Expectation' and 'The Expectation of an Eternal Blessedness', which describe respectively how the Messianic hope of the prophetess Anna and the apostle Paul's eschatological expectation give them a power and a freedom to endure all things and to do all things: that is, fully to engage with the difficult and often bitter realities of their lives.

In this regard, it is striking that in a crucial passage in *The Concept of Anxiety* in which he spells out the structure of the moment of vision, Kierkegaard alludes to one of Paul's most definitive eschatological statements: namely, the verses in which Paul speaks of how, 'at the last trumpet' 'we shall all be changed' 'in a moment, in the twinkling of an eye' (1 Corinthians 15.51–2). Contrasting his favoured category of the moment of vision (*Øjeblikket*) with the Latin 'momentum', Kierkegaard asserts that whereas the latter denotes merely the vanishing of time, the former refers precisely to the 'fullness of time' that is, he says, an 'atom of eternity' not an 'atom of time' and, as such, 'eternity's first reflex in time'.[29] But Kierkegaard's term 'atom' is in fact a simple transliteration of the Greek term translated in most English versions as 'moment' (as above; cf. Danish 'i et nu'). In this regard, Heidegger is correct to say that Kierkegaard defines the moment of vision by reference to eternity; however, this is not the timeless eternity of the *nunc stans* but the active eternity of the eschatological future, a point that Heidegger seems to have missed. Precisely by becoming present in time, in this atom, this 'now', this moment of vision, such an eternity is so far from negating time as to make possible an experience of time that is more than mere vanishing; it is to give time the possibility of becoming the medium of a meaningful and fulfilled human life. In this regard, then, Kierkegaard's eschatology is a kind of eschatology-in-the-process-of-realization. That is to say, it is not a matter of offering consolation for the sufferings of life by looking away from this world toward an imagined future happiness (which we might call apocalypticism) but of making the promised future an active element in the now.[30]

Probably, there *have* been versions of mysticism, Christian and non-Christian, marked by a flight from time. The mysticism of Plotinus and, arguably, Augustine might seem to be of this type. This is also likely to be the case in most versions of mysticisms that insist on non-dual ontological identity. However, it is also clearly the case that there are strong traditions of Christian mysticism (and, again, of non-Christian mysticism) that argue for a sense of the presence of God in, with, and under the conditions of temporal life. What we see in at least these Kierkegaardian texts is a new articulation of the metaphysics of time that makes better sense of such a worldly mysticism than was possible within the paradigm of Platonic thought. In this regard, then, Kierkegaard's rethinking of the question of time is itself tied up with his need adequately to articulate the possibility of an unmediated apprehension of divine presence under the conditions of temporality.

But there is one last objection: namely, that a mystical reading of Kierkegaard obfuscates the 'demand' character of the love commandment. Although K. E. Løgstrup's reading of Kierkegaard is generally acknowledged to be grossly one sided, it is fair to say that he did draw attention to the Kierkegaardian account of the self as determined by its response to a divine demand that comes from outwith the self's own consciousness, from a source the self can never plumb or adequately know.[31] And whilst Løgstrup himself seems simply to overlook Kierkegaard's own insistence in *Works of Love* that this demand is only adequately responded to by concrete works of love, it is clear that this is what Kierkegaard is in fact arguing for. But, like Løgstrup's own 'ethical demand' or Levinas's call to ethical responsibility, the love commandment is inexhaustible: we will never have done enough to fulfil all that it requires of us. In these terms, then, the God-relationship is not dependent on and is not best served by some kind of direct apprehension of divine presence but solely by obedience to the divine will: that is, by a conforming of our will to God's, which can as well be fulfilled in God's absence as in his presence.

Fully to answer this objection would take us into a lengthy consideration of Kierkegaard's anthropology as a whole. Undoubtedly there are passages in which he prioritizes the will as the faculty most directly relevant to religious life – 'purity of heart is to will one thing'. But apart from the fact that Kierkegaard's call for the purification of the will is entirely in keeping with salient elements in Christian mystical writings (as, e.g., in Fénelon's doctrine of the pure disinterested love of God), it is clear that although Kierkegaard's view of the human being is often explicated in terms of traditional faculty psychology, his own existential interpretation repeatedly bursts the constraints of such a psychology. Here it may well be the case, as Brandes thought, that Kierkegaard, like Columbus, saw the new world he had discovered through the concepts and categories of the old.[32] Minimally, it is clear that Kierkegaard's account of love involves what, in the traditional language, would have been called affective as well as purely volitional elements. As in the title of the 1844 discourse on the human being's highest perfection, the impulse to seek God is a 'Trang', a drive or need, that is not entirely the same as an act of deliberative volition. Likewise, the scenario of the sinful woman and Christ emphasizes that what is at work here, in her love, is not the 'will' in any ordinary sense but a need, a compulsion almost, that is as much passive as it is active; it is a love that is fulfilled in doing nothing, being nothing, just weeping.

But this, it might be said, is not the same 'love' that is at issue in *Works of Love*.[33] So how, then, does the soul's love of God relate to the demand to do works of love?

To answer this question, I turn to another of Kierkegaard's late discourses, again on Luke 7, specifically designated as a communion discourse focused on the saying that 'little is forgiven those who love little'. Parenthetically, it is worth noting that one of the 'sinful woman' discourses is also written as a communion address, and his depiction of her in both discourses as sitting, weeping, and seeking forgiveness at the Saviour's feet resonates with the communion context. 'Little is forgiven those who love little', then.

Kierkegaard begins with what seems to be a site-specific allusion to the Church of Our Lady in Copenhagen when he comments that 'Written by the altar is the invitation "Come to me all you who labor and are heavy laden and I will give you rest"'. But while this sentence encourages a person who comes to the altar deeply conscious of their sin and need of forgiveness, that same person might well be alarmed if, on leaving the altar, they were to be confronted with the words 'Little is forgiven those who love little'. Conscious of having loved little, they might then doubt the forgiveness seemingly offered at the altar. To resolve this paradox, Kierkegaard indulges in what some might see as typically Kierkegaardian grammatical hairsplitting:

> It does not say that those who are forgiven little *loved* little. No, it says, *love* little. Oh, when justice judges, it makes a reckoning, it draws a conclusion that takes into account all that is past and says, 'He loved little'. In saying that, it declares that the matter is once and for all decided: we two must part and have nothing more in common. The saying, the word of love, says on the contrary that those who are forgiven little, love little. They love little. They *love* – that is to say, that is how it is now, now in this moment. Love says no more than this. Infinite love, how true you are to yourself even in your smallest utterance. They love little now, in this 'Now'. But what is the now, what is the moment? Quickly, quickly, it passes and now, in the next moment, now everything has changed – now they love, even if not much, but they are trying to love much. Now everything has changed, only not 'Love'. Love is unchanged. Unchanged, it is the same love that lovingly waited for them, that lovingly refrained from reaching a decision about them, forbearing from seeking to divorce them but instead remaining with them. And now it is no longer justice that by way of conclusion says, 'They loved little', but it is love that with joy in heaven says, 'They loved little, but that was then, now it has changed, now, now they love much'.[34]

Grammatical hairsplitting? Perhaps, but the point it makes is a substantial one: namely, to return us to the time structure in which the eschatological possibility of forgiveness – that is, the possibility of liberation from a chain of compulsive causality – becomes present in a 'now' that is also, in this Eucharistic context, a moment of mutual presence between the self and Christ. This moment is a moment of temporal fullness, an atom of eternity in time, the twinkling of an eye in which we shall – or can – be changed. It is a moment of lived fullness that certainly does not elide the difference between divine and human or the distance between the present 'now' and the eschatological 'time to come' but that does allow divine and human, the now and 'to-come' present – in Danish literally 'near' – to one another. As such, it is also the moment that makes it possible for us both to receive the command and to act upon it, not through sheer exertion of will but through the movement of love in which the passive reception of divine love – prostrated, doing nothing, weeping – changes our lack of love into the possibility of love.

Again, the Eucharistic and Christocentric contextualization of this moment carries forward a long tradition of Christian mystical writing. The received assurance of God's love galvanizes the human capacity for love into action. In a later chapter we shall consider Tillich's distinction between Catholic mysticism and Protestant confidence, but for Kierkegaard at least, these are not antithetical. On the contrary, 'mysticism' (Catholic or otherwise) is the ground of confidence.

But where does this leave the issue of Kierkegaard's influence on the subsequent development of existentialism – not least in light of the fact that the discourses on which we have largely based our case were so widely neglected throughout the twentieth century? Heidegger, we know, esteemed Kierkegaard's edifying writings, although debate continues as to which exactly he meant. Jaspers, Shestov, Beauvoir, Sartre, Marcel, Weil, and others probably knew them hardly at all or, at least, don't cite them. However, our argument has not been that these mystical texts were themselves a direct source for later existentialist philosophy, simply that they are integral to the matrix in which Kierkegaard himself developed an existential anthropology that would set the direction for twentieth-century existentialism. In them, we see the appropriation and restatement of long-established tropes of mystical writing but also, especially with regard to the time structure that Kierkegaard develops in them, the projection of a new metaphysical horizon in which to interpret the spiritual resources of the past. In at least one decisive respect, Kierkegaard is at this point more radical than much of the literature about mysticism and religious experience that was characteristic of the early twentieth-century science of religion. Precisely because the God-relationship is reconceived within the temporal structure of human existence, 'God' is neither thought of as an object 'out there' to be known or ineffably sensed or intuited in a moment of pure mystical apprehension, nor is God an undifferentiated or non-dual 'Being' with which the self is ultimately identified. Both the model of subject-object experience and the model of non-duality of subject and object that lie behind such views of the mystical God-relationship fail to factor in the temporal structure of existence. In much of the literature, 'experience' is represented as some kind of correlation between two essentially static elements, the self and its object. Logics of identity tend ultimately to dispense with time altogether. But the fact that Kierkegaard's mysticism places the temporal structure of the self at the centre does not mean that it is not offering an 'experiential' account of the divine-human relationship, merely that it is offering a more adequate framework for thinking about that relationship than either empiricist or idealist accounts have been able to do.

Notes

1 The book is listed in the auction catalogue of Kierkegaard's books. Available in English translation in Hans Lassen Martensen, *Between Hegel and Kierkegaard: Hans L. Martensen's Philosophy of Religion*, ed. and trans. C. J. Thompson and D. J. Kangas (Atlanta, GA: Scholars Press, 1997), pp. 149–243. For further comment on this text and its relevance to Kierkegaard see Peter Šajda, 'Meister

Eckhart: The Patriarch of German Speculation Who Was a *Lebemeister*: Meister Eckhart's Silent Way into Kierkegaard's Corpus' in Jon Stewart (ed.), *Kierkegaard Research: Sources, Reception and Resources, Vol. 4: Kierkegaard and the Patristic and Medieval Traditions* (Farnham: Ashgate, 2008), pp. 237–53. Šajda also usefully sets Martensen's Eckhart book in the context of contemporary speculative theology. See Peter Šajda, 'Martensen's Treatise *Meister Eckart* and the Contemporary Philosophical-Theological Debate on Speculative Mysticism in Germany' in Jon Stewart (ed.), *Hans Lassen Martensen: Theologian, Philosopher and Social Critic* (Copenhagen: Museum Tusculanum, 2012), pp. 47–72.

2 Kierkegaard chose a verse from one of these hymns for his epitaph: 'In a little while, I shall have conquered, and will eternally, eternally, dwell in bowers of roses with my Jesus'.

3 Marie M. Thulstrup was a pioneer in the study of Kierkegaard's relation to mystical sources. See Marie M. Thulstrup, 'Kierkegaards møde med mystik gennem den spekulative idealismen', *Kierkegaardiana* 10 (1977): 7–69. More recently, this has been a theme in the work of younger scholars such as Christopher B. Barnett, who documents Kierkegaard's reading of Pietist and other devotional sources; Simon Podmore, who focuses on the 'abyssal' dimensions of Kierkegaardian spirituality; and David Kangas, who reads Kierkegaard from an Eckhartian perspective. See Christopher B. Barnett, *Kierkegaard, Pietism and Holiness* (Farnham: Ashgate, 2011); Christopher B. Barnett, *From Despair to Faith: The Spirituality of Søren Kierkegaard* (Minneapolis: Fortress, 2014); Simon D. Podmore, *Kierkegaard and the Self before God* (Bloomington: Indiana University Press, 2011); Simon D. Podmore, *Struggling with God: Kierkegaard and the Temptation of Spiritual Trial* (Cambridge: James Clarke, 2013); David J. Kangas, *Kierkegaard's Instant: On Beginnings* (Bloomington: Indiana University Press, 2007); David J. Kangas, *Errant Affirmations: On Kierkegaard's Religious Discourses* (London: Bloomsbury, 2017). See also the articles on Bernard of Clairvaux, Meister Eckhart, Tauler, and Thomas à Kempis in Jon Stewart (ed.), *Kierkegaard and the Patristic and Medieval Traditions: Kierkegaard Research: Sources, Reception and Resources*, vol. 4 (Farnham: Ashgate, 2008) and on Johann Arndt, Jacob Böhme, Fénelon, and Tersteegen in Jon Stewart (ed.), *Kierkegaard and the Renaissance and Modern Traditions: Theology: Kierkegaard Research: Sources, Reception and Resources*, vol. 5, Tome 2 (Farnham: Ashgate, 2009).

4 Søren Kierkegaard, *Either/Or*, trans. H. V. Hong and E. H. Hong, Part 2 (Princeton: Princeton University Press, 1987), p. 241.

5 Kierkegaard, *Either/Or*, p. 242.

6 Kierkegaard, *Either/Or*, p. 243.

7 Kierkegaard, *Either/Or*. Cf. François de Sales, *Traitté de l'Amour de Dieu* (Annecy: Niérat, 1894), Book 6, Chapter 8, pp. 330–1.

8 Kierkegaard, *Either/Or*, p. 243.

9 Kierkegaard, *Either/Or*, p. 243.

10 Kierkegaard, *Either/Or*, p. 244.

11 Kierkegaard, *Either/Or*, p. 244.

12 Kierkegaard, *Either/Or*, p. 246. In the light of this negative judgement, Peter Šajda has suggested that the figure of the aesthete is actually modelled on Martensen's account of the mystic, suitably secularized. See Šajda, 'Meister Eckhart'.

13 Søren Kierkegaard, *Eighteen Upbuilding Discourses*, trans. E. H. Hong and H. V. Hong (Princeton: Princeton University Press, 1990), p. 322.

14 Kierkegaard, *Eighteen Upbuilding Discourses*, p. 322 (translation adapted).

15 Kierkegaard, *Eighteen Upbuilding Discourses*, p. 399 (translation adapted).

16 Søren Kierkegaard, *Upbuilding Discourses in Various Spirits*, trans. H. V. Hong and E. H. Hong (Princeton: Princeton University Press, 2009), p. 121.

17 Søren Kierkegaard, *Kierkegaard's Spiritual Writings*, trans. George Pattison (New York: HarperCollins, 2010), p. 215.
18 Kierkegaard, *Upbuilding Discourses in Various Spirits*, p. 192.
19 Kierkegaard, *Upbuilding Discourses in Various Spirits*, p. 192.
20 Kierkegaard, *Upbuilding Discourses in Various Spirits*, p. 193.
21 Kierkegaard, *Upbuilding Discourses in Various Spirits*, p. 193.
22 In this regard, Kierkegaard's view has striking similarities to Henry Corbin's account of the teaching of Ibn Arabi, in particular in the notion of the *unio mystica* as *unio sympathetica*, which Corbin understands as the a priori relationship established between the soul and God such that God is presented to the soul as Lord and the soul as servant. See Henri Corbin, *Alone with the Alone: Creative Imagination in the Sūfism of Ibn 'Arabi* (Princeton: Princeton University Press, 1997), pp. 130–5.
23 In this regard we can assume that Kierkegaard's response to Martensen's book on Eckhart was negative, since Martensen portrays Eckhart as anticipating the speculative consciousness realized in Hegelianism in which human consciousness gains entire insight into the structure of the divine mind.
24 However we should also note that whilst the original form of the God-relationship is found in adoration, it may equally take other forms, such as what *Sickness unto Death* will describe as defiant self-assertion.
25 Kierkegaard, *Spiritual Writings*, pp. 262–3.
26 Kierkegaard, *Spiritual Writings*, pp. 274–5.
27 We could pursue these questions further in relation to the later Kierkegaard's emphasis on imitation of Christ's sufferings. But although this might seem to move us away from the mystical, meditation on Christ's sufferings and identification with them is a major theme of Christian mysticism, including sources such as Tauler with which Kierkegaard was familiar.
28 Kierkegaard, *Spiritual Writings*, pp. 223–4.
29 Søren Kierkegaard, *The Concept of Anxiety*, trans. R. Thomte (Princeton: Princeton University Press, 1980), p. 88.
30 This is the structure that many modern commentators have seen in the thought of Paul; it is nicely epitomized in the subtitle of a recent collection of essays on phenomenology and eschatology: namely, 'not yet in the now'. See Neal deRoo and John Panteleimon Manoussakis, *Phenomenology and Eschatology: Not Yet in the Now* (Farnham: Ashgate, 2009). The basic structure is well summed up by Rudolf Bultmann in his Gifford lectures on *History and Eschatology*: 'The man who understands his historicity radically, that is, the man who radically understands himself as someone future, or in other words, who understands his genuine self as an ever-future one, has to know that his genuine self can only be offered to him as a gift by the future'. See Rudolf Bultmann, *History and Eschatology* (Edinburgh: Edinburgh University Press, 1957), p. 150. However, for Bultmann, unlike for Kierkegaard, the possibility of this gift seems to be tied exclusively to the word of preaching rather than to a direct experiential immediacy vis-à-vis God.
31 Løgstrup's work is still only partially available in English translation. For a good overview of the issues his work raises, see Hans Fink and Robert Stern (eds.), *What Is Ethically Demanded? K. E. Løgstrup's Philosophy of Moral Life* (Notre Dame, IN: University of Notre Dame Press, 2017). The relevance of Løgstrup's thought to Kierkegaard is especially addressed in the articles by Pattison, Grøn, and Andersen.
32 Although this has not stopped many Kierkegaard commentators from seeing Kierkegaardian faith as primarily a matter of will.
33 Whilst Kierkegaard has often been seen as anticipating Nygren's strong distinction between erotic and agapic love, we are inclined to agree with the view

summarized by Pia Søltoft that there is 'only one love' in Kierkegaard, although actually tracing the ways in which the love that finds expression in erotic desire, preferential love of family and friends, love of God, and works of love can be thought within a common horizon is clearly a major challenge – whether we are limiting ourselves to the exegesis of Kierkegaard or to the topic of love more widely. From a growing literature see, for example, Pia Søltoft, *Kierkegaard og Kærlighedens Skikkelser* (Copenhagen: Akademisk Forlag, 2014); Sharon Krishek, *Kierkegaard on Faith and Love* (Cambridge: Cambridge University Press, 2009).

34 Kierkegaard, *Spiritual Writings*, pp. 286–7.

Works cited

Barnett, Christopher B., *From Despair to Faith: The Spirituality of Søren Kierkegaard* (Minneapolis: Fortress, 2014).

———, *Kierkegaard, Pietism and Holiness* (Farnham: Ashgate, 2011).

Bultmann, Rudolf, *History and Eschatology* (Edinburgh: Edinburgh University Press, 1957).

Corbin, Henri, *Alone with the Alone: Creative Imagination in the Sūfism of Ibn 'Arabi* (Princeton: Princeton University Press, 1997).

Fink, Hans and Stern, Robert (eds.), *What Is Ethically Demanded? K. E. Løgstrup's Philosophy of Moral Life* (Notre Dame, IN: Notre Dame University Press, 2017).

Kangas, David J., *Errant Affirmations: On Kierkegaard's Religious Discourses* (London: Bloomsbury, 2017).

———, *Kierkegaard's Instant: On Beginnings* (Bloomington: Indiana University Press, 2007).

Kierkegaard, Søren, *The Concept of Anxiety*, trans. R. Thomte (Princeton: Princeton University Press, 1980).

———, *Eighteen Upbuilding Discourses*, trans. E. H. Hong and H. V. Hong (Princeton: Princeton University Press, 1990).

———, *Either/Or*, trans. H. V. Hong and E. H. Hong, Part 2 (Princeton: Princeton University Press, 1987).

———, *Kierkegaard's Spiritual Writings*, trans. G. Pattison (New York: HarperCollins, 2010).

———, *Upbuilding Discourses in Various Spirits*, trans. H. V. Hong and E. H. Hong (Princeton: Princeton University Press, 2009).

Krishek, Sharon, *Kierkegaard on Faith and Love* (Cambridge: Cambridge University Press, 2009).

Martensen, Hans Lassen, *Between Hegel and Kierkegaard: Hans L. Martensen's Philosophy of Religion*, trans. and ed. C. J. Thompson and D. J. Kangas (Atlanta, GA: Scholars Press, 1997).

Podmore, Simon D., *Kierkegaard and the Self before God* (Bloomington: Indiana University Press, 2011).

———, *Struggling with God: Kierkegaard and the Temptation of Spiritual Trial* (Cambridge: James Clarke, 2013).

Roo, Neal de and Manoussakis, John Panteleimon, *Phenomenology and Eschatology: Not Yet in the Now* (Farnham: Ashgate, 2009).

Šajda, Peter, 'Martensen's Treatise *Meister Eckart* and the Contemporary Philosophical-Theological Debate on Speculative Mysticism in Germany', in Jon

Stewart (ed.), *Hans Lassen Martensen: Theologian, Philosopher and Social Critic* (Copenhagen: Museum Tusculanum, 2012).

———, 'Meister Eckhart: The Patriarch of German Speculation Who Was a *Lebemeister*: Meister Eckhart's Silent Way into Kierkegaard's Corpus', in Jon Stewart (ed.), *Kierkegaard Research: Sources, Reception and Resources, Vol. 4: Kierkegaard and the Patristic and Medieval Traditions* (Farnham: Ashgate, 2008).

Sales, François de, *Traitté de l'Amour de Dieu* (Annecy: Niérat, 1894).

Søltoft, Pia, *Kierkegaard og Kærlighedens Skikkelser* (Copenhagen: Akademisk Forlag, 2014).

Stewart, Jon (ed.), *Kierkegaard and the Patristic and Medieval Traditions: Kierkegaard Research: Sources, Reception and Resources*, vol. 4 (Farnham: Ashgate, 2008).

———, *Kierkegaard and the Renaissance and Modern Traditions: Theology: Kierkegaard Research: Sources, Reception and Resources*, vol. 5, Tome II (Farnham: Ashgate, 2009).

Thulstrup, Marie Mikulova, 'Kierkegaards møde med mystik gennem den spekulative idealismen', *Kierkegaardiana* 10 (1977): 7–69.

2 Buber and Heidegger

In search of Ur-experience

The philosophy of existence

If 'existentialism' is popularly associated with Sartre, de Beauvoir, and post-war Paris, it is clear that its distinctive philosophical development was strongly influenced by the 'philosophy of existence' that developed in the German-speaking world in the aftermath of the First World War and of which the key figures were Karl Jaspers and Martin Heidegger. This was itself associated with the theological development associated with Karl Barth, variously known as the theology of crisis or dialectical theology, as well as with various radical cultural movements. But although it was seen by some of its critics as merely a manifestation of the same kind of pessimism that informed Spengler's *Decline of the West*, it also, as we shall see, drew strongly on pre-war themes and questions. In philosophy, theology, and culture alike, the foregrounding of 'existence' was explicitly indebted to Kierkegaard, above all with regard to the very notion of 'existence' itself.[1] This movement would culminate in Heidegger's main early work, *Being and Time* (1927), in which Heidegger attempted to elucidate the meaning of being by means of an existential analysis of human Dasein (human beings as we find them living in the world) in terms of an anxious thrownness toward death that demands a resolute and courageous self-affirmation and an acceptance of what Heidegger calls 'guilt' for being the nullity that we are. This affirmation is made possible by a 'moment of vision' (*Augenblick*) in which we gain insight into the ineluctable and utter temporality of existence, such that time becomes the horizon for the meaning of being. In this situation there can be no appeal to the kinds of eternal truths or eternal values that nineteenth-century idealists and liberals liked to invoke and to which some versions of mysticism claimed to offer access. In these terms, the death of God is a presupposition of the new philosophy, although, in comparison with that of Sartre, Heidegger's atheism is more guarded and, he claimed, more purely methodological (and Jaspers remained a practising Christian). Nevertheless, not only the term 'existence' but also other key terms of the new philosophy, including 'anxiety', 'the moment of vision', 'guilt', and the idea of repetition (that is, that we do not just achieve authentic resolve once and for all but have to go on freely affirming it over and over again – precisely because even this entire self-affirmation is also itself subject to time) are also derived from Kierkegaard. These ideas in turn (as we saw in the last chapter) can be seem to have a strong affiliation to Christian spiritual traditions. But it was not only via Kierkegaard that the philosophy of existence had a certain affiliation to mystical sources. To understand the fuller picture, however, we have to turn back from the third to the first decade of the twentieth century and the appearance of what can be called a kind of proto-existentialism in the German-speaking world.

Mysticism in the Tyrol

As we have seen, the nineteenth century saw a growing interest in Christian mysticism, as reflected in the growing body of texts becoming available for personal use and scholarly research. At the same time, there was an even more rapid growth in the availability of Asian religious texts, which were widely seen as mystical. This view of a 'mystical East' was promoted both by those like Schopenhauer (the first Western philosopher to give serious attention to the religious traditions of India and who used the Vedas and Upanishads to critique the rationalism and optimism of modern liberal Christianity) and also by figures such as Vivekananda (1863–1902), who offered the ancient wisdom of Vedanta as offering a cure to the one-sided development of the West.[2] As in the case of Western mysticism, this also involved a range of publication ventures that made many primary sources readily accessible for the first time, notably Max Müller's fifty-volume collection of *Sacred Books of the East* (1879–1910) and Richard Wilhelm's early twentieth-century translations of Chinese classics into German (Lao Tse, *Tao Te Ching*, 1911 and *The Secret of the Golden Flower* [English title], 1912). But the interest in exotic traditions went beyond such mainstream translations, and the foundation of the Theosophical Society in 1875 is perhaps characteristic of a period that saw an exponential growth of interest in anything 'mystical' in the widest sense of the word, from the relative rationalism of Eckhart to magic and the revivifying of ancient mythologies. Even Evelyn Underhill, a theologically well-educated Anglican and author of one of the defining early twentieth-century works on Christian mysticism, was for a time a member of the esoteric society known as the Order of the Golden Dawn. This society saw itself as carrying forward an occult tradition going back to the mystery religions of the ancient world, and its members also included W. B. Yeats (probably the best-known member) and Aleister Crowley (1875–1947), the notorious Satanist who identified himself as the Beast of the Book of Revelation. That Underhill, Yeats, and Crowley could all at some point or other belong to the same order indicates something of the range and eclecticism of interest in 'the mystical' in the period leading up to the First World War. Importantly, this was a Europe-wide phenomenon, and one can see parallel developments in most European nations. Especially influential in the German-speaking world was Rudolph Steiner's anthroposophy, which mingled mysticism and science with a powerful educational philosophy.[3] What sympathetic Christian theologians might regard as an 'authentic' mysticism that could be seen to have developed in a clear line of descent from Augustine, and other Church fathers rubbed shoulders with tales of hidden Himalayan lamas, lost teachings of ancient wisdom, and new or reinvented techniques for gaining insight into cosmic truth. What seemed like entirely different and even incompatible discourses to philosophers and theologians often combined and multiplied in the imaginations of lay adepts. Especially, but not solely, in Russia, even Nietzsche, the avowed Antichrist and prophet of the death of God, could be read as a religious and even mystical writer. As Nel Grillaert writes, 'From 1900 on Nietzsche proves to be a prolific source of inspiration in Russian religious thought. For the younger generation of symbolists . . . [he] restored the Dionysian godhead in philosophy of culture and inspired them to draw parallels between the ancient Deity and Christ'.[4]

Writing in 1926, Paul Tillich could look back at this surge of 'mysticism outside the Churches' as a 'first reaction against the spirit of capitalist society', going on to list as examples 'Meister Eckhart, the women mystics of the Middle Ages, the stories of then saints, the Franciscan legend, the Protestant mysticism of Angelus Silesius . . . Soloviev's mystical philosophy and Dostoievski's descriptions of Russian monasticism . . . the Brahmanic religion of the Upanishads and the doctrines of Maya and Nirvana . . . Buddha . . . [and] early Buddhism', and ending with Lao Tse.[5]

This ferment had, unsurprisingly, a significant impact on the generation of students attending university in the decade leading up to the First World War, a generation including Heidegger, Barth, Tillich, Bultmann, Lukacs, and many other key figures of later twentieth-century thought. After the war Friedrich Gogarten would become a leading figure in the theology of crisis who attacked the previously dominant liberal theology and advocated a return to the Bible and, in a telling remark addressed to his erstwhile theological professors, commented that 'When we heard you, we heard the best and truest of intentions, but they sounded hollow, hollow to our ears . . . We never belonged to your period. . . . We were so far from this period that we had to look outside it; Nietzsche and Kierkegaard, Meister Eckhard [sic] and Lao-Tzu, have been our teachers more than you to whom we are indebted for all our intellectual training'.[6] This remark is indicative of the way in which what scholarship might regard as utterly heterogeneous materials could be combined in the experience of even – perhaps especially – the most intellectually engaged students.

This same period also saw the appearance of what has been described as a proto-existentialist current in the intellectual life of, especially, Austro-Hungary. This was connected with the confluent impact of Nietzsche, Russian literature (chiefly Dostoevsky and Tolstoy), the 'discovery' of Kierkegaard, and, not least, mysticism, especially 'outside the Churches'. It can also be connected with radical movements in art, literature, and music. Figures associated with this proto-existentialism in the Austro-Hungarian milieu include George Lukacs (later a leading Marxist theoretician), Rudolf Kassner (who published an influential monograph on Kierkegaard in 1905), Franz Kafka, Rainer Maria Rilke, Karl Kraus, and Martin Buber, to whom we shall shortly return. Also significant in this connection is the Tyrolean cultural journal *Der Brenner*, which ran from 1910 until after the war. Its leading contributor, Carl Dallago, articulated a passionate form of *Lebensphilosophie* (philosophy of life), in which Nietzsche, Laozi, and Kierkegaard all played a part and which he came to see as a kind of non- or even anti-ecclesiastical form of Christianity. Characteristic is an article entitled 'The Triumph of Insecurity' by Dallago himself in the first year of the journal, in which he wrote that 'I understand that the man as a whole, as the one who gives measure to life, is not an intellectual being but a being of nature, a mystical being, as all nature is in its basis mystical – all the reality of nature'.[7] The journal also included articles by Hermann Broch, Georg Trakl, and Theodore Haecker and translations of works by Kierkegaard, Dostoevsky, Strindberg, and Rabindranath Tagore.[8]

Martin Buber

Although the designation of Martin Buber as an existentialist writer is in some ways problematic, he is often seen as a representative of religious existentialism, and as we shall see, the themes with which he was already wrestling in the decade before the First World War were characteristic also of the philosophy of Existenz that emerged post-war – even if Buber would then develop these in a different direction.[9] In the 1920s he would also become a close collaborator of the Jewish philosopher Franz Rosenzweig, who identified his own thought as representative of what he called 'the new thinking'. This 'new thinking' was characterized by a new understanding of the relationship between subjectivity, time, and language, and when *Being and Time* was published in 1927, Rosenzweig saw in it a further example of this same development.

Buber belonged to a slightly older generation (b. 1878) than those who were students in the early 1900s. He was already a significant literary personality by this time and knew or was in correspondence with many of the leading figures of Austro-Hungarian cultural life. In relation to mysticism, he is perhaps best known through his rediscovery of the teaching of Hasidism, but he also collaborated on a selection of texts from Zhuangzi, published in 1910[10] and wrote about Laozi, seeing him as exemplifying the characteristically Chinese mode of instruction that he calls 'Teaching' and that he distinguishes from science and law. 'Such "teaching" and formal religion both relate to the whole of life, but whereas religion displays the seven colours of the spectrum in their separateness, teaching reveals them fused in one white light', he wrote. In its purest form, as in Laozi himself, such teaching is as concealed as its teacher's own life ('the most hidden, the most lacking in any comparison') and obscure and unrecorded death.[11]

Buber would later describe his own intellectual awakening as due to Kierkegaard and Dostoevsky, and Nietzsche also played a significant role. He also studied Jacob Boehme, Nicholas of Cusa, Meister Eckhart, and Angelus Silesius – a roll-call of mystical sources with which we are becoming familiar. His own vision as to where all these sources point can be seen in a 1909 essay, 'Ecstasy and Confession'. In this essay, Buber depicts human existence as exposed to an unremitting entrapment in multiplicity from which only occasional experiences (*Erlebnisse*) of unification are able to liberate it. The highest form of such experience is given to those in whom it is the result of fervent longing. For them it is a genuine 'ecstasy' in which the distinction between the 'I' and its world vanishes. As such it is 'unification with God. Ecstasy is original; entrance into God, enthusiasm: being filled with God'.[12] This ecstasy can only be expressed in such primordial symbols as eating, fire, eroticism, and rebirth. But, as Buber was quick to recognize, this creates a problem if we want to describe or define it verbally. Language is inherently complex and, of course, we owe it much. Language, Buber writes, 'has built up the Olympus of the human spirit by laying figure upon figure (*Bildwort*)' but it cannot express unity. 'Language is knowledge (*Erkenntnis*) . . . but the living experience (*Erleben*) of ecstasy is no act of knowing'.[13] The person who lives ecstatically will therefore be alone in 'the solitude of that which is without limits'. 'We keep silent about our experience and it is a star that transforms our way. We speak it, and it is thrown out to be trodden underfoot in the market-place'.[14] In ecstasy there is no longer a 'Thou' in the 'I', but as soon as the ecstasy comes to verbal expression, 'it already speaks [the existence of] the other'.[15]

But ecstasy is not only compromised by the other; it is also compromised by time. William James had already adduced transience as a salient feature of mystical experience, and a similar insight is reflected in Buber's view that ecstasy must inevitably succumb to time. Yet, he adds, an ecstatic experience will, even as it passes away, throw into time and into the common life of human beings living in time 'the word' that is burning within it. This word is unable of itself to bring about a repetition of the primordial experience (*Urerlebnis*) or express the primordial self (*Urselbst*). Just speaking about a primordial experience is never going to be capable of re-awakening it or awakening it in others. There seems to be at least a partial exception to this, however, in the truly great religious sources of humankind (in myth, the Vedas, the Upanishads, Midrash and Kabbalah, Plato, and Jesus). In these writings the word no longer consumes the prophet in question 'but is placed upon them like a father's hand'.[16] This tangled knot of experience, time, language, and the other will continue to feature throughout Buber's long career, although from the publication of *I and Thou* in 1923, he will affirm both the other and the word as being more properly basic to human existence than mystical experience, a point to which we shall return.

Hasidism, as Buber describes it in the pre-war writings, is precisely a way of life originating in fiery ecstasy and as such a 'way' without limits – 'The angels rest in God, but holy souls step forward in God'.[17] Here, too, language is scarcely adequate, and the discourse of the Hasidim is a 'stammering' passed from generation to generation but communicable to those who share the blood and spirit of its origin. But Buber is now starting to envisage the supreme moment as something more than the primordial self-experience of the 'I'. The teller of Hasidic 'legends' does so in response to an experience of vocation (*Berufung*), which requires both I and Thou.

The transition from Buber's early 'mysticism' to the philosophy of I and Thou is clearly underway in the 1913 dialogue *Daniel*, a unique text that exemplifies the extraordinary confluence of diverse existential and mystical elements that was possible and, if not typical, then characteristic of a young cultural radical of the time. *Daniel* consists of a sequence of imagined dialogues 'On Realization' entitled 'On Direction', 'On Reality', 'On Meaning', 'On Polarity', and 'On Unity'.

'Direction' is defined as 'that primal tension of a human soul which moves it to choose and realize this and no other out of the infinity of possibilities'.[18] It is what is needed by an existing being, facing a particular choice on the horizontal plane of earthly life. 'On Reality' emphasizes the actual realization of the particular direction that has been chosen: 'power is drawn from the depths and collected and moved to action and renewed in work' (*Dan*, p. 69). 'Realization' is a unifying force: 'The creative hours, acting and beholding, forming and thinking, are the unifying hours. The hero and the wise man, the priest and the prophet are unifying men' (*Dan*, p. 72). But such men are rare in the modern world. For the modern world is given over to 'producers', to the spirit of what Buber calls 'orientation', 'crafty economy', or 'shrewdness'. Our age, he laments, 'is the age that does not realize' (*Dan*, p. 74).

The third dialogue, 'On Meaning', contains a vivid account by Daniel's friend Reinold of an uncanny experience in which he was out at sea in a small rowing boat when, suddenly, he became aware of an imminent storm. The searchlight of a nearby cruiser sweeps across the shore, and although the illumination it provides is only momentary, it nonetheless helps him to orientate himself: 'for a moment I could compose myself and *knew* all' (*Dan*, p. 86). But then the storm arrives, and the lightning flashes that accompany it illustrate a very different kind of illumination: 'Spectral stretches of earth detached themselves from one another before me in a senseless service; not like parts of a shore, but like spectral shrieks. I "knew" that they were connected . . . but I *felt* no connection, rather shriek, shriek, and in between them the abyss' (*Dan*, p. 86). This experience has robbed Reinold of any sense of security – he is, we may say, undergoing an existential crisis. 'The abyss' revealed between the fragments of landscape illuminated arbitrarily by the lightning insinuated itself into every relationship 'between thing and thing, between image and reality, between the world and me' (*Dan*, p. 86).

Daniel advises him to abandon the quest for security and to take the anxiety of his experience into himself. 'All security which is promised, all security which is longed for and acquired, means to protect oneself. It is that which is promised to the believers of all old and new churches. But he who loves danger and practices realization does not want to protect himself but to realize himself' (*Dan*, p. 92). Even more forcibly, and striking unmistakable Nietzschean notes, he tells Reinold: 'your motto will be: God and danger. For danger is the door of deep reality, and reality is the highest price of life and God's eternal birth. . . . All creation stands on the edge of being; all creation is risk. . . . You must descend ever anew into the transforming abyss, risk your soul ever anew, ever anew vowed to the holy insecurity' (*Dan*, pp. 98–9). We might think again of Dallago's 'The Triumph of Insecurity'.

The next dialogue, 'On Polarity', is subtitled 'After the Theatre' and finds Daniel in deep discussion with another friend. Daniel is trying to explain an almost revelatory experience that had befallen him as he was watching the interaction of the characters on stage.

> What I saw was the spectacle of duality. But not good and evil; all valuation was only external dress. Rather the primal duality itself, being and counter being, opposed to each other and bound to each other as pole with pole, polar opposed and polar bound – the free polarity of the human spirit. . . . What they did only unfolded what they were . . . and what truly stood in the center between them was not something mediating but the I of the spirit whose primal secret duality they revealed.
> (*Dan*, pp. 104–5)

This revelation not only concerns the way in which the actors stand over against one another spatially but also the way in which they relate to each other in language. 'The drama is pure dialogue; all feeling and all happening has in it become dialogue' (*Dan*, p. 120). Nevertheless the drama is at the same time bound together by a principle of unity, and it is to this theme of unity that the final dialogue of the book, 'On Unity', is devoted. Here Buber argues the holy insecurity of those who risk the terrors of the abyss is not (versus Nietzsche's 'eternal recurrence') an eternally repeated acceptance of meaninglessness. The experience of duality (and even of fragmentation) may seem to militate against the final triumph of a unifying horizon of meaning, but Buber proclaims the paradox that 'he who genuinely experiences the world experiences it as a duality. . . . And to overcome this tension is his task' (*Dan*, p. 136). The experience of the divided self is resolved in the courageous act of one who truly realizes his direction: 'I had torn down the eternal wall, *the wall within me*. From life to death – from the living to the dead flowed the deep union' (*Dan*, p. 135). '[W]hoever truly lives (*erlebt*) the world, lives it as duality', Buber writes – yet also as one who is gripped by the longing for unity (*Dan*, p. 136). The solution is not overcoming the world (*Überwindung*) but consummation (*Vollendung*). In the closing lines of the dialogue, Daniel intimates to his friend that death has been the true subject of the dialogue all along: 'We have all the time spoken of nothing else' (*Dan*, p. 144). But precisely because 'the deep union' flows only for the one who has become open to his death, the ultimate symbol of the fruitlessness of all human endeavour, and which we cannot in any way manage, master, or control, Buber insists that 'True unity cannot be found, it can only be created' (*Dan*, p. 141).[19] Unity, in other words, is not a 'given' to be apprehended in a passive mystical vision. Unity can only exist for us in, and through, human freedom.

Buber himself would later see *Daniel* as too mystical, and in *Dialogue*, a short work published in 1929 that expanded on the themes of *I and Thou*, he explains how he eventually repudiated mysticism of this kind. In a section entitled 'Conversion', he describes how 'after a morning of "religious" enthusiasm' he was visited by an unknown young man.[20] Although outwardly polite and attentive, Buber realized that in a deeper sense he was not really 'there' for the young man. 'I omitted to guess the questions which he did not put', he wrote. Later he learns that the young man is no longer alive and that the questions he did not put were in fact questions that could have decided his destiny. 'Since then', he comments,

> I have given up the 'religious' which is nothing but the exception, extraction, exaltation, ecstasy; or it has given me up. I possess nothing but the everyday out of which I am never taken. The mystery is no longer disclosed, it has escaped or it has made its dwelling here where everything happens as it happens. I know no fullness but each mortal hour's fulness of claims and responsibilities.[21]

From here on Buber was to proclaim only a 'worldly' religiosity, although he would equally always insist that the word 'God' cannot be abandoned.[22] Indeed, even in the philosophy of *I and Thou*, in which temporality, language, and the inseparability of the I from its Thou in concrete historical existence are definitive themes, there remains a mystical aura that is hard not to miss. This is already apparent in the motto, taken from Goethe: 'So seeking I won from you the end: God's presence in each element'. Although understanding human existence in terms of the irreducible duality of I and Thou would seem to rule out strong versions of mystical union, unity remains a defining attribute of a self capable of giving itself in and to a relation of I and Thou. Moreover, every relationship that is genuinely a relationship of I and Thou – even though it occurs within the parameters of concrete historical life – is implicitly a relation of the self to God. 'Extended, the lines of relationships intersect in the eternal Thou. Every single Thou is a glimpse of that. Through every single You the basic word addresses the eternal Thou'.[23] Thus he can say that 'Of course, God is "the wholly other"; but he is also the wholly same: the wholly present . . . the mystery of the obvious that is closer to me than my own I'.[24] Neither mystical identity nor existential duality is on its own adequate to account for the lived reality of life, and what matters is not arriving at a formula but communicating a lived event, a spoken word that is realized in the life of the individual and that is not given to us as a 'content' to be explained, interpreted, or acted upon but as 'a presence as strength'.[25]

Buber is clearly attracted by the silence of the Buddha, but he nevertheless insists that there is a fundamental difference in goals between Buddhism and his own relational thought. The Buddha can teach the unification of the self, and he showed by the depths of his silence that he knows 'the Thou-saying to the primal ground',[26] but this capacity for saying 'Thou' is falsified by a teaching that negates the very condition for relating to the Thou: namely, life in the world. 'I know nothing of a "world" and of "worldly life" that separate us from God', insists Buber.[27] At this point it seems fair to say that Buber's purported rejection of mysticism is itself the outworking of a radical mysticism in which unity does, after all, provide the context for duality and not vice versa.

Mystical terror

Rudolf Otto's 1917 study of *The Holy* was influential across the field of religious and cultural studies and gave added impetus to seeing religion as essentially irrational. Although Otto cannot himself be regarded as an existentialist thinker, his thought was extremely influential on post–First World War movements in theology and philosophy that were or were close to the emerging philosophy of Existenz, as well as contributing to the growing field of phenomenological studies of religion. For these reasons it is appropriate to mention briefly some of his main insights as part of the larger picture of existentialism's relation to mysticism.

Otto did not deny that there was a rational element in religion but his study laid particular emphasis on the 'irrational' experience of what he called 'the numinous'.[28] Where William James spoke of the 'ineffable' quality of mystical experience, Otto stressed the awe- and fear-inspiring character of the encounter with the holy. This is an encounter in which God's 'majestas' comes especially to the fore, as in Isaiah's vision of God 'high and lifted up', causing him to cry out 'Woe is me! For I am lost; for I am a man of unclean lips . . . for my eyes have seen the King, the Lord of hosts!' (Isaiah 6, 1.5). Where Schleiermacher had spoken of religion as based on a 'feeling of absolute dependence', Otto spoke of a 'creature-feeling' characterized by awe and fear before the '*mysterium tremendum et fascinans*' of the numinous presence of the divine being, a presence that is 'wholly other' in relation to all other forms of human experience and thought. Where Buber's mystic experiences ecstatic and joyful self-transcendence, Otto's mystic shudders at the overwhelming power of his wholly other God, feeling himself to be but dust and ashes. This was a view that has often been taken as prophetic of the religious situation at the end of the war, when the foundations of metaphysical, cultural, and social order were shaken and, as Paul Tillich put it, 'self-sufficient finitude' yielded to 'the abyss of Being'. In these terms, although it clearly served a very different set of intellectual goals (*The Idea of the Holy* was, after all, an academic study), Otto's account seemed to give phenomenological backing to Kierkegaard's 'fear and trembling' as a basic feature of religious life.

In a later work, *Mysticism East and West*, Otto compared the Indian philosopher Śankara with Meister Eckhart (1260–1328?) in the light of a claim common (in his view) to both that (in words cited from the Chhandogya Upanishad) 'Being only was this in the beginning, one only, secondless'.[29] As Otto expounds this statement, it means that Being is equated with the unity of all things; it is that which is and as such absolutely simple, neither this nor that, and above all predicates. It does not become, it is above change, above death; it is 'nothing, silence'. In the light of this both Śankara and Eckhart pass beyond the personal God, distinguishing between God and Godhead or between Brahman and Iśvara.

Both also agree in seeing the issue not in terms of metaphysics but of salvation through knowledge. Being is not just 'being': that is, not just a purely philosophical category but 'blissful being'; it is ultimate 'value' (although Otto comments that for those formed by modern Western culture 'to dwell within [pure being] would be both tedious and valueless'). It is not an abstract idea but the concept that embraces all others. Importantly, it is also to be known primarily through the self. Knowledge of being is 'immediate self-perception'.[30] 'This intuition is not a result of dialectic but a firsthand and immediate fact and possession of the mystical mind', writes Otto.

Yet for all the similarities between his two subjects, Otto follows the prevailing opinion that Eastern mysticism sees the world as an illusion. Brahman is not a 'living God' as God is for Eckhart. For the latter, God is 'a wheel rolling out of itself' and 'a stream flowing into itself': 'God is in Himself a living process, not a static being',[31] a comment that finds support in Eckhart's category of 'ebullition', suggesting that the divine being is continually bubbling out over itself. In this perspective, 'being' means being that is manifest in the world, and whereas Śankara's quest is homesickness for an eternity outside the world, Eckhart's mysticism has an ethical character, affirming the world, justification, grace, and love. As Otto puts it, he is representative of 'Gothic man', reflecting 'the impulse that expresses itself in the Gothic Cathedral with its vaulted roofs and towers, and its restless upward striving into greater and greater heights'.

Mysticism and the genesis of *Being and Time*

It is now generally acknowledged (as Heidegger himself acknowledged) that religion and theology played a crucial role in what has been called 'the genesis of *Being and Time*' (1927). Augustine, Luther, and Kierkegaard are properly cited as major points of reference in this development, but mysticism is also an important early focus. As we shall see, Heidegger seems to move quite rapidly away from this mystical interest, but it then seems to make a striking return in his later writings, notably in connection with the Eckhartian concept of *Gelassenheit*. In what follows we shall therefore start by summarizing the 'mysticism' lecture notes before, secondly, considering why Heidegger (not unlike Buber) abandoned mysticism for a more secular or worldly version of existential philosophy and, thirdly and finally, looking at the return of mysticism in his later writings.

In August 1919 Heidegger made notes for a series of lectures on 'The Philosophical Bases of Medieval Mysticism'.[32] These lectures were never given, and the 1919–20 winter semester lectures were dedicated to 'Basic Problems of Phenomenology'. Heidegger returned to religion the following year when he lectured in the winter semester of 1920–21 on 'Introduction to the Phenomenology of Religion' (focused on Saint Paul), followed by summer semester lectures on 'Augustine and Neo-Platonism' (1921), but these do not explicitly engage questions of mysticism.

Four years previously (in 1915), Heidegger had completed a habilitation thesis on a text presumed to be by Duns Scotus, though now known to be by one Henry of Erfurt. The topic of the thesis was, in Heidegger's own words, 'the doctrine of categories and the goal is its fundamental grounding and organic completion, which has today become one of the clearly recognized tasks of philosophy'.[33] At its heart, this is said to be a problem '*of logic as such*', but, Heidegger adds, what he will present runs counter to 'the current evaluation of medieval scholasticism and its logic'.[34] The published conclusion of the thesis expands on these comments by showing how the study of medieval thought in general might be of service to contemporary philosophy.

In relation to German Idealism, we have already flagged up how the perceived separation of ideality and reality in Kantian thought was perceived by some as a philosophical problem to which mystical intuition might provide an 'answer' by offering an immediate and therefore incorrigible intuition of reality. As in the early nineteenth century, the early twentieth century was experiencing this same problem again, particularly in connection with the problem of value and how values might be brought into relation to reality. This was, as we have seen, the quest of Buber's Daniel: how can we ever be sure that the way in which we represent the world and the value judgements we make about it really do relate to the world as it is? As Heidegger would later come to see it, it is a question as to how mental life reveals the being of beings.

What Heidegger at this point (1919) sees in scholasticism and in the Middle Ages more generally is a kind of thinking for which this sort of dualism is not a problem. 'Precisely the existence of a theory of signification within medieval Scholasticism reveals a fine disposition for accurately giving ear to the immediate life of subjectivity and the nexus of meaning immanent to it without having acquired a refined concept of the subject', he writes.[35] And this, he thinks, can help him reach an understanding of the categories that are operative in the subjective self's own immediately experienced interpretation of the world prior to philosophical reflection. In other words, it is aimed at discovering the categories that life itself produces.

In this spirit logic should not be construed as a fully autonomous sphere of mental life but, instead, must be interpreted 'from a translogical perspective', which, in the first instance, indicates the need for metaphysical supplementation. 'For a theory of truth, this means that we must ultimately provide a metaphysical and teleological interpretation of consciousness. Value originates primordially in consciousness, insofar as consciousness is a "living deed" that is itself meaningful and actualizes meaning'.[36] But what is this 'living deed', and how can we get to know it?

Contemporary culture, he suggests, answers this question by saying that the synthesis of truth and value is reached by the construction of worldviews, such as the 'Catholic worldview' or 'Scientific worldview' but, in Heidegger's words, such worldviews are never more than 'an ever-provisional summary of what is knowable'. What is really needed, however, is 'a *breakthrough* to true actuality and actual truth'.[37] And, whether or not the use of the term 'breakthrough' is a deliberately Eckhartian gesture,[38] it is to effect such a breakthrough that Heidegger turns back to the medieval world that, in his view, was unencumbered by Neo-Kantian anxieties. Significantly, Heidegger at this point sees scholasticism and mysticism as essentially identical: 'For the medieval worldview', he writes, 'Scholasticism and mysticism stand essentially together'. Both have an essential attitude of 'absolute devotional and affective immersion in the received stuff of knowledge'. Unlike we moderns, post-Cartesian beings that we are, the medieval individual loses himself in the 'matter at issue', 'the material', and 'the universal'. The medieval thinker is not a 'subject' in the modern sense and has no clear sense of method or of the 'what' or the 'that' of knowledge but is concerned only with the 'how'. Even though Scotus is a logician, he is also concerned with real life, which Heidegger sees as the thrust of the renowned Scotist '*haecceitas* [thusness]'. And whilst modern textbook scholasticism has reduced the doctrine of analogy to 'a totally diluted concept', it can be seen to have originated as 'the conceptual expression of the *qualitatively* imbued, value-laden, and transcendently related world of experience of medieval humanity. It is the conceptual expression of that specific form of inner existence [Dasein] that is anchored in the transcendent, primal relationship of the soul to God – an inner existence as it was alive in the Middle Ages with rare concentration'.[39]

> The possibility and fullness of experience that results from this for subjectivity is thus conditioned by that dimension of the spiritual life that reaches out *for the transcendent* and not, like today, by the *breadth of its fleeting content*. The possibilities of growing uncertainty and complete disorientation are far greater and even limitless for this way of life of a fleeting surface existence [i.e. modernity], whereas the basic

> development of the form of life of medieval humanity from beginning to end does not in any way lose itself in the breadth of sensory reality and anchor itself there, but rather subordinates itself, as *something in need of anchoring*, to a transcendent and necessary goal.[40]

In this way, Heidegger sees medieval mysticism as a means of approaching what he has variously called the experiential fullness and the orientation toward transcendence of the medieval outlook. Nor should we regard it as irrational in this respect. On the contrary, it is precisely a means of helping us locate the point at which the rational finds its ground in the irrational in such a way that the categorial structure of subjective consciousness reveals the life that supports and informs it.

Lecture notes

Four years on from his habilitation, Heidegger turns again to the question of medieval mysticism. 'The driving problematic' of these lectures, he states at the outset, is the 'phenomenological investigation of religious consciousness' (GA60, p. 303), although in the light of the foregoing comments, it is striking that a couple of pages later, he restates this in terms of 'religious *life* [emphasis added]': 'What basic levels, forms, movements give themselves there [in religious life]? How does this life constitute itself?' he asks (GA60, p. 305). However, Heidegger's approach is now – as was not the case in the thesis – explicitly phenomenological, and in this regard, these notes offer an early example of how Heidegger understands phenomenological method.

Heidegger's notes are, of course, just that: notes. Some passages are fairly coherent, but others are little more than fragments and sketchy outlines. In the following interpretation we have rearranged the material under three headings that we think do justice to what Heidegger is attempting but which are not his own. These are (1) The Phenomenological Approach, (2) Key Concepts of Medieval Mysticism, and (3) Medieval Mysticism and Modernity.

(1) The phenomenological approach

At the start of the notes are several pages of methodological comments, largely concerned with clarifying what is involved in a phenomenological approach. 'The phenomenological researching of the religious consciousness' that we have heard him describe as the 'driving problematic' of the lectures requires the '(negative) renunciation of constructive philosophy of religion', refraining from purely historical enquiry (also described as 'negative'), and 'tracing the phenomena that have been genuinely clarified and genuinely seen to be primordial back to pure consciousness and its constitution' (GA60, p. 303). Consequently, the enquiry has a primarily metaphysical, ethical, and epistemological character, and it is this that determines the choice of historical examples rather than being guided by historical examples that have been chosen without any clarification of what, in this case, 'mysticism' is actually taken to mean.

This task (deciding what mysticism actually means) involves a number of preliminary observations that centre on the notion of *Erlebnis* or lived experience (we recall Heidegger's 1915 appeal to 'living spirit' as the ultimate point of reference for philosophical enquiry), which at one point Heidegger glosses simply as 'life' (GA60, p. 304). However, just as we have seen Buber distinguish between the living experience of ecstasy and the language in which we subsequently speak about it, Heidegger, too, distinguishes between the lived experience of the mystic and the theorizing of what has been lived, which is mystical theology and the metaphysical evaluation of mysticism. Philosophically, however, this means that we have to clarify what is actually meant here by *Erleben* or living experience. But, Heidegger says, the aim of such clarification is not simply to arrive at a *theory* of lived experience, but (to paraphrase) the directing (*Führung*) of lived experience in a manner appropriate to life itself, and it is this, firmly distinguished from (mere) 'theory', that constitutes phenomenological understanding.

But, Heidegger asks, why should focusing on medieval mysticism help us in this task, and which particular aspects of mysticism are relevant to such an enquiry? His answer is that mysticism shows religious life as concentrating itself on 'the movement brought about by the specific lived experience of finding God in detachment from self (*die Bewegtheit des spezifischen Erlebens des sich abscheidenden Gottfindens*)' (GA60, p. 304). However, although phenomenological interpretation is not aiming at mere theory but at directing lived experience in a manner appropriate to life itself (as we have just seen), the point is not to try to awaken such an experience in the student, which is the business of religion (perhaps). Yet if the researcher is to engage the topic in what Heidegger calls an *urwissenschaftlich* ('primordially scientific') manner, then he has to feel at home (*auf echtem Boden*) with the subject matter – which, Heidegger implies, is in any case a desideratum of all genuinely scientific work. If all we are aiming to achieve is an analysis or rational account of the logical component in a reported experience, we will not reach an understanding of the experience itself – but that is just what we must try to understand. In other words, the kind of understanding that phenomenological research is aiming at is not just any old understanding but is what Heidegger calls *Urverstehen* – 'primordial understanding'.

Just as Buber saw ecstasy as an *Urerlebnis* of the *Urselbst*, Heidegger, too, relies massively on the rhetorical force of the prefix *Ur-*, implying as it does a kind of qualitative primacy. We have already noted *urwissenschaftlich*, and as he now emphasizes, it is not just theory he wants but the *Urtheoretische*, something that involves an *Ursprungs-sehen*, a 'primordial seeing' or 'seeing of the primordial origin' *within* the theoretical. Indeed, it is not just a matter of the 'rhetorical force' of this prefix, since Heidegger is clearly gesturing toward a kind of intellectual operation of a distinctive and previously undeveloped kind – that is, previously undeveloped not only by

Heidegger himself but by the history of philosophy (although, as the parallel with Buber suggests, it is also rather typical of its time). By getting back to what is truly primordial through the phenomenon of the religious life, the philosopher will then also arrive at a new and more adequate understanding of the subject, the 'I' itself (GA60, p. 306) – more adequate, we are perhaps to assume, than the 'I' of the Cartesian cogito or the morally autonomous 'I' of modernity. Buber's *Urselbst* again, perhaps!

But all of this, as Heidegger had indicated at the outset, is 'without prejudice' regarding the truth claims of mystics or of mystical theology. What a philosophical (phenomenological) approach is interested in is how the articulation (*Gestaltung*) of the experience occurs, what he calls 'the means of the ways of *Erleben* itself' (i.e. how lived experience happens), and, the means of systematically conceptualizing this experience. Medieval mysticism is a form of expressing a lived religious experience, but the philosopher is interested only in what it shows us about the relationship between experience and the structuring of experience, extracting the constitutive moments of the experience so as to distinguish it from the, for example, Thomist or Augustinian interpretations that shape the mystic's own account of his experiences. In this way phenomenology seeks to identify the motivation, the moving force, behind the experience so that it becomes an *Ursachen-Lehre*, a doctrine of the *Ursache* (normally, and not incorrectly, translated as 'cause' but here probably bearing the full implication of the prefix and indicating something like the 'primordial matter or thing at issue').[41] The point is not to achieve some kind of taxonomy of mystical experience such as Heidegger could have seen in other contemporary studies of mysticism[42] but to see 'the concrete fullness precisely in the *eidos*' and as both concrete yet also relating to 'universal experiential structures and possibilities of modification' (GA60, p. 307). In a comment that Heidegger does not follow up on in these notes but that is clearly of extraordinary significance for his later development (and which, we shall suggest, is connected with the reasons for his abandoning the mysticism project), time is addressed 'freed from its linear spatial conception, not just as a framework for constructing [mental life] but as "*Motiv*"' (GA60, p. 307). In this context, we might take this as meaning motivating power: time, that is, precisely as part of the expressive structure that will be seen when we arrive at an *Ur-verstehen* of the 'primordial thing' at issue (GA60, p. 307).

As we shall see, Heidegger does not arrive at a clear articulation of this claim in these notes, and there are reasons why he does not do so. For now, he turns back to examining 'the constitution of religious objectivity' (*Gegenständlichkeit*, not *Objektivität*), but this immediately confronts us with the fundamental challenge of the relationship between experience and interpretation. Let us suppose that prayer is the defining feature of mystical life. If that is so, we then have to ask whether God is, in fact, 'constituted' in prayer. Does God exist for us because we pray to Him? Is 'God' simply the name of the One to whom we pray? Or is God already 'given' in some way in faith or love so that the act of prayer already presupposes some pre-understanding of who it is to whom we are praying? And, with regard to addressing such questions in relation to medieval mysticism, how are we to disentangle the material from its scholastic colouring?

All of this makes a phenomenological approach to religion very different from conventional philosophy of religion. From Heidegger's phenomenological point of view, such problems as those of faith and knowledge have been simply misconstrued. The problem is not the epistemological problem of how to know the object of religious experience but of how to interpret it as it is given in experience. In this regard, both Catholic and Protestant conceptions of faith are not themselves original data or elements of faith but involve the imposition of a presumed theological knowledge onto the actual lived quality of experience. Such faith is not an '*Ur-*' phenomenon of life but has an essentially secondary character.

The same can be said, Heidegger claims, about the distinction between rationalism and irrationalism as that is deployed in the philosophy of religion. Just because mysticism is not theoretical, it does not follow that it is formless or irrational. What phenomenology engages with is not the sublimation of experience into concepts but is a kind of *Zerstörung* that dismantles all sublimated conceptual interpretations of experience so as to ground them in what primordially motivated them.[43] And, once more, Heidegger returns to the question of history and whether and how history can illuminate the question as to the essence of a given phenomenon – a Hegelian question that Heidegger leaves unanswered.

Having identified these (as yet) unanswerable problems, Heidegger turns back to religious phenomena themselves, singling out silence and worship (*Anbetung*), characterizing the latter as a twofold wonderment involving both *Bewunderung*, the admiration of what is 'higher than' me, and *Verwunderung* or amazement. Using the term that will become characteristic of his usage in *Being and Time*, each Dasein is a locus of illumination, being what and as it is through specific illuminations, calling for a 'concept of primary luminosity' (GA60, p. 312) that is presupposed in any evaluative ordering of experience.

Is what Heidegger is seeking, then, something like a religious a priori? Perhaps – but such an a priori can only be understood in the horizon of transcendental philosophy: not in psychology of religion and not in Catholic theology, which he refers to as pseudo-philosophy. In fact, we have to get rid of systematizing in theology in order to address the sphere of genuine experience and action, which is subjectively determined. And whereas he had in 1915 seen scholasticism and mysticism as both expressive of the medieval world's pre-Cartesian realism, he now asserts that under the influence of Plato and Aristotle, scholasticism forgot religion and replaced it with theology and dogma. Nevertheless, he does concede that the problem of subject and object thrown up by scholasticism led to the search for a new mystical basis for understanding the subject and that this understanding is carried forward in the notion of the ethical 'ought': that is, a determination of the subject that cannot be derived from worldly experience and that thus corresponds to the 'detachment' of the medieval mystic.

The notes indicate the intention to offer a digression on contemporary Neo-Kantian approaches, especially Wilhelm Windelband's then much-discussed work *The Idea of the Holy*. Windelband sought a naturalistic explanation of what, in religion, contravenes norms of reason – that is, the Holy: 'The holy is the normal consciousness of the true, the good, and the beautiful, lived as transcendent reality', as Heidegger cites him. But although Heidegger does not develop this further in the notes, we can perhaps assume that he would have ultimately found Windelband's construction too rationalistic (cf. GA60, p. 334) and even as moving in the opposite direction from his own phenomenological *Zerstörung*, directed as that was to the '*Ur-*' experience of religion rather than to its 'highest' forms. Nevertheless, he does later comment that, in comparison with Rudolf Otto (whose similarly titled *Idea of the Holy* seems, according to Heidegger, to beg all the key questions regarding the relationship between categories and experience), Windelband is correct to see that 'what is decisive is the principle of posing the problem in the right way and that its division into groups of problems and the methodical points of departure are subordinate [to that]' (GA60, p. 334).

The key concepts of medieval mysticism

The lecture notes contain relatively little that draws specifically on medieval mystical texts themselves, at least in comparison with the more general methodological discussions. However, Heidegger does say enough to indicate the main lines along which he approached the primary material.

Heidegger defines the mystic's relation to the world as essentially one of detachment (Eckhart's *Abgeschiedenheit*), which he sees as the primordial (*Ur-*) motivation of this kind of religious life. But the relationship between detachment and the vision of God is unclear: is the negative form of detachment the constitutive element in a positive vision of God, or is it the other way round, such that the positive relationship to God is what causes the mystic to become detached from the world? Heidegger seems undecided at this point, although he remarks that detachment is not in the first instance a theoretical category but an emotional one, though, as such, genuinely religious.

But how is the lived experience of God (*Gotterleben*) or what mystics call mystical birth in God (*Gottesgeburt*) constituted? For the mystics themselves, he suggests, their experience of this divine birth presupposed the incapacity of nature and required a humble *Gelassenheit*, a term to which Heidegger will return many years later. All of this raises questions as to agency, such as how far mystical experience is to be ascribed to the sole agency of God working in the soul and how far divine grace is co-operant with the soul. In either case, Heidegger asserts that mystical experience precedes faith, a claim that, historically, is warranted by Luther's own formation in late medieval mysticism. Both in medieval mysticism and in Luther, humility and tribulation are the 'expression of personal certainty of salvation'.

Seen in this way, religious experience is manifest in such 'basic forms' of religion as revelation, tradition, and community. And, again, Heidegger pauses to comment on what is distinctive about a phenomenology of religion. What phenomenology seeks is an ontology of religion: it is 'no high-falutin religious philosophy' but an attempt to understand what happens at the very origins (*die echten Anfänge*) of religious life (GA60, p. 309). Although, as we have seen, the phenomenologist has to have a certain hermeneutic sympathy with the religious person, this does not mean that the phenomenologist has the same experience as such a person. What phenomenology is aiming at is not experience itself but an 'absolute view' (*Schau*) of that experience. For the religious person, on the other hand, 'life produces only life', and no external view on life is called for.

In these terms, Eckhart describes religious experience as immediate, as the uninhibited life of devotion to the holy, which, Heidegger says, is a historically distinct and new approach to what is at issue in the Christian life. What is decisive here is not that Eckhart added a new layer of theory but that he radically excluded reference to all particularities from the form of religious experience: the primordial object (*Urgegenstand*) of this experience is utterly without determination or specification (*bestimmungslos*). This detachment from the specificity of the experience in question leads to new insights into the nature of the 'I'. For if like can only be known by like, the same must hold true for the soul: it must be detached from everything that is multiple, so that subject and object may be united: I am it and it is I. As Heidegger will say, this also has an ethical aspect in that it countermands the restlessness of the soul. God and the ground of the soul are alike nameless, and there is no contradiction between them. There is not even a question as to whether intellect or will is primary since the ground of the soul is prior to the separation of willing and knowing. And (versus Windelband) it has nothing to do with the good, the true, and the beautiful. Even the distinction between realist and nominalist breaks down: Eckhart is an extreme realist, but he is atheoretical, and the living subject is the driving force of the mystical theoretical construction. The object is the highest value, but it is the highest value only for the mystical subject and not in itself. The one who is detached from contradictions knows the object without contradictions. Likewise, the eternal now of mystical experience means detachment from the multiplicity of time and place. The form of objectness as such without attributes is the absolute object: God-in-the-soul/the-soul-in-God 'as such'.

Medieval mysticism and modernity

Heidegger's notes do not account for the reasons behind his transitions from one subject to the next, but having focused on medieval mysticism, he now turns to Schleiermacher. Thinking back to the contrast between the medieval and modern worlds given in the conclusion of the Scotus thesis, it seems that Heidegger's implicit question here is whether such an experience and such a view are possible within modernity. For as he sees it, modernity is marked by the constant interaction of multiple worldviews, making it hard to hold fast to what is essential. Religion is seen either as a kind of theory or as a kind of practice: that is, in terms of its value for metaphysics or morals, and in both of these forms its distinctive sui generis nature is challenged. Schleiermacher (and Heidegger refers specifically to the second of the speeches *On Religion*) rightly sees the need to separate religion from these and focus on what is exclusive to it, thus paralleling the phenomenological *epochē*.[44]

'Piety', as Schleiermacher understands it, is not interested in 'knowing' God: piety wants only to withdraw from contemplation of the external in order to develop the inner sense and taste for the infinite. Infinite Being is not experienced conceptually but 'in the innermost sanctuary of life' where we find an 'original relation of feeling and intuition'. Everything individual is experienced in its uninterrupted continuity with the whole. The noetic moment is constitutive of the noematic 'total content of experience' (*Gesamtgehalt des Erlebens*). There is no privileged object of religion, but it is most fully realized in a living community of individuals as a holy music accompanying life.

The notes suggest that the discussion of Eckhart and Schleiermacher is to bring Heidegger to a position from which he can develop a more overarching account of the 'phenomenology of the religious *Erlebnis* and religion' in which he will discuss 'the typical forms and developed figures of religious life and historical consciousness' (GA60, p. 322). As both Eckhart and Schleiermacher suggest, religion has an entirely original and unique intentionality that can only be grasped from the perspective of the religious consciousness itself: it is totality rather than universality. Integral to this religious experience is historicity; that is, it is historically lived and only as historically lived is it meaningful (*Sinn*). If faith is *Vertrauen* (*fiducia*, not 'belief'), then it can only be understood by a phenomenological approach that focuses on the essence or *Wesen* – though not in the sense of some supra-historical essence but rather as an essence that is actual only in the reality of lived historical life. Only a phenomenology that holds fast to the 'radical moment of origin (*Ursprung*)' and refrains from theorizing its founding intuition or rationalizing the concept of essence in terms of universal validity can, Heidegger claims, answer to this philosophical need.

If faith in this sense is constitutive for the religious understanding of God, then God qua absolute cannot be adequately understood as 'the highest value' since the Absolute itself has to be understood in terms of its historicity as that is disclosed by phenomenological enquiry. Here, Heidegger finds inspiration in the work of Adolf Reinach, an *Assistent* of Edmund Husserl, who had been killed in the war. Reinach, as Heidegger notes, speaks of 'inwardly motivated transitions in the lived experience of diverse absolutes . . . in contrast to the usual logical development of these from each other' (GA60, p. 326). This presupposes what Reinach calls '[kinds of] knowledge that are immanent to lived experience' (GA60, p. 326). In the case of God, this is the feeling of being hidden (*Geborgensein*) in God, which he (Reinach) also glosses as 'the lived experience of an absolute dependence on God'. But this immanent knowledge is neither logical nor knowledge of a fact (*Tatsache*). Heidegger finds this very significant, but he remarks that this only brings us to the point at which the analysis needs to begin.

This leads Heidegger next to Hegel, noting the decisive Kantian element in Hegel's 'early theological writings' (then only relatively recently published for the first time). But precisely this Kantian element excluded a primary relation to the holy since it sees religion solely as a means to morality and Jesus as a teacher of morality. This reduction of religion as a means to a nonreligious end remains decisive for Hegel's whole approach to religion. And, Heidegger's notes imply, this is not unconnected to the limitations in Hegel's idea of the historical although (the notes are ambiguous here) this may also have to do with how, in Hegel (or perhaps for us, reflecting on Hegel), the historical becomes a philosophical question in its full originality (*Ursprünglichkeit*).

After two brief paragraphs on Hegel, Heidegger turns to a series of short discussions entitled 'Problems', 'Faith', and 'Piety/Faith cf. Psalms of Confidence', before returning again to Schleiermacher. These sections reprise questions with which we are by now familiar. Lived religious experience can only occur in historically specific lifeworlds – but how do these inform and how are they informed by that lived experience itself? Similarly, how is the *Urdoxa* (which Heidegger does not explain but which we may take to be the primordial lived experience of faith) modified in any given articulation of faith? Or how can the lived experience of waiting on God to which the psalms bear witness be related to the then-current *Religion in Geschichte und Gegenwart* definition of faith as 'the distinctive mythical-symbolic-practical religious forms of thought and knowledge, proceeding from historical personal impressions, believing in the [communal] myth for the sake of the practical religious powers dependent on [that myth] and that is only capable of articulating these powers, representing them and communicating them through that myth' (GA60, pp. 329–30). Heidegger is highly critical of this definition, although he scarcely discusses it, but we can now easily see how it fails to address what he sees as the main problem, namely, how an articulated view of faith (whether the Israelite's faith in Yahweh or the Greeks' faith in their manifold deities or the mystic's ascription of his experiences to divine grace) relates to the immediacy of lived experience.

Coming back to Schleiermacher, Heidegger asks (again): if piety is a determination of feeling or immediate self-consciousness, what is its *Sinn*-moment: that is, what makes it meaningful or (in the language of William James, to whom Heidegger does not refer) how does it acquire noetic content? The self, Heidegger says, is not a tabula rasa but has a certain orientation toward sense; religious life precedes the interpretation of life as religious as we have seen. However, although Schleiermacher's second speech aims precisely to raise awareness of this lived moment prior to the separation of feeling and intuition, the feeling of absolute dependence on God that his later theology develops is already an overinterpretation, objectifying what is given in primordial experience in the direction of a theory of Being (*Seinsteoretisk*). Why should the unknown on which we experience ourselves as dependent be identified with God? Instead of such a theological interpretation, what we need to find is the structure on the soul that allows for possibilities of fulfilment of various kinds. But such a fulfilment, qua historical, is not the pure reflection of the transcendental ego. It is the *Urform der Geöffnetheit für Wertvolles überhaupt* – the primordial form of openness toward whatever has value as such. Schleiermacher is right to reject Fichte's account of the 'I' as constituting itself through its own self-positing activity, but his own counterclaim that it is God who calls us is unwarranted by the phenomenological data. Schleiermacher reveals that the I exists as 'called' (a theme that will be of abiding concern to Heidegger's ongoing philosophical work).[45] Calling reveals the possibility of a form of consciousness that is both historical and fulfilled and that can only be understood from the perspective of a living consciousness. A concluding section on Saint Bernard, beginning with the abbot's exhortation that today we are to read in the book of experience (*Hodie legimus in libro experientiae*), returns us yet again to the persistent question that runs through the notes: 'Life as religious is already there', so what is the 'I' that it can always already find itself constituted in just this way and without having constructed itself as such?

The limits of mysticism

Why did Heidegger not go through with this lecture project? His own correspondence with the university suggests a lack of time, although Kisiel suggests that it was also likely to have involved the difficulty of resolving the questions he had set himself in them.[46] Yet there was, we suggest, another and in some ways simpler reason. One of the guiding questions for Heidegger was the question of the relationship between the given yet changing historical forms in which thinking is developed (Platonism, Aristotelianism, scholasticism, etc.) and the essentiality at which thinking aims. He seeks to address this question by tracing the historical form, in this case textual attestation to mystical experience, back to the primordial lived experience out of which it emerges. As we have seen, this is a view of mysticism that has been widely challenged since the 1970s, but in this regard Heidegger seems to be very much a man of his own generation, sharing the same kind of view as to the relationship between lived experience and theoretical understanding that we encountered in Buber. But, as for Buber (yet even more emphatically), there seems to be a tension between what mystical experience wants to claim regarding immediate union with the eternal and the ineluctable human experience of time. No matter how primordial, mystical experience is experience in which the subject's own experience of himself as a temporal being is radically occluded.

Heidegger himself seems never to have commented on this shortcoming in mystical literature. It is, however, telling that when he does return to religion in the 1920–21 lectures on Paul, it is precisely to texts that place the apostle's temporal experience of (as Heidegger interprets it) living in a time of tribulation between the crucifixion and the Parousia. In these lectures, Heidegger will interpret Pauline Christianity as the lived experience (now called the *faktische Lebenserfahrung*)[47] of time as such (GA60, pp. 67–125). 'Mysticism', then, enabled Heidegger to take a significant step beyond the impasse of Neo-Kantianism, even if it did not enable him to take the next step of relocating transcendence itself in time. In these terms, his criticism of Schleiermacher for pre-empting the outcome of a deeper enquiry into the 'Whence' of our being by naming this 'Whence' as 'God' identifies the point at which his own account of this "Whence' will be directed: namely, the account of Dasein as thoroughly temporalized thrownness toward death. In relation to this, Heidegger's insistence on avoiding interpreting time by means of its relation to eternity becomes a distinctive feature of the de-theologizing of those same theological sources that he acknowledged as 'philosophically essential'. It is the same point perhaps that lies behind the footnote in *Being and Time* in which Heidegger criticizes Kierkegaard for interpreting the moment of vision, the primordial experience of time, by reference to eternity.[48]

A mysticism of time-experience?

Our focus here has been on the way in which Heidegger's early preoccupation with medieval mysticism helped contribute to the genesis of *Being and Time*. But although that work would prove definitive of the 1920s' philosophy of existence (Existenz) and as such foundational for the future development of existentialism as a whole, Heidegger himself was always wary of being associated with philosophical fashions and, by the mid-1930s, most commentators agree that his philosophy had taken a very different turn – albeit one that retains considerable continuity with his earlier thought. He himself responded to Sartre's *Existentialism and Humanism* by the 1946 'Letter on "Humanism"', published in 1947. (It originally really was a letter to the French Heideggerian Jean Beaufret, although doubtless also intended for publication.) Here Heidegger made clear the distance between Sartre's emphasis on subjectivity and his own increasing orientation toward the primacy of being. As he writes, 'Only as far as the human being, ek-sisting into the truth of being, belongs to being can there come from being the assignment of those task that must become rule and law for human beings' – a statement that would be quite impossible on Sartrean assumptions.[49] Yet if there is clearly a sense in which the later Heidegger no longer belongs to the history of existentialism, it is interesting to us that in his end as in his beginnings Heidegger returns to a number of mystical motifs, drawing again on, especially, Meister Eckhart and Angelus Silesius.

Perhaps the best known and most striking example of this is his use of the Eckhartian term *Gelassenheit*, the subject of a lecture-cum-book published in 1959. The term is notoriously difficult to translate, sometimes appearing in English as 'releasment', since it relates not just to an attitude of letting-be but one in which we ourselves are 'let be' as a precondition of being able to let be. Heidegger sees in this a striking alternative to the attitude typified in contemporary technology. The technocrat manifests a kind of will to power in which the natural and human world is turned into an arsenal of resources that are to serve the needs of (supposedly) rational planning. Research carried out under the presuppositions of this technocratic mind-set is not research that deepens itself in a field in such a way as to become exposed to the possibility of experiencing something radically new. Instead, research is a matter of setting up a project that is to have predictable outcomes serving preprogrammed aims and objectives. The world, other human beings, and even our own bodies are turned into an ensemble of instruments to be honed into maximum serviceability for these same aims and objectives. *Gelassenheit*, by way of contrast, is being 'Let be towards things and openness to the secret', which Heidegger construes as essentially two sides of the same coin.[50] It does not seem that Heidegger imagines this to involve any mystical experience as such, yet the resulting orientation toward self and world seems to be very similar to Eckhartian detachment. However, whether this 'return' is to be interpreted as ultimately secularizing the idea of the mystical or as itself a kind of turn to mysticism is contestable.[51]

Angelus Silesius is the nom de plume of a seventeenth-century Catholic convert (Johannes Scheffler) who published a series of mystical verses under the title 'The Cherubic Wanderer'. Although verging on doggerel in literary terms, these verses give radical and startling expression to mystical themes of the interdependence of divine and human. Amongst the most vivid is the couplet 'I know that without me, God cannot live a single moment./ If I become nothing, he needs must give up the ghost'.

Heidegger turns to Angelus Silesius in a series of lectures on Leibnitz's principle of sufficient reason (*der Satz vom Grunde*) in 1955–56. According to this principle, nothing exists without there being a sufficient reason for its existence such that the task of science becomes the discovery and explication of this reason. In contrast to this, Heidegger finds Angelus Silesius stating that 'The rose is without why: it blooms because it blooms,/ It pays no attention to itself, asks not whether it is seen'.[52] This, we might say, is a perfect exemplification of Eckhartian *Gelassenheit*.[53] In any case, it serves Heidegger, both here and elsewhere, to show that the imperatives of technocratic reason are not the only option for human thinking. Thinking without a why is also possible.

That this connects with questions regarding the nature of religious consciousness is made clear in Heidegger's 1964 response to questions from a conference held at Drew University (New Jersey) in that year, addressing

'The Problem of a Nonobjectifying Thinking and Speaking in Today's Theology'. Heidegger does not cite Angelus Silesius directly, but the rose that blooms without a why seems to be present in his most extended example of what nonobjectifying thinking might be.

> Our everyday experience of things, in the wider sense of the word, is neither objectifying nor a placing over against. When, for example, we sit in the garden and take delight in a blossoming rose, we do not make an object of the rose, nor do we even make it something standing over against us in the sense of something represented thematically. When in tacit saying we are enthralled with the lucid red of the rose and muse on the redness of the rose, then this redness is neither an object nor a thing nor something standing over against us like the blossoming rose. The rose stands in the garden, perhaps sways to and fro in the wind. But the redness of the rose neither stands in the garden nor can it sway to and fro in the wind. All the same we think it and tell of it by naming it. There is accordingly a thinking and saying that in no manner objectifies or places things over against us.[54]

Heidegger makes the theological application of this clear with a second example, immediately following the discussion of the rose. This time it concerns a statue of Apollo that, as he says, can perfectly well be treated as an object of scientific representation. 'But this objectifying thinking and speaking does not catch sight of the Apollo who shows forth his beauty and so appears as the visage of the god'.[55] Thus he at least hints at the possibility of kinds of perception other than those employed in scientific analysis that seem in principle to allow for the appearing of divinity – mystical perception, perhaps?

Nevertheless, whatever sense of 'mystical' the later Heidegger might allow, he never renounces the insight of *Being and Time* that time sets the horizon for anything that can be humanly meaningful. Perhaps the closest he comes to accepting some value in the notion of the eternal comes in comments on the poetic imagery of the seventeenth-century preacher Abraham à Sancta Clara, who, like Heidegger, came from the Black Forest town of Messkirch. It is a quotation he describes as 'perhaps the most astonishing and beautiful poetic word-picture' left us by the preacher: 'Come hither, you silver-white swans, who, with your snow-defying wings, row round and about upon the water', to which he appends the further quotation, 'Do you not know that human life is like snow and clover, neither of which abide'.[56] But what does this juxtaposition of images mean? Heidegger's answer is as follows. We all know, he says, that snow will melt on water; yet, in the snow-white plumage of the swan, the preacher gives us an image of the transience of human life counterintuitively ('snow-defying') maintained in being as it moves on the surface of the water, itself a pure and universal image of temporal flux. In other words, the swan is a 'word-picture' of what abides in the midst of temporal change. In Heidegger's words, 'The movement of the white swans on the water is an image for what does not pass away in the midst of what passes away'.[57]

We are now perhaps a long way from existentialism, yet such an eternal consciousness would seem not to conflict with existentialism's defining acceptance of the encompassing ineluctability of time and death – although it certainly registers a very different view of what it is to be human from that which we find in *Being and Nothingness*. Watching the swans, pondering the poet's word-picture of their movement across the water, we are let be in the midst of things, open and receptive to the world and freed from remaking that world in the image of our own will. Perhaps we are as far from classic mysticism as we are from existentialism, but it is a view that has roots both in mysticism and in the philosophy of existence.

Notes

1 See Werner Brock, *An Introduction to Contemporary German Philosophy* (Cambridge: Cambridge University Press, 1935), pp. 72–86. Brock had been Heidegger's *Assistent*, but due to his Jewish origins left Germany after the Nazi rise to power. Heidegger himself will emphasize that the German *Existenz* has a different meaning from the Latin *existentia*, referring not to the fact that something (a tree, a cup, an atom) exists but to the distinctively human experience of existing.

2 It is worth noting that Vivekananda, like some other popularizers of Asian religions, including Iqbal and, later, D. T. Suzuki, had himself studied Western philosophy, especially in its nineteenth-century idealist variant.

3 On Franz Kafka's interest in anthroposophy see June O. Leavitt, *The Mystical Life of Franz Kafka: Theosophy, Cabala, and the Modern Spiritual Revival* (Oxford: Oxford University Press, 2012). Leavitt's subtitle is indicative of the Central European milieu in which interest in mysticism flourished in these years. Although Kafka was never a philosophical existentialist, his writings are often seen as exemplifying existential themes of anxiety, dread, and the absurd as well as an interest in fragmentary and altered states of consciousness.

4 See Nel Grillaert, *What the God-Seekers Found in Nietzsche: The Reception of Nietzsche's Übermensch by the Philosophers of the Russian Religious Renaissance* (Amsterdam: Rodopi, 2008), p. 36.

5 Paul Tillich, *The Religious Situation*, trans. H. Richard Niebuhr (New York: Meridian, 1956), pp. 161–3.

6 Friedrich Gogarten, 'Between the Times' in James Robinson (ed.), *The Beginnings of Dialectic Theology* (Richmond, VA: John Knox Press, 1968), pp. 277–8.

7 Carl Dallago, 'Der Triumph der Unsicherheiten', *Der Brenner* 1.2(18) (15 February 1911): 519. The title of the article also indicates Dallago's proximity to aspects of existentialist thought.

8 After the war it became rather more conventionally Catholic in orientation, with a lot of space given to John Henry Newman.

9 For Buber as existentialist, see Will Herberg, *Four Existentialist Theologians: A Reader from the Works of Jacques Maritain, Nicolas Berdyaev, Martin Buber, and Paul Tillich* (New York: Doubleday, 1958).

10 Martin Buber, *Reden und Gleichnisse des Tschuang-Tse* (Leipzig: Insel, 1910).

11 Martin Buber, *Die Rede, die Lehre und das Lied* (Leipzig: Insel, 1920), p. 58. In a three-part article on 'The Soul of the Far East', Dallago uses Buber to defend the essentially personalist character of the East against the views of Lafcadio Hearn, a then-fashionable writer on the East who became a naturalized Japanese citizen. See Carl Dallago, 'Die Seele des fernen Asiens' *Der Brenner* 1.2(20) (15 March 1911): 567–77, 1.2(21) (1 April 1911): 599–610, and 1.2(22) (15 April 1911): 631–42.

12 Buber, *Die Rede*, p. 18.
13 Buber, *Die Rede*, p. 22.
14 Buber, *Die Rede*, p. 24.
15 Buber, *Die Rede*, p. 26. These comments about language and ecstasy/mysticism reflect issues to the fore in other contemporary writers such as the novelist and theorist of language Fritz Mauthner and the anarchist mystic and Eckhart-translator Gustav Landauer, who was murdered in the aftermath of the Munich Soviet and whose letters Buber would edit.
16 Buber, *Die Rede*, p. 33.
17 Buber, *Die Rede*, p. 4.
18 Martin Buber, *Daniel: Dialogues on Realization*, trans. M. Friedman (New York: McGraw-Hill, 1965), p. 55. Further references are given as *Dan* in the text, followed by page number.
19 The motif of openness to death will also become a major theme of Heidegger's *Being and Time*.
20 In Martin Buber, *Between Man and Man*, trans. R. G. Smith (London: Fontana, 1961), p. 31.
21 Buber, *Between Man and Man*, pp. 31–2.
22 See Martin Buber, *The Eclipse of God* (London: Gollancz, 1953), pp. 15–18.
23 Martin Buber, *I and Thou*, trans. W. Kaufmann (Edinburgh: T. & T. Clark, 1970), p. 123.
24 Buber, *I and Thou*, p. 127.
25 Buber, *I and Thou*, p. 158.
26 Buber, *I and Thou*, p. 140.
27 Buber, *I and Thou*, p. 143.
28 See Rudolf Otto, *The Idea of the Holy*, trans. J. W. Harvey (Oxford: Oxford University Press, 1923).
29 Rudolf Otto, *Mysticism East and West: A Comparative Analysis of the Nature of Mysticism*, trans. Bertha L. Bracey and Richenda C. Payne (New York: Palgrave Macmillan, 1932), p. 4.
30 Otto, *Mysticism East and West*, p. 34.
31 Otto, *Mysticism East and West*, p. 170.
32 The notes are found in Vol. 60 of the collected works. See Martin Heidegger, *Phänomenologie des religiösen Lebens* (Frankfurt am Main: Vittorio Klostermann, 1995). Further references will be given as GA60 in the text. The apparatus to the *Gesamtausgabe* might seem to imply that what was being planned was a single lecture (see p. 348), although Kisiel treats the material as notes for a lecture series – see Theodor Kisiel, *The Genesis of Heidegger's Being and Time* (Berkeley: University of California Press, 1993), pp. 76–7, 108–11. Apart from other considerations, the scope and complexity of the notes seem to support the latter hypothesis.
33 Theodore Kisiel and Thomas Sheehan, *Becoming Heidegger: On the Trail of His Early Occasional Writings, 1910–1927* (Evanston, IL: Northwestern University Press, 2007), p. 77. For a fuller exposition see George Pattison, 'The Role of Mysticism in the Formation of Heidegger's Phenomenology' in David Lewin, Simon D. Podmore, and Duane Williams (eds.), *Mystical Theology and Continental Philosophy: Interchange in the Wake of God* (London: Routledge, 2017), pp. 131–46.
34 Kisiel and Sheehan, *Becoming Heidegger*, pp. 77–8.
35 Kisiel and Sheehan, *Becoming Heidegger*, p. 80.
36 Kisiel and Sheehan, *Becoming Heidegger*, p. 82.
37 Kisiel and Sheehan, *Becoming Heidegger*, p. 82.
38 Kisiel hints at the link between the philosophical and mystical sense of 'break-through' in Heidegger. See Kisiel, *Genesis*, pp. 102–3.

39 Kisiel and Sheehan, *Becoming Heidegger*, p. 84.
40 Kisiel and Sheehan, *Becoming Heidegger*, pp. 84–5.
41 There is very possibly also an allusion to Husserl's definition of phenomenology as attention to *die Sachen selbst*, 'the things themselves', now outbid by Heidegger as he wants to move beyond even the *Sachen* to the *Ur-Sache*, the primordial 'thing'.
42 Such as those of William James or Rudolf Otto.
43 We might compare this with the idea of a philosophical *Destruktion* of concepts that Heidegger will propose in *Being and Time* as a way of bringing philosophical concepts back into relation to the being that they are 'about'.
44 On Heidegger's interest in this speech, see Kisiel and Sheehan, *Becoming Heidegger*, pp. 86–91; see also Alexander S. Jensen, 'The Influence of Schleiermacher's Second Speech on Religion on Heidegger's Concept of Ereignis' *The Review of Metaphysics* 61(244) (June 2008): 815–26.
45 See, for example, Gertrud Heidegger (ed.), *"Mein liebes Seelchen!" Briefe Martin Heideggers an seine Frau Elfride 1915–1970* (Münich: Deutsche Verlags-Anstalt, 2005), p. 87. For further discussion see George Pattison, *Heidegger on Death: A Critical Theological Essay* (Farnham: Ashgate, 2013), pp. 129–45.
46 Kisiel, *Genesis*, p. 111.
47 This formulation evidences Heidegger's continuing desire to distance himself from the 'philosophies of life' that in his view lacked philosophical rigour. At the same time it also reveals his proximity to that same *Lebensphilosophie* orientation that we saw in Buber.
48 See Martin Heidegger, *Being and Time*, trans. J. Macquarrie and E. Robinson (Oxford: Blackwell, 1962), p. 497 (n. iii on p. 338 of the German text). For further discussion see George Pattison, *God and Being: An Enquiry* (Oxford: Oxford University Press, 2011), pp. 113–40.
49 In Martin Heidegger, *Pathmarks*, ed. William McNeil (Cambridge: Cambridge University Press, 1998), p. 274.
50 Martin Heidegger, *Gelassenheit* (Tübingen: Neske, 1959), p. 26.
51 For the former view, see John D. Caputo, *The Mystical Element in Heidegger's Thought* (New York: Fordham University Press, 1986), especially chapter 4, 'Heidegger and Meister Eckhart', pp. 140-217. For a more positive view of Heidegger's relation to Eckhart, see Reiner Schürmann, *Wandering Joy: Meister Eckhart: Mystic and Philosopher* (Barrington, MA: Lindisfarne Books, 2001), pp. 188–209 and, more recently, Duane Williams, 'Eckhart's Why and Heidegger's What: Beyond Subjectivistic Thought to Groundless Ground' in Lewin, Podmore and Williams, *Mystical Theology*, pp. 147–63.
52 Martin Heidegger, *The Principle of Reason*, trans. R. Lilly (Bloomington: Indiana University Press, 1991), p. 35.
53 See Williams, 'Eckhart's Why', pp. 151–6.
54 Heidegger, *Pathmarks*, p. 58.
55 Heidegger, *Pathmarks*, p. 58.
56 Martin Heidegger, *Reden und andere Zeugnisse eines Lebensweges, 1910–1976. Gesamtausgabe*, vol. 16 (Frankfurt am Main: Vittorio Klostermann, 2000), p. 607.
57 Heidegger, *Reden*, p. 607.

Works cited

Brock, Werner, *An Introduction to Contemporary German Philosophy* (Cambridge: Cambridge University Press, 1935).

Buber, Martin, *Between Man and Man*, trans. R. G. Smith (London: Fontana, 1961).

———, *Daniel: Dialogues on Realization*, trans. M. Friedman (New York: McGraw-Hill, 1965).
———, *The Eclipse of God* (London: Gollancz, 1953).
———, *I and Thou*, trans. W. Kaufmann (Edinburgh: T. & T. Clark, 1970).
———, *Die Rede, die Lehre und das Lied* (Leipzig: Insel, 1920).
———, *Reden und Gleichnisse des Tschuang-Tse* (Leipzig: Insel, 1910).
Caputo, John D., *The Mystical Element in Heidegger's Thought* (New York: Fordham University Press, 1986).
Dallago, Carl, 'Der Triumph der Unsicherheiten', *Der Brenner* 1.2(18) (15 February 1911): 515–25.
———, 'Die Seele des fernen Asiens', *Der Brenner* 1.2(20) (15 March 1911): 567–77, 1.2(21) (1 April 1911): 599–610, and 1.2(22) (15 April 1911): 631–42.
Gogarten, Friedrich, 'Between the Times', in James Robinson (ed.), *The Beginnings of Dialectic Theology* (Richmond, VA: John Knox Press, 1968).
Grillaert, Nel, *What the God-Seekers Found in Nietzsche: The Reception of Nietzsche's Übermensch by the Philosophers of the Russian Religious Renaissance* (Amsterdam: Rodolpi, 2008).
Heidegger, Gertrud (ed.), *"Mein liebes Seelchen!" Briefe Martin Heideggers an seine Frau Elfride 1915–1970* (Münich: Deutsche-Verlags-Anstalt, 2005).
Heidegger, Martin, *Being and Time*, trans. J. Macquarrie and E. Robinson (Oxford: Blackwell, 1962).
———, *Gelassenheit* (Tübingen: Neske, 1959).
———, *Pathmarks*, ed. William McNeil (Cambridge: Cambridge University Press, 1998).
———, *Phänomenologie des religiösen Lebens. Gesamtausgabe*, vol. 60 (Frankfurt am Main: Vittorio Klostermann, 1995).
———, *The Principle of Reason*, trans. R. Lilly (Bloomington: Indiana University Press, 1991).
———, *Reden und andere Zeugnisse eines Lebensweges, 1910–1976. Gesamtausgabe*, vol. 16 (Frankfurt am Main: Vittorio Klostermann, 2000).
Herberg, Will, *Four Existentialist Theologians: A Reader from the Works of Jacques Maritain, Nicolas Berdyaev, Martin Buber, and Paul Tillich* (New York: Doubleday, 1958).
Jensen, Alexander S., 'The Influence of Schleiermacher's Second Speech on Religion on Heidegger's Concept of Ereignis' *The Review of Metaphysics* 61(244) (June 2008): 815–26.
Kisiel, Theodor, *The Genesis of Heidegger's Being and Time* (Berkeley: University of California Press, 1993).
Kisiel, Theodore and Sheehan, Thomas, *Becoming Heidegger: On the Trail of His Early Occasional Writings, 1910–1927* (Evanston, IL: Northwestern University Press, 2007).
Leavitt, June O., *The Mystical Life of Franz Kafka: Theosophy, Cabala, and the Modern Spiritual Revival* (Oxford: Oxford University Press, 2012).
Otto, Rudolf, *The Idea of the Holy*, trans. J. W. Harvey (Oxford: Oxford University Press, 1923).
———, *Mysticism East and West: A Comparative Analysis of the Nature of Mysticism*, trans. Bertha L. Bracey and Richenda C. Payne (New York: Macmillan, 1932).
Pattison, George, *Heidegger on Death: A Critical Theological Essay* (Farnham: Ashgate, 2013).

———, 'The Role of Mysticism in the Formation of Heidegger's Phenomenology', in David Lewin, Simon D. Podmore, and Duane Williams (eds.), *Mystical Theology and Continental Philosophy: Interchange in the Wake of God* (London: Routledge, 2017).

Schürmann, Reiner, *Wandering Joy: Meister Eckhart: Mystic and Philosopher* (Barrington, MA: Lindisfarne Books, 2001).

Tillich, Paul, *The Religious Situation*, trans. H. Richard Niebuhr (New York: Meridian, 1956).

Williams, Duane, 'Eckhart's Why and Heidegger's What: Beyond Subjectivistic Thought to Groundless Ground', in David Lewin, Simon D. Podmore, and Duane Williams (eds.), *Mystical Theology and Continental Philosophy: Interchange in the Wake of God* (London: Routledge, 2017), pp. 147–63.

3 Blondel to Bergson
Mysticism and French philosophy

The history of mysticism in France is well known, in part – particularly its periods of protracted polemic – but other parts of it remain obscure. The case of its influence on existentialism is one example of the latter, and in order to demonstrate this influence, we will first turn to the resurgence of interest in mysticism at the turn of the twentieth century, as marked in France as in the German-speaking and Anglophone worlds.

In a 1900 issue of the *Revue de métaphysique et de morale*, Leon Brunschvicg wrote that the definitive question toward which human reflection is directed was 'to know if its being is reducible to the fragile particularities of its organism, and exhausted by its successive states of individual consciousness, or rather if there is for it a superior destiny'. Taking care to pose the problem 'without prejudging the solution', he wrote, the definitive question of human reflection was the question of religious life.[1] And central to that question in the public discourse of France in the early decades of the twentieth century was the nature and significance of *mysticism*. In 1902, Emile Boutroux wrote an article on the psychology of mysticism, claiming that a 'large and complete study of mysticism' did not just offer the interest of a curiosity, or even a scientific interest, but concerned 'very directly, life and the destiny of individuals and humanity'.[2]

Many histories of mysticism in France reach back, like Michel de Certeau's, to the early seventeenth century,[3] when (to borrow Henri Brémond's phrase) France was 'invaded' by mysticism, and a set of distinctly 'mystical' texts in French began to emerge, as we briefly considered in the introduction. By the end of that century, mysticism had been a vogue of courtly life only to be vehemently rejected, tainted by associations with quietism, mental ill-health, or fanaticism. Perhaps because its reputation suffered so much in the seventeenth century, in the eighteenth and nineteenth centuries mysticism was decidedly out of fashion:[4] Some went so far as to claim that Fénelon's condemnation had, to adapt André Bord's expression, 'beheaded religion'.[5]

In Anglophone scholarship on mysticism, another genealogy of the term focuses, as we have seen, on a different genesis: the early twentieth-century writings of William James, Evelyn Underhill, and Rudolf Otto, for example.

But as Eric Schmidt has shown, interest in mysticism didn't disappear altogether in these centuries: focusing on seventeenth-century France and the early twentieth-century developments in religious studies produces a 'gaping eighteenth- and nineteenth-century hole with only Schleiermacher to plug it'.[6]

The mystical sources of French existentialist thought can be traced back in part to the seventeenth-century 'quarrel of Augustinianisms', as mentioned in the introduction.[7] But the thinkers we will consider in the next three chapters were shaped by a generation of twentieth-century philosophers who were preoccupied by mysticism, and the primary aim of this chapter is to reconstruct that context. We begin by following Schmidt back to nineteenth-century America where, in May 1838, the Transcendentalist Club met to discuss the 'question of mysticism'. Bronson Alcott and Ralph Waldo Emerson were among those in attendance, and their subsequent interest in the subject produced several publications and conversations that crossed the Atlantic. Emerson wrote an essay on Swedenborg that, although critical, presented him as a paradigm mystic. Emerson's views influenced Walt Whitman and Henry James, Sr., among others.[8] This is significant because, as Schmidt observes, in the Transcendentalists' usage the meaning of the term, 'mysticism' deviated from its previous uses in Catholicism and the Enlightenment. 'It was neither an ancient form of Christian divinity nor part of a critique of enthusiasm and sectarianism; instead, it was becoming loosely spiritual, intuitive, emancipatory, and universal'.[9]

It is also significant because the emergence of this freshly reconnected term alongside the foundation of the field of comparative religions at Harvard in the 1870s and 1880s provided fertile soil for William James's interest in 'mysticism' and for *The Varieties of Religious Experience*. In the last decades of the nineteenth century, James travelled frequently to France, where he encountered the work and eventually made the acquaintance of Maurice Blondel[10] and the friendship of the philosophers Émile Boutroux (Blondel's supervisor) and Henri Bergson.[11]

In France in the nineteenth and early twentieth centuries, psychology was still taught as a subdiscipline of philosophy, and the 'psychology of religion' was therefore a philosophical topic. The educational reformer Victor Cousin had added psychology to the philosophy curriculum in 1830 (alongside logic, metaphysics, and morality), and it became the most important of the curriculum not long after.[12] Despite Cousin's efforts to laicize the teaching of philosophy, in the anticlerical context of the Third Republic reflection on religious emotions and the psychology of mysticism flourished in the secular academy. It was interdisciplinary, involving clergy (e.g. Maréchal and Bremond), philosophers (e.g. Delacroix and Blondel), sociologists (e.g. Durkheim and Mauss), and medical doctors (e.g. Janet and Dumas), to give a partial list. In 1899 Starbuck popularized the term 'psychology of religion',[13] but William James was the movement's most outspoken proponent. In 1896 James gave lectures at the Lowell Institute in Boston on 'exceptional mental states', which contributed to the now-famous *Varieties* (1902) and which drew attention from colleagues across the Atlantic. When the *Varieties* was published in French in 1906 – slightly later than expected and under the revised title *Religious Experience: An Essay of Descriptive Psychology* – Émile Boutroux's preface said that with mystics

> religious life is a continual experiment. They describe this inner work with extraordinary subtlety and penetration. What task is more worthy of a psychologist than to lean with love, no longer on doctrines and formulas, frozen residues of thought and action, but on life itself, taken from its pure and gushing source![14]

This chapter will focus primarily on the philosophical discussion of mysticism in the works of Maurice Blondel, Léon Brunschvicg, Henri Delacroix, Jean Baruzi, and Henri Bergson, since these writers' works on or rejection of mysticism were most important for the French existentialism that emerged a generation later. Not all of them were so effusive in their praise of mysticism: some saw it as obscurantist and opposed to reason. But in addition to attempting to study mysticism as a psychological phenomenon and to delineate criteria that could differentiate between 'good' and 'bad' mysticisms – for the taint of quietism and fanaticism was still strong – these thinkers each considered questions such as the noetic value of religious experience, the relationship between mysticism and philosophy, and the insights of particular mystics' thought on matters such as consciousness, temporality, desire, and the self.

The thinkers we will consider here drew on their own cultural repository of mystics and philosophers. Gary Gutting describes French philosophy during this period as 'very nearly autonomous'[15] and although the study of mysticism in early twentieth-century France was not limited to French mystics, its boundaries were drawn within an intellectual framework that assumed familiarity with the thinkers and debates: Pierre de Bérulle and the French School of spirituality, Descartes and Pascal, Madame Guyon, Fénelon, and Bossuet.

But when Blondel, Brunschvicg, Delacroix, Baruzi, and Bergson considered the question of religious life, they drew their philosophical interests in mysticism into dialogue with the work of James and their colleagues in the growing fields of the anthropology and sociology of religion. William James wanted to 'redeem religion from unwholesome privacy'; his pragmatism sought to give it 'public status' by the means of public, scientific investigation.[16] He argued that mysticism should be judged by its fruits, and if it produced the good fruits of saintliness and *active* habits, it was to be regarded as 'healthy-minded'.

This sat well with the tradition of French mysticism that emphasizes *action*. In this strand of mystical thought, contemplation and even *unio mystica* were seen as penultimate stages on the journey to mysticism's goal: transformative action. Long before James's pragmatism, Pierre de Bérulle argued that there should be no distinction between mystical and practical theology: 'All God's graces distributed upon earth are to enable us to act better'.[17]

This chapter cannot provide in-depth analysis of each philosopher's thoughts on mysticism: rather, our aim is to map this unfamiliar terrain of French thought, demonstrating through a discussion of the key works (i) that in the first quarter of the twentieth-century mysticism was high on the intellectual agenda of major French philosophers who, in turn, were important points of reference for the existentialist generation; (ii) that some 'mystics' were interpreted as systematic philosophers in their own right, worthy of other philosophers' attention; and (iii) that some 'philosophers' wrote mystical texts that are less well known on the standard English-speaking histories of philosophy. As we shall see in Chapters 4 through 6, philosophical interest in mysticism in the first quarter of the twentieth century continued into the second, featuring in French existentialists' educations and works in ways that have gone unrecognized.

Constraints of space prohibit a full consideration of work on literature and mysticism during this period, but it is nevertheless noteworthy that an important impetus to this resurgence of interest in mysticism was literary, including the recent discovery of Dostoevsky and Tolstoy in France. In 1897 Victor Charbonnel denounced a neo-mystic revival in French culture, attributing it to 'present literature' (including 'the Russian novel').[18] He described a 'renaissance of mysticism' all around, although in effect he considered it the resurgence of a disease, describing mysticism as 'obscure, indecisive aspirations, often lost in the vague confines of dilettantism and fantasy'. There had been a 'rebirth of the Religious Idea', he said, and consequently it was time to 'study one of the most strange crises of the contemporary soul'.[19]

By 1911, André Lalande's *Vocabulaire technique et critique de la philosophie* included an entry on mysticism that detailed four senses of the word:

1 the possibility of an intimate union between the human spirit (*l'esprit humain*) and the fundamental principle of being;
2 the affective, intellectual, and moral dispositions attached to this;
3 the great philosophical systems of the world that privilege feeling and imagination over reason;
4 beliefs and doctrines that are based on feeling and intuition as opposed to observation and reasoning.[20]

In what follows we will treat each thinker separately (proceeding chronologically), seeing how such mysticism was accepted, rejected, or modified in the works of Blondel, Brunschvicg, Delacroix, Baruzi, and Bergson.

Maurice Blondel

Maurice Blondel (1861–1949) was a philosopher whose work – especially *L'Action* (1893), his doctoral thesis supervised by Émile Boutroux – was intended to establish Christianity and philosophy in an appropriate relationship: he thought that philosophy's neglect of religion was mutually impoverishing. He was refused a post in Paris, however, because his views in *L'Action* were considered to be too Christian: that is, to compromise the autonomy of philosophical reason.

As has already been mentioned, Third Republic France was avowedly secular. Its Voltaire-infused stance on the role of religion in society was that religious beliefs were and ought to remain purely private, belonging to the domain of the individual conscience and not to public discourse. Philosophy – as a public discourse – should appeal only to reason. And human rationality, understood as a secular enterprise, required a neutral approach to claims to revealed truth.[21]

By way of contrast, Blondel's 1893 thesis maintained that action alone – the enactment of our aspirations in the natural realm – could never satisfy the human longing for more, for the transfinite. Like Pascal, he suggested that we should hope Christianity is true – whether it is or not – since human yearning could only be fulfilled by God, 'the first principle and the last term'. Anticipating Sartre, Blondel wrote that 'The substance of man is action; he is what he makes of himself'.[22]

But what we make of ourselves, for Blondel, is never enough: our own lives, alone, cannot generate the meaning we long for. Our action unfolds in a world that is social, a world which assigns meaning in the family, in the nation, in humanity. But all of these, Blondel says, can become idols – the recipients of misplaced worship, empty receptacles of unfulfilled desire. In Blondel's view, each stage of an individual's life involves the desire to find further levels of meaning, since there is a gap between what the will has accomplished already (the 'willed will', *volunté volue*) and the ineluctable 'willing will' (*volunté voulante*), which is what we will most profoundly of all. No matter how successful our 'willed will' is – no matter how many achievements we amass or objects we acquire – the will (*volunté voulante*) remains perpetually unsatisfied. His explanation for this continuous dissatisfaction is that my willing – the root of my own action itself – is not something I have willed.

> Suppose that man does everything as he wills it, obtains what he covets, vivifies the universe according to his liking, organizes and produces as he wishes the total ordering of conditions on which he rests his life: it remains that this will itself has not been posited or determined as it is by him . . . he wills, but he did not will to will.[23]

We would like to be self-sufficient, Blondel writes: we would like to be God. But we have a choice as to the manner in which we aspire to Godlikeness: we can choose 'to be God without God and against God' or 'through God and with God'.[24]

The latter route involves acknowledging that I am not the foundation of my own will and that my flourishing depends on recognizing its source. In union with this source (God) through supernatural grace, I can find the rest and self-sufficiency that meet the exigency of my *volunté voulante*. Philosophy, in Blondel's view, can take one only as far as the possibility of the supernatural. Its role is to 'prove that we cannot, in practice, not pronounce for or against the supernatural: "Is it or is it not?"'[25]

In Gary Gutting's excellent volume on French philosophy, he writes of Blondel that 'he published little until the 1930s, when his revision of *L'Action* appeared along with two major companion volumes'.[26] In 1934 he published a revised version of *L'Action*, following on from two treatises on thought (*La pensée*) and ontology (*L'Être et les êtres*). But as we shall see later when we discuss the works of Henri Delacroix, before these book-length works appeared, Blondel engaged in published debate with other philosophers on the value of mysticism. As Michael Conway writes, Blondel was 'keen to underline the legitimate and even essential role that philosophy plays in determining what exactly is true mysticism, and in differentiating this from a spectrum of false variations that had gained currency in the early decades of the twentieth century'.[27] For some of his contemporaries believed it to be obscurantist and against reason.

Leon Brunschvicg

Leon Brunschvicg was professor of philosophy at the Sorbonne from 1909 through 1939. His influence over the generation that included Sartre, Beauvoir, and Merleau-Ponty is well known, as is his representation of 'critical idealism'. Brunschvicg did not write a book-length work on religion or mysticism until the end of his career at the Sorbonne, when he published *La raison et la religion* [1939, *Reason and Religion*], but he wrote articles on the subject from the beginning (e.g. the aforementioned article from 1900, declaring *the* question of the time to be the question of religious life); co-founded the *Revue métaphysique et de morale* – a journal which included extensive discussion of the topic; and edited the edition of Pascal's *Pensées* that would remain standard until Louis Lafuma's edition in the 1960s. Brunschvicg was an intellectual giant, towering over Parisian philosophy.

Brunschvicg was a systematic philosopher known for work in epistemology as well as for studies of Descartes, Spinoza, and Pascal, whose *Pensées* Brunschvicg edited. Several of his works included discussions of God and religion, in which defended his own radical immanentism [*immanentisme radical*].[28] We only reach God, he wrote, 'by tearing ourselves away from the nostalgia of transcendence, the supernatural'.[29] Brunschvicg believed that humanity was gradually progressing toward shared, universal laws, and that part of that progress involved leaving behind hindering aspects of traditional religion. In his idealist view, the idea of God as a transcendent, independently existing being was incoherent, and the beliefs and practices that accompanied that idea – for example, dogmas, codes, and rites – were impediments to progress. In this sense Brunschvicg claimed that there was no place for religious consciousnesses in humanity's future. But he also wrote that 'where religions end, religion begins';[30] he contended that religious language could be used in defensible terms if God was understood as a value rather than a superhuman causal person.

As for mysticism, Brunschvicg condemned it as obscure, the shadowy substitute for the clear light of reason: 'an experience which detaches itself from clear and distinct consciousness refuses to justify the character of immediate authenticity which it claims for itself'.[31] Brunschvicg traced the rise of modernity to Montaigne's scepticism, outlining its influence on Descartes and Pascal in what he called the drama 'at the origins of French thought'.[32] Although Brunschvicg admired Pascal's scientific genius, he considered his interest in dogmas and rites a regression to childhood.

In the 1920s Brunschvicg supervised dissertations by both Simone de Beauvoir and Simone Weil; the latter he marked very harshly.[33] Weil had studied with Brunschvicg's contemporary Alain, whose views on the discipline of philosophy and the nature of time made his students unpopular with Brunschvicg for reasons that we shall see in Chapter 6.

Henri Delacroix

In 1900 Henri Delacroix[34] (1973–1937) published a book-length essay on fourteenth-century German mysticism: *Essai sur le mysticisme spéculatif en Allemagne au XIVe siècle*.[35] He introduced it by explaining that his interest in the movement surrounding Meister Eckhart was driven in part by a desire to clarify the origins of German philosophy.[36] But Delacroix claimed that Eckhart was more than instrumentally interesting: Eckhart's work had philosophical merit in itself. Yes, Eckhart was a religious thinker, whose work showed dubious debts to Neoplatonism and John Scotus Eriugenia. But Delacroix made clear that he took Eckhart to be a systematic thinker – which is to say, *a philosopher* – in his own right.

Delacroix's explicit intent in this work was to expound Eckhart as such.[37] His essay is worth dwelling on at some length since it includes – before James's *Varieties* and Bergson's *Two Sources* or even Delacroix's own 1908 *Les Grands mystiques chrétiens* – an account of a type of mysticism that is not contained to passive contemplation. Delacroix's study of mysticism includes a search for it in literature, life, and art, since 'it is rare that a rigorous doctrine, capable of creating a movement of the spirit, does not leave something of itself in other domains where pure speculation cannot penetrate'. In Delacroix's view, 'mysticism is particularly apt to penetrate emotions and hearts', and one can find examples and proofs of it in literary and material culture.[38]

Delacroix's introduction underscores that Eckhart's mysticism is *speculative* and *philosophical*. He knows many readers will recoil at the word 'mysticism', which has long served 'to designate so many chimeras, frenzies composed by weak or disordered imaginations'.[39] But Delacroix thinks their objections do not apply in the case of Eckhart. He distinguishes between 'degenerate mysticism', which ends in 'passionate and scrupulous idolatry'[40] and a superior variety he calls 'speculative'.

Eckhart's 'speculative' mysticism – unlike scholastic mysticism, which presupposes Christian piety – need not be linked to Christianity or to theology. What is more, Delacroix claims, it doesn't suppose any more than 'religious feeling' [*le sentiment religieux*]: that is, a much more widely accepted premise.[41] In his methodological prolegomena, Delacroix defines such mysticism as 'a solid and rational doctrine in its method if not in its principles. The historian of philosophy can approach it without peril; it is a real country, not an estate of phantasmagoria and dreams'.[42]

The philosophy Delacroix discovered in the 'real country' of Eckhart's works was a doctrine of 'annihilation [*anéantissement*], of decreated being [*la vie en l'increée*], of the loss of itself; he spoke of the absolute reality of being and of the contemplation which disappears in it'.[43] This mysticism is methodical, outlining a three-part method of negation, elevation [*eminence*], and causality as the means by which the soul raises itself to the knowledge of God.

After outlining Eckhart's method, Delacroix turned to his philosophy, in particular his ontology. The God Eckhart came to know was not 'one of the things that are'; rather, 'he encloses existence from beyond existence: he produces it without altering his fixity [*immobilité*]'.[44] God's 'Absolute Being is Being in itself' [*L'Être absolu est l'Être en soi*].[45] But despite his fixity and absoluteness Eckhart's God 'is not an immobile God, but a living one: he is not abstract Being, but the Being of Being'. Nothing can be negated in God; he is pure affirmation.[46] God 'is the subject of his own being, he can say: "I"'.[47]

Eckhart, Delacroix writes, wanted to awaken his audience 'to the art of the inner life'.[48] Human beings are 'conscious of living a life that is not reducible to any other, a personal life, an existence of their own'.[49] Cognizant that, in the French context, emphasis on the inner life frequently led to objections of quietism, Delacroix noted the importance of action in mystical life. In his definition, action 'is not essentially different from contemplation: it is its fulfilment and makes it fruitful; its movement still encloses rest, and doesn't alter the rest of the soul'. He goes on to say that action originates in the soul's rest, because movement and rest are eternally involved [in French, *s'impliquent*] in God; their discrepancy [in French, *contradiction*] is what makes the divine life so fertile.[50]

Delacroix's account of Eckhart's views is less noteworthy, for our purposes, than the way he positions them as philosophical and relevant to all, irrespective of religious commitments. Delacroix contended that Eckhart's mysticism was not circular and self-reinforcing in the way that (on his reading) scholasticism is. In Delacroix's definition, scholasticism is 'the science applied by religion to religion. Its first supposition is religion: it furnishes the lines and material of the system. But this religion, which gives itself as direct revelation, is at root the fruit of anterior systems, the end of a long theological elaboration, the influence of which reappears in the writings of the School'.

Delacroix singles out Augustine in particular, with his doctrines of God, predestination, sin, and grace, as dominating later theology (especially that of Thomas Aquinas). Whereas modern readers struggle to take the conclusions of earlier centuries as a gift from God in the way that scholasticism does, Delacroix argues that they can read Meister Eckhart with 'hardly any other supposition than human consciousness and the analysis of life'.[51] In making these statements, Delacroix claimed, he was employing the 'ordinary method of the history of philosophy': 'searching through the comparison and analysis of texts for the justification of our assertions'.[52]

In the years immediately thereafter, Delacroix published articles on Kierkegaard (1900), art and the inner life (1902), and a 27-page-long review of William James's *The Varieties of Religious Experience* (1903)[53] – as well as other work on Kant, Novalis, Hume, and more. In October 1905 he gave a report at a meeting of the *Société Française de Philosophie*, entitled 'The development of mystical states in Saint Teresa'. He presented his work in progress, the final shape of which was published in 1908 as *Études d'histoire et de psychologie du mysticisme*. In the meantime, the report was published in 1906 in the *Bulletins de la Société Française de Philosophie*, and the same year he published an analysis of Madame Guyon's mysticism in the *Revue Métaphysique et de Morale*.[54]

In 1906 Blondel published a reply to Delacroix's 1905 paper, agreeing with the latter that mysticism should be the object of critical study. But Delacroix went wrong, in Blondel's view, by studying mysticism as something *in – and therefore arising from* – the experiencing subject. Blondel charged Delacroix with the assumption that what is in consciousness is from consciousness. But this is a distorting lens through which to study mystical phenomena, for it leaves no criterion by which to distinguish between pathological and non-pathological cases. As Michael Conway puts it: 'You cannot discern the madman from the mystic!'[55]

In Blondel's reading, Delacroix treated Saint Teresa's mystical states in a reductionist manner, taking them to be neurotic. He does not contend that one should assume the opposite – one cannot assume that their origin is transcendent either. But rather, both assumptions – of a transcendent divine or pathological psychological origin – must be suspended in order to investigate the phenomenon without bias.

Michael Conway argues that in the 1908 volume we have 'for the first time, a method being applied to mystic states in all their complexity: historical, psychological, critical, rigorously objective, and, indeed, respectful of the fact in its alleged completeness'.[56]

But Delacroix's earlier work on Eckhart also exhibits these virtues. And in other publications from the period – for example, his 'Note sur Christianisme et mysticisme' (1908) – Delacroix wrote that he took himself to have established in *Études* that the great Catholic mystics were not satisfied with the momentary annihilation of individual life; for them there was no dissociation between contemplation and action. The superior state of the mystic was one in which 'without leaving the contemplation that absorbed them in God, they felt moved by God to act and led, by its immediate and continuous operation, to work in the world'. The consciousness of the self was definitively effaced before the consciousness of the divine – but also infused by an 'organizing energy' that gave birth to action 'without which it was not Christian life'.[57]

Ecstasy, in Delacroix's reading, was not the highest height of mystical life: it was a necessary step on the way to the true fruit of mystical life: action. In the next decade Delacroix continued to publish on the subject of mysticism, the psychology of religious experience, and other philosophical topics, engaging with Émile Durkheim and others.

Maurice Blondel also continued to ask methodological questions of his colleagues' approaches to mysticism in the years that followed. He engaged in correspondence with other members of the *Société Française de Philosophie* as André Lalande's *Vocabulaire* (1911) was in preparation. Concerning the entry on 'mystic – mysticism', Blondel objected to the idea that reason should be abrogated when examining mysticism, arguing instead that mysticism should be understood as, in Conway's words, 'a science, exercised in the laboratory of life'.[58] In response to sceptical colleagues, he made the point that mysticism, like any other historical reality, can be philosophically investigated – and should not be dismissed on the basis of its least credible instances or abuses of its alleged authority. In Conway's words, 'Mysticism in action, this "science of mysticism", is not to be reduced to a discourse on mysticism'.[59]

In the 1908 work Delacroix begins by saying that mysticism is quasi-universal: 'it is hardly linked to a single religion, people, or historical period', he writes; 'it is a human fact' that rests on 'certain dispositions of human nature'.[60] Delacroix looked far back into history in exploring problems with the intermediaries between prayer and ecstasy and heretical pursuits of the ecstatic: he considers the case of Montanism and its critics: Philo, Plotinus.[61] Delacroix does this because he recognizes the authority the Catholic church assigns to the fathers and because both Madame Guyon and Fénelon appealed to that authority in defence of their own views.[62]

Debates about ecclesial authority and the possibility of a scientific approach to mysticism had political implications in the first decade of the twentieth century; they were not limited to Blondel and Delacroix. Another outspoken and influential participant in this discussion was Jean Baruzi, a philosopher who had posts at the Collège Stanislas and the Faculty of Letters in Paris.

Jean Baruzi

Baruzi is best known for his major study of Saint John of the Cross, which was published in 1924 as *Saint Jean de la Croix et le problème de l'experience mystique*. In that work, he relates Saint John of the Cross to Fénelon and

Madame Guyon, the latter of whom claimed to have found much of her own doctrine in John of the Cross.[63] Baruzi's aim was not to assess their fidelity or departure from Sanjuanist texts, but rather to argue that 'they, for the first time, gave the doctrine of John of the Cross an expansion of a metaphysical character'.[64]

Baruzi first began publishing about mysticism nearly 20 years earlier. In January of 1905 he published *Three Mystical Dialogues* by Leibniz in the *Revue de métaphysique et de morale*. In 1907 he edited a collection of texts by Leibniz, entitled *Leibniz and the Religious Organization of the World: With Unreleased Texts*.[65] And in 1909 the book was reissued in a new edition. But Baruzi's book on Leibniz does not present him as contemporary Anglophone history of philosophy does: he is not merely one of the three great Continental rationalists. For in addition to propounding the doctrine of innate ideas, so-called Leibnizian 'optimism', and memorable phrases such as 'monads have no windows', Leibniz wrote extensively on matters of religion and *mysticism*. And, in fact, Baruzi includes extracts from a letter Leibniz wrote to Antoine Arnauld concerning nature and grace.[66] Another text selected by Baruzi treats Leibniz's appreciation of 'the beautiful thought' of Saint Theresa. In a letter to André Morell, Leibniz wrote that her idea that 'the soul should conceive of things as if there were only God and herself in the world' was an insight he has usefully employed in one of his own hypotheses.[67]

Baruzi presents Leibniz as 'in the modern sense of the word, a psychologist of mysticism': he offers his readers 'a psychological study of the mystical life',[68] taking an interest in the mystics of his time (including Antoinette Bourignon, Madame Guyon, Mademoiselle d'Assenburg) and those of earlier epochs (e.g. Perpetua and Felicitas). Like Delacroix with Eckhart, Baruzi defends Leibniz's relevance to the study of psychology as a subdiscipline of philosophy.

In the chapter entitled 'A psychology of mysticism' Baruzi's selection of texts shows that Leibniz asked questions including: what is the difference between meditation and contemplation? How can we be united with God? Were the causes of Theresa's and Catherine of Siena's visions purely natural, purely miraculous, or God working through nature? How should one understand the abnegation and annihilation of the Bohmists, quietists, and others?[69] In Leibniz's view, grace could not be reduced to either nature or miracle: 'Just as I believe it is false to say that all graces are natural, I believe it is no less false to sustain that they are entirely miraculous'.[70] Moreover, Leibniz's interest in the mystical life was personal rather than that of the detached observer. In another letter to Morell, Leibniz wrote that he had purchased the works of Saint Theresa and a life of Angela of Foligno, which made him recognize more and more that 'true theology and religion must be in our hearts by a pure abnegation of ourselves, in abandoning ourselves to divine mercy'.[71] But he could never approve of the view of some quietists who wish to reduce the soul to a passive state.[72]

Leibniz the mystic also wrote about the non-being of the human self and how to overcome it:

> Each creature can not be without a non-being; if not, it would be God. . . . In our personal being, there is an infinite, an image of the omniscience and omnipotence of God. . . . The negation of oneself is the hate of non-being in us, and the love of the source of our personal being, that is to say, of God. . . . It is in this that crucifying the old Adam consists: in taking Christ to myself, dying to Adam and living in Christ: this is how one renounces non-being and attaches oneself to being. Whoever knows how to prefer the interior light to sensible images, or personal being to non-being, loves God above all things.[73]

But Leibniz also lost patience with the lack of precision he found in Fénelon and Bossuet's arguments about the love of God: 'These gentlemen would have no need to argue if they had some distinct concepts, that is to say some good definitions, and if they would consider that when one truly loves one finds one's own pleasure in the happiness of the object loved, even if one would not derive any benefit from it'.[74]

Seventeen years later Baruzi published *Saint Jean de la croix et le problème de l'experience mystique* (1924), with a dedication to Henri Delacroix. In this work Baruzi discusses some of the methodological challenges that face scholars of 'mysticism', including the challenge of how to define it. Is it a matter of doctrine or experience? Saint John of the Cross, Baruzi suggests, provides a concrete link between experience and doctrine. John of the Cross was read by both Fénelon and Madame Guyon; Fénelon appealed to him in his arguments against Bossuet. Later French philosophers therefore often encountered Sanjuanist ideas through the *Maximes*.[75] Baruzi's methodology in *Saint Jean de la Croix* was descriptive. He drew from Bergson's concepts of the 'given' [*donné*] and mystical 'becoming'.[76] But he may also have drawn on phenomenology: as Margaret Simons writes, Baruzi refers to the question of whether the '"phenomenon" of mysticism issues from an "irreducible experience"'.[77] Baruzi did not think this question could be solved by a purely sociological, historical, or psychological method.

Rather, in *Saint Jean de la Croix* he describes his desire to attend to the 'rhythm of lived experience' [*experience vécue*],[78] which has been taken by some to support the idea that he was conversant in phenomenological parlance and method before Husserl's Paris lectures (February 1929) or first French translations (1931). In a 1925 presentation to the French Philosophical Society, entitled 'Saint John of the Cross and the Problem of the Noetic Value of Mystical Experience', Baruzi described what he was doing as a 'phenomenology' of mystical experience.[79] Jean-Louis Viellard-Baron writes that what would later be called the 'phenomenological approach' in French philosophy and in the study of religion is what Bergson called 'concrete metaphysics' [*métaphysique concrète*].[80]

Baruzi approached John of the Cross as a faithful reader of Bergson's *Time and Free Will*, in which Bergson wrote that few had known true liberty because most live at the level of the 'superficial self' [*le moi superficiel*] or the 'social self' [*le moi social*].[81] In Bergson's view, it took effort to attend to the inner life – a much greater effort than was required to acquire external knowledge. Although *The Two Sources of Morality and Religion* (1932) is probably Bergson's best-known work on religious matters, like the other philosophers discussed in this chapter Bergson did participate in debates about mysticism and interiority in shorter works in the decades before its publication. He gave a lecture course on Plotimus's *Enneads* (which Baruzi attended), and in a paper delivered in Spain in 1916 he wrote that mystics – 'the great mystics' – 'were men who had a clear and direct vision of the inner life' [*la vie intérieure*].[82] This claim prompted objections, including an objection from Baruzi, which would appear in the preface of his work on Saint John of the Cross: Mysticism, Baruzi wrote, is like life, in that it is lived by individuals; mystical experience differs from one mystic to another.

In the preface to Baruzi's first edition of *Saint Jean de la Croix* (1924), he sought to give 'a direct analysis of a mystical becoming': *becoming* rather than individual moments, *because each mystical experience* occurred in the context of a life that was experienced by the mystic as a continual process. Here Baruzi follows Bergson: the 'deep self' ['*moi profond*'] for Bergson is a process of becoming, a '*durée continue*'; attempts to refer to it as a thing fail because it is always becoming something new. The next year Baruzi explicitly brought his discussion of mysticism into dialogue with Kant's critical project: at a 1925 'séance' of the *Société Française de Philosophie*, Baruzi said that it is '*as if* John of the Cross invites us not to be content at the level of psychology. He brings us a logic of mysticism and even a critique of mystical experience. One could say that he is preoccupied with establishing the conditions of the possibility of mystical experience'.[83]

Aspects of Baruzi's approach do indeed seem to anticipate Husserl; it is possible that he was exposed to them through German readers in Paris.[84] But it is also possible that concepts and methods that look 'Husserlian' were present in other French philosophy of the late nineteenth century under other names. As Simone Pétrement has shown, Alain (Emile Chartier) and his even less-well-known teacher Jules Lagneau both objected to the discipline of psychology when it treated thought as the object of nature, instead of treating consciousness as the phenomenon of consciousness. Like Husserl, Pétrement writes, they took the task of philosophy not to be reasoning and proving by deduction, but to 'describe exactly what passes in perception'.[85] Epistemologically, Lagneau (1851–1894) claimed that 'all perception is the perception of an object' (much like Husserl's intentionality thesis). And ethically (much like Kierkegaard) he emphasized the necessity of choice, because choice bestows value on the chosen. In Lagneau's words: '*Il faut choisir*'.[86]

Before concluding our discussion of Baruzi and turning to Bergson, it is worth making a brief detour into the thought of Alain and Lagneau since, as we will see in Chapters 4 and 6, they were read and – to varying degrees at different times – respected by Beauvoir, Sartre, Bataille, and Weil. Alain has been remembered by posterity as 'not a philosopher properly speaking' but rather a moralist.[87] He was concerned with how life should be lived and believed that philosophy should be considered from the point of view of existence. His method of teaching his philosophy students (including Simone Weil) was not well liked by idealists such as Brunschvicg: Alain was interested in 'true men' rather than 'true ideas' and thought that the best philosophy was not to be found in the most comprehensive system, or the most rational analysis, or the best arranged argument, but rather in the work of people who had constructed philosophy in order to liberate human beings from their 'inner slavery'.[88]

Lagneau's posthumously published *De l'existence de Dieu* [*On the Existence of God*] contains a 'moral proof' for God's existence which is not a 'proof' in the demonstrative sense but rather a proof 'founded on the needs of our nature'.[89] Faith would not be faith if its truths could be demonstrated. But it can be supported by 'reasons of *sentiment*', the human desires for happiness and moral perfection.[90] The existence of God is shown, according to Lagneau, 'by the fact that we are capable of accepting our situation, and of finding contentment in it'.[91]

To return to Baruzi, his account of religion and humanity emphasizes the temporality of experience; he claimed that 'the true Church moves in time, or in this interior space which is the spiritual centre of humanity',[92] but he resisted the authoritarian approach to doctrine taken by the Catholic Church, instead insisting on freedom of intellectual research for himself and others. In letters to the Catholic thinker Peter Wust (who also wrote a substantial book on Kierkegaard) Baruzi expressed that religious anxiety [*angoisse*] was an indispensable part of his own religious experience. He wrote that 'Pascalian *angoisse*' was a good resumé of his religious attitude – with the qualification that it made his critical thought and his questions no less intrepid. In his lectures he drew on the theme of *angoisse* in Luther, Dürer, Augustine, Jerome, John of the Cross, and Kierkegaard.[93] Baruzi's emphasis on the becoming of all individuals in time, including mystics, clearly owes a debt to the early Bergson. But Baruzi's *Saint Jean de la Croix* also contributed to Bergson's late work: *The Two Sources of Morality and Religion*.[94]

Henri Bergson

Henri Bergson and William James, despite significant philosophical differences, felt deep and mutually acknowledged affinity with each other. After years of correspondence they met in person for the first time on 28 May 1905. In James's diary on that day he recorded 'Visit from Beautiful Bergson'. When Bergson remembered their meeting he remembered that James's visit question was 'how I envisaged the problem of religion'.[95]

We have already noted that Bergson did not publish a book-length work on religion until 1932 – but *The Two Sources of Morality and Religion* went through 17 editions between its first publication in French and its appearance in English in 1935.[96] We have already considered some of the implications of Bergson's 'concrete metaphysics' (which, as we'll see in the next chapter, influenced Sartre and Beauvoir), but before turning to the *Two Sources*, it is worth noting that Bergson has been described as 'liberating' the thought of many young listeners in the first decades of the twentieth century: listeners who included Jean Baruzi, Charles Blondel, Jacques Chevalier, Jacques Maritain, and Etienne Gilson. Jean-Louis Vieillard-Baron comments that this demonstrates a significant difference between Bergson and Husserl. Husserl 'wanted to found a philosophical school, the phenomenological school'; Bergson did not out of 'respect for the individuality of theoretical efforts'.[97]

Put simply, Bergson's argument in *The Two Sources of Morality and Religion* is that there are two kinds of 'morality', open and closed, and that these correspond to two kinds of religion: static and dynamic. Each of these has a different essence, or sine qua non. Bergson's *Two Sources* has many intertexts: Kant's *Groundwork for the Metaphysics of Morals*, clearly, as well as Durkheim and other French sociologists who were working to find an essence of religion, and William James. But it is mysticism that triumphs in dynamic religion: a mysticism of love that bears fruit in action.

Closed morality | static religion

The closed and static forms of morality and religion are what they are because they are motivated by social cohesion: since human beings are a species in which individuals cannot exist on their own, communal support is necessary in order to meet individual needs. Bergson takes such needs to be the source of Kant's categorical imperative – because the survival of the community requires obedience.

But the categorical imperative is not, Bergson argues, as universal as Kant takes it to be: it is limited and particular, concerning only *my society*. As such, closed morality is, in Bergson's words, 'perpetually read[y] for battle': 'its members hold together, caring nothing for the rest of humanity, on the alert for attack or defence'.[98] The form of religiosity that corresponds to closed morality is 'static', in Bergson's terms: it involves 'fabulation' or 'myth-making', the invention of gods to enforce our obedience to the strict morality that preserves the good of *my* society. In societies formed by static religion and closed morality Bergson writes that 'Humanity is asked to place itself at a certain level, higher than that of animal society, where obligation would be but the force of instinct, but not so high as the gods, where everything would partake of the creative impetus'.[99]

Bergson opens his chapter on static religion by saying that 'The spectacle of what religions have been in the past, of what certain religions are today, is indeed humiliating for human intelligence'. But human society has never been without religion. So why is it that *homo sapiens* 'the only creature endowed with reason, is also the only creature to pin its existence to things unreasonable?' Why is it, Bergson asks, that unreasonable beliefs and practices have been – and continue to be – accepted by reasonable beings?[100]

In the context of this discussion, Bergson engages with the works of Durkheim and Lévy-Bruhl concerning so-called 'primitive peoples', criticizing their notions of primitivity in light of his own philosophical psychology of the imagination. Bergson writes that 'superstitions' are often relegated to the faculty of imagination, implying that this is done with derogatory intent – *but*, he points out, under the heading 'imagination' we also find 'the discoveries and inventions of science and the achievements of art'. Bergson gives two reasons for this strange classification: convenience of speech and the negative reason that all these activities 'are neither perception, nor memory, nor logical operations of the mind'.[101]

He defines a faculty of mind he calls the 'myth-making function',[102] through which human intelligence protects itself from thinking only of itself: 'Primitive religion, taken from our first standpoint, is a precaution against the danger man runs, as soon as he thinks at all, of thinking of himself alone'.[103] He then gives three italicized definitions which we might take to be the sine qua non of static religion, demonstrating the two functions Bergson assigned to primitive religion: social preservation and defence against the inevitability of death.[104]

Amongst the key points Bergson goes on to make are that: (1) *Looked at from this first point of view, religion is then a defensive reaction of nature against the dissolvent power of intelligence*;[105] (2) 'The vital impulse is optimistic. All the religious representations which here arise directly from it might then be defined in the same way: *they are defensive reactions of nature against the representation, by intelligence, of a depressing margin of the unexpected between the initiative taken and the effect desired*';[106] and (3) '*It is a defensive reaction of nature against what might be depressing for the individual, and dissolvent for society, in the exercise of intelligence*'.[107]

But Bergson also defends 'primitives' against their anthropological interpreters, arguing that (i) there is not as much distance between the 'primitives' and us as the anthropologists imply; and (ii) that 'to connect religion with a system of ideas, with a logic or a "pre-logic", is to turn our remote ancestors into intellectuals'.[108]

Like William James, Bergson is critical of 'intellectualism', which is 'a valuation of or habitual preference for concepts as products of the intellect as opposed to percepts, sensation, or experience'.[109] Reflection, Bergson argues, 'cannot be relied upon to keep up th[e] selflessness' society requires:

> Intelligence. . . would more likely counsel egoism. . . That then is the office, that is the significance of the religion we have called static or natural. Religion is that element which, in beings endowed with reason, is called upon to make good any deficiency of attachment to life.[110]

In making his case Bergson critically engages with previous scholars' definitions of 'primitive' peoples, and dismisses Frazer's evolutionist view of magic as a primitive way of understanding causality, which eventually is superseded by religion, which in turn will give way to science.[111] Bergson offers his own definition of magic as 'the outward projection of a desire which fills the heart'[112] and argues that, on such a definition, there should be 'no talk . . . of an era of magic followed by an era of science'.[113] He also situates himself in the emerging conversation between substantivist and functionalist definitions of religion: whereas substantivists such as Tylor defined 'animism' as 'belief in spiritual beings', Bergson asserts that religion 'is not, in its beginnings a belief in deities',[114] and that 'there is no religion without rites and ceremonies'.[115] Nevertheless, he also criticizes Durkheim's functionalism, writing that 'the individual and society . . . condition each other, circle-wise'.[116]

In a sense, then, Bergson's analysis of static religion, like other early anthropological and sociological accounts, seems to provide a *reductio*, to reduce religion to a social or psychological function. But Bergson is not content to leave his analysis at that, and where dynamic religion is concerned we find a different, irreducible *sine qua non*. One early reader of Bergson's *Two Sources*, Hjalmar Sundén, writes that Bergson's distinctive contribution to the question of the nature of religion is his view that all religion appears to us to be a complement to our intelligence, but the distinction between open and closed reveals that some complements are more adequate than others.[117]

Open morality | dynamic religion

Open morality and dynamic religion, in Bergson's definitions, are creative and pursue progress. Rather than reinforcing the social cohesion of *my* society, they are open in the sense that they concern everyone and aim at peace for all. Bergson describes this open society as 'mystic', 'embracing all humanity and moving, animated by a common will, toward the continually renewed creation of a more complete humanity'.[118]

The mystic's attachment to life is inseparable from 'joy in joy, love of that which is all love': mysticism lifts the soul 'to another plane'.[119] Mysticism's ultimate end 'is the establishment of contact, consequently of a partial coincidence, with the creative effort which life itself manifests'.[120]

The language of 'mysticism', Bergson realizes, may be off-putting to some. So another way of framing his view is to say that Bergson locates the source of open morality in 'creative emotions'. In normal emotions we have a representation that causes feeling (I hear melancholy music and I feel sad). In creative emotion, the emotion precedes the representation. The example Bergson gives is of a musician whose emotion gives rise to a symphony, which is then represented in the music of the score. Likewise, Bergson thinks that genuine religious (i.e. mystical) experience, or open morality, must result in action. Unlike static religion, whose 'force' is obligation, dynamic religion's force is 'the impetus of love'. The creative emotions of dynamic religion – love, joy, sympathy – must express themselves in actions and representations.

Bergson argues that one of the problems for static religion and Kantian morality is the gap between the 'assent of the intellect and a conversion of the will'.[121] He writes:

> Our admiration for the speculative function of the mind may be great; but when philosophers maintain that it should be sufficient to silence selfishness and passion, they prove to us – and this is a matter for congratulation – that they have never heard the voice of the one or the other very loud within themselves. . . . [T]here can be no question of founding morality on the cult of reason.[122]

Dynamic religion, however, bridges the gap between intellectual assent and decision through 'the mystic way': imitation.[123]

'Beyond instinct and habit', Bergson writes, 'there is no direct action on the will except feeling'.[124] Affect brings about action. And mystical affect is inspired by example,[125] which provokes mystics to 'open their souls' to 'an onslaught of love': 'A love which thus causes each of them to be loved for himself, so that through him, and for him, other men will open their souls to the love of humanity'.[126] Heroism, he writes:

> cannot be preached, it has only to show itself, and its mere presence may stir others to action. For heroism itself is a return to movement, and emanates from an emotion – infectious like all emotions – akin to the creative act. Religion expresses this truth in its own way by saying that it is in God that we love all other men. And all great mystics declare that they have the impression of a current passing from their soul to God, and flowing back again from God to mankind.[127]

Dynamic religion, like static, draws on the faculty of myth-making, although in saying this again, Bergson warns his reader that he should not relegate the 'myths' to the 'imaginary' negatively connoted. 'We call imagination any concrete representation which is neither perception nor memory', Bergson writes, but myth-making is a faculty which 'creat[es] personalities whose stories we relate to ourselves'.[128]

Bergson's sine qua non of dynamic religion, which he describes as 'what is specifically religious in religion' is a 'state of soul'.[129] It is an affective state of creative emotion, which most often expresses itself in active joy[130] and love.[131] But such mysticism is rare. Religion is to mysticism, Bergson writes, as popularization is to science. And consequently 'The thing itself is confused with its expression or its symbol. This is the usual error of a sheer intellectualism'.[132]

Conclusion

We have now seen that mysticism was a subject of intense analysis and debate between French philosophers during the first decades of the twentieth century. Some claimed that mystics themselves were doing metaphysics; others that mystics were denigrating reason or defying revealed religion; and others still that mysticism overcame the Kantian gaps between assent, will, and action. It was into this intellectual context that Henri Brémond's eleven-volume *Histoire littéraire du sentiment religieux en France* was published between 1916 and 1933. It was during the interwar period that France had its second 'Nietzschean moment',[133] and its first Kierkegaardian one: from 1927 onward, Kierkegaard became a 'necessary' thinker in confronting the anxiety of modernity.[134] And it was into this intellectual context that a new wave of post-revolutionary translations of Dostoevsky appeared. These authors' emphases on individuality, moral perfectionism, and aestheticism – and their questions about the relationship between philosophy, religion, and modernity – mixed with the indigenous interests of the French philosophical elite to set the scene for the next generation of philosophers: the existentialists.

Notes

1 Léon Brunschvicg, 'La vie religieuse' *Revue métaphysique et de morale* 8 (1900): 1–22, here p. 1.
2 Emile Boutroux, 'La psychologie du mysticisme' *Revue bleue*, 15 mars 1902, cited in Paul Archambault, *Boutroux* (Paris: Vald. Rasmussen, 1928), p. 189.
3 Michel de Certeau, *The Mystic Fable, Vol. 1: The Sixteenth and Seventeenth Centuries*, trans. Michael B. Smith (Chicago: University of Chicago Press, 1992); *Heterologies: Discourse on the Other*, trans. Brian Massumi (Minneapolis: University of Minnesota Press, 1986).
4 See Amy Hollywood's introduction to *The Cambridge Companion to Christian Mysticism*, ed. A. Hollywood and P. Z. Beckman (Cambridge: Cambridge University Press, 2012), pp. 1–37.
5 André Bord, *Jean de la Croix en France* (Vendôme: Beauchesne, 1993), p. 145.
6 Leigh Eric Schmidt, 'The Making of Modern "Mysticism"' *Journal of the American Academy of Religion* 71(2): 273–302, here p. 275.
7 On seventeenth-century Augustinianisms in France, see Pierre Magnard, 'La querelle des augustinismes' in Denise Leduc-Lafayette (ed.), *Fénelon: Philosophie et Spiritualité* (Geneva: Librairie Droz, 1996).
8 Schmidt, 'The Making of Modern "Mysticism"', p. 285.
9 Schmidt, 'The Making of Modern "Mysticism"', p. 286.
10 Blondel, among others, is mentioned in the preface of James's *Pragmatism* (1907).
11 For more on the formation and character of these relationships, see Barbara Loerzer, 'William James, the French Tradition, and the Incomplete Transposition of the Spiritual into the Aesthetic' in Martin Halliwell and Joel D. S. Rasmussen (eds.), *William James and the Transatlantic Conversation: Pragmatism, Pluralism, and the Philosophy of Religion* (Oxford: Oxford University Press, 2014).
12 See Gary Gutting, *French Philosophy in the Twentieth Century* (Cambridge: Cambridge University Press, 2001).

13 Edwin Diller Starbuck, *The Psychology of Religion: An Empirical Study of the Growth of Religious Consciousness* (London: Walter Scott, 1899). With a preface by William James.
14 Émile Boutroux, 'Préface', to William James, *L'Expérience Religieuse: Essai de psychologie descriptive*, trans. F. Abauzit (Paris: Alcan, 1906), p. viii.
15 Gutting, *French Philosophy*, p. 8.
16 William James, *The Varieties of Religious Experience* (London: Penguin Books, 1982), p. 432.
17 'Some distinguish between a mystical and a practical theology, but this is a distinction which I do not wish to employ'. Quoted in William M. Thompson, 'Introduction' in Pierre de Bérulle, *Bérulle and the French School: Selected Writings*, ed. William M. Thompson and trans. Lowell M. Glendon (New York: Paulist Press, 1989), p. 32.
18 Victor Charbonnel, *Les Mystiques dans la literature présente* (Paris: Mercure, 1897).
19 Charbonnel, *Les Mystiques*, p. 8.
20 Michael Conway, 'With Heart and Mind: Maurice Blondel and the Mystic Life' in Louise Nelstrop and Bradley B. Onishi (eds.), *Mysticism in the French Tradition* (Farnham: Ashgate, 2015), p. 22, n. 16, citing André Lalande, *Vocabulaire technique et critique de la philosophie*, 6th ed (Paris: Presses Universitaires de France, 1988), vol. 1, pp. 662–5.
21 Eventually this would give rise to the well-known debate in the 1930s concerning the status and meaning of Christian philosophy, which included such luminaries as Émile Bréhier, Étienne Gilson, Maurice Blondel, Léon Brunschvicg, Jacques Maritain, Gabriel Marcel, Auguste Lecerf, Pierre Maury, and Henri de Lubac.
22 Cited by Jean Lacroix, *Maurice Blondel: Sa vie, son oeuvre, avec un exposé de sa philosophie* (Paris: Presses Universitaires de France, 1963), p. 33.
23 Maurice Blondel, *Action*, trans. Olivia Blanchette (Notre Dame, IN: University of Notre Dame Press, 1984), p. 303.
24 Blondel, *Action*, p. 328. This points forward towards an important theme in Sartre's, *Being and Nothingness*.
25 Blondel, *Action*, p. 328.
26 Gutting, *French Philosophy*, p. 84, n. 1.
27 Conway, 'With Heart and Mind'.
28 See Maurice Gex, 'L'idéalisme critique de Léon Brunschvicg' *Revue de théologie et de philosophie* 20 (1970): 145–64, especially pp. 153ff.
29 Léon Brunschvicg, *De la vraie et de la fausse conversion* (Paris: Presses Universitaires de France, 1950), p. 153.
30 Léon Brunschvicg, *De la connaissance de soi* (Paris: Felix Alcan, 1931), p. 55.
31 Léon Brunschvicg, *Héritage des mots, héritage d'idées* (Paris: Presses Universitaires de France, 1945), pp. 63–4.
32 Léon Brunschvicg, *Descartes et Pascal lecteurs de Montaigne* (Neuchâtel: Editions de la baconnière, 1942), p. 142.
33 See Hellen E. Cullen, *A Philosophical Anthropology Drawn from Simone Weil's Life and Writings* (Victoria, BC: Friesen Press, 2017), p. 16.
34 Delacroix studied under Bergson at the Lycée Henri IV and Boutroux at the Sorbonne.
35 Delacroix was a student of Henri Bergson, but Bergson's part in the revival of interest in mysticism came after his pupil's, so Bergson is discussed later in this chapter.
36 Henri Delacroix, *Essai sur le mysticisme spéculatif en Allemagne au XIVe siècle* (Paris: Alcan, 1900), p. 1.
37 Delacroix, *Essai sur le mysticisme spéculatif*, pp. 2–3. See the introduction to this work for further details of which Eckhart texts (or texts attributed thereto)

Delacroix considered. See also pp. 149–69 on his use and evaluation of Franz Pfeiffer's edition (1845, 1857).
38 Delacroix, *Essai sur le mysticisme spéculatif*, p. 4.
39 Delacroix, *Essai sur le mysticisme spéculatif*, p. 8.
40 Delacroix, *Essai sur le mysticisme spéculatif*, p. 9, n. 1.
41 Delacroix, *Essai sur le mysticisme spéculatif*, p. 11.
42 Delacroix, *Essai sur le mysticisme spéculatif*, p. 17.
43 Delacroix, *Essai sur le mysticisme spéculatif*, p. 144.
44 Delacroix, *Essai sur le mysticisme spéculatif*, p. 149. See also Chapter 7 for more on Eckhart's ontology.
45 Delacroix, *Essai sur le mysticisme spéculatif*, p. 171.
46 Delacroix, *Essai sur le mysticisme spéculatif*, p. 173.
47 Delacroix, *Essai sur le mysticisme spéculatif*, p. 181; "il est le sujet de son propre être, il peut dire: Moi".
48 In French: l'art de la vie intime (p. 146).
49 Delacroix, *Essai sur le mysticisme spéculatif*, p. 194.
50 Delacroix, *Essai sur le mysticisme spéculatif*, pp. 216–7.
51 Delacroix, *Essai sur le mysticisme spéculatif*, p. 275.
52 Delacroix, *Essai sur le mysticisme spéculatif*, pp. 5–6.
53 At the time it was expected to be published in French translation in December 1903; in fact it appeared in 1906.
54 Henri Delacroix, 'Le développement des états mystiques chez Sainte Thérèse' *Bulletins de la Société Française de Philosophie* 6 (1906): 1–42; 'Analyse du mysticisme de Mme Guyon' *Revue Métaphysique et de Morale* 15 (1906): 721–46.
55 Conway, 'With Heart and Mind', p. 20.
56 Conway, 'With Heart and Mind', p. 19.
57 Henri Delacroix, 'Note sur Christianisme et mysticisme' *Revue de Métaphysique et de Morale* 16 (1908): 771–82, here p. 771.
58 Conway, 'With Heart and Mind', p. 19.
59 Conway, 'With Heart and Mind', p. 23.
60 Henri Delacroix, *Études d'histoire et de psychologie du mysticisme* (Paris: Alcan, 1908), p. i.
61 Delacroix, 'Note sur Christianisme', p. 775.
62 Delacroix, 'Note sur Christianisme' pp. 780–1.
63 Jean Baruzi, *Saint Jean de la Croix et le problème de l'experience mystique* (Paris: Alcan, 1924), pp. 448, 450.
64 Baruzi, *Saint Jean de la Croix*, p. 452.
65 Jean Baruzi, *Leibniz et l'organisation religieuse de la terre, d'après des documents inédits* (Paris: Alcan, 1907).
66 Jean Baruzi, *Leibniz, avec de nombreux textes inédits* (Paris: Bloud et Cie, 1909), p. 312. (Hereafter *Leibniz*).
67 Leibniz to Morell, 10 December 1696, quoted in Baruzi, *Leibniz*, p. 326.
68 Baruzi, *Leibniz*, p. 327.
69 Baruzi, *Leibniz*, pp. 328–35.
70 Baruzi, *Leibniz*, p. 330.
71 Leibniz to Morell, 24 November 1696, cited in Baruzi, *Leibniz*, p. 337.
72 Leiniz to Morell, 1 October 1697, cited in Baruzi, *Leibniz*, p. 342. 'There are some philosophers, Arabs and others, who conceive of the soul as finally ruined [*abîmée*] in God, which is to say Kennica, the universal spirit, or in effect, annihilated. Such an abnegation, under beautiful words, overturns all piety and virtue' (p. 343).
73 Leibniz, *Von der wahren Theologia mystica*, cited in Baruzi, *Leibniz*, p. 375.
74 Leibniz to Morell, 11 May 1697, cited in Baruzi, *Leibniz*, p. 340.

75 See Jacques Le Brun, 'France: VI. Le Grand Siècle de la Spiritualité Française et ses Lendemains' in *Dictionnaire de spiritualité*, Tome 5 (Paris: Beauchesne, 1960), cols 921–3; see also Baruzi, *Saint Jean de la Croix*, pp. 732–7.

76 See, for example, Henri Bergson, *Time and Free Will: An Essay on the Immediate Data of Consciousness*, trans. F. L. Pogson (New York: Dover, 2001), p. 231.

77 See Margaret Simons, 'The Beginnings of Beauvoir's Existential Phenomenology' in W. O'Brien and L. Embree (eds.), *The Existential Phenomenology of Simone de Beauvoir*, Contributions to Phenomenology, vol. 43 (Dordrecht: Springer, 2001), p. 34. Baruzi's first direct reference to Husserl came in his inaugural lecture at the Collège de France in 1926: 'The problem of salvation in the religious thought of Leibniz'.

78 Baruzi, *Saint Jean de la Croix*, p. iv.

79 See Simons, 'Beginnings of Beauvoir's Phenomenology', p. 34.

80 Jean-Louis Vieillard-Baron, 'Présentation', to Jean Baruzi, *L'Intelligence mystique* (Paris: Berg International, 1985), p. 16.

81 See Bergson, *Time and Free Will*, pp. 132–3.

82 Bergson, cited in Juan-Miguel Palacios, 'Bergson en Espagne (1916). Les conférences des 2 et 6 mai 1916' *Les études bergsoniennes* 9 (1970): 13.

83 Jean Baruzi, 'Saint Jean de la Croix et le problème de la valeur noétique de l'éxpérience mystique' *Bulletin de la Société Française de Philosophie* (mai–juin 1925): 25–88, p. 64.

84 In a lengthy 1926 article on Husserl (who had not yet been translated into French), Lev Shestov wrote that the problem with Husserl's philosophy is that it takes humanity to need not wisdom, not depth of thought, but philosophy as 'a rigorous science'. See Lev Shestov, 'Memento Mori (a propos de la théorie de la connaissance d'Edmond Husserl' *Revue Philosophique de la France et de l'Etranger* 101 (janvier à juin 1926): 5–62, p. 10.

85 See Simone Pétrement, 'Remarques sur Lagneau, Alain et la philosophie allemande contemporaine' *Revue du Métaphysique et de Morale* 75(3) (juillet–septembre 1970): 292–300, here p. 295.

86 Cited in Pétrement, 'Remarques', p. 294.

87 See Pétrement, 'Remarques', p. 292.

88 See Pétrement, 'Remarques', p. 293.

89 Jules Lagneau, *De l'existence de Dieu* (Paris: Alcan, 1925), p. 2.

90 Lagneau's *De l'existence* also abounds in the language of annihilation and self-abnegation: even his reading of Kantian 'duty' is rendered an 'annihilation of the will' (p. 25).

91 Lagneau, *De l'existence*, p. 41.

92 Jean Baruzi, 'Leibniz et l'idée de schisme' *Revue catholique des Églises* (octobre 1907): 119.

93 Vieillard-Baron, 'Présentation', p. 25.

94 On the influence of Bergson on Baruzi and Baruzi on Bergson, see Vieillard-Baron, 'Présentation', pp. 28–30.

95 Henri Bergson, quoted in Ralph Barton Perry, *The Thought and Character of William James: As Revealed in Unpublished Correspondence*, 2 vols (Boston: Little, Brown, 1935), vol. 2, p. 614.

96 Henri Bergson, *The Two Sources of Morality and Religion*, trans. R. Ashley Audra and Cloudesley Brereton (Notre Dame, IN: University of Notre Dame Press, 1977), p. 5.

97 Vieillard-Baron, 'Présentation', p. 17.

98 Bergson, *Two Sources*, p. 166.

99 Bergson, *Two Sources*, p. 85.

100 Bergson, *Two Sources*, p. 102.

101 Bergson, *Two Sources*, pp. 107–8.
102 See Bergson, *Two Sources*, p. 108; for an explanation of the myth-making faculty as 'counteracting the work of intelligence' through 'the agency of intelligence itself', see p. 119.
103 Bergson, *Two Sources*, p. 123.
104 See Bergson, *Two Sources*, p. 129.
105 Bergson, *Two Sources*, p. 122.
106 Bergson, *Two Sources*, p. 140.
107 Bergson, *Two Sources*, p. 205.
108 Bergson, *Two Sources*, p. 176.
109 David C. Lamberth, '*A Pluralistic Universe* a Century Later: Rationality, Pluralism, and Religion' in Martin Halliwell and Joel D. S. Rasmussen (eds.), *William James and the Transatlantic Conversation* (Oxford: Oxford University Press, 2014), p. 138. Bergson discusses intellectualism in several places in *Two Sources*: for example, p. 40.
110 Bergson, *Two Sources*, p. 210.
111 See Bergson, *Two Sources*, pp. 163–73.
112 Bergson, *Two Sources*, p. 168.
113 Bergson, *Two Sources*, p. 173.
114 Bergson, *Two Sources*, p. 153.
115 Bergson, *Two Sources*, p. 201.
116 Bergson, *Two Sources*, p. 199. 'Each of us belongs as much to society as to himself' (Bergson, *Two Sources*, p. 14).
117 Hjalmar Sundén, *La théorie Bergsonienne de la religion* (Paris: Presses Universitaires de France, 1947), p. 292.
118 Bergson, *Two Sources*, p. 84. See also p. 267.
119 Bergson, *Two Sources*, pp. 212, 213.
120 Bergson, *Two Sources*, p. 220.
121 Bergson, *Two Sources*, p. 48.
122 Bergson, *Two Sources*, pp. 87, 89.
123 See Bergson, *Two Sources*, p. 97 on the two ways to 'get a hold over the will': training and 'the mystic way', imitation.
124 Bergson, *Two Sources*, p. 39.
125 Bergson, *Two Sources*, pp. 50, 52.
126 Bergson, *Two Sources*, p. 99.
127 Bergson, *Two Sources*, p. 53.
128 Bergson, *Two Sources*, p. 195.
129 Bergson, *Two Sources*, p. 268.
130 See, for example, Bergson, *Two Sources*, pp. 52, 58, 230, 317.
131 On love ('which absorbs and kindles the whole soul' [Bergson, *Two Sources*, p. 54]) see p. 78 on Gospels as message of overflowing love; as consuming 'which consumes him', 'through God he loves all mankind with a divine love' (p. 233 and see following). The mystic soul wants to become an instrument 'to be turned to some use by God' (p. 231). 'God is love, and the object of love: herein lies the whole contribution of mysticism. About this twofold love the mystic will never have done talking' (p. 252). On the mystic view: 'Beings have been called into existence who were destined to love and be loved, since creative energy is defined as love.' (p. 257).
132 Bergson, *Two Sources*, p. 269.
133 See Vincent Descombes, 'Le Moment français de Nietzsche' in Alain Boyer et al. (eds.), *Pourquoi nous ne sommes pas nietzschéens* (Paris: Grasset, 1991), p. 101.
134 See Margaret Teboul, 'La reception de Kierkegaard en France 1930–1960', *Revue des Sciences Philosophiques et Théologiques* 89(2) (2005): 315–36.

Works cited

Baruzi, Jean, *Leibniz, avec de nombreux textes inédits* (Paris: Bloud et Cie, 1909).
———, 'Leibniz et l'idée de schisme', *Revue catholique des Églises* (octobre 1907): 453–74.
———, *Leibniz et l'organisation religieuse de la terre, d'après des documents inédits* (Paris: Alcan, 1907).
———, *L'Intelligence mystique* (Paris: Berg International, 1985).
———, *Saint Jean de la Croix et le problème de l'experience mystique* (Paris: Alcan, 1924).
———, 'Saint Jean de la Croix et le problème de la valeur noétique de l'éxpérience mystique', *Bulletin de la Société Française de Philosophie* (mai–juin 1925): 25–88.
Bergson, Henri, *Time and Free Will: An Essay on the Immediate Data of Consciousness*, trans. F. L. Pogson (New York: Dover, 2001).
———, *The Two Sources of Morality and Religion*, trans. R. Ashley Audra and Cloudesley Brereton (Notre Dame, IN: University of Notre Dame Press, 1977).
Bérulle, Pierre de, *Bérulle and the French School: Selected Writings*, ed. William M. Thompson, trans. Lowell M. Glendon (New York: Paulist Press, 1989).
Blondel, Maurice, *Action*, trans. Olivia Blanchette (Notre Dame, IN: University of Notre Dame Press, 1984), p. 303.
Bord, André, *Jean de la Croix en France* (Vendôme: Beauchesne, 1993).
Boutroux, Émile, 'Préface' to William James, *L'Expérience Religieuse: Essai de psychologie descriptive*, trans. F. Abauzit (Paris: Alcan, 1906).
———, 'La psychologie du mysticisme', *Revue bleue* (15 mars 1902), cited in Paul Archambault, *Boutroux* (Paris: Vald. Rasmussen, 1928), p. 189.
Brunschvicg, Léon, *De la connaissance de soi* (Paris: Felix Alcan, 1931).
———, *De la vraie et de la fausse conversion* (Paris: Presses Universitaires de France, 1950).
———, *Héritage des mots, héritage d'idées* (Paris: Presses Universitaires de France, 1945).
———, 'La vie religieuse', *Revue métaphysique et de morale* 8 (1900): 1–22.
Certeau, Michel de, *Heterologies: Discourse on the Other*, trans. Brian Massumi (Minneapolis: University of Minnesota Press, 1986).
———, *The Mystic Fable, Vol. 1: The Sixteenth and Seventeenth Centuries*, trans. Michael B. Smith (Chicago: Chicago University Press, 1992).
Charbonnel, Victor, *Les Mystiques dans la littérature présente* (Paris: Mercure, 1897).
Conway, Michael, 'With Heart and Mind: Maurice Blondel and the Mystic Life', in Louise Nelstrop and Bradley B. Onishi (eds.), *Mysticism in the French Tradition* (Farnham: Ashgate, 2015).
Cullen, Hellen E., *A Philosophical Anthropology Drawn from Simone Weil's Life and Writings* (Victoria, BC: Friesen Press, 2017).
Delacroix, Henri, 'Analyse du mysticisme de Mme Guyon', *Revue Métaphysique et de Morale* 15 (1906): 721–46.
———, *Essai sur le mysticisme spéculatif en Allemagne au XIVe siècle* (Paris: Alcan, 1900).
———, *Études d'histoire et de psychologie du mysticisme* (Paris: Alcan, 1908).
———, 'Le développement des états mystiques chez Sainte Thérèse', *Bulletins de la Société Française de Philosophie* 6 (1906): 1–42.

———, 'Note sur Christianisme et mysticisme' *Revue de Métaphysique et de Morale* 16 (1908): 771–82.

Descombes, Vincent, 'Le Moment français de Nietzsche', in Alain Boyer et al. (eds.), *Pourquoi nous ne sommes pas nietzschéens* (Paris: Grasset, 1991).

Gex, Maurice, 'L'idéalisme critique de Léon Brunschvicg', *Revue de théologie et de philosophie* 20 (1970): 145–64.

Gutting, Gary, *French Philosophy in the Twentieth Century* (Cambridge: Cambridge University Press, 2001).

Hollywood, Amy, 'Introduction' to *The Cambridge Companion to Christian Mysticism*, ed. A. Hollywood and P. Z. Beckman (Cambridge: Cambridge University Press, 2012).

James, William, *The Varieties of Religious Experience* (London: Penguin, 1982).

Jones, Rufus, *New Studies in Mystical Religion* (New York: Macmillan, 1927).

Lacroix, Jean, *Maurice Blondel: Sa vie, son oeuvre, avec un exposé de sa philosophie* (Paris: Presses Universitaires de France, 1963).

Lalande, André, *Vocabulaire technique et critique de la philosophie*, 6th edition (Paris: PUF, 1988).

Lamberth, David C. '*A Pluralistic Universe* a Century Later: Rationality, Pluralism, and Religion', in Martin Halliwell and Joel D. S. Rasmussen (eds.), *William James and the Transatlantic Conversation* (Oxford: Oxford University Press, 2014).

Lagneau, Jules, *Célèbres leçons de Jules Lagneau* (Nîmes: Imprimerie Coopérative La Laborieuse, 1928).

———, *De l'existence de Dieu* (Paris: Alcan, 1925).

Le Brun, Jacques, 'France: VI. Le Grand Siècle de la Spiritualité Française et ses Lendemains', in *Dictionnaire de spiritualité*, tome V (Paris: Beauchesne, 1960).

Loerzer, Barbara, 'William James, the French Tradition, and the Incomplete Transposition of the Spiritual into the Aesthetic', in Martin Halliwell and Joel D. S. Rasmussen (eds.), *William James and the Transatlantic Conversation: Pragmatism, Pluralism, and the Philosophy of Religion* (Oxford: Oxford University Press, 2014).

Magnard, Pierre, 'La querelle des augustinismes', in Denise Leduc-Lafayette (ed.), *Fénelon: Philosophie et Spiritualité* (Geneva: Librairie Droz, 1996).

Palacios, Juan-Miguel, 'Bergson en Espagne (1916). Les conférences des 2 et 6 mai 1916', in *Les études bergsoniennes*, tome IX (Paris : Presses Universitaires de France, 1970).

Perry, Ralph Barton, *The Thought and Character of William James: As Revealed in Unpublished Correspondence*, 2 vols (Boston: Little, Brown, 1935).

Schmidt, Leigh Eric, 'The Making of Modern "Mysticism"', *Journal of the American Academy of Religion* 71(2) (2003): 273–302.

Shestov, Lev, 'Memento Mori (a propos de la théorie de la connaissance d'Edmond Husserl', *Revue Philosophique de la France et de l'Etranger*, trans. B. de Schoelzer 101 (janvier à juin 1926): 5–62.

Simons, Margaret, 'The Beginnings of Beauvoir's Existential Phenomenology', in W. O'Brien and L. Embree (eds.), *The Existential Phenomenology of Simone de Beauvoir*, Contributions to Phenomenology Vol. 43 (Dordrecht: Springer, 2001).

Starbuck, Edwin Diller, *The Psychology of Religion: An Empirical Study of the Growth of Religious Consciousness* (London: Walter Scott, 1899).

Sundén, Hjalmar, *La théorie Bergsonienne de la religion* (Paris: Presses Universitaires de France, 1947).

Teboul, Margaret, 'La reception de Kierkegaard en France 1930–1960', *Revue des Sciences Philosophiques et Théologiques* 89(2) (2005): 315–36.
Thompson, William M., 'Introduction' to Pierre de Bérulle, *Bérulle and the French School: Selected Writings*, ed. William M. Thompson, trans. Lowell M. Glendon (New York: Paulist Press, 1989).
Vieillard-Baron, Jean-Louis, 'Présentation' to Jean Baruzi, *L'Intelligence mystique* (Paris: Berg International, 1985).

4 Beauvoir and Sartre

Love and value in the phenomenal world

We come now to the two figures who, more than any others, are identified with the term 'existentialism': Simone de Beauvoir and Jean-Paul Sartre. As such, they are probably generally regarded as being remote from anything 'mystical', and we have already noted Sartre's surprise at being called 'a mystic'. However, even if it is the case that neither is 'a mystic', we shall see that mysticism, especially as mediated by the figures considered in the previous chapter, played a significant role in their intellectual evolution and left positive as well as negative traces in their mature work.

Simone de Beauvoir

Simone de Beauvoir is often presented as Jean-Paul Sartre's derivative double – as a distinguished novelist, memoirist, and feminist, but one whose distinction resulted primarily from popularizing Sartre's ideas rather than from philosophical insights of her own. The recent publication of Beauvoir's student diaries in French, however, has revealed that Beauvoir's philosophical formation shared many significant features with Sartre's, including the reading of theological and mystical sources, and that Beauvoir formed some convictions and distinctions which would later be known as 'existentialist' *before* she met Sartre in 1929.[1] For example, she defined her central philosophical question as the opposition between self and other as early as 1927,[2] and distinguished between what she called 'the view from within' and the 'view from without',[3] which closely resemble Sartre's being-for-itself and being-for-others. These recent publications also illuminate the reasons why, as Joseph Mahon observed, 'For someone who so vehemently rejected God, Simone de Beauvoir wrote an extraordinary amount about Him'.[4]

Beauvoir was raised in a decreasingly haute bourgeois family in Paris, by a Catholic mother and a *laïque* father. Like other existentialists, she was prolific, and her works span many genres: she wrote five novels, two collections of short stories, a play, four volumes of autobiography and two memoirs, interviews, philosophical essays, feminist essays, political essays, reviews, prefaces, and *The Second Sex*. *The Second Sex* was published in English in 1953 in a much abridged and unphilosophical translation by

H. M. Parshley and, apart from *The Ethics of Ambiguity*, which was published in English translation in 1976, significant parts of Beauvoir's philosophy have not been available in English.

Even in French, the student diaries were not published until 2008. They show that love – a theme that runs throughout Beauvoir's works, literary, philosophical, and feminist – was one of her earliest philosophical preoccupations. In particular, Beauvoir is concerned about the relation between concepts of love and value, action and justice. In her 1944 essay *Pyrrhus and Cinéas*, for example, she discusses the 'love command' of the New Testament: Christ's injunction to 'love your neighbour as yourself'. When the disciples asked Christ 'Who is my neighbour?', Beauvoir writes, he did not respond by giving them an abstract enumeration of an ethics. He told them the parable of the Good Samaritan, who made a neighbour of the man abandoned on the roadside by covering him with his coat. In Beauvoir's view, 'One *is* not the neighbour of anyone. One *makes* the other a neighbour by treating him as a neighbour in action'.[5]

In the same work, Beauvoir cites the mystic Angelus Silesius with approval: 'God needs me, just as I need him'.[6] In order to demonstrate the mystical sources informing Beauvoir's thought, this section will compare her published autobiographical writings with her student diaries, showing some of the ways in which her public persona involved an erasure of Beauvoir's study of mystics and struggling with mysticism, epistemological and experiential. It will also argue that Beauvoir's later work distinguished between types of mysticism and mystification and that this distinction clarifies some of the tensions that earlier readers of Beauvoir have perceived in the chapter of *The Second Sex* entitled 'The Mystic'.

Mysticism in autobiography

Simone de Beauvoir's first published volume of autobiography, *Memoirs of a Dutiful Daughter*, describes her childhood from her birth in 1908 until her student days, during which she met Jean-Paul Sartre in the summer of 1929. In *Memoirs of a Dutiful Daughter*, she describes her Catholic upbringing and realization of her loss of faith at the age of 15. However, she also alludes to a period in her student years, prior to meeting Sartre, during which she was 'tempted by mysticism'. As she recounts the period in her memoirs, it was a time of despair, characterized by feeling that

> The earth was nothing to me any more; I was 'outside life'. I didn't even want to write any more; the horrible vanity of all things had me by the throat again; but I had had enough of suffering and weeping in the past year; I built a new hope for myself. In moments of perfect detachment when the universe seems to be reduced to a set of illusions and in which my own ego was abolished, something took their place: something indestructible, eternal; it seemed to me that my indifference was a negative

> manifestation of a presence which it was perhaps not impossible to get in touch with.[7]

In the memoirs she wrote that it was not the Christian God she experienced, adding that she was increasingly disgusted by Catholicism.[8] But the certainty of the voice in the memoirs – a careful narrative crafted for public consumption – differs markedly from the spiritual and intellectual wrestling Beauvoir expressed in her diary at the time. In the memoirs, Beauvoir acknowledged that she had been in conversations with 'Mademoiselle Lambert' (a pseudonym for Jeanne Mercier) and 'Pradelle' (Maurice Merleau-Ponty), both of whom affirmed the idea that it was possible to attain true 'being'. Beauvoir wrote that she

> read Plotinus and books about mystical psychology; I began to wonder if, beyond the limitations of reason, certain experiences were not susceptible to revealing the absolute to me; I was seeking fulfilment in this desert of abstraction in which I was reducing the inhospitable world to sand. Why shouldn't a mystical theology be possible? 'I want to touch God or become God', I declared in my journal. All through that year I abandoned myself intermittently to these deliriums.[9]

Jeanne Mercier (1896–1991) was one of the first female *agrégées* in philosophy. She went on to publish reviews on Bergson and Blondel and wrote articles on Blondel, including a commentary on his book *Action*.[10] Better known to philosophical posterity, Merleau-Ponty had sought out Beauvoir's conversation after she attained excellent results on a competitive exam, and her student diaries include reflections on many of their conversations about God, faith, and reason. We will return to explore these conversations from 1927 at greater length. But the diaries begin earlier, in 1926, and contain a significant episode that illuminates the persistent questions Beauvoir had about what it meant to love another as oneself and whether one could do so without sacrificing oneself and justice.

In August 1926 Beauvoir made a pilgrimage to Lourdes with her aunt. When she saw the physical suffering of the sick who sought healing, she was overwhelmed, feeling 'disgust at all the intellectual and sentimental elegance before the invalids'. Her own sorrows seemed nothing compared to their physical pain and distress. She felt ashamed and thought that a life of complete self-giving – even 'self-abnegation' – was the only appropriate response.[11]

But in a later diary entry she reflected that she had been wrong to reach this conclusion. She urged herself not to be ashamed of living: she was given a life, and so it was her duty to live it in the best possible way. To give herself away completely, in fact, would be 'moral suicide'. But it would also be easier than deciding how much of herself to give and how much to keep. She called what was needed 'equilibrium': in which people gave themselves without 'annihilat[ing] the consciousness of themselves in order to serve others'.[12]

Six days later she returned to this theme in her diaries, discussing two poles of possibility: devotion and egoism. Although the word 'devotion' takes on negative connotations in *The Second* Sex, at this stage Beauvoir wrote that she wanted to be devoted to others because she had 'a liking for beings'. But she also recognized her own uniqueness and desire to be individual:

> Certainly, I am very individualistic, but is this incompatible with the devotion and disinterested love of others? It seems to me that there is one part of me that is made to be given away, another that is made to be kept and cultivated. The second part is valid in itself and guarantees the value of the other.[13]

Two decades later Beauvoir would write *The Ethics of Ambiguity*, claiming that it offered an ethics that was individual but not solipsistic.[14] An injunction to 'love', in Beauvoir's reading, leaves room for vices of excess and deficiency for both the other and the self, and equilibrium (or reciprocity)[15] is not something that can be achieved once and for all but rather something that must always be pursued.

Beauvoir's memoirs mention childhood reading of Catholic devotional texts such as *The Imitation of Christ* and some lives of the saints, but the primary focus here will be her philosophical education in the late 1920s. Each of her notebooks opens with epigraphs that give some indication of her intellectual diet: Alain, Valéry, Schopenhauer, Lagneau, Bergson, Baudelaire, Nietzsche, Claudel, Mauriac, Péguy, and many others feature. As Margaret Simons has noted, although Beauvoir refers to her earlier loss of faith, her sustained interest in mysticism and spirituality is evident.[16] She took some solace in the 'cult of self' advocated by Maurice Barrès and by Charles Péguy's commitment to social justice and spirituality in action. But gradually her confidence in their value waned.

In May 1927 Beauvoir wrote in her diary that she knew that

> There is only one problem and one that has no solution, because it does not perhaps make sense. It is the one formulated by Pascal . . . I would want to believe in something – to meet with total exigency – to justify my life. In short, I would want God. Once formulated as such, I will not forget this. But knowing that this noumenal world exists, that I cannot attain, in which alone it can be explained to me why I live, I will build my life in the phenomenal world, which is nevertheless not negligible. I will take myself as an end.

But despite pronouncing this resolution, the diaries show the extent to which Beauvoir wrestled with it: 'Oh! My God, my God, is this being whom we would like to love and to whom we would give all, does this being truly not exist? I know nothing, and I am weary, weary. Why, if he is, does he make seeking him so difficult?'[17]

Multiple times she expressed frustration with her critical mind and the way it hindered what she called 'This need to be, this duty, in relationship to whom, in relationship to what?'[18] Jules Lagneau had taught that God could not be proven by intuition or by demonstration, but rather was known by an intimate *realization*.[19] In her diaries she discusses a phrase from Lagneau – 'I have no support but my absolute despair' – and resolved that her despair would be the basis on which she finds joy in life.[20]

Jeanne Mercier tried to convert Beauvoir, and Beauvoir admitted that she found some aspects of the prospect tempting:

> This morning while racing in vain to St. Cloud, I passionately desired to be the young girl who receives communion at morning mass and who walks with a serene certainty. Mauriac's and Claudel's Catholicism . . ., how it has marked me and what a place remains in me for it! And yet, I know that I will no longer know this; I do not desire to believer. An act of faith is the greatest act of despair that could be and I want my despair to preserve at least its lucidity. I do not want to lie to myself. Besides, this infinite God saves me only as a *person*; and it is my entire individual that I want to save.

Consequently, Beauvoir resolved to spell out her 'philosophical ideas . . . The theme is almost always this opposition of self and other . . . Now has come the time to make a synthesis of it'.[21]

In her memoirs Beauvoir wrote that in addition to talking with Mercier and Merleau-Ponty, she 'also went to hear Jean Baruzi, the author of a thesis that was very well thought of on St John of the Cross'.[22] But in fact Beauvoir did more than 'go to hear' Baruzi; she wrote a thesis under his supervision. Beauvoir liked Baruzi because, among other reasons, he would criticize her and took her seriously.[23] But in the memoirs Beauvoir is curiously silent about the philosophical content of her thesis, saying only that it treated 'the personality'.[24] The diaries show that her work for Baruzi included discussions of the concept of love.[25] The *Memoirs* report that Baruzi returned it to her with 'copious praise'; he told her that it was 'the basis of a serious work'.[26]

The 'personality' was a concept discussed by, among others, Henri Bergson, whom Beauvoir was reading during this period. In her diaries she quotes several lines from his works, including comments on mysticism and metaphysics: 'The metaphysician is a mystic who restrains himself. It is perhaps not normal to philosophize'.[27] Bergson would later write about an 'eruption' of mysticism 'in action'. But his conceptions of freedom and philosophy influenced the development of Beauvoir's thought. In *Time and Free Will*, Bergson wrote that 'we are free when our acts spring from our whole personality, when they express it, when they have that indefinable resemblance to it which one sometimes finds between the artist and his work'.[28]

Beauvoir would go on to write a thesis on the philosophy of Leibniz for the Diplôme d'Études Superieures under the supervision of Léon Brunschvicg. As we saw in Chapter 3, Leibniz had written (and Baruzi included in his edition) that the *place of the other* [*la place d'autrui*] is the true point of perspective in politics and in ethics.[29] Leibniz's discussion of is framed in terms of Christ's command to love one's neighbour.

Beauvoir's private reading and philosophical instruction both provided ample material for reflection on the 'opposition of self and other' and the compatibility of love and justice since, in the Jansenist view of sin and salvation, sin's antonym was *caritas*, which was given by grace to the few. In the eyes of its objectors this 'love' was famously arbitrary and therefore unjust and unloving. We know that Beauvoir's conversations with Merleau-Ponty included discussions of grace and of love and judgement. After recounting their difference of opinion in a passage from July 1927, Beauvoir describes having been 'tempted by mysticism':

> I know nothing, nothing; not only no answers but no presentable manner of posing the question. Scepticism, indifference are impossible, a religion is impossible for the moment – mysticism is tempting: but how will I know the value of a thought which leaves no place for thought? On what can I base my rejection or acceptance of it? Accept to spend two years in reading, conversations, fragmentary meditations. I am going to work like a brute: I don't have a minute to lose. And neglect nothing: link up with Baruzi, do my homework, try to know, to know.[30]

Beauvoir's diaries employ the word 'mysticism' in epistemological and experiential senses, and it is clear that at this stage she identifies – at least reluctantly – with both.

Epistemologically, Beauvoir writes,

> All explicative philosophy puts us in front of a remainder. Reason gives only the human element, necessity of a mysticism. Isn't the first crime to think? That is why I do not believe that philosophy will ever tell us the secret of the world; we are enclosed in reason and can judge reason only with itself: vicious circle. . . .
>
> Ponti [Merleau-Ponty] supports his [philosophy] with faith in reason, I on the powerlessness of reason. Who proves that Descartes prevails over Kant? I am maintaining what I wrote for the Sorbonne – use your reason, you will end up with remainders and irrational elements.
>
> But precisely in religion there is a mysticism, 'act of faith' – act of defiance in reason. If I am logical with myself, I must admit it. I have understood the act of faith, for at least a split second.[31]

At the age of 19, two years before meeting Sartre, Simone de Beauvoir was re-reading issues of *l'Ésprit* and studying mysticism, Kant, Bergson, Plato,

Leibniz, and Thomism.[32] That summer she concluded that she could not love God and the world at the same time – that somehow, loving God meant renouncing all the other things she loved and dreamed of loving, including herself as an 'individual'.[33]

But by the autumn her diary includes some very realist-looking references to God; her resolution to restrain herself to the phenomenal world was not kept at all times.[34]

Pyrrhus and Cinéas

In *Pyrrhus and Cinéas*, Beauvoir confronts the apparent absurdity of human projects in the absence of transcendent values; human projects 'seem absurd because they exist only by setting limits for themselves, and one can always overstep these limits, asking oneself derisively, "Why as far as this? Why not further? What's the use?"'[35]

Candide and Christ open her discussion: for Candide suggests that we must 'cultivate our garden', and Christ that we should 'love our neighbour'. But what, she asks, is my garden? Who is my neighbour? And how should I act, to love him? Beauvoir's essay includes references to Camus, Dostoevsky, Claudel, Hegel, Kant, Spinoza, Leibniz, and Pascal, among others. In the absence of God, Beauvoir writes, only I 'can create the tie that unites me to the other'; and only I can determine what is my garden, choosing 'its location and its limits'.[36] As we have seen already, it is through action that Beauvoir thinks one *makes* a neighbour of the other. Every human must decide what place to occupy in the world and how they will shape the world that others inhabit.

Beauvoir's ethics – which she will go on in the *Ethics of Ambiguity* to call 'ambiguous' in order to distinguish it from Camus's 'absurd' – is defined in contrast to what she calls 'the serious mind', which claims that there are values in the world that exist prior to the human bestowal of value upon them. Beauvoir credits Spinoza and Hegel with exposing the illusion of false objectivity which 'denies that any value exists in the world because it denies man's transcendence and wants to reduce him to his immanence alone'.[37]

In the section on God, Beauvoir distinguishes between different conceptions of God – as (i) plenitude of being and (ii) Catholic naturalism (which she finds in Paul Claudel), which she explores with reference to the German mystic Angelus Silesius. On the first view, in which God is 'infinity and the plenitude of being', Beauvoir writes that 'there is in him no distance between his project and his reality. What he wills is; he wills what is. His will is only the immobile foundation of being; one can barely still call it a will. Such a God is not a singular person. He is the universal, the unchangeable and eternal everything. And the universal is silence'. Pascal's 'eternal silence of these infinite spaces' is not explicitly invoked by Beauvoir here, but he is invoked to demonstrate the perpetually elusive nature of human desire.

On the second view, in which, as Paul Claudel put it, 'all is grace', Beauvoir writes that it is difficult to call any action evil because whatever exists is good. Beauvoir thinks that Claudel and likeminded Christians do not think through the consequences of this position. It is well and good for a gourmand priest to say that God would not have invented delicacies if they were not meant to be eaten. But, Beauvoir objects, 'he is carefully forgetting that God also invented woman. There was an old woman who, outraged, refused to put butter on her soft-boiled egg. "I eat it like the dear Lord made it", she said. And she reached for the salt shaker'.[38] In this view, virtue is to be found in the will of God. But how does one know which earthly vessel has accurately understood it?

There is another understanding of the relationship between God and man that Beauvoir thinks is 'conceivable'. As long as 'God is not all that has to be', Beauvoir says, 'man can found him'. Then man is in situation with respect to God. This is what Silesius means, by writing that 'God needs me as I need him'. If the Christian God is a living person for whom one can act, then this mystical, singular, personal God 'could satisfy the aspirations of human transcendence'.[39]

But this God is no longer the absolute, universal. And even a formal decision to want the will of God does not, as Beauvoir puts it, 'dictate any actions to man'. To the confident assertions of believers that we must listen to the voice of God, Beauvoir replies: 'God could manifest himself only through an earthly voice because our ears can hear no other. But how, then, does one recognize the divine nature?'[40] Beauvoir draws on Kierkegaard's *Fear and Trembling* to reiterate the point that what may be 'the voice of God' could be the devil's: 'The Catholic Church and the Protestant individualist can rightly reproach each other for taking the echo of their personal convictions as a divine inspiration'.[41]

Instead of God, whose will cannot be known on earth by anything but earthly means, Beauvoir suggests that human actions can be motivated by human others. Beauvoir does not assert the non-existence of God; in fact, she is openly uncertain: 'I don't know if God exists, and no experience can make him present for me'.[42] Beauvoir's proposal is that in the absence of God, actions should be oriented to the human other, because here, too, they can take on an infinite dimension by being witnessed and becoming the foundation of others' projects. When a child finishes a drawing, she writes, he is eager to show it to his parents – his accomplishment gains reality when it is beheld by their eyes. Although solitude can be enjoyable, Beauvoir says, no one is satisfied with it for entire life; we need witnesses: 'Even Saint Teresa wrote *The Interior Castle* and St John of the Cross his canticles'.[43]

The human need for affirmation by others often follows one of two wayward patterns she calls 'devotion' and 'self-interest'. Devotion has been the wish of 'many men, and even more women'. In Beauvoir's view, human beings must be justified, and devotion provides 'rest' from this exigency; devotion justifies one's existence because the devoted person takes her life to meets the need of another being who has value. Devotion does not escape the problems of Candide's garden or Christ's neighbour; it still raises the question 'To whom shall I devote myself?' But problematically, in devotion, the devoted person takes the end of the other as their own end – and wants it 'without him and against him'.[44] Devotion can be tyrannical – it claims to want the good of the other, but in fact it imposes a value on the other that may not be of his or her choosing. 'The fundamental error of devotion is that it considers the other as an object carrying an emptiness in its heart that would be possible to fill'.[45]

On the other hand, the 'ethics of self-interest' also assumes that there is 'an emptiness' – a *néant* – in the other person that can be filled by my action – and only my action. What is needful, in Beauvoir's view, is that the other is respected *as a freedom*, to choose their own values and pursue their own becoming.

Importantly, Beauvoir argues – in longstanding disagreement with Sartre, although he would later change his view – that Descartes's distinction between 'freedom' and 'power' must be upheld because while all human beings are free, they do not all have the same power to exercise their freedom.[46]

This theme of intersubjective dependence on the freedom of others is developed further in *The Ethics of Ambiguity*, where Beauvoir writes that no existence can be fulfilled if it is limited to itself. 'A man who seeks being far from other men, seeks it against them at the same time that he loses himself'.[47] And so is the theme of human constraint and oppression – Beauvoir repeatedly emphasized, against Sartre, that abstract freedom and the concrete power to exercise it were not equally distributed in the world: 'every individual may practice his freedom inside his world, but not everyone has the means of rejecting, even by doubt, the values, taboos, and prescriptions by which he is surrounded'.[48] *The Ethics of Ambiguity* draws on Husserl and Hegel to present an ethics of intersubjectivity that is individualist without solipsism. The aim of her student diaries, to find 'equilibrium' between self-giving and self-loss, remained a central philosophical concern. And such equilibrium was dependent on the *situation* of human action.

Attending to the 'situation' of women was a major motivation behind the writing of *The Second Sex*. At the end of the second volume, there is a chapter entitled 'The Mystic'. Along with 'Narcissism' and 'The Woman in Love', it is one of three chapters in a section entitled 'Justifications'. Beauvoir thinks that the 'traps of bad faith and the mystifications of seriousness' await both men and women, and that freedom belongs to each. But because the *situations* occupied by men and women have been such that men have had disproportionate power to exercise their freedom, Beauvoir took it to be the case that 'in woman this freedom remains abstract and empty'. For women to become truly free, a collective liberation of what she calls 'the feminine condition' was required.[49]

In order to achieve this collective liberation, Beauvoir held that 'mystifications' of love must be revealed for what they are. The term 'mystification' has several uses in the work of Marx, each of which indicates a collective obfuscation of the kind that benefits a select group of people: for example, the mystification of commodities and the mystification of history (e.g. about the emergence of capitalism) that benefited the bourgeoisie. Philosophical mystification, for Marx, occurs when philosophers are complicit in the practical building of power relationships in the domain of thoughts and ideas, instead of turning to the reality in which they are lived. Marx accused Hegel of such mystification, which legitimized state and empire, and determined to 'discover the rational kernel within the mystical shell'.[50]

In *The Second Sex*, Beauvoir discusses 'mystification' many more times than 'mysticism' because mysticism is only one possible form of mystification that has been used to perpetuate the oppression of women. She argues that '[women today] want transcendence to prevail over immanence in themselves as in all of humanity; they want abstract rights and concrete possibilities to be granted to them, without which freedom is merely mystification'.[51]

Unlike the student diaries, in which Beauvoir discussed mysticism in both epistemological and experiential senses, in *The Second Sex* her focus is on 'mystics', their experiences, and their actions. As in *Pyrrhus and Cinéas*, as we have seen, Beauvoir rejects the 'mystifications of seriousness' here because they assume ready-made values – in *The Second Sex*, the ready-made values she calls into question are the value of 'woman' and the ideals of the feminine. Alongside the mystifications of seriousness and devotion, which Beauvoir explicitly rejected in her earlier works and again rejects here, we find the mystifications of motherhood and religion as well. Of the latter she writes:

> There is a justification, a supreme compensation, that society has always been bent on dispensing to woman: religion. There must be religion for women as for the people, for exactly the same reasons: when a sex or a class is condemned to immanence, the mirage of transcendence must be offered to it. It is to man's total advantage to have God endorse the codes he creates: and specifically because he exercises sovereign authority over the woman, it is only right that this authority be conferred on him by the sovereign being. Among others, for Jews, Muslims, and Christians, man is the master by divine right: fear of God will stifle the slightest inclination of revolt in the oppressed. . . . If she throws herself so willingly into religion, it is because religion fills a profound need. In modern civilization, where freedom plays an important role – even for the woman – religion becomes less of an instrument of constraint than of mystification. The woman is less often asked to accept her inferiority in the name of God than to believe, thanks to him, that she is equal to the male lord; even the temptation to revolt is avoided by pretending to overcome injustice. The woman is no longer robbed of her transcendence, since she will dedicate her immanence to God; souls' merits are judged only in heaven and not according to their terrestrial accomplishments; here below, as Dostoevsky would have said, they are never more than occupations: shining shoes or building a bridge is the same vanity; over and above social discriminations, equality of the sexes is reestablished.[52]

Despite the dangers of mystification in religion, Beauvoir acknowledges the striking fact that religion is the cultural field in which women have been the most successful in asserting themselves. In particular, *mystics* are conspicuous exemplars of female agency.

In cases of royalty and religion, Beauvoir notes, there have been women who were 'neither male nor female': Catherine of Siena and Saint Teresa, she says, are 'saintly souls' whose 'lay life and their mystical life, their actions and their writings, rise to heights that few men ever attain'. It is legitimate to conclude on this basis, Beauvoir writes, that 'if other women failed to mark the world deeply, it is because they were trapped by their conditions'.[53]

Beauvoir's discussion of mystics in 'The Mystic' and in earlier passages of *The Second Sex* shows that she distinguishes between 'authentic' and hysteric mystics, calling some reports of mystical experience 'pathological'.[54] Beauvoir holds 'mystics of action' in higher esteem than mystics of contemplation – Teresa of Avila, Catherine of Siena, and Joan of Arc all belong to the former category and are deemed praiseworthy, but their contemplative counterparts are called 'lesser sisters'. This discrepancy has been noted by, among others, Pamela Sue Anderson and Amy Hollywood.[55] The latter writes that 'despite Beauvoir's predominantly negative attitude toward mysticism, she claims that, for Teresa, mysticism served as a support not for narcissism but for a transcendent and active form of subjectivity'.[56]

The Second Sex is a long text written in a famously difficult voice: it is not always clear when Beauvoir is advancing her own view, recounting the view of another, or articulating objections to others' views. She uses generalizing language and is not always consistent in her use of terms or clear in her distinctions. But it is clear that while some mystics are negative female exemplars, others are positive. Beauvoir writes that 'every mystic is aiming for' 'the source of supreme values'.[57] And yet she distinguishes between the narcissistic mysticism of Madame Guyon and Angela of Foligno and the self-annihilating 'devotion' of Marie Alacoque, which was lived out in extreme forms of bodily asceticism.[58]

What distinguishes Teresa from her 'lesser sisters', in Beauvoir's view, is that she understood that the value of mysticism was not the subjective experience of it. In Beauvoir's reading, the phenomena of ecstasy are almost identical in Saint Teresa and Marie Alacoque. But their messages are significantly different. Teresa's is intellectual and concerned with the relationship between the individual and God, the transcendent Being: the subjective experience has an objective scope.

Moreover, while interior mystical experience was enough for some women mystics, others were moved to action, leading to a further distinction:

> The connection between action and contemplation takes two very different forms. There are women of action like St Catherine, St Teresa and Joan of Arc who are well aware of the goals they set themselves and who lucidly invent the means to reach them: their revelations merely

> give an objective form to their certainties; they encourage them to take the paths they have carefully planned.

Narcissistic mystics, by contrast, don't care very much what they do as long as they do *something*; it flatters their self-love to feel that they are God's chosen. Beauvoir concludes the chapter by leaving open the possibility of an 'active and independent' life that includes 'mystical fervour'. But the only way for the mystic to accomplish her freedom in the world authentically 'is to project it by a positive action into human society'.[59] In Beauvoir's view, neither 'narcissism' nor 'devotion' – the cult of the self or the cult of its sacrifice – is compatible with love, which 'must be founded on the reciprocal recognition of true freedoms'.[60]

The indebtedness of these distinctions to Beauvoir's earlier work on love has significant explanatory power. Amy Hollywood argues that in *The Second Sex* 'as in her novels, Beauvoir insists that women, like men, desire to be everything'. Hollywood's argument draws on *She Came To Stay*, a metaphysical novel published in 1943. In the novel, Beauvoir explores the *desire to be* and the desire to disclose being; its main character, Françoise, says outright at one point that she wants 'to be all'. But this novel was Beauvoir's first, written in the early 1940s, and presents a solipsistic ethics which Beauvoir later deemed bad faith; the conclusion of the novel is a murder, and its epigraph and philosophical leitmotif is from Hegel – 'Each consciousness seeks the death of the other'. From *Pyrrhus and Cinéas* onward, Beauvoir articulated her disagreement with the Sartrean existentialism that valued radical freedom at the expense of others and saw all human relationships as the wrestling of subjects and objects, relentlessly captive to the master-slave dialectic. Instead, Beauvoir argued that the particularity of the individual can be valued without solipsism because the individual's actions in the world create being that will live beyond her in the lives of others.

In Hollywood's reading of Beauvoir, women were 'unable to act directly on the world, with the consequence that women can only seek transcendence and the justification of their existences through others (although, as we will see, these others are ultimately effaced in women's love for themselves)'.[61] However, as outlined above, Beauvoir's position is that everyone, male or female, seeks justification in the eyes of others, and that *no one*, male or female, can flourish alone. It is bad faith to think this is possible. It is also bad faith to desire to be 'all', for oneself or another – such desire leads us to either pole of failed love, narcissism, or devotion. Hollywood's reading of Beauvoir makes the central human project 'to be all', instead of, as Beauvoir outlined in *Pyrrhus and Cinéas*, to choose my place in the world and acknowledge my role as a shaper of the world others inhabit.

Hollywood claims that Beauvoir 'recreates Teresa as an existentialist hero',[62] but that what 'remains to be clarified is why some women's actions count as authentic when others are deemed narcissistic'.[63] In Hollywood's reading, it is Teresa's foundation of an order (the reformed Carmelites), active engagement in establishing convents in Castille, and writing that distinguish her from her peers. But Beauvoir's praise of Teresa leaves open another possibility. Beauvoir describes Teresa as being one of the only women who has

> lived the human condition for herself, in total abandonment: we have seen why. Placing herself beyond earthly hierarchies, she, like St John of the Cross, felt no reassuring sky over her head. For both of them it was the same night, the same flashes of light, in each the same nothingness, in God the same plenitude. When finally it is possible for every human being to place his pride beyond sexual difference in the difficult glory of his free existence, only then will woman be able to make her history, her problems, her doubts and her hopes those of humanity.[64]

Hollywood argues that it is Teresa's 'totalizing autonomous subjectivity' that draws Beauvoir's admiration, interpreting the lack of a 'reassuring sky' as 'a site of absolute freedom from and transcendence of the limitations of situatedness', a return to the '(male) narcissistic subject'.[65] But in light of Beauvoir's longstanding desire for the absolute and references to God as an absence or silence, another interpretation is possible in which the freedom Beauvoir admired in Teresa was not freedom from the limitations of situatedness, but her living the human condition of 'night', acting transformatively in the world despite the absence of the comfort of ready-made values, if not God.

This reading absolves Beauvoir of the charge that she uses Teresa to reinforce the 'myth that subjects can successfully assert themselves independently of the world's recognition'.[66] And it also explains the 'slippage' that Hollywood astutely observes between the 'love of God and love of self [that] runs throughout Beauvoir's discussion of religion'.[67] Love of other and love of self are difficult to disentangle when love is a middle way between devotion and egotism, an equilibrium which I cannot maintain alone because it involves another freedom.

Read as such, Beauvoir's philosophical project seems much more like a revaluation of values – in particular, the value of love – than an appropriation or application of Sartre's ideas. Sartre's philosophy, as we shall see, rejected this value as an unrealizable ideal.

Jean-Paul Sartre

Over the last decade the relation between Sartre and mysticism – like the relation between Sartre and theology more generally – has received increased attention in English-speaking research. Although there were some twentieth-century studies of the theological or mystical themes in Sartre's works – notably Francis Jeanson's *Sartre Devant Deiu*, Thomas King's *Sartre and the Sacred*, Jacques Sylvan's *The Scandalous Ghost*, Christina

Howells's 'Sartre and Negative Theology' – the posthumous publication of Sartre's early works, the *Notebooks for an Ethics*, letters, working drafts, and unpublished manuscripts has given scholars an even fuller picture of Sartre's voluminous corpus.[68] But although these new publications have offered some illumination of Sartre's works, they have also raised new questions.

Simone de Beauvoir wrote in *The Prime of Life* that during the 1930s Sartre 'took an interest in the psychology of mysticism', which prompted Beauvoir herself to read Catherine Emmerich and Angela of Foligno. We have seen already that her interest in mysticism predates this. And Sartre's interest in mysticism also stretched back much further than is commonly acknowledged; his *mémoire* for the *Diplôme d'Études Supérieures* included a section on mystics, including Teresa of Avila and John of the Cross.

Margaret Simons's research on Beauvoir demonstrates that Sartre may in fact have encountered phenomenology for the first time not in the famous apricot-cocktail conversation with Raymond Aron in the early 1930s, but in discussions with Beauvoir about mysticism. During the 1920s, as we have seen, Beauvoir wrote a dissertation under the supervision of Jean Baruzi, who may have drawn on phenomenology.[69] Just two years later, Sartre's dissertation (*mémoire*) for the *Diplôme d'Études Supérieures* was supervised by Henri Delacroix. The subject was the 'image', and it contained a chapter on 'attitudes toward the image' that included a section on mystics. Sartre's work drew not only from Baruzi's book on John of the Cross, but also from Delacroix (*Le Mysticisme en Allemagne au XIVe siècle*; *Etude de psychologie et d'histoire du mysticisme*), Gilson, and mystics themselves: Tauler and Saint Teresa.

The young Sartre, like Beauvoir, was attracted to philosophy through the work of Bergson – even though its fashionability was waning. In Bergson, Sartre wrote, 'I immediately found a description of my own psychic life'.[70] In the *mémoire* he discusses the question of whether 'intuition' is an 'image', and draws on mystics whose lives, he says, 'guarantee that they did not have intuitions of fantasy [*intuitions de fantasie*]: Saint Teresa, John of the Cross, and Eckhart'.[71] Sartre argues that he is little qualified to make psychology of philosophy. But nevertheless, he notes that other authors are writing in support of the view that philosophy is reducible, in some sense, to psychology:

> James speaks of a sub-universe that we carry within us, Jaspers considers all metaphysicians paranoiacs. Behind these exaggerations, there is the incontestable fact that any philosophical system is the construction of a reality which has no guarantee apart from itself, which one cannot even call a point of view, but the image of a point of view on the universe.[72]

Consequently, Sartre concluded that every philosophical theory is an arbitrary limitation of the exterior world, the production of a sub-universe by means of images. One of the examples he gives is the mental effort that is required to read a text in order to understand its author's position. The example he gives is Jules Lagneau's *De l'existence de Dieu*.[73] As discussed in Chapter 3, Lagneau's 'moral proof' for the existence of God started with human need. Need gives birth to belief, in Lagneau's view, and – as Victor Hugo put it – the doubt of philosophers can constructively clear the way to this recognition:

> Ces douteurs ont frayé la route
> Et sont si grands sous le ciel bleu
> Que, désormais, grâce à leurs doutes,
> On peut enfin affirmer Dieu.
>
> These doubters have cleared the route
> And are so great under the blue sky
> That now, thanks to their doubts
> We can finally affirm God.[74]

Before Beauvoir met Sartre, and before either of them became famous atheists, their philosophical interests in freedom, 'personality', and philosophical methodology overlapped significantly and drew heavily from sources including mystics, their philosophical readers, and their literary interpreters – for example, the novelists Péguy, Bernanos, and Claudel, among others. This philosophical formation clarifies the origins of the mystical themes in Sartre's work. But Sartre was an atheist who objected to being called 'a mystic'. So let us turn now to consider the senses in which Sartre has been accused of and rejected this term.

In Sartre's memoir, *Words* (1964), he refers to his young self as a 'militant' and a 'mystic' and as 'prey to two opposing mystical theologies'. One made him a 'gift from heaven' and another 'the child of my works'.[75] In Sartre, as in Beauvoir, there is a distinction to be made between the *unio mystica* that begins and ends in the inner life and the mysticism of action that bears fruit in the world. But during the war, when the critic Émile Bouvier called Sartre 'a mystic', he expressed astonishment and indignation in his diary, writing 'I'd never believed that anyone would consign me to mysticism'.[76]

More recently, Jerome Gellman argued that Sartre is a 'mystical atheist',[77] for experiential and epistemological reasons. Gellman claims that Sartre's atheism is mystical because (i) Sartre describes having a 'momentary intuition' that God does not exist; and (ii) because of the mystical language Sartre used in his 1938 novel *La Nausée*.

The experience Gellman draws on to support the former claim is recounted in biographical literature by and about Sartre twice, once in *Words* and once in *Adieux* (by Simone de Beauvoir). Gellman cites the latter, where we read:

> When I was about twelve . . . in the morning I used to take the tram with the girls next door . . . One day I was walking up and down outside their house for a few minutes waiting for them to get ready. I don't

> know where the thought came from or how it struck me, yet all at once I said to myself, 'God doesn't exist' . . . As I remember very well, it was on that day and in the form of a momentary intuition that I said to myself, 'God does not exist'.[78]

But as has been argued elsewhere, the extent to which Sartre's novels – or, indeed, 'autobiography' – can be taken to accurately represent Sartre's lived experience or philosophical commitments is difficult to determine. Given that Sartre gives contradictory accounts of the origins of his unbelief – and holds the existentialist view that the self is always free to renounce its past commitments (to atheism, for example) – the story of Sartre's atheism is less clear cut than Gellman suggests.[79] In *Being and Nothingness*, for example, Sartre mentioned having had a 'mystic crisis in my fifteenth year'.[80] It is beyond contest that Sartre does use mystical language in his literature and ontology in his philosophy – and we will discuss this further shortly. But despite his youthful 'momentary intuition' and later 'mystic crisis', Sartre was highly critical of certain types of mystical experience (for example, that of Georges Bataille's *Inner Experience*) and epistemological 'mysticism' insofar as it is conveys an experience, knowledge, or grace that is the purview only of the few or where mysticism is, as André Gide defined it, 'whatever presupposes and demands the abdication of reason'.[81]

The notion that mysticism was a departure from reason was particularly important in the 1930s, when the word 'mysticism' took on connotations of National Socialism. It was the anti-philosophy: where philosophy emphasizes doubt and critical reflection, mysticism was a kind of being carried away, often against reason.[82] When Sartre called Georges Bataille 'A New Mystic' in 1943, it was decidedly not a compliment. Reviewing *Inner Experience*, Sartre wrote that this book was 'an adventure beyond philosophy'. In Sartre's reading, Bataille rejected the power of reason in the formation of beliefs; for Bataille, conviction 'does not arise from reasoning, but only from the feelings which it defines'.[83] Sartre writes that Bataille is 'neither a scholar nor a philosopher, [though he] has, unfortunately, a smattering of science and philosophy'.[84] No: 'it is for the mystic's apprentice that M. Bataille writes', and his offering is 'a little holocaust of philosophical words'.[85]

It is not just his adulterous treatment of language that Sartre objected to, however, but the implications of Bataille's view concerning epistemic access. Bataille's 'non-knowledge' is, like efficacious grace, not the preserve of all but only of the few. *Inner Experience* is, 'like most mystical writings, the product of a *re-descent*. M. Bataille is returning from an unknown region; he is coming back down among us'.[86] 'He is on high, we are down below. He delivers a message and it is for us to receive it if we can'.[87] In Sartre's view, when 'mystics' refuse to express themselves in reasoned argument, they evade responsibility for their positions.

'Mysticism', as Sartre defines it in 1943, 'is ek-stasis or, in other words, a wresting from oneself toward, and intuitive enjoyment of, the transcendent'.

But, Sartre asks, 'How can a thinker who has just asserted the absence of any transcendence achieve, in and by that very move, a mystical experience?' That is the question he believes Bataille must – yet fails to – answer.[88] On this topic it is worth quoting at length from Sartre's review:

> There are people you might call survivors. Early on, they lost a beloved person – father, friend, or mistress – and their lives are merely the gloomy aftermath of that death. Monsieur Bataille is a survivor of the death of God. And, when one thinks about it, it would seem that our entire age is surviving that death, which he experienced, suffered, and survived. God is dead. We should not understand by that that He does not exist, nor even that he now no longer exists. He is dead: he used to speak to us and he has fallen silent, we now touch only his corpse. Perhaps he has slipped out of this world to some other place, like a dead man's soul. Perhaps all this was merely a dream.[89]
>
> God is dead, but man has not, for all that, become atheistic. Today, as yesterday, this silence of the transcendent, combined with modern man's enduring religious need, is the great question of the age.[90]

The problem, then, which Sartre poses to Bataille is: how can one deny the transcendent and yet affirm mysticism? Beauvoir's answer is that the mysticism of apotheosis is bankrupt, but the mysticism of action is not. She argues that we should seek the infinite in the other through reciprocal recognition of their freedom and the power of our own freedom to shape the world.

In *Being and Nothingness*, Sartre does not leave room for any such compatibility. For Sartre love is an impossible ideal and 'mysticism' is a form of bad faith, because both of these pursuits – like all human projects – are at root 'the desire to be God'. So central is this desire that Sartre defines man as 'the being whose project is to be God'; 'To be man means to reach toward being God. Or if you prefer, man fundamentally is the desire to be God'.[91] But we will never accomplish this project, in Sartre's view, which means that an honest appraisal of our condition is that we are condemned to freedom, to our 'useless passion'.

Sartre rarely uses the term 'mystic' or 'mysticism' in *Being and Nothingness*. But it does appear in discussions of existence with others and the idea of God. When Sartre discusses being-for-others, he writes that this fundamental relation cannot be made with reference 'to any mystic or ineffable experience':

> It is in the reality of everyday life that the Other appears to us, and his probability refers to everyday reality. The problem is precisely this: there is in everyday reality an original relation to the Other which can be constantly pointed to and which consequently can be revealed to me outside all reference to a religious and mystic unknowable.[92]

By contrast, 'mystic experiences of the presence of the Other, the notion of God as the omnipresent, infinite subject *for whom* I exist' is something which Sartre thinks lacks 'proved reality'.[93]

Like Beauvoir in *Pyrrhus and Cinéas*, in *Being and Nothingness* Sartre argued that human beings exist 'for a witness'. In his student notebooks from the 1920s (*Carnet Midy*), we read that 'All men need a witness. Without a doubt it is a sociological necessity. Some therefore invent God, others conscience (personified), others appear in the world, can't think without saying what they think, and still others go mad, obscurely imagining the beautiful women who watch them'.[94]

In *Being and Nothingness* Sartre rejected the existence of a transcendent witness (God) and even an immanent, loving gaze to be found in human others. Sartre criticized Heidegger for focusing on too narrow a range of experiences of Nothingness, for failing to see its presence in everyday life and the ecstatic temporalization of the for-itself. Sartre's translator, Hazel Barnes, wrote that it was conspicuous, given this criticism, that Sartre himself excluded 'an entire set of special experiences in which the idea of Nothingness is tremendously important; namely, the whole history of mysticism'.[95]

The works of Thomas King, Jacques Sylvan, Christina Howells, and Stephen Wang all discuss aspects of Sartre's ontology, taking it to resemble numerous theological antecedents including Augustine, Aquinas, and Eckhart as well as more recent philosophical antecedents in Hegel, Kierkegaard, and Heidegger. However, Sartre's education in French philosophy and literature exposed him to more local theological traditions of mysticism as well, from Pierre de Bérulle and the French School of spirituality to Descartes, Pascal, and Fénelon (among others). He was well versed in debates about Jansenism,[96] also exposed to late nineteenth- and early twentieth-century advocates of intuitionism and 'Christian philosophy'. On this basis, Kirkpatrick has argued that Sartre's concept of nothingness and its epistemological and ethical implications is indebted to Augustinian (more specifically, Jansenist) ontology in which the human being exists between being and nothingness.[97]

In one sense, therefore, Hazel Barnes was correct to acknowledge that there is 'no room' in Sartre's atheist existentialism for mysticism. She notes several divergences between Sartre's concept of nothingness and what she calls 'the mystic's, namely:

1 'Applying the concept in the form of negative definition to the ultimate reality, The One;
2 Presenting the loss of personality, which is a species of Nothingness, as an ideal goal;
3 Giving an irrational (one might almost say sensational) cast to the whole experience'.[98]

But while Barnes is correct to be suspicious of this ostensible absence, the mysticism that haunts Sartre's existentialism is not the *unio mystica* that would absorb individuality in The One. It is not the stasis of Plotininian contemplation. It is the mysticism of action in which human beings are individuals, cocreators of a world that is perpetually being remade.

To better understand the ontology of this mysticism, it may be useful to consider the thought of Pierre de Bérulle. In an anthology of French mysticism published in Paris in 1941, Bérulle is introduced as someone who has been 'neglected' by 'official literary history'.[99] Despite his historical significance in both philosophical and theological circles – as Descartes's spiritual director,[100] an influence on Malebranche,[101] the founder of the Oratory of France, for example – his political fall from grace (in a dispute with one of the better-known cardinals of his epoch, Cardinal Richelieu) led to the association of his name with various errant parties and resulted in a prolonged period of neglect. It was only when Henri Brémond published the third volume of his *Histoire littéraire du sentiment réligieux en France* in 1921 that Bérulle and the school of spirituality he founded – referred to by Brémond as 'l'école française'[102] – began to receive recognition as one of the 'masters of the masters' of French mysticism, and introductory volumes began to proliferate.[103]

For example, Baruzi's book on John of the Cross mentions 'Bérullian elevation', citing Brémond's third volume, and also mentions Bérulle in connection with Etienne Gilson's 1913 work on Cartesian freedom and theology.[104] In what follows it must be emphasized that there is only space to paint a partial portrait of Berullian spirituality; Bérulle is renowned for his 'theocentrism' and for rejecting the 'abstract mysticism' of his predecessors on account of its 'Christological gaps' – that is to say, for ignoring the humanity of Jesus. For Bérulle, theology and spirituality are inseparable. In his own words: 'Some distinguish between a mystical and a practical theology, but this is a distinction which I do not wish to employ', says Bérulle. 'All God's graces distributed upon earth are to enable us to act better'.[105] But rather than focusing on God or Christ, however, what concerns us is Bérulle's anthropology and the role nothingness plays in it.[106]

For Bérulle, the first quality of being human is to be in a relation of inferiority or superiority with the world, in a relationship of *dependence*.

> There is nothing better known in the world, by the senses or by reason, than the difference between and condition of being master and servant. It is the most general and applicable quality in the world. It applies to all men: it enters into their sentiments and affections; it enters into or even invades every state and condition . . . and if they are masters of some, they are servants in the eyes of others.[107]

For Bérulle, the condition of dependence and servitude is inseparable from being human. We are creatures, and our creaturely origin is such that, though made *by* God, we were made *from* nothing.[108] Throughout Bérulle's works nothingness – *néant* – plays a profound role; it is widely acknowledged to be one of the most frequent of his themes. It is a question of debate whether this emphasis on nothingness resulted from 'an excessively pessimistic interpretation of St Paul and St Augustine' or 'as a reaction to the unwarranted exaltation of human nature and freedom at the hands of the humanists', but Bérulle looked on man as 'the most vile and useless creature of all; indeed, as dust, mud, and a mass of corruption'.[109]

Bérulle clearly distinguishes between the order of nature and that of grace. One of the differences separating humanity from other creatures 'is that they were created perfect in their state and without the expectation of a further new degree which they lack; but man's nature was not created to remain in the limitations of nature; it was made for grace, and destined for a state raised above its power'.[110]

Bérulle describes human beings as 'a nothingness that tends to nothingness'.[111] But in his account there are three types of nothingness: the nothingness of nature, the nothingness of sin, and the nothingness of grace.[112] With respect to the first, the created nature of humanity contains the traces of the nothingness whence it came: humanity is 'pulled out of nothingness'.[113] But in addition to the consequences of creation *ex nihilo*, as a result of the Fall, Bérulle writes that 'our being is full of nothingness; our understanding is full of ignorance, our power is full of weakness and impotence; because there is more nothingness than being in our being'.[114] Bérulle's account of the nothingness of sin is Augustinian: sin is the absence of good; it is explicitly presented in ontological terms as the privation of being: a spiritual death. This nothingness reveals the creature's weakness. It is worse than the nothingness of nature in the sense that it rejects grace; in sin nothingness opposes the being of God. What is needful, in Bérulle's view, is that we recognize that – 'on all sides we are nothing but impotence, indigence, nothingness . . . and this nothingness must be surrounded by grace on all sides'.[115] If humanity seeks its origins outside of God, we will find nothing but the nothingness from which we issue.[116]

The third form of nothingness, the nothingness of grace, appears in this context. After original sin, our nature includes inclinations to evil – and indulging in actual sins does nothing but exacerbate this inclination. Salvation is ours in Christ, but on the condition that we fight our flaws, whether hereditary or personal. In doing so grace becomes more active, and we find ourselves *anéanti*. But the nothingness reclaimed by grace is, like the grace of nature, a relative nothingness. By making ourselves nothing – through *anéantisation* – we are released from the spell of egoism and can glimpse the perfection of Christ. But in this state of grace we realize that 'our being is a *relation* [rapport] to God'; of ourselves, we are nothing.[117] But in the right relation to our creator, we *are*; we share in God's being.

Human life, therefore, rests on two principles: nothingness and divine power (puissance). Both are present in creation and perdure in the creature who, in consequence, constantly tends toward nothingness and is always kept from it by divine intervention. There is nothing between us and nothingness but the creative hand of God.[118] Human existence is *essentially* precarious. In each moment of his life, man is on the point of falling back into nothingness, but at the same moment the [divine] power of continual creation keeps him from it: God perpetually wills being into being.

Bachmann suggests that this 'spiritual climate' paved the way for the *Meditations* of Descartes, writing that

> After having discovered existence in the moment, Descartes drew the consequences with full rigour. The cogito detaches a unique moment of existence, a moment which does not rely in any way on that precedes it neither on anything that follows in the course of its existence . . . The Cartesian man also must be conserved; to be recreated at each instant. In the nakedness of the Cartesian moment one unerringly arrives at the notion of continual creation.[119]

Denise Leduc-Lafayette notes Fénelon's indebtedness to Bérulle and also to the Spanish mystics whose thought Bérulle introduced to France: Teresa and Saint John of the Cross. In particular, she highlights the conceptual scheme Fénelon inherited, including 'creaturely dependence', the 'first nothingness' which is creation, and also the second nothingness into which sin cast humanity.[120]

Fénelon's relevance has already been noted in the introduction. But it is worth delving into in greater depth here with respect to Sartre's mystical sources. For Fénelon, the nature of created beings is dependent, for 'that which has no being except by another cannot keep it by itself'.[121] Human existence is not essential; it is accidental, contingent,[122] and subject to the ravages of time. The notion of time plays an important role in Fénelon's thought: he calls it 'the change of created being', 'the negation of a very real and supremely positive thing that is the permanence of being'. Unlike God, human beings continually change; they are subject to '*la défaillance de l'être*'.[123] In Fénelon's view, 'everything which is not truly being is nothingness'.[124] Consequently, human beings require a '*don actuel*' to be kept from nothingness.[125] But we are kept from nothingness because there is a link – a *rapport* – between the Creator and the created.[126]

It is in the context of this discussion on time we find the text Jacques Salvan uses as an epigraph for his chapter on Sartre and mysticism:

> I am not, O my God, what is; alas, I am almost what is not. I see myself as an incomprehensible intermediate between nothingness and being. I am the one who has been; I am the one who will be; I am the one who is no longer what he has been; I am the one who is not yet what he will be; and, in this in-between that I am, something unknowable that cannot be held in itself, that has no consistency, that flows away like water; something unknowable that I cannot seize, that flees from my hands, that is no longer as soon as I wish to grasp or perceive it; something

> unknowable that finishes at the very instant in which it begins; so that I can never at any moment find myself stable and present to myself, so as to say simply that I am. Thus my duration is nothing but a perpetual failure/lack [*défaillance*] of being.[127]

For Fénelon, being eludes us because humans exist between being and nothingness.[128] In this respect, Fénelon follows the trajectory of Bérulle, writing: 'I do not know how to assure myself that the me [*le moi*] of yesterday is the same as today's. They are not necessarily linked together. One could be without the other'.[129] For Fénelon, the lack of a link between moments results in a loss of consistency of the self. The self escapes its own self-knowledge at each instant, its fluidity eludes definition. Over the course of the seventeenth century, the nothingness of the created was asserted with greater and greater intensity. According to Bachmann, 'If Bérulle and Descartes could still say, in knowing themselves in the present moment, "I am", the driving force of being unmade [*entraînement de la défaillance*] was too great for Fénelon; he did not discover that he was, but rather that he was lacking [*défaillant*]'.[130]

In *Being and Nothingness*, where Sartre discusses the elusive nature of the self, we hear a distinctly Fénelonian refrain:

> [A] nothingness has slipped into the heart of this relation; I *am* not the self which I will be. First I am not that self because time separates me from it. Secondly, I am not that self because what I am is not the foundation of what I will be. Finally I am not that self because no actual existent can determine strictly what I am going to be. Yet as I am already what I will be (otherwise I would not be interested in any one being more than another), *I am the self which I will be, in the mode of not being it.*[131]

This is why to be human, in Sartre's view, is to be anxious – and why we attempt to take flight from our anxiety through bad faith. Sartre continues to say that in order for any resolution – to continue in writing this book, for example – 'to come to my aid once more, *I* must remake it *ex nihilo* and freely'.[132] For Sartre, consciousness is 'always predisposed to find something lacking'; indeed, he describes freedom as 'really synonymous with lack'.[133] And although the French word *manque* is usually behind the English 'lack',[134] Sartre also uses Fénelon's theological language, *défaut*.[135]

The difference, for Sartre, is that while there exists a nothingness of nature and (arguably) a nothingness of sin, there is no nothingness of grace. Bérulle writes that self-knowledge can be found – but only '*par le regard pur de Dieu*', by the pure gaze of God.[136] Clearly Sartre rejects such a regard, and such a resolution to the problems of nothingness. Every negation, for Sartre, is an estrangement from being. Sartre asserts that anxiety manifests human 'freedom in the face of self', showing that we are always 'separated by a nothingness' from our essence'.[137] Without grace, there is nothing that can 'ensure me against myself, cut off from the world and from my essence by this nothingness which *I am*'.[138] Sartre accepts the mystics' diagnosis but rejects their cures: in *Being and Nothingness* both being and love are 'unrealizable ideals' – useless passions.

Notes

1 Simone de Beauvoir, *Cahiers de jeunesse, 1926–1930*, ed. Sylvie le Bon de Beauvoir (Paris: Gallimard, 2008). The 1926–27 diaries have been published in English as *Diary of a Philosophy Student, Vol. 1: 1926–27*, ed. Barbara Klaw, Sylvie le Bon de Beauvoir, and Margaret A. Simons (Chicago: University of Illinois Press, 2006). The later diaries are forthcoming in the same Beauvoir Research series.
2 Beauvoir, *Diary of a Philosophy Student*, p. 279, 10 July 1927.
3 For more on the way even leading Beauvoir scholars have read Beauvoir as Sartre's philosophical follower, see Margaret Simons, 'Confronting an Impasse: Reflections on the Past and Future of Beauvoir Scholarship' *Hypatia* 25(4) (2010): 909–26.
4 Joseph Mahon, *Simone de Beauvoir and Her Catholicism: An Essay on Her Ethical and Religious Meditations* (Galway: Arlen House, 2002), p. 165.
5 Simone de Beauvoir, 'Pyrrhus and Cinéas' in Simone de Beauvoir, *Philosophical Writings*, ed. Margaret A. Simons, Marybeth Timmermann, and Mary Beth Mader (Chicago: University of Illinois Press, 2004), p. 93.
6 Beauvoir, *Pyrrhus and Cinéas*, p. 104.
7 Simone de Beauvoir, *Memoirs of a Dutiful Daughter*, trans. James Kirkup (London: Penguin Books, 2001), p. 261.
8 On Beauvoir's Catholicism, see Mahon, *Simone de Beauvoir and Her Catholicism*.
9 Beauvoir, *Memoirs*, p. 261.
10 See Marguerite Léna, 'Jeanne Mercier, lectrice de Maurice Blondel: Une correspondence philosophique' in Marie-Jeanne Coutagne, *Maurice Blondel et la quête du sens* (Paris: Beauchesne, 1998), p. 109. See also Margaret A. Simons, 'Beauvoir's Early Philosophy' in Simone de Beauvoir, *Diary of a Philosophy Student, Vol. 1: 1926–27* (Chicago: University of Illinois Press, 2006).
11 Beauvoir, *Diaries*, p. 55, 6 August 1926.
12 Beauvoir, *Diaries*, p. 55, 6 August 1926.
13 Beauvoir, *Diaries*, p. 63, 12 August 1926.
14 Simone de Beauvoir, *The Ethics of Ambiguity*, trans. Bernard Frechtman (New York: Citadel Press, 1976), p. 156.
15 See Beauvoir, *Diaries*, p. 266, 28 May 1927.
16 See Margaret A. Simons, 'Beauvoir's Early Philosophy' in *Beauvoir and the Second Sex: Feminism, Race, and the Origins of Existentialism* (New York: Rowman and Littlefield, 2001), p. 188.
17 Beauvoir, *Diaries*, p. 289.
18 Beauvoir, *Diaries*, p. 263. On the same page, Beauvoir lamented being 'so ironically conscious that the forty-nine positions that I have left out have just as much worth as the fiftieth that I have adopted? Barrès or Lagneau? The N.R.F. or *L'Esprit*? Ah! If only I could sometimes have tunnel vision!'
19 See André Bremond, 'La Religion de Lagneau', *Revue Philosophique de Louvain*, 14(1949): 266–78, p. 271.
20 Quoted at the opening of the Fourth Notebook, Beauvoir, *Diaries*, p. 225, 17 April 1927.
21 Beauvoir, *Diaries*, p. 279, 10 July 1927.
22 Beauvoir, *Memoirs of a Dutiful Daughter*, p. 262.
23 Beauvoir, *Diaries*, p. 277, 7 July 1927.
24 Beauvoir, *Memoirs*, p. 314.

25 Beauvoir, *Diaries*, p. 277, 7 July 1927.
26 Beauvoir, *Memoirs*, p. 265.
27 Beauvoir, *Diaries*, p. 226 (beginning of Fourth Notebook; preceding first dated entry, 17 April 1927).
28 Henri Bergson, *Time and Free Will: An Essay on the Immediate Data of Consciousness*, trans. Frank Lubeck Pogson (Mineola, NY: Dover, 2001), p. 172.
29 See 'La Place d'autrui est le vrai point de perspective' in Jean Baruzi, *Leibniz: Avec de nombreux textes inédits* (Paris: Bloud et cie, 1909), p. 363.
30 Beauvoir, *Diaries*, p. 296, 29 July 1927.
31 Beauvoir, *Diaries*, pp. 286–7, 19 July 1927.
32 Beauvoir, *Diaries*, p. 288, July 1927. *L'Esprit* was a journal of the group that included Pierre Morhange, Paul-Yves Nizan, Georges Friedmann, Georges Politzer, Henri Lefebvre, and Norbert Guterman. They promoted a rethinking of Marxism and the relationship between the individual and the universal, arguing that self-definition was based on one's actions in the world. They were heavily influenced by Pascal, Spinoza, and Nietzsche as well as Schelling and Hegel; they were opposed by Bergson, Mounier, Louis Aragon, Breton, Marcel, and others. (See Thorpe, review of *French Marxism between the Wars*, pp. 1–3, cited in *Diaries*, p. 222, n. 308).
33 Beauvoir, *Diaries*, p. 291, 22 July 1927.
34 See Beauvoir, *Diaries*, p. 314, 29 September 1927: 'It is imperative to work, to become again as in my attic at Meyrignac, myself and God, and the others only inasmuch as they are with God'.
35 Beauvoir, *Pyrrhus and Cinéas*, p. 90.
36 Beauvoir, *Pyrrhus and Cinéas*, pp. 93, 95.
37 Beauvoir, *Pyrrhus and Cinéas*, p. 99. On 'the serious', see also p. 127: 'The serious mind considers health, fortune, education, and comfort as indispensable goods whose worth is written in heaven. But he is duped by an illusion; ready-made values whose hierarchy is imposed upon my decisions do not exist without me. What's good for a man is what he wants as his own good'.
38 Beauvoir, *Pyrrhus and Cineas*, p. 103.
39 Beauvoir, *Pyrrhus and Cinéas*, p. 104.
40 Beauvoir, *Pyrrhus and Cinéas*, p. 104.
41 Beauvoir, *Pyrrhus and Cinéas*, p. 105.
42 Beauvoir, *Pyrrhus and Cinéas*, p. 116.
43 Beauvoir, *Pyrrhus and Cinéas*, p. 116.
44 Beauvoir, *Pyrrhus and Cinéas*, p. 118.
45 Beauvoir, *Pyrrhus and Cinéas*, p. 122.
46 Beauvoir, *Pyrrhus and Cinéas*, p. 124.
47 Beauvoir, *Ethics of Ambiguity*, p. 66.
48 Beauvoir, *Ethics of Ambiguity*, p. 98.
49 Simone de Beauvoir, *The Second Sex*, trans. Constance Borde and Sheila Malovany-Chevallier (London: Vintage, 2011), p. 680.
50 Karl Marx, *Capital: A Critique of Political Economy*, vol 1, trans. Ben Fowkes (New York: Penguin Books, 1990). [Originally published in 1867], p. 103.
51 Beauvoir, *The Second Sex*, pp. 154–5.
52 Beauvoir, *The Second Sex*, pp. 674–5.
53 Beauvoir, *The Second Sex*, p. 152.
54 See Beauvoir, *The Second Sex*, p. 727, and Amy Hollywood, *Sensible Ecstasy: Mysticism, Sexual Difference, and the Demands of History* (Chicago: University of Chicago Press, 2002), p. 131.
55 See Pamela Sue Anderson, 'An Eruption of Mystical Life in Feminist Action: Mysticism and Confidence after Bergson' in Louise Nelstrop and Bradley B.

Onishi (eds.), *Mysticism in the French Tradition: Eruptions from France* (Farnham: Ashgate, 2015).
56 Hollywood, *Sensible Ecstasy*, p. 134.
57 Beauvoir, *The Second Sex*, p. 728.
58 See Beauvoir, *The Second Sex*, pp. 730–1.
59 Beauvoir, *The Second Sex*, p. 734.
60 Beauvoir, *The Second Sex*, p. 723.
61 Hollywood, *Sensible Ecstasy*, p. 122.
62 Hollywood, *Sensible Ecstasy*, p. 144.
63 Hollywood, *Sensible Ecstasy*, p. 134.
64 Beauvoir, *The Second Sex*, pp. 766–7 (translation adapted).
65 Hollywood, *Sensible Ecstasy*, p. 143.
66 Hollywood, *Sensible Ecstasy*, p. 145.
67 Hollywood, *Sensible Ecstasy*, p. 132.
68 See François Jeanson, *Sartre devant Dieu* (Paris: Éditions Cécile Defaut, 2005 [1966]); Thomas King, *Sartre and the Sacred* (Chicago: University of Chicago Press, 1974); Christina Howells, 'Sartre and Negative Theology' *Modern Language Review* 76(3) (July 1981): 549–55; Stephen Wang, *Aquinas and Sartre: On Freedom, Personal Identity, and the Possibility of Happiness* (Washington, DC: Catholic University of America Press, 2009).
69 See Chapter 3 for more on Baruzi's methodology and phenomenology.
70 Sartre, cited in Annie Cohen-Solal, *Sartre: A Life* (London: Heinemann, 1987), p. 57.
71 Jean-Paul Sartre, *mémoire*, unpublished MS, p. 145.
72 Sartre, *mémoire*, p. 146.
73 Sartre, *mémoire*, p. 149.
74 Victor Hugo, *Rupture avec ce qui amoindrit*, cited in Jules Lagneau, *De L'existence de Dieu* (Paris: Alcan, 1925), p. 12.
75 See Jean-Paul Sartre, *Words*, trans. Irene Clephane (London: Penguin Books, 2000), pp. 156, 108.
76 Jean-Paul Sartre, *The War Diaries: November 1939–March 1940*, trans. Quintin Hoare (New York: Pantheon, 1984), p. 158.
77 Jerome Gellman, 'Jean-Paul Sartre: The Mystical Atheist' *European Journal for Philosophy of Religion* 1(2) (2009): 127–37.
78 Simone de Beauvoir, *Adieux: A Farewell to Sartre*, trans. Patrick O'Brian (New York: Pantheon, 1984), p. 437.
79 Kate Kirkpatrick, 'Jean-Paul Sartre: Mystical Atheist or Mystical Antipathist?' *European Journal for Philosophy of Religion* 5(2) (2013): 159–68.
80 Jean-Paul Sartre, *Being and Nothingness*, trans. Hazel E. Barnes (London: Routledge, 2003), p. 520.
81 André Gide, *Journals 1889–1949* (London: Penguin Books, 1967), p. 414.
82 Peter Tracey Connor, *Georges Bataille and the Mysticism of Sin* (London: John Hopkins University Press, 2000), p. 129.
83 Cited in Jean-Paul Sartre, 'A New Mystic' in *Critical Essays*, trans. Chris Turner (London: Seagull Books, 2010 [1943, *Cahiers du Sud*]), p. 223. For more on Bataille, see Chapter 6.
84 Sartre, 'New Mystic', p. 240.
85 Sartre, 'New Mystic', pp. 232, 239.
86 Sartre, 'New Mystic', p. 230.
87 Sartre, 'New Mystic', p. 233.
88 Sartre, 'New Mystic', p. 274.
89 Sartre, 'New Mystic', p. 234.
90 Sartre, 'New Mystic', p. 235.

91 Sartre, *Being and Nothingness*, p. 587.
92 Sartre, *Being and Nothingness*, p. 277.
93 Sartre, *Being and Nothingness*, p. 305.
94 Jean-Paul Sartre, *Carnet Midy*, p. 455. See John Gillespie's recent articles, which show that the theme of having a witness (*témoin*) is recurrent in Sartre's works, often appearing in contexts where Sartre is discussing the death of God. (John Gillespie, 'Sartre and God: A Spiritual Odyssey, Part 2' *Sartre Studies International* 20(1) (2014): 45–56; 'Sartre and God: A Spiritual Odyssey, Part 1' *Sartre Studies International* 19(1) (2013): 71–90.
95 Hazel Barnes, 'Translator's Introduction' in Hazel Barnes (trans.), *Being and Nothingness* (New York: Washington Square Press, 1992), p. xxv.
96 See Jean-Paul Sartre, 'Liberté-Égalité', posthumously published manuscript (probably written in 1952) *Études Sartriennes* 12 (2008), in which Sartre discusses Jansenism and disputes about universal versus efficacious grace.
97 See Kate Kirkpatrick, *Sartre on Sin: Between Being and Nothingness* (Oxford: Oxford University Press, 2017).
98 Barnes, 'Translator's Introduction', p. xxv.
99 Henri Daniel-Rops (ed.), *Mystiques de France* (Paris: Corrêa, 1941), p. 133. All translations from French texts are the author's own unless otherwise stated.
100 Jackob Bachmann, *La notion du temps dans la pensée de Pierre de Bérulle* (Winterthur: Éditions P. G. Keller, 1964), p. 44.
101 See Paul Cochois, *Bérulle et l'École française* (Paris: Éditions du Seuil, 1963), p. 158.
102 Although this term gained currency following Brémond's use, it had been employed earlier; Thompson attributes its coinage to the Sulpician G. Letourneau around 1913 (1989, p. 89, n. 1).
103 Daniel-Rops, *Les Mystiques de France*, p. 37 quotes Brémond referring to de Sales and Bérulle as 'les maîtres des maîtres'. See Claude Taveau, *Le Cardinal de Bérulle: Maître de vie spirituelle* (Paris: Desclée de Brouwer, 1933) on Bérulle's reception.
104 Baruzi, *Saint Jean de la Croix*, citing Henri Brémond, vol. 3, pp. 117–26.
105 William Thompson, 'Introduction', cited in William M. Thompson (ed.), Lowell M. Glendon, SS (trans.), *Bérulle and the French School: Selected Writings* (New York: Paulist Press, 1989), p. 32.
106 It is worth noting, nonetheless, that Bérulle's notion of God is thought to be 'pseudo-Dionysian and Platonic, as transmitted by Saint Augustine and the Rhineland mystics'. Like Augustine, he considered unity the principal attribute of God (Jordan Aumann, OP, *Christian Spirituality in the Catholic Tradition* (London: Sheed & Ward, 1985), p. 223).
107 Bérulle, *Opuscules*, p. 1145.
108 Pierre de Bérulle, *Discours de l'Etat des Grandeurs de Jésus* (Paris: Gauine, 1859), p. 219.
109 See Jordan Aumann, OP, *Christian Spirituality in the Catholic Tradition* (London: Sheed & Ward, 1985), p. 221, latterly citing Pierre de Bérulle's *Œuvres complètes* (Paris: Migne, 1856), col. 880.
110 Bérulle, *Opuscules*, pp. 132, 3, 27, 3, cited in Henri de Lubac, *Augustinianism and Modern Theology*, trans. Lancelot Sheppard (London: Geoffrey Chapman, 1969), p. 270.
111 Nous sommes un néant qui tend au néant, qui cherche le néant, qui s'occupe du néant, qui se contente du néant, qui se remplit du néant, et qui enfin se ruine et se détruit soi-même pour un néant. A lieu que nous devons être un néant à la vérité – car cela nous convient par nature – mais un néant en la main de Dieu, un néant destiné à Dieu, un néant consacré à Dieu; un néant rempli de Dieu, et enfin un néant possédé de Dieu et possédant Dieu, et cela nous convient par grâce. (Bérulle, *Opuscules*, p. 1129).

112 Claude Taveau, *Bérulle*, pp. 248–51.
113 Bérulle, *Discours*, p. 219; 'tirée du néant'.
114 Bérulle, *Opuscules*, p. 1014.
115 Bérulle, *Opuscules*, p. 1140.
116 'Je vous [dis] que le fonds de votre esprit est a Dieu . . . Si vous contemplez votre origine sans regarder Dieu, vous ne trouverez que le néant, duquel nous sommes tous issus, et qui est notre unique et premier état hors la main de Dieu, et ainsi le néant nous appartient par le fond de la nature; le néant, dis-je, absolu, néant d'être.' (Bérulle, *Opuscules*, p. 1237).
117 Bérulle, *Opuscules*, p. 1150: 'Notre être est un rapport à Dieu'.
118 Bérulle, *Opuscules*, p. 1165.
119 Bachmann, *La notion du temps*, p. 45.
120 Denise Leduc-Lafayette, 'Vouloir ne vouloir pas' in Denise Leduc-Lafayette (ed.), *Fénelon: Philosophie et Spiritualité* (Geneva: Librairie Droz, 1996), p. 98, citing Pierre de Bérulle, *Opuscules de Piété* (Paris: Aubier-Montaigne, 1944), p. CXXXVI.
121 Fénelon, *De l'Existence*, p. 123. [*Ce qui n'a l'être que par autrui ne peut le garder par soi-même.*]
122 Fénelon, *De l'Existence*, p. 132.
123 Fénelon, *De l'Existence*, p. 176.
124 Fénelon, *De l'Existence*, p. 140. [*Tout ce qui n'est point réellement l'être est le néant*].
125 Fénelon, *De l'Existence*, p. 76.
126 Fénelon, *De l'Existence*, p. 183.
127 '*Je ne suis pas, ô mon Dieu, ce qui est: hélas! je suis presque ce qui n'est pas. Je me vois comme un milieu incompréhensible entre le néant et l'être; je suis qui a été, je suis celui qui sera, je suis celui qui n'est plus ce qu'il a été, je suis celui qui n'est pas encore ce qu'il sera; et dans cet entre-deux que suis-je? . . . un je ne sais quoi que je ne puis saisir . . .; un je ne sais quoi qui finit dans l'instant même où il commence, en sorte que je ne puis jamais un seul moment me trouver moi-meme fixe et présent à moi-même pour dire simplement: Je suis. Ainsi ma durée n'est qu'une défaillance perpétuelle*'. (Fénelon, *De l'Existence*, p. 180; English translation adapted from Salvan).
128 Fénelon, *De l'Existence*, p. 180.
129 Fénelon, *Œuvres*, ed. Gaume 1851, vol. 1, p. 117, cited in Bachmann, *La notion du temps*, p. 45.
130 Bachmann, *La notion du temps*, p. 46.
131 Sartre, *Being and Nothingness*, pp. 55–6.
132 Sartre, *Being and Nothingness*, p. 57.
133 Sartre, *Being and Nothingness*, p. 586; see also pp. 109ff., 124, 222.
134 For example, in cases like Sartre, *Being and Nothingness*, p. 586. In French "*le pour-soi se décrit ontologiquement comme manque d'être*"; Jean-Paul Sartre, *L'être et le néant* (Paris: Gallimard, 1972), p. 652.
135 See, for example, Sartre, *Being and Nothingness*, p. 109. In French: "*le pour-soi ne peut soutenir la néantisation sans se determiner comme un* ***défaut d'être*** "; Sartre, *L'être et le néant*, p. 128; emphasis original.
136 Bérulle, *Un néant capable de Dieu* (Paris: Arfuyen, 1987), p. 32.
137 Sartre, *Being and Nothingness*, p. 59.
138 Sartre, *Being and Nothingness*, p. 63.

Works cited

Anderson, Pamela Sue, 'An Eruption of Mystical Life in Feminist Action: Mysticism and Confidence after Bergson', in Louise Nelstrop and Bradley B. Onishi (eds.), *Mysticism in the French Tradition: Eruptions from France* (Farnham: Ashgate, 2015).

Bachmann, Jakob, *La notion du temps dans la pensée de Pierre de Bérulle* (Winterthur: Éditions P. G. Keller, 1964).
Baruzi, Jean, *Leibniz: Avec de nombreux textes inédits* (Paris: Bloud et cie, 1909).
———, *Saint Jean de la Croix et le problème de l'experience mystique* (Paris: Alcan, 1924).
Beauvoir, Simone de, *Adieux: A Farewell to Sartre*, trans. Patrick O'Brian (New York: Pantheon, 1984).
———, *Cahiers de jeunesse, 1926–1930*, ed. Sylvie le Bon de Beauvoir (Paris: Gallimard, 2008).
———, *Diary of a Philosophy Student, Vol. 1: 1926–27*, ed. Barbara Klaw, Sylvie le Bon de Beauvoir, and Margaret A. Simons (Chicago: University of Illinois Press, 2006).
———, *The Ethics of Ambiguity*, trans. Bernard Frechtman (New York: Citadel Press, 1976).
———, *Memoirs of a Dutiful Daughter*, trans. James Kirkup (London: Penguin, 2001).
———, 'Pyrrhus and Cinéas', in Simone de Beauvoir, *Philosophical Writings*, ed. Margaret A. Simons, Marybeth Timmermann, and Mary Beth Mader (Chicago: University of Illinois Press, 2004).
———, *The Second Sex*, trans. Constance Borde and Sheila Malovany-Chevallier (London: Vintage, 2011).
Bergson, Henri, *Time and Free Will: An Essay on the Immediate Data of Consciousness*, trans. Frank Lubeck Pogson (Mineola, NY: Dover, 2001).
Bérulle, Pierre de, *Bref discours de l'abnégation intérieur*, in Pierre de Bérulle, *Œuvres Complètes* (Paris: Migne, 1856).
———, *Discours de l'Etat des Grandeurs de Jésus* (Paris: Gauine, 1859).
———, *Opuscules Divers de Piété*, ed. Gaston Rotureau (Paris: Aubier, 1944).
———, *Un néant capable de Dieu* (Paris: Arfuyen, 1987).
Bremond, Andre, 'La Religion de Lagneau', *Revue Philosophique de Louvain* 14 (1949): 266–78.
Cohen-Solal, Annie, *Sartre: A Life* (London: Heinemann, 1987).
Connor, Peter Tracey, *Georges Bataille and the Mysticism of Sin* (London: John Hopkins University, 2000).
Daniel-Rops, Henri (ed.), *Mystiques de France* (Paris: Corrêa, 1941).
Fénelon, François, *De l'existence de Dieu, Lettres sur religion, etc.*, avec introduction par le Cardinal de Bausset (Paris: Garnier Frères, 1880).
Gellman, Jerome, 'Jean-Paul Sartre: The Mystical Atheist', *European Journal for Philosophy of Religion* 1(2) (2009): 127–37.
Gide, André, *Journals 1889–1949* (London: Penguin, 1967).
Gillespie, John, 'Sartre and God: A Spiritual Odyssey, Part 1', *Sartre Studies International* 19(1) (2013): 71–90.
———, 'Sartre and God: A Spiritual Odyssey, Part 2', *Sartre Studies International* 20(1) (2014): 45–56.
Hollywood, Amy, *Sensible Ecstasy: Mysticism, Sexual Difference, and the Demands of History* (Chicago: University of Chicago Press, 2002).
Howells, Christina, 'Sartre and Negative Theology', *Modern Language Review* 76(3) (July 1981): 549–55.
Jeanson, François, *Sartre devant Dieu* (Paris: Éditions Cécile Defaut, 2005 [1966]).
King, Thomas, *Sartre and the Sacred* (Chicago: University of Chicago Press, 1974).

Kirkpatrick, Kate, 'Jean-Paul Sartre: Mystical Atheist or Mystical Antipathist?', *European Journal for Philosophy of Religion* 5(2) (2013): 159–68.

———, *Sartre on Sin: Between Being and Nothingness* (Oxford: Oxford University Press, 2017).

Lagneau, Jules, *De L'existence de Dieu* (Paris: Alcan, 1925).

Leduc-Lafayette, Denise, 'Vouloir ne vouloir pas', in Denise Leduc-Lafayette (ed.), *Fénelon: Philosophie et Spiritualité* (Geneva: Librairie Droz, 1996).

Léna, Marguerite, 'Jeanne Mercier, lectrice de Maurice Blondel: Une correspondence philosophique', in Marie-Jeanne Coutagne (ed.), *Maurice Blondel et la quête du sens* (Paris: Beauchesne, 1998).

Mahon, Joseph, *Simone de Beauvoir and Her Catholicism: An Essay on Her Ethical and Religious Meditations* (Galway: Arlen House, 2002).

Marx, Karl, *Capital: A Critique of Political Economy*, vol. 1, trans. Ben Fowkes (New York: Penguin Books, 1990).

Salvan, Jacques, *The Scandalous Ghost: Sartre's Existentialism as Related to Vitalism, Humanism, Mysticism, Marxism* (Detroit: Wayne State University Press, 1967).

Sartre, Jean-Paul, *Being and Nothingness*, trans. Hazel E. Barnes (London: Routledge, 2003).

———, *L'être et le néant* (Paris: Gallimard, 1972).

———, 'A New Mystic', in Chris Turner (trans.), *Critical Essays* (London: Seagull Books, 2010 [1943, *Cahiers du Sud*]).

———, *The War Diaries: November 1939–March 1940*, trans. Quintin Hoare (New York: Pantheon, 1984).

———, *Words*, trans. Irene Clephane (London: Penguin, 2000).

Simons, Margaret, 'Beauvoir's Early Philosophy', in Simone de Beauvoir (ed.), *Diary of a Philosophy Student, Vol. 1: 1926–27* (Chicago: University of Illinois Press, 2006).

———, 'Beauvoir's Early Philosophy', in *Beauvoir and the Second Sex: Feminism, Race, and the Origins of Existentialism* (New York: Rowman and Littlefield, 2001), p. 188.

———, 'The Beginnings of Beauvoir's Existential Phenomenology', in W. O'Brien and L. Embree (eds.), *The Existential Phenomenology of Simone de Beauvoir*, Contributions to Phenomenology Vol. 43 (Dordrecht: Springer, 2001).

———, 'Confronting an Impasse: Reflections on the Past and Future of Beauvoir Scholarship', *Hypatia* 25(4) (2010): 909–26.

Thompson, William M., 'Introduction' to Pierre de Bérulle, *Bérulle and the French School: Selected Writings*, ed. William M. Thompson, trans. Lowell M. Glendon (New York: Paulist Press, 1989).

Wang, Stephen, *Aquinas and Sartre: On Freedom, Personal Identity, and the Possibility of Happiness* (Washington, DC: Catholic University of America Press, 2009).

5 Marcel and Camus

Mystery and the affirmation of the absurd

Marcel

At the start of the lecture 'Existentialism and Humanism', Sartre acknowledges that alongside the atheistic humanism of which he is himself the prime representative, there is also a Christian existentialism, in this case represented by Gabriel Marcel (1889–1973). However, it is clear that he regards atheism as the more rigorously consistent response to the basic ontological insights of existentialist philosophy. Nevertheless, it was not only Sartre's opinion but that of many other commentators that Marcel was, in fact, a prime exponent of Christian existentialism. Indeed, according to Simone de Beauvoir, he was the first to use the expression 'existentialism' as opposed to the 'philosophy of existence' associated with Heidegger and Jaspers.[1]

Marcel's thought was avowedly Christian and specifically Catholic. (Coming from a secular background, he converted to Catholicism as an adult after a 'Protestant' period, effectively inverting Heidegger's passage from Catholicism via Protestantism to atheism.) Yet whilst ideas such as mystery and presence (ideas that are strongly associated with mystical thought) play a prominent role in the overall structure of his thought, it would be plausible to say that he is not only amongst the least philosophically systematic but also amongst the least mystical of existentialist thinkers, secular or religious.[2] Why is this?

We have argued that existentialism shared with modern conceptions and practices of mysticism a sense of frustration at the seemingly unbridgeable gap between thought and reality or between the inner subjective life of the individual and the external objective life of the world. In its most radical formulations, this was glossed as the gap between non-being (nothingness) and being or between human existence and God. Both existentialism and mysticism offered strategies for overcoming this gap, whether of a theoretical or experiential kind (which might, of course, include eliminating one or other side of the equation). Marcel's thought, too, offers a way of conceptualizing the unity of self and other or humanity and being, but in his case this amounts neither to a radical identification of the two aspects nor to the elimination of one or other pole, and, insofar as it is a matter of unity, it is a unity that is always internally differentiated. Rather than requiring a transition from difference to identity, the two poles remain in a dynamic state of differentiated tension, although it is a tension marked by faith, hope, and love rather than anxiety and despair. Part of the reason for this is that Marcel seems never to have experienced the mutual alienation of the polarities of existence (as they will be called by Tillich) with the same intensity as did, for example, Kierkegaard, Sartre, or Tillich himself. Marcel's thought-world is a world of mixed light and shadow and is in every one of its moments far from the extremes of pure light and utter darkness. To the extent that mysticism promises release from darkness into pure light or a transformation of nothingness through the power of being, Marcel is decidedly non-mystical.

At the same time, however, Marcel is far from any kind of rationalism, and in face of the mystery of being, he tells us that even for the most faithful and loving person the mystery will remain just that, a mystery, never to be resolved into the clarity of thought. Our primary relation to the world is not one of knowledge but existence, and the crucial choices are not between knowledge and ignorance but between existential comportments of which 'having' and 'being' are amongst the most important. Only when we cease thinking of ourselves as subjects who 'have' various properties or have such and such a relation to the world or to others and understand ourselves in the perspective of being can we learn what it means to live in faith, hope, and love and to be in a mode that Marcel calls *disponibilité*. *Disponibilité* means letting oneself be at the disposal of (or perhaps available for) the world, others, and God – or, quite simply, available for being in all its dimensions. Against a self defined as the Sartrean self is defined through its actions, a self that is *disponible* is a self that understands itself as much in terms of passivity as of activity and that is therefore defined as much by what it receives as by what it does. In these terms it has some analogy to the Heideggerian *Gelassenheit* and, like *Gelassenheit*, reflects a view of the self that has strong precedents in Christian spiritual literature. In terms of recognizing the importance of passivity in the constitution of the self, then, Marcel reveals significant continuities with what we find in mystical sources, though also (we should add) in non-mystical religious literature.[3]

As we shall also see in the cases of Berdyaev and Tillich, Schelling played a significant formative role in Marcel's development, being (with Coleridge) the joint subject of an early dissertation (1909). Both Schelling and Coleridge, he concluded, were moving toward an idea of freedom that was very different from the mere freedom we have of discovering the necessary laws of nature that rule the world in which we live. Rather, theirs was a freedom shaped by the idea of the world as created and therefore contingent in its entirety. However, whilst such a strong notion of the world as created might seem to weigh against any possibility of identity in the relationship between human beings and God, it does allow for a different kind of affinity: namely, one grounded in mutual freedom. As he writes:

> this exigency of freedom . . . [is] essential . . . to a philosophy that, simultaneously refusing to look on the world either as an ensemble of abstract relations or as subjected to a process of blind development, affirms that that in us which is better and superior cannot be absolutely without relation to what lies at the basis of things and some profound analogy must subsist between the inner principle that animates our actions and the energy at work in them.[4]

From early on, then, it is a consistent principle of Marcel's thought that, in the words of the dissertation, there is 'some profound analogy' between human beings and 'what lies at the basis of things': that is, what he will come to call being. However, perhaps more than many of its theological defenders, Marcel seems to have implicitly understood that analogy is just that – analogy – and not identity. As the Thomist doctrine itself acknowledges, analogy may involve as much or more of unlikeness as likeness. Analogy, then, is not a formula for objective or scientific knowledge but, at best, for what we might call a sense of God.

Inevitably, Marcel needed to make his own reckoning with Cartesianism, and 20 years later, we see his idea of analogy reformulated in terms of the relationship between essence and existence. Marcel says that this was a problem that had always preoccupied him. Now, however, he believes it to be based on an illusory way of representing the relationship between thought and reality. This relationship, he says, is conventionally treated as if thought were somehow outside of reality and had to be brought into relation to it. But 'in fact we have there simply two distinct modalities of being' and it is simply impossible for thought ever to get outside of existence. If thought really were outside of existence, then the transition from thought to existence would be entirely unthinkable and meaningless. As it is, what philosophers call the transition from essence to existence is 'a specific intra-existential reformulation', and he concludes the formula '*es denkt in mir*' provides a better defence against pure subjectivity than the Cartesian cogito.[5] A couple of weeks later, he writes that he has finally eliminated and even 'exorcized' all residues of idealism from his thinking and with that made possible a more adequate approach to what he at this stage calls 'the problem of being'. This new approach is based on the insight that '[a] blindfold knowledge of Being in general is implied in all particular knowledge'.[6] And that, as he considers some weeks later, means that '[t]hought, far from being a relation with itself, is on the contrary essentially a self-transcendence'.[7]

For Marcel, then, there is no fundamental split between self and world, thought and being that needs to be overcome through some exceptional experience or deed. We are always already in relation to being, and the question then is only how. Are we to recognize its claim (or, as Marcel likes to put it, its exigency) and respond with fidelity to what is revealed to us of being, making ourselves *disponible* (available) to being and responding in love and hope to its intimations, or are we to withdraw in pride, contempt, and vilification as Marcel believes we see in Sartre?

It is precisely this choice that is the ultimate issue in the duality of having and being that becomes a major theme of Marcel's mature thought. When I exist in the mode of 'having', I relate to the world, to my body, and even to my thoughts as things that belong to me and that I am free to use as I choose for the realization of my subjective purposes. This involves what Marcel calls 'a thickening, a sclerosis' of the body and of the ensemble of relations to the world and to others that are grounded in my embodied life in the world.[8] To see my life in the world in terms of having is to see it as if my life were something that has to be managed, and in these terms the distinction between being and having is more fundamental than the opposition between autonomy and heteronomy that is so characteristic of modernity. Achieving autonomy simply means being able to run my affairs for myself, but this, as Marcel puts it, is 'still administration'.[9] He writes

> 'I want to run my own life' – that is the radical formula of autonomy. It refers essentially to *action* and implies . . . the notion of a certain province of activity circumscribed in space and time. Everything belonging to the order of interests, whatever they are, can be treated with relative ease as a province, a district marked off in this manner. Furthermore, I can administer, or treat as something to be administered . . . everything that can be compared . . . to a *possession* – something *I have*. But where this category of *having* becomes inapplicable, I can no longer in any sense talk about administration, whether by another or myself, and therefore I cannot talk about autonomy either.[10]

We are perhaps not surprised to discover that it is precisely the transition from having to being that makes it possible for us to love as opposed to merely desiring others (for which the motto is: 'I want you!'), and similarly, true creativity can only be based in being rather than having: 'A man *is* a genius, but *has* talent' as Marcel puts it.[11]

We have seen that whilst Marcel supposes that we are in some way always already in relation to being, he does not think that our relation to being can be fully known. It is a relation that is always intrinsically mysterious and, as such, very different from what we refer to as a problem (although, as we noted, Marcel himself had earlier referred to the 'problem of being'). Paralleling the relationship between having and being, he offers the following distinction between 'problem' and 'mystery':

> A problem is something which I meet, which I find complete before me, but which I can therefore lay siege to and reduce. But a mystery is something in which I am myself involved, and it can therefore only be thought of as *a*

> *sphere where the distinction between what is in me and what is before me loses its meaning and its initial validity.* A genuine problem is subject to an appropriate technique by the exercise of which it is defined: whereas a mystery, by definition, transcends every conceivable technique.[12]

This has a fairly clear application to questions of theology – and it is not only the mystery of God but also the mystery of evil that is misconceived when it is turned into a 'problem' to be solved. However, at the same time it is important to note that the distinction is not exclusive to what we might think of as metaphysical or supernatural relationships. Precisely because it relates to being as such, it potentially concerns every aspect of our relation to being: that is, our existence or life in the world as a whole. Ultimately, my relation to myself, to my body, to others, and to the cosmos is as much and as properly a 'mystery' as my relation to God.

This becomes clear in a further distinction Marcel makes, this time between presence and object. To relate to the world in the mode of being is to relate to it as presence, whereas a relationship founded in the mode of having will only ever know the world as object. Marcel writes:

> We can, for instance, have a very strong feeling that somebody who is sitting in the same room as ourselves, sitting quite near us, someone whom we can look at and listen to and whom we could touch if we wanted to make a final test of his reality, is nevertheless far further away from us than some loved one who is perhaps thousands of miles away or perhaps, even, no longer among the living. We could say that the man sitting beside us was in the same room as ourselves, but that he was not really *present* there, that his *presence* did not make itself felt.[13]

Such a situation is 'communication without communion'. Someone to whom I am talking but whom I do not feel to be present 'understands what I say to him, but he does not understand *me*'.[14] 'Presence' in this sense partakes of the quality of mystery, and whilst there are procedures that can be learned for dealing with objects, openness to presence cannot be taught. There is no such thing, Marcel thinks, as the art of making one's presence felt or (another favourite example) of being charming.

The encounter with the mystery of being, then, is in one sense not so very mysterious. It is or can be a part of our everyday life in the world, and we could say of Marcel's philosophical persona that, like Sartre and Aron, it, too, can do philosophy over cocktails. Indeed, in the Gifford lectures, he uses a self-conscious young man's experience at a cocktail party to illustrate what is involved in discovering the other as genuinely present and losing the kind of self-consciousness that arises when we think of our self, our ego, as something we have to protect from the 'malevolent lucidity of other people's glances'.[15] Of course, this is not of itself a reason for seeing it as non-mystical. Not least in the tradition of François de Sales, the preferred site of

Christian mysticism is not the monastery but life in the world, 'amongst the pots and pans' as Brother Lawrence put it.[16]

Nor does Marcel's insistence on 'incarnation' as a fundamental given of human existence make his thought non-mystical.[17] Perhaps the contrary. Although this means that being 'bound to a body', I can never become entirely transparent to myself and must always somehow remain a riddle and a mystery to myself, this is precisely to figure the self in ways deeply congruent with key currents of Christian mysticism. Yet, again, we do not find an insistence on entire union or entire self-giving in Marcel. The self that I am, quite concretely, in my world, at work, and at the cocktail party after work, is the self that I am, and I am not called to be other than that, neither to negate nor to transcend myself. I am called simply to be myself, responsible, attentive, and available in relation to others.

Marcel's philosophy is, rightly, as well described as personalist as existentialist. Even before the publication of Buber's *I and Thou*, Marcel was wrestling with the challenge of knowing the other, the Thou, in such a way as not to reduce him or her to a mere 'it' and, at the same time, how to inflect the 'we' with a quality of Thou-ness.[18] The integrity of the human person is central to his thought, and it is one of his main objections to Sartre that the philosophy of *Being and Nothingness* involves the 'vilification' of the human person.[19] In this regard there are analogies to Camus, who similarly takes human beings as they are in their being in the world, and to Berdyaev, whose work at several points reflects a commonality of interest with Marcel, not least regarding the possibility of a common life in which the value of the person as 'Thou' is preserved.[20] Yet precisely where (as we shall see) Berdyaev's personalism supposes a radically dualistic transcendence of spiritual life over all worldly conditions, including the body, Marcel, as we have seen, insists on life in the world as the sole locus of authentic existence or, as he might put it, faithfulness to being. In these terms, it is not coincidental that whereas Berdyaev explicitly relates his thought to Christian mystical traditions, Marcel rarely does. If, however, we consider the Marcellian self in characterological terms, it nevertheless shows a strong analogy with the kind of self modelled in much Christian mystical literature. As we have seen, it is not a self defined by action or by autonomous sovereignty over itself and its world, but by its *disponibilité*, its openness and receptivity toward the world; toward others; and in, with, and under every encounter with the world (with being) also *disponible* in relation to God.

Camus

On Camus's view, by contrast, there is no God to whom to be available. And yet despite his rejection of the transcendent and view of the world as indifferent he sought harmony with it, seeing the appeal of – if not succumbing to – a 'mystic affirmation of the world'.[21] In 1953 Camus translated the Spanish Baroque dramatist Calderon's drama *The Devotion of the Cross* for a production at the festival of drama held at the Château d'Angers. The play offers a full-blooded affirmation of Counter-Reformation values, complete with miracles, a resurrection, and an ascent into heaven. Camus himself calls it an 'extravagant chef d'œuvre' and a 'religious melodrama', noting also its having been originally written for performance in a sacral context.[22] Yet he concludes his brief translator's introduction with a contemporary reference, noting that 'It is more than three centuries before Bernanos that Calderon enunciated and illustrated in a provocative manner that "All is of grace", which offers a response for the modern mind to the unbelievers' "Nothing is just"'.[23] The comment, though not further developed by Camus himself at this point, opens a fascinating window onto possible, if elusive, resonances between Calderon's world of mysticism and miracles and the modern world's atheism. To explore this further we shall now briefly examine Calderon's play and the Bernanos text to which Camus refers (*The Diary of a Country Priest*), perhaps prompted by the eloquent film version by Robert Bresson, released in 1951.

Without going into every twist of its complex Baroque plot, Calderon's story concerns Eusebio and Julia, twins born on a wild mountainside at the foot of a wayside cross. Their mother has been driven out and mortally wounded by her husband, Curcio, who is jealously convinced that the children are not his – although her dying words persuade him otherwise. He leaves her as dead before the children are born, but she revives, gives birth, and manages to bring Julia back to him before dying, and he raises her as his daughter. Eusebio, however, is left on the mountainside, where he is rescued by peasants, but Curcio never learns that he is his son. Various astonishing events persuade Eusebio of the prophylactic power of the cross, although this scarcely mitigates his wild lifestyle. He and Julia, unaware of each other's identity, fall in love, but when this is discovered by her other brother, Lisardi, the inevitable duel follows and Lisardi is killed by Eusebio – although the latter mercifully bears the dying Lisardi to a monastery where he can make his confession. Curcio insists that Julia, dishonoured by Eusebio's advances and now by the killing of Lisardi, must enter a convent. Despite Eusebio's entreaties, she does so. However, her love for Eusebio has not died entirely, and when he breaks into the convent to carry her away, she consents to his advances. At the very last moment, however, he has a vision of blazing lights, perhaps the blazing lights of hell, shining from her eyes, and he flees. She follows but, not finding him, is now excluded both from the convent and from his love. Driven by a fierce instinct for survival, she kills several of those she encounters in the wild and even challenges Eusebio himself to a duel. In a chaotic sequence of events, Eusebio is mortally wounded by a mob and collapses at the foot of the cross where Curcio had long ago abandoned him. It is at this point that Curcio finally recognizes that Eusebio is his son and Julia's brother. Eusebio dies but comes back to life to make his confession. Julia, too, now discovers the truth and, appealing to the cross on behalf of Eusebio, disappears into heaven.

Nothing, it seems, could be further from the atmosphere and worldview of post-war French existentialism. Yet, as we have seen, Camus relates it via Bernanos to the cry of contemporary atheism that 'nothing is just'. The link to Bernanos is pivotal to understanding what is going on here, so we turn next to this radical Catholic author and, in particular, his novel *The Diary of a Country Priest*, first published in 1936, which ends with the words to which Camus alludes, 'All is grace'.[24]

As we have just indicated, Bernanos wrote as a committed Catholic, and *The Diary*, like his other work, promotes a Catholic critique of the modern world and, indeed, one developed from the viewpoint of a strongly conservative, anti-democratic version of Catholicism associated with extreme right-wing politics in the interwar years. Nevertheless, Bernanos's opposition to Franco gained him no little respect from many who were otherwise on the opposite political wing, including Simone Weil.[25]

Unlike in Calderon's world of miracles, Bernanos recognizes that the modern world is not likely to find direct revelations of the supernatural persuasive. As in Dostoevsky's novelistic universe (the Russian writer being a significant influence on Bernanos), even the saints may be unrecognized and ignored, and, as in the case of the Elder Zosima, their bodies may rot after death instead of, as expected, being miraculously preserved. The eponymous Curé of the novel is very much a saint living under the conditions of an incognito sanctity. In many respects, he is a holy fool, who, even when he does good, does so through inadvertence.

In a key passage, the Curé meets with the wife of the local squire, whose family is well connected in the ecclesiastical hierarchy. She is embittered over the death of a son and, beneath a veneer of conformity to public religious practice, cannot forgive God. Through their conversations she is transformed and becomes able to forgive – however, the upheaval of this experience precipitates a heart attack, and from the point of view of her husband and family, who are unaware of the personal transformation that took place in her, she has simply been worked on by the Curé in such a way that he is responsible for her death.

Given the influence of the squire in both community and Church, this leads to the increasing ostracism and isolation of the Curé. Suffering from an undiagnosed stomach cancer, he lives almost solely on bread and watered-down wine, a diet that readers may understand in the light of the Christian sacrament of Christ's body and blood but which feeds rumours in the village as to his alcoholism. He himself feels close to being abandoned by God and recounts experiences of spiritual dereliction that, we may say, bring him close to the experience of radical atheism: 'The same solitude. The same silence. And no hope this time of turning away the obstacle. Besides, there isn't any obstacle. Nothing. God! I breathe, I inhale the night, the night is entering into me by some inconceivable, unimaginable gap in my soul. I, myself, am the night'.[26]

Strangely, amongst the few friendly overtures he receives is that of the squire's cousin, a soldier in the foreign legion. He recognizes that, at a certain level, he and the Curé are men of the same kind, men who have to go on, facing forward, even in situations of utter hopelessness.

Finally, the Curé dies, having gone to Lille to seek medical treatment. At the end he lodges with an acquaintance from seminary days who has lost his faith. Nevertheless, at the Curé's urging, it is he who, in describing the priest's last hours, gives him absolution – even though he himself no longer sees anything supernatural in it, merely a gesture of 'humanity and friendship'.[27] He records the Curé's last words as follows: '"What does that matter. All is grace"'.[28]

How, then, does this relate to the atheists' view that 'nothing is just'? The point of contact, it seems, is simply this: that we live in a world in which affairs are not ordered according to any humanly comprehensible criteria of justice. In other words, the world is marked by a fundamental moral absurdity or ambiguity; it simply is as it is and cannot be explained but only be accepted or rejected in its entirety. Entire acceptance is the view that all is grace (thus Bernanos); entire rejection is Ivan Karamazov's intention to 'return the ticket'.

But what of Camus? Camus seems to hint at the possibility of a third option, an option of world acceptance that, nevertheless, does not presuppose any divine justice. The world is indeed absurd, but this does not require us to reject it. In *The Outsider*, Meursault states at one point that he 'looked up at the mass of signs and stars in the night sky and I laid myself open for the first time to the benign indifference of the world'.[29] The world is indifferent – 'nothing is just' – but it can also be experienced as benign – 'all is of grace' (a position, of course, that would have been impossible for Sartre to affirm).

This is the kind of vision that, in its most positive rendering, finds expression in the essay 'Summer in Algiers':

> Unity expresses itself here in terms of sea and sky. The heart senses it through a certain taste of the flesh that constitutes its bitterness and greatness. I am learning that there is no superhuman happiness, no eternity outside the curve of the days . . . Not that we should behave as beasts, but I can see no point in the happiness of angels. All I know is that this sky will last longer than I shall. And what can I call eternity except what will continue after my death? What I am expressing here is not the creature's complacency about his condition. It is something quite different. It is not always easy to be a man, even less to be a man who is pure. But to be pure means to rediscover that country of the soul where one's kinship with the world can be felt, where the throbbing of one's blood mingles with the violent pulsations of the afternoon sun.[30]

This may seem like – it is – sheer worldliness, and perhaps not many would immediately want to categorize it as in any way 'mystical'. Nevertheless, the emphasis on unity, on the simple clear perception and acceptance of everything being just as it is, could remind us that Camus's own academic studies culminated in a master's dissertation on Plotinus and Augustine, and the sentiment we find in this passage and elsewhere (as in the notion of 'benign indifference') seems especially compatible with Plotinus's fundamental view of the world.

The thesis is what it is, a relatively short master's thesis that largely relies on standard literature. However, the choice of subject shows the young Camus's interest in religion and, as we shall see, illuminates aspects of Plotinus in particular that point toward the passage from 'Summer in Algiers' and confirm that Camus's existentialism drew on mystical sources. Moreover, against Nietzsche's claim that Christianity's ascetic ideal involved 'saying no to life', Camus's exploration of the relation between Christianity, Hellenism, and modernity led him to conclude that there was a mystical way of saying yes to life, a 'mystic affirmation of the world'.[31]

Christian Metaphysics and Neoplatonism

Before Camus completed his university studies and left Algeria for France, on 8 May 1936, he submitted his *mémoire* for the *Diplôme d'Études Supérieure* at the University of Algiers. Entitled *Christian Metaphysics and Neoplatonism*, it was written under the official supervision of René Poirier, while Camus continued to receive unofficial guidance from Jean Grenier.[32]

As Camus introduced it, the *mémoire's* guiding question was: In what respect is Christianity original?[33] Camus framed his study with reference to the contemporary debate about Christian philosophy that was unfolding in the pages of the *Bulletin de la Société Française de Philosophie* and the *Revue de Metaphysique et de Morale*. On the basis of Christianity having contributed a great deal to the thought of the first centuries after Christ, Camus concluded that 'it is difficult to exclude all notion of a Christian philosophy'.[34]

Camus's later philosophical writings illustrate the aptness of his point. Although commentators have noted the presence of immanent or nature mysticism in Camus's literature, due to constraints of space and the contested status of novels and plays as philosophy, the focus here will be primarily Camus's well-known essays *The Myth of Sisyphus* (1942) and *The Rebel* (1951).[35] Throughout these works, several commentators have noted, Camus is interested in the relation of Greek thought, Christianity, and modernity. And as Hardré notes, *Christian Metaphysics* 'shows very definitely the interest that the young Camus had in 'the development of early Christian thought and in the influence on this development of late Greek philosophy'.[36]

But Camus assigns 'mystic reason' a significant chapter in both his *mémoire* and his later analyses of politics and philosophy. In order to understand what Camus means by this, a summary of his *mémoire's* argument will be made. The following summary is not intended to raise questions about the accuracy or originality of Camus's characterizations of Greek thought or early Christianity (both of which are likely to raise the eyebrows of classicists and scholars of the early church).[37] Rather, it is to draw attention to the Pascalian framing of his Nietzschean project and to illuminate the conceptions of 'mysticism' Camus will employ in the later works.

In Camus's introduction to *Christian Metaphysics and Neoplatonism* he states that Christian thought adopted and transformed Greek thought and that in order to understand the originality of Christianity, he will return to its sources. What he finds in those sources – an impressive range of patristic theologians, even if largely dependent on secondary literature – is that Christianity's original contribution to human thought is 'on the affective plane where problems arise and not in the system that tries to respond to them'.[38] *In its beginnings*, Camus continues, 'Christianity is not a philosophy that is opposed to a philosophy, but an ensemble of aspirations, a faith, that moves to a certain plane and seeks its solutions within that plane'.[39]

The Greeks, in Camus's reading, were content to claim that their kingdom was of this world. The world as they conceived it was eternal and necessary.[40] In such a world sin and salvation made no sense; here any evil could be attributed to ignorance or error. But in the Greco-Roman world 'the desire for God' grew stronger and 'the problem of the Good' lost ground; what Camus calls 'the aesthetic plane of contemplation' was concealed by a 'tragic plane where hopes are limited to the imitation of a God'.[41]

The Greeks thought that virtue could be learned. But Christianity's rule was love, not virtue. And Christianity could 'do nothing but embody this idea, so little Greek in nature, that the problem for man is not to perfect [the world], but to escape it'.[42]

Camus divides the course of this evolution into four stages – (i) Evangelical Christianity, (ii) Gnosticism, (iii) Neoplatonism, and (iv) Augustinianism – arguing that the contribution of Greek thought to Christianity was to orient it to metaphysics and universality. For Camus, Neoplatonism was 'the ultimate effort of Greek thinking',[43] which attempted 'to reconcile rationalism and mysticism'. And after it Christianity 'blossoms', as Camus puts it, 'in the second revelation that was Augustinian thought'.[44]

(i) Evangelical Christianity

Evangelical Christianity as Camus depicts it was ignorant and characterized by 'disdain of all systematic speculation'.[45] In the view of the earliest Christians, 'one must choose between the world and God'.[46] Camus ascertained two stages in evangelical Christianity: pessimism and hope. He divides the chapter into subsections, one on 'The Tragic Plane' and another on 'Hope in God'. But curiously, Camus's examples of tragic Christianity draw on much later sources than the period under discussion: he includes some biblical texts and Ernst Renan's *Life of Jesus* on death. And then he cites Pascal as an example of the pessimistic strand in Christian thinking: 'We are laughable to remain in the company of our fellow men: miserable like us, powerless like us, they will not help us: one dies alone'.[47] Having introduced the 'misery' pole of the Pascalian *misère/bassesse* duality in this way, Camus returns to Romans 7 and Augustine's interpretation of the human 'incapacity not to sin'. Again, Camus cites Pascal on the tragedy of the human condition in the shackles of sin.[48] But the passage Camus cites is called by Pascal *an image* of man's condition:

> Let us imagine a number of men in chains and all condemned to death, of which some each day have their throats cut in the sight of the others, and those who remain see their true condition in that of their fellows, and looking at each other with sorrow and hopelessness, await their turn. This is an image of man's condition.

The section on hope, too, begins with Augustine – the Augustine of the *Soliloquies*, who desires to know nothing less than God and the soul.[49] The kingdom of Christianity, in Camus's reading, has nothing terrestrial about it. Whereas Greek wisdom conceived of itself as a science in which an orderly world could be understood and people in it could be instructed, Christian salvation is a state of affairs: 'one must be Greek in order to believe that wisdom is learned'.[50] The strangeness of Christianity's hope in the Incarnate God as a means of redemption from the impending doom of fate and death is illustrated by the reactions of such pagans as Celsus and Porphyry – how could these two worldviews become synthesized in the way that they did? Camus attempts to answer this question by offering summaries of the key Apostolic Fathers and apologists, showing how someone like Justin Martyr could combine a 'spirit, which education had made Greek, and their heart, which Christian love had penetrated'.[51]

(ii) Gnosticism

Gnosticism, though 'a Greek reflection on Christian themes', actually demonstrated a mutual failure of assimilation, ending with 'an outrageous Christianity, woven from oriental religions and Greek mythology': it 'reveals to Christianity the path not to follow'.[52] Here Camus builds on the distinction between earned and given salvation. Christian grace is arbitrary; what gnostic conceptions of initiation offer is an 'influence over the divine kingdom' – for the gnostic salvation is learned and earned; for the Christian, salvation is given.[53] At the root of Gnostic thought[54] – and 'all Christian thought',[55] in Camus's view – is the problem of evil. The meaning of history is also a problem, but Camus sees it as one of lesser significance in the thinkers he considers. 'It is evil that obsessed the Gnostics. They are all pessimists regarding the world'.[56]

(iii) Mystic reason

In the chapter entitled (significantly for us) 'Plotinus and Mystic Reason', Camus discusses Plotinus's *Enneads*. We noted at the outset of this section that Camus saw the main issue in the relationship between Hellenism and Christianity as one of feeling or affectivity rather than ideas, narrowly understood. He argues that there are two aspirations in ancient Greek thought that Plotinus sought to reconcile: mystical longing for God and an associated concern with the destiny of the soul[57] and a need for rationality or coherence, associated with a view of the world as orderly and therefore apt to be understood in such terms.[58]

Plotinus writes against the Gnostics: 'against those who say that the . . . universe is evil'.[59] Plotinus's solution to the apparent irreconcilability of the Greek desire for coherence and longing for God is to give Christian thought not a doctrine but 'a method and way of seeing things'. 'The desire for God is what animates Plotinus'. But Plotinus is also Greek; he wants rational explanations and intellectual satisfaction. His solution, Camus writes, depends on his conception of Reason: 'To know is to worship in accordance with Reason'.[60] Here Camus returns again to Pascal, claiming that to a certain extent: 'Plotinian Reason is already the "heart" of Pascal'.

Pascal's 'heart' – the little-understood subject of the widely cited *Pensée* 'the heart has its reasons that reason does not know' – is a cognitive faculty that perceives moral value. Its function is closely linked to that of the imagination: whereas the heart perceives value through feeling or intuition (*sentir*), the imagination bestows it by construing objects in certain ways when it represents them. The postlapsarian imagination, however, does not always represent objects in the world accurately; it can apply magnifying or minimizing lenses, distorting the true worth of the things it claims to see. The heart perceives value, and it has its own form of reasoning which Pascal calls *finesse*.

> We know the truth not only through our reason but also through our heart. It is through the latter that we know first principles, and reason, which has nothing to do with it, tries in vain to refute them. . . . For knowledge of first principles like space, time, motion, and number is as solid as any derived through reason, and it is on such knowledge, coming from heart and instinct, that reason has to depend and base all its argument.[61]

Moreover, it is not just first principles that the heart perceives; it is the faculty that is capable of knowing God and seeing Jesus.

> It is the heart which perceives God, and not the reason. That is what faith is, God perceived by the heart, not by the reason.[62]
>
> Jesus without wealth or any outward show of knowledge has his own order of holiness . . . With what great pomp and marvelously magnificent array he came in the eyes of the heart, which perceive wisdom.[63]

Although in some readings of Pascal, the heart aims at truth and desires it because it is beautiful,[64] Camus reads early Christian thought as divorcing Reason from Beauty.

When Christianity separates Reason and Beauty, he writes, 'Reason is reduced to its role of logical legislator. And thus conflicts between Faith and Reason become possible. For a Greek, these conflicts are less acute because Beauty, which is both order and sensitivity, economy and the object of passion, remains a ground of agreement'.[65]

In Camus's reading of Plotinian 'knowledge', it is 'not an experience but an effort and a desire, in a word, a creative evolution'.[66] Like the Pascalian heart (and Bergsonian intuition), it is cognitive and affective. It replaces Greek reason (with the logic of contradiction) with a 'Mystic Reason' governed by the logic of participation. Seven times in the *mémoire* Camus refers to participation as homecoming: 'to know the One is to return to one's homeland'.

Plotinus criticizes the Christian view of Salvation for being irrational and unmerited, writing that it is

> evidence of their indifference to virtue, that they have never made any treatise about virtue . . . for it does no good at all to say 'look to God', unless one also teaches how one is to look. In reality it is virtue which goes before us to the good and when it comes to exist in the soul along with wisdom, shows God; but God, if you talk about him without true virtue, is only a name.[67]

Plotinus thus advocated an attitude toward the world rather than a doctrine. It is a 'mystic reason', a dialogue between the heart and reason, in which, as Camus writes 'truth can only be expressed through images'.[68]

Plotinus's 'sentiment' is ultimately not that of the believer but of the artist: 'if things are explained it is because the things are beautiful', he comments.[69] Naturally, in the light of our knowledge that this young master's student would go on to become known primarily as a writer of fiction and drama, these words cannot but acquire additional force. A further approximation of Plotinus to Camus's own novelistic world is also suggested, albeit (perhaps necessarily) enigmatically, when we read that 'It is not the appearance that Plotinus seeks but rather the inside of things which is his lost paradise. Each thing here below is made a living reminder of this solitary homeland of the wise. This is why Plotinus describes intelligence in a sensual way'.[70] The task of the soul – a task at once philosophical and religious, specifically mystical – is thus to seek its origin in a voyage 'From God to God': that is, from God manifest in the world to the God, the One, beyond image and discourse. That, he adds, 'is its prayer' and 'this union, so complete and so rare, is ecstasy'.[71]

Camus himself seems almost to shift to ecstatic mode when he describes the culminating 'ecstasy' of this 'voyage' and this 'prayer': 'Solitary meditation, in love with the world to the extent that it is only a crystal in which the divinity is reflected, thought wholly penetrated by the silent rhythm of stars, but concerned about the God who orders them, Plotinus thinks as an artist and feels as a philosopher, according to a reason full of light and before a world in which intelligence breathes'.[72] Camus, philosophy student and future artist, may be writing as much of his own vocation as of Plotinus. So, too, when he speaks of the opposition but also the need to balance 'mystical reason, sensible Intelligence, God, who is both immanent and transcendent', a balance that, he says, 'can only be expressed through images'.[73]

Nevertheless, it would be a mistake to think of Plotinus as 'more Christian than he is'. Plotinus remained a Greek philosopher adhering to the aristocratic virtues of his calling and disdaining the Christian's vulgarity in embracing even 'vile men' as his brothers and, at a more theoretical level, dismissive of any view of salvation that was disconnected from the practice of virtue.[74]

(iv) Augustine's 'second revelation'

Augustine was – like his evangelical, gnostic, and Neoplatonic predecessors – obsessed by the problem of evil. But his obsession was 'fecund'.[75] 'Greek in his need for coherence, Christian in the anxieties of sensitivity . . . What Augustine demanded beside faith was truth, and beside dogmas, metaphysics'.[76] Augustine's metaphysics introduced evil as the privation of good, developing an account of evil, grace, and freedom. Unlike Plotinus, Camus's Augustine claims that there must first be grace, and only after grace can there be virtue'.[77] Consequently Camus concludes that our only freedom 'is precisely the freedom to do evil'.[78]

Camus finds it curious that the author of the *Confessions* takes his own experience to be 'the perpetual reference for his intellectual pursuits'.[79] If Christianity teaches the escape from the world, why does this infamous naysayer want the world to be intelligible?

Augustinian reason must be enlightened by faith to be illuminating; otherwise philosophy is inadequate to the pursuit of truth. That was Neoplatonism's gift: Augustine's doctrines of humility and faith. Neoplatonism's role in the development of Christian thought was 'to assist this relaxing of Reason, to lead Socratic logic into religious speculation, and in this way to pass on this ready-made tool to the Fathers of the Christian church'.[80]

At the end of the book Camus returns to Nietzsche, writing that if Nietzsche was correct that 'pessimistic Greece, deaf and tragic, was the mark of a strong civilization, it is necessary to admit that Christianity in this regard is a rebirth in relation to Socraticism and its serenity'.[81] But as in Camus's introduction, Nietzsche's words in his conclusion are quickly followed by Pascal's: '"Men", says Pascal, "being unable to cure death, are wise not to think about it"'.[82]

When Srigley's translation of *Christian Metaphysics and Neoplatonism* was published in 2007, he noted that with the exception of McBride's earlier translation and discussion in *Albert Camus: Philosopher and Littérateur*, commentators on Camus's work have been notably silent about this book and its relationship to Camus's mature thought'.[83] Perhaps this is because Camus's atheism has led to the assumption that his early research on patristic Christianity would be irrelevant. But it is all the more surprising given that Camus's *mémoire* raised several questions to which his later work would return: the problem of evil; whether we say yes or no to the world in Nietzschean affirmation of Christian negation; whether we belong to it; the desire for God and the need for coherence; the role of reason, whether 'rational' or 'mystic'; whether the only freedom available to us is the freedom to sin.

One commentator who has considered the relation of the thesis to later work, Paul Archambault, writes that 'If it be a Christian disease to feel dispossessed and cast adrift in a hostile universe, it is fair to say that, although Camus fought that disease tooth and nail, he never entirely convalesced'.[84] Roger Quillot's introduction to the 1965 French edition of *Christian Metaphysics* agrees: Camus was 'seduced by the tragic anguish of Saint Augustine'.[85] But it was not only anguish that attracted Camus to this tradition of Christian thought.

Before turning to *The Myth of Sisyphus*, it is worth noting that between the writing of the *Christian Metaphysics and Neoplatonism* and *The Myth of Sisyphus*, entries from Camus's notebooks show us that he continued to think about – and wanted to return to – ways of knowing that were not 'rational': images, ethical and aesthetic conceptions of reason.

> April 1934: 'I believe that the judgement that a man makes about life is too complex to be enclosed in the category of pessimism or optimism'.[86]
>
> January 1936: 'People can only think in images. If you want to be a philosopher, write novels'.[87]
>
> September 1938: 'Resume work on Plotinus. Theme: Plotinian reason. Reason – not an unambiguous concept. Interesting to see how it behaves in history at a time when it must either adapt itself or perish. Cf. *Diplôme*. It is the same reason, and it is not the same, because there are two kinds of reason, the one ethical and the other aesthetic. Pursue further: images in Plotinus as the syllogism of this aesthetic form of reason. The image as a parable: the attempt to express the undefinable nature of feeling by what is obvious and undefinable in concrete things'.[88]

One of Camus's examiners, René Poirier, commented that his dissertation was the work of an author 'more a writer than a philosopher'.[89] Sartre would be the first to make this criticism of Camus publicly, in his 'Explication of the Stranger'.[90] In hindsight, it is interesting to note that Sartre also claimed that Nietzsche was a poet 'who had the misfortune to be taken for a philosopher' and that Sartre would also face such charges.[91] These philosophers used images and exemplars to pose philosophical problems or – as some would have it – 'mysteries' of existence.

The Myth of Sisyphus

The Myth of Sisyphus (written in 1940 and published in 1942) introduces itself as an attempt to resolve the problem of suicide; Camus wrote that it 'marked the beginning of an idea' which he would pursue further in *The Rebel* in relation to murder.[92] Its epigraph, taken from Pindar, reads: 'O my soul, do not aspire to immortal life, but exhaust the limits of the possible'. Camus was committed to the view that philosophy should be *lived*. He followed Nietzsche in claiming that 'a philosopher, to deserve our respect, must preach by example'.[93]

In this work, Camus returns to the theme of 'desire for God'. He writes that there is 'a nostalgia for unity', which is the 'essential impulse of the human drama'. But: that we have the desire does not imply that it can or will be met.[94] The problem that Augustine faced – to reconcile the desire for coherence and this longing – is the root of the absurdity of the world.

> I said the world is absurd but I was too hasty. This world in itself is not reasonable, that is all that can be said. But what is absurd is the confrontation of the irrational and the wild longing for clarity whose call echoes in the human heart.[95]

The Myth of Sisyphus discusses 'a family of minds related by their nostalgia but opposed by their methods or aims' – namely Nietzsche's Zarathustra, Kierkegaard (on despair), Jaspers, Heidegger, Shestov, and Scheler. Camus writes that they have 'persisted in blocking the royal road of reason and in recovering the direct paths of truth'.[96] But none of these philosophies succeeds in offering hope; instead, they offer merely escape.

Camus's discussion of the shortcomings of these 'existentialists' shows that he thinks they succumb to 'mystic reason'. Their preoccupation with the irrational is 'reason becoming confused and escaping by negating itself'. What he offers in the absurd, by contrast, is 'lucid reason noting its limits'.[97]

A page earlier Camus introduced the human and divine aspects of reason, writing that 'Since Plotinus, who was the first to reconcile it with the eternal climate, [reason] has learned to turn away from the most cherished of its principles, which is contradiction, in order to integrate into it the strangest, the quite magic one of participation'.[98] At several points in *Myth of Sisyphus* Camus speaks of mystics and existentialists in the same breath. Mystics, he says,

> find freedom in giving themselves. By losing themselves in their god, by accepting his rules they become secretly free. In spontaneously accepted slavery they recover a deeper independence. But what does that freedom mean? It may be said above all that they *feel* free with regard to themselves and not so much free as liberated. . . . It can be seen at this point that the initial themes of existential philosophy keep their entire value.

> The return to consciousness, the escape from everyday sleep represents the first steps of absurd freedom.[99]

Among the 'initial themes' of existentialism, Camus praises Kierkegaard's depiction of despair ('nothing is more profound'), agreeing with Augustine and later interpreters of the doctrine of sin that 'sin is what alienates from God'. 'The absurd' Camus writes, 'is sin without God'.[100]

> 'Prayer', says Alain, 'is when night descends over thought'. 'But the mind must meet the night', reply the mystics and the existentials.[101]

But the mind that meets the night here is soothed by mystic reason – such as Kierkegaard's leap – which requires 'the sacrifice of the intellect'.[102]

The Rebel

After *The Myth of Sisyphus* his interest in the relation between Hellenism, Christianity, and modernity persisted and shifted. In a 1947 entry in Camus's *Notebooks* he wrote that: 'If, to outgrow nihilism, one must return to Christianity, one may well follow the impulse and outgrow Christianity in Hellenism'.[103] This would seem to support the Nietzschean reading that sees Camus's philosophy as midway between optimism and pessimism, a 'saying yes to life'.

In *The Rebel* Camus turns his consideration from individual uses of mystic reason in existentialists' illuminations of the question of suicide to the interpersonal questions of murder and genocide. Again Camus's discussion of Christianity and modernity draws on Nietzsche. But Camus thinks philosophers have misread Nietzsche and that Christianity has misread Christ.

Camus's Nietzsche sees Christ's doctrine as 'total consent' and 'non-resistance to evil'. The injunction not to kill extends even to the prevention of killing. All must be accepted. 'Not faith but deeds' is the message of Nietzsche's Christ, and 'from then on, the history of Christianity is nothing but a betrayal of this message'.[104] The nineteenth century produced degenerate forms of Christianity in socialism[105] and mysticism (here understood as a crude antipathy to reason) in Nazism – which restored 'idolatry and a debased deity to the world of nihilism'.[106]

Camus is explicit that he reads Nietzsche in the light of Pascal: 'The *Will to Power* ends, like Pascal's *Pensées* of which it so often reminds us, with a wager. Man does not yet obtain assurance but only the wish for assurance which is not at all the same thing'.[107]

In Marx and Nietzsche Camus sees the difference between the Christian and the Greek: Marx wants to subjugate nature in order to obey history; Nietzsche to do the contrary. Marxism agrees with Christianity that human history is unique. But both are hostile toward nature, considering it as an 'object not for contemplation but for transformation. For the Christian, as for the Marxist, nature must be subdued. The Greeks are of the opinion that it is better to obey it'.[108]

In the degenerate Christianity that is socialism, Marx is 'the Jeremiah of the god of history and the Saint Augustine of the revolution'.[109] He understood that 'a religion which did not embrace transcendence should properly be called politics'.[110] Camus disagrees with 'the fanatical Marxists' who claimed that Marx was 'the beginning and end of the prophecy' because they fail to see the extent to which Marx was an heir. Camus cites the 1844 manuscripts to show the indebtedness of Marx to the conceptual inheritance of the Christian tradition and in particular to the way Marx promises to overcome the estranging effects of the 'absurd' situation that is sin without God:

> *Communism* as the *positive* transcendence of *private property* as *human self-estrangement*, and therefore as the real *appropriation* of the *human* essence by and for man; communism therefore as the complete return of man to himself as a *social* (i.e. human) being – a return accomplished consciously and embracing the entire wealth of previous development. This communism, as fully developed naturalism, equals humanism, and as fully developed humanism equals naturalism; it is the *genuine* resolution of the conflict between man and nature and between man and man – the true resolution of the strife between existence and essence, between objectification and self-confirmation, between freedom and necessity, between the individual and the species. Communism is the riddle of history solved, and it knows itself to be this solution.[111]

Well before Marx, in Camus's analysis, Rousseau's *Social Contract* replaced the 'mystic body of temporal Christianity' with the 'mystic idea' of civil religion. The year 1789 was the birth year of the reign of 'holy humanity', 'our Lord of the human race'.[112]

In the absence of God, history has assumed the role of supreme judge:[113] 'Totality is . . . the ancient dream of unity common to both believers and rebels, but projected horizontally on to an earth deprived of God'.[114]

The tortuous question of the twentieth century, Camus wrote, therefore, was: 'how to live without grace and without justice?'[115] Camus's answer is that the rebel cannot exist without 'a strange kind of love': 'Those who find no rest in God or in history are condemned to live for those who, like themselves, cannot live: in fact, for the humiliated'.[116] And, alongside the struggle for justice and in face of the absence of God – and if only at the margins of Camus's thought – there is, as we have also seen, the possibility to which *Summer in Algiers* bears witness. This is the possibility that, however momentarily, nature itself may offer a pledge of the lost and sought for unity, the One to which Plotinus thought we were journeying home. That possibility should not be taken as 'softening' Camus's atheism, but it should not be forgotten either.

Notes

1 According to Beauvoir, the term 'existentialism' was coined by Marcel to refer to Sartre's philosophy and – by extension – hers. Both Beauvoir and Sartre were irritated by it; Beauvoir claimed that her inspiration 'came from [her] own experience, not from a system' (Simone de Beauvoir, *Force of Circumstance*, trans. Richard Howard (London: Penguin Books, 1987), pp. 44, 45).
2 Philosophy in the narrow sense was only one aspect of Marcel's life work; he was also active as a dramatist and critic, and much of his philosophical work is in the form of his 'metaphysical journals', essays, and reviews rather than in systematic expositions. The most substantial of these are his Gifford lectures at the University of Aberdeen, published as *The Mystery of Being, Vol. 1: Reflection and Mystery* (London: The Harvill Press, 1950) and *Vol. 2: Faith and Reality* (London: The Harvill Press, 1951).
3 In relation to Marcel's focus on the actual comportment of the self in its world, it is also worth mentioning that the American pragmatist Josiah Royce was another important focus of his early work.
4 Gabriel Marcel, *Coleridge et Schelling* (Paris: Aubier-Montaigne, 1971), p. 242.
5 Gabriel Marcel, *Being and Having*, trans. Katharine Farrer (London: Fontana, 1965), p. 32. Metaphysical Journal 12th June 1929. However, we should note that in a remark added in 1934 Marcel later regarded this way of putting it as 'rather too categorical'.
6 Marcel, *Being and Having*, p. 33.
7 Marcel, *Being and Having*, p. 36.
8 Marcel, *Being and Having*, p. 181.
9 Marcel, *Being and Having*, p. 142.
10 Marcel, *Being and Having*, p. 143.
11 Marcel, *Being and Having*, p. 188.
12 Marcel, *Being and Having*, p. 127.
13 Marcel, *The Mystery of Being*, vol. 1, p. 205.
14 Marcel, *The Mystery of Being*, vol. 1, p. 205.
15 Marcel, *The Mystery of Being*, vol. 1, pp. 176–8.
16 Brother Lawrence, *The Practice of the Presence of God* (London: H. R. Allenson, 1906).
17 See, for example, Marcel, *Being and Having*, p. 16.
18 See, for example, Gabriel Marcel, *Metaphysical Journal*, trans. Bernard Wall (London: Rockliff, 1952) pp. 286–7 (entry for 8 July 1922).
19 See the essay on Sartre in Gabriel Marcel, *Homo Viator* (London: Victor Gollancz, 1951).
20 See especially Nicholas A. Berdyaev, *Solitude and Society*, trans. George Reavey (London: Geoffrey Bles, 1938).
21 Camus, *The Rebel*, p. 188.
22 Albert Camus, 'Introduction' to Pedro Calderon de la Barca, *La Dévotion à la Croix* (Paris: Gallimard, 1953), pp. 11–2.
23 Camus, 'Introduction', p. 12.
24 The connection here is slightly obscured by Pamela Morris's rendering 'Grace is . . . everywhere'. See Georges Bernanos, *The Diary of a Country Priest*, trans. Pamela Morris (London: Collins, 1956), p. 253.
25 See Simone Weil, *The Need for Roots*, trans. Arthur Wills (London: Routledge, 2003), pp. 167–8.
26 Bernanos, *Diary of a Country Priest*, pp. 91–2.
27 Bernanos, *Diary of a Country Priest*, p. 253.
28 Bernanos, *Diary of a Country Priest*, p. 253.
29 Albert Camus, *The Outsider* (London: Penguin Books, 2000), p. 117.

30 Albert Camus, *Lyrical and Critical Essays*, ed. Philip Thody (New York: Vintage, 1970), p. 90.
31 Albert Camus, *The Rebel*, trans. Anthony Bower (London: Penguin Books, 1986), p. 188.
32 Grenier encouraged Camus to read Kierkegaard, Chestov, and Berdiaev alongside Plotinus and Augustine. See Oliver Todd, *Camus: A Life*, trans. Benjamin Ivry (New York: Knopf, 1997), p. 43.
33 Albert Camus, *Christian Metaphysics and Neoplatonism*, trans. Ronald Srigley (Columbia: University of Missouri Press, 2007), p. 44.
34 CMN 44. Camus's notes here refer to the March 1931 *Bulletin de la societé française de Philosophie*; and in the *Revue de métaphysique et de morale*, Bréhier, in April 1931; and Souriau in July 1932.
35 See, for example Ronald D. Srigley, *Albert Camus' Critique of Modernity* (Columbia: University of Missouri Press, 2011), p. 12 (on Camus's nature mysticism in *The Fall*).
36 Jacques Hardré, 'Camus' Thoughts on Christian Metaphysics and Neoplatonism' *Studies in Philology* 64 (1967): 97–108, here p. 97.
37 Moreover, as Srigley notes, Camus was careless in his quotations and references (Srigley, 'Introduction', to Camus, *Christian Metaphysics*, p. 14).
38 Camus, *Christian Metaphysics*, p. 39.
39 Camus, *Christian Metaphysics*, p. 40.
40 Camus, *Christian Metaphysics*, p. 40.
41 Camus, *Christian Metaphysics*, p. 43.
42 Camus, *Christian Metaphysics*, p. 43.
43 Camus, *Christian Metaphysics*, p. 41.
44 Camus, *Christian Metaphysics*, p. 45.
45 Camus, *Christian Metaphysics*, p. 47.
46 Camus, *Christian Metaphysics*, p. 47.
47 Cited in Camus, *Christian Metaphysics*, p. 49. Because the MS for Pascal's *Pensées* was left unfinished, different editions have proliferated and citations are usually to fragment number rather than page. Louis Lafuma's edition respects the provisional classification suggested by the order of MS copies, whereas Léon Brunschvicg rearranged the fragments thematically, rejecting the possibility of any 'true' ordering. In the following references to the *Pensées* I have provided both the Brunschvicg and Lafuma fragment numbers; the latter because Lafuma's edition is still widely respected, and the former because it was the prevailing edition in the period under consideration here. Camus uses Léon Brunschvicg's numbering, and in this instance cites: Brunschvicg 211; Lafuma 151.
48 Cited in Camus, *Christian Metaphysics*, p. 50; Pascal, *Pensées*, Brunschvicg 199; Lafuma 434.
49 Camus, *Christian Metaphysics*, p. 50.
50 Camus, *Christian Metaphysics*, pp. 53, 55.
51 Camus, *Christian Metaphysics*, p. 63.
52 Camus, *Christian Metaphysics*, pp. 67, 86.
53 Camus, *Christian Metaphysics*, p. 69.
54 Camus, *Christian Metaphysics*, p. 70.
55 Camus, *Christian Metaphysics*, p. 84.
56 Camus, *Christian Metaphysics*, p. 86.
57 As Srigley notes, sometimes Camus argues that longing for fulfilment or the 'home' of the soul is a constant in human nature; at other times he says that such a longing is foreign to the Greeks – although one wonders on this basis whether he had read Plato's *Symposium*.
58 Camus's discussion of Plotinus is indebted to Emile Bréhier's *La Philosophie de Plotin* and René Arnou's *Le désir de Dieu dans la Philosophie de Plotin* (see

Archambault, *Hellenic*, pp. 44–53). The influence of Bréhier may explain the rationalist reading of Plotinus in *Christian Metaphysics*, which contrasts with the more intuitive Plotinus we encounter in the *Myth of Sisyphus*.
59 Ennead II. 9, cited in Camus, *Christian Metaphysics*, p. 67.
60 Camus, *Christian Metaphysics*, p. 89. See also p. 101 on 'the sight of intelligence', brought about through the conversion that finds its source in desire for God.
61 Pascal, *Pensées*, Brunschvicg, p. 282; Lafuma, p. 110.
62 Pascal, *Pensées*, Brunschvicg, p. 278; Lafuma, p. 424.
63 Pascal, *Pensées*, Brunschvicg, p. 793; Lafuma, p. 308.
64 See William Wood, *Blaise Pascal on Duplicity, Sin and the Fall* (Oxford: Oxford University Press, 2013), Chapter 4, for a reading of the heart and the imagination in Pascal that links the pursuit of the true and the beautiful.
65 Camus, *Christian Metaphysics*, p. 91.
66 Camus, *Christian Metaphysics*, p. 92.
67 *Enneads* II.9.15; as cited in Camus, *Christian Metaphysics*, p. 108.
68 Camus, *Christian Metaphysics*, p. 111.
69 Camus, *Christian Metaphysics*, p. 90.
70 Camus, *Christian Metaphysics*, p. 90.
71 Camus, *Christian Metaphysics*, p. 106.
72 Camus, *Christian Metaphysics*, p. 106.
73 Camus, *Christian Metaphysics*, p. 111.
74 Camus, *Christian Metaphysics*, p. 107.
75 Camus, *Christian Metaphysics*, p. 99.
76 Camus, *Christian Metaphysics*, p. 117.
77 Camus, *Christian Metaphysics*, p. 120. Camus's study cites Gilson's *Introduction à l'étude de Saint Augustin*.
78 Camus, *Christian Metaphysics*, p. 120.
79 Camus, *Christian Metaphysics*, p. 118.
80 Camus, *Christian Metaphysics*, p. 129.
81 Srigley suggests that apart from his teachers Nietzsche was the greatest influence on Camus's thought during the early 1930s, on the basis that his name appears frequently in Camus's notebooks and because *The Birth of Tragedy* is taken to be a reference point for Camus's analysis of the departure of Christianity from the Greeks. In *The Birth of Tragedy*, Nietzsche claimed that the Greeks 'knew and felt the terror and horror of existence'. But Socrates's introduction of the 'theoretical man' heralded the death of the tragic sense. 'Apollonian contemplation' and 'Dionysian ecstasies' gave way to 'cool, paradoxical thoughts' and 'fiery effects', which were pale imitations of their forebears. See Friedrich Nietzsche, *The Birth of Tragedy*, trans. Walter Kaufmann (New York: Vintage, 1987), Sections 15, 12.
82 Camus, *Christian Metaphysics*, p. 133.
83 Srigley, 'Introduction', p. 8. See Srigley, p. 9 n. 27 for a list of works that treat Camus and Christianity; see also pp. 15 ff. for Srigley's discussion of I. H. Walker, Jacques Hardré's 'Camus' Thoughts', and Paul Archambault's works on *Neoplatonism and Christian Metaphysics*.
84 Paul Archambault, *Camus' Hellenic Sources* (Chapel Hill: University of North Carolina Press, 1972), p. 104.
85 Roger Quillot, 'Inroduction' to Albert Camus, *Essais* (Paris: Pléiade, 1965).
86 Letter to Grenier, 17 April 1934, "Je crois que le jugement qu'un homme porte sur la vie est trop complexe pour etre enfermé dans un catégorie pessimisme ou optimisme." Albert Camus, *Correspondence 1932–1960* (Paris: Gallimard, 1981), p. 18.
87 In Albert Camus, *Notebooks 1935–1942*, trans. Philip Thody (New York: Knopf, 1963), p. 10.
88 Camus, *Notebooks*, p. 103. (Cited in S?).

89 The examiner was Poirier: see Herbert R. Lottman, *Camus: A Biography* (New York: George Braziller, 1981), p. 109.
90 Jean-Paul Sartre, 'An Explication of *The Stranger*' in *Literary and Philosophical Essays of Jean-Paul Sartre*, trans. Annette Michelson (New York: Criterion Books, 1955).
91 Jean-Paul Sartre, *Carnet Midy*, in Jean-Paul Sartre, *Écrits de jeunesse*, ed. Michel Contat et Michel Rybalka (Paris: Gallimard, 1990), p. 471.
92 Albert Camus, 'Preface' to *The Myth of Sisyphus*, trans. Justin O'Brien (London: Penguin Books, 2013), p. ix. [On life as a work of art see 'Everyone tries to make his life a work of art' (Albert Camus, *The Rebel*, trans. Anthony Bower (London: Penguin Books, 1986), p. 227)].
93 Camus, *Myth*, p. 5.
94 Camus, *Myth*, p. 15.
95 Camus, *Myth*, p. 17.
96 Camus, *Myth*, p. 19.
97 Camus, *Myth*, p. 37.
98 Camus has a note here which reads 'A. At the time reason had to adapt itself or die. It adapts itself. With Plotinus, after being logical it became aesthetic. Metaphor takes the place of the syllogism' (Camus, *Myth*, p. 36).
99 Camus, *Myth*, p. 44. In *The Rebel* Camus refers to the 'The mystic slogan "Die and become what you are"' as being 'taken up once more by Hegel' (Camus, *The Rebel*, p. 108).
100 Camus, *Myth*, p. 31.
101 Camus, *Myth*, p. 48.
102 See *Myth*, p. 37. In both *Myth* and *Rebel* Camus discusses Ignatius of Loyola's third sacrifice: 'the sacrifice of the intellect' (Camus, *Myth*, p. 29).
103 Albert Camus, *Notebooks 1942–1951*, trans. Justin O'Brien (New York: Paragon House, 1991), p. 183.
104 Camus, *The Rebel*, p. 60.
105 Camus, *The Rebel*, p. 61.
106 Camus, *The Rebel*, p. 151. Also a reference to 'Fascist mystics' on p. 155.
107 Camus, *The Rebel*, p. 66.
108 Camus, *The Rebel*, p. 158.
109 Camus, *The Rebel*, p. 159.
110 Camus, *The Rebel*, p. 164.
111 Karl Marx, *Economic and Philosophical Manuscripts of 1844*, section 3, www.marxists.org/archive/marx/works/1844/manuscripts/comm.htm.
112 Camus, *The Rebel*, pp. 86, 87.
113 Camus, *The Rebel*, p. 207.
114 Camus, *The Rebel*, p. 199.
115 Camus, *The Rebel*, p. 192.
116 Camus, *The Rebel*, p. 268.

Works cited

Archambault, Paul, *Camus' Hellenic Sources* (Chapel Hill: University of North Carolina Press, 1972).

Beauvoir, Simone de, *Force of Circumstance*, trans. Richard Howard (London: Penguin, 1987).

Berdyaev, Nicholas A., *Solitude and Society*, trans. George Reavey (London: Geoffrey Bles, 1938).

Bernanos, Georges, *The Diary of a Country Priest*, trans. Pamela Morris (London: Collins, 1956).

Bréhier, Emile, *La Philosophie de Plotin* (Paris: Boivin, 1928).
Camus, Albert, *Christian Metaphysics and Neoplatonism*, trans. Ronald Srigley (Columbia: University of Missouri Press, 2007).
———, *Correspondence 1932–1960* (Paris: Gallimard, 1981).
———, 'Introduction' to Pedro Calderon de la Barca, *La Dévotion à la Croix* (Paris: Gallimard, 1953).
———, *Lyrical and Critical Essays*, ed. Philip Thody (New York: Vintage, 1970).
———, *The Myth of Sisyphus*, trans. Justin O'Brien (London: Penguin, 2013).
———, *Notebooks 1935–1942*, trans. Philip Thody (New York: Knopf, 1963).
———, *Notebooks 1942–1951*, trans. Justin O'Brien (New York: Paragon House, 1991).
———, *The Outsider* (London: Penguin, 2000).
———, *The Rebel*, trans. Anthony Bower (London: Penguin, 1986).
Hardré, Jacques, 'Camus' Thoughts on Christian Metaphysics and Neoplatonism', *Studies in Philology* 64 (1967): 97–108.
Lottman, Herbert R., *Camus: A Biography* (New York: George Braziller, 1981).
Marcel, Gabriel, *Being and Having*, trans. Katharine Farrer (London: Fontana, 1965).
———, *Coleridge et Schelling* (Paris: Aubier-Montaigne, 1971).
———, *Homo Viator*, trans. E. Craufurd (London: Victor Gollancz, 1951).
———, *A Metaphysical Journal*, trans. B. Wall (London: Rockliff, 1952).
———, *The Mystery of Being, Vol. 1: Reflection and Mystery*, trans. G. S. Fraser (London: The Harvill Press, 1950).
———, *The Mystery of Being, Vol. 2: Faith and Reality*, trans. R. Hague (London: The Harvill Press, 1951).
Nietzsche, Friedrich, *The Birth of Tragedy*, trans. Walter Kaufmann (New York: Vintage, 1987).
Quillot, Roger, 'Introduction' to Albert Camus, *Essais* (Paris: Pléiade, 1965).
Ross, Michael, 'Transcendence, Immanence, and Practical Deliberation in Simone Weil's Early and Middle Years', in E. Jane Doering and Eric O. Springsted (eds.), *The Christian Platonism of Simone Weil* (Notre Dame: University of Notre Dame Press, 2004).
Sartre, Jean-Paul, *Écrits de jeunesse*, ed. Michel Contat et Michel Rybalka (Paris: Gallimard, 1990).
———, 'An Explication of *The Stranger*', in Annette Michelson (trans.), *Literary and Philosophical Essays of Jean-Paul Sartre* (New York: Criterion Books, 1955).
Srigley, Ronald D., *Albert Camus' Critique of Modernity* (Columbia: University of Missouri Press, 2011).
———, 'Introduction' to Albert Camus, *Christian Metaphysics and Neoplatonism*, trans. Ronald Srigley (Columbia: University of Missouri Press, 2007).
Todd, Oliver, *Camus: A Life*, trans. Benjamin Ivry (New York: Knopf, 1997).
Weil, Simone, *The Need for Roots*, trans. Arthur Wills (London: Routledge, 2003).
Wood, William, *Blaise Pascal on Duplicity, Sin and the Fall* (Oxford: Oxford University Press, 2013).

6 Weil and Bataille

Mystic exemplars?

In this chapter we turn to two figures whose lives and work are intertwined with those of key representatives of existentialism and, in different ways, express similar concerns to other existentialists. At the same time, their fundamental philosophical commitments sometimes seem in tension with those of, for example, Heidegger and Sartre. In the case of Simone Weil, this has to do with her affinities to Platonism; in the case of Bataille, the opposite tendency, toward a naturalizing of subjectivity. As we have indicated in the introduction, we do not think it profitable to define the boundaries of philosophical movements such as existentialism too narrowly, and by including Weil and Bataille here we hope, at the very least, to give a fuller picture of the immediate intellectual, cultural, and religious world in which existentialism took shape. We shall address further issues regarding their respective relations to particular figures and themes of existentialist thought as they arise, and we begin now with Simone Weil.

Simone Weil: a 'secular saint'?

Simone Weil is an ambiguous thinker who deliberately employed contradictions in her philosophy. Consequently, there are several senses in which she could be considered to belong – or not to belong – to the categories 'existentialist' or 'mystic'. As we have seen already, the existentialists Sartre and Beauvoir emphasized the lack of a human essence, emphasizing the centrality of action to becoming who we are: we are what we make of ourselves. Weil's thought also emphasized action and a commitment to *living* her ideas. Unlike Sartre and Beauvoir, however, Weil claimed to have had many mystical experiences. These experiences seem to place her in the category of 'mystic', but her philosophical descriptions of mysticism arguably emphasize Plato more than the Gospels. Where the Left Bank existentialists drew on Christian mystics as exemplars of love in action (in Beauvoir), bad faith (in Sartre), or an immanent affirmation of the world (Camus), Weil's philosophy can be read both as world affirming and as taking annihilation to ascetic extremes. She has been taken by many to be an exemplar, in the inspiring Nietzschean sense of the term, but is her example positive or negative?

Weil was neither a constructor of systems nor a defender of doctrines. She was, as her recent biographer Maria Clara Bingemer put it, 'undoubtedly, a mystic'.[1] Few scholars contest this, but their qualitative judgements (in particular, with respect to its sources, orthodoxy, or origin in mental health) vary widely. On the one hand, Weil was praised by her early Catholic editors on account of her mysticism having 'nothing in common with those religious speculations divorced from any personal commitment which are all too frequently the only testimony of intellectuals who apply themselves to the things of God'.[2] But on the other, the way Weil *lived* her mysticism concluded in a self-inflicted death that was 'apparent[ly] senseless': why, as Irwin puts it, did she commit this 'obscure self-squandering in an English tuberculosis hospital'?[3] Stuart Jesson's answer is that Weil's mysticism is 'a mysticism of death, not Resurrection'.[4] And while some deem this a laudable or even 'logical consequence of her love of God',[5] its logic and its laudability are disputed.

Because Weil's thought shaped her life and death and because both her life and death shaped the way her contemporaries received her thought and action, this section will begin biographically before turning to a thematic investigation of her engagement with mystical sources and themes in her later works. Some divisions of Weil's written works refer to her 'pre-mystical' and 'mystical' periods,[6] although as we shall see, the influence of Plato and Descartes on her early thought render this distinction problematic. Biographically, however, the dividing line between Weil's earlier and later works is a mystical experience that has been ranked among 'the most beautiful and moving that we possess'.[7] It occurred in 1938 while reciting George Herbert's poem 'Love', which Weil had committed to memory. During a recitation of it, Weil wrote in a letter (the 'Spiritual Autobiography') of May 1942, 'Christ himself came down and took possession of me'.[8] She described the experience as neither sensory nor imaginative: 'I only felt in the midst of my suffering the presence of a love, like that which one can read in the smile on a beloved face'.[9]

Prior to that moment, Weil had considered the problem of God insoluble. She had heard of 'real contact' between human beings and God but had not believed in them. But Weil also wrote that she had not read any mystical works because 'I had never felt any call to read them. . . . God in his mercy had prevented me from reading the mystics, so that it should be evident to me that I had not invented this absolutely unexpected contact'.[10]

After her pivotal reading of Herbert, Weil began to recite the Our Father in Greek daily, with 'absolute attention'. She reported that this produced the effect of being transported 'to a place outside space where there is neither perspective nor point of view'; here she described Christ as 'present with [her] in person' in an even more moving way than during her first mystical experience.[11]

But the claim that she had never read any mystics before is a curious one, given her philosophical education and her later claim that Plato was 'an authentic mystic and even the father of Occidental mysticism'.[12] She studied under Alain at the Lycée Henri IV (which she entered in 1925) and aspired to study at the École Normale Supérieure. As a woman, she was admitted to study at the ENS at Sèvres, and she would go on to take seventh place in the *agrégation* of 1931. According to her classmate and later biographer Simone Pétrement, Weil's thought was born in the lectures of Alain (Émile Chartier, 1868–1951) in particular.[13] As Pétrement wrote: 'Just as an artist starts with a work of art and not with the natural world itself, every philosopher starts with a previous philosophy'.[14]

Where the mystical sources of Weil's thought are concerned, there are obvious Christian 'mystics' who appear in her works, most notably Saint John of the Cross and Pascal. The former is usually cited approvingly, whereas her evaluation of the latter is mixed, as we shall see. Weil also discusses Augustine, La Rochefoucauld, and Plato in her late works. But Weil's method of writing and stance on the history of philosophy complicate claims of 'provenance' or inheritance. For in addition to the usually acknowledged difficulties with Weil's work – that it is sometimes epistolary, aphoristic, contradictory, and almost entirely posthumously published – she rarely cited the secondary material with which she engaged, which gives the appearance that her reading of, for example, Plato, had no mediation through the competing philosophical lenses of her day or earlier receptions.[15]

Admitting the relevance of such considerations is in fact contrary to her understanding of the history of philosophy. In Weil's view, 'Philosophy . . . is one, eternal and not susceptible to progress. The only renewal of which it is capable is that of expression', which is required by new epochs and new publics.[16] As Miklos Vetö has shown, Weil understood Descartes and Kant to be 'two incarnations of the same being' and Plato to have synthesized the thought of both: Plato, Descartes, and Kant, are 'the three fixed stars' in Weil's early philosophy. But in her mature writings, Vetö writes, all but Plato are subject to a 'spectacular eclipse'.[17]

Like Simone Pétrement's biography, Vëto's insightful genealogy locates Weil's 'eternal' perspective on philosophy in Weil's studies with Alain. Alain discouraged the use of secondary sources; he didn't want to develop historians of philosophy but rather held that 'the true method for forming the notion of philosophy is to think that there were philosophers' (where, by 'philosophers', Alain meant 'les grands philosophes' – the great thinkers of the past).[18]

Weil largely shared Alain's disdain for the contemporary. While she did acknowledge the importance of Husserl, she rejected the works of Bergson and Nietzsche as repulsive, rarely cited Kierkegaard or Marcel, and never cited Heidegger. Weil also followed Alain's advice to 'defy systems' and their obsession with clarity and coherence.[19] But there were three 'more recent thinkers' of whom Weil did think well: Lagneau, Alain, and Husserl.[20] In fact, in the French secondary literature Weil has been called the 'last representative of French spiritualism' (a Catholic movement of the Third Republic).[21]

Where Weil's reception of mystical sources is concerned, it is important to begin by outlining a perennial debate about the value of and right relationship between contemplation and action. In the *Enneads*, Plotinus wrote that action is for weak contemplators:

> In the same way, human beings, when weak on the side of contemplation, find in action their trace of vision and of reason: their spiritual feebleness unfits them for contemplation; they are left with a void, because they cannot adequately seize the vision; yet they long for it; they are hurried into action as their way to the vision which they cannot attain by intellection. They act from the desire of seeing their action, and of making it visible and sensible to others . ... Everywhere, doing and making will be found to be either an attenuation or a complement of vision-attenuation if the doer was aiming only at the thing done; complement if he is to possess something nobler to gaze upon than the mere work produced.[22]

Plotinus does not see why, when we can contemplate 'the Authentic', anyone chases after its mere 'image' in action. Meister Eckhart, by contrast, sees action as the fulfilment and achievement of contemplation. Reversing the common reading of the story of Mary and Martha in Luke 10:38–42, Eckhart claimed that Martha was the more mature sister, who realized that Mary's contemplation was a stage on the way to fruition in work.[23] And for Bérulle and Bergson, as we have seen, mysticism is incomplete if it does not lead to action: it must keep the neighbour in its vision, or it collapses into egotism or quietism.

Because Weil's early philosophy is commonly acknowledged to emphasize praxis and to be Marxist in so doing, it is also important to consider the role Marx's thought played in shaping this emphasis. In a 1933 essay published in *Critique sociale*, Weil cites Marx's *Theses on Feuerbach* on the problematic prioritization of contemplation in philosophy:

> The chief defect in all the materialistic doctrines that have so far been elaborated, including Feuerbach's, lies in the fact that the real, the sensible, are conceived only in the form of object, of contemplation, and not as sensible human activity, as *praxis*, in a subjective way. That is why the active side has been developed – in an abstract way, it is true – in opposition to materialism, by idealism, which, of course, does not know real, sensible activity as such.[24]

Weil agrees with Marx that what is needed in a 'synthesis in which a radical opposition between passive nature and human activity is preserved'. But she writes that Descartes was 'more socialist, in the matter of culture, than all Marx's disciples have been' because he founded a School of Arts and Crafts – he wanted to teach artisans the theoretical bases of their crafts.[25] Weil's engagement with Marx's followers was critical, and the instrument of her criticism was a Cartesian praxis.

In Weil's late works, she offers negative definitions of mysticism, prayer, and friendship with God, which demonstrate her position on the question of contemplation and action. So we shall now turn to her discussions of false mysticism, false prayer, and what we will call 'false friendship' with God as a way into introducing their 'true' alternatives.

False mysticism

For Weil 'false mysticism' is the 'search for a special state',[26] whether through literal or metaphorical drugs. It seeks to escape the world rather than to love it. On Weil's view, the search for God is not a search for a special state, but neither is it a quest of 'muscular will'; the latter is the problem Weil diagnoses in Pascal, who perpetuated the view that one could will oneself into faith because he confused 'faith and autosuggestion'.[27] What is needful, on Weil's view, is that we should love the world despite its resistance to love.[28]

False prayer

False mysticism is closely related to false prayer. Again Weil couches her objections as objections to Pascal: in *Waiting for God* Weil claimed that she never prayed because she was afraid of the prayer's 'power of suggestion', the 'power for which Pascal recommends it. Pascal's method seems to me one of the worst for attaining faith' (WG 28). True prayer, by contrast, consists instead of 'attention'.[29] Attention, in Weil's definition, is a human faculty which, when directed toward God, 'is the very substance of prayer'.[30] Its antithesis is contempt.

In *Gravity and Grace*, Weil wrote that in attention, 'all that I call "I" has to be passive. Attention alone – that attention which is so full that the "I" disappears – is required of me. I have to deprive all that I call "I" of the light of my attention and turn it on to that which cannot be conceived'.[31]

False friends of God

In Letter IV of *Waiting for God* Weil chastises her friend – a priest – for what she sees as a sinful partisanship. She borrows an image from Saint John of the Cross to make her point: namely that her priest's fidelity to the institution of religion renders him unfaithful to the spirit of it. 'Such an attachment [to the Church as to an earthly country] is perhaps for you that infinitely fine thread, of which Saint John of the Cross speaks, which so long as it is not broken holds the bird down on the ground as effectively as a great metal chain'.[32] In Weil's view, love 'should stretch as widely across all space, and should be equally distributed in every portion of it, as is the bright light of the sun'.[33] We are to imitate Christ, Weil argued, in bestowing light 'indiscriminately' and seeing the world through the gaze of God.

In *Letter to a Priest* Weil makes a similar point, writing that when she reads the catechism of the Council of Trent she finds 'nothing in common with the religion there set forth'. Rather, it was the faith of the New Testament and 'the mystics' that she claimed as her own.[34]

'Genuine friends of God' – among whom Weil mentions Eckhart as an example – do not confuse the 'words they have heard in secret amidst the silence of the union of love, and these words are in disagreement with the teaching of the Church'. Instead, they recognize that 'the language of the marketplace is not that of the nuptial chamber'.[35] In Weil's view, the church abuses its power and fails to love properly when it attempts to force the language of faith onto inappropriate domains.[36]

True mysticism, true prayer, true love: action

Weil's writings make clear that she evaluated mystics not only on the basis of their teachings, but also on how they lived their lives: she thought Saint Francis and Saint John of the Cross succeeded in ordering their loves for God and creation. Rightly ordered love, in Weil's view, is a *seeing*. It is sight freed from the illusion that the self is the centre of the world:

> A transformation then takes place at the very roots of our sensibility, in our immediate reception of sense impressions and psychological impressions. It is a transformation analogous to that which takes place in the dusk of evening on a road, where we suddenly discern as a tree what we had first seen as a stooping man; or where we suddenly recognize as a rustling of leaves what we thought at first was whispering voices. We see the same colors; we hear the same sounds, but not in the same way.[37]

Whether and to which 'mystical' sources Weil is indebted here is a difficult question to answer for the reasons already given: her debts to almost all but Plato have been eclipsed. In Weil's essay on Plato's *Republic* she says that sight is the faculty which is in relation to the good and that love is a seeing. On Weil's reading, Plato's allegory of the cave illustrates this; the image of love as seeing 'makes the impossibility of egoism evident, for the eyes cannot see themselves'.[38] But Weil's 'intimations' of Christianity in ancient Greek sources frequently read Christian doctrines into pre-Christian texts in question-begging ways.

Weil's *Intimations* makes reference to other literary and philosophical depictions of 'love' as a kind of seeing. In particular, she refers to seventeenth-century French moralists including La Rochefoucauld and playwrights Molière and Racine.[39] In Racine's play *Phèdre*, for example, Weil writes that 'human misery is revealed in its nakedness in connection with love. That was a strange century in which, contrary to what happened in the epic age, man's misery could only be revealed in love'.[40]

This seventeenth-century French tradition has deep and well-documented roots in Augustinian thought. But while Weil's writings do include direct references to Augustine,[41] she dwells at length on the *ordo amoris* she finds in Plato. In *Intimations*, she cites *The Symposium* on the healing qualities of well-ordered love:

> Love, the orderer, is divine Love. The love of disorder is demoniac love. (188d)
>
> Of all the Gods, love is the greatest friend of men, their defender and the physician of those ills whose healing would be the supreme felicity for the human species.
>
> (189d)[42]

Weil's analysis of love starts from Aristophanes's claim (in Plato's *Symposium*) that we are missing our other half and seek it: 'This quest is Love'. But Weil then qualifies that in addition to being a quest, love is

> the feeling of our radical insufficiency in consequence of sin, and the desire, coming from the very sources of our being, to be reintegrated into the state of completion. Love is thus the right physician for our original illness. We need not ask ourselves how to have love, it is in us from birth to death, imperious as hunger. We need only know in what direction to direct it.[43]

Plato's wisdom, according to Weil, consisted in orienting the soul toward grace, which is the only source of salvation.[44]

For Weil, the *seeing* of love is neither a philosophy nor a state of contemplation: true-sighted love must be directed to our neighbour. In *Gravity and Grace* Weil acknowledges that attention is more difficult to achieve in the presence of other humans. She writes that the value of solitude consists of being 'in the presence of mere matter', which produces 'the greater possibility of attention'.[45] But in 'Forms of the Implicit Love of God' Weil writes that love of neighbour is made of 'creative attention' – of 'giving attention to what does not exist'. Much like Beauvoir's in *Pyrrhus and Cineas*, Weil's analysis of the parable of Good Samaritan offers it as an injunction to act – but to act by attending:

> Humanity does not exist in the anonymous flesh lying inert by the roadside. The Samaritan who stops and looks gives his attention all the same to this absent humanity, and the actions which follow prove that it is a question of real humanity.[46]

For Weil, love 'sees what is invisible' – in this case, humanity – and brings it into existence. In this respect the creativity of human love is an image of the continuous creativity of divine love.[47]

Weil recognizes and warns against the dangers of instrumentalizing the neighbour: she claims that expressions like loving our neighbour 'in God' are 'misleading and equivocal'. When one sees a fallen person at the side of the road, one should not turn her thoughts to God but turn her actions to the person before her. If the neighbour is *seen* as an opportunity to do good, then 'God is not present'. The neighbour, Weil writes, 'may even be loved on this account, but then they are in their natural role, the role of matter and of things. We have to bring them in their inert, anonymous condition a personal love'.[48]

In *Letter to a Priest* Weil singles out John of the Cross, whose 'very lofty spirituality . . . seized simultaneously and with an equal force both the personal and the impersonal aspects of God', unlike lesser souls who tend to focus on one at the expense of the other.[49] In section 15 of *Letter to a Priest* Weil returns to the love command, writing that following it is the criterion of true belonging to Christ.[50] True religion, for Weil, 'is nothing else but a looking'.[51] 'By loving our neighbour we imitate the divine love which created us and all our fellows. By loving the order of the world we imitate the divine love which created this universe of which we are a part'.[52]

But this 'looking' is not exclusive to Christianity – and, indeed, many who go by the name of 'Christian' do not *see* truly. Weil's writings refer to many mystical traditions other than Christianity, including Zen koans and pre-Socratic mystery cults because, in her view, all truth is God's, and the coincidence of mystical accounts is so extensive that 'they can hardly be distinguished'. She draws on John of the Cross in articulating her understanding of other religions:

> St John of the Cross compares faith to reflections of silver, truth being gold. The various authentic religious traditions are different reflections of the same truth, and perhaps equally precious. But we do not realize this, because each of us lives only one of these traditions and sees the others from the outside. But, as Catholics are forever repeating – and rightly – to unbelievers, a religion can only be known from the inside.[53]

Despite her 'outsider' status in relation to many of the religions of which she spoke, Weil claimed that:

> The contemplation practised in India, Greece, China, etc., is just as supernatural as that of the Christian mystics. More particularly, there exists a very close affinity between Plato and, for example, St John of the Cross. Also between the Hindu Upanishads and St John of the Cross. Taoism too is very close to Christian mysticism.[54]

But statements of 'affinity' and being 'very close' are not statements of identity. And it is noteworthy that Weil singles out *contemplation* for this exercise in comparison.

In the 'Spiritual Autobiography' Weil writes that love, faith, and intelligence are 'three strictly individual faculties'.[55] And in *Letter to a Priest* she claims that the 'mysteries of the faith' are not an object for the intelligence since, according to Weil, they are not 'of the order of truth, but above it'. She writes that the only faculty that is 'capable of any real contact with them is the faculty of supernatural love'.[56]

Weil is adamant that one cannot argue or will oneself into intellectual adherence to a religion: she criticizes Pascal's wager as a degradation of faith that makes way for doubt and 'temptations of faith'. Such 'mistaken conceptions' of intellectual obligation weaken faith, encourage unbelief, and stifle the soul.[57] At heart, Weil's objection to Pascal is that 'The love and the knowledge of God cannot really be separated'.[58] Moreover, the love of God cannot be separated from loving the order of the world God created.

In Alexander Irwin's study of Weil and Georges Bataille, *Saints of the Impossible*, he convincingly documents the conviction of both thinkers that the best way to communicate a message is to *be* the message – we might, with Kierkegaard, say to live it *in existence*.[59] But in Weil's case, although the life she lived demonstrates a mysticism of action it is unclear whether that mysticism – and her message – was one of loving the world unto death or of loving death itself. Kempfner says that Weil's self-starvation should be attributed to 'the despair of being reduced to inaction';[60] in this reading we might say that Weil succumbed to tragic interpretation of the ideal of John 15:13, that there is no greater love than to lay down one's life for friends.

But in Plato's *Phaedo* we find a different account of the *telos* of wisdom's pursuit, one which Weil cites in *Intimations of Christianity among the Ancient Greeks*: 'Those who devote themselves as they should to the pursuit of wisdom, have no other goal than to die and to remain dead. . . . Death being nothing else than that state of the soul when it is separated from the body'.[61]

Weil's notion of decreation, as presented in *Gravity and Grace*, can be read as suggesting that loving the order of the world did extend to loving one's own place in it. In this reading, Weil's philosophy may admit what Camus called the 'mystical affirmation' of the world. But here, as in other cases, her use of contradiction makes it possible to deny any world-affirming character in her thought. For Weil also writes that decreation involves making 'something created pass into the uncreated'. Our existence is contingent, and in Weil's view each moment that we exist demonstrates God's sustaining love for us. But, Weil continues, 'God can only love himself. His love for us is love for himself through us. Thus, he who gives us our being loves in us the acceptance of not being'.[62] Depending on their understanding of divine love, adherents of Abrahamic religions may recoil from the idea that God *only* loves Godself, such that we must (as Weil enjoins) 'turn all our disgust into a disgust for ourselves'.[63] Passages such as this support the view of Stuart Jesson and Anne Loades that Weil's mysticism was 'deadly'.[64]

In *Intimations* Weil wrote that there was a 'double image' of 'death and nakedness' in Christian spirituality: death in Saint Paul and nakedness in Saint John of the Cross and Saint Francis.[65] The question of which image her life and thoughts reflect – whether it is a mysticism of affirmation or an ascetic ideal that literally says no to life – is impossible to ascertain. But it is indubitable that her mysticism was a mysticism of *action* and, as such, existential. Before and after her death her life – as written and as lived – inspired those who encountered it.

Georges Bataille

In Georges Bataille's novel *Le bleu du ciel* (1935) the narrator, Henri Troppmann, is in the apartment of a revolutionary activist when he becomes part of a discussion about the political responsibility of intellectuals.[66] The activist's name is Louise Lazare; she is ill-kempt, her clothing is masculine, and her life ascetic. Troppmann, who has stopped by unannounced, finds her in discussion with her stepfather – a professor of philosophy decrying the 'collapse of socialist hopes'. Lazare's view, softly spoken, is that 'Whatever happens, we must stand by the oppressed'.

> I thought: She's a Christian. Obviously! . . . 'We must'? In the name of what? What for?'
>
> 'One can always save one's soul', said Lazare.[67]

Louise Lazare – Jewish, idealist, socialist – is widely acknowledged to be a literary portrait of Simone Weil.[68] And as Alexander Irwin has noted, in the 1930s both Weil and Bataille believed that positive political renewal 'depended on a transformation for which the language of religion provided the least inappropriate vocabulary'.[69] But precisely what they did with religious vocabulary is a matter of dispute: was it borrowing or parody? A turn to the sacred or the profane?

After spending the 1920s as a 'virtually unknown librarian',[70] in the 1930s Bataille was, like Weil, known for being militantly of the left, an intellectual whose politics committed him to fight oppression in the street. But in the late 1930s his thought underwent a volte-face. In his *Guilty*, begun in September 1939, Bataille writes that despite current events he will not talk about war, but about 'mystical experience': 'I began to read, standing in a crowded train, the *Book of Visions* of Angela of Foligno'.[71] While the Resistance formed and resisted, Bataille practiced yoga and meditation, pursued romantic relationships, and wrote. Between 1941 and 1942 he penned *Inner Experience*, the first work of what he would later call his 'Summa Atheologica' (*La Somme athéologique*).[72]

In the *Summa Theologica* Aquinas wanted to demonstrate the harmony between faith and reason: using the dialectical methods of Aristotle, Aquinas brought philosophical speculation to bear on his belief in the Divine origin of the world and revelation of truth. Similarly, Bataille's unfinished *Summa Atheologica* is guided by a question about the compatibility of seemingly dissonant commitments – the compatibility of religiosity and atheism. Atheology, for Bataille, 'places thought before the worst and the best of what is God, but the same fact before the absence of God'.[73] Similarly, as Andrew Hussey has noted, Bataille's stated aversion to the word 'mysticism' (although Bataille did not always object to the word, sometimes employing it himself) is derived from an emphatic affirmation of the possibility of direct experience of the *absence* of God.[74]

Alexander Irwin describes mysticism as a 'queasy subject' in the study of Bataille.[75] Andrew Hussey's 2000 study, *The Inner Scar*, describes Georges Bataille as the 'avatar of limitless irrationalism'[76] and identifies mysticism as a 'blind spot' of contemporary Bataille criticism. In addition to Hussey's work, the publication of Peter Tracey Connor's *Georges Bataille and the Mysticism of Sin* (2000) and Amy Hollywood's *Sensible Ecstasy* (2002) have improved our vision of this question in depth that cannot be replicated in this brief section. But because Bataille's 'mysticism' drew other existentialists into sustained debate, taking questions about reason and philosophy in directions that no one else did and influencing significant subsequent thinkers of twentieth-century France, we have included a brief analysis of the most important themes arising from his engagement with Shestov and Nietzsche and from *Inner Experience* (1943).[77]

As we saw in Chapter 3, early twentieth-century French philosophers disagreed about the value of mysticism. Some saw it as obscurantist, anathema to reason, and therefore anathema to philosophy; others saw it as quietist, anathema to action, and therefore anathema to the earthly pursuit of justice. There were many possible responses to these charges: for example, rejecting the allegation of obscurantism by claiming that mysticism was a complementary faculty to reason (e.g. the Pascalian 'heart' or [in one reading] Bergson's intuition) or rejecting charges of quietism by claiming with Eckhart and l'École Française that action was the fruition of contemplation. But Bataille chose to accept the premises of mysticism's critics and to assign 'inner experience' value precisely on the basis that it was neither reason nor action. In *Inner Experience*, Bataille wrote, 'I didn't fulfil the rules. I wrote what a philosopher never writes, a book without rigor, more an expression, a debauchery of thought'.[78] Inner experience, by his definition, was 'the opposite of action'.[79]

In this Bataille's example might be seen to be diametrically opposite to Weil's desire for a concrete philosophy that was worked out in life. But Bataille's renunciation of action was half-hearted. French intellectuals had, for centuries, perceived writers to be exemplars – secular saints who championed the immanent trinity of liberty, equality, and fraternity. The French literary canon included spiritual polemics, including – famously – those of Pascal against the Jesuits in *Les Lettres Provinciales*. Pascal's 1923 anniversary brought him a renaissance, as did Lev Shestov, who was an important influence on Bataille during the same period. It is important to note that

Bataille did not have the education of an *agrégé* in philosophy: unlike Beauvoir, Sartre, Marcel, and Weil, he did not write dissertations under the tutelage of the Parisian philosophical elite. In 1913, at the age of 16, he dropped out of school and converted to Catholicism. Seven years, later, however, he lost his faith. He trained to become a medievalist librarian and obtained a position at the Bibliothèque Nationale in 1922. Shortly thereafter, from 1923 to 1925, Bataille's reading was guided by Lev Shestov, who introduced him to Nietzsche and Dostoevsky.

As Amy Hollywood has observed, Bataille's Nietzsche was a mystical Nietzsche.[80] In the words of Bataille's biographer, Michael Surya, Bataille's Nietzsche was made up of 'Pascal, Plotinus, and Tertullian'.[81] But it was mediated by Shestov, who read Nietzsche alongside *les romans Russes*. We saw in Chapter 3 that by the end of the nineteenth century, commentators such as Charbonnel were denouncing the resurgence of interest in 'mysticism' and attributing it to the 'mysticism of present literature' – such as Dostoevsky and Tolstoy.

In the 1920s a new wave of translations of Russian novels appeared in France, following the wave of emigrations prompted by the Russian Revolution. Lev Shestov arrived in Paris in the spring of 1921 and began to teach at the Sorbonne's Institute of Slavic Studies. In 1922 he published 'The Conquest of the Self-Evident: Dostoevsky's Philosophy' in the *Nouvelle Revue Française*, after which Shestov began to receive offers from French publishers. And in 1923 he met Georges Bataille at the Institute of Oriental Languages in Paris, where Bataille was studying Chinese and Russian. Bataille's interest in Shestov's work became so deep that he planned to write a book about him (though he did not do so) and worked with Tatiana Rageot (Shestov's daughter) to translate Shestov's *The Good in the Teachings of Tolstoy and Dostoevsky* into French. In addition to exposing Bataille to Dostoevsky as philosopher, Shestov also represented a way of conceiving of philosophy as a way of life. Berdyaev – a friend of Shestov's – claimed that Shestov 'philosophized with his whole being'; for him 'philosophy was not a matter of academic specialization, but a matter of life and death'.[82] Shestov's book on Kierkegaard, significantly entitled *Kierkegaard et la Philosophie Existentielle*, published in French in 1936, played a major role in introducing Kierkegaard's thought to France and, thanks to its very one-sided presentation, did much to shape the image of Kierkegaard as a kind of proto-existentialist and extreme irrationalist.[83]

In the context of a contemporary disciplinary dispute about what counted as philosophy, Shestov knew that 'mysticism' was a term that designated impurity or outright exclusion from the discipline. On learning that a reviewer had called him a 'great Russian mystic', he replied that 'They write "mystic" in order to dismiss me, and they add "great" to settle the matter. Then there's nothing left to say . . . By "mystic", one understands clearly that the questions one is asking are outside of philosophy, and that there is no need to go to the trouble of understanding them'.[84]

Bataille denounced the purported purity of philosophy; in his 1932 essay 'The Critique of the Foundations of the Hegelian Dialectic' Bataille writes that it is disingenuous to insist on it. The Hegelian dialectic has a 'long experimental history' – but its origins are not only to be found in Heraclitus, Plato, or Fichte: 'It is linked even more essentially to currents of thought such as Gnosticism, Neoplatonic mysticism, and to philosophical phantoms such as Meister Eckhart, the Cardinal Nicholas of Cusa, and Jackob Boehme'.[85]

In the next decade works would emerge in France calling Hegel's philosophy 'a reflection upon a mystical experience'.[86] But in the context of the mid-1930s, when the connotations of 'mysticism' were increasingly tainted by Nazism and political mystification, some philosophers wanted to keep a distance. In the late 1930s a shift of connotations occurs in Bataille's use of the word 'mysticism': as Alexander Irwin shows, his use of the word changes from negative to positive meanings in 1939 – particularly when Bataille experiments with early uses of 'spiritual exercises' in the style of Saint Ignatius in 1939.[87] Bataille's borrowing records from the Bibliothèque Nationale in the early 1940s give some indication of the intellectual appetites during the period that shaped *Inner Experience*: he borrowed Heidegger's *What is Metaphysics?*, Kierkegaard's *The Concept of Anxiety* and *Philosophical Fragments*, Jean Wahl's *Études Kierkegaardiennes*, Karl Jaspers. At the turn of 1941–42 he read mysticism and psychology, including books by and on the subject of mystics: John of the Cross, Teresa of Avila, Pseudo-Dionysius, Janet's *De l'angoisse à l'extase*.[88]

There are passages in Bataille's works from the 1930s that use the language and discuss themes that are found in these authors and in other French mystics.[89] For example, in a 1939 lecture to the College of Sociology Bataille took it to be one of 'the most widely accepted results of man's efforts to discover what he really is' that human beings 'lack unity of being'.[90] In an earlier work, 'Sacrifices' (1933), Bataille described 'living the death of the *me*' (in French, *le moi*, or 'the self'):

> In the course of the ecstatic vision, at the limit of death on the cross and of the blindly lived *lamma sabactani*, the object is finally unveiled as *catastrophe* in a chaos of light and shadow, neither as God nor as nothingness, but as the object that love, incapable of liberating itself except outside of itself, demands in order to let out the scream of lacerated existence.[91]

Bataille defines '*catastrophe*' as 'lived time', going on to say that 'the nature of time as the object of ecstasy reveals itself in accordance with the ecstatic nature of the *me* [*le moi*] that dies': 'Time is not the synthesis of being and nothingness if being or nothingness are only found in time and are only arbitrarily separated notions. There is, in fact, neither isolated being nor isolated nothingness; there is time'.[92] Bataille also claimed that 'existence sometimes weakens and sometimes accomplishes being', that 'different beings "are" unequally';[93] he employs the language of self-annihilation.[94]

Despite having lost his faith in 1920, Bataille wrote in 'The Sacred Conspiracy' (1936) that 'WE ARE FEROCIOUSLY RELIGIOUS'. Modernity, for Bataille, had resulted in a world in which value was measured by utility; being 'reasonable and educated' had led to 'a life without appeal'.[95] It was largely to Nietzsche that Bataille turned for illumination about the relationship between religion, value, and modernity. Bataille admired Nietzsche for his 'flagrant disregard for the senile Idealism of the establishment' and for resisting the bleak utilitarianism of modernity, which only valued things if they were useful.[96] Nietzsche, in Bataille's reading, did not see 'his experiences and perceptions as useful; instead, he saw them as an end'. And he valued them as an end because they were not just *any* experience: In 'Nietzsche and the Fascists' (1937) Bataille wrote that 'Nietzsche, speaking of the death of God, used a disordered language that manifested the most excessive inner experience'.[97] And in 'The Obelisk' (1938) we read that Nietzsche's eternal return (or recurrence) was a 'sudden ecstatic vision' which should not be compared to 'profound reflection'.[98] Bataille was not alone in reading Nietzsche as a mystic: in 1931 Charles Andler wrote that 'Nietzsche's doctrine of eternal recurrence is a great mystical intuition . . . the synthesis of all the most profound religions and of all the most noble philosophies'.[99]

In 'Propositions' (1937), Bataille wrote that Nietzsche's works demand 'that life, joy, and death be brought into play, and not the tired attention of the intellect'. The revaluation of values, for the person undergoing it, is 'is tragedy itself; there is little room left for repose'.[100] Although the revaluation of values is tragic for Bataille, the practice of 'joy before death' is the only way to truly affirm the world in the absence of transcendent values. In his 1939 essay 'The Practice of Joy Before Death' (the title of which seems likely to have deliberately mirrored Brother Lawrence's 'The Practice of the Presence of God') Bataille includes poetic texts which, he claims, 'cannot alone constitute an initiation into the *exercise* of a mysticism of "joy before death"'. He tells his reader that he can only give a 'vague representation' of that 'which by nature cannot be grasped'. He uses the word 'mysticism' to refer to the practice of joy before death but clarifies that he means only to imply an 'affective resemblance' between this practice and religions. There is no beyond for those who seek joy before death, no source of transcendent joy, only the pursuit of immanent ecstasy. How, he asks: 'could a *beyond*, a God or what resembles God, still be acceptable? No words are clear enough to express the happy disdain of the one who "dances with the time that kills him" for those who take refuge in the expectation of eternal beatitude'.[101]

He does not claim that joy before death is equivalent to a foretaste of eternal beatitude. But it is the way to say yes to life, where that Nietzschean affirmation is understood to be a mystical practice:

> Only a shameless, indecent saintliness can lead to a sufficiently happy *loss of self*. 'Joy before death' means that life can be glorified from root to summit. It robs of meaning everything that is an intellectual or

> moral *beyond*, substance, God, immutable order, or salvation. It is an apotheosis of that which is perishable, apotheosis of flesh and alcohol as well as of the trances of mysticism. The religious forms it rediscovers are the naïve forms that antedate the intrusion of a servile morality: it renews the kind of tragic jubilation that man 'is' as soon as he stops behaving like a cripple, glorifying necessary work and letting himself be emasculated by the fear of tomorrow.[102]

Inner Experience was published by Gallimard in 1943 and must be understood in the context of this Nietzschean desire to 'glorify life from root to summit'. A second edition was published in 1954, including *Method of Meditation* (1947) and 'Post-Scriptum 1953', and presented as part of the multivolume project *La Somme Athéologique* (*Summa Atheologica*).

Inner Experience is a famously elusive text, one translator of which described it as 'a dark corridor of distorting funhouse mirrors'.[103] It has been read as a critical engagement with surrealism, as a critique of the 'spirit of rationality' that reigned over Paris in the 1930s and 1940s, and as an 'aggressively anti-idealist philosophy which refuses all attempts at reduction or simplification'.[104] But whether it is a reasoned critique of rationalism or a rejection of rationalism in favour of 'experience' as the bedrock of human knowing, Bataille's case is made with explicit reference to a wide range of mystics: Ignatius of Loyola, Angela of Foligno, Meister Eckhart, Dionysius the Areopagite, John of the Cross, and Teresa of Avila all figure – as well as references to non-Western mystical traditions.[105]

Bataille would go on to write that a methodology of mysticism 'cannot be communicated in writing'[106] – rather, it must be lived. *But* – and this makes clear that his renunciation of action is not as thoroughgoing as he states – Bataille thought that one way of embodying mysticism was to produce it in writing as an exhortation or invitation for others to follow. In this, we see echoes of Nietzschean exemplars, Shestov's insistence that philosophy must be lived, and Bergson's claim that mystics don't preach, they practice.

In the methodology of *Inner Experience*, experience is primary – it is an end in itself. Mystics refuse to be reduced to argument or to debase experience by claiming to bring it entirely into the realm of the intellect. As a result, for Bataille, mysticism is the 'repressed other' of philosophy[107] – the denied party not only in Hegelian dialectics but also in human experience. The method Bataille recommends in *Inner Experience* is 'dramatization' or 'dramatic mimicry'; it is indebted to the spiritual exercises of Ignatius of Loyola in which the seeker imaginatively identifies with the sufferings of Christ. Bataille explicitly draws on Ignatius's *Spiritual Exercises* in introducing the method, claiming that it is an error to see the *Exercises* as belonging to discursive thought. They do rely on discursive thought, Bataille admits, but they do so in the mode of drama: 'Discourse exhorts: represent yourself, it says, the place, the characters in the drama, and remain there as one among them'.

Bataille uses words that are familiar in the vocabulary of both mystics and existentialists, writing for example that 'NONKNOWLEDGE COMMUNICATES ECSTASY. Nonknowledge is first of all ANGUISH'.[108] But he rarely spends time clarifying concepts. Rather, his interest in mysticism seems to be in the kind of imaginative engagement it produces, in particular through the method of 'dramatization'.

Nietzsche figures prominently in the early pages of this work, where Bataille compares his own mysticism to that of Nietzsche. Nietzsche was solitary in his saying yes to life (his 'affirmation'), Bataille comments, and 'a feeling of community' drives Bataille to write about inner experience for others because he has tended even further toward 'the night' than Nietzsche did. For while 'Nietzsche had the experience of the eternal return in a mystical form, properly speaking', it was also 'confused with discursive representations'.[109]

Salvation, according to Bataille, is 'the perspective of value perceived from the point of view of personal life'.[110] And in order to achieve this, one must attain a nondiscursive inner experience. In the section of the second edition of *Inner Experience* called 'Post-Scriptum to the Torture (Or a New Mystical Theology)', Bataille clarifies that the method by which this can be achieved is 'dramatization':

> To dramatize is what the devout people who follow the *Exercises* of Saint Ignatius do (but not them alone). If one were to imagine the place, the characters of the drama and the drama itself: the torture to which Christ is led. The disciple of Saint Ignatius offers himself a theatrical representation. He is a peaceful room: he is asked to have the feelings he would have on Calvary. He is told that despite the peacefulness of his room, he *should* have these feelings. One desires that he should get out of himself, deliberately dramatizing this human life, of which one knows in advance that it is likely to be a half-anxious, half-dozing futility. But not yet having had a properly inner life, before having shattered discourse within him, he is asked to project the point about which I have spoken, similar to him – but even more similar to that which he wants to be – in the person of Jesus agonizing. The projection of the point, in Christianity, is attempted before the mind has its inner movements at its disposal, before it has become free of discourse. It is only the rough projection, which one attempts, starting from it, to attain non-discursive experience.[111]

Bataille, in extrapolating the method of dramatization, wanted to communicate the means of achieving 'inner experience'. His writing, therefore, can be understood as a way of *acting* in order that others might achieve inner experience. In Bataille's view, fiction is a mode of experience.[112]

Every French existentialist discussed in this book wrote fiction with the explicit intention of raising philosophical questions: in *Le bleu du ciel* Troppmann and Lazare (Bataille and Weil) represent diametrically opposed approaches to manners, morals, and metaphysics. Bataille had no philosophical education, admired Sade and Nietzsche, and gloried in the profane. Weil, by contrast, was educated at the prestigious École Normale, admired Plato above all, and lived a life famous for its asceticism. André Breton called Bataille an 'excremental philosopher'; Weil has been called – and Bataille's own novel calls Lazare – a 'saint'. But in the context of the philosophy outlined in Chapter 3, it is clear that Bataille and Weil both turned to *mystics* on account of their mysticism rather than their sainthood. In Weil's view, it is false mysticism to 'search for a special state';[113] in Bataille's view, 'inner experience' is precisely such a state.

Drawing on Edith Wyschogrod's *Saints and Postmodernism*, Alexander Irwin has argued that Weil's and Bataille's literary and political strategies in the 1930s and 1940s – to live their philosophy in person and in writing – were motivated by the failure of moral theories to 'nurture real moral action in society'. Wyschogrod's proposal was to turn away from conventional moral theory to 'human exemplars – saints – as concrete embodiments of active virtue'.[114] Weil and Bataille shared a commitment to the view that philosophy should be *lived*. But in styling their lives as exemplary they were not concerned solely with 'active virtue', but with its conditions in the human imagination. In particular, they described attention and dramatization in writing as methods that help human beings 'see' value where they otherwise would not. For Bataille, the resulting 'salvation' was the ability to see value 'from the point of personal life'[115] despite the catastrophe of lived time; for Weil, it was to see that 'Each perfect existence is a parable written by God'.[116]

Notes

1 Maria Clara Bingemer, *Simone Weil: Mystic of Passion and Compassion* (Cambridge: Lutterworth Press, 2015), p. 65.
2 Gustave Thibon, 'Introduction' to Simone Weil, *Gravity and Grace*, trans. Emma Crawford and Mario von der Ruhr (London: Routledge, 2002), p. ix.
3 Alexander Irwin, *Saints of the Impossible: Bataille, Weil, and the Politics of the Sacred* (Minneapolis: University of Minnesota Press, 2002), p. xxv.
4 Stuart Jesson, 'Traces of Resurrection: The Pattern of Simone Weil's Mysticism' in Thomas Cattoi and Christopher Moreman (eds.), *Death, Dying, and Mysticism: The Ecstasy of the End* (London: Routledge, 2015), p. 49.
5 Gaston Kempfner, *La Philosophie Mystique de Simone Weil* (Paris: La Colombe, 1960), p. 24.
6 See, for example, Marie Cabaud Meaney, *Simone Weil's Apologetic Use of Literature: Her Christological Interpretation of Classic Greek Text* (Oxford: Clarendon Press, 2007), which employs a 'pre-mystical' and 'mystical' period distinction (p. 191).
7 Kempfner, *La philosophie mystique*, p. 12.
8 The experience was reported in two letters to close friends, Joe Bousquet and P. Parrin.
9 Simone Weil, *Waiting for God*, trans. Emma Craufurd (London: Harper Perennial, 2009), p. 27. (Hereafter WG).
10 Weil, *Waiting*, p. 27.

11 Weil, *Waiting*, p. 29.
12 Simone Weil, 'God in Plato' in *Intimations of Christianity among the Ancient Greeks* (London: Routledge, 1998), p. 77. (From *La Source Grecque*, pp. 65–77).
13 Simone Pétrement, *La Vie de Simone Weil*, 2 vols. (Paris: Fayard, 1973) tome 1, p. 63.
14 Pétrement, *Vie de Simone Weil*, tome 1, p. 64.
15 See Miklos Vetö, 'Simone Weil et l'histoire de la philosophie' *Archives de Philosophie* 72(4) (2009): 581–606.
16 Simone Weil, *Oeuvres complètes*, 4 tome (Paris: Gallimard, 1988 et suivantes), vol. 1, p. 58.
17 Vetö, 'Simone Weil', p. 597.
18 Alain, *Élements de Philosophie*, p. 15, in Georges Pascal, *Pour connaître la pensée d'Alain* (Paris: Bordas, 1957), p. 41.
19 See Vetö, *Simone Weil*, pp. 583–4.
20 Weil, *Oeuvres complètes*, p. 58.
21 See Elodie Wahl, '"J'ai eu faim, et vous m'avez nourri . . ."/Faim, assistance et charité/ Charité, agapé' *Terrain (revue)* 51 (septembre 2008). Wahl's examples of Third-Republic French spiritualism include Ravaisson, Lachelier, Blondel, Lagneau, Alain, and Bergson.
22 Plotinus, *Enneads* III.8.4.
23 Meister Eckhart, Sermon 9, in *Complete Mystical Works of Meister Eckhart*, trans. Maurice O'C Walsh, revised by Bernard McGinn (New York: Crossroad Publishing, 2009).
24 Karl Marx, *Theses on Feuerbach*; cited in Simone Weil, 'Reflections on Technocracy, National-Socialism, the USSR and Certain Other Matters' in *Oppression and Liberty*, trans. Arthur Wills and John Petrie (London: Routledge, 2002), p. 31. [Originally published in *Critique sociale*, November 1933].
25 Weil, 'Reflections on Technocracy', p. 34.
26 Weil, *Waiting*, p. 111.
27 Weil, *Waiting*, p. 127.
28 Weil, *Waiting*, p. 114.
29 Weil, *Waiting*, p. 57.
30 Weil, *Waiting*, p. 58.
31 Weil, *Gravity and Grace*, p. 118.
32 Weil, *Waiting*, p. 49.
33 Weil, *Waiting*, p. 50.
34 Simone Weil, *Letter to a Priest*, trans. A. F. Wills (London: Routledge, 2002 [1942]), p. 1.
35 Weil, *Waiting*, p. 35.
36 See Weil, *Waiting*, p. 36.
37 Weil, *Waiting*, p. 100.
38 Weil, 'The Republic' in *Intimations*, p. 134.
39 Weil, *Intimations*, p. 135.
40 Weil, 'The *Iliad*, Poem of Might' in *Intimations*, p. 55.
41 See Weil, 'The Pythagorean Doctrine' in *Intimations*, p. 171; see also her discussion of Manichaeanism in *Letter to a Priest*, p. 24.
42 These are English translations of Weil's translations from Greek to French. Weil's translation of the 188d is rendered in much more Augustinian language than, for example, in the Alexander Nehamas and Paul Woodruff English version. See *Symposium*, in Plato, *Complete Works* (Indianapolis: Hackett, 1997).
43 Weil, 'The *Symposium* of Plato' *Intimations*, p. 109.
44 The Plato Weil discusses in *Intimations* is the Plato of the *Phaedo, Timaeus, Symposium, Republic, Philebus* . . . Weil sees some of Plato's ideas (e.g. his 'transcendent

conception of Providence' in the *Timaeus*) to be 'revelation' (see 'Divine Love in Creation' *Intimations*, p. 105). In 'God in Plato', Weil writes that 'It is impossible to affirm more categorically that grace is the unique source of salvation, that salvation comes from God and not from man. . . . The wisdom of Plato is not a philosophy, a search for God by means of human reason. Such a research was made as well as it can be made by Aristotle. Plato's wisdom is nothing but an orientation of the soul toward grace'. ('God in Plato' *Intimations*, p. 85).

45 Weil, *Gravity*, p. 121.

46 Weil, 'Forms of the Implicit Love of God', WG 92.

47 See Weil, *Waiting*, p. 92: 'God *thought* that which did not exist, and by this thought brought it into being. At each moment we exist only because God consents to think us into being, although really we have no existence'.

48 Weil, *Waiting*, p. 93.

49 Weil, *Letter to a Priest*, p. 20. Weil gives Thérèse de Lisieux as an example of someone whose God was personal at the expense of the impersonal.

50 Weil, *Letter to a Priest*, p. 24.

51 Weil, *Waiting*, p. 130. Although the 'nothing else' is challenged by what she has already written on p. 127, where she writes that 'Religion on the contrary corresponds to desire, and it is desire that saves'; on p. 125 she writes that 'looking is what saves us'.

52 Weil, *Waiting*, p. 99.

53 Weil, *Letter to a Priest*, p. 19.

54 Weil, *Letter to a Priest*, p. 29.

55 Weil, *Waiting*, p. 34.

56 Weil, *Letter to a Priest*, p. 37.

57 Weil, *Letter to a Priest*, pp. 38–9.

58 Weil, *Letter to a Priest*, p. 42.

59 See Irwin, *Saints of the Impossible*, p. xviii.

60 Kempfner, *La philosophie mystique de Simone Weil*, p. 36.

61 Plato, *Phaedo*, 64a–67d, cited in 'God in Plato' *Intimations*, p. 82.

62 Weil, *Gravity*, p. 32. On God's love see also p. 62.

63 Weil, *Gravity*, p. 179.

64 Ann Loades, *In Search of Lost Coins: Explorations in Christianity and Feminism* (London: SPCK, 1987), p. 55.

65 *Intimations*, p. 83; Weil returns to 'spiritual nakedness' in Saint John of the Cross in her discussion of social prestige (and La Rochefoucauld) on p. 137. (The discussion begins on p. 135.)

66 *Le Bleu de ciel* was written in 1935 but not published until 1957. The title (*Blue of Noon*) is likely indebted to Victor Hugo's *Rupture avec ce qui amoindrit*, cited in Chapter 4.

67 Bataille, *Œuvres Complètes*, tome 3 (Paris: Gallimard, 1974), p. 424.

68 See Simone Fraisse, 'La représentation de Simone Weil dans *Le bleu du ciel* de Georges Bataille', *Cahiers Simone Weil* 5(2) (1982): 81–91; see also Michael Surya, *Georges Bataille: An Intellectual Biography*, trans. Krzysztof Fijalkowski and Michael Richardson (London: Verso, 2002), pp. 214–5.

69 Irwin, *Saints of the Impossible*, p. xvi.

70 Allan Stoekl, 'Introduction' to *Visions of Excess: Selected Writings 1927–1939*, trans. Allan Stoekl, Carl R. Lovitt, and Donald M. Leslie, Jr. (Minneapolis: University of Minnesota Press, 1985), p. xi.

71 Bataille, *Le coupable*, *Œuvres Complètes*, tome 5, p. 245.

72 The texts comprising the 'summa' are: *L'éxperience intérieure* (1943), *Méthode de meditation* (1947), *Le coupable* (1944), *L'Alléluiah* (1947), and *Sur Nietzsche* (1945). NB: the chronology of composition differs from the dates of publication.

See Hussey, *The Inner Scar*, pp. 24ff. on chronology of writing and Bataille's intentions for the summa.
73 Bataille, *Oeuvres Complètes*, tome 6 (Paris: Gallimard, 1973), pp. 265–74.
74 See Andrew Hussey, *The Inner Scar: The Mysticism of Georges Bataille* (Amsterdam: Rodolpi, 2000), p. 25f.
75 Irwin, *Saints of the Impossible*, p. 156.
76 Hussey, *Inner Scar*, p. 1.
77 See, for example, Derrida's 'From Restricted to General Economy: A Hegelianism without Reserve' in *Writing and Difference*, trans. Alan Bass (Chicago: University of Chicago Press, 1978).
78 Georges Bataille, *Unfinished System of Non-Knowledge*, trans. Michelle Kendall and Stuart Kendall (Minneapolis: University of Minnesota Press, 2001), p. 174.
79 Bataille, *Oeuvres Complètes*, tome 5 (Paris: Gallimard, 1973), p. 59.
80 Amy Hollywood, 'Bataille and Mysticism: A "Dazzling Dissolution"' *Diacritics* 26(2) (1996): 75.
81 See Michel Surya, *Georges Bataille*, p. 58.
82 N. Berdyaev cited in Vrozhikhina, 'Shestov's Ideas', p. 368.
83 See Léon Chestov, *Kierkegaard et la Philosophie Existentielle. Vox Clamantis in Deserto* (Paris: Vrin, 1936). Interestingly, Shestov had been prompted to read Kierkegaard by Edmund Husserl after they had attended a lecture by Heidegger. The occasion of Shestov's visit was to invite Husserl to lecture in Paris. The lectures, published as Husserl's Cartesian Meditations, were also an important milestone of existentialism in France by virtue of exposing a French public to the thought of modern phenomenology's founding father. For discussion see George Pattison, 'Lev Shestov: Kierkegaard in the Ox of Phalaris' in Jon Stewart (ed.), *Kierkegaard's Influence on Existentialism: Kierkegaard Research: Sources, Reception and Resources*, vol. 9 (Farnham: Ashgate, 2011).
84 Cited in Bejamin Fondane, *Rencontres avec Léon Chestov* (Paris: Plasma, 1979), pp. 95–6.
85 Georges Bataille, 'The Critique of the Foundations of the Hegelian Dialectic' in *Visions of Excess*, p. 109.
86 See Henri Niel, *De la Mediation dans la Philosophie de Hegel* (Paris: Aubier-Montaigne, 1945), p. 57.
87 See Irwin, *Saints of the Impossible*, pp. 130ff.
88 See Jean-Pierre Le Boulet et Joëlle Bellec Martini, 'Emprunts de Georges Bataille à la Bibliothèque Nationale (1922–1950)' in Bataille, *Oeuvres completes*, tome 12, pp. 616–8; cited in Kendall, 'Introduction' to Bataille, *Inner Experience*, p. xxiii, n. 4.
89 See introduction and Chapter 3 of this volume.
90 Bataille, 'The College of Sociology' in *Visions of Excess*, p. 248.
91 Bataille, 'Sacrifice' in *Visions of Excess*, p. 134.
92 Bataille, 'Sacrifice', p. 135.
93 Bataille, 'The Labyrinth' in *Visions of Excess*, p. 171.
94 See Bataille, 'The Practice of Joy before Death' in *Visions of Excess*, p. 237.
95 Bataille, 'The Sacred Conspiracy' in *Visions of Excess*, p. 179.
96 Georges Bataille, 'The "Old Mole" and the Prefix *sur* in the Words *Surhomme* [Superman] and Surrealist' in *Visions of Excess*, p. 36.
97 Bataille, 'Nietzsche and the Fascists' in *Visions of Excess*, p. 191.
98 Bataille, 'The Obelisk' in *Visions of Excess*, p. 220. As we saw in Chapter 2, there was a tradition of reading Nietzsche as a kind of mystic going back at least to the beginning of the twentieth century.
99 Andler, Charles, *La dernière philosophie de Nietzsche: Le renouvellement de toutes les valeurs* (Paris: Bossard, 1931), pp. 60–1.

100 Bataille, 'Propositions' in *Visions of Excess*, p. 197.
101 Bataille, 'The Practice of Joy before Death' in *Visions of Excess*, p. 236.
102 Bataille, 'The Practice of Joy before Death', p. 237.
103 Stuart Kendall, 'Introduction' to Georges Bataille, *Inner Experience*, trans. Stuart Kendall (Albany: SUNY Press, 2014), p. xv.
104 See Peter Tracey Connor, *Georges Bataille and the Mysticism of Sin* (Baltimore: Johns Hopkins University Press, 2000), p. 8ff. on the difficulty of situating Bataille in the intellectual tradition; Hussey, *The Inner Scar*, p. 23 reads Bataille as anti-idealist.
105 Passages such as IE p. 25 suggest that Bataille saw Hinduism, for example, as impoverished: 'the poverty of these people is that they are concerned with a salvation, however different from Christian salvation'.
106 Georges Bataille, *Œuvres Complètes*, tome 5 (Paris: Gallimard, 1973), p. 265.
107 See Connor, *Georges Bataille*, p. 31.
108 Bataille, *Inner Experience*, p. 120.
109 Bataille, *Inner Experience*, p. 33.
110 Bataille, *Inner Experience*, p. 29.
111 Bataille, *Inner Experience*, p. 120.
112 See Kendall, 'Introduction', p. xix.
113 Weil, *Waiting*, p. 111.
114 Irwin, *Saints of the Impossible*, p. xx.
115 Bataille, *Inner Experience*, p. 29.
116 Simone Weil, *La Conaissance surnaturelle* (Paris: Gallimard, 1950), p. 121.

Works cited

Andler, Charles, *La dernière philosophie de Nietzsche: Le renouvellement de toutes les valeurs* (Paris: Bossard, 1931).

Bataille, Georges, *Inner Experience*, trans. Stuart Kendall (Albany: SUNY Press, 2014).

———, *Œuvres Complètes*, tome III (Paris: Gallimard, 1971).

———, *Œuvres Complètes*, tome V (Paris: Gallimard, 1973).

———, *Œuvres Complètes*, tome VI (Paris: Gallimard, 1971).

———, *Unfinished System of Non-Knowledge*, trans. Michelle Kendall and Stuart Kendall (Minneapolis: University of Minnesota Press, 2001).

———, *Visions of Excess: Selected Writings 1927–1939*, trans. Allan Stoekl, Carl R. Lovitt, and Donald M. Leslie, Jr. (Minneapolis: University of Minnesota Press, 1985).

Bingemer, Maria Clara, *Simone Weil: Mystic of Passion and Compassion* (Cambridge: Lutterworth Press, 2015).

Chestov, Léon, *Kierkegaard et la Philosophie Existentielle. Vox Clamantis in Deserto* (Paris: Vrin, 1936).

Connor, Peter Tracey, *Georges Bataille and the Mysticism of Sin* (Baltimore: Johns Hopkins University Press, 2000).

Derrida, Jacques, 'From Restricted to General Economy: A Hegelianism without Reserve', in Alan Bass (trans.), *Writing and Difference* (Chicago: University of Chicago Press, 1978).

Eckhart, Meister, *Complete Mystical Works of Meister Eckhart*, trans. Maurice O'C Walsh, revised by Bernard McGinn (New York: Crossroad Publishing, 2009).

Fondane, Benjamin, *Rencontres avec Léon Chestov* (Paris: Plasma, 1979).

Fraisse, Simone, 'La représentation de Simone Weil dans *Le bleu du ciel* de Georges Bataille', *Cahiers Simone Weil* 5(2) (1982): 81–91.

Hollywood, Amy, 'Bataille and Mysticism: A "Dazzling Dissolution"', *Diacritics* 26(2) (1996).
Hussey, Andrew, *The Inner Scar: The Mysticism of Georges Bataille* (Amsterdam: Rodolpi, 2000).
Irwin, Alexander, *Saints of the Impossible: Bataille, Weil, and the Politics of the Sacred* (Minneapolis: University of Minnesota Press, 2002).
Jesson, Stuart, 'Traces of Resurrection: The Pattern of Simone Weil's Mysticism', in Thomas Cattoi and Christopher Moreman (eds.), *Death, Dying, and Mysticism: The Ecstasy of the End* (London: Routledge, 2015).
Kempfner, Gaston, *La Philosophie Mystique de Simone Weil* (Paris: La Colombe, 1960).
Kendall, Stuart, 'Introduction' to Georges Bataille, *Inner Experience*, trans. Stuart Kendall (Albany: SUNY Press, 2014).
Loades, Ann, *In Search of Lost Coins: Explorations in Christianity and Feminism* (London: SPCK, 1987).
Meaney, Marie Cabaud, *Simone Weil's Apologetic Use of Literature: Her Christological Interpretation of Classic Greek Text* (Oxford: Clarendon Press, 2007).
Niel, Henri, *De la Mediation dans la Philosophie de Hegel* (Paris: Aubier, 1945).
Pascal, Georges, *Pour connaître la pensée d'Alain* (Paris: Bordas, 1957).
Pattison, George, 'Lev Shestov: Kierkegaard in the Ox of Phalaris', in Jon Stewart (ed.), *Kierkegaard's Influence on Existentialism: Kierkegaard Research: Sources, Reception and Resources*, vol. 9 (Farnham: Ashgate, 2011).
Pétrement, Simone, *La Vie de Simone Weil*, 2 vols (Paris: Fayard, 1973).
Plato, *Complete Works* (Indianapolis: Hackett, 1997).
Stoekl, Allan, 'Introduction' to *Visions of Excess: Selected Writings 1927–1939*, trans. Allan Stoekl, Carl R. Lovitt, and Donald M. Leslie, Jr. (Minneapolis: University of Minnesota Press, 1985).
Surya, Michael, *Georges Bataille: An Intellectual Biography*, trans. Krzysztof Fijalkowski and Michael Richardson (London: Verso, 2002).
Thibon, Gustave, 'Introduction' to Simone Weil, *Gravity and Grace*, trans. Emma Crawford and Mario von der Ruhr (London: Routledge, 2002).
Vetö, Miklos, 'Simone Weil et l'histoire de la philosophie', *Archives de Philosophie* 72(4) (2009): 581–606.
Vorozhikhina, Ksenia V., 'Lev Shestov's Ideas in the French Philosophical and Cultural Context', *Russian Studies in Philosophy* 55(5) (2017): 364–75.
Wahl, Elodie, '"J'ai eu faim, et vous m'avez nourri . . ."/Faim, assistance et charité/Charité, agapé', *Terrain (revue)* 51 (septembre 2008).
Weil, Simone, *Gravity and Grace*, trans. Emma Crawford and Mario von der Ruhr (London: Routledge, 2002).
———, *Intimations of Christianity among the Ancient Greeks* (London: Routledge, 1998).
———, *La Conaissance surnaturelle* (Paris: Gallimard, 1950).
———, *Letter to a Priest* (1942), trans. A. F. Wills (London: Routledge, 2002).
———, *Oeuvres complètes* (Paris: Gallimard, 1988 et suivantes).
———, *Oppression and Liberty*, trans. Arthur Wills and John Petrie (London: Routledge, 2002).
———, *Waiting for God*, trans. Emma Craufurd (London: Harper Perennial, 2009).

7 Berdyaev

A mysticism of freedom

Berdyaev and existentialism

Although N. A. Berdyaev (1874–1948) has remained a consistent point of reference for non-Soviet Russian thought since the early twentieth century (in Imperial Russia, in exile, in underground literature, and in the post-Glasnost period), it is perhaps difficult today to estimate the kind of reputation he came to enjoy in the West in the 1930s and 1940s. Reviewing *Slavery and Freedom* in the journal *Theology* in May 1945, D. R. Davies wrote that 'Berdyaev, as has been said, is one of the most important Christian thinkers of our time. Whatever, therefore, he writes must be read'.[1] Paul Tillich, reviewing the same work, spoke of it as 'the expression of an unusual wisdom, profundity and universality'.[2] In 1947 the Russian writer was awarded an honorary doctorate of divinity by Cambridge University (the first Russian to receive an honorary doctorate there since Tchaikovsky) and was referred to in the orator's address as a new Socrates. Often spoken of as a 'prophet', he was also appreciated as a thinker and philosopher, albeit not as practicing the kind of philosophy cultivated in university departments of philosophy. As he himself freely admitted, he wrote in an aphoristic and anti-systematic style, refusing membership of any school and not especially troubled by apparent or real contradictions and inconsistencies – a feature that irritated many of his reviewers.

This makes it more than usually difficult to categorize Berdyaev's thought, and if D. R. Davies could describe him as a prophet, others spoke of him as a philosopher, a gnostic, and a theologian – but he can also be regarded as, in some sense, an existentialist writer. Although Berdyaev had already arrived at his most characteristic positions by the time existential philosophy emerged as a distinctive movement in ideas, he himself was quick to see an affinity between existentialism and his own thought – at least, that version of existentialist philosophy that allowed for 'the existence of spiritual experience as primary and qualitatively distinct and as preceding all objectification'.[3] Although he himself emphasized that he never encountered Kierkegaard until late in his life (probably prompted by his friend Lev Shestov), he also stated that he was an existentialist before he ever encountered the writings of Kierkegaard.[4] He was also prepared to adopt at least some of the key terms of existentialism for further working out his own position, as long as this did not involve compromising the kind 'spiritual experience' he most valued and that, as we shall see, he also found in (some) mysticism.

Others, too, saw existentialism as an appropriate framework in which to place the Russian thinker. In 1965 Donald A. Lowrie (a translator of Berdyaev's work) published an anthology of writings by Berdyaev under the title *Christian Existentialism.*[5] Lowrie was not the only one to see Berdyaev as, precisely, a Christian existentialist, and a number of other books and articles reflect this view.[6]

We have seen that existentialism spanned a range of currents and tendencies, and not every representative of existential philosophy can be neatly fitted in to the template of 1940s Left-Bank Sartrean existentialism and this may be especially true in the case of Berdyaev. For Berdyaev, as we have observed, was an anti-systematic thinker par excellence, even suspecting existentialism of its own version of systematic thought. If we were to categorize him under any one single movement of thought, personalism might be the most plausible contender. The category of 'personality' that was already a strongly developed theme in Russian thought in the late nineteenth century is a central theme in Berdyaev. Yet the boundaries between personalism and existentialism are themselves fluid – Marcel, for example, could be assigned to either camp – and Berdyaev would certainly have rejected those elements in personalism that tended toward a naturalization of human subjectivity. As he writes in *Slavery and Freedom*

> The human being, the only human being known to biology and sociology, man as a natural being and a social being, is the offspring of the world and of the processes which take place in the world. But personality, the human being as a person, is not a child of the world, [but] of another origin. . . . Personality is a break through, a breaking in upon this world; it is the introduction of something new. Personality is not nature. . . . Man is a personality not by nature but by spirit.[7]

Such passages (and there are many in the Russian thinker's often-repetitive writings) indicate why and how he could see an affinity between his own thought and that of existential philosophy, which (in his view) also dealt with 'the whole human being, spiritual and transcendental' and not just with what can be known of human beings in the perspective of one or other of the positive sciences – biology, sociology, psychology, or even certain kinds of philosophy and theology.[8] In our approach to the human being, he insisted, 'The fundamental antithesis is between spirit and nature, between the existential scheme of things and that of objectification'.[9] But objectification not only encompasses the attitude inherent in any scientific approach that reduces the human subject to a phenomenon of nature, but (as the contents page of *Slavery and Freedom* paradigmatically indicates) it also extends to the subordination of spiritual life to the state, to war, to nationalism, to aristocratic culture, to bourgeois materialism, to revolution, to collectivism, to utopianism, to sex, and to art. It can even extend to the enslavement of human subjectivity by philosophies and theologies that prioritize being over freedom (as, Berdyaev thinks, occurs in Thomism) or that one-sidedly absolutize the demand of God over the freedom of the human response (of which he sees an example in the theology of Karl Barth). Elsewhere he also dwells on technology as an especially salient form of modern slavery.[10]

What Berdyaev says about 'spirit' could easily be glossed with another key word in his vocabulary: freedom. As he puts it in *Freedom and the Spirit*, 'Spirit is freedom unconstrained by the outward and objective, where what is deep and inward determines all. . . . Freedom is the freedom of the spirit . . . it is the inner dynamic of the spirit, the irrational mystery of being, of life, and of destiny . . . it is not natural to the human being; it is rather a new birth in which the spiritual human being makes [its] appearance and which is only revealed in the experience of the spiritual life'.[11] Again, the emphasis on freedom as a primary and unqualifiable characteristic of authentic life indicates Berdyaev's natural affinity for existentialism – although where Sartre followed the logic of Dostoevsky's fictional nihilist Kirillov, who thought that one or other but not both of God and human beings must be the source of freedom, Berdyaev held that, in fact, the mutuality of divine and human freedom is intrinsic to the character of freedom itself. Whereas many have followed the argument that if God is free then only God can truly create and human beings can only ever be imitators, makers rather than creators, Berdyaev argued that it is precisely because human beings are made in the image of God the creator that they, too, are free and freely creative. Freedom is not a fixed quantity that must be fought over by rival claimants, but freedom elicits freedom in the free response of love.

Berdyaev's mysticism

All this sets the stage for Berdyaev's view of mysticism. Vladimir Lossky, another thinker of the Russian emigration, argued that the Eastern Church had always understood theology as essentially mystical rather than doctrinal or ethical.[12] In other words, Eastern theology is grounded in the direct experience of God rather than in a teaching mediated by scripture and tradition. However, for Lossky himself and others associated with what became known as the Neo-Patristic synthesis, this was not intended to provide leverage for a critique of Church teaching but rather as a kind of interpretative pointer aimed at showing Church teaching for what it really is, a kind of mystagogy. In the sometimes virulent and invariably intricate debates that marked the life of the Russian Church in exile, Berdyaev and Lossky represent two very different tendencies. Where the thinkers of the Neo-Patristic synthesis sought to repristinate theology through a return to the Fathers, renewing the spiritual life of the Church through a deeper immersion in its own tradition, Berdyaev looked to a more fundamental and far-reaching reformulation of Christian life and thought capable of responding to the civilizational crisis of the modern world. In other words, Berdyaev was not looking to a return to the past but to a new kind of Christianity and a new kind of Christian spirituality appropriate to the emerging new age.

This last comment also flags up a further feature of Berdyaev's thought that merits being mentioned before we turn explicitly to the topic of mysticism. This is that his thinking is fundamentally eschatological and, as such, oriented toward the irruption into history of something radically new, a Kingdom of God that cannot be anticipated or understood in terms of purely historical social and political categories. This eschatological orientation is already evident in *The Meaning of History*, the first book that he published in the West, in 1923 (the year after he had been sent into exile on the 'philosophy steamer').[13] Here he writes that 'the elaboration of a religious philosophy of history would appear to be the specific mission of Russian philosophical thought, which has always had a predilection for the eschatological problem and apocalypticism'.[14] In *The Meaning of History* itself this is developed in terms of human life having a kind of twofold temporality, the temporality that belongs to what we conventionally call history, events unfolding in time, and a temporality that Berdyaev refers to as 'super-history' and which he later comes to call 'existential time', time that 'happens in the vertical and not the horizontal'.[15] This is a history that, unlike conventional historical time, has an intrinsic relation to eternity. This is why the true time of existence is apocalyptic time, for 'time [i.e. time in the normal, chronological sense] is not the image of eternity . . . time is eternity that has collapsed in ruins'.[16] But whilst Berdyaev continues to maintain that we already here and now participate in super-history and thus in apocalyptic time, he increasingly suggests that this participation does not exclude a chiliastic belief in and a commitment to a radical transformation of world history and the advent of a new age.

Berdyaev's existentialism, then, is an existentialism of personality, of spirit, of freedom, and of eschatology, gesturing toward a radical creativity truly capable of bringing about something new within the continuum of human historical time. So what role does mysticism play in this vision?

We have referred to the unsystematic, aphoristic, and repetitive nature of Berdyaev's style, and references to themes and figures associated with mysticism are ubiquitous in his writings. Nevertheless, there are several points at which he sets out a more sustained account of the topic, notably in the chapters 'Mysticism: Its Contradictions and Achievements' in *Spirit and Reality* and 'Mysticism and the Way of the Spirit' in *Freedom and the Spirit*. Also relevant is the introduction he wrote to an edition of *Six Theosophic Points* by Jacob Boehme, who, as we shall see, was amongst the most – if not the most – important of the mystical sources inspiring Berdyaev's thought. Perhaps the most substantial of these texts is 'Mysticism: Its Contradictions and Achievements', and it is therefore to this that we turn first.

At the outset of *Spirit and Reality*, Berdyaev contrasts his own approach to that of German Idealism, which he refers to as 'spiritualistic ontology'. Such an ontology 'claims that authentic or essential being is spirit; and that spirit is being, objectified being'. This, however, is to reduce spirit to 'an objectified concept', to something 'universal [and] impersonal'. By way of contrast, Berdyaev states that 'Spirit inheres only in the subject, who alone is existential'. But this is not to make spirit into a mere idea, since spirit has an 'immeasurably greater' and 'a more primal' reality than that of so-called 'objective being'. Spirit, in short, penetrates human existence 'with the highest quality of existence, with an inner independence and unity' and 'is the agency of super-consciousness in consciousness. Spirit exercises a primacy over being'.[17]

Berdyaev's reflections on mysticism follow on from a discussion of evil and suffering. In the light of the lived reality of evil and suffering, it is clear that the primacy of spirit over being is not a simple given. In the world as it is, spirit is constantly threatened and frustrated. Life in the world, Berdyaev consistently teaches, is inherently tragic. Nor is this something that social or scientific progress can ultimately alleviate. In fact, he suggests, 'the increasingly rationalized organization of social life' is likely only to intensify 'the tragic conflict between the personality and society, between the personality and the cosmos, between the personality and death, between time and eternity'.[18] Nor can utopian projects (which, in his view, include Marxism) do more than express an ultimately nostalgic hope for a better and happier life. They cannot of themselves bring about the conditions for such a life. A better way, it seems, is offered by the mystics.

The chapter on mysticism opens by effectively distinguishing mysticism from asceticism. Asceticism, Berdyaev says, is only the first stage of three in the mystical life. It aims only at purification, but illumination and contemplation (*theōria*), which he also calls 'inspired intuitive knowledge', cannot be achieved by ascetic practice.[19] Ultimately, it seems (Berdyaev is not entirely clear on this point), any kind of mysticism framed by ascetic practice is going to be limited to the relationship between God and the soul, ascending to God through the soul. Truly theoretic or contemplative mysticism, on the other hand, is not focused on the individual but on what Berdyaev calls the 'cosmic drama . . . within the Godhead', a 'divine mystery-drama'.[20] In these terms, mysticism is not a matter of subjectivity versus objectivity (which could perhaps be said of the way to God through the soul), but it is essentially beyond the duality of subjectivity and objectivity, or as Berdyaev says, it is 'a preoccupation with primal realities, with the existential mystery' – that is, with the reality that, as we have seen, he finds exclusively in spirit and in freedom.[21] We shall return to what Berdyaev might mean in calling contemplative mysticism a mysticism oriented toward the divine mystery-drama, but first we note a number of other distinctions he makes between various kinds or aspects of mysticism.

The paradoxical character of Berdyaev's style is, perhaps unsurprisingly, well to the fore. On the one hand he claims that 'mysticism is a transcendence of the created world' whilst simultaneously rejecting what he calls an 'abstract anti-human spirituality'.[22] But if mysticism transcends the created world, must it not therefore also transcend the human and therefore become, in these terms, 'abstract' and 'anti-human'? The question leads to a key theme in Berdyaev's version of mysticism: namely that, as he puts it in the same passage, 'there is a greater affinity between God and the human being than between the human being's spiritual and natural natures'.[23] In other words, the line between nature and spirit is not identical with the line between the human and the divine. Instead, it is a line found within the human and, qua spirit, the human being exists in a relation to God that stands outside the order of nature. In this relationship both God and the human being exist and relate to each other in mutual spiritual freedom.

These comments relate to a further theme that Berdyaev indicates at this point, when he says that mystics are often accused of immanentism: that is, reducing God to the world and consequently denying significant transcendence to God. This, Berdyaev thinks, is also the result of applying mistaken categories, since the unity of divine and human is not the kind of unity found in philosophical monism. 'Spirituality is the immanence of the divine in the human', he writes, 'but this does not infer [sic] undifferentiated identity'.[24] Rather, 'the idiom of mysticism is founded on love rather than on precepts'.[25] Commenting on Angelus Silesius's teaching that God could not exist without the human being, Berdyaev explains that it is a case of the lover not being able to exist without the beloved. It is in the sense of love's reciprocity then that 'God and the human were reciprocal. . . . If there were no human being, then there would likely be no God. When the human being was born, then God, too, was born. That is the most profound truth of spiritual experience, a truth revealed in spiritual freedom'. It is a truth expressed by Saint Symeon the New Theologian, whom Berdyaev hails as 'the greatest mystic of the Christian East', when, addressing God, he affirms 'I thank thee, O God that Thou . . . art now in very truth and unchangeably one spirit with me'.[26]

An implication of seeing the unity of divine and human in terms of the unity of lover and beloved is that it is not a unity that is simply given as a part of the human constitution, which would be the position of what Berdyaev here calls immanentism or monism. It is not a fact of nature that could be made the object of any science such as a metaphysical anthropology. On the contrary, it is something that can only be discovered by being achieved through free decision and therefore also through temporal becoming – although we should remember that, as has been pointed out, Berdyaev believed there to be different kinds of time, and the temporality of mysticism is a topic to which we must and shall return.

Berdyaev turns next to the question of apophaticism, which he affirms. God cannot be made into an object of knowledge, although proper apophaticism, he says, is something very different from the kind of agnosticism that he associates with Herbert Spencer and that merely indicates a limit to human knowledge. Apophaticism in the Christian sense is a positive response to the essential mysteriousness of God. In these terms it is actually affirmative rather than negative, affirming 'that the human being is capable of experiencing the Divine, of communing with It, of being one with It'.[27] Again, this marks a point of distinction between the apophaticism of a philosopher such as Plotinus and authentic religious apophaticism, although, Berdyaev claims, Neoplatonic mysticism has, via Pseudo-Dionysus, been reflected in Christian figures such as Maximus the Confessor, Thomas Aquinas, and even Meister Eckhart.[28] In this tradition, apophaticism could come to be incorporated into 'German intellectualist mysticism', as in the distinction between *Gottheit* (Godhead or God-ness) and God found in Eckhart.[29]

However, this could also lead in another direction, as in the idea of the *Ungrund*, the 'un-ground', that is the origin of all things in Jacob Boehme's theogonic visions. This is inherently apophatic, since it is '*nothingness* as distinct from *something* in the order of being'.[30] Only something that actually 'is' something, the implication is, can properly be named. Something that is not must remain nameless. Being beyond or outside being, this *Ungrund* is 'the primal pre-existential freedom. For freedom precedes being. Freedom is not created'; it is 'beyond the world of causality'.[31] However, the fact that something very different is going on here from what we see in earlier Christian apophaticism is indicated by Berdyaev's view that Boehme's thought is ultimately Cabalistic rather than Neoplatonic, a view that is undoubtedly contentious in terms of historical lineage and, for that matter, systematic implications – but in Berdyaev's own context it serves the purpose of underlining the distinction between an apophaticism oriented toward ontology and defined in terms of its implication for knowledge and an apophaticism oriented toward a positive experience of the divine mystery in, with, and under the mystery of human freedom.

With these comments on Boehme we can start to see what Berdyaev is thinking of when he speaks of the mysticism of the cosmic or divine drama, since Boehme's vision is nothing if not dramatic. We shall return to Berdyaev's interpretation of Boehme, but first follow the remainder of the present expositions of the 'contradictions and achievements of mysticism'.

Having argued in favour of apophaticism, at least of a certain kind, Berdyaev next distinguishes between the kind of mysticism which 'deifies the cosmos or the human being' (which he approves) and that which 'repudiates the cosmos or the human being' (which, predictably, he rejects).[32] Yet his affirmation of the deification not just of the human being but of the cosmos does not extend to endorsing what he sees as the 'orgiastic' or Dionysian kind of mysticism that he sees in Nietzsche, in the Russian thinker Rozanov, or in D. H. Lawrence. In the terms of *Slavery and Freedom*, this is to subordinate the freedom of personality to the impersonal force of cosmic powers. Yet, equally, he rejects the 'austere and unloving mysticism' that he sees in Plotinus and in Hindu doctrines of identity.[33]

What is called for is not the annihilation of the self in relation to nature, God, or the One. Such annihilation is, as he sees it, epitomized in the movement known as quietism and which culminates in the claim that human action is entirely suspended in the God-relationship to the point at which the devout soul is not even required to repent. In contrast to such doctrines of annihilation, Berdyaev states that 'the spiritual life is both dualistic and monistic; it is a confrontation, a dialogue, an interaction, an agency of one upon the other; it is in short, divinely human'.[34] Expressly opposing himself to Barth, Berdyaev declares that there is a double genesis, of the divine in the human and of the human in the divine: 'there is speech – not only of God, but also of the human being replying to Him. There is the human nostalgia for God; and there is also God's nostalgia for the human, God's need of the human'.[35]

Always important for Berdyaev is the mutual distinctiveness of Eastern (i.e. Russian) and Western thought, and he now maps some of the distinctions he has been making onto this cultural typology. In terms of the opposition made between an ascetic mysticism moving via the human soul to God and a theoretic mysticism contemplating the divine drama unfolding in cosmic life and history, he now suggests that the West is particularly characterized by a focus on the ascent of the human toward the divine. This focus is exemplified in the 'confessions, diaries, autobiographies, accounts of the spiritual lives saints and mystics' that, he says, are typical of the West.[36] This kind of literature is lacking in the East, which turns instead to the contemplation of divinity in the Incarnate Jesus.

This same distinction recurs early on in the essay on 'Mysticism and the Ways of the Spirit' in *Freedom and the Spirit*. Here Berdyaev draws attention to the current popularity of mysticism stemming from the kind of late-nineteenth/early-twentieth-century developments that we considered in the introduction and that are exemplified by William James, amongst others. But this, Berdyaev says, has set the understanding of mysticism on a false trail. What he calls the psychologism of this kind of approach 'is in conflict with the real significance of mysticism'.[37] The difference, he suggests, is condensed into the difference between 'soul' and 'spirit'. The field in which the psychologist chooses to operate is by definition that of the 'soul' or *psyche*, which Berdyaev understands as referring to the somatic, emotional, and experiential life of the individual. Spirit, by way of contrast, is not only (as we have seen) defined by its relation to a higher reality than that of everyday worldly life, but is also 'an escape from individualism'.[38] Only the depths and heights of the spiritual life deserve the name of mysticism', he writes, for it is there that the human being penetrates to the ultimate mystery'.[39] And although he then goes on to describe this as 'the inexhaustible and ineffable', terms that James would presumably have had no problem endorsing, he is clearly wanting to suggest something different to what he sees as resulting from any purely psychological approach.

Once more he insists that authentic mysticism is not dualistic. In mysticism, 'the natural becomes supernatural and the creature is deified'.[40] This, however, puts mysticism on a crash course with institutional religion, since religion is characteristically committed to dualism, insisting on the difference between God and creature, between Church and world, between flesh and spirit. When Berdyaev says that 'mysticism is the overcoming of creatureliness', then, he does not so much mean the annihilation or abandonment of creatureliness in favour of a life separated from life in the world but a refusal to see creaturely life otherwise than in the light of its inherent relation to God.[41] As he finds especially forcefully expressed in ideas of transfiguration and deification typical of Eastern Christian mysticism, 'mysticism frees us from the natural and historical world which lies outside us, and brings the whole evolution of material nature and history within the sphere of the spirit'.[42] Later, he will comment that 'the Eastern fathers . . . have never regarded the non-divinity of the natural as absolute'.[43] This position leads to panentheism, which he describes as deification through grace and freedom.

The unitive aspect of this vision is stressed when Berdyaev states that in mystical life 'there is no separation between things and no one thing is external to another. Nothing is external to me, everything is in me and with me, within the very depths of myself'.[44] In such a perspective 'everything forms a part of my own inner destiny and transpires at a level so deep that it is nearer to me than my own self . . . the whole history of the world is the history of my spirit . . . I only acquire being, reality, and personality when everything about me has ceased to be external, strange, impenetrable, or lifeless and then the Kingdom of Love is realized'.[45]

In both the essays we are considering, Berdyaev expresses the view – common to most writers on mysticism in his time – that mysticism is ecumenical both within and beyond Christianity and, as he says, that 'there are greater affinities between the mystics of various religions than between the religions themselves'.[46] In *Freedom and the Spirit* he claims that mystics and mystical movements as diverse as Orphism, Plotinus, Hinduism, Sufism, Saint Symeon the New Theologian, John of the Cross, Meister Eckhart, and Jacob Boehme 'speak to one another, each from his own world, and their language is often the same' – often, but not always. Not always, since (as we have already hinted) Berdyaev undoubtedly gives a special prominence to the mystical traditions of the Eastern Church.

Catholic mysticism is again seen as essentially a kind of 'sacramental mysticism' which, in Berdyaev's view, is inherently conservative. It is Christocentric, anthropological, and Eucharistic, emphasizing the structuring of mystical life through the threefold way of purgation, illumination, and union.[47] Also, it lacks a sufficient understanding of the role of the Holy Spirit in stimulating spiritual freedom in the human being. Ultimately, Catholic mysticism is a mysticism for those living the religious life as monks or nuns.[48] This can also lead, as in Loyola, to the mechanization of ascetic practice. Even Eckhart is now said to place detachment above love.[49] These tendencies are not unknown in the East, and Berdyaev charges the Philokalia, a collection of sayings and stories of the desert fathers, with operating at a purely ascetic level. Yet the basic and anti-ascetic idea of Orthodox mysticism is 'the transfiguration of everything created'.[50] This transfiguration is worked by the Spirit in moments of direct illumination. Nevertheless, this kind of typology of Eastern and Western mysticism is not absolute, and there are exceptions in each tradition. Bonaventure is cited as a Western theologian who affirms such illuminative intuition, and Francis of Assisi is set alongside Seraphim of Sarov as manifesting a kind of spirituality deeply at one with cosmic life.

At the same time, and as has been indicated above, Berdyaev saw the human condition as essentially historical and, in the light of that, believed that the present age was being presented with the demand for an epochal transformation in the understanding of religion. Of the inherited forms of religious life, however, it is mysticism that comes closest to anticipating the new kind of spirituality that is now being called for. Only this will not be a sacramental mysticism concerned with the remembrance of things past but a prophetic mysticism, dynamically open toward and engaged with the eschatological demand of the present.

Fully to respond to this demand, however, will mean sifting the mystical inheritance of Christianity in the kinds of ways that Berdyaev's distinctions between the varieties of mystical experience suggest. The mysticism that is now required will be a mysticism freed from asceticism, not seeking intellectual insight into the unity of all things in the manner of monism nor hypothesizing the immanence of the divine in the world. Neither will it be a mysticism geared to the needs of the Church and the ecclesiastical task of separating out the true sons and daughters of the Church from their worldly brothers and sisters. It will, precisely, be a mysticism of spirit and freedom, of vision and love, and ecumenical in the fullest sense, embracing not only the manifold of Churches and religions but even the manifold of cosmic life itself, 'a mysticism of creation' that is not a strategy of orgiastic immersion in the material life of the world but the perception of and love for 'divine creation' and for the world and for the human being as differentiated elements within the unity of that divine creation.[51]

Dostoevsky

For an example of this 'more luminous type of mysticism' Berdyaev turns to Dostoevsky, who, he says, was 'the prophet of a totally different spirit and quite another form of mysticism' from that of earlier ecclesiastical Christianity.[52] In particular, he turns to Dostoevsky's portrayal of the saintly Elder Zosima in *The Brothers Karamazov*. Dostoevsky was, in fact, a major and constant point of reference for Berdyaev throughout his career, and it is therefore worthwhile to look briefly at how his reading of Dostoevsky fed into his views on mysticism. This is also important in the present context, however, because Dostoevsky was in his own right a major influence on religion, philosophy, and culture in the era of existentialism. From amongst the French existentialists, it is perhaps Camus who most obviously uses the Russian novelist in his own work, including his adaptation of *The Possessed* for the stage.[53] But Sartre, too, makes significant references to Dostoevsky, speaking of Ivan Karamazov's saying that 'If God does not exist then everything is permitted' as 'the starting-point' of existentialism.[54] Heidegger, who rarely mentions Dostoevsky in his published work, is said to have kept a photograph of the novelist on his desk.[55] Amongst the 'religious' existentialists, references are still more common. Berdyaev's close friend Lev Shestov, like Berdyaev, gave a central place in his thought to the writer whom he regarded as Kierkegaard's 'twin'.[56] Martin Buber ascribed his intellectual awakening to the influence of Kierkegaard and Dostoevsky (often linked in the literature of the period). Karl Barth (to the extent that the early Barth of the theology of crisis is 'existentialist') speaks of Dostoevsky as highly influential on the reworking of his commentary on Romans for its second edition, while his collaborator Eduard Thurneysen published a study of Dostoevsky.[57] Tillich admits to Barth's characterization of his own theology as an incessant struggle against the Grand Inquisitor,[58] whilst amongst Catholic theologians of the period Romano Guardini devoted an especially influential study to 'the religious figures' of Dostoevsky's novels.[59] Oswald Spengler, author of *The Decline of the West*, said that 'The next two thousand years would belong to the Christianity of Dostoevsky', and though Spengler was no existentialist (anything but), his view is indicative of the kind of status that Dostoevsky achieved in the early- to mid-twentieth century in the West.

Although, as has just been said, references to Dostoevsky are found throughout Berdyaev's writings, his study *Dostoevsky* brings his main insights into a single text, and we therefore turn next to this, looking at it, of course, with particular emphasis on what it can tell us about Berdyaev's view of the new spirituality, the new mysticism, of which Dostoevsky was the forerunner.

Berdyaev makes clear at the outset that his is neither a literary nor a psychological study but an interpretation of Dostoevsky as a spiritual writer, and his task is to present the core of what he calls Dostoevsky's 'world-vision'. In Berdyaev's opinion Dostoevsky was not only a great artist but also 'a great thinker and a great visionary . . . a dialectician of genius and Russia's greatest metaphysician'.[60] But this is not to turn the writer into a systematic thinker since, for Dostoevsky, 'ideas are fiery billows, never frozen categories; they are bound up with the destiny of man, of the world, of God himself'.[61] Given Berdyaev's own emphasis on freedom, it is not surprising that he understands the Russian writer, too, as an apostle of freedom. 'It was a controlling idea of Dostoevsky', he writes, 'that there could be no world harmony except through an experience of freedom that embraced both good and evil, that it could not be based on compulsion, whether theocratic or socialistic'.[62] Yet in Dostoevsky's negative characters this freedom becomes the occasion for self-deification, with some regarding themselves as no longer bound by the same moral laws as the rest of humanity. As Sartre would pick up on, Ivan Karamazov sums up this possibility when he states that if there is no immortality and no God then everything is permitted.

It is precisely in the face of this danger that Christianity must develop a new and more interior experience of freedom that is also a rediscovery of the 'secret of Jesus Christ'.[63] In the perspective of this freedom the main human task is not self-deification but love, and for Dostoevsky, Christianity is the Johannine religion of love, and his 'Russian Christ' is 'the messenger of unbounded love'.[64] This reaches its culminating expression in the portrayal of the saintly Elder Zosima in *The Brothers Karamazov* who becomes a prototype of the new and coming form of Christianity. Although Zosima is modelled on some of the actual elders encountered in his own life and in Russian Church history, Berdyaev thinks that Dostoevsky's fictional elder goes beyond anything that any actual elder could have taught, citing Zosima's words to his monks:

> Brothers, do not fear men's sin but love them even in their sin, for then will your love resemble divine love and be greater than any other on earth. Love all God's creation, the whole of it and each tiny grain of sand. Love every leaf, every ray of God's light, love the animals, love the plants, love everything. Love all things and you will find the mystery of God in all things. . . . Love to throw yourself upon the ground and kiss it. Kiss it and love it with a tireless and insatiable love. Love all men. Love all things. Seek this rapture and ecstasy. Water the earth with the tears of your joy and love those tears that you have shed.[65]

At the end of humanity's 'tragic journey', 'a new holiness' appears and 'from the Karamazov world' – that is, the world of human beings driven by compulsive, fleshly, and violent desires – 'the new man has been born'.[66] Novelistically, this is revealed in Alyosha Karamazov's dream of his departed elder sharing in the light and joy of the wedding feast at Cana, as Christ turns the water of earthly life into the joy of heaven.

Berdyaev is not uncritical of Dostoevsky, however, especially with regard to the writer's nationalism and hostility to non-Orthodox forms of Christianity. Nevertheless, he writes that he knows 'no more profoundly Christian writer' and his study includes the often-quoted words that 'So great is the worth of Dostoievsky [*sic*]that to have produced him is by itself sufficient justification for the existence of the Russian people in the world; and he will bear witness for his countrymen at the last judgement of the nations'.[67]

Jacob Boehme

Dostoevsky confirms the 'Russian' credentials of Berdyaev's approach to mysticism. However, the influence of the German Protestant thinker Jacob Boehme is no less significant for an overall view of Berdyaev's mysticism.

As in the case of Dostoevsky, references to Boehme are scattered throughout Berdyaev's writings, although most concentrated in the brief introduction he wrote to an edition of Boehme's *Six Theosophic Points*.[68]

We have already touched on Berdyaev's judgement that Boehme's thought was of Cabalistic rather than Neoplatonic origin. Also, he quite correctly observed the importance of Boehme's thought in the genesis of German Idealism, although, to paraphrase his rather vague argument, German Idealism essentially incorporated Boehme back into a kind of Neoplatonic way of thinking and pressed him into the service of a 'spiritualistic ontology' that ultimately subordinated the freedom of the spirit to a philosophical concept of being. At the same time, it is clear that Schelling probably played some role in alerting Berdyaev to the significance of Boehme's thought although, unlike in the case of Tillich, his reading of Boehme seems to have been in large part independent of Schelling.

Although Berdyaev's early pre-exilic work already shows familiarity with Boehmian themes, the particular impulse to engage more explicitly may be associated with the influential study on the man Hegel called 'the first German philosopher' by Alexander Koyré, another Russian exile, published in Paris in 1929. Berdyaev opens his introduction by declaring that Boehme was 'one of the greatest of Christian gnostics' (Ungrund, v), although he immediately goes on to qualify the latter term and to make clear that he is not aligning Boehme with the Gnostics of the early Church. On the contrary, that kind of Gnosticism is in its own way guilty of the kind of privileging knowledge over freedom that Berdyaev saw as typical of philosophical approaches to spiritual life. Boehme, by way of contrast, showed 'a wisdom more contemplative than discursive' (again downplaying the possibility of any 'scientific' conclusions being drawn from his work) and, as a person, was marked by 'great simplicity of heart and childlike purity of soul' (Ungrund, v). Again, as we have already noted, he insists that Boehme's mysticism is not Neoplatonic but, he now says, biblical. It is also in line with his distinction between a psychological and individualistic kind of mysticism on the one hand and a mysticism of the divine drama on the other that he says that 'Boehme speaks of what pertains to God, the world, and the human being, and not of what happens to himself' (Ungrund, viii). For Boehme, 'To know God means to see him being born in one's own soul' (Ungrund viii-ix). Perhaps most fundamental is the intuition of God as fire (Ungrund, ix) and the accompanying recognition that 'light cannot reveal itself without darkness, nor good without evil, nor the Spirit without the resistance of matter' (Ungrund, xi). In other words, the revelation of God cannot be described without showing how God, so to speak, becomes God through his interaction with darkness, evil, and matter. In terms we have seen Berdyaev use elsewhere, this indicates an essentially panentheistic vision in which God and world are integrated in a single overarching process.

Berdyaev thus (rightly) sees Boehme as implicitly rejecting the medieval notion of God as pure act and turning instead to what he calls a 'theogonic process' (Ungrund, xii). It is within the unity of this process, that the admission of a certain darkness 'in' God is not to be conceived dualistically but as an element within the 'internal life' of God, a life that exposed God, no less than creation, to the 'tragic nature that belongs to all life' (Ungrund, xiii).

As Boehme describes the theogonic process, everything begins in a state of complete non-differentiation, what he calls the *Ungrund*, a state void of all attributes, an ultimate nothing that is even more empty than the kind of non-being (meontic non-being) inherent in beings that have not yet attained their full actuality. That the acorn is not yet an oak means that it is marked by a certain kind of lack, but it is not nothing. The *Ungrund*, then, is not, as it were, the potential world; it is simply nothing. This, for Boehme, is all that is 'given'. How then does anything arise? In the first instance merely as a blind desire or will toward becoming something.

This is rather obviously something that is extremely difficult to say anything about, but Berdyaev resists the temptation to which Schelling resorts of rendering *Ungrund* as *Urgrund*: that is, as the primordial or original ground or basis of things, rather than as the *Un-* or non-ground. For whilst such an *Urgrund* may similarly be said to precede all particular qualification as this or that (matter perhaps, or primordial chaos), it does not seem impossible to say that it is something. The *Ungrund*, however, as Berdyaev understands it, is precisely entire non-being. It is, he says, 'an absolutely original freedom, something that is not even the meontic freedom determined by God' (Ungrund, xii). In other words, it is a nothingness that in some sense precedes God or over which God has no control.

An important consequence that flows from this is that whereas rational theology turns the relationship between God and the world into a comedy, in the sense that God can from the beginning guarantee its good outcome, 'a game that God plays with himself' (Ungrund, xv), Boehme's vision is essentially tragic, in that God's own life is put at stake in the struggle to transform the utter indifference of the *Ungrund* into a living and good creation, and there can be no advance guarantee of the desired happy ending.

Boehme was 'perhaps the first man in the history of human thought to recognize that the foundations of being, prior to being, are unfathomable freedom, the passionate desire of nothing to become something, the darkness in which light and fire are burning' (Ungrund, xx). Will and freedom are no longer conceived of as divine attributes (perhaps, for example, also bestowed on human beings insofar as these are created in the image and likeness of God) but reside 'in the depths of divinity and before divinity . . . [in] the abyss, the free nothingness which extends below God and beyond God' (Ungrund, xx). Again, apophaticism seems appropriate in attempting to speak of such nothingness, whereas 'the God of cataphatic theology is already a something' (Ungrund, xxi). The primordial character of the *Ungrund*, however, means that the 'eternal beginning' of creation is not a divine idea but 'a passion' (Ungrund, xxv).

As Berdyaev at many points suggests, all of this implies that the process by which God becomes God is ultimately inseparable from the process by which we become human. As in the case of freedom, the distribution of freedom between God and human beings is not a zero-sum game, such that whatever is gained by one is lost by the other. So, too, here: human beings do not gain their humanity at the expense of God, but, on the contrary, the more fully human we become, the more God, too, is able to become God. Divine identity and human identity are mutually productive and mutually affirming. Theogony and anthropogony are the same process seen from two different but related perspectives. As he will say in *The Divine and the Human*

> The old doctrine according to which God created human beings and the world, having in no respect any need of them and creating them only for His own glory, ought to be abandoned as a servile doctrine which deprives the life of human beings and the world of all meaning. God with human beings and the world is a greater thing than God without human beings and the world. Human beings and the word are an enrichment of the divine life.[69]

This, as he adds in a Nietzschean flourish, is 'a radical transvaluation of the traditional doctrine of divine Providence', and although (he concedes) this can lead to atheism, this need only be so if we tie the cause of God to that of classical theism.

If, for Sartre, existentialism is a humanism, so, too, for Berdyaev, Christianity – or, at least, Christianity in the transfigured and transvalued form of a new mysticism of freedom – is likewise a humanism, a divine humanism, we may say. Whether Berdyaev's thought is also an 'existentialism' will depend on exactly how we read him. Is he offering a kind of theosophical speculation, perhaps extending the philosophical appropriation of Jacob Boehme seen in Schelling into more explicitly theological territory? Or is he attempting a symbolic and perhaps poetic expression of a struggle for freedom and creativity in human existence that, whilst acknowledging the radical lack of ontological foundation at the heart of human existence, nevertheless insists that something is to be struggled *for*? Or, to bring the matter to perhaps its simplest point, whether Berdyaev's whole adventure of thought is simply (in the best sense of the term) an argument for the possibility of love in face of the ineluctable tragedy of existence?

Berdyaev never embraced the method of existential phenomenology which, as we have seen, allows for a certain staging of the question as to whether despair (Sartre) or hope (Marcel and, differently, Camus) is the most appropriate way of characterizing the basic meaning of human beings' being-in-the-world. Berdyaev's 'method' (to the extent that he had one) is essayistic and is largely played out on the field of the history of ideas where, as in his discussion of mysticism, philosophers of all periods and schools rub shoulders with mystics and novelists. It may seem rather indiscriminate. Yet, in his own way, Berdyaev brings the issue between atheistic and religious existentialism round to the same question at which those such as Marcel and, more recently, Paul Ricoeur and Jean-Luc Marion have also arrived. This is, essentially, the question as to whether such theological responses as faith, hope, and love are ultimately appropriate ways of responding to the thrown tragedy of human existence or whether, as Heidegger and Sartre suspected, they are merely a painted veil flung over an entirely indifferent world. Berdyaev himself would have been the first to acknowledge that such questions cannot be decided as matters of science. We cannot say whether or not love is an objective feature of the real world, an attribute, as it were, of being. We can only decide the question to the extent that we think and speak from out of the honest evidence our own free – and Berdyaev would say spiritual – subjectivity. It is, in any case, to this question that he sees the new mysticism foretold by Dostoevsky as leading us. Insofar as this is a mysticism that is world- and life-affirming and, as such, also a mysticism of love, it may, in fact, also be regarded as a restatement of what is already implied in many earlier forms of mysticism. It is, of course, then up to us whether we decide for love or against. That is and can only be a matter of freedom, which, in Berdyaev's account, is no less fundamental than the freedom praised in Sartrean humanism. And if that is so, then Berdyaev can count not only as a Christian existentialist but more particularly as a Christian existentialist formed by the tradition and transformation of Christian mysticism.

Notes

1 David R. Davies, 'Review *Slavery and Freedom*' *Theology Today* (May 1945): 115.
2 Paul Tillich, 'Review *Slavery and Freedom*' *Theology Today* 2(1) (April 1945): 132.
3 Nicholas A. Berdyaev, *Truth and Revelation*, trans. R. M. French (London: Geoffrey Bles, 1953), p. 14.
4 See Nicholas A. Berdyaev, *Dream and Reality*, trans. K. Lampert (London: Geoffrey Bles, 1950), pp. 287, 102 respectively.
5 Nicholas A. Berdyaev, *Christian Existentialism. A Berdyaev Anthology*, ed. and trans. Donald A. Lowrie (London: George Allen & Unwin, 1965).
6 The titles of David Bonner Richardson's *Berdyaev's Philosophy of History: An Existentialist Theory of Social Creativity and Eschatology* (The Hague: Martinus Nijhoff, 1968) and Fuad Nucho's *Berdyaev's Philosophy: The Existential Paradox of Freedom and Necessity: A Critical Study* (London: Victor Gollancz, 1967) are eloquent in this regard. Will Herberg included Berdyaev in an anthology of *Four Existentialist Theologians: A Reader from the Works of Jacques Maritain, Nicolas Berdyaev, Martin Buber, and Paul Tillich* (New York: Doubleday, 1958). Katarzyna Stark wrote of 'The Idea of God-Man in Nicolas Berdyaev's Existentialism' in Anna-Teresa Tymieniecka (ed.) *Phenomenology and Existentialism in the Twentieth Century, Book One: New Waves of Philosophical Inspirations: Analecta Husserliana: The Yearbook of Phenomenological Research*, vol. 103 (Dordrecht: Springer, 2009), pp. 217–30. James McLachlan identified 'Nicolas Berdyaev's Existentialist Personalism' in *The Personalist Forum* 8(1) (Spring 1992): 57–65, whilst his monograph *The Desire to Be God: Freedom and the*

Other in Sartre and Berdyaev (New York: Peter Lang, 1992) compared the Russian thinker with the foremost representative of French existentialism. It should not be forgotten that Berdyaev was personally acquainted with many of the key figures associated with existentialism in France. In Jean Wahl's *A Short History of Existentialism*, for example, we find him as a round-table member of the concluding discussion alongside Gabriel Marcel and Emmanuel Levinas (amongst others). See Jean Wahl, *A Short History of Existentialism*, trans. F. Williams and S. Maron (New York: The Philosophical Library, 1949), pp. 35–56. The notes on participants describe Berdyaev as a '"personalist" philosopher who often verged on mysticism' (Wahl, *A Short History of Existentialism*, p. 56).

7 Nicholas A. Berdyaev, *Slavery and Freedom*, trans. R. M. French (London: Geoffrey Bles, 1943), p. 21.
8 Berdyaev, *Truth and Revelation*, p. 20.
9 Berdyaev, *Truth and Revelation*, p. 21.
10 In a particularly emphatic statement Berdyaev says that 'the chief cosmic force which is now at work to change the whole face of the earth and dehumanize and depersonalize man is not capitalism as an economic system, but technics, the wonder of our age'. N. A. Berdyaev, *The Fate of Man in the Modern World*, trans. Donald Lowrie (London: SCM Press, 1935), pp. 80–1. For discussion of Berdyaev's views on technology see George Pattison, *Thinking about God in an Age of Technology* (Oxford: Oxford University Press, 2005), pp. 42–4.
11 Nicholas A. Berdyaev, *Freedom and the Spirit*, trans. O. F. Clarke (London: Geoffrey Bles, 1935), pp. 117–21.
12 See Vladimir Lossky (anonymous trans.), *The Mystical Theology of the Eastern Church* (Cambridge: James Clarke, 1957).
13 On the circumstances of Berdyaev's exile and his role in the collective expulsion of writers and intellectuals on the philosophy steamer, see references in Leslie Chamberlain, *The Philosophy Steamer: Lenin and the Exile of the Intelligentsia* (London: Atlantic, 2006).
14 Nicholas A. Berdyaev, *The Meaning of History*, trans. G. Reavey (London: Geoffrey Bles, 1936), p. vii.
15 Nicholas A. Berdyaev, *The Beginning and the End*, trans. R. M. French (London: Geoffrey Bles, 1952), p. 163.
16 Berdyaev, *The Beginning and the End*, p. 207.
17 All quotations in this paragraph are from N. A. Berdyaev, *Spirit and Reality*, trans. George Reavey (London: Geoffrey Bles, 1939), pp. 2, 2, 4, 5, 5, 5, 15 respectively.
18 Berdyaev, *Spirit and Reality*, p. 127.
19 Berdyaev, *Spirit and Reality*, p. 129.
20 Berdyaev, *Spirit and Reality*, pp. 129–30.
21 Berdyaev, *Spirit and Reality*, p. 131.
22 Berdyaev, *Spirit and Reality*, p. 132.
23 Berdyaev, *Spirit and Reality*, p. 132.
24 Berdyaev, *Spirit and Reality*, p. 133.
25 Berdyaev, *Spirit and Reality*, p. 135.
26 All quotations in this paragraph from Berdyaev, *Spirit and Reality*, p. 135.
27 Berdyaev, *Spirit and Reality*, p. 138.
28 However, he also argues that a new position is reached with Nicholas of Cusa's teaching on the coincidence of opposites, a position that, he says, advances beyond both Greek and scholastic traditions.
29 Berdyaev, *Spirit and Reality*, p. 140.
30 Berdyaev, *Spirit and Reality*, p. 144.
31 Berdyaev, *Spirit and Reality*, p. 145.

32 Berdyaev, *Spirit and Reality*, p. 146.
33 Berdyaev, *Spirit and Reality*, pp. 149–50.
34 Berdyaev, *Spirit and Reality*, p. 155.
35 Berdyaev, *Spirit and Reality*, p. 155.
36 Berdyaev, *Spirit and Reality*, p. 157.
37 Berdyaev, *Freedom and the Spirit*, p. 240.
38 Berdyaev, *Freedom and the Spirit*, p. 240.
39 Berdyaev, *Freedom and the Spirit*, p. 241.
40 Berdyaev, *Freedom and the Spirit*, p. 243.
41 Berdyaev, *Freedom and the Spirit*, p. 243.
42 Berdyaev, *Freedom and the Spirit*, p. 247.
43 Berdyaev, *Freedom and the Spirit*, p. 256.
44 Berdyaev, *Freedom and the Spirit*, p. 267.
45 Berdyaev, *Freedom and the Spirit*, p. 268.
46 Berdyaev, *Spirit and Reality*, p. 149.
47 Berdyaev, *Freedom and the Spirit*, p. 255.
48 Berdyaev, *Freedom and the Spirit*, p. 259.
49 Berdyaev, *Freedom and the Spirit*, p. 261.
50 Berdyaev, *Freedom and the Spirit*, p. 255.
51 Berdyaev, *Freedom and the Spirit*, p. 263.
52 Berdyaev, *Freedom and the Spirit*, p. 263.
53 Albert Camus, *Les possédés: pièce en trois parties adaptée du roman de Dostoïevsky* (Paris: Gallimard, 1959).
54 Jean-Paul Sartre, *L'Existentialisme est un Humanisme* (Paris: Les Editions Nagel, 1970), p. 36.
55 However, he does mention reading both *The Brothers Karamazov* and the *Political Writings* (collected in volume 2 of the German edition of the collected works) in letters to his wife. See references in Gertrud Heidegger (ed.), *"Mein liebes Seelchen!" Briefe Martin Heideggers an seine Frau Elfride 1915–1970* (Munich: Deutsche Verlags-Anstalt, 2005).
56 See, for example, the essay by Léon Chestov, 'En guise d'Introduction: Kierkegaard et Dostoievsky' in Léon Chestov, *Kierkegaard et la philosophie existentielle* (Paris: Vrin, 1972), pp. 9–34.
57 See references in Karl Barth, *The Epistle to the Romans*, trans. E. Hoskyns (Oxford: Oxford University Press, 1933); Eduard Thurneysen, *Dostoevsky*, trans. K. Crim (Louisville: John Knox Press, 1964).
58 Paul Tillich, 'On the Boundary: An Autobiographical Sketch' in Paul Tillich, *The Interpretation of History* (New York: Charles Scribner's Sons, 1936), p. 26.
59 Romano Guardini, *Der Mensch und der Glaube. Versuch über die religiöse Existenz* (Leipzig: Hegner, 1933).
60 Nicholas A. Berdyaev, *Dostoevsky*, trans. D. Attwater (New York: Meridian, 1957 [1934]), p. 11.
61 Berdyaev, *Dostoevsky*, p. 12.
62 Berdyaev, *Dostoevsky*, p. 77.
63 Berdyaev, *Dostoevsky*, p. 79.
64 Berdyaev, *Dostoevsky*, p. 127.
65 Berdyaev, *Dostoevsky*, p. 206.
66 Berdyaev, *Dostoevsky*, pp. 206–7.
67 Berdyaev, *Dostoevsky*, p. 227.
68 Jacob Boehme, *Six Theosophic Points and other Writings*, trans. John Rolleston Earle with an introductory essay, 'Unground and Freedom', by Nicolas Berdyaev (Michigan: University of Michigan Press, 1958). Further reference will be given in the text as 'Ungrund', followed by page number. Strikingly, Berdyaev endorses

Boehme's category of theosophy, although he wants to distinguish this from the modern theosophy of Madame Blavatsky and her followers, influential on many of his Russian contemporaries. Although it could in principle be helpful at this point to offer a summary of Boehme's 'theosophy', it would in practice probably take us too far afield from the main focus of this study. Hopefully the most relevant elements in his thought will be sufficiently explained with regard to their function in Berdyaev's thought. For a fuller exploration of Boehme's thought and its influence on and further development in subsequent religious and philosophical speculation see Ariel Hessayon and Sarah Apetrei, *An Introduction to Jacob Boehme: Four Centuries of Thought and Reflection* (London: Routledge, 2014), including the article 'The Russian Boehme' by Oliver Smith (Hessayon and Apetrei, *An Introduction to Jacob Boehme*, pp. 196–223).

69 Nicholas A. Berdyaev, *The Divine and the Human*, trans. R. M. French (London: Geoffrey Bles, 1949), p. 7.

Works cited

Barth, Karl, *The Epistle to the Romans*, trans. E. Hoskyns (Oxford: Oxford University Press, 1933).

Berdyaev, Nicholas A., *The Beginning and the End*, trans. R. M. French (London: Geoffrey Bles, 1952).

———, *Christian Existentialism: A Berdyaev Anthology*, ed. and trans. Donald A. Lowrie (London: George Allen and Unwin, 1965).

———, *The Divine and the Human*, trans. R. M. French (London: Geoffrey Bles, 1949).

———, *Dostoevsky*, trans. D. Attwater (New York: Meridian, 1957 [1934]).

———, *Dream and Reality*, trans. K. Lampert (London: Geoffrey Bles, 1950).

———, *The Fate of Man in the Modern World*, trans. D. Lowrie (London: SCM Press, 1935).

———, *Freedom and the Spirit*, trans. O. F. Clarke (London: Geoffrey Bles, 1935).

———, *The Meaning of History*, trans. G. Reavey (London: Geoffrey Bles, 1936).

———, *Slavery and Freedom*, trans. R. M. French (London: Geoffrey Bles, 1943).

———, *Spirit and Reality*, trans. G. Reavey (London: Geoffrey Bles, 1939).

———, *Truth and Revelation*, trans. R. M. French (London: Geoffrey Bles, 1953).

———, 'Unground and Freedom', in Jacob Boehme (ed.), John Rolleston Earle (trans.), *Six Theosophic Points and Other Writings* (Michigan: University of Michigan Press, 1958).

Camus, Albert, *Les possédés: pièce en trois parties adaptée du roman de Dostoïevsky* (Paris: Gallimard, 1959).

Chamberlain, Leslie, *The Philosophy Steamer: Lenin and the Exile of the Intelligentsia* (London: Atlantic, 2006).

Chestov, Léon, 'En guise d'Introduction: Kierkegaard et Dostoievsky', in idem. (ed.), *Kierkegaard et la philosophie existentielle* (Paris: Vrin, 1972).

Davies, David R., 'Review *Slavery and Freedom*', *Theology* (May 1945): 115.

Guardini, Romano, *Der Mensch und der Glaube. Versuch über die religiöse Existenz* (Leipzig: Hegner, 1933).

Heidegger, Gertrud (ed.), *"Mein liebes Seelchen!" Briefe Martin Heideggers an seine Frau Elfride 1915–1970* (Munich: Deutsche Verlags-Anstalt, 2005).

Herberg, Will, *Four Existentialist Theologians: A Reader from the Works of Jacques Maritain, Nicolas Berdyaev, Martin Buber, and Paul Tillich* (New York: Doubleday, 1958).

Lossky, Vladimir, *The Mystical Theology of the Eastern Church*, trans. anon. (Cambridge: James Clarke, 1957).

McLachlan, James, *The Desire to Be God: Freedom and the Other in Sartre and Berdyaev* (New York: Peter Lang, 1992).

———, 'Nicolas Berdyaev's Existentialist Personalism', *The Personalist Forum* 8(1) (Spring 1992): 57–65.

Nucho, Fuad, *Berdyaev's Philosophy: The Existential Paradox of Freedom and Necessity: A Critical Study* (London: Victor Gollancz, 1967).

Pattison, George, *Thinking about God in an Age of Technology* (Oxford: Oxford University Press, 2005).

Richardson, David Bonner, *Berdyaev's Philosophy of History: An Existentialist Theory of Social Creativity and Eschatology* (The Hague: Martinus Nijhoff, 1968).

Sartre, Jean-Paul, *L'Existentialisme est un Humanisme* (Paris: Les Editions Nagel, 1970).

Smith, Oliver, 'The Russian Boehme', in Ariel Hessayon and Sarah Apetrei (eds.), *An Introduction to Jacob Boehme: Four Centuries of Thought and Reflection* (London: Routledge, 2014), pp. 196–223.

Stark, Katarzyna, 'The Idea of God-Man in Nicolas Berdyaev's Existentialism', in Anna-Teresa Tymieniecka (ed.), *Phenomenology and Existentialism in the Twentieth Century: Book One: New Waves of Philosophical Inspirations: Analecta Husserliana: The Yearbook of Phenomenological Research*, vol. 103 (Dordrecht: Springer, 2009), pp. 217–30.

Thurneysen, Eduard, *Dostoevsky*, trans. K. Crim (Louisville: John Knox Press, 1964).

Tillich, Paul, 'On the Boundary: An Autobiographical Sketch', in idem. (ed.), *The Interpretation of History* (New York: Charles Scribner's Sons, 1936).

———, 'Review *Slavery and Freedom*', *Theology Today* 2.1 (April 1945): 130–2.

Wahl, Jean, *A Short History of Existentialism*, trans. F. Williams and S. Maron (New York: The Philosophical Library, 1949).

8 Tillich

From being to love

In the post-war period, Paul Tillich became one of the best known and most influential of those seen as representing a theological version of existentialism. He was often grouped with Rudolf Bultmann, the New Testament scholar who promoted what he called a demythologized version of Christianity, developed through his collaboration with Heidegger in the 1920s. But although both Bultmann and Tillich offered wide-ranging reinterpretations of Christian doctrine in the light of existential thought, they were in many respects thinkers of very different kinds. This is not least the case with regard to mysticism, since whereas Bultmann's position is essentially anti-mystical, Tillich gives mysticism an important, not to say central role in his theological system. And if it might seem surprising to encounter a Christian theologian embracing both existentialism and mysticism, perhaps it is even more surprising to encounter an existentialist thinker who is explicit about also attempting to offer a 'systematic theology' – but this, as the title of his three-volume magnum opus unashamedly announces, is precisely what Tillich aims to do. No less paradoxical is the fact that Tillich writes very much as a Protestant theologian but, against the mainstream of Protestant thought, also affirms the legitimate role of philosophical and even metaphysical thought in developing his theological system. Let us disentangle some of these apparent contradictions, beginning with the last.

Regarded as philosophy or philosophical theology, Tillichian thought is centred on the question of being, which was also the question that Heidegger had sought (successfully, it seems) to reanimate in *Being and Time*. For Tillich it is axiomatic that God is being itself.[1] This is a reprise of the scholastic formulation *ipsum esse*. However, Tillich also glosses this definition as 'the power of being', which, since it is 'the power of resisting non-being', immediately intimates that being itself can only be thought of in the perspective of a struggle to maintain itself in and as being against the possibility of falling away from its own actuality into non-being (ST1, p. 261). But God is also 'the ground of being', indicating that whatever structures we may identify in the very being of being, these are grounded in and by God in such a way that God is not, as it were, contained or limited by them (ST1, p. 264).[2] All this entails that God is not 'a' being (ST1, p. 261). Furthermore, the statement that God is being itself is the one non-symbolic statement we can make about God (ST1, pp. 264–5). Everything else we might say about God – such as that God is Father, Trinity, creator, and living – is symbolic and therefore shaped at least in part by our human cognitive capacities.

Because God is not 'a' being, God does not exist in the normal sense in which we say that planets, atoms, and we ourselves qua animal individuals exist. But, for Tillich, to exist is already to stand out from essential being (the kind of being proper to the being of God as being itself) into a domain in which the power of being is radically threatened by non-being. As Tillich puts it, to exist means, literally, to stand out. In the first instance this means standing out from non-being. Something that exists 'is', it has being, it is not nothing. But it does not have the absolute being of God. As existing, it exists in the constant tension of being and non-being.[3] As a finite something, it is not everything and therefore finds itself limited and even threatened by other finite beings – 'everything finite is innately anxious that its substance will be lost . . . every change reveals the relative non-being of that which changes' (ST1, p. 219).

In this situation, a philosophy such as that of Hegel recognizes the inherent estrangement of everything actually existing from its divine ground but also sees this estrangement as merely provisional. As Tillich puts it, Hegel believed 'that, in spite of everything unreasonable, the rational or essential structure of being is providentially actualised in the process of the universe. The world is the self-realisation of the divine mind; existence is the expression of essence and not the fall away from it' (ST2, p. 27).

However, as this last phrase implies, Tillich sees existence itself as necessarily involving a kind of falling away from essential being. 'The transition from essence to existence is the original fact', he writes (ST2, p. 41). And, as he explains, it is recognition of this fact that separates all forms of existential philosophy from the kind of essentialism seen in Hegel. Going further, and drawing on Kierkegaard's analysis of anxiety, this transition is also a transition into a state in which the existing creature is exposed to temptation; to guilt; and, potentially, to self-loss, physical, and moral. It is this that Christian doctrine expresses in the myth of the Fall and points to the human situation as inherently tragic (ST2, p. 33). Nevertheless, Christian doctrine teaches that we can be restored to our relation to essential being, in, with, and under the conditions of finite being. This possibility, Tillich says, is given in the revelation of what he calls 'the new being' manifest in Jesus as the Christ. Restoration to this new being is made effective in love: firstly, the love of God for human beings ('Agape', Tillich says, 'characterizes the divine life itself, symbolically and essentially')[4] and then also in human beings' love for God, in which love is manifest as 'the drive toward the reunion of the separated' (ST3, p. 147).

This is, obviously, only a thumbnail sketch of a large and complex body of thought, and we have only identified a few of its defining features. Nevertheless, this may be enough to show something of the tensions between Tillich's philosophical theology and more traditional Protestant thought. Perhaps the first and most obvious point is that whereas traditional Protestant theology (and for that matter other forms of Christian thought) speaks of God as a divine, personal agent, Tillich seemed to many of his critics to reduce 'God' to a symbol for absolute being. Then, traditional theology, both Catholic and Protestant, has seen the Fall as a non-necessary event. The original creation, it was taught, was in and of itself good. It was spoiled only by an act of disobedience on the part of human beings, an act that was in itself neither forced nor necessary. Adam was free not to sin. But Tillich seems to present sin and fall as necessary features of existence. He does, as we have indicated, go on to talk of salvation through the revelation of the new being, but here we stumble on another difficulty connected with defining God in terms of being: namely, whether God's love for us and our reunion with God through love is 'merely' a symbolic way of speaking about what is really an ontological rather than a personal relationship. Furthermore, since we experience and live out our God-relationship in existence, it would seem that even if we do achieve renewal through the love of God, we still do not escape the tragedy inherent in the fact of existing. Faith, in this view, might enable us to endure life in a finite, tragic world, but it does not offer any final salvation from it.

Such issues made the reception of Tillich's thought controversial, in his own time and since. However, by seeing the drama of creation, fall, and redemption in ontological terms, Tillich was able to redescribe this drama in non-theological terms, opening a way for theology to engage with and to correlate its doctrinal myths and symbols with the actual existential questions and anxieties of contemporary men and women – not least as they were formulated by both German and French versions of existentialism. At the same time, the ontological structure of Tillich's thought provides us with a key to its relation to mysticism – though here, too, we encounter a significant tension between what we might call a mysticism of being and a mysticism of love.

As we now move to look more specifically at the role of mysticism in Tillich's thought, we shall take a broadly developmental view, noting how mysticism features differently at different stages in his career.

Mysticism and guilt-consciousness

Interest in mysticism goes right back to the start of Tillich's career, as evidenced by his 1911 licentiate dissertation on *Mysticism and Guilt-Consciousness in Schelling's Development*. We have already sketched the general outline of the argument of this dissertation in our introduction and noted that it not only offered a reading of Schelling but also established a template for his own future theological development. Let us now look at it a little more closely.[5]

Schelling's argument, as set out by the young Tillich, involved supposing a point of original unity standing in dialectical tension with the differentiated and alienated lives of human beings living in finite space and time. Schelling's presentation of this has a strongly intellectualist character. The ambition is to start with the self-evident formula of identity, A=A, and from this to deduce the manifold of the appearances of the world. If this can be achieved then it can also serve to vindicate the claim that when we know something we really do know it as it is in itself and not just some more or less distorted appearance. No less importantly, it underwrites the possibility that we can be at one with ourselves in our volitional acts. We have already at several points considered the epistemological aspect of this. Let us briefly say more about the volitional aspect, since it becomes crucial to Tillich's distinctive mystical existentialism.

The problem that Schelling is wrestling with, Tillich contends, comes from Fichte's account of action. When I want to do something, such as reach out and pick up a glass, my 'I' is necessarily involved in what is 'not-I'. But this 'not-I' is not simply the glass sitting out there, two feet away on the table. It is the whole ensemble of the laws of physics that makes it possible for the glass to be there at all, for physical movement such as the movement of arm and hand to take place. At the same time all the biological laws governing the existence and behaviour of a being such as I am are also involved and in play – to which we could add all the historical and economic processes that have brought about the situation in which I am sitting comfortably at a table with a glass of water to hand, a situation that not all human beings everywhere have been able to enjoy even though they, too, are subject to the laws of physics and biology.

Fichte himself had an essentially optimistic view of this situation, holding that the 'I' is, in fact, capable of fulfilling whatever projects it sets itself. Nor are these limited to simple physical interactions with the world, such as picking up a glass of water; they extend to the moral project of creating a society of mutually respectful moral agents. In Schelling's own early nature philosophy, this view is further supported by the idea that nature is not an indifferent realm of 'not-I' standing over against the 'I' but is itself a manifestation of divine spirit, albeit in unconscious form, such that the impulses of our human volition have an inherent affinity with the world in which we live and move and have our being. Especially, as we have seen, the early Schelling saw this revelation of nature as paradigmatically manifest in art. The poet and painter show us nature as it truly is, confirming that human beings are essentially at home in and at one with their world.

Yet the idea of nature and, even more, the experience of history seem to suggest that simple unity is an impossible ideal. If all there is to reality is A=A or, in theological terms, the divine I AM THAT I AM, then there is really no world, only (perhaps) an eternal, timeless event of divine self-enjoyment. In the world in which we find ourselves, however, it seems that difference, separation, and alterity are unavoidable. I can reach out and pick up the glass, but in doing so my hand encounters something cold and alien, a formed piece of inorganic matter, devoid of life (even if the water it contains is essential for the continuation of my life). You are not me, and I am not you. And even though you and I may get on very well together, we are never the same person. And even though you and I may get on very well together, not everybody does. In fact, the actual history of human relationships is a history of disagreements, quarrels, and, ultimately, war.

From mysticism to eschatology

Already in 1911 Tillich was aware that the experience of separation (the 'guilt-consciousness' of the dissertation's title) would have to be integrated into whatever experience of unity was possible for human beings. However, his first-hand experience of the First World War as a frontline chaplain seemed to drive out any possible unity on the plane of historical life. As he would say in a later sermon, what the war revealed was the omnipresence of death: that is, that human beings have been delivered over to their ultimate separation from the divine ground. In these terms, Tillich's war experience seems to mark the extinction of the mystical element in his earliest thought and its replacement by an emphasis on radical eschatology. Writing back from the battle of Verdun, he wrote that 'I am an utter eschatologist . . . I am experiencing the actual death of this our time. I preach almost exclusively "the end"'.[6] This was both the 'death of our time' and 'the revelation of death': that is, the return of the medieval vision of death as the decisive power in human life, which, at the same time, Tillich could gloss as the revelation of non-being and, as such, the revelation that most profoundly moves us to raise the question of being at all. As Tillich states in a radical formulation of the interdependence of being and non-being, 'There can be no world unless there is a dialectical participation of non-being in being' (ST1, p. 208). Perhaps even God cannot be being itself unless being itself is also participated in by non-being and is therefore no longer simple being, *ipsum esse*, being itself? Or, to put it in more traditional doctrinal terms, God cannot be God except by suffering and dying in the world, as Christians claim occurred in the crucifixion of Jesus, Son of God.

Thinking under the twin signs of eschatology and death would seem to render mysticism virtually impossible. The basic idea of human life as definable only in relation to an eschatological judgement already inscribes the possibility of difference into every worldly configuration of events. The good man may prove to be bad, the bad man good, the king a beggar, and the beggar be clothed with a glory greater than Solomon's. We just do not know what God's judgement will be, and we can therefore never delete the 'not' from every eschatological 'not yet'. And if, for us, God is who God will be in the final eschatological revelation, then God, too, is 'not yet' all that He is or may be.

In the interwar years, Tillich typically articulated his turn to eschatology in terms of the correlation between the Christian symbol of the Kingdom of God and the Marxist symbol of the coming classless society. In Tillich's interpretation of Marxism, this coming classless society would not result from a linear unfolding of historical laws. The classless society was a 'transcendent symbol' as much as an 'immanent fact' and, as such, could only be approached in an attitude of active expectation and enacted through fateful decisions that were not prescribed in existing historical conditions.[7]

We may in large measure see this turn to a prophetically anticipated future as a turning away from the 'mystical' solution to human beings' experience of alienation. Yet even in his religious socialist period, Tillich's thought is not simply 'eschatological'. In a reworking of the Schellingian pattern, he argues that genuine revolution presupposes some experience of the humanity of the proletariat for whose benefit the revolution is to be effected. It is because we recognize this humanity and because the worker recognizes himself as having a right to all that belongs to authentic humanity that the idea of revolution is at all possible. An utterly degraded, utterly dehumanized proletariat would be incapable of revolutionary action. It is only when the victim can say 'Am I not also a man?' that he finds the power for authentic action. Translated into the vocabulary of Tillich's philosophical theology, this means that it is only by virtue of having some participation in being that the worker is able to overcome the manifestations of non-being that threaten his life in the world. Being never 'exists' without non-being, but non-being likewise cannot exist unless it has some relation to being.

Nevertheless, at the height of his socialist period, in the time leading up to Hitler's accession to power, Tillich is prepared to gloss the 'being' in which the worker participates in terms of material needs such as food, housing, access to education, political power, et cetera. Even if we can recognize the same formal structure of participation in being that is described in the Schelling dissertation as 'mysticism', the content of this participation seems to be thoroughly concrete and material and not (in any usual sense) 'mystical'.

In the course of the 1930s and 1940s, however, a further shift seems to have taken place in Tillich's thinking. One obvious factor here is that the socialist revolution for which he had hoped in 1933 didn't happen. Instead, the world was plunged into what he regarded as the 'demonic' power of a new barbarism. And whilst he seems to have hoped that an Allied victory would provide the opportunity for rebuilding a socialist Germany, the reality of events proved otherwise. Indeed, his own wartime broadcasts for the Voice of America were curtailed due to what was perceived as their overly leftist orientation. The post-war situation of the Cold War thus seemed to inaugurate a time in which active hope of social transformation was indefinitely deferred. As Tillich put it in a sermon entitled 'Waiting': 'Our time is a time of waiting; waiting is its special destiny'.[8] As such it is a relation to God 'through not having Him'.[9]

Mysticism and the courage to be

Does this then mean that human beings are left suspended in a kind of neutral, featureless nothingness? Certainly that seemed to be the testimony of the radical art of the period that Tillich identified as revelatory of the truth of the historical human condition – we might think of works such as Beckett's *Waiting for God*, Camus's *Outsider*, or the black-and-maroon abstracts of Mark Rothko. In short, this is the situation disclosed in the culture of post-war existentialism. Yet at the same time, the vision and courage that enabled such artists to depict the human condition with such unwavering honesty also, Tillich surmised, testified to a kind of paradoxical courage. It was this courage that he explored in what would probably be his most widely read work of the post-war years, *The Courage to Be*. And whilst his writings of this time frequently appeal to examples from art and culture, *The Courage to Be* argues that this is fundamentally a religious crisis and, as we shall see, one in which mysticism once more plays a significant role.

Tillich sees courage as a response to anxiety, itself occurring as the irruption of non-being into the realm of human being or, in Tillich's formulation, the fact that we stand out into non-being simply by virtue of existing. However, he also argues that anxiety and the courage that is able to respond to and overcome it take different forms in different historical epochs. In the ancient world, anxiety was focused on the seemingly ineluctable power of fate, which, as in ancient tragedy, was seen to rob human beings of power over their own lives. In the period of the late Middle Ages and Reformation, by way of contrast, anxiety was generated by a sense of guilt and condemnation. In Luther this form of anxiety took an extreme form, at least until he broke through to his new idea of faith and his discovery of a gracious and forgiving God. In the modern era, anxiety takes a different form again. This is the form that Tillich calls 'the anxiety of emptiness and meaninglessness', which he says 'is anxiety about the loss of an ultimate concern, of a meaning which gives meaning to all meanings. This anxiety is aroused by the loss of a spiritual centre, of an answer, however symbolic and indirect, to the question of the meaning of existence'.[10]

This is the form of anxiety most prevalent in the post-war period, in this time of waiting, when humanity seems no longer to have answers to ultimate questions and, of course, the time when existentialism becomes definitive of European and North American culture. Perhaps confusingly, Tillich invests existentialism with a number of overlapping meanings. At one level, as in the case of mysticism, he sees existentialism as an element found in many different cultural moments. Plato's idea of the separation of the soul from its true home and the Christian doctrine of the Fall are both expressions of an existentialist point of view.[11] At the same time the existentialist attitude (as he calls it) demands an involved or participative answer, rather than a merely theoretical or doctrinal solution.[12] Whenever the sense of estrangement is ignored or suppressed or explained at a purely theoretical level, however, existentialism finds itself having to protest, as in Kierkegaard's protest against the Hegelian system. This was also a protest against an experience 'in which people were transformed into things, into pieces of reality which pure science can calculate and technical science can control'.[13]

Rejecting both conformism and collectivism, modern existentialism emerges as 'the expression of the anxiety and meaninglessness and of the attempt to take this anxiety into the courage to be as oneself'.[14] As such, 'it has become a reality in all of the countries of the Western world', writes Tillich. 'It is expressed in all the realms of man's spiritual creativity, it penetrates all educated classes' and it can do so because 'twentieth-century man has lost a meaningful world and a self which lives in meanings out of a spiritual centre'.[15] Existentialism faces this crisis and yet finds the courage to go on existing in the very energy of despair.

This crisis of meaninglessness is not just a crisis of culture, however. It is also and most fundamentally a metaphysical and religious crisis. In other words, it is not just a loss of faith in social institutions or cultural traditions, but a sense of lacking any ontological basis and of the entire irrelevance of the God of theism. Invocations of God no longer have power to reassure those experiencing this crisis, since 'God' is as meaningless as everything else.

It is in this situation that mysticism emerges as a possible source of a renewed courage to be. As we have seen, Tillich always remained true to the basic Schellingian insight that human beings never entirely lose an element of identity with that 'Being Itself' that is their ground of being. Normally, this identity is mediated through symbols, such as the symbol 'God'. Such mediation, however, is precisely what is lacking in the present age of anxiety. The stage is thus set for the appearance of the mystic, a religious type who relates to God or to Being directly and without symbolic mediation. Moreover, whereas mysticism is often glossed in terms of self-surrender, Tillich sees it as, specifically, a form of courage: 'That which from the point of view of the finite world appears as self-negation is from the point of view of ultimate being the most perfect self-affirmation, the most radical form of courage'.[16]

As the most radical form of courage, mysticism is able to conquer each of the historical forms of anxiety.

> Its limit is the state of emptiness of being and meaning, with its horror and despair, which the mystics have described. In these moments the courage to be is reduced to the acceptance of even this state as a way to prepare through darkness for light, though emptiness for abundance. As long as the absence of the power of being is felt as despair, it is the power of being which makes itself felt though despair. To experience this and to endure it is the courage to be of the mystic in the state of emptiness.[17]

Moreover, Tillich immediately goes on to say, mysticism is not just one form of religious experience alongside others; 'it is an element of every form' of 'the relation to the ground of being', and 'the element of identity on which mysticism is based cannot be absent in any religious experience'.[18]

Returning to 'Waiting', it is thus the case that even in the state of waiting, knowing our lack of God, perhaps even waiting as Eliot put it 'without hope', there is a mystical moment. This is because, as Tillich puts it there, 'if we know that we do not know Him, and if we then wait for Him to make Himself known to us we then really know something of Him, we then are grasped and possessed by Him'.[19] In the language of *The Courage to Be*, 'The faith which makes the courage of despair possible is the acceptance of the power of being, even in the grip of non-being'.[20]

As it becomes manifest in the contemporary crisis of meaninglessness, however, such faith has no particular content. It is not faith 'in God' or 'in Jesus', still less in 'communism' or 'prosperity'. It is simply faith in being, as such, above and beyond any particular symbolism or mediation. As such, it is, Tillich says, *absolute* faith. The content of this absolute faith, he adds, is 'the "God above God". Absolute faith and its consequence, the courage that takes the radical doubt, the doubt about God, into itself, transcends the theistic idea of God'.[21]

Although he does not cite Eckhart at this point, it seems likely that Tillich knew the expression 'God above God' to be Eckhartian. Certainly he would acknowledge the analogies between what he was saying and the testimony of historical mysticism. As he writes in his *History of Christian Thought*, based on lectures given in 1953, the God of Pseudo-Dionysius

> is beyond even the highest names which theology has given to him . . . He is not the highest being but beyond any possible highest being. He is supra-divinity, beyond God, if we speak of God as a divine being. Therefore, he is 'unspeakable darkness' . . . Thus, all the names must disappear after they have been attributed to God, even the holy name 'God' itself. Perhaps this is the source – unconsciously – of what I said at the end of my book, *The Courage to Be*, about the 'God above God', namely, the God above God who is the real ground of everything that is, who is above any special name we can give to even the highest being.[22]

Mysticism in history

It is interesting that Tillich here interjects 'unconsciously', implying that he had not been thinking of specific historical examples at the time of writing *The Courage to Be*. However, it is at this time – that is, in the immediate post-war period – that he begins to make mysticism a central topic in his teaching and does so with specific regard to its role in the history of Christian thought. This is evident in *A History of Christian Thought* itself, but other lecture series from the early- to mid-1950s give even greater prominence to the role of mysticism. Course titles occur in various forms in his papers, but it seems that at Union Theological Seminary he taught a course entitled 'The Theology of the Christian Mystics' in the spring term of 1952 (February through May, possibly giving a longer version at some later point) as well as a course on 'Mysticism in the System of Origen'. Four years later at Harvard he offered both a seminar in Christian mystics, running from

September 1956 through April 1957, and a lecture course 'Christian Mystics in Church History', probably reusing materials from the Union course, running roughly at the same time, from October 1956 through April 1957.[23] The seminar was attended, at least for relevant sessions, by George Florovsky, Gershom Scholem,[24] and Martin D'Arcy, and student presenters included John Zizioulas and Carl Braaten. This was undoubtedly a stellar intellectual event. Although he would never publish 'A History of Christian Mysticism', it seems that he was assembling materials for such a publication and that this is an important sub-theme in the *History of Christian Thought*.

In terms of Tillich's overall development, it is striking that it is at this point that he turns to specifically historical studies and does so with a level of sustained application that is significantly different from what we find in his pre-war writings. It is as if having achieved the systematic position he wanted to occupy he now sets about giving it historical support.[25] This comment could be understood in a cynical sense, but that is not how it is meant. Rather, it illustrates from another angle the interdependence of the systematic and historical elements in Tillich's thought, where the systematic element points toward the ultimate conceptual unity of what is to be understood and the historical element to its dispersion in time and space. It is a fundamental and enduring 'Hegelian' trait in Tillich that his confidence in the basic correlation of both elements never wavers. And even if from our later point of view it is not hard to see that his historical work sometimes forces the material into what the system requires, it is equally the case that the system requires historical corroboration. Let us see how this works out in the case of mysticism.

Although the 1956–57 Harvard seminar was focused on the student presentations, Tillich used the first session to give a general introduction to the topic, still referred to in his notes by the Germanic 'Mystik', and this introduction therefore makes a useful start for his overall view of mysticism in this period.

Tillich starts off with some etymological observations. Initially, he suggests, the term comes from *musis*, meaning shutting the eyes so as to exclude sensation and receive divine illumination, but at the same time, it implied closing the mouth and keeping the knowledge thus received secret. *Mustikos* thus becomes everything that cannot be pronounced, and the term embraces all kinds of symbolism in which what is said is said only indirectly so that mystical theology is very often also symbolic theology.

The term is then extended to those activities directed toward experiencing a unity with the divine that cannot be had in ordinary consciousness. These include holy meals, weddings, intoxication, emptying, concentration, ecstasy, and speculation or gnosis. Thus, in Christianity, it is the ritual event, as in baptism and the Lord's Supper, that is the mystery and not the doctrine. To this, Tillich adds that seeing the Christian faith as a mystery is not a response to persecution but testimony to the sense that 'words cannot explain the real meaning outside the real experience. It *cannot* belong to the daily life experience'. In mystical language, 'God' is not qualified by conventional predicates (as in 'God is loving') but by the identification of two nouns or substantives (as in 'God is love'), which, Tillich says, points to the mystical sense of the identity of everything in God.

If mysticism is not a response to persecution, it is also not a kind of irrationalism. On the contrary, 'the great mystics' were mostly very good ('geniuses' even) at rationalizing the world and their own experience. Mysticism is not something 'dark, arbitrary, without criteria' nor is it a kind of minority report within religious life. Rather it is '1) the one great type of high religious experience all over the world and in all religions' and '2) A special quality which cannot be denied in any religious experience'. In this latter sense it is a category that is constitutive of all types of religious experience and life rather than one exclusive type. Yet there have been persistent moves to remove the mystical element from Christianity (Tillich elsewhere picks out Ritschl, Barth, and Brunner as especially culpable in this respect). Instead, theistic and personalistic elements are emphasized to the exclusion of mysticism. 'The consequences for all realms of theology seem tremendous', Tillich comments: 'mysticism is attacked as negating sin and justification, community and personality, moral[ity] and history, Christ and eschatology!' But he questions whether this is possible, pointing out not only the existence of perennial currents of Christian mysticism but also the accepted orthodoxy of the notion of a *unio mystica*.

The fullest account of how this works out historically is in the notes for 'Christian Mystics through Church History'. The lectures can scarcely be attacked for not being sufficiently inclusive in scope. After introductory remarks the course tackles Plotinus (two sessions), prophetism, Paul, and John (a precursor of Greek Catholic mysticism, as Tillich calls it). From John the development proceeds to the Alexandrian School (gnosis, Clement, and Origen – and Plotinus again), Pseudo-Dionysus, mysticism and monasticism (dealing with Basil the Great and, perhaps surprisingly, Alyosha from Dostoevsky's *Brothers Karamazov*), and mysticism and the cult, including icons. Tillich next turns to Roman Catholic mysticism, where he runs through Augustine, the Victorines, Bernard of Clairvaux, Julian of Norwich, Bonaventure, Aquinas, Eckhart, and lay mysticism (where he places Tauler and Thomas à Kempis). In a slightly odd sequence, Tillich apparently skips to the apocalyptic radical Thomas Münzer, then moves to the Counter-Reformation mysticism of Theresa of Avila, Francis of Sales, quietism, Molinos, and Fénelon before turning back to Protestant mysticism, starting with Luther and including Schwenkenfeld, Frank and Weigel, Jacob Boehme, George Fox, American denominationalism and the Wesleys, Jonathan Edwards, Pietism (Zinzendorf), and, finally, mysticism and modern theology, including Kant's relation to Pietism, Schleiermacher, Ritschl, Troeltsch, Otto, and von Hügel, ending with Barth's and Brunner's attacks on mysticism.

Tillich's own notes are extremely sketchy. For some lectures we find lists of numbered points, for others unnumbered quotations and key phrases.

The lecture on icons is extremely thin on detail, but we know that he used reproductions of icons in class, so presumably spoke to them without notes. And although the selection itself and some of the points of interpretation clearly support a particular view of mysticism, the aim seems to be to present the primary sources with limited commentary concerning Tillich's own point of view (although it seems at least possible that he would have offered this in addition). Although the course never matured into a book, unlike *History of Christian Thought* (developed from lectures at Union Theological Seminary in 1953 and with which the mysticism course contains significant overlaps), it is minimally clear that Tillich was reading widely in mystical literature and, as a result, was also aware of and attentive to the varieties of mystical experience and theology whilst (as we have seen) insisting on some common elements.

In many respects, perhaps inevitably, Tillich's assumptions about mysticism often represent views that we have already encountered in German Idealism. These include both the idea of mysticism as a universal form of consciousness involving a direct apprehension of the absolute and the view of the Middle Ages as having a special propensity for mystical thinking, Thus, in the *History of Christian Thought*, he writes that 'Every medieval scholastic was a mystic; that is, he experienced what he was talking about in personal experience. . . . There was no opposition between mysticism and scholasticism Mysticism was the experience of the scholastic message. The basis of dogma was union with the divine in devotion, prayer, contemplation, and ascetic practices'.[26]

Tillich gives an especially important role to Bernard of Clairvaux, referring in the *History of Christian Thought* to a seminar in which, as he says, 'we have dealt with the question, "Can mysticism be baptized?" Can it be Christian?', adding that 'In our seminar we came to the conclusion that mysticism can be baptized if it becomes concrete Christ-mysticism, very similar to the way it is in Paul – a participation in Christ as Spirit. This is just what Bernard of Clairvaux did. The importance of Bernard is that he is the "baptizing father" in the development of Christian mysticism'.[27]

This seems a slightly odd claim, given that we have already heard Tillich cite Pseudo-Dionysius as foreshadowing the position he himself describes as mystical in *The Courage to Be*. However, it is clear enough that he sees Bernard as introducing (or, as the reference to Paul suggests, reintroducing) something new: namely a mysticism focused specifically on Christ. This has important implications for the relationship between mysticism and love and mysticism and eschatology, to which we shall return.

A different (and, we might say, more 'ontological') kind of mysticism is found in Meister Eckhart. In the *History of Christian Thought* Tillich says explicitly that 'Meister Eckhart was the most important representative of German mysticism', adding that Eckhart 'unites the most abstract scholastic concepts – especially that of being – with a burning soul, with the warmth of religious feeling and the love-power of religious acting'.[28] And if we are in any doubt that Tillich's Eckhart is made in Tillich's own image, he continues by quoting (though without naming a source) Eckhart himself: 'Nothing is so near to the beings, so intimate to them, as being-itself. But God is being-itself'.[29] In the lectures on mysticism there are further notes on this theme: 'God is nearer to me than I myself am' and 'God is more within the things than they themselves are within themselves'.[30] The thought here also strikingly correlates with another archived note on 'Our Eternal Ground. Estrangement and Reunion': 'In mysticism that which is our own ultimate concern, that which we call God, is at the same time, we ourselves. In looking at him, we are looking at his being in us'.[31]

Tillich further notes in the *History* lectures that by speaking of God as being he himself might seem to have turned God into something static, but he denies this, both on his own behalf and on that of Eckhart. His and Eckhart's being, he says, 'is life and has dynamic character'.[32] Also, as in his own case, Eckhart is able to distinguish between God and divinity (that is, in terms of *The Courage to Be*, between the theistic God and the God above the God of theism). This latter, divinity, is 'the simple ground, the quiet desert' and 'has no nature'.[33]

All of this becomes actual in the spiritual life of the mystic, who lets go his finitude, even himself, for God to be born in him. The moment in which God comes to such a soul is 'the *nunc aeternum*, the eternal now', an idea to which we shall shortly return.

Rather strangely, the *History of Christian Thought* contains no chapter on Jacob Boehme, whose mysticism had an undoubted influence on Tillich. Perhaps even more strangely, while the mysticism lectures were scheduled to contain a lecture on Boehme, no notes actually survive. Given that we have already given an outline of Boehme's thought in connection with Berdyaev (a connection of which Tillich, too was aware [ST1, p. 210]), it will perhaps be sufficient here simply to flag up the points at which Boehme's influence is most apparent in Tillich's own thought. These are the idea of the original *Ungrund* or (as Tillich sometimes refers to it) *Urgrund*, which, Tillich argues, imbues reality from the ground up with a dynamic quality (ST1, p. 198). It also shows being as inextricably entangled with non-being in the actuality of life (ST1, p. 210). As we have seen, this is not a duality that can be resolved by rational thought alone, as in Hegelian essentialism, but one that demands action by the will (ST1, p. 257). This further connects to Tillich's controversial views regarding the coincidence of creation and Fall, since although he does not specifically mention Boehme in the section of the *Systematic Theology* dealing with this, it, too, is an idea associated with Boehmian thought. Looking back over our earlier summary of Tillich's theology, we can see that the parallels between Boehme and Tillich are by no means marginal but belong at the very heart of Tillich's overall system.

In picking out Bernard of Clairvaux, Eckhart, and Jacob Boehme, we have had to be very selective with regard to what we have shown was Tillich's very extensive treatment of mysticism. They seem, however, to highlight three particular features of mysticism that arguably stand in tension: namely, love, being, and the dynamics of being, non-being, and will. In these terms they pose a question to Tillich's own mysticism, a question that can be regarded as a version of the more general question about the relationship between Tillich's deeply ontological theology and the more personal vocabulary of conventional Christian doctrine. At its simplest, we might say the question is simply a question as to the relative priority of love and being.

However, before we return to this question there is a further dimension that we need to examine: namely, the relationship between mysticism and eschatology. As we have considered this issue thus far, we have seen a tension between the eschatological-prophetic orientation of Tillich's interwar religious socialism and his turn to mysticism in the post-war years. We can condense this tension into the question as to the relationship between the expectation of the Kingdom of God and the experience of the Eckhartian 'eternal now'. But does this tension amount to an actual contradiction? Must Tillich's turn to mysticism be seen as a renunciation of eschatological hope for the coming Kingdom of God?

In some respects, these questions point to themes we have already considered in relation to Berdyaev, themes that in turn flag up what is perhaps a fundamental question with regard to the relationship between existentialism and mysticism. This is the question as to how a thoroughly temporal or historical account of the constitution of human subjectivity can also allow for a mystical view that seems inherently to relate to what is, in some sense, beyond time. Yet what is beyond time (or time as we know it, historical time) need not necessarily be construed as timeless, still less immutably timeless. Some such possibility of history and therefore time being in some way incorporated into what is beyond history and time could be seen as implied in the basic idea of the Kingdom of God itself: that is, a kingdom that is to come on earth but that will also be the manifestation of the eternal design of God.

Tillich in any case includes the radical Protestant visionary Thomas Münzer in the 1955–56 mysticism course, and the notes are amongst the fullest in the series, listing a first set of fourteen and a second set of six points to be covered in the lecture. Many of these relate to the messianic elements in Münzer's thought and his violent and violently suppressed attempt to inaugurate the coming of the Kingdom of God on earth. Like some other left-wing interpreters (such as Ernst Bloch), Tillich sees Münzer's uprising as anticipating his own religious socialism and other later radical political movements. Münzer, he suggests, taught democracy 'in the sense of the old Germanic rights' against the claims of the princes, calling for the abolition of oaths, trials, war, servitude, and private property. Yet this is also a kind of mysticism since a basic assumption of Münzer's teaching is that God's Word is not limited to Scripture (as Luther was claiming) but is spoken individually to each person 'within', in their own inner experience of the cross. Tillich amplifies this point in the *History of Christian Thought*: 'God has not spoken only in the past, and has now become silent. He always speaks; he speaks in the hearts and depths of any man who is prepared by his own cross to hear. The Spirit is in the depths of the heart, although not of ourselves but of God'.[34] But Tillich also connects this mystical moment to existentialist experience: 'The cross is, we could say, the boundary situation. It is internal and external. In an astonishing way Münzer expressed this in modern existentialist categories. If a man realizes his human finiteness, it produces in him a disgust about the whole world. Then he really becomes poor in spirit. The anxiety of creaturely existence grasps him, and he finds that courage is impossible. Then it happens that God appears to him and he is transformed'.[35]

In this account, then, the historically and socially transformative aspect of Münzer's apocalyptic thought turns out to be rooted in an inner and mystical experience. However, an arguably more radical figuring of the relationship between the future Kingdom of God and mystical experience is offered by Albert Schweitzer's *The Mysticism of Paul the Apostle*. In separate notes from the 1955–56 lectures, Tillich observes that, according to Schweitzer, Paul's 'sacramental mysticism' was 'active and historical, directed towards the future'. The Greek 'metaphysical mysticism', by way of contrast, was 'individualistic' and 'directed towards the past, without collectivistic elements'.[36] Paul's mysticism is not 'Hellenistic' but 'eschatological', based on 'an experience in which the difference between the temporal and the eternal is overcome and a man living in time has *already* reached eternity'. At the same time, Paul's mysticism is only Christ-mysticism, not God-mysticism. In related notes apparently connected to the New Testament scholar Lohmeier, Tillich writes that 'In Christ not mystical but participation in the metaphysical reality of the eschatological event' and 'The ego the place in which Spirit, God, Christ are effective not a subjectively faithful or mystical ego. . . . Not mysticism but metaphysics'.[37] Whether this disowning of mysticism is Tillich's own or reflects his source, it seems nevertheless clear that the basic notion of participation now in the eschatological event is a notion that he is elsewhere happy to let count as mystical. If the comments are his own, we might speculate that the force of 'metaphysical' here is not to negate the 'mystical' aspect but to argue for its being something not merely subjective, a revelation of being, of ontological and not merely emotional participation.

There is clearly a tension here. But does it amount to a contradiction? Certainly there is a difference in tone between the social revolutionary writings of the 1920s and 1930s, focused as they are on a future Kingdom of God as the defining symbol of human beings' God-relationship, and the vision of 'the eternal now' as that came to expression in the eponymous sermon of a 1963 collection. Here we read that

> Whenever we say 'now' or 'today', we stop the flux of time for us. We accept the present and do not care that is it gone in the moment that we accept it. We live in it and it is renewed for us in every new 'present'. This is possible because every moment of time reaches into the eternal.

> It is the eternal that stops the flux of time for us. It is the eternal 'now' which provides for us a temporal 'now'.[38]

However, this is not simply a tension between an eschatological faith that is oriented toward a future irruption of God into the continuum of historical time and a more Plotinian mysticism that looks instead to an 'eternal now', but a tension within Tillichian mysticism itself. Bultmann's demythologized view of faith as the capacity to awaken the eschatological possibility within every historical moment through self-acceptance and love is, we suggest, resolutely non-mystical. This is evident in his insistence that this possibility can only be actualized as a response to the (human) preaching of the word. Tillich, however, insists on the essentially mystical idea that we each have immediate access to the source of such a possibility. The question then is whether that access is, as it were, refracted through a relation to the future that is made effective in present existential decision or whether it is a present experience that empowers us to go toward what is to come.

This is by no means a marginal issue in the overall thrust of Tillich's thought since it is a tension that emerges in the final pages of his *Systematic Theology* when he considers the religious symbols of 'the end of history' and 'eternal life'. Here we read that 'Time is the form of the created finite . . . and eternity is the inner aim, the telos of the created finite, permanently elevating the finite into itself' (ST3, p. 426). Consequently, the transition from time to eternity is not itself a temporal event. If this is so, then neither the Kingdom of God nor individual eternal life is merely some kind of future event or an extension of current temporal experience. Rather, it is a matter of experiencing our present experience of time otherwise. Tillich calls the position for which he is arguing 'eschatological pan-en-theism', meaning that eternal life is a dimension of what is occurring now, in time (ST3, p. 450). Yet because God's eternity is not timeless eternity, it is also an eternity in which the relationships between past, present, and future also have a place – even if we can only speak of this in poetic metaphors (ST3, p. 426). Therefore it is possible and arguably as legitimate to relate to God by means of images, metaphors, and experiences that are oriented toward the future as it is to see the time/eternal relationship in terms of the eternal now. Without the inflection of the future (and, indeed, the past), the eternal now expresses only one part of what is possible with God.

Whether the position that Tillich is attempting to articulate and propose here is coherent with classical Christian theology and whether it is internally coherent or metaphysically persuasive are matters that would call for another – and another kind of – enquiry. Our focus here is on the particular conjunction of existentialism and mysticism in Tillichian thought, and here it would seem that we are led back to another basic tension in his system: namely, the tension between the scientific ambition of the system and its claim to do justice to existential experience. With regard to the latter, we may perhaps concede to Tillich that it is possible to envisage a kind of lived experience in which we become vividly aware of our temporal thrownness toward death (to borrow Heidegger's phraseology) but, at the same time, find an unsummoned and even unhoped-for courage that seems to well up from within the depths of our own life and, at the same time, offers a new future – perhaps even when 'all seems lost'. In such moments, time is no longer experienced solely as the relentless attrition of being but becomes a locus for courageous and hopeful action. But do – can – such experiences offer anything like knowledge? Can we move from such lived experiences to the ontological claim that, in God (being itself) being eternally triumphs over non-being? Can mysticism become theology? Again, we cannot pursue this question further here, other than to say that Tillich's system may be read as a sustained effort to give a positive answer that, nevertheless, maintains the existential pathos of its own mystical moment.

Being and love?

These last considerations relate also to the final point to which we now turn, namely, whether Tillich's mysticism is, in the end, to be counted as a mysticism of being or a mysticism of love. We have seen how he gave an emphatic place to Bernard in the history of Christian mysticism, a place connected both with Bernard's Christocentrism and with his emphasis on love. These are essentially interconnected, since Christ is himself the revelation of God's love, and our relation to Christ is to be a relation of love rather than obedience. As man (*homo*) Christ is *amor carnalis*, as Word (*Verbum*) he is *amor spiritualis* so that whether we are relating to him as man or as God, that relation must be a relation of love. The relationship between God and the soul is not 'consubstantial', such that the soul shares the divine substance, but a relationship of 'consent', and in this way God and the soul become '*unus spiritus in amore*' (one spirit in love).[39]

Yet, at least in Bernard, this theme of love is, according to the *History of Christian Thought*, also qualified as 'abstract' since it abstracts from the lived concreteness of life in the world. However, for Tillich, the new being revealed and made effective in Christ must enable us to accept ourselves in our concrete existential life circumstances and to be reconciled with whatever and whoever threatens the integrity of our individual and social being. And this is a further meaning of the transformation of time through its relation to eternity.[40] Where classic Christian love-mysticism turns away from the world to be absorbed in the beloved God (thus the prevalence of Song of Songs imagery in this type of mysticism), Tillich's existential mysticism requires the love relationship to take shape in and through how we are and what we do in the world. In this connection, whilst morality emphasizes our freedom to act according to what the moral law teaches us to be right, the Christian *agapē* reveals the content and ultimate norm of freedom, to live not for ourselves but for the other (ST3, p. 51).

As in relation to time, futurity, and the eternal now, the question of love again highlights the question as to the kind of knowledge claims implied in Tillichian mysticism. Just as the dimension of futurity in our relation to the eternal seems to set a limit on what we can know, so, too, the fact that what is demanded is love seems to relegate the imperative of knowledge to (at least) second place. In this regard, it is striking that in the sermon 'The Power of Love', which immediately follows that on 'The New Being', Tillich does not go further down the path of doctrinal and metaphysical explanation but turns instead to retell the life story of a saintly woman, Elsa Brandström, who devoted her life to working with orphans, prisoners of war, and refugees in Russia, Germany, and the United States. Here, it seems, is the point where ontological speculation has to stop.[41]

Is such speculation then pointless? To say so would render Tillich's whole intellectual enterprise pointless, and whilst this might please his critics, we can scarcely imagine he would easily have accepted such a claim. Perhaps Tillich offers a bridge from the immediate, practical example of saintliness seen in Elsa Brandström to the more metaphysical claim implied in the primacy of love in another sermon, 'Love is Stronger than Death'. Here he points not just to the need for love in the specific individual circumstances of life, but to the importance of love with regard to the global crises of modern humanity, inclusive of war, terror, and mass migration, events that, as he says, constitute a revelation of the power of death over us all. Earlier in this chapter we noted that Tillich sometimes glosses being itself as 'the power of being', and so, too, love is not to be understood as an abstract category but as a power in life. So, in relation to the crises of his time (which are, of course, not entirely dissimilar from the crises of our own time), Tillich speaks of love as the power, implicitly the one power, that is able to break the power of death. 'Love is the infinite which is given to the finite. Therefore we love in others, for we do not merely love others, but we love the Love that is in them and which is more than their or our love. In mutual assistance what is most important is not the alleviation of need but the actualization of love'.[42] Love, in other words, is the power of the new being as that becomes manifest in the mutual assistance that human beings exposed to the otherwise omnipotent power of death give one another.

In these reflections on love, the discussion may seem to be moving away from mysticism. However, this is minimally a necessary footnote to any consideration of Tillichian mysticism, since it reminds us that the point of such mysticism is not the attainment of some esoteric knowledge of God but the transformation of our lives in the world: that is, the transformation of our existential possibilities. As such it is both a worldly mysticism and a mysticism of love.

Notes

1 Paul Tillich, *Systematic Theology*, vol. 1 (Welwyn Garden City: James Nisbet, 1953), p. 261. Further references are given in the text as ST1 followed by page number.

2 Given that 'Grund' is a German term regularly translated as 'reason', as in Leibnitz's 'principle of sufficient reason' (*Satz vom Grunde*) it is striking that, Tillich says in an archived note, 'ground' 'is a mystical term. It is neither sense nor substance, not a category derived from nature, but it includes both of them. It is the sense of sense, the substance of substance. It is more a symbol than a concept, pointing to the dimension of depth in all things'. *Paul Tillich Papers, 2894–1974*, bms649/54 (34) 2.
3 Paul Tillich, *Systematic Theology*, vol. 2 (Welwyn Garden City: James Nisbet, 1957), p. 22. further references are given in the text as ST2 followed by page number.
4 Paul Tillich, *Systematic Theology*, vol. 3 (Welwyn Garden City: James Nisbet, 1964), p. 146. Further references are given in the text as ST3 followed by page number.
5 For a fuller summary and discussion see George Pattison, *Paul Tillich's Philosophical Theology* (London: Palgrave Macmillan, 2015), pp. 9–17.
6 Cited in Wilhelm Pauck and Marion Pauck, *Paul Tillich: His Life and Thought*, vol. 1: *Life* (London: Collins, 1977), p. 51.
7 See Paul Tillich, *The Socialist Decision* (New York: Harper and Row, 1977), p. 111.
8 Paul Tillich, *The Shaking of the Foundations* (London: SCM Press, 1949), p. 152. Tillich's treatment of this theme bears comparison with Eliot's reflections on waiting in 'East Coker', lines 122–8 in T. S. (Thomas Stearns) Eliot, *Four Quartets* (London: Faber and Faber, 1944), likewise with the treatment of waiting in Simon Weil (see Chapter 6).
9 Tillich, *Shaking of the Foundations*, p. 151.
10 Paul Tillich, *The Courage to Be* (London: Collins, 1952), pp. 54–5.
11 Tillich, *Courage*, pp. 126–7.
12 Tillich, *Courage*, p. 124.
13 Tillich, *Courage*, p. 136.
14 Tillich, *Courage*, p. 138.
15 Tillich, *Courage*, p. 138.
16 Tillich, *Courage*, pp. 154–5.
17 Tillich, *Courage*, p. 156.
18 Tillich, *Courage*, p. 156.
19 Tillich, *Shaking*, p. 151.
20 Tillich, *Courage*, p. 171.
21 Tillich, *Courage*, p. 176.
22 Paul Tillich, *A History of Christian Thought* (London: SCM Press, 1968), p. 92.
23 The lecture notes are on A5 Union Theological Seminary paper, but some are dated to 1956 or 1957 when Tillich was teaching at Harvard.
24 Despite the title of the seminar series, one session was dedicated to Jewish mysticism.
25 The lectures slightly postdate the first publication of *The Courage to Be* and are concurrent with work on the first two volumes of his *Systematic Theology*.
26 Tillich, *History*, p. 136. This is a view we have already encountered in Heidegger. (See Chapter 2.) However, it is clearly intension with, for example, Thomas's own view that we can have no direct experience of God in this life.
27 Tillich, *History*, p. 173.
28 Tillich, *History*, p. 201.
29 Tillich, *History*, p. 201.
30 *Paul Tillich Papers*, bMS 649/56. Notes for lecture on February 7, 1957.
31 *Paul Tillich Papers*, bMS 649/54 (34). 5.
32 Tillich, *History*, p. 202.

33 Tillich, *History*, p. 202. The mysticism notes add: 'untouchable quietness' to this characterization of divinity, adding that 'God is his own nothing' and 'a superessential nothingness'.
34 Tillich, *History*, p. 239.
35 Tillich, *History*, p. 239.
36 *Paul Tillich Papers*, bMS 649/56 (8).
37 *Paul Tillich Papers*, bMS 649/56 (8).
38 Paul Tillich, from 'The Eternal Now' in *The Boundaries of Our Being* (London: Collins, 1973), p. 107.
39 *Paul Tillich Papers*, bMS 649/56 (19).
40 See, for example, the sermon 'The New Being' in the collection 'The New Being' in Tillich, *Boundaries*, pp. 162–70.
41 See Tillich, *Boundaries*, pp. 170–3.
42 Tillich, *Boundaries*, p. 280.

Works cited

Pattison, George, *Paul Tillich's Philosophical Theology* (London: Palgrave Macmillan, 2015).

Pauck, Wilhelm and Pauck, Marion, *Paul Tillich: His Life and Thought, Vol. 1: Life* (London: Collins, 1977).

Tillich, Paul, *The Boundaries of Our Being* (London: Collins, 1973).

———, *The Courage to Be* (London: Collins, 1952).

———, *A History of Christian Thought* (London: SCM Press, 1968).

———, *Papers, 1894–1974* (Andover-Harvard Theological Library, Harvard Divinity School, Harvard University, 1886–1965).

———, *The Shaking of the Foundations* (London: SCM Press, 1949).

———, *The Socialist Decision* (New York: Harper and Row, 1977).

———, *Systematic Theology*, vol. 1 (Welwyn Garden City: James Nisbet, 1953).

———, *Systematic Theology*, vol. 2 (Welwyn Garden City: James Nisbet, 1957).

———, *Systematic Theology*, vol. 3 (Welwyn Garden City: James Nisbet, 1964).

Conclusion

We have examined a range of ways in which the key figures of philosophical and theological existentialism drew on mystical sources. This does not necessarily make them 'mystics', and in some cases (as, notably, Sartre), there is an explicit rejection of what these sources offered. However, as the case of Kierkegaard illustrates, an explicit rejection of mysticism does not exclude the use of mystical tropes – what's in a name? At the same time, a positive attitude to mysticism does not of itself imply endorsement of theological claims, especially not those of classical Christian doctrine. This is clearly true in the case of Bataille, but even a God-seeking thinker such as Simone Weil arrives at a kind of mysticism that sits uncomfortably with key Christian doctrinal positions and with Christian attitudes to the body and to life in the world.

What these and other possible qualifications amount to is that we must take each case on its own terms and merits and wherever the word 'mystical' is used be attentive to just what is being meant by it. This is perhaps disappointing if one imagines 'existentialism' to be a cohesive movement in ideas and 'mysticism' to be a clear and distinct category. But neither of these is in fact the case. Like many other movements in ideas and in culture, existentialism developed a variety of forms, as Sartre's acknowledgement of a Christian existentialism alongside his own atheistic version already indicated. This should not surprise us. In the introduction we commented on the internally pluralistic character of most major philosophical movements, but we might also consider the equally relevant development of modern art. Impressionism, cubism, expressionism, new realism, and abstract expressionism are not strictly uniform movements. Monet and Renoir are as distinct as Marc and Schmidt-Rotluff or Rothko and Newman – yet, at the same time, few would confuse Pissarro with Braque or the latter with Jackson Pollock. Perhaps (and perhaps for obvious reasons) existentialism was more strongly marked by the individual personalities and life-views of its main representatives than some other intellectual movements, but whilst these differed amongst themselves, they also appear as, in many ways, a distinctive group. The analogy with art also reminds us that there are always those who represent a movement in its purest, most radical, or most distinctive form, whilst others retain or develop elements from other schools and traditions – and nearly all major thinkers, like nearly all major artists, show significant developments in the course of their careers.

These comments do not mean that no general conclusions are to be drawn. What is certainly clear is that, from early Romanticism onward, 'mysticism' became a term invested with positive as well as negative meanings and, especially in relation to what were perceived as limitations of Kantian philosophy, could be seen as contributing to the solving of some philosophical problems. This was especially the case with regard to what is variously called 'the absolute', 'ultimate reality', or (of course) God. Although variously articulated, if there is a single core mystical claim, it is, then, that we have some kind of direct consciousness of this reality. However, the claim is immediately qualified by the acknowledgement by most of the thinkers we have been considering that this consciousness cannot be regarded as establishing 'knowledge' in any conventional sense. As regards what is known (which is, of course, not properly spoken of as a 'what' or an 'object'), this seems to appear more in the mode of non-being than being and, in this regard, may require the annihilation or emptying out of everything that we normally associate with subjectivity. The 'I' that has become open to the absolute or to God is no longer a thinking subject, any more than the absolute or God is an object amongst objects.

It is not difficult to portray such claims as paradoxical, absurd, or, quite simply, meaningless. However, we are taking it that for most of the figures we have been considering, the language of religion is being bent and stretched in order to testify to something that has been lived. But here we need to add further cautions. For despite clear echoes of the kind of language used by William James and the mystics to whose testimonies he appeals, the issue here is not Jamesian 'experience'. Rather, it is, as Tillich liked to say, more like a 'dimension of depth' in life as it is lived, a quality of existence more than a kind of experience. Thus we might say that to the extent that existentialist thinking is informed by mystical sources, these are taken up and developed in such a way as to endorse rather than to abstract from the living existing self's engagement in its world.

We see this in the French existentialists' preoccupation with imagination – with ways of seeing and being seen – and, in some cases, with seeking sources of value after the death of God. Whereas Nietzsche dismissed Christianity's ascetic ideal as a perpetual saying no to life, many existentialists saw in mysticism a way of saying yes to it – even in the face of nothingness, injustice, and absurdity.

If, as a result of this transformative appropriation of mystical sources, what we arrive at is a kind of worldly or life-affirming mysticism rather than a mystical flight from the world, however, this doesn't of itself rob the term 'mystical' of all purchase. In fact, it can be seen as the reanimation of themes deeply embedded in Christian (and some non-Christian) mystical literature itself. Against the flow of much medieval commentary, it is Meister Eckhart himself, generally regarded as epitomizing the most radical kind of Christian mysticism, who declares Martha, busy about her household chores, to be preferred to Mary, sitting at the feet of the Lord in contemplation of his sublime teaching. A similar fusion of mysticism and worldliness can be tracked through the literature of the modern devotion, the devout life tradition of François de Sales and Archbishop Fénelon. Commentary on Teresa of Avila (including that of Beauvoir) is consistent in pointing to the evidence of her practical engagement in the world, and she herself repeatedly downplays the importance of the ecstasies and visions that she certainly did experience. In this regard it is perhaps a paradox of the history of ideas that the very way in which post-Kantian Romanticism took up and popularized the idea of mysticism lost or occluded what had been an important and even crucial dimension in the late medieval and early modern development of Christian spirituality. In returning mysticism to the world, the existentialists returned it to where it has always belonged, to what French philosophers of the twentieth century defined as the sphere of 'action'. But as far as Christianity is concerned, the roots of this are clearly to be found in the New Testament itself, for how can we say we love God whom we have not seen if we do not love the brother and sister whom we do see?

This has been an essentially historical study, but we may be allowed to conclude by raising the question as to whether the story we have told has had any continuing impact. Certainly, the wider post-war culture was often indiscriminate in mixing 'existentialist' and 'mystical' themes, with or without direct reference to historical philosophical and religious sources. We noted in the introduction that Colin Wilson, a significant popularizer of existentialism in Britain, linked it to figures such as William Blake. At the same time, in the 1950s, writers like Jack Kerouac mixed existential themes of alienation and outsiderdom with mystical experience in ways that anticipate the counterculture of the 1960s – and although these mostly relate to Buddhism, Christian themes are also apparent.[1] Another contemporary, the popular monastic writer Thomas Merton (who also mixed Christian with Buddhist references), drew on existential accounts of anxiety and nothingness in describing the inner development of the soul.[2] Such writers and the movements with which they are associated live on in the burgeoning literature of spirituality, Christian, Buddhist, and secular, which continues to reflect both existential and mystical currents, even if philosophical precision and explicit references are (in the nature of the case) lacking. But we might also draw attention to another line of development, leading through the 'secular' or 'worldly' or 'religionless' Christianity of the post-war period, to which

Buber, Berdyaev, and Tillich were major contributors. In exponents of this new kind of Christianity, both mystical and philosophical antecedents were often downplayed, as is the case in the writings of Dietrich Bonhoeffer, a key point of reference in this literature. In others, such as Ronald Gregor Smith in Britain or Thomas Altizer in the United States, both existentialist and mystical sources are clearly foregrounded. Precisely because of the avowedly worldly nature of this theology, many of its inheritors are living thoroughly secular lives – yet it is maybe thanks to them that references to, for example, Angelus Silesius and Meister Eckhart continue to turn up in surprising places.

And, of course, there are the existentialist writers themselves. Even if it is now a long time since they could individually or collectively be taken as representing the avant-garde of contemporary thought, they remain widely read – and not only in the academy. In varying degrees, all have a continuing presence in cultural life and are finding new generations of readers. Whether or not their mystical sources are noticed (and it is clear that they are often not) it is, we think, impossible fully to understand their accounts of the human condition without reference to them. There is undoubtedly much work still to be done in further expanding the account we have given, but it is, we believe, a beginning that is worth following.

These comments prompt a further and final reflection. Contemporary society is strongly divided between those who insist that ours is a secular age and those who plead for the legitimacy of religious insights in shaping our common world. What the history of existentialism's complex relation to its mystical sources strongly suggests is that the line of division between secular and religious is by no means as clear as many think. If what we have just claimed about the worldly character of Christian mysticism is true, it implies that, in fact, the more religious or the more mystical a given individual is, the more they will be involved in the world and attendant to its claims and obligations. In this respect Buber's turn from mysticism to worldliness is paradigmatic – only Buber himself misdescribed it when he saw it as a matter of renouncing mysticism.

Pointing up false dichotomies is no mere intellectual exercise. The assumed line of division between secular and religious plays out at multiple levels of contemporary life: in politics, in education, in debating the major moral questions of the day, and even in the funding of university research. Fully to realize the possibilities given us in our being human, we need to be maximally open to all that our intellectual and religious traditions have bequeathed us. Fully cognizant of their manifold differences, the figures we have considered are, for the most part, paradigmatic in the way in which they pioneered ways of being modern while at the same time drawing on what some of their contemporaries regarded as no more than useless history. But as many tales, legends, and teachings suggest, it is often in the detritus that the jewel of great price is to be found.

Notes

1 See, for example, chapter 19 of *The Dharma Bums*, which recounts the narrator's thoughts during Christmas. Jack Kerouac, *The Dharma Bums* (New York: New American Library, 1958).
2 See, for example, Thomas Merton, *Contemplative Prayer* (London: Darton, Longman, and Todd, 1973).

Works cited

Kerouac, Jack, *The Dharma Bums* (New York: New American Library, 1958).
Merton, Thomas, *Contemplative Prayer* (London: Darton, Longman, and Todd, 1973).

Index

ARGONAUTA

PERIPECIAS MODERNAS ENTRE EL OCÉANO Y EL CAMBIO CLIMÁTICO

PABLO RODRÍGUEZ ROS

Raspabook

Primera edición, septiembre 2020

www.raspabook.com
correo@raspabook.com

I.S.B.N.: 978-84-121458-2-3
D.L.: MU 618-2020

Edición a cargo de Raspabook

A mis hermanos y primos,
por el tiempo que estas vivencias nos han restado

«Cuando la culpa es de todos,
la culpa no es de nadie».
Concepción Arenal

«Cuando emprendas tu viaje a Ítaca
pide que el camino sea largo,
lleno de aventuras, lleno
de experiencias».
Ítaca, *Constantino Cavafis*

«Nuestra imaginación solo se
sorprende por lo grande, pero el amante
de la filosofía natural debe reflexionar
igualmente sobre las pequeñas cosas.»
Alexander von Humbolt

«-No es encesario haber estado en
un sitio para saberlo todo sobre él
—respondía Abdul—; si no, los marineros
serían más sabios que los teólogos.»
Baudolino, *Humberto Eco.*

Índice

PRÓLOGO

ANDREU ESCRIVÀ

Conocí a Pablo Rodríguez Ros casi por azar, como casi todo lo que sucede en la vida y vale la pena. El algoritmo de Twitter nos juntó hace ya bastantes años, y a partir de ahí empezamos a hablar a través de la red social. Muy pronto me di cuenta de que compartíamos desvelos científicos, preocupaciones políticas y sociales, esperanzas climáticas y también un sentido del humor que nos permitía afrontarlo (¡menos mal!) entre risas y bromas. Aunque suene a psicología de taza de café, resultó evidente que conectamos.

En febrero de 2019 coincidimos en Barcelona, otra vez por azar, y pude por fin conocer a Pablo en persona, estrecharle la mano y darle un abrazo; gestos que ahora parecen casi de ciencia ficción, en este mundo que transita a tientas hacia la nueva normalidad que nos ha impuesto la COVID-19. También nos encontramos ese mismo año en la Cumbre del Clima COP25 de Madrid, aunque yo iba desde València y él desde California. Nos quedamos charlando un buen rato, en una cafetería inhóspita e incómoda, tomando un refresco aguado en una inexplicable penumbra, en lo que quizás era un símil no buscado de la cumbre climática. No sé cuántas horas estuvimos hablando, pero sí sé que me dijo que estaba escribiendo un libro. Me alegré, y mucho, porque si algo he aprendido a detectar después de muchos años de conversaciones con gente a la que apenas conozco en persona es quién tiene algo que contar, y quién no. Pablo, se le notaba a la legua, tenía una historia. O eso pensaba yo entonces, porque hoy sé que en realidad tiene varias.

Argonauta no es un libro de divulgación científica, tampoco uno de viajes. No es un libro activista, ni uno de historia. Tampoco un ensayo sobre el cambio climático. Es todo eso, y mucho más. Hay poesía, hay manifiestos del plancton (¡en serio!), hay ciencia que se puede tocar con los dedos, muchas olas y una preocupación latente por el cambio global y el impacto de las actividades humanas sobre la naturaleza. Y mucho humor, por supuesto, porque es un ingrediente fundamental para contar cualquier historia. El libro que tienes en tus manos es un relato vital y honesto, en el que el autor se desnuda a cada página (literalmente, incluso; espérate a leer sobre los preparativos del viaje a la Antártida) y se percibe el latido que le ha empujado a escribirlo: enseñar, concienciar, compartir. Y seguro que disfrutar mientras lo hacía.

Pablo estudió Ciencias Ambientales, como yo, y si uno se fija se puede descubrir cómo aflora el ambientólogo que lleva dentro en cada capítulo, mezclando historia con bioquímica, geología con leyendas o a Bradley Cooper con pólipos y zooxantelas. En un mundo diverso que se enfrenta al reto poliédrico del cambio climático —más bien, incluso, cambio global, como acertadamente puntualiza— aquello que conseguirá que tengamos éxito no es solo la ciencia, sino la capacidad de transmitirla, de remar todos juntos en la misma dirección, de señalar a los culpables sin dejar de calafatear un barco en el que quepamos todos. Y sin tampoco olvidar la reivindicación, constante y sentida, de la ciencia. Porque este es un libro de ciencia, en el sentido más amplio del término. Es un libro cuyo motor se alimenta de curiosidad, la del autor y la del lector.

Pablo tiene la virtud de transmitir de forma palpable algo tan etéreo como el nerviosismo antes de una expedición científica. Incluso yo, que hice la tesis en ecología de lagunas de agua dulce, sentía una cierta y vaga emoción recorriéndome el cuerpo antes de subir al coche, camino a Albacete, Castellón o Teruel. ¡Cómo no va a hormiguearte todo el cuerpo si al día siguiente embarcas rumbo a la Antártida! El libro se convierte, en algunos párrafos, en el mejor alegato en pro de la ciencia que pueda existir: el que consiste en humanizarla. Frente a discursos alienantes e incapaces de conectar con la gente, centrados en la excelencia y alejados de la realidad cotidiana, Pablo abre el foco desde el Mar Menor, que tan bien conoce a nivel ecológico y humano, y nos muestra camarotes, zodiacs, legionarios, albóndigas rusas, copépodos y albatros, madrugones y pingüinos. Es un libro que llega a hacerte pensar que aún hay rincones indómitos en el planeta, que queda mucho por descubrir. Que quizás ya no hay expediciones como las del siglo XIX, pero que sin duda vale la pena seguir explorando e investigando este pedazo de roca (¡y agua!) en el que hemos tenido la suerte de nacer. Y, desde luego, es un libro en el que se aprende, y utilizando la máxima contraria a aquello de «La letra con sangre entra». Aquí el agua marina refresca conceptos y, casi sin darnos cuenta, estamos aprendiendo cómo se muestrea una columna de agua en medio del Atlántico, los procesos que llevan a la formación de las nubes o la amenaza que suponen las especies invasoras en latitudes polares.

Reconozco también que es un libro que, pese a provocarme una tremenda envidia, me ha servido para viajar sin traspasar las paredes de mi casa. Lo he leído durante las semanas del confinamiento debido a la COVID-19, encerrado en un piso de ciudad viendo cómo pasaba por delante de mi ventana la primavera. Si bien uno llega a empatizar con Pablo en su particular confinamiento en los distintos camarotes de este libro, es aún más intensa la sensación de libertad que provoca su vívida descripción de los animales y paisajes con los que se encuentra.

Lo que cuenta el autor en este libro me ha evocado, a ratos, a algunas biografías contenidas en el libro de 1880 de Gaston Tissandier, Los mártires de la ciencia. Allí están descritas, con todos los pormenores, las trayectorias vitales de distintos exploradores que se embarcaron una y otra vez en aventuras hacia lo desconocido. Que querían llegar más alto, más profundo, más lejos. Afortunadamente, Pablo no es un mártir, sino un millenial con muchas ganas de escribir y poderosos aliados: la Biodramina y el café. Estoy seguro de que seguirá navegando por los mares o incluso tierra adentro, y de que la inquietud científica y las ganas de escribir le acompañarán siempre. Quizá en el siglo XXI las expediciones no se tiñen de la épica de otras épocas, pero desde luego sí de compañerismo, diversión, emoción e incluso miedo. De humanidad y descubrimientos, de curiosidad permanente. De todo lo que encontrarás en este libro.

Escribía Juan Goytisolo, en *Campos de Níjar*: «En el horizonte, el mar es solo una franja de plomo derretido». Un plomo con el que Pablo ha forjado un relato vibrante y consistente, capaz de resistir el oleaje y anclar el lector a sus palabras. Ponte cómodo, porque en cuanto pases la página, vas a empezar a notar el oleaje. Palabra.

València, 10 de junio de 2020

Andreu Escrivà es ambientólogo, Doctor en Biodiversidad y técnico ambiental de la Fundació València Clima i Energia, del Ajuntament de València. También es autor de los libros *Aún no es tarde: Claves para entender y frenar el cambio climático* (PUV, 2016) y *Y ahora yo qué hago* (Capitán Swing, 2020).

OS PREGUNTARÉIS CÓMO HE (HEMOS) LLEGADO HASTA AQUÍ

«Los valores de la ciencia y los valores de la democracia son concordantes, en muchos casos indistinguibles».
Carl Sagan (1934-1996), científico y divulgador

Diciembre de 2019. A unos diez mil metros de altitud, sobrevolando el océano Atlántico rumbo a España desde América, no hago más que reflexionar acerca de los retos que tenemos que afrontar como sociedad global en el presente siglo XXI. Uno de estos retos, el mayor de todos según Naciones Unidas, es el motivo de mi viaje: el cambio climático. Y es que nos equivocaríamos si pensáramos que esto del cambio climático va únicamente de osos polares y de lo bien o mal que nos cae la líder adolescente Greta Thunberg que insiste en algo tan «radical» y ofensivo como que la política escuche y haga caso a la ciencia. Sin embargo, no podemos perder el tiempo desmintiendo a los «terraplanistas del aire», ya que el cambio climático es un problema del presente y, si no se producen grandes cambios cuanto antes, todo apunta a que seguirá siendo un problema para generaciones futuras. Es por ello por lo que muchos decidimos dedicarnos profesionalmente al análisis de este gran reto global, en mi caso desde el estudio de los mares y océanos del planeta. Como aquellos Argonautas (Argó: nombre de la nave, naútēs: marinero) de la mitología griega a los que se enviaba a un viaje lleno de peligros para resolver una tarea, a priori, imposible, los científicos trabajamos para conseguir nuestro objetivo de combatir el cambio climático sirviéndonos también de nuestras habilidades y aliados inesperados. Tenemos por delante el reto de descubrir y comprender fenómenos desconocidos a bordo de nuestras argo, desde las más evidentes como los buques oceanográficos modernos hasta las más inesperadas como la Cumbre de Naciones Unidas sobre el Cambio Climático (COP25).

He interrumpido la escritura de mi tesis doctoral para poner rumbo a Madrid y participar en la COP25 como observador acreditado por Naciones Unidas e integrante de la Delegación de la Universidad de California, junto a representantes de todos los actores involucrados en la lucha contra el cambio climático: gobiernos, ONG, investigadores, empresas, etc. Todos ellos reunidos en una COP que ha sido bautizada como la COP Azul debido a su compromiso con la conservación de los mares y océanos y su papel como agentes clave contra el cambio climático.

La humanidad depende de manera directa o indirecta de los mares y océanos, que cubren casi tres cuartas partes de la superficie terrestre, alrededor del 70% de la superficie total, y contienen el 97% del agua de la Tierra. Los océanos son, por tanto, parte irrenunciable y esencial de nuestro hogar. Este planeta Tierra, que deberíamos de llamar «Océano», es fascinante, peligroso y complejo a partes iguales. Si solo pensásemos en el océano como una masa de agua, tenderíamos a creer que es parte de la hidrosfera; pero también hay seres que lo habitan (biosfera), nutrientes químicos que sustentan los ecosistemas (geosfera) y, a veces hay cobertura de hielo (criosfera), que tiene un papel fundamental en la regulación del clima global (atmósfera). En definitiva, la relación existente entre el agua, la vida y nuestro planeta es compleja, pero científicamente tangible y es, posiblemente, nuestro mayor bien.

La vida surgió en el agua de los océanos y, aún hoy en día, el mar es vital para las sociedades humanas; de hecho, la mayoría de la población mundial vive a menos de trescientos cincuenta kilómetros del mar. Sin embargo, aunque es una contradicción de dimensiones bíblicas, nuestros mares y océanos sufren de manera constante la desidia de aquellos cuyas sociedades dependen de estos. Y, como es de esperar, al final todos acabamos, y acabaremos, pagando las consecuencias. Y el precio a pagar es tanto en euros, dólares, etc.; como en otras magnitudes no tan fáciles de cuantificar. Por ello, cualquier impacto sobre estos y sus dinámicas, inevitablemente provoca un cambio en la sociedad humana. Queda claro que a todos nos interesa que estos impactos sean mínimos para el planeta Tierra, ya que como suele decirse *al hogar, como a la nave, le conviene la mar suave*.

Volver a Europa también significa dejar mi vida en Estados Unidos y mi lugar de trabajo en la playa de La Jolla (San Diego, California) durante unas semanas. En esta zona costera, los surfistas comparten «hábitat» con especies como tiburones leopardo, rayas, delfines, cormoranes, pelícanos y leones marinos. Justo delante de esta singular fauna está Scripps Institution of Oceanography (Universidad de California San Diego), la institución líder en oceanografía y cambio climático de la costa oeste de Estados Unidos, donde trabajo. Desde mi departamento, se ve el «muelle de Scripps» adentrarse varios cientos de metros en el océano Pacífico con numerosos aparatos e instrumentación científica para medir, entre otros, los cambios de temperatura y salinidad del agua. Aquí, ciencia, naturaleza y seres humanos conviven desde hace más de cien años en un escenario que ha sido testimonio de gran parte del conocimiento que poseemos acerca de cómo funcionan los océanos y su papel en el planeta Tierra. Fue en Scripps donde se empezaron a medir las concentraciones de CO_2 en la atmósfera desde el Observatorio de Mauna Loa (Hawaii) en 1956, como parte de un proyecto de investigación liderado por el científico Charles David Keeling. Esta molécula de dos átomos de oxígeno y uno de carbono es, posiblemente, la más mencionada en los medios de comunicación, ya que es la principal causa del calentamiento global provocado por las emisiones procedentes de la quema de combustibles fósiles. Y, por desgracia, va a seguir siendo una molécula que vamos a tener «hasta en la sopa», pues su concentración atmosférica sigue creciendo de forma ininterrumpida. Como consecuencia de ello, la temperatura media global del planeta ya ha aumentado 1°C con respecto a niveles preindustriales. El aumento de 1°C es un promedio global, es decir, en unos lugares ha aumentado menos, incluso disminuido, y en otros ha aumentado más de 1°C. Por ejemplo, en la región ártica este calentamiento supone entre el doble y el triple que la media global, es decir, entre 2°C y 3°C. Además, el propio calentamiento se está acelerando, cada año que pasa no solamente nos calentamos un poco más, sino que lo hacemos más rápido; el ritmo actual es de un aumento de 0,2°C por década.

Muchos habréis oído hablar del Acuerdo de París (2015) que se firmó en la COP21. Este acuerdo pretende evitar que la temperatura media global aumente 1,5°C en los próximos años y evitar una subida de 2°C, que es el verdadero camino que llevamos. Sobre todo, si tenemos en cuenta que, si las emisiones continúan al ritmo actual, el temido aumento de 1,5°C sucedería entre 2030 y 2052. Como podréis suponer, es un objetivo ciertamente ambicioso. Otra cosa que hay que tener en cuenta es que el calentamiento originado por las emisiones de gases de efecto invernadero no cesaría de manera automática si parásemos de emitir, de la misma manera que si redujésemos nuestras emisiones la temperatura no disminuiría a la misma velocidad. De hecho, el calentamiento que ya hemos causado persistirá durante siglos y milenios, con las implicaciones que esto tendrá para la subida del nivel del mar o el aumento en la frecuencia e intensidad de fenómenos meteorológicos extremos, como lluvias torrenciales. Por ello, el problema del Acuerdo de París es que no es suficiente para limitar el calentamiento global a 1,5°C. Incluso si se aplicaran medidas ambiciosas a gran escala a partir de 2030, se prevé que el Acuerdo de París nos lleve inexorablemente hasta un aumento de 3°C para el año 2100 respecto a niveles preindustriales.

Muchos os estaréis preguntando que por qué es importante limitar este aumento de temperatura a 1,5°C. Es más, que suba la temperatura media a 2°C o a 3°C tampoco es tanto, ¿no? Es un grado y medio más, como mucho. El problema es que esto no es tan simple y la realidad no es muy halagüeña. Si tuviera que utilizar un símil diría que todos hemos tenido fiebre alguna vez en nuestra vida y sabemos que un aumento en nuestra temperatura corporal de 37°C a 39°C, pese a ser una diferencia de tan solo 2°C, supone un gran cambio. Del mismo modo, muchos de los riesgos asociados al cambio climático serían mayores con un aumento de 2°C que de 1,5°C. Estos riesgos son: el aumento de la frecuencia e intensidad de fenómenos meteorológicos extremos como tormentas y lluvias torrenciales, la destrucción de la biodiversidad, los impactos negativos en los ecosistemas, la ganadería y la agricultura, en los suministros de agua, en la salud y la seguridad humanas, en las infraestructuras y en el crecimiento económico. Además, entre un aumento de 1,5°C y 2°C se superarían muchos puntos de no retorno (o *tipping points*, en inglés) de nuestro sistema climático. ¿Qué es esto? Pues límites en algunos de los componentes del sistema climático de nuestro planeta que si se superan no tienen marcha atrás y estaremos a merced de sus efectos. Esto originaría pérdidas irreversibles en muchos ecosistemas, así como cambios en la cobertura helada de algunas regiones del planeta que provocarían que el nivel del mar subiera incluso varios metros en una escala de cientos o miles de años.

Incluso si consiguiéramos limitar el calentamiento a 1,5°C, muchos de los impactos serán irreversibles y continuarán a partir del año 2100. Medio grado importa, no podemos olvidarlo. Por ejemplo, con un aumento de 1,5°C, se reducirá entre el 70% y el 90% la superficie ocupada por los arrecifes de coral de aguas cálidas. En cambio, si este aumento es de 2°C prácticamente desaparecerán, al reducirse más del 99% su área de distribución. Además, en concreto, la región mediterránea también sufrirá los impactos del cambio climático; de hecho, constituye uno de los ejemplos más claros de alta vulnerabilidad. Principalmente estaríamos hablando del aumento de las sequías fruto de la disminución de la escorrentía (agua de lluvia que discurre por la superficie) en un 17% si alcanzamos el aumento de temperatura media global de 2°C, y en un 9% si lo limitamos a 1,5°C ; así como del aumento de la evapotranspiración por dicho aumento de temperatura. Además, fácilmente podemos deducir que esto no nos saldrá gratis, solo hay que pensar en sectores clave para la economía como la agricultura o el turismo. De hecho, un reciente estudio apunta a que el cambio climático en España puede suponer un coste de hasta el 12% de su PIB.

Así las cosas, limitar el aumento a 1,5°C de temperatura supone una ventana de oportunidad para poder adaptarnos y mitigar los efectos del cambio climático, sobre todo en las regiones y poblaciones más vulnerables. En general, limitar el calentamiento a 1,5°C implica realizar una transición energética/ecológica en todos los países a corto plazo. Lo cual significa cambiar el funcionamiento de los sistemas de energía, transporte, etc.; así como los usos del suelo. Asimismo, sería necesaria una reducción en el consumo de energía, de recursos materiales y de consumo de alimentos que tengan una menor huella de carbono. Por otro lado, la tecnología para retirar CO_2 de la atmósfera aún no ha demostrado su eficacia a escala global, por lo que es prematuro contar con ella, aunque se incluye en algunas proyecciones de cambio climático. Por lo tanto, tal vez estamos, de nuevo, infraestimando sus efectos negativos. Para limitar el calentamiento a 1,5°C, mientras seguimos la senda del desarrollo sostenible y de la erradicación de la pobreza (no podemos combatir el cambio climático dejando en la estacada a los más débiles), son necesarias transiciones que únicamente serán posibles si invertimos en adaptación y mitigación, nuevos instrumentos políticos, aceleración de la innovación científica y tecnológica (mediante el incremento de la inversión en ciencia) y cambios en las conductas. Para ello, necesitamos cooperar internacionalmente y reforzar las capacidades institucionales de las autoridades locales y nacionales, pero también de la sociedad civil, el sector privado, las ciudades, las comunidades locales y los grupos indígenas. Se necesita, por tanto, de una colaboración transversal e internacional que no tiene precedentes.

Y esto es precisamente lo que persigue la COP, una cita que nos permite mostrar a todas aquellas personas interesadas, desde políticos europeos hasta representantes de pueblos indígenas amazónicos, cuáles son los nuevos avances en ciencias del mar, para qué sirven y cómo nos ayudan a comprender mejor algunos procesos de nuestro planeta. Resulta sorprendente ver que la ciencia y la tecnología tienen un potencial enorme para solucionar problemas en lugares lejanos a donde han sido concebidas. Así, la instrumentación oceanográfica utilizada en Scripps, en la costa de California, puede ser adaptada para poder solucionar problemas de contaminación del agua en lugares como Brasil. Además, los científicos también participamos en algunos debates de la toma de decisiones como asesores expertos en el clima y el océano. Y es que muchos no nos cansamos de insistir en que la lucha, la mitigación y la adaptación del cambio climático es un asunto esencialmente político. La comunidad científica internacional lleva décadas repitiendo lo mismo basándose en la mejor evidencia posible, pero, desgraciadamente, la valentía política para tomar las decisiones vitales casi siempre brilla por su ausencia, como ha ocurrido en España con el Prestige, en Galicia, o el Mar Menor, en la Región de Murcia.

Sin embargo, en la lucha contra el cambio climático no estamos solos. La naturaleza posee diversos mecanismos conocidos, y otros aún desconocidos, para poder paliar sus efectos. No podemos olvidar que el cambio climático es un problema principalmente para el ser humano, y no tanto para el planeta Tierra que tiene sus propios mecanismos de autorregulación y está preparado para cuando nosotros hayamos «desaparecido», si es que eso llega a suceder. Sin embargo, este aprendizaje de la naturaleza requiere de un esfuerzo científico colectivo de estudio y comprensión. En esta línea, los mares y océanos del planeta juegan numerosos papeles clave; por ello son (o deberían de ser) nuestros mejores aliados. Por ejemplo, son capaces de captar parte del exceso de CO_2 atmosférico derivado de las actividades humanas o el calor (energía) en exceso que es consecuencia del calentamiento global. Sin embargo, para poder captar este exceso de CO_2 de manera eficiente, el océano debe gozar de buena salud y esto solo se consigue si garantizamos la conservación de la biodiversidad marina, la disminución de la contaminación y la reducción de la emisión de gases de efecto invernadero.

No obstante, muchas de estas herramientas con las que los océanos nos ayudan a luchar contra el cambio climático están llegando al límite a una velocidad nunca antes vista. El primero y más evidente es que el océano también se está calentando, no solo la atmósfera. Desde 1970, el océano ha absorbido más del 90% del exceso de calor en el sistema climático fruto del calentamiento global. Al absorber este calor es cuando el océano se calienta. Y no solo eso, sino que desde 1993 la velocidad de calentamiento se ha multiplicado por dos, es decir, el calentamiento se está acelerando. Por otro lado, las olas de calor marinas (sí, también hay olas de calor en el océano, aunque no oigamos a los peces quejarse) han duplicado su frecuencia y aumentado su intensidad desde 1982, lo cual tiene impactos significativos sobre, por ejemplo, los corales de aguas cálidas, pero los problemas no se quedan solo en el calor. Como os decía, el océano tiene una gran capacidad para absorber CO_2 atmosférico. Y es tan eficiente que desde 1980 ha absorbido entre el 20% y el 30% de las emisiones de CO_2 realizadas por el ser humano, pero esto no está exento de consecuencias. Cuando el CO_2 pasa al agua marina se agrava el proceso de acidificación, así como la disminución del oxígeno presente en el agua. Además, no podemos olvidarnos de la estrella de la corona del cambio climático y los océanos: la subida del nivel del mar. Pues el ritmo al que asciende el nivel del mar, sorpresa, también se está acelerando. Esto se debe a varios factores, principalmente a la pérdida de hielo en lugares como Groenlandia o la Antártida, pero también a un fenómeno del que se habla poco: la expansión térmica del agua. Veréis, es muy simple. El agua marina es un fluido y, como tal, cuando se calienta aumenta en volumen, es decir, se expande. Por lo tanto, si los océanos se calientan, se expanden. Y si se expanden, sube el nivel del mar.

Obviamente todos estos procesos tienen sus impactos sobre los seres vivos que viven en los océanos. Así, desde la década de los cincuenta del pasado siglo, muchas especies marinas han comenzado a migrar desde el ecuador hacia los polos en búsqueda de aguas más frías. Sin olvidar los impactos que sufren los ecosistemas costeros, de los más sensibles al cambio climático, fruto de la combinación de la subida del nivel del mar, el aumento de las temperaturas o la acidificación. Además, aparte de los seres vivos marinos, los humanos también sufren sus efectos. Para las comunidades humanas, conforme más tiempo pasa, más complejo es actuar y los esfuerzos e iniciativas de adaptación y mitigación van quedando desfasados progresivamente.

Los ecosistemas marinos y la criosfera nos proporcionan un sinfín de servicios y funciones sin los cuales no podrían entenderse el pasado y presente desarrollo de la humanidad. Por ello, es vital que se tomen medidas en cuanto a la protección y restauración de dichos ecosistemas, no solo poniendo énfasis en la precaución y la prevención, sino también en el fomento del uso de recursos renovables y en la reducción de los niveles de contaminación actuales. Las comunidades humanas costeras se enfrentan a un riesgo que es principalmente económico. No nos engañemos, no despertaremos un día bajo dos metros de agua por el efecto del calentamiento global. Lo que sí sucederá es que nuestras infraestructuras costeras se verán cada vez más dañadas por fenómenos meteorológicos extremos, como las marejadas ciclónicas que se agravan con la subida del nivel del mar, por lo que no podrán cumplir su función. Evitarlos depende de elaborar respuestas para la subida del nivel de mar y de la protección de ecosistemas costeros que amortigüen fenómenos meteorológicos extremos en zonas vulnerables como los manglares y marismas. Así como, en última instancia, trasladar las poblaciones humanas en otros lugares. Por ejemplo, países como Nueva Zelanda están diseñando programas específicos para acoger a refugiados climáticos que tengan que abandonar islas del Pacífico por la subida del nivel del mar.

Como veis, no estamos hablando de cambios que se hayan producido en cientos de años, estamos narrando fenómenos que se vienen produciendo durante los últimos cuarenta o cincuenta años. Lo importante es tener claro que el problema no radica en el «cambio» *per se*, sino también en la velocidad a la que se produce. Los mares y océanos del planeta son nuestros grandes aliados para luchar contra numerosos de los problemas ambientales del presente, pero no podemos olvidar que también están sufriendo los efectos no solo del cambio climático, sino también de la contaminación, la pérdida de biodiversidad, la sobreexplotación pesquera, etc. Ante este reto la ciencia debe aportar un análisis constante que debe ir actualizándose progresivamente. Desgraciadamente, las acciones políticas no van al mismo ritmo que los avances científicos y esto, en momentos en los que no hay tiempo que perder, es letal tanto para numerosos sistemas humanos como para los ecosistemas naturales. Vivimos tiempos convulsos en los que pese a que la ciencia, por lo general, es valorada por los ciudadanos en los distintos países del mundo, no suele ser escuchada por quienes han de regir los designios de la *argo* en la que todos navegamos: el planeta Tierra.

Por si esto fuera poco, el reto de abordar el cambio climático y otros problemas relacionados con las múltiples crisis ambientales globales es aún más complicado, puesto que nos encontramos en un contexto de auge global de movimientos políticos reaccionarios que niegan el cambio climático y otros problemas ambientales; negando, por tanto, la evidencia científica. Además del beneplácito de muchos líderes políticos que tienen a bien de llegar a acuerdos normalizando y asimilando estos postulados pseudocientíficos. Y es que es bastante contradictorio, a la par que imposible, intentar solucionar un problema yendo de la mano de aquellos que niegan la existencia de este. Urge desconfiar, en general, de aquellos que se oponen a la ciencia, pues es algo recurrente en la historia y suele ser el lado equivocado. Ya nos lo advirtió en su día el científico y divulgador Carl Sagan: «los valores de la ciencia y los valores de la democracia son concordantes, en muchos casos indistinguibles». Así pues, no es de extrañar que quienes atenten contra una, tarde o temprano acabarán atentando también contra la otra. Y es aquí donde todas las formas de vida de la Tierra perdemos, incluidas las de mares y océanos, pero, sobre todo, los seres humanos. Y, entre ellos, especialmente los más débiles.

Para ayudarnos a mejorar nuestra comprensión del cambio climático como fenómeno y proponer soluciones basadas en la evidencia científica más rigurosa, científicos y científicas de todo el mundo publican sus investigaciones cada día. Con el objetivo de hacer accesible todo el conocimiento que generan, el Panel Intergubernamental de Expertos sobre el Cambio Climático (IPCC), una entidad científica perteneciente a la Organización Meteorológica Mundial (OMM) y el Programa de Naciones Unidas para el Medio Ambiente (PNUMA) creada en 1988, se encarga de proporcionar información objetiva, clara, equilibrada y neutral del estado actual de los conocimientos sobre el cambio climático a los responsables políticos y otros sectores interesados. Es decir, recopila toda la ciencia conocida de este tema mes a mes, año a año, y la transmite a otros sectores que mayoritariamente no pertenecen al sector científico, como el político. El IPCC emite informes cada varios años. En septiembre de 2019, publicó el *Informe Especial sobre cambio climático y océanos y criosfera*, que evalúa el estado actual de los océanos en cuanto a los impactos del cambio climático, pero también en su capacidad de lucha contra el propio cambio climático. El próximo informe del IPCC, el denominado AR6 de 2021 está en camino y no es nada halagüeño, pero mientras lo esperamos os voy contando qué pinta tiene el panorama. Es posible que cuando muchos de los lectores de este libro lean estas líneas, dicho informe ya haya visto la luz y, como es de esperar, todo será un poco más negro de lo que voy a exponer a continuación. Así que intentad leer estas líneas con la melancolía de lo que pudo haberse evitado, y que dicha melancolía alimente la esperanza contra el cambio climático. Y ojalá sirva esto como un revulsivo en la conciencia de muchos ciudadanos que les inste a movilizarse, de alguna de las múltiples maneras posibles, para luchar y exigir las medidas urgentes que necesitamos.

Tras unas semanas de intensas negociaciones, la COP25 va llegando a su fin (si me permitís la metáfora futbolística) en el segundo tiempo de la prórroga del partido de fútbol más importante que hemos jugado nunca: la lucha contra cambio climático. Y nadie quiere llegar a los penaltis. ¿O sí? En mi humilde opinión, jugárselo todo en los penaltis no es buena idea. La historia nos ha demostrado que la épica es algo que no suele acabar bien. Escribo estas líneas desde la Residencia de Estudiantes de Madrid, en la que residieron figuras como Federico García Lorca, José Ortega y Gasset, Luis Buñuel o Salvador Dalí, tras otra jornada intensa en la cumbre y mientras los compromisos ambiciosos necesarios para no superar el aumento de temperatura media global de 1,5°C siguen sin llegar. En base a lo que dicen los informes científicos del IPCC, estamos seguros de que se nos acaba el tiempo. En el minuto ciento dieciséis de la prórroga, sigue sin llegar un Iniesta que meta el gol decisivo para la victoria.

Es más, no parece que exista ningún Iniesta del cambio climático. Nuestra última esperanza es el tiempo añadido de la prórroga, es decir, la COP26 aplazada a 2021 por la COVID-19. Allí veremos si la década que acabamos de empezar es la de la lucha contra el cambio climático o es otro tramo del tobogán sobre el que llevamos décadas deslizándonos.

Sin renunciar a la esperanza, lo que viene en las siguientes páginas es una narración de diez años de experiencia de investigación de los mares y océanos, y su relación con el cambio climático y otros problemas ambientales, por muchos de los rincones de nuestro planeta. Abordaremos numerosos procesos y fenómenos naturales, desde una óptica científica, pero sin olvidarnos del aspecto humano, para poder entender los impactos de la crisis ambiental global en todas sus dimensiones. Nos introduciremos en el mundo de la investigación y exploración científica contemporánea, ahondando en las penurias y alegrías de poder dedicarse a una de las profesiones más fascinantes del mundo, pero con la idiosincrasia de hacerlo en el siglo XXI. Todas las historias de ciencia o exploración científica que merecen ser recordadas empiezan o acaban con algún momento épico. A veces, consiste en una serie de coincidencias imposibles que virtuosamente llevan a sus protagonistas a lugares o eventos insospechados. Otras veces, sin embargo, se da pie a la aventura tras varios infortunios que siempre, por supuesto, acabarán bien. Esta historia, en cambio, no es ninguna de ellas. Todo sucede de manera bastante normal, incluso banal. Los accidentes, las decisiones y el azar a veces nos llevan adonde queremos ir; y, muchas otras, adonde no teníamos pensado. Esta es una historia de cómo la curiosidad, la pasión por el medio ambiente y la ciencia pueden empujarte, a veces de forma poco glamurosa, a los confines de la Tierra, haciendo honor al título de este libro. Aunque también es un viaje a los enclaves geográficos más cercanos, ya que los descubrimientos y el aprendizaje de la naturaleza, en ciencia y exploración científica, se pueden encontrar hasta en los lugares más comunes. Tomaos esta narración como una invitación a descubrir una pequeña parte del conocimiento científico y de los lugares más remotos de la Tierra que no suelen aparecer en las narraciones científicas habituales, pero, sobre todo, os emplazo a acompañarme en algunas peripecias que nunca antes han sido narradas, puesto que le han sucedido a un pequeño grupo de personas. Bienvenidos a este viaje moderno por los mares y océanos de la Tierra.

HORIZONTE DOBLE

«(...) Las praderas azules de las aguas,
y la tierra mollar que el sol embebe.

Una sola mirada abarca el todo:
el milagro del pan y de los peces.
Andando está el pastor sobre las aguas,
y el árbol de su cruz muy cerca crece (...)».

Los poemas de Mar Menor, *Carmen Conde*

La primavera acababa de llegar al Campo de Cartagena. Las margaritas llenaban las lindes de los campos de almendros, que ya habían florecido hacía semanas, y el tomillo y el romero se preparaban para lo mismo. Las primeras lluvias de la primavera habían despertado a los caracoles que con el frío de la mañana aparecían cubiertos de gotas de rocío. A los frutos de la sabina mora, o ciprés de Cartagena (*Tetraclinis articulata*), aún les quedaban unos meses para madurar. El 1 de abril de 1941, Paco Martínez se levantó muy temprano por la mañana, como casi siempre. Sin embargo, aquella vez tenía motivos para el optimismo. Tras una vida de calamidades, trabajos esclavos y luchar en la Guerra Civil, por fin encontró el trabajo que él definía como su gran objetivo vital: ser fogonero, concretamente del Tren Chicharra, llamado así por el ruido que hacía en marcha y lo lento que iba (una media de veinte kilómetros por hora). Se trataba de un viejo tren de vapor que hacía el trayecto Cartagena-Los Blancos y que recorría parte del Campo de Cartagena pasando por el municipio de La Unión.

A lo largo de su trayecto, el Tren Chicharra transportaba tanto a trabajadores de las minas de la Sierra Minera de Cartagena y La Unión como a los habitantes de los pequeños pueblos agrícolas de la zona. Por aquel trabajo, Paco Martínez obtenía un salario de 2400 pesetas al año; una «fortuna» con la que lo primero que hizo fue comprar materiales para fabricarse un mueble en el que guardar garbanzos, judías, arroz, lentejas y de todo lo que pudo. La agricultura predominante en aquella época era la de secano, puesto que el clima de la zona es el correspondiente a una región semiárida. Muchos de los habitantes de la zona, sin embargo, también se sustentaban de la abundante pesca que les proporcionada un lugar único que tenían muy cerca: el Mar Menor. Y es que la comarca del Campo de Cartagena no podía, ni puede, entenderse sin la relación entre pesca, agricultura y minería.

Lo que escribo de Paco Martínez me lo contaron de pequeño porque yo soy uno de sus bisnietos. Sin embargo, hoy en día, no escribo estas líneas desde el Campo de Cartagena, sino desde California, durante la segunda semana del mes de septiembre de 2019. Mientras que por aquellos pueblos por donde circulaba el Tren Chicharra, el agua discurre con ferocidad. La gota fría o DANA ha originado una serie de tormentas concatenadas que han sido consideradas las más catastróficas del sureste peninsular español en las últimas décadas. Todo el Campo de Cartagena se ha visto afectado, ocasionando muchas pérdidas materiales por las inundaciones y unos daños estimados de varias decenas de millones de euros.

Sin embargo, la catástrofe no solo ha sido económica, sino también ambiental (si es que hay alguna diferencia). Las lluvias han arrastrado todo lo que encontraban a su paso y sus efectos se han podido ver incluso desde los satélites del programa *Copernicus* de la Agencia Espacial Europea. Plásticos de los cultivos de agricultura intensiva que han sustituido a los de secano, metales pesados aún presentes en los suelos como vestigios de siglos de minería y sedimentos, muchos sedimentos. Y todo ello se ha dirigido a lo largo de varias ramblas hacia su lugar natural de descarga: el Mar Menor, cuya costa occidental ha quedado totalmente anegada. Muchas personas han sufrido enormes daños en sus casas y las playas que veían desde sus ventanas han desaparecido. El nivel del agua ha subido tan rápido (unos sesenta centímetros en promedio, en solo seis horas) que al Mar Menor no le ha dado tiempo de evacuarla y en algunas zonas los barcos están sobre los muelles a los que estaban amarrados. Playas desaparecidas a las que se une la tragedia de las costas, a las que llegan peces muertos, caballitos de mar, cangrejos... resultado de una vida que lucha por su supervivencia y que al mismo tiempo se apaga lentamente, la del Mar Menor.

El Mar Menor

El Mar Menor es una laguna costera hipersalina situada en el sureste de la península Ibérica, en el lado oriental del Campo de Cartagena (Región de Murcia), y es considerada la mayor laguna de agua salada de España y una de las más grandes de Europa. Para los oriundos de la zona, tiene un valor especial, pues hemos pasado muchos días de nuestra infancia en sus aguas. De hecho, hace años era bastante común que los ciudadanos de Cartagena fueran en tren o en coche para refrescarse en la laguna durante las vacaciones de verano. Allí recuerdo cómo mi abuelo cogía caracolas y almejas del fondo para comérnoslas, solas o con un buen chorro de limón. El método de recolección era curioso. Mi abuelo no sabía nadar, y sigue sin saber. Sin embargo, las aguas del Mar Menor son tan someras (la profundidad máxima ronda los seis metros) que puedes ir andando sobre el fondo y seleccionando las capturas si miras desde la superficie con las gafas de bucear, y a veces sin ellas. Obviamente esto exponía la espalda de los «valientes» pescadores al sol abrasador del sureste peninsular. Por ello, era común ver a la gente en esa postura tan curiosa, con el agua a la altura de la barriga, llevando una camiseta puesta con el logo de alguna marca comercial internacional. Esta práctica no por ser tradicional significa que no fuera nociva para el ecosistema, ya que muchas especies fueron despareciendo de algunas playas por el «marisqueo» en exceso que realizaban algunos ciudadanos, llegando a llenar varias bolsas de plástico de supermercado de individuos.

El Mar Menor ha sido la cuna, y también el vertedero, de muchísimas culturas (fenicios, cartagineses, romanos, árabes, etc.). Las explotaciones mineras de la zona se remontan siglos atrás en el tiempo y muchos de los residuos generados (la «ganga») de la extracción de los minerales deseados (la «mena») se acababan vertiendo al Mar Menor. Esta explotación minera duró muchos siglos de forma más o menos ininterrumpida, lo que originó que durante todo ese tiempo se fueran vertiendo gran cantidad de metales pesados que se iban acumulando por densidad en el fondo de la laguna. ¿Y quienes viven en los fondos arenosos alimentándose gracias al filtrado del agua que también transportan estas partículas? Efectivamente, moluscos como las caracolas y almejas que nos comíamos de pequeños. Al menos yo ya no lo hago, pero ha habido gente que durante toda su vida ha estado comiendo esporádicamente algunos de estos organismos, pese a que en numerosas ocasiones superan los niveles de metales pesados permitidos para que sean considerados saludables; tal y como se alerta periódicamente desde las administraciones competentes, pero... «¡Y lo buenas que están!», como dirían algunos.

El poco intercambio de aguas del Mar Menor con el Mar Mediterráneo comparado con otras lagunas costeras, debido a que sus tres canales de comunicación son estrechos y someros, hace que la temperatura y la salinidad entre ambas masas de agua sea distinta, pese a estar separados solo por una barrera arenosa de varios cientos de metros de ancho: La Manga del Mar Menor. Sobre esta manga de arena se encuentra una de las mayores aberraciones urbanísticas que se han cometido en la costa española. Esta barrera, ahora prácticamente llena de cemento, era hace unos sesenta años una península formada por dunas llenas de biodiversidad, que también servían de destino ideal para muchas aves migratorias, así como de zona de desove de tortugas marinas, aunque estas especies lo siguen intentando hoy en día. Las islas que rodean La Manga, sobre todo Isla Grossa, son una reminiscencia de lo que fue en el pasado esta zona para las aves. En cuanto a las tortugas marinas, los últimos años se están sucediendo avistamientos nocturnos de tortuga boba (*Caretta caretta*) por parte de los habitantes de la zona cuando se encuentran disfrutando de la actividad nocturna. De hecho, a finales de septiembre de 2019, nacieron en las costas de

Cartagena, concretamente en el Parque Regional de Calblanque, las primeras tortugas boba de los últimos cien años.

Eutrofización (o «empacho» de nutrientes)

Además de todo lo mencionado hasta ahora, existe un riesgo adicional para el Mar Menor bien conocido por los habitantes de la zona: la eutrofización. La eutrofización es un proceso íntimamente relacionado con la disciplina científica llamada «biogeoquímica», siendo uno de sus campos de estudio todos aquellos procesos y efectos consecuencia de incrementar en exceso la concentración en nutrientes en sistemas acuáticos. El proceso sería el siguiente, de manera resumida. Primero, necesitamos un gran aporte de nutrientes en un ecosistema acuático, que puede ser un lago o una laguna costera; por ejemplo, uno que mantenga poco intercambio de agua con sistemas adyacentes como otros lagos o el océano, lo cual hace muy difícil la renovación de sus aguas. Este aporte de nutrientes hace que los productores primarios, principalmente las microalgas del fitoplancton que viven en la superficie del agua, crezcan de manera desmesurada. Este crecimiento en exceso no trae nada bueno para el ecosistema, aunque así lo parezca a primera vista. Lo que sucede a continuación es que estas microalgas copan la superficie impidiendo que la luz solar pase al fondo del sistema acuático. Es decir, la fotosíntesis de las macroalgas y plantas que viven en el fondo se ve muy mermada. Eventualmente, deja de haber fotosíntesis en el fondo, por lo que dichos organismos fotosintéticos mueren, dando paso a que proliferen las bacterias anaeróbicas, es decir, aquellas que basan su metabolismo en otros compuestos que no son el oxígeno, ya que este empieza a escasear. La muerte de estas praderas de macroalgas y plantas de los sistemas acuáticos tiene otros importantes efectos sobre la salud del ecosistema. Uno de ellos, posiblemente el más conocido, es que las larvas de muchas especies de peces, que se refugiaban en estas pequeñas plantas y macroalgas, no tienen donde esconderse y acaban muriendo por falta de comida o sirven de alimento para los peces más grandes.

Hoy en día vivimos en un contexto global de cambio climático, el cual tiene mucho que ver en fenómenos como la eutrofización o los fenómenos meteorológicos extremos, como tormentas o lluvias torrenciales. Sin embargo, ligar estos fenómenos directamente al cambio climático requiere lo que los científicos llamamos «estudios de atribución», por lo que es algo arriesgado plantearlo en estos términos. Sin embargo, lo que sí que sabemos es que la frecuencia e intensidad de los fenómenos meteorológicos extremos aumentarán en todo el mundo, así como la temperatura de las aguas. Imaginemos por un momento esta misma fuerza destructiva que hemos visto con la gota fría en la comarca de Cartagena, qué efectos originaría en un mar cuyo nivel está subiendo, o los efectos de una eutrofización permanente del Mar Menor sobre el turismo, la pesca o la agricultura de la zona.

En septiembre de 2010, aún con diecinueve años, me encontraba cursando tercero de la Licenciatura en Ciencias Ambientales de la Universidad de Murcia. Por aquel entonces, llevaba sobre mi espalda la losa de la angustia común de todos los estudiantes de esta carrera, y de quien tiene intereses afines, de cómo luchar contra la crisis ecológica global y el cambio climático. Día tras día presenciábamos cómo la evidencia científica aportaba datos cada vez más contundentes acerca del daño que el ser humano infringe en numerosos lugares de nuestro planeta de maneras muy variopintas. Era ciertamente frustrante y deprimente, el asistir a clase y escuchar toda esa serie de evidencias científicas que te recordaban una y otra vez que muchas especies estaban despareciendo (algunas posiblemente antes de ser descubiertas y descritas por la ciencia) o que la contaminación de los ríos y mares afectaba no solo a la fauna y la flora del lugar, sino también a poblaciones humanas. Desde entonces ha transcurrido una década y en cuanto a la concienciación medioambiental de la sociedad, la situación ha mejorado bastante. Sin embargo, factores como la escasa valentía de los gobiernos (sean locales, nacionales, etc.) junto a la de la mayoría de grandes empresas y la complacencia de muchos ciudadanos, así como las nuevas alertas que aporta la ciencia diariamente, no nos muestran un futuro a medio o largo plazo al que mirar con demasiado optimismo. Aquel año dejábamos atrás los 2000, una década en la que no se acabó el mundo, pero en la que muy probablemente empezamos a ser conscientes de que muchas cosas de nuestro planeta estaban cambiando y que nosotros éramos los responsables, aunque también podíamos ser la solución.

Es común que a los estudiantes de las carreras universitarias se les ofrezcan oportunidades de colaboración durante el desarrollo de sus estudios, con el objetivo de profundizar en algún área de conocimiento de su interés. A estas colaboraciones se les dan nombres distintos en cada universidad. En la mía, era «alumno interno». Estos periodos de investigación no remunerados y movidos por la combinación de juventud, vocación y un puñado de créditos necesarios para obtener el título, han sido y seguirán siendo el inicio de la carrera investigadora de muchísimas personas. En mi caso, llevaba desde que empecé la carrera dándole vueltas a colaborar en un departamento de investigación científica en la Facultad de Biología. Aunque, sinceramente, sabía muy poco de qué iba todo esto de la ciencia. A mí me gustaban el deporte y la naturaleza, sobre todo el mar. Tras pensarlo mucho eché la solicitud para colaborar con el Departamento de Ecología e Hidrología de la Universidad de Murcia, concretamente en el grupo de Ecología Marina y Ordenación de Ecosistemas Marinos Costeros. Un mes más tarde me comunicaron que me aceptaban como colaborador mientras estaba acabando de jugar un partido de la liga universitaria con el equipo de mis compañeros de clase, el cual, como casi siempre, perdimos. Así empezó todo. Más o menos.

A partir de ese momento, entré a formar parte de un grupo de investigación. En él, había investigadores predoctorales (aquellos que realizan su tesis doctoral) y postdoctorales (investigadores que ya tienen el doctorado), personal técnico y los investigadores principales (personal científico estable). Con los integrantes de este grupo de investigación, aparte de una gran amistad, mantuve algunas de las mejores conversaciones científicas que he tenido en mi vida. Al ser la primera vez que entraba en un grupo de investigación y empezaba a hacer un poco de «ciencia», tenía el cuerpo lleno de ilusión e impulsividad y la cabeza llena de ideas y reflexiones, la mayoría de ellas seguramente irrealizables o erróneas. Por ello, mirándolo en perspectiva, seguramente yo no parase de repetir tonterías o perogrulladas, pero a ellos no parecía importarles. Me explicaron en qué consistiría mi trabajo: trabajaría directamente con varios de los investigadores predoctorales del grupo. Llegué una mañana a las ocho de la mañana al departamento, puesto que así habíamos quedado unos días antes con los investigadores que iban a ser mis «jefes» y «jefas». Ahí aprendí la primera lección en ciencia: es bastante poco probable que haya alguien trabajando antes de las nueve en cualquier departamento del mundo, a no ser que haya algún experimento en marcha. Tal vez exagere, puesto que no he estado en todos los países del mundo, pero he estado en bastantes y, como se dice en los artículos científicos, con un «intervalo de confianza del 90%» esto es así. Y esto no es debido a que se trabaje poco, sino más bien a todo lo contrario, ya que también es muy raro ver a alguien abandonar su puesto de trabajo antes de las seis de la tarde (eso si no tiene que dar clase después de esa hora). Finalmente, mis supervisores llegaron a su hora, es decir, alrededor de las nueve y media.

En ese momento empecé a recibir las instrucciones de lo que me iba a deparar ese año trabajando con ellos. Aparte de «conocimiento científico», mi trabajo también consistiría en bucear, pasar frío, madrugar y pasar muchas horas en el laboratorio haciendo trabajo mecánico. Todo esto en el Mar Menor, un ecosistema que yo conocía bien por haber pasado muchos días de mi vida allí, pero del cual desconocía sus aspectos científicos más complejos. Y con ese cóctel de ingenuidad e ilusión (cosas que, por cierto, siempre suelen ir juntas) me comunicaron que iba a pasarme el curso trabajando en el Mar Menor. Mis primeras tareas como alumno interno fueron bastante distintas. Por un lado, debía ayudar en los muestreos de larvas de peces para el doctorado de uno los estudiantes del grupo. Por otro, debía también colaborar en los muestreos de fanerógamas y macroalgas para otra de las tesis doctorales. Dos trabajos bien distintos, pero con muchas similitudes.

La mayoría desconoce el ciclo larvario de muchos de los peces que llegan a su plato, lo cual he de reconocer que es bastante comprensible. En el Mar Menor existen larvas de numerosas especies de peces que luego son pescados recreativamente o por pescadores profesionales. Algunas de ellas son bien conocidas por la mayoría de los ciudadanos, como las doradas o lubinas; aunque también hay otros menos conocidos comercialmente como son el raspallón (*Diplodus annularis*), la vidriá (*Diplodus vulgaris*) o los sargos (*Diplodus sargus*). Muchas de estas especies desarrollan su estadio larvario en las someras y tranquilas aguas del Mar Menor, donde residirán hasta que alcancen un tamaño superior y abandonen la laguna costera rumbo al mar Mediterráneo. Muchas de estas larvas se esconden para no ser predadas entre las hojas de la *Cymodocea nodosa*, una planta marina (fanerógama) muy parecida pero más pequeña que la *Posidonia oceanica*. Allí estarán seguras al menos durante un tiempo hasta que se conviertan en juveniles. Es fascinante sumergirse en las aguas del Mar Menor con unas simples gafas y un tubo y poder observar a todas estas pequeñas larvas de peces que se esconden allí. Son prácticamente réplicas en miniatura de los individuos adultos y es bastante fácil identificarlas. También es común encontrar entre esas praderas otros seres muy curiosos como son los caballitos de mar (*Hippocampus ramulosus*) o la aguja mula (*Syngnathus typhle*). Sin embargo, el proceso de eutrofización intermitente, con riesgo de ser permanente, que existe en el Mar Menor, origina que muchas de estas especies de algas y plantas desaparezcan de ciertas zonas de la laguna. De esta manera, los lugares donde se pueden esconder las larvas para no ser depredadas cada vez son más pequeños, disminuyendo así también las poblaciones adultas de estos organismos. Lo cual, aparte de ser un problema para los ciudadanos que dependen de la pesca como modo de trabajo, también supone un impacto negativo sobre los propios ecosistemas.

Los equilibrios ecológicos en los ecosistemas marinos en ocasiones son frágiles, aunque muchos sean muy resilientes, es decir, que ante una perturbación o impacto pueden recomponerse relativamente rápido y con cierta facilidad. Hay un ejemplo muy simple que se da en nuestras costas que ilustra claramente el gran grado de interconexión entre los distintos organismos marinos. Mucha gente es aficionada a la pesca y muchos de ellos la practican desde la orilla con cañas de pescar. Yo mismo pasé muchos días de mi infancia y adolescencia pescando de esa manera en las costas de Cartagena. Quien haya pescado así, sabe que muy pocas veces se capturan peces grandes de determinadas especies, como pueden ser los sargos, las vidriadas, los raspallones, etc. Entonces, lo que se suele hacer es que cuando se capturan individuos pequeños de estas especies, se sueltan de nuevo. Sin embargo, suelen suceder dos cosas. Por un lado, muchas de estas capturas no sobreviven y no pueden ser devueltas al medio. En segundo lugar, mucha gente hace caso omiso a las regulaciones pesqueras y vuelven a casa con cubos llenos de peces que no llegan a los diez centímetros de longitud muchas veces. *A priori*, uno podría pensar que, bueno, como se siguen pescando estos individuos año tras año, esto no tiene ningún efecto sobre los ecosistemas. Sin embargo, lo que debemos preguntarnos es: ¿qué papel juegan estos peces en el ecosistema que estamos explotando? La respuesta no es simple, ya que no solo juegan un papel; sino muchos, y de ellos, es posible que algunos no se conozcan aún. Lo que sí sabemos es que la desaparición de muchos individuos de especies como los sargos hace que estos no se alimenten de los erizos de mar, que son los principales depredadores de muchas de las especies de algas que viven sobre las rocas. De esta manera, las poblaciones de erizos aumentan exponencialmente cubriendo las rocas en las que crecen las algas. Esto puede observarse de manera muy simple buceando en cualquier zona donde la gente habitualmente pesque con caña. Cualquiera que tenga unas gafas puede adentrarse en las numerosas calas de la costa mediterránea y verá que, en muchas ocasiones, las rocas se encuentran prácticamente desnudas de especies de algas y los erizos crecen sobre ellas de manera masiva. La disminución de las poblaciones de estas algas puede originar, por ejemplo, que la cantidad de oxígeno en el agua disminuya, ya que se realiza menos fotosíntesis en el ecosistema. Si unimos este ejemplo con el caso del Mar Menor, es fácil darse cuenta del grado de interconexión existente entre los sistemas marinos. Ya que, la desaparición de macroalgas y plantas del Mar Menor puede originar que las larvas no encuentren refugio y haya menos individuos de especies que, fuera de la laguna costera, actúen como controladores de las poblaciones de erizos marinos, originándose también un decrecimiento de la biodiversidad de algas fuera del Mar Menor. Acabar con una especie vegetal en una laguna costera puede implicar que se acabe con otras especies fuera de ella. Los impactos de los fenómenos y alteraciones humanas no tienen, por tanto, por qué darse en el mismo lugar donde se producen.

Precisamente, uno de los proyectos en los que participaba en los inicios de mi carrera investigadora consistía en evaluar la dispersión larvaria entre el Mar Menor y el Mar Mediterráneo de muchas de las especies de peces. Para ello, depositábamos por la noche unas «trampas de luz». Dichas trampas consistían en cubos blancos, como los de pintura, con agujeros a los lados. En cada uno de estos agujeros se introducía un vaso de plástico en perpendicular, como los que se usan en las fiestas de cumpleaños (y esperemos que dejen de usarse pronto) que a su vez tenían un pequeño orificio en el fondo. Por último, dentro del cubo se introducía una luz LED dentro de un *tupper* cerrado herméticamente. Estos cubos se ponían en el fondo de algunas de las playas del Mar Menor cada noche y por la mañana había que ir a recogerlos. ¿Cómo funcionan estas trampas? Es muy simple. Resulta que las larvas de los peces se comportan de manera semejante a los insectos en tierra firme: se sienten atraídas por la luz. Todos hemos visto, sobre todo durante los meses de verano, que cuando encendemos un farol en la puerta de casa o el balcón se arremolinan junto a él muchísimas especies distintas de insectos. Pues con las larvas de los peces sucede lo mismo. La pequeña lámpara de luces LED que estaba dentro de las trampas emitía luz constante durante toda la noche. Como consecuencia, alrededor de ella se arremolinaba un frenesí de larvas de numerosas especies de peces, aunque también de crustáceos y moluscos. Imaginad qué pequeña maravilla en una playa ínfima del Mar Menor: una luz que emerge de un cubo de pintura reutilizado que es capaz de concentrar toda la vida larvaria de esa zona. Cómo una sola luz puede atraer las generaciones futuras de multitud de especies que son tan importantes para nosotros, los seres humanos, ya que forman parte de nuestra dieta. Sin embargo, esta danza larvaria alrededor de la luz tenía un fin inesperado para ellas. Las pequeñas larvas primero se acercaban al vaso de plástico, donde la luz era un poco más intensa, para finalmente adentrarse por el pequeño agujero del fondo del vaso y quedar atrapadas, junto a otras muchas, en la «trampa de luz». A la mañana siguiente, cogíamos la furgoneta del Departamento de Ecología e Hidrología de la Universidad de Murcia e íbamos a recoger las trampas. Una a una, las vaciábamos en botes con formol para proceder a su identificación, cuantificación y, en general, estudio.

Sin embargo, la ciencia no es tan apasionante, idílica y evocadora como puede parecer y mucha gente se esfuerza en perpetuar. Depositar estos cubos que emitían luz relativamente cerca de la orilla, en uno de los lugares con más actividad nocturna de la Región de Murcia, entrañaba sus riesgos. En varias ocasiones, grupos de jóvenes que acababan su noche de desenfreno en algún local cercano, se acercaban a la playa y, claro, se encontraban que en el agua había algo que emitía luz. «Huevos de alienígena», escuchamos decir a uno de ellos. Por ello, algunas noches había que quedarse vigilando los cubos porque, aunque llevasen el logo de la Universidad de Murcia estampado y pusiera claramente «NO TOCAR», a según qué horas de la noche esas indicaciones no están claras para muchos. No obstante, no de todo se debe culpar a los jóvenes, ya que observamos un comportamiento generacional dual con este experimento. En la zona existen muchos ancianos jubilados que pasan sus mañanas pescando con caña desde la orilla del Mar Menor algunas de las especies que se usan en los platos de la zona: mújoles (*Mugil cephalus*), doradas (*Sparus aurata*) o lubinas (*Dicentrarchus labrax*). Y, claro, los jubilados madrugan mucho. Madrugan tanto que a veces llegaban antes que nosotros a recoger las trampas y sucedía lo inevitable. Más de una vez nos encontramos con que se habían metido en el agua, habían sacado las trampas y las tenían a su lado mientras pescaban. Recordemos que las trampas estaban totalmente agujereadas, por lo que carece totalmente de sentido cogerlas para darles uso como cubo de pesca. Aún a fecha de hoy desconocemos las motivaciones que llevaban a los jubilados del Mar Menor a recoger nuestras trampas recurrentemente y ni siquiera esconderlas de nuestra vista. Esto queda pues como uno de los misterios no resueltos del Mar Menor. O, tal vez, hace honor a esa ley escrita del mar que establece que «el primero que se encuentra algo en el mar se lo queda».

Las muestras que recolectábamos de dichas trampas las llevábamos al laboratorio del Departamento de Ecología e Hidrología, donde las analizábamos una a una. Como os podéis imaginar, la mayor parte del proceso que os describo a continuación no era demasiado agradable. El formol ya de por sí tiene un olor característico, aunque lo eliminásemos lavando con agua la muestra de larvas de peces que quedaban retenidas en un colador. Posteriormente se secaban utilizando papel absorbente de laboratorio y, larva a larva, se procedía a la identificación de la especie y a medir sus dimensiones. De esta manera, año tras año, se puede llevar la cuenta de qué especies desarrollan su estadio larvario en qué zonas del Mar Menor y qué tamaño alcanzan. Pese a lo que pueda parecer en una primera impresión, el número de larvas recolectadas es ínfimo en comparación con el total de esas playas en particular y del Mar Menor en general. Por lo que no conviene alarmarse por el impacto de esta práctica científica sobre las poblaciones pesqueras del Mar Menor.

En otro de los proyectos en los que colaboré, estudiábamos las poblaciones de fanerógamas marinas y macroalgas. Aunque ya las hemos mencionado con anterioridad, lo primero que debemos explicar es qué diferencia hay entre las fanerógamas marinas y las macroalgas. La fanerógamas son plantas, es decir, son organismos que se reproducen por reproducción sexual y al ser angiospermas también tienen flores. Sí, estas especies florecen para reproducirse como sus parientes terrestres. De hecho, evolutivamente hablando, son plantas terrestres que en su viaje evolutivo volvieron al mar. Entre las especies de este tipo se encuentra la famosa *Posidonia oceanica* que se agrupa en grandes praderas por el Mediterráneo y es fuente de vida de los ecosistemas marinos. En cuanto a nuestra laguna salada, el Mar Menor, la fanerógama más común es la *Cymodocea nodosa,* morfológicamente muy parecida a la *Posidonia oceanica*, pero más pequeña en tamaño. En contraposición, las macroalgas son seres asexuales que se reproducen por otras vías, como puede ser la bipartición (un organismo se divide en dos que son formas genéticamente iguales a su «progenitor»). Una especie de alga muy común en el Mar Menor es la *Caulerpa prolifera*, un alga invasora que ya se ha hecho con el control de gran parte de los fondos marinos tras su entrada en la laguna hace varias décadas y que por la zona se conoce como «Oreja de liebre», ya que su forma recuerda a ellas. Sin embargo, entraña riesgos para muchos organismos, pues es tóxica y hace que los fondos sean anóxicos (carentes de oxígeno). Es curioso que, aunque evolutivamente la *Caulerpa prolifera* y la *Cymodocea nodosa* distan mucho una de la otra, conformen de manera conjunta las praderas marinas en numerosos ecosistemas marinos, entre ellos, los fondos del Mar Menor. Esto se debe a que algunas de sus funciones en el ecosistema son bastante similares, aunque compitan entre ellas por los recursos y la *Caulerpa profilera* deba ser erradicada del Mar Menor, según los expertos. Como ya hemos comentado, actúan como guardería para muchas de las larvas de peces y sirven de hábitat de muchas especies de moluscos, crustáceos o nemátodos. Pero ¿cómo podemos estudiar científicamente estas especies? Pues de diversas maneras, todo depende de cuál sea nuestro objetivo. En nuestro caso, queríamos estudiar la diversidad y abundancia de estas especies en las comunidades que viven en los fondos marinos del Mar Menor y, para ello, una de las técnicas que utilizábamos implicaba el uso de una «draga». Este instrumento consiste en algo semejante a las palas que utilizan las excavadoras para cavar un agujero y sacar toda la tierra. Sin embargo, la principal diferencia es que en vez de ser una pala son dos, a modo de valvas. La draga se tira desde el barco y, cuando toca en el fondo, ambas valvas se cierran llevándose una pequeña porción de fondo marino, con todas las especies que lo habitan. Posteriormente se usa una cuerda para izar la draga a bordo y de esa porción de fondo marino se retiran aquellas piedras y otros materiales grandes para recolectar solo las especies vegetales que finalmente se guardan, bien limpias, en frascos con agua marina y formol. Finalmente, en el laboratorio, se extraen todas las especies vegetales, se clasifican, se miden y se pesan. De esta manera podemos saber cuántas hay, pero también cuánto pesan (lo que nosotros llamamos «biomasa») y cuánta superficie de fondo marino ocupan. Pero no solamente de dragas vive la *biología bentónica* (aquella que estudia los organismos que viven fijos al sustrato marino), muchas veces había que mojarse. Concretamente, realizábamos otro tipo de muestreo, el conocido como «muestreo por cuadrantes», que consistía en lo siguiente: en primer lugar, ataviarse con un buen traje de neopreno, ya que la temperatura del Mar Menor desciende por debajo de los 10°C en invierno (investigadores de la Universidad Politécnica de Cartagena han llegado a medir temperaturas de 8°C). Después, sumergirse a pulmón hasta el fondo y allí contabilizar las especies que había dentro de un cuadrante de plástico que transportábamos con nosotros y que tenía un área de superficie conocida. De esa manera, eramos capaces de conocer cuántos organismos de cada especie había por cada metro cuadrado. Es lo que se conoce como «densidad poblacional».

Como os decía, estas praderas marinas son esenciales para la vida en el Mar Menor, pero, sin embargo, pueden llegar a desaparecer por muchos factores distintos. Por un lado, el proceso de eutrofización al que se ha visto sometida la laguna en los últimos años y, por otro, el cambio climático que a su vez aumenta el riesgo y la severidad del primero. En los últimos años, el Mar Menor ha sufrido episodios más o menos graves de eutrofización. El peor de todos ellos fue el que sucedió en verano de 2016, el cual fue tan intenso que, según un estudio del Instituto Español de Oceanografía, más del 90% de las praderas de macroalgas y plantas, como *Cymodocea nodosa* o *Caulerpa prolifera*, desaparecieron. Sin embargo, la eutrofización, como muchos otros procesos que se dan en los ecosistemas, es un fenómeno reversible si no se superan puntos de no retorno, es decir, cuando ya no hay vuelta atrás. Los denominados puntos de no retorno (o *tipping points*, en inglés) son una de las terminologías más utilizadas en disciplinas científicas relacionadas con el cambio global. Imaginemos por un momento que estamos subiendo una escalera, escalón tras escalón. Si queremos, podemos bajar o seguir subiendo, es decir, podemos modular nuestras acciones con nuestra voluntad. Sin embargo, un día decidimos seguir subiendo, y seguir, y seguir. Llega un momento que llegaremos a un punto en el que los escalones se acaban. Sin embargo, allí no hay una gran planicie idílica, sino un pozo. Un pozo con las paredes resbaladizas y un fondo que no se alcanza a ver. Llegados a este punto, a todos nos parecería totalmente absurdo intentar seguir subiendo los escalones, ya que no hay; es más, ¡hay un maldito pozo! Desgraciadamente, todos conocemos el comportamiento del ser humano, «aquel animal que tropieza dos veces con la misma piedra» (muchas más de dos, diría yo). Finalmente, se toma la decisión de no dar la vuelta, de seguir subiendo, con la consecuencia inevitable de precipitarse hasta lo más hondo de ese pozo del que ya no se puede salir. El punto de no retorno es ese último escalón, esa última oportunidad que por una mala decisión se supera llevándonos a un lugar nuevo del que no podremos volver. A un lugar que, sin haber sido, será. En el caso del Mar Menor aún podemos albergar esperanzas, parece que no hemos superado el punto de no retorno. Aunque tal vez haya llegado el momento de dejar de «subir escalones».

No obstante, también hay motivos para la esperanza. La crisis del Mar Menor es un ejemplo perfecto de que se necesita de todo el mundo para salir de ella, no solo de científicos que propongan soluciones técnicas o políticos que las apliquen, sino también de la sociedad civil en sus múltiples formas de organización y acción. En esta línea, este mismo año, antes de la desgracia de la inundación, tuve la oportunidad de conocer a los alumnos del C.E.I.P. La Asomada, en Cartagena, concretamente a la clase de Paco Ruíz. Estos niños y niñas no son unos alumnos cualesquiera, sino que son las cabezas pensantes de El Mar Menor de los Niñ@s, como ellos mismos han bautizado la iniciativa. Durante dos cursos académicos han estado divulgando y aprendiendo sobre el Mar Menor, con el objetivo de despertar conciencia ciudadana y colaborar en su protección y conservación. Así, han llevado a cabo decenas de medidas y propuestas para mejorar el estado de la laguna que han hecho llegar a las autoridades locales y regionales, que incluso han llegado a visitarles en persona. Otros profesionales también hemos tenido la enorme fortuna de poder asistir y compartir con ellos un rato escuchando sus ideas. Desde habilitar un carril cicloturista alrededor del Mar Menor hasta construir un tranvía a lo largo de la Manga o mover a los turistas por el Mar Menor en un barco eléctrico solar. Las nuevas generaciones parece que están mucho más concienciadas que las anteriores. Uno esperaría que esas pequeñas semillas que sus maestros y maestras ayudan a que germinen, dentro de unos años sean robustos árboles de conocimiento dispuestos a echarnos una mano. Y para robustas, no podemos olvidarnos de las actividades de recuperación de ecosistemas que llevan a cabo desde hace décadas los voluntarios de la Asociación de Naturalistas del Sureste (ANSE) como, por ejemplo, la restauración de parte de las Salinas de Marchamalo o la promoción de la recuperación de la actividad salinera tradicional. Para que el Mar Menor vuelva a ser lo que era, o incluso sea una mejor versión, los necesitamos a todos y a todas. Esperemos que aún estemos a tiempo.

DONDE SE MEZCLAN LAS AGUAS

«Que inadecuado es llamar al planeta Tierra,
cuando en realidad es Océano».
Arthur C. Clarke

Las orcas gaditanas

Las costas de Europa y África se miran la una a la otra en un lugar muy especial: el Estrecho de Gibraltar. Es a través de este lugar donde se ha producido el comercio entre distintas civilizaciones durante milenios. Pero no solo eso, también es un lugar muy importante para la vida marina. Todos los años, en primavera, los atunes rojos (*Thunnus thynnus*) cruzan el océano Atlántico, provenientes de las frías aguas del círculo polar ártico, de camino hacia el Mar Mediterráneo para desovar. Posteriormente, emprenden el viaje de vuelta durante el verano. Desde hace centenares de años, los pescadores del Estrecho de Gibraltar se han lanzado a sus aguas en busca de estos grandes peces migratorios. Sin embargo, la sobrepesca provocada por el paso de la pesca tradicional (principalmente la *almadraba,* utilizada desde tiempos prerromanos y que consiste en instalar un laberinto de redes en el paso de los atunes, normalmente próximo a la costa) a la industrial en 1960 ha mermado sus poblaciones y, actualmente, es mucho más difícil encontrarlos. Si bien, los pescadores no son los únicos conocedores de esta migración, de hecho, nunca han estado solos en su cacería. Existe una comunidad de orcas (*Orcinus orca*) residente en el Estrecho de Gibraltar, cuya presa más codiciada es el atún rojo. Durante muchos años, los pescadores y las orcas se han repartido el botín sin problema alguno. Las orcas cazan cerca de los barcos aprovechándose de las artes de los pescadores y estos a veces se sirven de dichos animales para conocer la situación de los atunes. Sin embargo, el declive en las poblaciones de atún hace qué ahora las orcas sean mucho más vulnerables, al no tener comida suficiente, y les sean molestas a los pescadores. La competencia por el atún rojo ya no es «virtuosa», ahora es voraz y desde la comunidad científica se requieren medidas drásticas para salvar a estas poblaciones de orcas locales, así como del atún rojo. Esto es vital no solo para el Estrecho de Gibraltar, sino también para las poblaciones de atún rojo de todo el Mar Mediterráneo. Ya que es en estas aguas dónde, en cierto modo, empieza el Mar Mediterráneo.

En julio de 2011, mientras me preparaba para realizar una inmersión de submarinismo en aguas de Barbate, varias aletas negras largas asomaron en la lejanía. Salí corriendo hacia uno de los muelles con el café todavía ardiendo en la garganta. Allí conversé con unos pescadores que practicaban la pesca de almadraba. Según me contaron, esa era una de las pocas orcas que veían ese verano por allí, que cada vez eran menos frecuentes, pero casi que mejor, ya que se comían muchos atunes rojos y estos escaseaban. Volví al club de buceo y nos pusimos los trajes, cargamos el material y zarpamos desde el puerto pensando que tal vez nos las podríamos encontrar más de cerca. Nos sumergimos en un agua que era muy turbia, comparada con las que yo estaba acostumbrado a ver en la costa cartagenera. De repente, uno de mis amigos me tocó el brazo y me señalo hacia arriba. Unas manchas negras pasaron muy rápido varios metros por encima de nuestras cabezas. Eran muy grandes. No recordaba haber visto nada moverse tan rápido en el agua en mi vida. Fue un instante y luego desaparecieron. Era un grupo de atunes rojos, tal vez unos que habían logrado escapar de las almadrabas o las orcas. Este es un espectáculo que esperemos que siga pudiendo verse en las aguas del Estrecho de Gibraltar. Sin embargo, la importancia de este lugar es mucho mayor.

Biogeoquímica y campañas oceanográficas

Tras estar muchos meses trabajando en aguas del Mar Menor, me surgió la oportunidad de poder trabajar durante el verano de 2011 en el Consejo Superior de Investigaciones Científicas (CSIC), concretamente en el Instituto de Ciencias Marinas de Andalucía, en Cádiz (ICMAN-CSIC, de ahora en adelante). Para poder conseguir este contrato de dos meses de duración tuve que competir a escala nacional para poder optar a una de las codiciadas becas JAE Intro, que en aquella edición fueron unas diez para todo el país. Tocaba hacer las maletas y abandonar la Región de Murcia por primera vez en mi vida, y encima para hacer ciencia de primer nivel e intentar no hacer el ridículo. Con veinte años iba a poder participar en un proyecto de investigación en oceanografía en el CSIC, algo que nunca hubiera imaginado antes. Iban a ser solo dos meses, pero aún no sabía lo importantes que iban a ser para todo lo que vendría después.

El proyecto que desarrollaría en el ICMAN-CSIC versaría sobre una disciplina que estaba estudiando en la carrera y me encantaba: la biogeoquímica. A primera vista, escuchar un término así de extraño, «biogeoquímica», a mucha gente le llama la atención. Mi experiencia me ha enseñado que la mayoría de los ciudadanos piensan que las personas que nos dedicamos a investigar en los mares u océanos solemos trabajar con cetáceos (delfines, ballenas, etc.), corales o pesquerías. Muy pocas personas son conscientes de que la investigación de los mares y océanos también se hace desde otras disciplinas como la química, la física o la geología. Y muchas menos son conscientes de la importancia que tienen estos estudios para entender nuestro planeta y nuestro impacto sobre él. La biogeoquímica puede entenderse como el estudio científico del «viaje» que realizan los distintos elementos químicos de la tabla periódica por los distintos subsistemas del planeta Tierra (biosfera, atmósfera, hidrosfera y geosfera). Por ejemplo, cómo el carbono de una molécula de CO_2 que exhalamos cuando respiramos es incorporado por una planta a través de la fotosíntesis para finalmente ser transformado en glucosa y ser consumido en forma de néctar por un insecto que se dispone a polinizarla. En los mares y océanos del planeta existen otros muchos procesos y fenómenos que se estudian desde la disciplina de la biogeoquímica. Como puede intuirse, es en estos subsistemas y en sus interacciones donde tiene lugar el cambio global, y cada ínfimo dato científico acerca de estos es vital, ya que, como se suele decir, «el diablo está en los detalles». En nuestro planeta existen numerosos equilibrios entre los distintos subsistemas que provocan que la vida del ser humano y otras muchas especies sea posible. Al fin y al cabo, la evolución por selección natural hace que las especies se vayan adaptando de forma progresiva al medio ambiente y a sus cambios. Sin embargo, si la velocidad a la que se producen los cambios es muy elevada, estos mecanismos adaptativos no son suficientes. Estos equilibrios entre los distintos subsistemas no son especialmente frágiles, pero el ser humano tiene la capacidad de romperlos, desplazarlos, modificarlos... o cualquier otro eufemismo para referirse a los efectos de los impactos del ser humano en el planeta. Tal vez los casos más conocidos por los ciudadanos son el calentamiento global por efecto invernadero y el agujero (mejor dicho, «debilitamiento») de la capa de ozono estratosférico. Para sorpresa de mucha gente, el efecto invernadero es un fenómeno esencial para que surgiera la vida en el planeta Tierra, tal y como la conocemos, gracias a él la temperatura media en la superficie de nuestro planeta es de unos 15°C, muy superior a la que tendríamos sin dicho efecto que sería de -18°C. Sí, «menos» 18 °C, 33°C menos. El problema viene cuando este equilibrio se rompe y, debido a la emisión de gases de efecto invernadero, el efecto invernadero se refuerza y provoca un calentamiento progresivo de la atmósfera de la Tierra que hace que esa temperatura media se eleve. Así llegamos al conocido calentamiento global antropogénico por efecto invernadero producido por unos gases que, en un alarde de ingenio y creatividad, se denominaron «Gases de Efecto Invernadero» (GEIs, de aquí en adelante). Entre ellos se encuentran el famoso dióxido de carbono (CO_2), el metano (CH_4), el óxido nitroso (N_2O) o el vapor de agua (H_2O), entre otros. Por otro lado, la destrucción de la capa de ozono se produjo por la emisión de una serie de gases llamados CFCs que se usaban, por ejemplo, en sistemas de refrigeración. Estos son capaces de reaccionar un número muy elevado de veces con el ozono estratosférico y destruirlo y, por ello, también son considerados gases de efecto invernadero. Gracias al Protocolo de Montreal de 1992, se prohibió el uso en la fabricación y la emisión de estos gases en todo el mundo. Como consecuencia, la capa de ozono se ha recuperado en los últimos años, aunque a una velocidad más lenta de la esperada. Pero, a pesar de que siempre se ha usado el ejemplo del Protocolo de Montreal para mostrar que los esfuerzos internacionales en materia de protección ambiental son capaces de generar consensos y solucionar retos de la humanidad, se han vuelto a detectar grandes emisiones de estos gases en Asia en 2019.

Al llegar al ICMAN-CSIC mi primera tarea fue de lo más definitoria en cuanto a en qué consiste muchas veces la oceanografía. Tras estar una semana estudiándome un libro de biogeoquímica marina de más de quinientas páginas, me llamaron para que bajara al sótano. Había que preparar algunos materiales para las campañas oceanográficas que se iban a realizar ese verano. Al bajar, ante mí encontré una boya oceanográfica de color naranja casi como yo de alta. Me explicaron que dicha boya en concreto se situaría en el Estrecho de Gibraltar y se le anudaría una cadena en su parte inferior de la que colgarían una serie de instrumentos científicos valorados en decenas de miles de euros. Estos aparatos serían los encargados de medir si las aguas del Estrecho de Gibraltar están cambiando por los efectos del calentamiento global. Para ello, se medirían variables como la temperatura, la salinidad o el CO_2 disuelto. Tras dicha explicación pensé que mi tarea consistiría en programar alguno de estos instrumentos o analizar los datos. Sin embargo, lo que me esperaba era algo bien distinto: «Tienes que pintar la boya. Has de poner el logo del CSIC, el nombre del centro de investigación y el número de teléfono de contacto. Aquí tienes *spray* negro y hojas de acetato para hacer las plantillas». Así fue como comenzó mi carrera en el mundo científico fuera de la Región de Murcia. Había quedado entre los diez primeros de toda España y ahí estaba, pintando una boya con *spray* en un sótano en el mes de julio. Lo peor es que disfruté haciéndolo durante tres días. Han pasado muchos años desde aquello y las que fueran mis jefas aún siguen recordándomelo.

Sin embargo, lo mejor estaba por llegar. A los pocos días se me comunicó que participaría en una campaña oceanográfica en aguas del Estrecho de Gibraltar. Desde bien pequeño siempre había soñado con participar en una campaña oceanográfica, sobre todo cuando paseaba por el puerto de Cartagena y veía el Buque de Investigación Oceanográfica (BIO) Hespérides atracado en alguno de sus muelles. Esta vez no iba a ser en ese buque, sino en el García del Cid. Y tampoco iba a ser una expedición muy larga, solo un par de días. Pero bueno, qué más se podía pedir, participar en una campaña oceanográfica con solo veinte años era todo un logro. Si hay algo que defina a la oceanografía como disciplina científica son precisamente las campañas oceanográficas. A lo largo de la historia de la oceanografía, numerosos investigadores e investigadoras han realizado investigaciones navegando a bordo de los distintos buques oceanográficos. Meses alejados de sus familiares y seres queridos adentrándose en alguno de los mares u océanos del planeta dispuestos a hacer avances en el conocimiento científico.

Estas campañas oceanográficas tienen una serie de dificultades idiosincráticas añadidas si las comparamos con otras ciencias u otras maneras de investigar. Lo primero es que el trabajo se realiza dentro de un barco. Esto puede parecer una perogrullada, pero tiene una serie de implicaciones técnicas, sociales y laborales que mucha gente no se imagina. Uno podría pensar que, al fin y al cabo, en los buques también hay laboratorios, como en cualquier centro de investigación en tierra firme. Sin embargo, no es lo mismo ni de lejos. Para empezar, la instrumentación científica en los laboratorios de los buques de investigación no suele estar integrada, sino que hay que transportarla desde los laboratorios en tierra firme. Sí, transportar instrumentación científica que vale decenas o centenas de miles de euros al puerto donde se encuentre el buque de investigación. Y, al llegar, montar el laboratorio de nuevo dentro de un buque, que no siempre es el mismo. Sucede a veces que si los buques son extranjeros pueden existir incompatibilidades con el voltaje de la corriente, la grifería, las conducciones de gases, etc. Es decir, desmontar y montar un laboratorio entero, aquí tenemos la primera gran diferencia. Podríamos pensar que, una vez montado el laboratorio, el trabajo sería igual que en tierra firme. Error. Nos encontramos en un barco, es decir, el suelo se mueve. Y siempre se mueve. Más o menos, pero se mueve. Esto quiere decir que toda la instrumentación científica hay que atarla a aquellas superficies posibles para que no se caiga. Puede parecer que exageramos, pero yo he visto sillas literalmente volando de una punta a otra de los laboratorios con olas relativamente pequeñas. La manera de atar los instrumentos a las mesas, paredes o techo es diversa y algunas de las técnicas son de lo más ingeniosas. La manera más común suele ser atar los instrumentos con cuerdas o «pulpos» (cuerdas elásticas con un gancho en cada extremo) a las asas de los muebles, pequeños orificios o asas de las mesas. También suelen usarse «cinchas» como las que usan los transportistas en los camiones para transportar la mercancía en palés. Sin embargo, para objetos más pequeños se usan otras técnicas más curiosas como el velcro. Se pega una de las caras del velcro a la mesa y la otra, por ejemplo, a la base de un ordenador portátil. Luego se pone el portátil encima y seguro que no se mueve sean como sean las olas de grandes. También se suelen utilizar alfombrillas antideslizantes de cocina para poner cosas encima. Toda idea es buena para fijar objetos cuando el suelo se mueve bajo tus pies.

Que el suelo se mueva, obviamente, no solo tiene implicaciones para los objetos, sino también para las personas. Y sí, llegan los mareos. Me gustaría recalcar que todo el mundo, absolutamente todo el mundo, se marea cuando navega. La diferencia es que hay gente que aguanta más y gente que aguanta menos, pero yo he visto a marinos profesionales de color amarillo, y no pasa nada. Puedes marearte y dedicarte a la oceanografía, mucha gente se marea y se seguirá mareando. Por suerte, tienes una gran ayuda para luchar contra ello, ¿tu vocación? No, la Biodramina (con cafeína si es posible). El hecho de estar mareado y que el suelo se mueva origina que numerosos aspectos de tu día a día se compliquen. Existen acciones que todos realizamos en tierra firme que nos parecen increíblemente simples, pero que en un barco son una auténtica odisea. Lo primero, trabajar en un laboratorio o muestreando (cogiendo) agua para analizarla. El trabajo de laboratorio, por lo general, supone dos cosas: estar sentado, moverte lentamente y fijar mucho, mucho la vista. Si a esto le sumamos que la mayoría de los laboratorios de buques de investigación no tienen ventanas, pues tenemos el cóctel perfecto para marearnos más aún. Calor, luz artificial, trabajo forzando la vista, nula presencia de un horizonte lejano al que aferrarse... las náuseas están más que aseguradas. En alguna expedición yo mismo he trabajado con un cubo bajo la mesa, pero eso es otra historia que os contaré más adelante. De hecho, que el suelo se mueva no solo afecta al trabajo, sino también al resto de tu vida dentro de un buque. Así, las duchas y los inodoros tienen asas a las que aferrarse mientras los usas. Sí, te puedes caer mientras haces de vientre o te duchas, de hecho, es bastante común que esto le suceda a alguien en alguna campaña con la consiguiente fractura de algún hueso o esguince. Las sillas del buque (comedor, salón, etc.) están ancladas con una cadena al suelo para que no se caigan, al igual que los sofás o las mesas. Nada se puede mover de su sitio. Salvo las sillas de los laboratorios, que a veces, como os decía, vuelan. En general, el barco se mueve siempre y no es nada cómodo pasar semanas o meses en un entorno que está en continuo movimiento, incluso mientras duermes o lo intentas. A todo esto, hay que sumarle el trabajo científico arduo e incesante dentro de un buque de investigación. Las jornadas muchas veces son de seis horas con descanso de otras seis. Eso quiere decir que nunca se duermen ocho horas y llega un momento en que uno pierde la noción del tiempo. Asimismo, es bastante común trabajar de manera intensa durante muchas horas seguidas. Aunque estos temas los abordaremos más adelante, cuando lleguemos a campañas oceanográficas en regiones más lejanas del planeta.

El movimiento del barco, la dificultad del trabajo científico, el espacio reducido y, por qué no decirlo, vivir, trabajar y pasar tu tiempo libre en el mismo espacio donde están tus jefes durante semanas, seguramente no es el mejor ambiente para tu salud mental. Para embarcarse en una expedición oceanográfica larga, aparte de tener buena salud e ir a diversos médicos, se requiere ser apto psicológicamente. Para ello, ha de pasarse una evaluación psicológica en formato entrevista con un profesional, el cual decidirá en base a su criterio si eres apto o no. Creedme si os digo que pasar mucho tiempo encerrado con tanta gente no es nada fácil. De hecho, muchos compañeros están de acuerdo en que es posiblemente lo más difícil de una expedición oceanográfica. Pensad que el único espacio que es tuyo, sobre el cual tienes posesión absoluta y puedes dar rienda suelta a tu intimidad es tu cama. Una cama que, casi siempre, se encuentra en un camarote que compartes con una o varias personas. Si te estresas, te agobias, quieres relajarte... en un barco no puedes dar un paseo sin encontrarte a nadie, siempre hay alguien, nunca estás solo. Esto agobia a mucha gente, sobre todo a aquellas personas que no son muy sociables habitualmente. Sobre todas estas cuestiones, volveremos más adelante, no os penséis que os vais a quedar sin conocer todos los eventos y anécdotas contados con sus pormenores que a veces rozan la indignidad humana.

Como decía, iba a participar en una campaña oceanográfica en el García del Cid. Había escuchado hablar de ese buque, era el más antiguo que tenía el CSIC en esos momentos y, a fecha de octubre de 2019, con cuarenta años de vida, aún sigue en activo. Es un buque pequeño, de treinta y siete metros de eslora (menos de la mitad que el BIO Hespérides que alcanza los noventa y dos metros) y su puerto base es el de Barcelona, pese a que su mantenimiento se hace en Vigo. Y muchos os preguntaréis, ¿y a qué iba ese barco a Cádiz? La respuesta es muy simple: los buques oceanográficos navegan mucho cada año y se desplazan, según el proyecto científico, por muchos lugares distintos de las costas españolas o de otros países. Este buque en concreto puede encontrarse la mayor parte del tiempo que no está en el mar, en el Puerto de Barcelona, justo detrás del centro comercial del Maremágnum. Es ciertamente gracioso, a la par que idiosincrático de una ciudad hiperturística como es Barcelona, que un buque de investigación oceanográfica se encuentre atracado delante de franquicias de comida rápida por donde circulan cada día cientos o miles de turistas que no reparan en su presencia. «Un barco rojo más», pensarán, «pero este no nos lleva a ver la puesta de sol mientras bebemos una copa de cava».

Situémonos de nuevo en Cádiz. La preparación de una campaña oceanográfica suele llevar mucho más tiempo que la propia campaña. En el caso de la que yo me disponía a embarcar, era de solo dos días, por lo que el tema logístico no era tan complejo. Así, preparamos todo bastante rápido en el ICMAN-CSIC en unas cuarenta y ocho horas de intenso trabajo. El proyecto de investigación en el que se enmarcaba dicha campaña tenía como objetivo estudiar si las corrientes marinas predominantes en el Estrecho de Gibraltar estaban viéndose alteradas de una manera u otra por el cambio climático o perturbaciones originadas por la actividad humana. Las aguas del Estrecho de Gibraltar no solo están repletas de historia desde hace milenios y suponen la frontera entre dos continentes, sino que en ellas también se dan muchos fenómenos interesantes en términos oceanográficos. Si mirásemos un mapa del Mar Mediterráneo nos daríamos cuenta de que es la única zona donde se produce el intercambio de agua con el océano Atlántico (mientras que el Canal de Suez intercambia agua con el Mar Rojo). Este intercambio de masas de agua en el Estrecho de Gibraltar no es nada simple, ya que no se produce una mezcla homogénea de ambas, la atlántica y la mediterránea. Es más complejo. La radiación solar hace que en el Mediterráneo se evapore mucha cantidad de agua, lo que provoca que la salinidad sea más elevada que en el océano Atlántico. Sin embargo, esto no se debe solamente a la evaporación, sino que también se produce debido a que los aportes de agua dulce (lluvias, ríos, etc.) desde tierra firme no consiguen compensar la evaporación en esa zona. Esto es bastante simple de comprender si tenemos en cuenta que el sur de la península ibérica y el norte de África no son zonas que se caractericen por su gran cantidad de lluvias. En contraposición, las aguas que provienen del océano

Atlántico tienen una salinidad menor que las del Mediterráneo, y es en esta diferencia de salinidad donde reside la explicación del intercambio de aguas en el Estrecho de Gibraltar. Así, las aguas que provienen del Mar Mediterráneo, cuando se encuentran con las atlánticas se hunden, puesto que su densidad es mayor. A su vez, las aguas atlánticas se sitúan por encima de las mediterráneas. Finalmente, tenemos dos flujos de agua en direcciones opuestas y profundidades distintas: las aguas muy saladas procedentes del Mediterráneo pasan al Atlántico en profundidad, mientras que las aguas del Atlántico pasan al Mediterráneo en superficie. Posteriormente las aguas atlánticas siguen diversos caminos por el Mediterráneo, principalmente en paralelo a la costa española, francesa e italiana; mientras el agua se va evaporando y se vuelve más salina, para finalmente convertirse también en agua del Mediterráneo y emprender el camino de vuelta hacia el océano Atlántico. Como podéis suponer, este proceso es bastante complejo y existen otras masas de agua que juegan papeles relevantes en este intercambio. Sin embargo, para eso iba a servir la boya que había estado varios días pintando. Se colocaría dentro de unas semanas en un punto central del Estrecho de Gibraltar y a ella se atarían «colgando» una serie de instrumentos oceanográficos para estudiar la evolución de estas corrientes marinas a lo largo del año. Es curioso pensar acerca de estas corrientes y la cantidad de agua, vida, etc. que transportan de un lugar a otro del planeta. Podríamos afirmar que las masas de agua no son de un océano u otro, sino que pasan de un lugar a otro de los océanos del planeta por acción del sol. Que una molécula de agua en cualquiera de los mares del planeta en otro tiempo pudo pertenecer al océano más lejano, haber formado parte de una nube o discurrido por algún río (o de la orina de algún vecino tuyo, por decir algo menos épico e igual de posible).

La campaña oceanográfica tuvo lugar a finales de julio y empezó muy, muy temprano. Me desperté a eso de las cuatro de la madrugada en mi habitación alquilada en Playa Victoria, muy cerca del estadio de fútbol Ramón de Carranza. Los nervios no me dejaron desayunar, así que con un triste café me preparé la mochila con todo lo necesario y salí de casa. En la avenida general me esperaban mis compañeros con la furgoneta del centro de investigación. Desde allí, nos dirigimos al puerto de Cádiz mientras comentábamos el tiempo que iba a hacer ese día en el mar y ultimábamos algunos detalles.

Llegamos al Puerto de Cádiz cuando todavía era de noche y por fin pudimos atisbar el buque de investigación. El García del Cid estaba amarrado a uno de los muelles con una pequeña pasarela para acceder a él. Unos pequeños faroles alumbraban los escalones para evitar caídas y resbalones. Ya en el interior, nos indicaron cuales serían nuestros camarotes. La mayoría de los cuales eran iguales, salvo el del jefe científico. Mientras que la mayoría de los camarotes tienen una litera y un baño, el del jefe de la campaña suele ser un camarote individual. Claro está, para hacer cosas importantes, cosas de jefes.

Dejé mi mochila en una de las camas y fui directo al laboratorio del barco. Teníamos un par de horas para montar algunos de los instrumentos y material necesario para la campaña. Así que, desempaquetamos todo lo que habíamos traído desde el centro de investigación y nos pusimos manos a la obra. Preparamos varias bandejas profundas en las que dejar los frascos de vidrio para las muestras de agua y las fijamos a las mesas. También montamos algunos instrumentos y los atamos a las mesas y paredes. Como sabéis, los buques siempre se mueven, lo que sucede es que cuanto más pequeño es un buque más se mueve, como es el caso del García del Cid.

Una vez que habíamos montado todo el laboratorio, nos informaron de que el desayuno ya estaba listo. Nos dirigimos al comedor y allí nos encontramos con varias cafeteras de café, zumos de varios tipos, cereales, cruasanes, napolitanas de chocolate y ensaimadas recién hechas en una pastelería cercana al puerto. La verdad es que el día no podía empezar mejor y, puesto que no había desayunado nada, me comí varios de los pasteles y un par de tazas de café. Los primeros rayos del día entraban por los ojos de buey cuando nos informaron de que zarparíamos en una media hora.

En mi caso, soy una persona que se marea bastante en los barcos, cosa que me sucede desde pequeño. Nada importa el tipo de barco, la altura de las olas o la longitud del trayecto, ya que tengo tendencia a acabar vomitando. Sin embargo, los meses de navegación me han hecho descubrir algunos trucos que hacen que me maree poco o casi nunca. Y es que en esto de no marearse «cada maestrillo tiene su librillo», por lo que es posible que estas técnicas no funcionen en todos los casos (por favor, como dicen en la tele «no intenten esto en casa», ni en un barco, yo no soy médico y no os debéis fiar del «a mí me funciona»). El primero de los trucos es mantenerte siempre activo, muy activo. Para ello, es necesario tomar café y evitar sentarte; es decir, no parar de trabajar, aunque ello implique ayudar en tareas que no sean las tuyas o pasearte por la cubierta de los barcos. El caso es no parar y mantenerse activo. El otro truco es mantener siempre el estómago algo lleno, cada poco tiempo comer algo para no tener sensación de hambre. En mi caso, tener el estómago vacío hace que me maree mucho más rápido. Por ello, siempre llevo en los bolsillos frutos secos o galletas. Lo que me lleva al tercer y último truco, evitar las comidas grasas en cualquier momento. Cualquier alimento o comida susceptible de provocarme una digestión pesada, al final me acaba mareando. Por ello, siempre es mejor comer alimentos ligeros, pero que llenen. Aparte de los frutos secos y las galletas, la fruta y el pan funcionan bastante bien. Sin embargo, aquella era mi primera campaña y aún lo desconocía, por lo tanto, recurrí al mejor de los inventos de la historia para los marinos: la Biodramina. Pero cometí un grave error, era la primera vez que la compraba y era sin cafeína. Es conocido que uno de los efectos secundarios de este medicamento es adormecimiento, que es más o menos fuerte en función de la persona. En mi caso, la Biodramina me tumba en menos de una hora y puedo estar durmiendo durante bastantes horas sin parar. Y, bueno, eso fue lo que sucedió. Zarpábamos en media hora, tiempo justo para que la Biodramina hiciera efecto. Si te la tomas demasiado tarde, cuando empiezas a notar el mareo, no te hace ningún efecto. Nos informaron de que habría algo de oleaje, no mucho, pero sí bastante. Así que nos recomendaron que descansáramos pues muy posiblemente la jornada de trabajo fuera más difícil y nos cansaríamos bastante. El trayecto hasta nuestra zona de trabajo sería de unas tres o cuatro horas, por lo que tampoco teníamos mucho que hacer durante ese tiempo. Así que me tomé una pastilla y me fui a mi camarote a leer un libro. Informé a mis compañeras de que en un rato saldría al comedor general por si querían jugar a algún juego de mesa o salir a cubierta para ver si podíamos ver algún cetáceo. Era época de orcas en el Estrecho de Gibraltar y suelen verse también delfines y calderones. Sin embargo, lo que sucedió es que nunca fui al comedor ni a ver cetáceos. Me puse a leer y me quedé durmiendo sin previo aviso por efecto de la Biodramina. De hecho, me dormí todo el trayecto hasta la zona de trabajo sin percatarme de nada. Por lo que de repente desperté con un sobresalto en mi camarote debido a los golpes que estaban dando en mi puerta para que me despertase. Empezábamos a muestrear en diez minutos y aún no me había quitado la ropa de calle. Para trabajar en un buque de investigación hay que calzarse botas de seguridad (de esas que llevan la punta reforzada con acero) y, en función de la tarea, también hay que usar guantes, gafas, casco y chaleco salvavidas. Así que salté de la cama y me vestí corriendo. No estaba mareado, pero lo primero que note fue que todo se movía muchísimo. Al andar por el pasillo en dirección al laboratorio me pegué varias veces con todas las paredes. Dentro de un barco casi nunca puedes saber cuándo viene una ola, por lo que no puedes prepararte para el impacto. Aparte, uno de los efectos de la Biodramina es que, aunque notas el movimiento, pierdes un poco de equilibrio, lo que hace que te muevas algo torpe. Cuando llegué al laboratorio mis compañeras me indicaron el protocolo y nos preparamos para aplicar una serie de técnicas que ya conocíamos.

Nuestra tarea consistiría básicamente en muestrear agua, es decir, coger agua y analizar diversos parámetros físicos, químicos y biológicos. Como podéis suponer, coger agua no es tan simple como utilizar un cubo con una cuerda, aunque, que tire la primera piedra el oceanógrafo u oceanógrafa que no lo haya tenido que hacer alguna vez. En esta campaña muestreábamos agua con un instrumento muy curioso que es posiblemente el más famoso, y útil, de la oceanografía: la «roseta-CTD». El nombre compuesto de este instrumento indica su función. *Roseta* hace alusión a su estructura. Una roseta es un conjunto de botellas especiales, llamadas «niskin», que se disponen de manera concéntrica alrededor de una estructura metálica. De esta manera, quedan dispuestas de manera semejante a las balas en el revolver de una pistola. CTD hace alusión a conductividad, temperatura y profundidad, por sus siglas en inglés. Son una serie de sensores que se adhieren a la roseta para medir dichas variables. El funcionamiento de la roseta-CTD es muy curioso. Toda la estructura está sujeta mediante un cable de acero al buque de investigación. Dicho cable está enrollado como si fuera el sedal de un carrete de una caña de pescar, ya que el procedimiento de trabajo es algo parecido. La roseta-CTD se lanza por la borda y va descendiendo en profundidad sujeta al cable. Conforme va bajando, podemos conocer la profundidad y la temperatura, y otras variables, gracias a los sensores sujetos a ella. Estos datos pasan a los ordenadores del buque desde donde se monitorizan. Por lo tanto, mientras desciende podemos conocer las propiedades del agua, si hay algún cambio brusco, alguna zona más cálida, etc. Cuando llega hasta la profundidad deseada, que en algunos buques pueden ser varios miles de metros, se para y se procede a su ascensión. Y aquí es donde entran en juego las botellas niskin. Lo «especial» que tienen estos recipientes es que desde el barco podemos abrirlas y cerrarlas a voluntad herméticamente. En la bajada, las botellas van abiertas, pero durante el ascenso podemos seleccionar cuándo cerrarlas, «cogiendo» agua de la profundidad deseada. Y podemos realizar este procedimiento con cada una de ellas, ya que se suelen seleccionar varias profundidades para el muestreo dado su interés científico. No solo es importante lo más profundo o lo más superficial. A todo el conjunto de aguas en profundidad se le conoce coloquialmente como «columna de agua». De esta manera, conseguimos coger agua de distintas profundidades de la columna de agua sin mojarnos un pelo. Una vez la roseta-CTD llega a superficie, con ayuda de un sistema de poleas se saca del agua y se pone en cubierta. *Et voilá!* Ya tenemos a nuestra disposición una o varias decenas de botellas con agua de distintas profundidades.

El siguiente paso es recolectar el agua de las botellas una a una y analizar diversos parámetros. Aparte de variables como la temperatura o la salinidad, es importante conocer algunos de los parámetros biológicos de la columna de agua. El más famoso es un pigmento fotosintético: la clorofila, una molécula que se encuentra en los cloroplastos de las células capaces de realizar la fotosíntesis, tanto en las plantas terrestres como en las marinas, y, por supuesto, en el fitoplancton marino. Por ello, si conocemos el contenido en clorofila del agua podemos saber si el fitoplancton es más o menos abundante y si, por tanto, las aguas son más o menos productivas, biológicamente hablando. Para medir la clorofila, lo primero que se hace es filtrar el agua a través de unos filtros especiales que tienen un tamaño de poro muy pequeño. La succión se realiza con sistemas de succión por vacío, lo que hace que toda el agua se vea forzada a atravesar los filtros. Finalmente, los organismos fitoplanctónicos se quedan recogidos en el filtro que se pliega y guarda en un vial pequeño a una temperatura de -20°C. Posteriormente, en tierra firme, se analiza mediante técnicas de fluorimetría y así somos capaces de conocer, a posteriori, cuál es la concentración de clorofila en la columna de agua, en este caso la del Estrecho de Gibraltar.

Trabajar en un buque de investigación es bastante complicado y entraña bastantes riesgos. Sin ir más lejos, ese mismo día me hice un corte bastante feo en la mano al muestrear porque debido al movimiento del barco caí y se me rompió un pequeño utensilio de vidrio en la mano. Por lo que tuve que pasar el resto del día con la mano vendada y desinfectándola constantemente. Sin embargo, pudimos acabar nuestra jornada laboral, que duró más de las ocho horas «normales» que, por cierto, casi nunca se trabajan en ciencia; de manera exitosa. Finalmente nos dispusimos a ir al comedor para cenar y ahí cometí uno de mis grandes errores.

Estaba hambriento, así que de primero tomé ensaladilla rusa y fideuá de segundo. Posiblemente lo más grasiento que había. Debido a ello, después de comer y sin volver a tomarme otra Biodramina, me mareé de una manera muy intensa y el resto ya lo imaginaréis. No dormí mucho, pero todo había salido bastante bien en el trabajo, aunque personalmente estuviera mareado y tuviera un corte en la palma de la mano. ¿Habéis escuchado o sentido alguna vez eso de «qué mareado estoy, todo me da vueltas»? Pues en un barco, aparte de las vueltas del mareo, es que todo da «vueltas» de verdad. Así aprendí a evitar las comidas grasas y a tomar la Biodramina con cafeína. Sin embargo, fue una campaña muy corta, de solo un par de días. La cosa es muy distinta cuando el tiempo embarcado se mide en semanas o en meses, como os contaré más adelante.

Pasadas unas horas de trayecto de vuelta llegamos al Puerto de Algeciras, pues el García del Cid tenía que partir a otro lugar y les venía mejor dejarnos allí en lugar de en el de Cádiz. De hecho, el desembarco lo realizamos en zódiac, sin ni siquiera atracar en el puerto. Así, descargamos todo el material y lo introdujimos en la furgoneta del centro de investigación, ya que habían venido a recogernos. En el trayecto de vuelta pasamos por el Parque de los Alcornocales, situado al sur del Parque Natural de la Sierra de Grazalema (que es sorprendentemente el lugar más lluvioso de España). En el trayecto pudimos ver un ciervo que asomaba el cuerpo cerca de la carretera. Algo es algo. Las orcas tendrían que esperar.

DE ESTUARIOS Y CORRIENTES

«Los antiguos llamaban al hombre un mundo menor, designación justa, porque está compuesto de tierra, agua, aire y fuego como el cuerpo terrestre, y a él se asemeja. Si el hombre tiene sus huesos, que le sirven de armadura y sostienen su carne, el mundo tiene sus rocas que sostienen su tierra; si el hombre tiene dentro de sí un lago de sangre, donde crece y decrece el pulmón para su respiración, el cuerpo de la tierra tiene su mar océano que, cada seis horas, crece y decrece también para su respiración; si de aquel lago de sangre derivan las venas que van ramificándose por todo el organismo, análogamente el mar océano llena el cuerpo terrestre con innumerables venas de agua; pero faltan a nuestro globo los nervios, que no le han sido dados porque ellos están destinados al movimiento, y el mundo, en su perpetua estabilidad, carece de movimiento, y donde no hay movimiento los nervios son inútiles. Pero, en todo lo demás, el hombre y el mundo son semejantes».

Aforismos, Leonardo da Vinci, s.xv

La etapa universitaria ofrece muchas oportunidades a los jóvenes que invierten en ella algunos de los años más valiosos de su vida. Una de ellas es, sin duda alguna, la posibilidad de participar en un programa de estudios en otra universidad del país o en uno extranjero. En España existen varias becas, muy escasas económicamente, que te permiten hacerlo. En mi caso, quería aprender inglés así que tras pensarlo mucho elegí solicitar una Beca Erasmus. Quería irme a un país del norte de Europa, y tras dudar entre Suecia, Dinamarca o Reino Unido, me decanté por solicitar una plaza en mi último curso de Licenciatura para ir a estudiar Biología Marina a la Universidad de Aberdeen en Escocia.

Aberdeen es la ciudad más grande al norte de Reino Unido. Situada en el extremo nororiental de Gran Bretaña, sus aguas están bañadas por el mar del Norte. En dicho mar, entre las costas escocesas y las de la península escandinava, se encuentran multitud de plantas petrolíferas que extraen crudo. Estas actividades tienen un gran impacto en la actividad económica de la ciudad que, de hecho, en su calle principal cuenta con numerosas sedes de las distintas compañías petrolíferas que explotan la zona. Es por ello, por lo que la variación en los precios del petróleo tiene sobre esta ciudad unos efectos notables, lo que provoca grandes fluctuaciones de su población. Esta ciudad es conocida también como «The Granite City» («la ciudad de granito»), aunque en la jerga local se le suele llamar también «la ciudad gris». El tiempo del lugar es muy lluvioso y suele estar nublado casi siempre. Así su color siempre es grisáceo y no es, digámoslo así, la ciudad más bonita de Reino Unido.

Pero, si abandonamos la ciudad, los parajes son preciosos. En dirección al oeste se encuentran las famosas Highlands escocesas y sus grandes prados verdes, bosques y formaciones rocosas. Allí también está el Lago Ness, que visité hasta en cuatro ocasiones sin ver al famoso monstruo. Debido a la actividad bacteriana y a los sedimentos de color muy oscuro que flotan en sus aguas, en ocasiones, el fondo es muy difícil de ver incluso en aguas poco profundas. De hecho, si metes los pies es prácticamente imposible vértelos. Esta ha sido una de las características que ha dotado de tanto misticismo al lugar.

En otra dirección, la costa norte de Aberdeen, formada por playas de arenas sobre las que sopla un potente viento, es el hogar de cientos de especies de aves, migratorias o residentes, que gozan de una presencia humana muy baja y una gran cantidad de alimento marino (sobre todo crustáceos y moluscos, fáciles de cazar cuando baja la marea). También existen grandes poblaciones de focas, principalmente de foca gris (*Halichoerus grypus*) o foca del puerto (*Phoca vitulina*).

Así que, en esta ciudad gris, rodeada de grandes extensiones y una fauna que no había visto en mi vida, tendría que pasar seis meses estudiando. Me preparé una maleta que iba a reventar con todo lo necesario para esos meses. Seguramente no calibré muy bien el tema del frío al elegir destino. Subestimé lo que es vivir en un sitio en el que prácticamente llueve todos los días y sale poco el sol. Pero bueno, la experiencia merecía la pena y, total, solo iban a ser seis meses. O no. Y digo esto porque nada más llegar conseguí otra beca, llamada Erasmus plus, para poder quedarme los tres meses de verano a trabajar allí también. Concretamente, en el OceanLab (laboratorio oceánico) situado en el precioso pueblo de Newburgh, a media hora en autobús de Aberdeen en dirección Norte. Y eso es lo que os voy a contar.

Newburgh es un pueblo costero fundado en el año 1261 que cuenta con una población de unos mil quinientos habitantes. En sus alrededores existen unos enormes ecosistemas dunares que atraen a «pajareros» (aficionados a la ornitología) de numerosos lugares del mundo a observar sus aves favoritas. Pero no solo eso, también existe una gran colonia de focas que descansan sobre dichas dunas tras darse sus atracones diarios de diferentes tipos de crustáceos y moluscos. Estas focas fueron las primeras que vi en mi vida. Para quien no haya visto focas en su estado natural, son unos animales muy interesantes. De hecho, aún recuerdo al primer ejemplar que vi. Fui con unos amigos en primavera a ver si podíamos encontrarlas y, de repente, vimos algo en el agua a bastante distancia de nosotros. No sabíamos qué era y uno de mis amigos dijo «es un perro nadando». Y es que ciertamente parecen perros nadando cuando lo hacen con la cabeza fuera del agua, pero no era un perro, era una foca que nos ayudó a encontrar la colonia mientras íbamos tras ella, corriendo por la orilla gracias a que seguía sacando la cabeza de vez en cuando del agua. Encontrar una colonia no es tarea fácil, pues suelen moverse de un sitio a otro de la costa de Newburgh y las dunas, dependiendo del viento, las olas y las mareas, y a veces puede llevarte un par de horas. Aparte de todo esto, lo interesante que tiene Newburgh es que se encuentra situada en un estuario, es decir, un lugar donde desemboca un río, pero sin formar un delta (como, por ejemplo, sí que hace el Ebro). Los estuarios suelen tener forma de embudo, es decir, conforme llegan al mar sus riveras se van alejando una de la otra y las mareas facilitan el intercambio entre aguas fluviales, las que lleva el río, y marinas. Concretamente, este río tiene el nombre de Ythan y es un lugar de contrastes.

Como os comentaba al principio, en este lugar del mar del Norte existen varias plataformas petrolíferas. Una de las razones es que este mar es muy somero, es decir, poco profundo. Por ello, pueden instalarse estas infraestructuras mediante grandes columnas fijas al fondo marino. En el proceso de extracción de petróleo existen varias situaciones en las que se pueden producir fugas que se vierten al medio marino. La peligrosidad de estos vertidos en términos biológicos, según el tipo, lugar o momento en el que se produzcan, etc., ha de evaluarse. Muchos de estos vertidos se producen a través del propio sustrato marino, y pueden tener un grave impacto en las distintas especies de organismos que allí viven. A las especies que desarrollan su ciclo de vida, por entero o casi en su totalidad, dependientes del sustrato marino se las conoce como «bentónicas». Almejas, caracolas, erizos de mar, estrellas de mar, pepinos de mar, fanerógamas marinas (como la *Posidonia oceanica*), etc., son ejemplos de algunas de ellas.

Sin embargo, no nos podemos olvidar de otros seres mucho más pequeños que viven en el sustrato marino: las bacterias, organismos unicelulares procariotas, es decir, no son células eucariotas como las que forman nuestro cuerpo. Entre las diferencias que se pueden enumerar de ambas tipologías celulares destaca el hecho de que el núcleo (donde se localiza el ADN) no se encuentra rodeado de la membrana nuclear, sino que está más o menos disperso por el interior de la célula (citoplasma); o que poseen, aparte de la membrana celular, otra estructura llamada «pared celular». Lo interesante de las bacterias es que participan en multitud de procesos aún desconocidos. De hecho, uno de ellos fue el que estuvimos investigando durante todo un verano. Veréis, a veces algunos restos de petróleo pueden llegar a los estuarios cercanos y, en trabajos científicos anteriores como el del «OceanLab» se había constatado que el petróleo en los estuarios se degradaba de una manera mucho más rápida que en el mar. ¿Quiénes podrían estar detrás de esa degradación tan eficiente? Nosotros creíamos que las bacterias. Aunque, como os imaginaréis, intentar responder a una pregunta así no es nada simple. Para ello, preparamos una serie de experimentos, cada uno de varias semanas de duración.

La ciencia, por lo general, no es una profesión glamurosa; sobre todo cuando implica trabajar en el medio natural. En nuestro caso, íbamos a trabajar en el estuario del río Ythan, lo que suponía dos elementos que tener en cuenta: las mareas y el fango. Lo que queríamos era identificar las bacterias que son capaces de degradar el petróleo en el fango de dicho estuario. Para ello, necesitábamos coger muestras próximas a la orilla y lo más cerca posible del límite inferior del río, cuando la marea lleva al estuario a su nivel más bajo. La única forma de hacerlo era ir a pie, es decir, no podíamos utilizar ningún barco de muestreo o semejante, lo cual complicaba un poco el asunto. Además, debía hacerse cuando la marea estuviera lo más baja posible, fuera a la hora del día que fuera. Antes de salir al estuario nos poníamos unos pantalones con las botas incorporadas, los mismos que usan los pescadores en los ríos, y nos abrigábamos con guantes y gorro para no pasar frío. La mayoría de días llovía y el viento era también una tónica habitual en el estuario del río Ythan. Para coger las muestras utilizábamos unos cilindros de metacrilato de un metro de longitud y unos diez centímetros de diámetro. Gracias a un GPS podíamos conocer el punto exacto al que teníamos que ir. Y allí nos dirigíamos tres o cuatro personas con tubos de metacrilato y vestidos como si fuéramos a pescar. El proceso para extraer las muestras era bastante simple y, a su vez, complicado. Consiste en introducir casi la totalidad del tubo de metacrilato en el fango a base de hacer fuerza presionando o dando golpes con un pequeño martillo. Posteriormente, el cilindro se extrae y se le pone una tapa en cada uno de los extremos, para que el contenido no se salga. Este proceso había que realizarlo en cada una de las zonas del río seleccionadas, que eran unas diez en total. El único problema era que conforme más se avanzaba en el río, más inestable se volvía el fango y yo, que en aquel momento debería pesar unos ochenta kilos, era el principal damnificado. En una ocasión, cuando aún nos quedaban un par de puntos de muestreo antes de llegar a los límites del río, me empecé a hundir, como si fueran arenas movedizas. Ya nos habían avisado de que aquello podía pasar, así que sabíamos lo que teníamos que hacer. Cuando tenía el fango por encima de las rodillas me tiré de boca hacia un lado, y empecé a sacar las piernas poco a poco. Creo que nunca he estado tan sucio en mi vida. Cuando conseguí liberarme, como no podía avanzar más, inicié el camino de vuelta hacia el centro de investigación. Mientras lo hacía, pequeños pollitos de correlimos (*Calidris alpina*), una especie de ave muy común que también habita en España, salieron corriendo en todas direcciones. Era muy curioso porque los veía moverse, pero no veía de dónde venían y adónde iban, hasta que me detuve y empecé a observarlos con atención. Debía de haber cientos o miles, se camuflaban entre las algas que quedaban al aire libre cuando bajaba la marea, su plumaje tenía un color muy parecido. Es de los mejores camuflajes que he visto en mi vida. Iban de un alga a otra muy rápido, se pegaban a ella y se quedaban inmóviles.

Una vez que llegábamos al laboratorio, utilizábamos los cilindros de metacrilato que contenían en su interior las muestras para los experimentos. Básicamente, llenábamos de agua del estuario el cilindro y le introducíamos un tubo con el que burbujeábamos aire. Una vez hecho esto, introducíamos una determinada cantidad de petróleo crudo en cada cilindro. De esta manera, solo sobrevivirían aquellos organismos capaces de degradar el petróleo. Y eso era lo que nosotros queríamos averiguar. Pasados unos días, cogíamos una muestra de cada cilindro y procedíamos a hacer cultivos bacterianos en placas *petri*, una técnica muy utilizada en microbiología. Finalmente, mediante técnicas de ecología molecular estudiábamos cuántas especies había o cuáles eran sus funciones. Es increíble la cantidad de especies distintas de microorganismos que hay en una porción de fango. Los análisis nos indicaron que había unas cuatro o cinco especies potenciales capaces de degradar el petróleo en condiciones naturales.

Actualmente, una persona realiza su doctorado en este mismo laboratorio clasificando cuáles son exactamente estas especies y analizando si de sus genes se puede extraer alguna información relevante, o no, para el desarrollo de organismos modificados genéticamente que sean capaces de limpiar el petróleo en aguas marinas; lo cual sería un avance increíble para la sostenibilidad del medio marino.

Más al norte todavía

Si la costa este de Escocia da al mar del Norte, su costa oeste da al océano Atlántico norte. Y, desde luego, no tiene nada que envidiar. En esta zona se encuentran muchos de los parajes más alucinantes que se puedan contemplar. Entre ellos, un lugar muy famoso es la Isla de Skye. Entre sus paisajes de tonos verdes, azulados o violetas se pueden visitar sitios únicos como «The Old Man of Storr»: una gran masa volcánica de roca desnuda que tiene un lago a sus pies, a unos cuatrocientos metros por encima del nivel del mar. Acerándose a la orilla de este enclave se atisba el océano Atlántico y, más allá, el océano Atlántico norte e Islandia. Un lugar muy importante para nuestro planeta pese a que no mucha gente lo conoce.

Vivimos en un planeta tremendamente diverso, formado por multitud de parajes en distintas localizaciones geográficas, y con sus propias peculiaridades. En cualquier lugar cercano a nosotros podemos encontrar paisajes o ecosistemas que no nos dejan indiferentes. Sin embargo, siempre es interesante conocer también aquellos lugares recónditos que poseen una idiosincrasia particular, digna de ser apreciada de cerca. Para mí, uno de esos lugares es, sin duda alguna, Islandia. Esta isla precede a la región Ártica, y atendiendo a su latitud, en términos oceanográficos podría considerarse que gran parte de las aguas que bañan las costas de Islandia son aguas árticas.

Islandia, también conocida como la «Tierra de hielo y fuego», ha sido uno de los lugares que más visitantes ha recibido en los últimos años, todo un lugar de peregrinaje para los aficionados a la aventura, la naturaleza y el riesgo. Un lugar con cierto aire de misticismo, donde Julio Verne se inspiró para escribir su famoso libro *Viaje al centro de la Tierra* mientras observaba el volcán Snæfellsjökull (cuyo glaciar podría desaparecer en 2100 por los efectos del cambio climático). De hecho, la estancia del escritor es lo que le confiere su mayor atractivo turístico. El papel que tenía dicho volcán en el libro era esencial, ya que era la entrada al centro de la Tierra. Actualmente, en la cima existe un glaciar con el mismo nombre que suele estar cubierto de nieve durante todo el año.

También es el lugar de la tierra que da nombre a los géiseres, pues la localidad islandesa Geysir es donde se observaron por primera vez. No extrañará pues que este sea uno de los lugares del mundo donde más géiseres se pueden encontrar (con perdón del Parque Nacional de Yellowstone, que es el lugar del mundo en el que hay más géiseres). Sin embargo, estos no son los únicos secretos que esconde este país, ya que aquí es dónde empieza el clima de la Tierra.

En Pinvellir (o Thingvellir, en islandés), un paraje natural protegido, muy cerca de Reikjiavi, la capital, es posible bucear en un lago de aguas cristalinas. Aunque, lo importante de este lago no es la claridad de sus aguas, sino que cada una de sus orillas es una placa tectónica: la euroasiática y la americana. De hecho, si se desciende lo suficiente, es posible poner una mano en cada placa, es decir, tocar un continente con cada mano. La denominada dorsal mesoatlántica atraviesa Islandia aproximadamente de norte a sur, haciendo de este país una de las pocas regiones del planeta donde la geología está viva. Esta dorsal no solo divide a Islandia, también el océano.

Hay muchos otros lugares en la isla de gran interés ambiental. Es increíble la variedad de fauna que encierran estas tierras, por ejemplo, las colonias de foca moteada (*Phoca vitulina*) o aves como el cormorán moñudo (*Phalacrocorax aristotelis*), el arao aliblanco (*Cepphus grylle*), el eider común (*Somateria mollissima*) o la gaviota sombría (*Larus fuscus*), y los curiosos caballos islandeses. En lugares como Húsavík, es posible salir en uno de los pocos barcos que tiene el pueblo a avistar ballenas. Las especies que se pueden observar van desde orcas (*Orcinus orca*) hasta la ballena azul (*Balaenoptera musculus*), el animal más grande del mundo; aunque lo más común es ver ballenas jorobadas (*Megaptera novaeangliae*).

Otro lugar fascinante es el lago Mývatn, donde existen multitud de parajes volcánicos y piscinas de aguas termales naturales donde bañarse. Si bien, el agua caliente de las emanaciones termales de la isla huele a ácido sulfhídrico (H_2S), o lo que es lo mismo, a huevos podridos. Aunque lo peor es que el agua caliente de las casas huele también así, ya que aprovechan esa misma agua caliente y la capacidad calorífica del subsuelo para el abastecimiento doméstico. Es decir, si te duchas con agua caliente te estarás duchando con un agradable y permanente olor a huevos podridos. Así que, la próxima vez que veáis fotos de gente bañándose en aguas termales en Islandia recordad que, por mucho que sonrían, lo hacen con ese embriagador aroma.

Otro paisaje digno de mención lo encontramos en el norte de Islandia, en la región de Krafla, donde se encuentra una caldera volcánica de alrededor de diez kilómetros de diámetro. Un increíble paraje geotermal plagado de volcanes de lodo hirviente, solfataras y fumarolas humeantes. En esta zona, la NASA vino a probar los vehículos («rovs») no tripulados que ha enviado a sus misiones en Marte. Lo que más llama la atención en este lugar es que existen multitud de colores, en un paraje en el que a priori podríamos esperar encontrar tonalidades muy lúgubres. Así, tenemos piedras cubiertas de azufre, planicies cubiertas de vegetación de un verde intenso y montañas con tonalidades que van desde el amarillo al marrón, pasando por el naranja.

Otros de los lugares interesantes de Islandia son el lago Jökulsárlón y el glaciar Vatnajökull. Vatnajökull es, de hecho, el segundo glaciar más grande de Europa. Y no solo eso, sino que este glaciar supone el 8% de toda la superficie de Islandia. La laguna se comunica con el mar a través de un breve cauce por el cual discurren los hielos hasta encontrar el agua salada. De hecho, en las proximidades se encuentra una playa en la cual quedan varados muchos de estos hielos y pueden tocarse con los dedos de la mano. Para los más valientes, la zona es propicia para pegarse un baño, llevando mucho cuidado con las corrientes, que son tremendamente fuertes y, además, también es bastante fácil ver aves como el charrán ártico (*Sterna paradisaea*). Si nos adentramos por la parte sur de la isla se puede llegar a Vík í Mýrdal. Esta zona es famosa por sus playas de arena volcánica de increíble color negro. Aquí también se pueden observar los pájaros más famosos de la isla: el frailecillo común (*Fratercula arctica*), que puede verse nadando en la propia playa de Vík, aunque en unos acantilados colindantes es posible hacerlo con mayor facilidad. Los frailecillos comunes son unas aves muy curiosas, con un plumaje de colores semejante al de los pingüinos y un pico rojizo y blanco característico. Asimismo, son unos grandes buceadores y se zambullen sin parar en el agua intentando pescar.

Este país, por tanto, no deja indiferente a quienes lo visitan, y es que no podemos olvidar que nos encontramos en una isla, lo que quiere decir que el mar puede explicar muchos de los fenómenos ambientales que aquí se producen. Islandia es una isla peculiar en cuanto a océanos se refiere. Así, las costas de su parte sur, y la mayor parte de la costa este y oeste, están bañadas por las aguas del océano Atlántico. Sin embargo, al norte de la isla, cerca de Húsavík (pueblo famoso por los avistamientos de ballenas), encontramos el inicio del océano Ártico. Por ello, Islandia, aparte de tener mil caras y paisajes en tierra firme, es el país de los dos océanos: de la transición oceánica de las cálidas aguas atlánticas hasta las gélidas aguas polares en las que habitan osos, morsas y ballenas, entre otros seres vivos. Este choque e intercambio de aguas frías y cálidas no solo es importante para los organismos polares, sino que también lo es para nosotros, los humanos.

Si hablamos de fronteras en el mar, estas no tienen sentido científicamente hablando. Clasificamos las masas de agua con distintos nombres como mares u océanos y sí es cierto que para algunos mares tiene sentido, puesto que tienen cierto aislamiento como el Mar Mediterráneo; sin embargo, el océano solo es uno y, por eso mismo, está totalmente conectado, pero ¿cómo es esta conexión? En dos palabras: corrientes oceánicas. Gracias a las grandes corrientes oceánicas, el océano es el mayor transportador de calor del planeta Tierra. De esta manera, la radiación solar que incide sobre el ecuador calienta el agua marina superficial, que se vuelve más salada. Si nos centramos en el océano Atlántico, vemos cómo esta agua ecuatorial cálida se desplaza hacia el norte, recorriendo miles de kilómetros, mientras que por debajo fluyen aguas más frías y con un menor contenido en sal. Estas aguas que viajan por debajo de las cálidas tienen una historia compartida con las mismas aguas cálidas que circulan por arriba: han hecho exactamente el mismo recorrido, pero ya hace algún tiempo. Si nos fijamos, podemos identificar tres regiones que son especialmente curiosas, pues allí se produce el hundimiento o ascensión de las aguas cálidas: la zona norte del océano Índico, entre la Península Arábiga y la India, donde las aguas frías que provienen de la Antártida afloran a la superficie; al norte de las islas Hawái, donde sucede algo semejante; y, por último, la zona del océano Atlántico norte, concretamente en las aguas de Islandia, donde las aguas cálidas que provienen de las zonas ecuatoriales de todo el planeta inician un descenso vertical al enfriarse. Ya podéis ir haciéndoos una idea de lo importante que es este fenómeno para el clima de nuestro planeta.

El movimiento horizontal que se produce desde estas regiones oceánicas a otras supone el mayor mecanismo conocido de transporte de calor que existe en el planeta. Y, como es de esperar, este perpetuo ir y venir de las aguas de un océano a otro del planeta, en superficie o profundidad, afecta también a las propiedades de la atmósfera. Por ejemplo, la corriente del Golfo desplaza una gran masa de agua cálida procedente del golfo de México y que se dirige al Atlántico Norte. Como consecuencia, la corriente del Atlántico Norte originada a partir de la corriente del Golfo hacia el noreste suaviza las temperaturas en Europa, mientras que la corriente de Azores fluye hacia el sureste suavizando las temperaturas en la península Ibérica.

Podríamos pensar que aquí ya son bastante suaves las temperaturas. Sin embargo, ¿qué pasaría si os digo que Nueva York está aproximadamente a la misma latitud que Madrid? Todos pensaríamos en los inviernos que hemos visto en numerosas películas, en cómo la gente juega con la nieve en Navidad por las calles de la «ciudad que nunca duerme». Mientras tanto, en nuestro país nunca llegamos a tener temperaturas tan frías. Este fenómeno se debe fundamentalmente a que dicha corriente marina calienta Europa, mientras que la corriente de aguas frías desciende desde el Atlántico Norte por toda la costa americana, haciendo que las temperaturas sean mucho más frías.

En este punto tan interesante para la circulación oceánica y el clima de nuestro planeta, que se encuentra ubicado en las aguas de Islandia, se produce la transformación y conexión entre agua superficial caliente fluyendo hacia el norte y agua profunda fría rumbo sur. Sin embargo, más interesante aún es lo que sucede algo más al sur: la AMOC (Atlantic Meridional Overturning Circulation). Este es uno de los fenómenos más estudiados por los científicos marinos y atmosféricos del mundo. Este lugar esconde información de unos de los episodios periódicos más importantes del planeta Tierra: los procesos de glaciación-desglaciación. Ya que, cuando esta corriente se ha parado o ralentizado en la zona AMOC, se han producido episodios de glaciación en todo el planeta. De hecho, algunos científicos han propuesto que el cambio climático puede detener esta corriente y llevarnos, paradójicamente, a una glaciación. Al fin y al cabo, ahora estamos viviendo un periodo climático denominado como interglacial y, al ser un proceso cíclico, la glaciación llegará antes o después.

El área del Atlántico Norte donde se produce la AMOC es mucho más curioso de lo que pueda parecer. ¿Qué tal si hacemos un *zoom*? Lo que observamos es que el sistema que esconden las aguas de Islandia y de Groenlandia, que juega también un papel esencial, es mucho más complejo de lo que esperaríamos. Así, si observamos la sección este de la dorsal, nos daremos cuenta de que la misma dorsal oceánica que parte a Islandia en dos también divide las aguas; sin necesidad, por cierto, de poseer poderes bíblicos como Moisés. De esta manera, por ambas laderas de la dorsal fluye, por la parte inferior, una corriente de aguas frías y, por la parte superior, una corriente de aguas cálidas. De hecho, también vemos lo mismo si observamos lo que sucede con Groenlandia. Aunque, esto es un fenómeno bastante esperable al tratarse de territorio emergido. Pero ¿quién podría imaginarse que una dorsal oceánica que apenas llega a la superficie en casi todo el océano Atlántico puede dividir las grandes masas de aguas transportadas por las corrientes marinas que condicionan el clima global? Honestamente, muy pocos. Por suerte, una de las maravillas de la ciencia moderna es poder comprender estos fenómenos tan esenciales para nuestra vida en el planeta Tierra. Ya que, entender cómo funcionan estos procesos es crucial a la hora de tomar medidas de mitigación y adaptación a fenómenos globales como el cambio climático. No solo es importante la velocidad de esta corriente, así como evitar que se pare, sino que además existen otros procesos importantes que allí se dan lugar, como la acidificación oceánica.

La acidificación oceánica es un proceso global que se enmarca dentro de aquello que llamamos cambio global, en el que se incluyen procesos que van desde la pérdida de biodiversidad hasta el cambio climático. La acidificación de los océanos se produce debido al exceso de CO_2 que está presente en la atmósfera como producto de las actividades humanas. Por lo tanto, el CO_2 acumulado en la atmósfera en exceso, cuya concentración es mucho mayor que en el agua marina, tiende a pasar de la atmósfera al agua por difusión; un fenómeno que se produce entre la atmósfera y el océano al intentar mantener en equilibrio químico los compuestos que comparten. Cuando el CO_2 pasa a la fase acuosa, es decir, al mar, reacciona con el agua y se forma ácido carbónico (H_2CO_3). Posteriormente, este ácido carbónico se descompone liberando protones de hidrógeno (H^+), lo que produce un descenso en el pH del agua marina, acidificándose y volviéndose así menos básica, ya que su pH sigue por encima de siete.

La acidificación de los mares y océanos tiene múltiples efectos negativos sobre los ecosistemas y la vida marina. El proceso más conocido es la disminución de carbonato cálcico ($CaCO_3$) disponible en el agua necesario para las estructuras calcáreas de organismos marinos como corales o moluscos. Esto, a su vez, disminuye la capacidad de desarrollo de muchas especies distintas pertenecientes a dichos grupos.

Un reciente estudio publicado en *Nature* con participación del Instituto de Investigaciones Marinas de Vigo (perteneciente al Consejo Superior de Investigaciones Científicas), titulado

Meridional overturning circulation conveys fast acidification to the deep Atlantic Ocean, ha demostrado que los efectos de la acidificación oceánica no solo se restringen a la superficie de los océanos, sino que también afectan a sus profundidades. Las aguas de la corriente del Golfo, que fluyen de manera superficial hacia el Atlántico Norte, acumulan CO_2 atmosférico en su recorrido. Este gas reacciona con el agua y así acidifica las cálidas aguas de la corriente del Golfo. Posteriormente, dicha corriente llega a las zonas de Islandia y Groenlandia donde se empieza a enfriar. Este enfriamiento eventualmente produce que las aguas empiecen a hundirse, por diferencia de densidad. Sin embargo, el pH no se ve prácticamente afectado, lo que origina que esta agua más ácida que discurría por la superficie del océano, ahora viaje por las capas más profundas. Y lo que es más preocupante: en sentido inverso.

Los resultados de este estudio son a todas luces impactantes. Estas aguas que viajan en profundidad de norte a sur por el océano Atlántico son capaces de alterar aquellas estructuras de los organismos formados por carbonato cálcico. Con frecuencia, se desconoce que, en las profundidades oceánicas, de quinientos a mil quinientos metros bajo la superficie del océano, existen corales. No son tan coloridos como los que estamos acostumbrados a ver en los documentales de televisión, pero son igual de importantes. Estos corales de agua fría suelen tener colores blanquecinos y juegan un papel esencial en los ecosistemas marinos. Posiblemente, el más importante para los seres humanos: en estos corales ponen sus huevos y pasan la primera parte de su vida en forma larvaria numerosas especies de interés pesquero, como la merluza. A la destrucción de estos corales por la conocida pesca de arrastre, ahora se suman unas aguas ácidas y frías que vienen del norte. Las conclusiones de este estudio no son nada halagüeñas ni llaman al optimismo. De hecho, según el Dr. Marcos Fontela, coautor del estudio, las consecuencias serán devastadoras. «La cantidad de iones carbonato disponibles para las comunidades de corales de aguas profundas es casi un 50% menor que hace doscientos cincuenta años. Y si el ritmo de emisión de CO_2 se mantiene como hasta ahora, un 70% de las comunidades de corales de aguas profundas del Atlántico Norte van a encontrarse viviendo en un medio que no es el adecuado para su crecimiento y desarrollo antes de final de siglo», explica Fontela. Otro de los alarmantes resultados de este estudio es que sus efectos pueden llegar a notarse hasta en el «banco de Galicia», uno de los principales caladeros de la flota pesquera española, con el impacto económico que eso supondría.

El cambio climático es un fenómeno que afecta a múltiples aspectos de nuestra vida. En algunos lugares del planeta Tierra ya vemos las consecuencias en la acidificación de los mares y océanos, la contaminación del medio ambiente o en la pérdida de biodiversidad, entre muchas otras. Por sus singulares características y ubicación, Islandia es uno de esos lugares que merecen ser estudiados y, como suele decirse en jerga científica, monitorizados. Por suerte, proteger nuestro medio ambiente, con pequeñas y grandes acciones, es cada vez más fácil gracias a las numerosas herramientas que nos brinda la ciencia y la tecnología. Por ejemplo, las aguas al sur de Islandia son uno de los puntos de interés para muchos de los satélites dedicados a la observación de la Tierra desde las distintas agencias espaciales. Los satélites pueden aportarnos valiosísimos datos en forma de imágenes con las cuales poder conocer la temperatura de las aguas, su salinidad o su contenido en clorofila, entre otros. Con estos datos, podemos estimar dónde se está produciendo el hundimiento de aguas cálidas en la AMOC e, incluso, saber su velocidad. Existe un pensamiento que se ha extendido por ciertos sectores que establece que invertir dinero público en los programas espaciales es algo absurdo pudiendo gastarlo en la protección de nuestro planeta. Sin embargo, gracias a los satélites y otros instrumentos espaciales podemos cuantificar en tiempo real qué está pasando en muchos lugares del planeta. No es solo que podamos monitorizar la AMOC, sino que también podemos medir el avance o retroceso de los bosques, la humedad de los campos de cultivo o el avance y el retroceso de las grandes masas de hielo de los glaciares. Un sinfín de oportunidades que brindan cientos de ojos que nos observan desde el espacio.

¿Podrá salvarnos la ciencia y la tecnología de la ralentización de la AMOC? ¿Podrán tomarse medidas políticas a tiempo para reducir nuestras emisiones de CO_2? ¿Podremos utilizar lo mejor de la política y de la ciencia para afrontar los retos que nos trae el presente siglo? Estas son algunas de las preguntas que deberíamos hacernos para evitar que nuestras acciones locales tengan efectos en regiones remotas del planeta, como el Atlántico Norte, y que estas, a su vez, agraven y potencien problemas como el cambio climático que nos afecta a todos. ¿Estaremos a la altura?

Podría parecer que es fácil ya que tenemos todo en nuestra mano. Sin embargo, muchos países se están echando atrás en la lucha contra el cambio climático, como los Estados Unidos de América que han abandonado el Acuerdo de París. Por ello, es más necesaria que nunca la cooperación internacional en la lucha contra el cambio climático. Es vital comprender que la atmósfera, los océanos, etc., no entienden de fronteras y, por ello, no debemos restringir las acciones según sea nuestra ciudad, región o país. Se ha de cooperar internacionalmente, como hacemos los científicos, para que se tomen medidas para la reducción de emisiones de GEIs y la mitigación y adaptación al cambio climático más allá de nuestros países. El éxito de la lucha contra el cambio climático solo lo conseguiremos juntos. En contraposición, su fracaso puede depender solamente de la inacción de unos pocos países, para desgracia de todos.

LOS ERRANTES INVISIBLES

El Pi de Formentor

«Mon cor estima un arbre! Més vell que l'olivera,
més poderós que el roure, més verd que el taronger,
conserva de ses fulles l'eterna primavera,
i lluita amb les tormentes que assalten la ribera,
com un gegant guerrer.

No guaita per ses fulles la flor enamorada;
no va la fontanella ses ombres a besar;
mes Déu ungí d'aromes sa testa consagrada
i li donà per trone l'esquerpa serralada,
per font l'immensa mar.

Quan lluny damunt les ones renaix la llum divina,
no canta per ses branques l'aucell que encativam;
el crit sublim escolta de l'àguila marina,
o del voltor que passa sent l'ala gegantina
remoure son fullam (...)».

Miquel Costa i Llobera
(Versión de 1907)

El Pino de Formentor

«Hay en mi tierra un árbol que el corazón venera:
de cedro es su ramaje, de césped su verdor;
anida entre sus hojas perenne primavera,
y arrastra los turbiones que azotan la ribera,
añoso luchador.

No asoma por sus ramas la flor enamorada,
no va la fuentecilla sus plantas a besar;
mas báñase en aromas su frente consagrada,
y tiene por terreno la costa acantilada,
por fuente el hondo mar

Al ver sobre las olas rayar la luz divina,
no escucha débil trino que al hombre da placer;
el grito oye salvaje del águila marina,
o siente el ala enorme que el vendaval domina
su copa estremecer (...)».

Miquel Costa i Llobera
(Versión castellana del autor en Líricas, 1899)

Tras pasar nueve meses viviendo en el frío y lluvioso norte de Escocia, no tenía muchas ganas de pasarme otro año «a la sombra». Por ello, decidí mudarme a las Islas Baleares para realizar un máster en Cambio Global, que después me abriría las puertas a un doctorado. Así que, tras estar trabajando con bacterias que se «comían» el petróleo, me marché a Mallorca a seguir estudiando los océanos. Aunque no solo los océanos y sus procesos internos, sino también qué papel juegan estos en el clima de nuestro planeta y, de manera inversa, cómo los cambios en el clima afectan a nuestros océanos y las formas de vida que los habitan.

El cambio climático es el mayor reto al que ha de enfrentarse la sociedad global a lo largo del presente siglo XXI y, muy probablemente, también durante los siglos venideros. Este fenómeno global, cuyos impactos son locales, es el principal motor de un conjunto de fenómenos y procesos más amplio, el llamado cambio global, que no solo involucra al cambio climático y sus efectos, sino también a todos aquellos procesos globales cuyo agente causante es, en mayor o menor grado, el ser humano. Así, dentro de este concepto se engloban también la contaminación (del agua, suelos, aire, etc.), la pérdida de biodiversidad o las enfermedades emergentes. Sin embargo, todos estos procesos que suceden dentro del planeta Tierra están íntimamente relacionados y, por tanto, mantienen fuertes relaciones de interdependencia que se traducen en numerosos bucles de retroalimentación positiva. Por ello, la lucha contra el cambio global no puede realizarse sin la correcta comprensión de cada uno de los procesos individuales que lo conforman y cómo estos interactúan entre sí.

No podemos olvidar que el ser humano pertenece al sistema Tierra, por lo que no solo es agente causal de esta serie de problemas globales, sino también receptor de sus impactos negativos. Los distintos agentes del cambio global interactúan de múltiples maneras con respecto al sistema socioeconómico de las sociedades humanas en un mundo cada vez más globalizado. Por tanto, este reto no es solo científico, sino también económico, político y social. Es más, las soluciones, aunque previamente investigadas por el sistema científico, deben ser ejecutadas en forma legislativa en todos los ámbitos desde lo local a lo global.

Es por ello que ahora están surgiendo numerosas visiones distintas acerca de cómo afrontar nuestro gran reto global (como, por ejemplo, el famoso *Green New Deal* en los Estados Unidos de América). Este «galimatías» de interacciones entre ciencias naturales, economía, política, etc., hacen del estudio del cambio global un campo apasionante a la par que arduo.

Un buen ejemplo para comprender lo complejo y vital de las interacciones entre naturaleza y actividades humanas, lo encontramos en el primer capítulo de este libro. Como comentábamos, del 12 al 15 de septiembre de 2019, la gota fría o DANA asoló numerosos pueblos y ciudades del Levante peninsular, ocasionando graves daños y pérdidas humanas, materiales y ambientales. Es de esperar que, como consecuencia del cambio climático, este tipo de fenómenos vean incrementada su frecuencia e intensidad en las próximas décadas, según el Panel Intergubernamental de Expertos sobre el Cambio Climático (IPCC). Estos fenómenos meteorológicos extremos provocan importantes daños que no se deben únicamente a las condiciones meteorológicas, sino que también son fruto de otras razones como la más que cuestionable planificación urbanística, que ha ocupado zonas inundables en numerosos puntos del país. Sirva de ejemplo la Región de Murcia, donde la DANA ha provocado catorce mil siniestros y daños materiales estimados en ochenta y dos millones de euros, para ser conscientes del potencial de impacto negativo que tendrá el cambio climático en nuestro país. Sus consecuencias afectarán a sectores tan estratégicos para nuestra economía como la agricultura o el turismo. Y es que el impacto del cambio climático en la región mediterránea no es un asunto baladí, pues se prevé que en España pueda afectar a un 12% del PIB. Pecaríamos de ingenuos si pensáramos que nos vamos a librar de estos impactos. Ya que, como decíamos, el cambio climático es un fenómeno global, cuyos impactos son locales (esto lo repito a conciencia puesto que es una idea clave). Los mares y océanos que bañan las costas españolas también sufrirán las consecuencias. Actualmente, los ecosistemas marinos ya nos revelan cómo los impactos del cambio climático están afectando a las especies que los habitan. Por ejemplo, en las Islas Baleares, las idílicas aguas transparentes del mar balear se deben a una característica biogeoquímica en su composición: la *oligotrofia*. Este término significa literalmente «poco alimento», es decir, en estas aguas hay pocos nutrientes, lo cual hace que las comunidades de microorganismos que viven en ellas sean más reducidas. Esto contrasta con otras zonas en las que se dan procesos de eutrofización, como el Mar Menor, donde las aguas no son tan trasparentes. Sin embargo, en estas aguas tan transparentes sí que ocurren muchos procesos interesantes que pasan desapercibidos para el ojo humano. Y es que el mundo que forman los microorganismos marinos es impresionante.

En tierra firme los organismos encargados de hacer la fotosíntesis son las plantas (árboles, hierba, arbustos, etc.). Sabemos que las plantas son organismos fotosintéticos capaces de captar CO_2 y emitir O_2, utilizado la luz solar y los nutrientes del suelo. A estos organismos se les conoce como los «productores» dentro de un ecosistema. Gracias a este proceso tan importante, las plantas no solo eliminan parte del CO_2 atmosférico, sino que inician las redes tróficas en el planeta Tierra. Esto puede parecer una exageración, pero no lo es. Posteriormente los «consumidores primarios» se alimentan de las plantas. Sin embargo, esta explicación es demasiado simplista para entender la realidad que sucede en los ecosistemas naturales. Tradicionalmente se ha explicado como si las relaciones tróficas entre los organismos fueran «lineales» y «unidireccionales»: el conejo se come la hierba y el zorro se come al conejo. Así, para definir esta relación trófica, durante muchos años se usó el término «cadena trófica». ¿Esto qué quiere decir? Pues que todos los eslabones de los ecosistemas están unidos a modo de cadena. Sin embargo, la realidad es mucho más compleja, como siempre. Lo correcto no es hablar de cadenas, sino de «redes tróficas». Para entender esto pensemos en un ecosistema mediterráneo típico de la península Ibérica. Plantas herbáceas brotan del suelo en una zona campestre, pero no todas ellas son de la misma especie. Llega un grupo de conejos europeos (*Oryctolagus cuniculus*) a alimentarse de ellas. Sin embargo, no están solos; a unos metros también hay un ejemplar de liebre ibérica (*Lepus granatensis*), que también se alimenta de esas plantas. Por el momento tenemos a muchas especies de plantas y a dos especies de consumidores primarios: el conejo europeo y la liebre ibérica, pero aquí no acaba la historia. Si algún individuo de ambas especies se despistase podría ser depredado por un «consumidor secundario». Y en este grupo también hay variedad, ya que las liebres o los conejos podrían ser presa de especies como el búho real (*Bubo bubo*), el lince ibérico (*Lynx pardinus*), el zorro (*Vulpes vulpes*) o el águila ibérica (*Aquila adalberti*). ¿Veis la «cadena trófica» por algún lado? Yo tampoco, porque es una «red» de interacciones.

En los mares y océanos, las redes tróficas son también muy diversas y complejas. Pese a que en tierra firme estamos acostumbrados a estudiarlas y comprenderlas usando ejemplos de seres vivos visibles a simple vista, en los ecosistemas marinos también existen redes tróficas, pero en este caso, microscópicas. Aparte de las algas y fanerógamas (plantas) marinas, en los océanos el fitoplancton marino también es capaz de hacer la fotosíntesis. Estos organismos son unicelulares y existen multitud de tipos diferentes. Así tenemos a las diatomeas, los cocolitofóridos o las algas clorofíceas unicelulares. Todos ellos viven en la columna de agua, es decir, «flotan» en el océano y están sujetos a las condiciones físicas del medio, como las corrientes marinas o el oleaje. A estos organismos que viven en la columna de agua los llamamos «plancton» (del griego *planktos* que significa «errante»). Así, a grandes rasgos, el plancton marino estaría formado por el fitoplancton (organismos planctónicos capaces de hacer la fotosíntesis), pero también por el zooplancton (organismos planctónicos que se alimentan del fitoplancton), bacterioplancton (bacterias marinas, algunas incluso hacen la fotosíntesis), virioplancton (virus patógenos de otros organismos planctónicos) y el plancton gelatinoso (medusas y ctenóforos). Y, tal y como sucede en los ecosistemas terrestres, las relaciones entre ellos son múltiples y complejas. Recordemos que son redes, no cadenas. De momento, nos centraremos en el caso del fitoplancton.

El fitoplancton marino, pese a que habita en los océanos del planeta, tiene un papel esencial para la vida en tierra firme. A través de la fotosíntesis, produce el 50% del oxígeno que estáis respirando mientras leéis esta frase y absorbe CO_2 atmosférico a través de la fotosíntesis y lo acumula en capas profundas del océano. Además, también mantiene las redes tróficas de los ecosistemas marinos (incluidos los peces, crustáceos, moluscos, etc., de los que nos alimentamos los seres humanos). Estos organismos «errantes» se encuentran en todos los mares y océanos del planeta, pero sus especies y abundancia difieren de un lugar a otro. Así, en los mares polares las especies de fitoplancton no son las mismas que en las zonas tropicales, aunque sí que hay algunas que cubren gran parte de los océanos. Entre todas las especies distintas de fitoplancton hay una que tiene una historia muy interesante, el *Prochlorococcus*. A finales de los años 80, un grupo de investigadores descubrió un género de bacterioplancton, que incluye varias especies muy semejantes entre sí, capaz de hacer la fotosíntesis que, por tanto, también formaría parte del fitoplancton (sí, estas categorías a veces son un poco liosas). Estos organismos habitan sobre todo en las aguas superficiales de todos los océanos tropicales del planeta y no suelen encontrarse en aguas muy frías. Es decir, es un organismo que vive en más del 50% de la superficie de los océanos y hasta hace cerca de treinta años lo desconocíamos. Pero no solo eso, la particularidad de estos organismos unicelulares es que son los más pequeños del planeta Tierra capaces de hacer la fotosíntesis.

Si tenemos en cuenta la superficie en la que habitan y su tamaño, nos daremos cuenta rápidamente, como se dieron cuenta los investigadores, que *Prochlorococcus* es el organismo fotosintético más abundante del planeta Tierra. Es decir, hay más *Prochlorococcus* en el mundo que margaritas o pinos. De hecho, muchísimos más. Este es uno de los múltiples secretos que esconde el fitoplancton marino y que refleja lo mucho que aún nos queda por conocer. Es sorprendente que hace treinta años, cuando ya habíamos pisado la Luna, inventado Internet o descendido en submarinos a algunas de las zonas más profundas de los océanos, aún no supiéramos de la existencia del organismo fotosintético más abundante de la Tierra. Un organismo que produce alrededor de una quinta parte del oxígeno que estamos respirando ahora mismo.

Aunque queda mucho por descubrir de estos microorganismos, la ciencia nos ha permitido avanzar enormemente en su conocimiento, así sabemos que el fitoplancton marino vive en aquellas partes de la columna de agua donde puede hacer la fotosíntesis, es decir, donde llega la luz del sol. A esta porción de radiación solar que participa en el proceso fotosintético la conocemos como «radiación fotosintéticamente activa». Sin embargo, no toda la radiación que llega del sol puede usarse para realizar la fotosíntesis. El sol también irradia radiación ultravioleta que es nociva para multitud de organismos, incluidos nosotros, los humanos. Esta radiación es la que potencialmente puede producirnos cáncer de piel. Esto es debido a que la radiación ultravioleta incide directamente en el ADN de las células de nuestra piel produciendo mutaciones. Imaginemos por un momento los efectos que tiene esta radiación sobre el fitoplancton, que son organismos unicelulares. La radiación ultravioleta hace inviable la vida de los organismos fitoplanctónicos a determinados niveles. Entonces, ¿cómo sobrevive el fitoplancton? Pues de múltiples maneras distintas. Una de las más conocidas es su capacidad para producir determinadas moléculas que actúan como «protector solar». Sin embargo, lo más sencillo para estos organismos es evitar que la radiación ultravioleta les incida directamente. Para ello, el fitoplancton se desplaza varios metros bajo la superficie del agua, donde llega menos cantidad de radiación ultravioleta. Esto origina un fenómeno muy curioso, ya que uno esperaría encontrar a los organismos que realizan la fotosíntesis lo «más cerca» posible de la superficie del océano, pero esto no es así. Es más, esto es un problema que se ha acentuado en las últimas décadas debido al debilitamiento de la capa de ozono. De esta manera, actualmente llega más radiación solar a las capas superficiales del océano, lo que hace que los organismos fitoplanctónicos no puedan desarrollar su ciclo vital de manera óptima a determinadas profundidades.

Pero no solo la radiación ultravioleta tiene impactos negativos sobre los microorganismos marinos, también existen multitud de procesos relacionados con el cambio global que tienen efectos nocivos comparables. Uno de ellos es la acidificación de los océanos, que ya hemos visto. Otro sería el aumento de la temperatura de las aguas oceánicas como consecuencia del calentamiento global. Pensad por un momento en vosotros mismos. El ser humano está «preparado» para vivir en un rango de temperatura determinado. Imaginad ahora que fuésemos desnudos por el mundo, ¿qué rango de temperatura podríamos soportar? Tendríamos una temperatura mínima a partir de la cual entraríamos en hipotermia y moriríamos, así como una temperatura máxima a partir de la cual también moriríamos. Pues al fitoplancton marino le sucede exactamente lo mismo: cada especie tiene un rango de temperatura en el que puede vivir. Si la temperatura del agua aumenta, determinadas especies no pueden vivir y se ven obligadas a desplazarse a regiones más frías.

Uno podría intentar estudiar estos fenómenos de manera aislada, es decir, analizar primero cuáles son los efectos de la acidificación sobre el fitoplancton, luego ver los de la radiación ultravioleta y finalmente los del aumento de la temperatura del agua. Sin embargo, en la naturaleza 1+1 no siempre es 2. Me explico. A partir de nuestro ejemplo, podemos considerar a estos tres fenómenos (radiación ultravioleta, subida de la temperatura y acidificación) como tres agentes de estrés para el fitoplancton marino. Estos agentes de estrés, o estresantes, cuando actúan de manera conjunta multiplican sus impactos, no los suman. Imaginad una única célula fitoplanctónica que flota en la inmensidad del mar. La temperatura empieza a subir y se desplaza a una zona más fría, pero sigue recibiendo la misma cantidad de radiación ultravioleta y esa masa de agua en la que ahora se encuentra es más ácida. Cuando los tres agentes de estrés inciden sobre el fitoplancton su potencial de impacto negativo se multiplica, es decir 1+1+1 no sería 3, sino más.

Esto es lo que llamamos sinergia entre agentes de estrés. En contraposición, puede producirse que la acción de diversos estresores sobre nuestros organismos fitoplanctónicos no multiplique los impactos, sino que los «divida» y los disminuya; esto es lo que conocemos como antagonismo entre agentes de estrés. Por ejemplo, un aumento de la temperatura y un exceso de nutrientes de un tipo determinado puede beneficiar a unas especies de fitoplancton mientras que, a la vez, perjudica a otras. Por tanto, un conjunto de agentes de estrés puede ser *sinérgico* o *antagónico* dependiendo de las especies, aunque estas se encuentren presentes en el mismo sitio. Este es otro ejemplo de lo compleja que es la naturaleza, no solo en su estudio fundamental, sino también a la hora de evaluar los impactos de las actividades humanas sobre las especies que habitan en un determinado ecosistema.

Para explorar las distintas respuestas de estos microorganismos a agentes de estrés, durante mi Trabajo Fin de Máster realicé prácticas de investigación en el Instituto Mediterráneo de Estudios Avanzados, IMEDEA (CSIC-UIB), estudiando durante un año cómo la radiación ultravioleta influía en el crecimiento de una especie de fitoplancton llamada *Tetraselmis suecica*. Para ello, sometíamos a cultivos de esta especie de fitoplancton a distintas intensidades de radiación ultravioleta y medíamos el tamaño de sus poblaciones cada día. De esta manera, podíamos conocer si la supervivencia de esta especie se veía amenazada a partir de una cantidad de radiación ultravioleta determinada o si simplemente crecían más o menos lentamente, pero no solo eso, también queríamos investigar si dichos organismos podían adaptarse a unas condiciones elevadas de radiación ultravioleta, incluso a unos niveles que nunca podrían darse en la naturaleza. Sorprendentemente, esta especie podía soportar niveles muy altos de intensidad de radiación ultravioleta, y es aquí donde llegaba la tercera pregunta de nuestro trabajo: Vale, pueden adaptarse, pero ¿a cambio de qué? Nosotros pensábamos que tal vez algunas de sus propiedades cambiarían en detrimento de dicha adaptación. Concretamente nos centramos en una de ellas, la *palatability*, que en castellano no tiene una traducción fácil, pero sería algo así como la apetencia o sabor agradable para sus depredadores, es decir, el zooplancton. Por tanto, queríamos ver si dicha adaptación generaba algún cambio en su composición que hiciera que los organismos zooplanctónicos se las «comieran» más o menos. Para ello, teníamos que introducir algunos organismos de zooplancton en los cultivos de fitoplancton. Es bastante difícil mantener el zooplancton en condiciones de laboratorio, hay que alimentarlos, controlar la temperatura, evaluar si mueren algunos o no cada día, etc. Concretamente para nuestro estudio seleccionamos especies del género *Calanus*, que se engloban dentro de los copépodos (si alguien ha visto *Bob Esponja*, el «señor Plancton» es en realidad un copépodo). La ventaja que nos aportaban estos pequeños crustáceos es que podíamos encontrarlos en las aguas de Mallorca, así que solo había que ir a buscarlos. Aunque esto no iba a ser tan fácil.

Para cazar a los copépodos o, mejor dicho, muestrearlos, lo primero que teníamos que hacer era comprobar que nuestros instrumentos de muestreo funcionaban bien. La manera de muestrear estos organismos es utilizar un instrumento semejante a un embudo del estilo de un copo de pesca, hecho con una malla de poro muy, muy pequeño; concretamente de doscientas micras, es decir 0,2 milímetros (una quinta parte de un milímetro, que es una décima parte de un centímetro). Es algo semejante a una manga pastelera, con la diferencia de que en vez de ser una bolsa de plástico que retiene el líquido, es una malla porosa que deja salir el agua. El procedimiento de muestreo es bastante sencillo: se tira el copo al agua, se sumerge y se recoge para hacerlo volver a la superficie con una cuerda. Una vez que tenemos el copo en superficie, se deja escurrir el agua a través de los poros. De esta manera, se recogen aquellos organismos planctónicos que haya en el agua, ya que estos no pueden pasar por un tamaño de poro tan pequeño. Posteriormente se retiran del fondo del copo los organismos muestreados, con suerte algunos copépodos, y se trasfieren a un recipiente con agua marina para su posterior traslado al laboratorio. Este proceso se realiza tantas veces como sea necesario para conseguir la cantidad óptima de copépodos necesarios para los experimentos en laboratorio. Aunque, como casi siempre, esto no está exento de dificultades. La primera vez que probamos este dispositivo, nos fuimos a una cala perteneciente al pequeño pueblo de Banyalbufar, en la cara norte de la Sierra de Tramuntana. Allí muchas de las calas tienen rocas frente a las cuales a veces hay más de cinco metros de profundidad, por lo que son un lugar idóneo para realizar las pruebas del copo de zooplancton. Para llegar hasta una de las rocas, tuve que bajar trepando con todo el material por una pendiente bastante pronunciada. Una vez que logré llegar a la roca idónea para el «lanzamiento de copo», me di cuenta de que las olas pasaban por encima, no muy fuerte, pero el suelo estaba totalmente empapado, así que me tuve que quedar en bañador y descalzo. Durante alrededor de una hora repetí el proceso una y otra vez: «copo para arriba, copo para abajo». Cada vez que lo recogía miraba si se estaban recolectando copépodos o no y, sorprendentemente, estaba funcionando. Así que nuestro método estaba en disposición de poder usarse de una manera más óptima en los próximos días. Me dispuse a recoger todo el material, pero no tuve en cuenta que llevaba una hora en una posición muy incómoda y se me había dormido un poco una pierna. Al levantarme, me resbalé por el suelo empapado de agua por las olas y me caí de espaldas sobre la roca haciéndome varias heridas. Fue una caída de las más ridículas de mi vida, el resbalón fue tan grande que mientras caía vi el cielo y uno de mis pies entre él y yo. Todos los copépodos que había muestreado se me cayeron y tuve que empezar de nuevo a muestrear, esta vez con dolor y un poco de sangre. Nadie dijo nunca que la ciencia no fuera dolorosa y ridícula a partes iguales. Como esta prueba fue un «éxito», unas semanas después nos dispusimos a hacer el muestreo real. Para ello, nos fuimos un día entero a la Bahía de Pollença, en el noreste de Mallorca, para llevar a cabo el muestreo desde la zódiac. Esta vez todo fue sobre ruedas y no hubo ningún percance, salvo que hizo mucho sol y nos quemamos la cara. Volvimos al IMEDEA (CSIC-UIB) cargados de copépodos para llevar a cabo los experimentos. Y, finalmente, descubrimos que cuanta más radiación ultravioleta incidía sobre el fitoplancton, algunos de nuestros organismos de estudio sobrevivían. Sin embargo, su contenido nutricional era mucho menor, lo cual hacía que los copépodos depredaran un mayor número de ellos hasta llevarlos a desaparecer de los cultivos, desencadenando también la muerte por inanición de los copépodos. Los copépodos son el alimento de algunas especies de peces y de sus larvas, siendo por ello también muy importantes en las redes tróficas marinas. Estos resultados nos sirven de ejemplo para comprender que determinados estresores, como la radiación ultravioleta, pueden producir fenómenos de cascada trófica que afecten a otros organismos de las redes tróficas. O, lo que es lo mismo, cómo el aumento de la radiación ultravioleta, en determinadas circunstancias, puede disminuir las poblaciones de peces de interés para el ser humano con la pérdida de algunas especies de organismos fitoplanctónicos y, consecuentemente, el zooplancton que se alimenta de ellas. De nuevo, la complejidad de los ecosistemas y los organismos que los habitan se pone de manifiesto y nos debería hacer reflexionar sobre la importancia de investigar estos fenómenos que, a priori, parecería que no son muy importantes.

Conscientes de ello, tras acabar el máster muchos alumnos deciden continuar con la carrera investigadora. En mi caso, tenía mucho interés en realizar un doctorado para, en un futuro, llegar a ser investigador y poder dedicarme profesionalmente a estudiar los océanos. Había trabajado en muchos sitios antes de acabar mi máster y tenía distintas oportunidades para emprender un doctorado, sin embargo, ninguna de ellas me convencía del todo. ¿Debía emigrar como hicieron muchos compañeros y compañeras en busca de oportunidades en el extranjero? ¿Tendría oportunidades equivalentes en España y debía apostar por quedarme? Viendo las dificultades de la carrera investigadora en el ámbito nacional e internacional, ¿merecía la pena emprender este camino profesional? En un primer momento, estuve preparando mi candidatura para irme a hacer el doctorado a Nueva Zelanda, a las antípodas de la península Ibérica. Preparé todo lo necesario y el nivel de inglés que exigían, pero ocurrió algo asombroso. Uno de mis profesores del máster, el Dr. Rafel Simó del Institut de Ciències del Mar de Barcelona (ICM-CSIC), con quien había hablado de mi interés en realizar un doctorado, me notificó que estaba dispuesto a acogerme en los próximos meses para poder planificar cómo hacer la tesis doctoral bajo su supervisión (el tema de estudio, posible financiación, etc.). Pero no solo eso, se me presentaba una oportunidad única para participar en dos campañas oceanográficas que cambiarían mi visión de las ciencias marinas y de nuestro planeta para siempre. Así que, dos semanas antes de acabar el máster, ya me había mudado a Barcelona. Y solo un mes después de acabarlo, me preparaba para una de las expediciones oceanográficas que serían parte de mi investigación doctoral. Volvía al océano Atlántico, pero esta vez por mucho más tiempo.

CLIMA Y ALGODÓN DE AZÚCAR

«Por diferentes motivos se marchan los hombres a los confines abandonados del mundo. A algunos les impele solamente el afán de aventuras, otros sienten una intensa sed de saber, los terceros obedecen a la seductora llamada de unas voces quedas, al encanto misterioso de lo desconocido que les aleja de los senderos rutinarios de la vida cotidiana».

Ernest Shackleton (1874-1922), explorador polar

Hoy en día quienes se dedican a la investigación científica no viajan de un sitio a otro en buques tan interesantes como el Endurance (el buque de la expedición Imperial transantártica de Shackleton) o el Beagle (el famoso barco con el que Darwin dio la vuelta al mundo). Hoy en día, las «naves» que te llevan de una expedición a otra suelen tener nombres tan corrientes como Vueling o Ryanair, y fue en una de esas donde me embarqué rumbo a Barcelona con un par de mochilas, mucha ilusión y una incertidumbre laboral inversamente proporcional. Pasaba de trabajar en un centro de investigación situado en el corazón de la Serra de Tramuntana a currar en el centro de la Barceloneta y la Vila Olimpica de Barcelona, el epicentro de la gentrificación, el turismo y el consumo desacerbado. El cambio, a simple vista, parecía que no iba a ser a mejor en algunos aspectos.

Nada más llegar a Barcelona me tenía que embarcar en dos expediciones científicas que me llevarían más lejos de lo que nunca había estado y donde seguramente tampoco ha llegado nadie de mi familia. La preparación de una campaña oceanográfica es un proceso muy largo y complejo. Lo primero que hay que tener en cuenta es que para realizar una expedición científica hace falta financiación, es decir, dinero. Los investigadores científicos por lo general consiguen dicho dinero de fuentes de financiación públicas, normalmente dependientes de los ministerios o gobiernos regionales competentes en ciencia de cada estado, o bien, de entidades supranacionales como la Unión Europea, y como podréis imaginar, conseguir un proyecto de investigación es un proceso muy competitivo. En España, tras casi diez años de recortes en ciencia e investigación fruto de la crisis económica más reciente, el panorama no es nada halagüeño. Sin embargo, aún se sigue haciendo ciencia de nivel, aunque es una situación que requiere de un viraje importante si no queremos quedarnos atrás con respecto a otros países de nuestro entorno o, peor aún, perder la batalla científica global que está teniendo lugar contra fenómenos como el cambio climático. Una vez que se consigue financiación, la expedición científica que queda enmarcada dentro de un proyecto no tiene lugar en unas semanas o meses, sino en un periodo de años. Por lo general, si una expedición involucra a un gran número de científicos de distintos países y tiene lugar en algún rincón remoto del planeta, pueden tardarse dos o tres años en prepararla. Durante ese tiempo se trabaja en la obtención de permisos para faenar aguas de otros países (sí, el océano a veces también tiene fronteras políticas), aprender o mejorar las técnicas científicas que se van a implementar en la expedición y seleccionar al equipo. Una vez completados todos estos pasos, y otros que os iré contando más adelante, la expedición científica puede comenzar y un buque oceanográfico suelta amarras desde el puerto para marcharse en dirección a algún lugar del gran azul.

Mi director de tesis había conseguido un proyecto científico en el año 2012 y así en 2014 y 2015 iban a tener lugar las campañas oceanográficas de dicho proyecto, cuyos resultados tendría que incluir en mi tesis doctoral. En mi caso, iba a participar en ambas expediciones científicas: una en el océano Atlántico y otra en el océano Antártico, en ese orden. Sinceramente lo afronté con el vértigo que puede esperarse de alguien de tan solo veintitrés años de edad, el integrante más joven de un equipo de treinta investigadores nacionales e internacionales, que acaba de finalizar sus estudios de máster las semanas anteriores a la partida hacia el océano Atlántico para unos meses después ir al Antártico. Y lo que era aún más impresionante, las expediciones iban a tener lugar a bordo del buque insignia de la investigación polar española: el BIO Hespérides. Nos preparábamos para visitar cinco puertos distintos y estar más de setenta y cinco días encerrados con varias decenas de científicos y personal de la Armada Española entre las mamparas de hierro del BIO Hespérides. Para un proyecto de científico como yo, todo esto parecía un escenario casi ilusorio. Es bastante extraño ver cómo tu sueño de niño se torna real y, a la vez, intuyes que solo es la punta del iceberg de lo que queda por venir.

El nombre del proyecto de investigación era PEGASO, aunque en realidad es el acrónimo de *Plankton-derived emissions of trace gases and aerosols in the Southern Ocean*. ¿Qué significa este título tan complejo y qué íbamos hacer al frío océano Antártico? Vamos por partes. De manera muy resumida os diré que este proyecto tenía muchos objetivos distintos, pero, a grandes rasgos, se trataba de investigar cómo el océano es partícipe de los procesos atmosféricos de formación de nubes y, por lo tanto, de qué manera esto puede afectar al sistema climático global. Es decir, desentrañar qué importancia tienen estos procesos en la regulación del clima del planeta Tierra. El proyecto PEGASO se subdividía en dos campañas oceanográficas distintas a bordo del BIO Hespérides: Trans-PEGASO y PEGASO. La campaña Trans-PEGASO zarparía de Cartagena (España) el 20 de octubre de 2014 y finalizaría unos treinta días después, el 22 de noviembre, en Punta Arenas (Chile). Pese a que el Hespérides investiga todos los años en las frías aguas del océano Antártico, durante lo que se conoce como *Campaña Antártica*, su base permanente es el Puerto de Cartagena. Por ello, todos los años ha de cruzar el océano Atlántico hasta llegar generalmente a los puertos de Chile o Argentina. Así que, la campaña Trans-PEGASO aprovecharía la «bajada» del Hespérides en su tránsito desde Cartagena hasta Punta Arenas previo a la campaña antártica de ese año. En dicha campaña embarcamos un grupo reducido de investigadores junto a los instrumentos científicos necesarios para afrontar la campaña PEGASO que tendría lugar varios meses después en aguas del océano Antártico. Durante treinta días en el Atlántico, nuestro trabajo sería poner a punto los equipos para la mencionada campaña PEGASO, averiguar qué problemas podrían surgir y cómo solucionarlos, y; como no, muestrear agua y aire para tener datos valiosos en las remotas regiones del océano Atlántico. Posteriormente, a primeros de enero de 2015 zarparíamos desde el Puerto de Ushuaia (Argentina) para pasar cuarenta y cinco días en el océano Antártico y volver al mismo puerto a mediados de febrero de 2015.

El principal objetivo de la campaña PEGASO era investigar la producción por el fitoplancton marino de sustancias formadoras de aerosoles (unas partículas que juegan un papel clave en la atmósfera), principalmente gases que se encuentran en una concentración muy pequeña que llamamos *gases traza*, así como partículas biológicas producidas también por el fitoplancton. Una de las razones por las que debíamos estudiar estos procesos en el océano Antártico era que durante el verano austral (es decir, cuando es invierno en el hemisferio norte), se producen abundantes proliferaciones de plancton marino.

Y es que en nuestro maravilloso planeta Tierra existen multitud de fenómenos increíbles que aún permanecen ocultos. Procesos que influyen más de lo que nos imaginamos en nuestro día a día. Como os contaba anteriormente, la vida en el planeta no puede entenderse sin la luz del sol; ya que, gracias a ella, las plantas y algas realizan la fotosíntesis y elaboran elementos orgánicos que sirven para iniciar el flujo de alimento hacia el resto de seres vivos, incluido el ser humano. Debido a esto, no podemos entender el desarrollo de nuestra vida cotidiana y de nuestros hábitos y costumbres sin el sol. Existen muchísimos más procesos y fenómenos en la naturaleza que no pueden entenderse el uno sin el otro y que, a pesar de todos los avances científicos, aún carecen de una explicación completa que nos ayude a entenderlos. Por este motivo, un grupo muy numeroso de científicos embarcamos en el Proyecto PEGASO, a bordo del BIO Hespérides rumbo al Atlántico y a la Antártida. ¿Por qué? Porque aún desconocemos en gran medida cómo se forman las nubes en regiones remotas del océano. Tal vez esto resulte chocante, pero es así. Para que una nube se forme, pese a lo que nos explican en la escuela, no se necesita solamente vapor de agua. Se necesita también algo muy importante, sin lo cual no puede existir absolutamente ni una gota de rocío, lo que nosotros conocemos como «núcleos de condensación de nubes». Se trata de pequeñas partículas, a las cuales se les pega el agua alrededor hasta formar pequeñas gotas que poco a poco van uniéndose hasta formar las nubes.

Imaginémonos la típica feria en la que se hace algodón de azúcar. Alrededor del palo se unen pequeñas fibras de azúcar hasta formar el ansiado dulce. Sin ese palo, no se podría formar el algodón de azúcar, sería una masa deforme. Pues algo muy semejante es lo que pasa con las gotas que forman las nubes. Ahora bien, ¿qué son estas partículas?, ¿de qué están formadas? Pues prácticamente de todo lo que podamos imaginar dentro de un rango de tamaño determinado: desde partículas de humo de fábricas o emisiones de volcanes; hasta, incluso, bacterias o sal marina. ¿Y qué es lo que hacíamos los científicos en este proyecto? La respuesta es tan simple como el hecho de que para que se forme una nube se necesita agua, y ¿dónde hay más agua que en el océano? Prácticamente en ningún sitio. Y allí estábamos nosotros, pero ¿cuáles son esas partículas?, ¿cuál es «palo» que emite el océano para que se formen los «algodones de azúcar», que nosotros llamamos nubes?

En nuestro caso nos dedicamos a estudiar a los responsables de parte de este fenómeno: el fitoplancton marino. Estos pequeños organismos emiten millones y millones de pequeñas moléculas (de muchos tipos y muy distintas en su composición), que llamamos *gases traza.* Estos gases salen del agua y pasan a la atmósfera para que el agua se condense en torno a ellos transformándose en gotas de rocío, que formarán las nubes. Este proceso en realidad es mucho más complejo, ya que, estos gases traza han de reaccionar en la atmósfera con otros compuestos para que se formen las partículas que potencialmente pueden actuar como núcleos de condensación de nubes. Pero ¿por qué ir hasta la Antártida? Pues muy simple, porque allí no hay ni emisiones de volcanes ni fábricas ni chimeneas... ni nada que interfiera en el papel que desempeña la biología marina. Por lo tanto, permite averiguar cómo se forman las nubes de la Antártida, para posteriormente conocer hasta qué punto el ser humano interfiere en este proceso a través de las emisiones industriales, de hogares, medios de transporte, etc. En resumen, podría decirse que el objetivo era averiguar en qué grado interferimos en la naturaleza y en el clima global, y qué riesgos asociados pueden producirse en nuestras vidas y las de nuestro maravillo planeta Tierra si continuamos alterando estos procesos.

La preparación de la campaña Trans-PEGASO fue verdaderamente frenética. Más de cien cajas baúles y cajas de material científico se distribuían por los pasillos del Institut de Ciències del Mar de Barcelona. Cada uno de los investigadores que participaban en ambas expediciones tenía que estar seguro de que no se olvidaba nada de lo necesario para llevar a cabo su trabajo, en la Antártida no hay tiendas donde adquirir material científico. Asimismo, los investigadores internacionales también tenían que preparar su material científico y tenían dos opciones: o enviarlo a Barcelona para que nosotros los transportásemos hasta el puerto, o directamente enviarlo allí. Una vez que todo el material estuvo listo lo cargamos en un camión que partió rumbo a Cartagena, mientras que los investigadores hacíamos el mismo recorrido con las furgonetas del centro de investigación. Como ya habéis visto, *glamour* y ciencia no suelen ir de la mano y, aunque así fuera, lo importante es que todo esté a punto antes de la expedición. El capitán James Cook, uno de los exploradores polares más famosos de la historia, lo tenía bien claro:

«Para su tiempo, James Cook iba magníficamente equipado. En buena parte debió sus éxitos al hecho de que nunca levó anclas hasta haberse preocupado con todo detalle del abastecimiento de la dotación y los barcos, no dejando nada al azar».

La lucha por el polo sur, *K. W. L Bezemer, 1952.*

Durante la primera semana, estuvimos en el puerto de Cartagena realizado las labores previas a Trans-PEGASO a bordo del BIO Hespérides. Hay que tener en cuenta que en un buque de investigación no solo navegan científicos, nosotros solemos ser bastante inútiles fuera de nuestro campo de trabajo y, como ya imaginaréis, si dependiera de los investigadores el mantenimiento y navegación de un buque de más de ochenta metros de eslora; la historia no acabaría bien. Sería graciosa, eso sí. Por ello, en las campañas oceanográficas a bordo del BIO Hespérides suelen embarcar tres grupos de personas distintas: los científicos (que realizan labores de investigación, enmarcadas en proyectos científicos financiados nacional e internacionalmente), el personal de la Armada (que se encarga de la navegación y es responsable del mantenimiento del buque) y el personal técnico de la Unidad de Tecnología Marina (responsables del mantenimiento del equipamiento científico del buque y del apoyo para la realización de las campañas oceanográficas). Como podéis suponer, cada uno de estos tres grupos se debe encargar, antes del inicio de la campaña Antártica anual, de preparar todo el material necesario para llevar a cabo sus labores durante la navegación. Mientras se está en puerto antes de zarpar, en el buque se trabaja sin cesar durante la mayor parte del día poniéndolo todo a punto. No recuerdo jornadas más extenuantes que las de ese tipo. En concreto, los científicos estuvimos preparando material todos los días desde, aproximadamente, las 8.00 a. m. hasta las 23.00 p. m.; solo parando para comer. Sin embargo, un par de días antes de zarpar ya lo teníamos todo listo. Solo quedaban los últimos preparativos acompañados de nervios e ilusión.

Esta ilusión, en mi caso, hacía muchos años que se forjaba. El BIO Hespérides tiene para mí un significado muy especial. Yo crecí en Cartagena, de donde es mi familia y donde residí hasta los diecinueve años. Mi madre, que es maestra, me enseñó casi todo lo que un niño podía necesitar saber acerca del medio que le rodea y desde muy pequeño potenció en mí la curiosidad. Mi habitación siempre estuvo llena de libros de naturaleza, viajes y ciencia; por cierto, no muy diferente a como la tengo ahora que rondo los treinta. Desde bien pequeño me gustó el mar, aprendí muy, muy pronto a nadar y bucear; aparte de pasar innumerables amaneceres pescando con mi padre por algún lugar de la costa cartagenera, principalmente cerca del Faro de Navidad. Desde allí, veíamos muchas veces al BIO Hespérides saliendo a hacer alguna maniobra o adentrándose en el Mar Mediterráneo para volver muchos meses después procedente del frío océano Antártico. Es curioso, ya que el BIO Hespérides fue botado y empezó a realizar su función como buque científico en 1990, prácticamente cuando yo nací. Mi padre, como el suyo y parte de nuestra familia, es trabajador de astilleros y, concretamente, participó en la construcción de este buque. Lo cual tiene su gracia, podría decirse que mi padre «nos hizo» al BIO Hespérides y a mí prácticamente a la vez. Así que, tanto el Hespérides como yo, somos *millennial*. Además, por parte materna, mi abuelo era marino de la armada y durante mi infancia siempre me contaba sus historias de cuando estuvo embarcado y navegando por distintos lugares; poniendo especial énfasis, de nuevo, en este buque. Supongo que él quería que yo fuera en el BIO Hespérides de mayor, pero como militar. Una opción que, por cierto, descarté de muy joven. Seguramente se sentiría orgulloso, aunque nunca lo sabré porque falleció algunos años antes de que yo embarcase. Para poner la guinda al pastel, desde los ocho años formé parte del Grupo Scout San Ginés, donde aprendí acerca del medio natural que me rodeaba y a convivir con mucha gente aislados en mitad del monte; y gracias a esa experiencia, mis ganas de explorar se fueron haciendo más y más grandes. Y todo eso, en una ciudad como Cartagena suponía el cóctel perfecto para que a un joven le entrase «el gusanillo» de cómo sería vivir y trabajar a miles de kilómetros de casa en pleno océano. Históricamente, los puertos siempre han sido las puertas de entrada a la exploración y el descubrimiento, de aventuras y hazañas de los más intrépidos. No es de extrañar, pues, que esta aventura científica comenzara en uno de ellos.

Estando aún en el puerto de Cartagena, y ultimando los preparativos para zarpar con destino al océano Atlántico, podíamos sentir el peso de la historia de esta ciudad marítima. Desde su fundación en el 227 a. C. por Asdrúbal el Bello, los destellos cristalinos de la superficie del agua han despertado a los habitantes de Cartagena. Entre praderas de *Posidonia oceanica*, sus fondos arenosos llenos de restos arqueológicos son una reminiscencia de todo lo que allí ha acontecido. Es en este puerto natural, formado por los surcos esquistosos de la costa mediterránea, donde empieza, acaba y, por suerte, aún perdura la historia; cuyo nexo común es una de las mayores incógnitas y motivos de fascinación del ser humano: el mar. Y aquí era justamente donde comenzaba la historia de nuestra campaña de exploración oceanográfica.

Pero, antes de adentrarnos de lleno en cómo fue nuestra campaña, vale la pena aprovechar la oportunidad que nos brinda este enclave para echar la vista atrás hasta la exploración del pasado, el paso previo a la investigación científica moderna. Su origen seguramente reside en la imperiosa necesidad del ser humano de ver algo con sus propios ojos antes de plantearse preguntas acerca de ello. Los viajes en aras de conocer los límites y recursos naturales de nuestro planeta, llevaron a numerosos exploradores oriundos de Cartagena a adentrarse en lugares del globo terráqueo nunca antes visitados. La apertura directa al mar y una cultura empapada por el olor a salitre, hicieron de esta ciudad una cuna de exploradores y marinos. Algunas de las misiones que llevaron a cabo, contemporáneamente olvidadas, recogen la esencia misma de la acción de descubrir, y es que el mar siempre ha sido un cajón de misterios, actuando como una suerte de canto de sirena para los exploradores. Así, el marino cartagenero Juan Fernández posiblemente descubrió Nueva Zelanda en el siglo XVI. De confirmarse, habría sido el primer europeo en poner pie en dichas islas (aunque este es un hecho histórico controvertido). Es más, habría sido el primer español en visitar sus antípodas, es decir, aquel lugar que está lo más lejos posible en el globo terráqueo. ¿Qué debe sentir una persona al descubrir sus antípodas? Pues seguramente hambre y frío, si no se estaba muriendo de escorbuto. Desgraciadamente, no queda nadie a quien preguntárselo.

Otra empresa admirable fue la llevada a cabo por Marcos Jiménez de la Espada, también cartagenero, que cruzó Sudamérica de este a oeste durante varios años (1862-1866) descubriendo numerosas especies animales y contribuyendo a cimentar la historia del conocimiento de la naturaleza por parte del ser humano.

Antes, se había licenciado en Ciencias Naturales en la Universidad Central de Madrid, focalizando sus posteriores investigaciones en el estudio y taxonomía de los anfibios; de suma importancia en sus posteriores expediciones por el mundo. A mediados del siglo XIX nos encontrábamos todavía en un periodo en el que las exploraciones, para la captación de recursos naturales, y el establecimiento de colonias, se sucedían sin cesar desde los países que llevaban varias décadas «industrializándose». Por ejemplo, tengamos en cuenta que no se descubrió que la Antártida era un continente hasta 1820-1821. Por no hablar de que se tardaron cien años más en llegar al Polo Sur. No en vano, la reina Isabel II de España creó la Comisión científica del Pacífico, una expedición de naturalistas, humanistas y fotógrafos españoles enviada al continente americano entre 1862 y 1865 en aras de incrementar el conocimiento de la humanidad. Dicha tarea la realizarían con la ayuda de marinos del ejército español que se encargarían de transportarlos, mientras imponían la política colonial del gobierno de la época en las zonas por las que pasaban.

Para la Comisión científica del Pacífico, tras un arduo proceso de selección, fueron escogidos ocho expedicionarios: Patricio María Paz y Membiela, Fernando Amor, Francisco de Paula Martínez y Sáez, Marcos Jiménez de la Espada, Manuel Almagro, Juan Isern, Rafael Castro y Ordóñez, y Bartolomé Puig y Galup. En total eran seis profesores vinculados al Museo de Ciencias Naturales de Madrid (tres zoólogos, un geólogo, un botánico y un antropólogo), entre los que se encontraba Jiménez de la Espada, y dos ayudantes: un taxidermista y un dibujante-fotógrafo. Estos ocho expedicionarios embarcaron a bordo de las fragatas Nuestra Señora del Triunfo y Resolución, y la goleta Covadonga rumbo a América, zarpando del puerto de Cádiz el 10 de agosto de 1862. Fue la aventura científica más importante emprendida por un gobierno español hacia tierras sudamericanas durante el siglo XIX, y la primera en la historia de la que existe material fotográfico.

A su llegada a América, en primer lugar, centraron sus actividades en Brasil, el Río de la Plata y Chile. El siguiente objetivo era llegar a la ciudad chilena de Valparaíso, para el que unos irían por tierra y otros por mar. De esta manera, Paz, Amor, Isern y Almagro optaron por la vía terrestre, cruzando las pampas argentinas y atravesando los Andes. Por otro lado, Jiménez de la Espada atravesó el difícil estrecho de Magallanes en la goleta Covadonga; y sus colegas Martínez, Puig y el fotógrafo Castro hicieron la travesía por el Cabo de Hornos tras repostar en Puerto Stanley, en las islas Malvinas. Una vez se reencontraron los ocho expedicionarios en Valparaíso, pretendían continuar su exploración con la intención de llegar hasta el océano Atlántico, es decir: cruzar América de oeste a este por el mismísimo corazón de la selva amazónica. ¡Y vaya si lo consiguieron! Pero no todos ellos. Evidentemente, no fue un camino de rosas y se encontraron numerosas adversidades, principalmente motivadas porque su medio de transporte eran los buques de guerra. Además, al mismo tiempo estalló un conflicto entre España y Chile. Por ello, solo cuatro de los expedicionarios (los zoólogos Martínez y Jiménez de la Espada, el antropólogo Almagro y el botánico Isern), se dispusieron a realizar el autodenominado «Gran viaje». El nombre se queda corto, cortísimo. Primero cruzaron el continente americano desde Guayaquil a Belém. En ese trayecto, pudieron visitar y dibujar el volcán Izalco (El Salvador), donde Jiménez de la Espada se perdió durante tres días para finalmente ser rescatado por sus compañeros; hasta cruzar la cordillera Andina. En la segunda etapa, se dirigieron hacia el Amazonas siguiendo el curso del Río Napo, para finalmente llegar al ansiado océano Atlántico. Durante toda la expedición científica, que al final duró cuatro años (1862 y 1866), no solo buscaban muestras zoológicas y botánicas, sino también geológicas. Además, hicieron importantes hallazgos arqueológicos y estudiaron tribus sudamericanas aún desconocidas por la antropología. Respecto a Marcos Jiménez de la Espada, su contribución a la zoología fue admirable, tal y como se destaca en el archivo de dicha expedición en el Consejo Superior de Investigaciones Científicas (CSIC), aunque también hizo numerosas contribuciones a la geografía, historia y antropología:

«Espada destacó, sobre todo a su regreso a España, como estudioso de la fauna sudamericana. Dio a conocer nuevas especies de mamíferos del área del alto Amazonas, e hizo un extenso estudio sobre los 786 ejemplares de anfibios que recolectaron los comisionados. Su principal obra, publicada en 1875, Vertebrados del viaje al Pacífico. Batracios, recibió los plácemes de sus coetáneos. Considerada un clásico de la literatura zoológica, ha merecido una reciente reedición —en 1978— auspiciada por la Society for the Study of Amphibians and reptiles. En ella hizo la redescripción de dieciocho géneros y veinticuatro especies previamente conocidos, y describió dos géneros, doce especies y tres subespecies nuevos, a lo que añadió interesantes observaciones sobre la biología de las especies».

De vuelta a tierra firme, si hablamos del conocimiento universitario y la inherente dispersión del conocimiento científico por la ciudad de Cartagena, no podemos olvidar a Carmen Conde, primera mujer en la Real Academia Española de la Lengua y fundadora de la Universidad Popular de Cartagena en el siglo pasado. Tal vez, esta última fue la tarea más ardua de las tres, ya que, para prevalecer en el mundo del conocimiento, una mujer no solo tenía que romper barreras geográficas, sino también sociales.

Hoy, los tiempos han cambiado, la exploración ya no ocupa un lugar tan prominente entre las prioridades de la sociedad. Quizá porque queda menos por explorar de nuestro planeta a la antigua usanza, salvando cuevas y galerías bajo tierra o los fondos oceánicos. O tal vez porque, en ocasiones, la exploración manifestó una intención meramente geopolítica, que poco aportó al conocimiento del mundo natural. Sea por la razón que sea, hoy en día, vivimos una época en la cual es ridículamente simple establecer contacto físico u obtener información con lugares remotos del planeta. ¿Qué pensarían los antiguos exploradores de que ahora nos baste con un par de clics y varios *scrolls* para descubrir el número de habitantes, la dieta o el nombre del equipo de fútbol de una isla del océano Pacífico sur? Actualmente, nos desenvolvemos en una época donde la ciencia es el paradigma que rige el rumbo de nuestras sociedades y también el de la nueva exploración. A simple vista podría parecer que la exploración se encuentra en su momento más decadente, incluso obsoleto, que solo goza de cierto brillo épico vestigial. Sin embargo, muchos sostenemos que la exploración no ha acabado, sino todo lo contrario. ¿Qué es la investigación científica sino la exploración de nuestros tiempos? ¿Qué otra actividad enarbola la bandera del descubrimiento y la exploración como esta? ¿Qué otra manera de entender el mundo reta nuestros límites intelectuales y físicos como especie? Vivimos en la época dorada de la exploración y desarrollo del conocimiento científico. Y yo, personalmente, prefiero catalogar la actividad de muchos autoproclamados «exploradores» modernos como «viajes» o «gestas deportivas» (¡muy admirables, faltaría más!); pero, lo siento, sin ciencia no existe tal exploración. No hay exploración sin que los avances científicos obtenidos moldeen a los seres humanos exigiéndoles una readaptación dinámica y continua en sus infraestructuras, tecnología y, por consiguiente, su estilo de vida, en su manera de relacionarse con el medio que les rodea.

Volviendo a nuestra campaña, mientras miraba las aguas del puerto de Cartagena justo antes de zarpar, no podía olvidar todas esas historias. El agua del mediterráneo de ese puerto aún impregna las vidas y las vocaciones de los habitantes actuales como ya lo hizo con sus predecesores, pues sobre el mismo suelo hemos seguido desenvolviendo nuestras vidas. Por suerte, la aventura, la exploración y el conocimiento ya no están en manos solo de los ricos o poderosos que podían permitírselo casi como una afición. Ya no somos solo marineros o exploradores, ahora muchos de los que hemos crecido sintiendo la brisa marina en nuestra piel, somos científicos. Y resulta poético pensar en que es así cómo los buques de investigación surcan las aguas de ese puerto eterno como si nada hubiera cambiado, camino de los lugares más remotos del planeta. Y que, en ellos, viajan investigadoras e investigadores para aventurarse de nuevo en los secretos que aún guarda el mar, que por ahora estaba en calma, aunque ya vendría la «tempestad».

DONDE LOS PECES PLANEAN

«Espléndido día para la partida. Sol brillante, cielo sin nubes, leve viento del Norte; en resumen, cuanto pudiéramos desear para un principio cuajado de esperanzas».

Ernest Shackleton, el 29 de octubre de 1908

El día previo a cualquier campaña oceanográfica supone un frenesí de emociones. La alegría, las ganas de aventura y de aprender se convierten en un torbellino que a más de uno no nos deja pegar ojo en toda la noche. En mi caso, pasé la noche antes de zarpar dentro del BIO Hespérides, para ir acostumbrándome. Y allí, con el buque aún atracado en el puerto encontré un poco de tranquilidad en algo que nunca creí posible: hacer la cama. En un buque oceanográfico todo es un reto. Aunque lo normal es compartir camarote, en el Hespérides, solo íbamos a ser diez investigadores para esta expedición, por lo que disponíamos de camarote propio provisto de un escritorio con estantería, una litera, un armario y un aseo con ducha. Todo un lujo cuando uno lee las condiciones en las que los antiguos exploradores zarpaban durante meses o años.

Es cierto que a veces nos solemos quejar, pero los investigadores marinos que hemos tenido la suerte de participar en expediciones de este tipo lo tenemos muy claro: somos unos privilegiados. Puede ser que no seamos ricos (y nunca lo seremos dedicándonos a esto), que trabajemos alrededor de dieciocho horas diarias en un laboratorio que se mueve bajo nuestros pies e incesantemente prueba nuestra resistencia (física y mental), puede ser que el extrañar a nuestros amigos y seres queridos se convierta en una de las consecuencias más desagradables del aislamiento... Incluso, puede que sentirte como un pequeño punto en el océano te haga ser consciente de lo insignificante que eres, al igual que situar nuestro planeta Tierra en un universo infinitesimal de estrellas. Pero todo eso merece la pena. En los buques oceanográficos suelen congregarse un grupo de personas que, casi todas, tienen una característica en común, un simple sentimiento que es el primer paso para cambiar el mundo: la ilusión. Y es que seguramente nunca debemos de dejar de creer en nosotros mismos ni en nuestros objetivos, aunque esto sea cada vez más difícil cuando nos hacemos mayores. Nunca debemos de dejar de ser unos niños que se hacen preguntas y encuentran respuestas que, *a priori*, pudieran parecer locuras. Y, sobre todo, nunca debemos hacer que alguien deje de soñar y pierda la ilusión. Esto último también va dirigido a muchos profesores, que deben elegir entre ser catalizadores de vocaciones o, todo lo contrario. Cualquier sueño, por descabellado que parezca, como el de un niño que de mayor se quiere embarcar en el BIO Hespérides, ha de tomarse como una declaración de intenciones que rompa con los muros de la apatía y el conformismo de los que están a su alrededor, sobre todo de quienes deben orientarle. Y tal vez ahí resida una de las claves de la ciencia: no conformarse con lo que ya se sabe. Queremos saber más y, sobre todo, saber mejor. Y todo ello en nuestro caso empieza con el inicio de una campaña oceanográfica.

Al día siguiente zarpamos desde Cartagena y la despedida no pudo ser más emocionante. A diferencia de los científicos, los militares pasarían muchos más meses lejos de sus casas. Por ello, nos despidieron con todos los honores. Una banda de música nos acompañó mientras el personal de la armada se despedía de sus seres queridos. Bueno, y yo también, ya que tuve la inmensa suerte de que gran parte de mi familia pudiera venir a decirme adiós. No creo que muchos investigadores marinos de Cartagena hayan vivido algo así. Que te despidan con honores en tu ciudad es algo verdaderamente bonito. Sin embargo, hay otras cosas no tan bonitas. Las autoridades de la ciudad también vinieron a despedirnos, la mayoría de ellas fueron muy educadas y pudimos conversar con ellas. Desgraciadamente, la por aquel entonces alcaldesa de la ciudad, «mi» alcaldesa, pasó por delante de los científicos sin ni siquiera girar la cabeza y se fue directa a hablar con los altos cargos militares. Supongo que no lo hizo por mala fe, sino por ignorancia, quizá porque no íbamos vestidos de gala. Cuando volvió a pasar por delante de nosotros tampoco dijo «adiós». Ni siquiera lo comenté con el resto de investigadores, ya que creo que era el único que sabía que dicha persona era la alcaldesa; haciendo de dicho encuentro un perfecto ejercicio de ignorancia recíproca. Por ello, aún a día de hoy, este me sigue pareciendo un hecho bastante simbólico de la relación real entre ciencia y política. Una vez abandonaron el buque las autoridades, soltamos amarras, la música de la banda se escuchaba cada vez más lejana y en pocos minutos todo lo que se oía era el mar. Ahora había que poner el laboratorio en marcha cuanto antes.

Además del instrumento científico roseta-CTD, existen otras muchas maneras de recolectar agua. Si el buque es lo suficientemente grande y cuenta con los medios suficientes, también disponemos de un sistema de bombeo continuo de agua hacia el laboratorio. Sí, como lo oís, simplemente abriendo un grifo en el laboratorio sale agua marina. Esto se produce gracias a un mecanismo de bombeo desde una toma hecha en el casco del buque que suele situarse en torno a los cinco metros de profundidad, pero, como podéis suponer, está profundidad varía puesto que el buque oscila con el movimiento de las olas. En nuestros laboratorios solemos tener instrumentos que nos permiten medir directamente numerosos parámetros en continuo de esa agua, es decir, podemos conocer en tiempo real y a una resolución de segundos cuál es la concentración de clorofila, la temperatura o la salinidad del agua. En cierto modo, es como si tuviéramos una aguja como la que usan los médicos, pero en vez de extraer sangre y analizar la cantidad de glóbulos blancos, por ejemplo, lo que hacemos es medir otros parámetros para conocer la «salud» de los océanos. Así que, cuando se puso en marcha el Hespérides fuimos corriendo al laboratorio a comprobar que el sistema de bombeo en continuo funcionaba y podíamos poner nuestros instrumentos en funcionamiento. Pese a algunos problemas iniciales todo funcionaba y ya nos encaminábamos rumbo al Estrecho de Gibraltar, pero esta vez no nos detendríamos, sino que pasaríamos de largo a una velocidad de unos doce nudos, que es a la que suele ir el Hespérides cuando hace buen tiempo.

La entrada al océano Atlántico digamos que se «notó» bastante. Pasamos del tranquilo Mar Mediterráneo, en el que las olas se rompían ante la imponente proa del buque, sin ocasionar prácticamente ningún movimiento; a los fuertes vaivenes de las aguas atlánticas. Y fue en esos momentos cuando empezaron a surgir los primeros mareos. Así que lo que tocaba era tomarse una buena dosis de Biodramina con cafeína, Coca-Cola y café. Si creéis que ingiriendo esa gran cantidad de cafeína y azúcar diaria por las noches no se puede dormir, nada más alejado de la realidad, personalmente caer como un tronco cada noche es lo que más recuerdo de mis meses embarcado.

Nuestro siguiente destino eran las Islas Canarias, a las que llegamos pocos días después de zarpar. Cuando se recorren kilómetros y kilómetros tan despacio, uno se da cuenta de lo grandes que son las distancias del planeta Tierra. Mientras que en avión habría tardado unas tres horas en llegar, en barco eran varios días. Y un buque nunca para de navegar, de día y de noche, dejando agua atrás, y parece que nunca llegas, que todo está muy lejos. En cuanto al laboratorio, todos los aparatos científicos funcionaban perfectamente y no había mucho trabajo, es decir, no más de ocho horas diarias. Así que tuvimos tiempo para realizar otro tipo de actividades. En el BIO Hespérides la interacción entre científicos y militares es fluida y mucho más afable de lo que mucha gente podría esperar. El aprendizaje es mutuo y, por tanto, es una experiencia enriquecedora. Una de las actividades que se suelen hacer son las charlas y debates. Por nuestra parte, una vez por semana nos encargábamos de preparar una serie de charlas de divulgación científica sobre nuestro trabajo y el proyecto PEGASO. Era algo semejante al festival internacional Pint of Science en el que los científicos van a los bares a hablar de su investigación. Sin embargo, nosotros lo hacíamos sin cerveza, ya que el alcohol no está permitido salvo en ocasiones especiales. Por parte del personal de la armada, recibíamos cada dos días charlas formativas acerca de la actuación en situaciones de emergencias, protocolos de seguridad, normas de convivencia, navegación, organización del buque, etc. En esta línea, una de las experiencias más importantes, a la par que divertidas, son los simulacros de incendios. ¿Qué hacer en caso de incendio? Dentro de cada camarote disponemos de casco, traje de supervivencia y linternas. Es decir, cada uno de nosotros tenemos nuestro propio equipo y tenemos que cuidar de él. El traje de supervivencia es ciertamente curioso por varias razones. La primera es que es de talla única para personas que miden entre 1,50 y 2,00 metros, y pesan entre cuarenta o ciento veinte kilogramos. Es decir, para prácticamente la totalidad de los adultos. ¿Esto que quiere decir? Que a no ser que midas dos metros y peses cien kilogramos el traje siempre te va a quedar ridículamente grande. Por dentro está recubierto por completo de un tejido semejante al forro polar y, además, las botas y guantes están incorporados en el traje. Por fuera, está recubierto de una capa de un par de milímetros de plástico impermeable. Por ello, son cariñosamente llamados *Teletubbies*, ya os imagináis por qué. Un traje de estas características puede ser todo un lujo si hay un incendio y hay que evacuar en aguas polares, ya que es muy cálido y permitiría sobrevivir más tiempo. Sin embargo, lo que no es tan divertido es tener que aprender a ponerse y quitarse el traje en menos de dos minutos frente a Gran Canaria a treinta grados de temperatura. Después, hay que dirigirse a las balsas de supervivencia siguiendo una ruta individualizada, es decir, uno no puede ir a la balsa que le apetezca: tienes que ir a la tuya y tienes que seguir una ruta fija. Si no lo hacemos así, se pueden ocasionar atascos en la evacuación del buque, lo cual puede ser letal para ti y para otros. Una vez llegados a las balsas de supervivencia, ¡hay que tirarlas al agua!, vamos, una auténtica yinkana. Dentro de las balsas hay de todo: pastillas potabilizadoras, GPS, comida, mantas térmicas... todo lo necesario para sobrevivir unos veintiún días, ocho personas en la mar. Sin embargo, si nos encontramos en aguas polares la cosa cambia, hay que utilizar la embarcación de supervivencia polar. Esta embarcación es vital si nos encontramos en la Antártida, ya que nos informaron de que los equipos de rescate de los países adyacentes (Argentina, Chile, Sudáfrica) no vuelan si el viento es superior a cuarenta millas por hora en el Paso de Drake, el tramo de mar que separa América del Sur de la Antártida. Lo cual, dicho sea de paso, es bastante probable, aunque ya hablaremos de esto más adelante.

Tras varios días de navegación con unas condiciones de mar difícilmente mejorables, alcanzamos el Archipiélago de Cabo Verde. En ese momento me puse a reflexionar acerca de que era la primera vez en mi vida que bajaba de los 20°N. Nunca había estado tan al sur. También es cierto que fuera de mi trabajo nunca había viajado muy lejos. Aunque la geografía de la Península Ibérica sí que la conocía como la palma de mi mano; Escocia, algunos lugares de centro Europa y Canarias eran los únicos sitios que había visitado. Sirva un ejemplo que siempre suelo poner cuando doy alguna charla o alguna clase a mis alumnos: pisé la Antártida antes que Francia. Y aunque esto pueda sonar un poco a chovinismo español por la rivalidad con Francia y todo eso, la verdad es que es un simplemente hecho casual.

La vida a bordo del BIO Hespérides, y en cualquier otro buque de investigación, es intensa y llena de sorpresas a cada segundo. Esto conlleva que una semana allí embarcado parezca ser muchísimo más tiempo. Y, si juntamos esto con el hecho de que durante Trans-PEGASO tuvimos las cuatro estaciones concentradas en un mes, era parecido a disfrutar de un «miniaño» a bordo del buque. Si lo pensamos por un momento, partimos de Cartagena en otoño. Al ir navegando hacia el sur, llegamos a las Islas Canarias con su preciado clima subtropical; y aquí es donde empezó nuestro verano. Desde las Islas Canarias, fuimos hasta Cabo Verde y con rumbo al ecuador, es decir, más calor y humedad. Posteriormente, nos dirigimos a Buenos Aires tras costear Brasil, donde, al estar ya en el hemisferio sur, disfrutaríamos de una agradable primavera. Finalmente, llegaríamos a Punta Arenas (Chile) en la cual, pese a ser primavera, las temperaturas son muy bajas y es mucho peor que cualquier invierno en Cartagena. Todo ello enmarcado en una rutina diaria que puede resumirse de la siguiente manera:

07.30 a. m. Suena el despertador. Diez minutillos de «remoloneo». Retiras la cortina azul que cubre la ventana del camarote. Un cielo grisáceo y un mar azul te dan los buenos días. A vestirse y a salir del camarote.

08.00 a. m. Hora del desayuno en el comedor. Café, zumo de naranja recién exprimido, bizcocho recién hecho del día por el panadero y tostadas. Entra el personal que ha estado de guardia por la noche, ahora les toca dormir a ellos.

09.00 a. m. Empieza el primer muestreo del día. Los científicos bajamos a nuestro laboratorio a pasar el resto de la mañana. entre risas, música y mucho trabajo.

10.30 a. m. Pequeño descanso para tomarnos el bocadillo. Subimos a la camareta de Oficiales, justo debajo del Puente, una de las zonas más elevadas del barco. Nos sobrevuelan albatros viajeros y petreles mientras nos tomamos el café y bocadillo correspondientes. Hay que coger fuerzas hasta la hora de comer.

13.15 p. m. Hora de la comida, a ver con qué nos sorprende Don Paco, el jefe de cocina oriundo de Pliego (Murcia). Hoy toca caldero del Campo de Cartagena, lacón con grelos o fideuá. Van entrando todos a comer. Después de comer toca un poco de siesta, a trepar de nuevo hasta la litera.

16.00 p. m. Empieza de nuevo el muestreo. Última salida a cubierta para respirar un poco de brisa marina. Al laboratorio de nuevo. Suena la música otra vez, los Artic Monkeys amenizan el turno.

18.30 p. m. Un poco de ejercicio en el gimnasio del barco para liberar tensión y no salir del BIO Hespérides hechos una «bola», pese a los esfuerzos diarios de Don Paco.

19.15 p. m. Toca cenar. Cada dos noches de acompañamiento tenemos las famosas patatas fritas del Hespérides, peladas a mano, no de las congeladas. Como primer plato, hay de todo: judías salteadas con jamón, chuleta de cordero, sopa, etc. Si comparamos esta hora de cenar con la vida en tierra firme es temprano, pero ya hay sueño.

21.00 p. m. Anochece, subimos al puente de mando; los atardeceres desde aquí son increíbles. Casi todas las noches en uno de los televisores se pone una película para ver en grupo. Muchos traemos una gran cantidad de películas y series en discos duros, por lo que no es problema encontrar algo que ver. Aunque sí decidirlo.

23.00 p. m. Subimos al puente de mando a ver cómo están los ánimos, para que el barco siga navegando hace falta gente que siga trabajando por las noches, no solo por el día.

24.00 p. m. A trepar a la litera, cierro la ventana para que no me entre luz a las cinco de la madrugada (los días cada vez son más cortos). Toca leer un poco e intentar descansar si el movimiento del barco lo permite. Y entre las páginas de algún libro de exploración o naturaleza, pienso en que ya queda un día menos para llegar a la Antártida, el próximo mes de enero.

La vida en un barco no solo transcurre entre compañeros de fatigas, ya que también suelen unirse a la rutina unos invitados muy curiosos. Alrededor del buque se congregan toda clase de cetáceos y aves marinas, aunque también existen otra serie de animales que se sirven de los barcos para alimentarse y buscar cobijo. En nuestro caso, desde que cruzamos el Estrecho de Gibraltar nos dimos cuenta de que estaba ocurriendo algo extraño ya que, a veces, aparecían pequeños pájaros muertos en la cubierta. Sin embargo, tardamos varios días en localizar al culpable. Con nosotros había embarcado también durante varias centenas de kilómetros un ejemplar de cernícalo vulgar (*Falco tinnunculus*). Aunque cada vez eran menos frecuentes las pequeñas aves marinas de las que se alimentaba conforme nos alejábamos de la costa africana, «no solo de pájaros vive el cernícalo». Uno de los fenómenos más alucinantes que se producen en los océanos, y que he tenido la suerte de vivir en varias ocasiones, son los peces voladores. Una vez que se alcanzan las aguas tropicales están por todos lados. Salen del agua volando durante varios segundos y recorriendo a ras de agua distancias de incluso cien metros o más. Son como balas plateadas. Cada vez que el barco se cruza con ellos se pueden ver escapar por babor y estribor del buque. El océano en esas latitudes es prácticamente un «desierto», pero en su superficie sigue habiendo fauna. Por desgracia para ellos, y suerte para el cernícalo que venía con nosotros, en muchas ocasiones se estrellaban contra el barco si volaban demasiado alto y caían sobre la cubierta. Entonces era cuando el halcón bajaba a toda velocidad y se llevaba su presa antes de que algún marinero lo retirase rápidamente para que el buque no oliera mal. Y creedme, hacía tanto calor y humedad que no era conveniente tener peces pudriéndose. Para que os hagáis una idea, a unos 10°N la temperatura del agua y del aire rondaban los 30°C.

Si hay una cosa de la que uno se da cuenta cuando navega en mitad del océano Atlántico es de lo lejos que están Europa y África de América. Y de lo solo que se siente uno en mitad de sus aguas. No recuerdo haber sentido una sensación de aislamiento más intensa que en mitad del Atlántico. Mires a donde mires solo hay agua y apenas hay olas, el mar casi siempre está en calma. Es como un desierto plano e infinito de color azul, bastante aburrido y ciertamente tétrico. Sin embargo, incluso en las calmas ecuatoriales, Neptuno ya resopla por los rincones. Cerca del ecuador nos encontramos varias tormentas que originaron los primeros mareos fuertes entre la tripulación, no solo a los científicos. Eso sí, el cernícalo aún seguía con nosotros, aunque en algún momento cerca del ecuador nos abandonó. Fuese a donde fuese a partir de ese momento, el viaje de vuelta tuvo que ser impresionante.

En un punto de la navegación nos encontramos justo por encima de la dorsal centro-oceánica atlántica que se encuentra en mitad del océano Atlántico a lo largo del mismo. Esta dorsal divide Islandia en dos. A lo largo de esta, se liberan progresivamente ingentes cantidades de magma ígneo procedentes del manto terrestre. La estructura geológica interna de la tierra se constituye, a grandes rasgos, por tres partes: corteza, manto y núcleo; en orden de exterior a interior del planeta. Esta liberación de magma ocasiona la formación de nuevas rocas y, por tanto, el crecimiento de la corteza oceánica. Debido a este proceso, Europa y África se separan progresivamente del continente americano. Resulta curiosa la sensación de estar justo encima de uno de los lugares de donde brota el magma caliente que configura poco a poco, a escalas de millones de años, los continentes que nosotros llamamos hogar.

Poco después, cruzamos por fin el ecuador y pasamos al hemisferio sur, es decir, el otro lado del planeta. Que, por cierto, siempre se suele escribir como 0°N y casi nunca 0°S, pese a ser lo mismo. Ay, ¡cómo somos los del hemisferio norte! Aquí las estaciones son las opuestas, los ciclones y los anticiclones giran en sentido contrario, y solo vive alrededor del 10% de la población mundial ya que la mayor parte de su superficie corresponde a los océanos. Lo que muchos no sabíamos era que cruzar el ecuador y adentrarnos en el hemisferio sur no solo iba a significar seguir con el calor y el mar en plano típico de las calmas ecuatoriales. Así que una mañana nos despertamos con el barco lleno de papeles con el siguiente texto:

«No hay buque que mares surque sin que Yo, Neptuno, dueño y señor de todas las aguas marinas, conozca su travesía. Un año más, el Hespérides ha puesto rumbo a la Antártida, y debo suponer que, como el año pasado no lo hicisteis, este osáis cruzar el ecuador con el buque repleto de neófitos por Mí no bautizados, sin pago de tributos y sin rendir la debida pleitesía. ¡Insolentes mortales! Ante tal desvergüenza, debería descargar mi gran ira sobre todos vosotros, pero seré benevolente y por ello anuncio:

El próximo viernes 31 de octubre, tomaré el mando de mi querido Hespérides, con el beneplácito de mi viejo amigo Javier Moreno para que aquellos neófitos que puedan acreditar su valía como Marinos sean por Mí bautizados, obtengan Mi gracia, y seguir así la travesía con los buenos vientos que al Hespérides regalaré.

Para todo ello, vendré acompañado de mi Corte de Ninfas, Verdugos y Negros, quiénes como Yo, esperan tras finalizar el acto ser agasajados con un fastuoso banquete en el que abunden las viandas, los buenos vinos y los licores espirituosos.

Dado en el Océano Atlántico, a 28 de octubre de 2014»

Y es que en todo buque que se precie, existe la tradición marinera de que la primera vez que cruzas el ecuador debes pasar una serie de pruebas para ser bautizado y convertirte en «marinero». A grandes rasgos, consistió en la realización de pruebas y demás actos varios por parte de los «neófitos» (aquellos que nunca habíamos cruzado el ecuador navegando). Dichas pruebas fueron encargadas por el Dios Neptuno, que tomó el mando del Buque a las 10.00 a. m. Aparte de dichas pruebas, el personal de tripulación de la armada se cambió los rangos entre ellos, es decir, los marineros pasaron a ser oficiales, los oficiales, cocineros, estos a comandantes, los comandantes a panaderos... A algunos se les veía mucho más felices con su nueva función en el BIO Hespérides. Tras la finalización de las pruebas y el bautizo de los neófitos, todos disfrutamos de una barbacoa al aire libre en un, no tan calmado, océano Ecuatorial. Más de uno nos sentíamos en la universidad de nuevo. Al final del día todos éramos marineros y marineras, puesto que superamos las pruebas y las expectativas. ¡Incluso nos dieron un diploma!

Sin embargo, no todo iban a ser buenas noticias. La entrada en el hemisferio sur también supuso el comienzo de algunos problemas con las telecomunicaciones. Muchos os preguntaréis qué tipo de conexión a Internet o teléfono existe en un buque de este estilo. En aquella ocasión, disponíamos de una sala común con cuatro ordenadores con conexión a Internet, que era el único sitio en el que se podía consultar el correo electrónico y poco más. Era imposible utilizar cualquier red social, por ejemplo. También teníamos wifi en la zona de camarotes, pero solo se podía utilizar WhatsApp sin enviar ni imágenes o vídeos. Por último, teníamos un teléfono que todos los científicos podíamos usar en todo momento. Es decir, las comunicaciones eran bastante escasas y esto significaba básicamente decir adiós a las redes sociales durante varias semanas. Lo cual, imaginaréis, para un grupo de *millennials* no es tan simple; aunque en un buque lo llevas sorprendentemente bien. Hay mucho trabajo y suelen pasar cosas interesantes. Aparte, si te gusta leer, una campaña oceanográfica es el paraíso. En el BIO Hespérides existe una biblioteca con muchos libros que puedes coger prestados. Recuerdo, por ejemplo, haber leído la trilogía completa de *Memorias de Idhun* en unas dos semanas.

Coincidencias de la vida, justo el día después de cruzar el ecuador, el día 1 de noviembre, fue mi cumpleaños. Y, posiblemente, tuvimos el día con peores condiciones de mar hasta el momento, con olas de hasta seis metros de altura. Nunca habría podido imaginar que disfrutaría de un cumpleaños a bordo del Hespérides, prácticamente en el ecuador. Es en estos momentos cuando te das cuenta de lo importante que es la gente en el buque. A fin de cuentas, los grupos de investigadores embarcados somos como una pequeña familia. Sin embargo, a mí me gusta más definirlo como una suerte de pequeño Gran Hermano, en el cual no hay cámaras grabándolo todo. Es decir, es aún peor que *Gran Hermano*... ¡y encima no hay premio! Esta buena relación, tanto entre científicos, como entre científicos y personal de la Armada, se traduce en eventos ocasionales tan especiales como hacerle una fiesta sorpresa al más pequeño del buque que cumple su primer año en el hemisferio sur, al que hay que sumarle los otros 23 en el hemisferio norte. Hubo tarta e, incluso, regalos. El más especial un frasco de agua embotellada del ecuador con la inscripción: 00° 00′ 00″N (o «S», según cómo se mire).

La entretenida vida a bordo, entre celebraciones, contrastaba con la poca vida fuera del buque. Los océanos, pese a que pueda parecer lo contrario, tienen grandes extensiones de superficie que pueden considerarse «desiertos» de vida, un ejemplo son los llamados «giros subtropicales» que se encuentran en las zonas centrales de los océanos, alejadas de los continentes. Los ecosistemas están principalmente dominados por unos pequeños organismos microscópicos planctónicos, aunque también hay especies más grandes en tamaño como peces o mamíferos marinos en rutas migratorias. Durante estas tres primeras semanas, navegamos por una de esas zonas «desérticas» y la verdad es que, como era de esperar, vimos muy, muy poca vida, salvo algunos avistamientos de cetáceos por parte de la tripulación desde el puente de mando. Este tipo de avistamientos, en parte, es lo que otorga encanto a las campañas oceanográficas: puedes ver cosas increíbles. Aunque, claro, estas zonas sin mucha vida también tienen otros fenómenos increíbles como cielos rosados, púrpuras y puestas de sol increíbles.

Sin embargo, al ir acercándonos a la costa de Uruguay y situándonos en la desembocadura de un río de tales dimensiones como el Río de la Plata, el asunto cambió. Aparte de que los avistamientos de cetáceos se iban incrementando, desde el puente de mando del BIO Hespérides veíamos algo semejante a troncos que flotaban en superficie. Y había bastantes, pero de momento no estaban tan cerca del buque como para poder saber qué eran. Mientras los militares hacían maniobras de izado de embarcaciones, ni más ni menos que un ejemplar de tortuga verde (*Chelonia mydas*) asomó la cabeza por encima del agua dejándose ver y rápidamente se zambulló huyendo de un, más que posible, choque con el buque. Poco después empezamos a entender qué eran esos «troncos» grisáceos que estaban cerca del buque, ya que cada vez se acercaban más. Y fue bastante fácil porque tenían aletas, concretamente aletas de tiburones martillo (Familia *Sphyrnidae*). No dejaron de acercarse al buque mientras nos adentrábamos en el Río de la Plata rumbo a Buenos Aires (Argentina) donde haríamos una parada de varios días antes de llegar a Chile. Durante dicho trayecto, los tiburones martillo se acercaban al buque intentando encontrar algo de comida que cayera del BIO Hespérides. Había muchísimos y medían alrededor de dos metros.

Y por fin, tras veintún días de travesía por el océano, atracamos en nuestro primer destino: Buenos Aires. Fondeamos en el marrón Río de la Plata la noche del 9 de noviembre, para a las 05.00 a. m. zarpar y atracar en el puerto de Buenos Aires. Tras tantos días en el océano abierto resultaba muy impresionante volver a ver la civilización. Nos acercamos de manera lenta, pero ordenada, poco a poco; atisbando a lo lejos los primeros edificios. Buques inmensos llenos de contenedores y cruceros de turistas se arremolinaban a la entrada del Río de la Plata. Parece que todo el mundo tiene las mismas prisas por llegar a los puertos tras semanas en el gran azul. Para llegar al puerto de Buenos Aires, hay que atravesar varias millas por la desembocadura del río, esto implica navegar a unos diez kilómetros por hora rozando un fondo, previamente dragado, de diez metros de profundidad (a veces incluso menos). Los edificios se iban haciendo más grandes, ya estábamos en América, a punto de pisarla. Era bastante mágico haber llegado a este continente por mar, como hicieron antes otros muchos. Conforme íbamos entrando en el puerto, la alegría iba creciendo. Muchos días sin pisar tierra, gente con ganas de beber y comer sin que se mueva el suelo bajo sus pies. Muchos marineros tenían familiares en Argentina y a otros les esperaba su familia que había viajado desde España. A los científicos, en cambio, no nos esperaba nadie; por lo que tuvimos tiempo de sobra para planificar qué hacer en Buenos Aires y cómo sería el trabajo una vez zarpásemos de nuevo rumbo a Chile. Por fin, llegamos al muelle naval de Argentina, donde, gracias una maniobra de cirujano, atracó el BIO Hespérides. Durante todo el proceso sonaban las trompetas de la orquesta que nos daba la bienvenida. Allí nos esperaban también el embajador de España en Argentina, la secretaria de Estado de Investigación de España y algunos curiosos. Unos días después, el 15 de noviembre, disfrutamos de nuestra última comida de carne argentina, última cerveza Quilmes y última pisada en tierra firme. Levamos anclas. Otra vez sonó la orquesta, pero esta vez para despedirnos y seguir navegando hacia el sur.

Los últimos días de la expedición trascurrieron a lo largo de la península Valdés. Esta zona es enormemente famosa debido a las numerosas especies de cetáceos que habitan sus aguas. De hecho, en muchos documentales televisivos se muestra que en esta parte del planeta las orcas se han especializado en cazar leones marinos adentrándose en la propia orilla. Así, aprovechan las olas para sorprender a los leones marinos y devorarlos posteriormente aguas adentro. No tuvimos la suerte de ver orcas, pero sí varios ejemplares de yubarta, también conocida como ballena jorobada (*Megaptera novaeangliae*), que son bastante comunes en esta zona. Los últimos días de la expedición fueron muy, muy fríos. Era el momento de sacar la ropa de invierno. Se notaba que nos acercábamos cada vez más al océano Antártico y la temperatura del agua bajaba más de 10°C. Por fin, tras más de cuatro semanas navegando, llegamos al puerto de Punta Arenas en Chile. Allí no hubo orquesta y el único recibimiento fueron los gélidos vientos que soplaban desde la Patagonia. Volvíamos a España unas semanas a descansar, después nos esperaba el océano Antártico. Uno de los sueños de cualquier investigador marino.

TIERRA DE NADIE, TIERRA DE TODOS

Manifiesto planctónico por unas nubes dignas

Por la presente, notificamos a los humanos que hoy, de nuevo, ha vuelto a salir el sol. «Menuda novedad», pensaréis. Somos conscientes de que vosotros no sois seres unicelulares que os movéis erráticamente por la superficie del agua de todo el planeta, sujetos a los vaivenes de las corrientes marinas y al paso de grandes buques que remueven nuestro hábitat. Por ello, os pedimos un poco de empatía para entender lo que os vamos a contar a continuación.
Para nosotros, el fitoplancton marino, el sol supone un velo diario que se vierte sobre nuestras cabezas que trae a partes iguales vida y destrucción. La misma luz necesaria para poder realizar la fotosíntesis, que sustenta las redes tróficas del océano, y vuestras queridas pesquerías, también están compuestas por radiación ultravioleta. Y cuando esta incide sobre nuestro ADN (nuestras membranas celulares son fáciles de atravesar), se producen mutaciones que nos llevan, en última instancia, a la muerte. Para colmo, habéis destruido parte de la capa de ozono e impacta aún más radiación que hace solo unas décadas sobre la superficie del océano. Aunque firmasteis un protocolo a final de los años ochenta y dejasteis de emitir muchos de esos gases nocivos, los niveles de ozono estratosférico aún no se han recuperado.
Algunos de nosotros al menos tenemos flagelos y podemos movernos en vertical, escapando así a capas más profundas cuando llega la radiación. Sin embargo, muchos de nuestros iguales no tienen tanta suerte. Cada noche nos despedimos de ellos, ya que sabemos que muy posiblemente mañana no estarán. Y hemos constatado que cada día sobreviven menos individuos, pero no hagamos de esto un drama, somos seres unicelulares que nos reproducimos por clonación bastante rápido. Ciertamente, no sabemos muy bien si a quienes vemos a la mañana siguiente, son o no nuestros congéneres; bueno, en verdad siguen siendo ellos. Aunque, eso sí, con alguna modificación genética parte del proceso evolutivo. Ay, ¡qué calvario supone la inmortalidad intermitente! Y luego decís vosotros que tenéis crisis existenciales. Si no morimos por la radiación, nos comen los copépodos, aunque después a ellos se los comen las larvas de los peces. La venganza, decís los humanos, no es buena; pero en el océano es inevitable. Y para qué negarlo, sienta bastante bien.
Seremos seres unicelulares, pero sabed que ya hace millones de años que encontramos una solución a nuestros problemas ambientales.

Leednos con atención, pues tal vez aprendáis algo. Obviamente, no podemos evitar que llegue radiación a la superficie del océano, ni tampoco somos capaces de evitar que los humanos sigan alterando la atmósfera. Lo que sí podemos hacer es usar un paraguas. Sí, un paraguas, como habéis oído. No sois los únicos seres vivos a los que se os ocurren inventos. Lo que sucede es que nuestro paraguas es algo especial. Nuestros ancestros descubrieron que algunos de los gases que producimos, aunque suene raro, pueden ayudarnos a luchar contra la radiación ultravioleta. Cuando liberamos estos compuestos en el agua tienden a acercarse a la superficie y pasan a la atmósfera. Su camino no es fácil, ya que deben evitar ser convertirse en el alimento de las bacterias y atravesar la capa más superficial del océano, pero una vez en la atmósfera, hemos constatado que reaccionan con otros compuestos mediante complejas reacciones de oxidación-reducción. Como producto final, se obtienen algunas partículas muy, muy pequeñas que llamamos aerosoles. Alrededor de estos aerosoles, se condensan moléculas de agua una y otra vez, hasta formar microgotitas. Estas gotas se aglutinan en la troposfera para formar nubes. Y estas nubes evitan que llegue tanta radiación solar a la superficie del océano. ¿Lo habéis adivinado? Las nubes son nuestros paraguas, y nos cuesta mucho esfuerzo producirlas. Por otro lado, también os ayudan a vosotros, ya que reflejan parte de la radiación solar y hacen que el calentamiento global, que también habéis provocado los humanos, no sea tan severo.

Por todo lo explicado en este manifiesto, todas las formas unicelulares marinas que habitan la superficie de los océanos, con flagelos o sin ellos, autótrofas o heterótrofas, instamos a los seres humanos a que se comprometan a cumplir, ya no nuestras exigencias, sino aquellas que formen parte de vuestros «Derechos Humanos». Concretamente la parte en la que se establece que: «Cada mujer, hombre, joven y niño tiene derecho a un medio ambiente seguro y saludable, así como a otros derechos humanos fundamentales relacionados con un medio ambiente saludable». Exigimos a la humanidad que cese en sus emisiones de gases de distinta índole a la atmósfera en aras de mantener nuestra cobertura nubosa y así evitar el apocalipsis planctónico global y, de paso, garantizar la supervivencia del ser humano uniéndonos en la lucha contra el cambio climático.

¡El plancton unido jamás será vencido!
Un saludo fraternal interespecífico,
Federación Planctónica Global
Océano, 2020

Conseguir trabajar en la Antártida es, a grandes rasgos, bastante complicado. Si bien es cierto que actualmente los investigadores, técnicos y militares que desarrollan sus labores profesionales en la Antártida no sufren las penurias de los tiempos iniciales de la exploración polar, llegar hasta aquí sigue entrañando múltiples dificultades. Uno de los obstáculos más curiosos, pero que es imprescindible superar, es el reconocimiento médico. Por lo general, en la mayoría de las expediciones científicas, uno debe cumplir con una serie de requisitos físicos y de salud, así como de vacunación. Imaginemos, por ejemplo, que una expedición va a navegar cerca de las aguas de Brasil, donde hay enfermedades tropicales. En caso de que a algún integrante de la expedición le sucediera algo, lo más probable es que haya que socorrerlo desde dicho país y trasladado a alguno de sus hospitales. Esto implica un riesgo de contagio de enfermedades muy alto. En mi caso tuve que pasar la aptitud técnica en más de diez especialistas médicos. Este tipo de revisiones médicas se pueden hacer en centros especializados sin ningún problema. Sin embargo, a mí me ofrecieron hacerlo de forma gratuita en el Hospital Central de la Defensa Gómez Ulla en Madrid. Y allí que fui, pensando que encontraría a más científicos como yo. Nada más lejos de la realidad. Pasé una entretenida mañana con un grupo de unos cuarenta legionarios que se marchaban de misión al Líbano, y a mí hasta me daba vergüenza decirles dónde me iba yo. No solo por el riesgo que corren, sino también por el calor que iban a pasar en Líbano mientras yo estaba en aguas antárticas. El procedimiento médico era de lo más peculiar. Íbamos pasando a cada especialista en grupos de cuatro personas. Cada especialista aplicaba el mismo chequeo protocolario, eso sí, con todos a la vez semidesnudos en la misma consulta. Bueno, y no tan «semi», porque uno de los especialistas que tuvo que darnos el famoso «apto» fue el urólogo. Ya os podéis imaginar el cuadro. Otro especialista que requiere especial mención es el psicólogo. El protocolo consiste en una entrevista individual de unos treinta minutos en la que se te pregunta por posibles antecedentes de problemas psíquicos o psicológicos. Aparte, te hacen una serie de preguntas que plantean dilemas que pueden tener lugar trabajando en el océano Antártico. Por ejemplo, «si estás muestreando agua desde la zódiac entre los hielos antárticos y tu compañero se cae al agua por un lado y las muestras, de las que depende todo el proyecto de investigación, por el otro, ¿qué o a quién salvarías primero?». Esto os parecerá obvio, pero el psicólogo me dijo que me sorprendería si supiera cuánta gente afirma que salvaría las muestras. También me preguntó si alguna vez en mi vida había experimentado una situación semejante de aislamiento, pero no solo de aislamiento, sino de estar confinado en un espacio pequeño con mucha gente, día sí y día también. En un simple ejercicio retrospectivo llegué a la conclusión de que la única situación semejante que había vivido en mi vida fue en los campamentos de verano. Vale que un campamento no es lo mismo, pero no hay comunicaciones puesto que no hay cobertura ninguna. También supone trabajar y convivir con la misma gente durante un par de semanas, te caigan bien o mal; lo cual origina muchas situaciones conflictivas. El psicólogo, obviamente, se rio ante tal comparación. Tenía fuera esperando a cuarenta legionarios que iban a batirse el cobre al Líbano y ahí estaba yo hablándole de los scouts. Una vez obtuve el apto en el reconocimiento médico, la Antártida me estaba esperando.

El BIO Hespérides estaba en un lugar cercano a Punta Arenas (Chile) donde lo habíamos dejado hacía un par de meses. Concretamente, se encontraba en Ushuaia, la ciudad más austral del planeta que, entre otras cosas, es la única ciudad de Argentina al otro lado de los Andes cuyas aguas pertenecen al océano Pacífico. Ushuaia es una ciudad muy singular, antiguamente no mucha gente quería vivir allí debido a las condiciones meteorológicas, pese a ser un puerto importante para la exploración y el comercio marítimo. El puerto de la ciudad nos recibió con una enorme pancarta: «Fuera piratas británicos de nuestras aguas» (el conflicto de las Islas Malvinas allí sigue latente). Tras unas horas por la ciudad uno se da cuenta rápidamente de cuál es su motor económico: el turismo. Por un lado, la Patagonia es uno de los lugares más deseados por muchos viajeros y, además, desde Ushuaia es posible ir a muchos lugares de manera relativamente fácil, como a la Antártida. Sí, aunque mucha gente lo desconozca, el turismo antártico existe y es cada vez más numeroso. De hecho, hace un par de años el número de turistas que visitó el gran continente helado superó al de investigadores. Uno se da cuenta rápidamente también de la rentabilidad de este negocio, no solo por los precios, sino también por el tipo de barcos turísticos que llegan a sus costas. Casualmente, el BIO Hespérides estaba atracado delante de uno de ellos, el de National Geographic, que tenía más plantas y era casi el doble de largo que el Hespérides. El turismo antártico es un tema muy controvertido ya que conlleva numerosos riesgos e impactos sobre el medio ambiente. Por ejemplo, pueden producirse vertidos difusos o localizados de hidrocarburos. Además, existen otros más sutiles y desconocidos como es el caso de las especies invasoras. Existen especies en la región Ártica, y otras regiones polares de alta montaña o incluso la cercana Patagonia, que están perfectamente adaptadas a las bajas temperaturas y la escasa precipitación. Por ello es muy fácil que muchas de estas especies se establezcan en el continente Antártico, por ejemplo, a través de semillas que se adhieren a las botas de los visitantes y terminan germinando gracias a esas condiciones climáticas. Por otro lado, el calentamiento global está provocando que, en algunas zonas de la Antártida, como la Península Antártica (la zona más próxima a Chile y Argentina), la temperatura esté subiendo. Esto, aparte de facilitar el establecimiento de especies invasoras por efecto humano, también provoca que especies del continente cercano puedan colonizar y establecerse en la Península Antártica. Incluso recientemente un grupo de investigación español llamado MicroAirPolar ha descubierto que los microorganismos son capaces de viajar del Ártico a la Antártida y colonizar uno u otro ambiente si las condiciones son propicias. Obviamente, muchos de estos riesgos también los entraña la propia exploración científica, pero seguramente no sea lo más prudente llevar a la mayor cantidad de gente posible por motivos meramente económicos y especulativos. Aunque ¿podemos limitar el acceso a la Antártida como si fuera un país? O, dicho de otra manera, ¿a quién pertenece la Antártida?

El tratado Antártico fue firmado en Washington D. C. el 1 de diciembre de 1959 y, en resumen, establece que la Antártida y las aguas que la bañan no son de nadie, es decir, que son de todos. Asimismo, no puede desempeñarse en ella ningún tipo de explotación de recursos naturales. Es, a grandes rasgos, un lugar dedicado a la exploración, a la ciencia y al turismo (ya he comentado mis discrepancias acerca de los términos *turismo* y *exploración* contemporáneos, ya que muchas veces son sinónimos), que supone un gran ejemplo de cooperación internacional.

Sin embargo, este acuerdo de duración indefinida no está exento de polémica para algunos países que quieren lucrarse de sus recursos naturales, lo que echaría por tierra el compromiso internacional del tratado. Durante estas casi siete décadas muchos países han establecido bases de investigación en la Antártida. España, por ejemplo, posee dos. Pero, aunque estas bases tienen una función eminentemente científica, no puede obviarse su intencionalidad geopolítica. Ya que, en caso de que en un futuro se rompa el acuerdo, existirán numerosos países que reclamen su «porción» de la Antártida. Lo cual sería más simple si ya existen asentamientos humanos que pertenecen a esos países tan interesados en reclamar. Por cierto, tampoco puede olvidarse que la Antártida es la mayor reserva de agua dulce del planeta. Lo cual, en un contexto que vaticina conflictos cada vez más intensos relacionados con la escasez de agua, refuerza el papel geopolítico internacional que puede llegar a desempeñar. Según los expertos, este tipo de diatribas legales que ocurren en torno a la Antártida se consideran como algo semejante a lo que sucederá cuando la humanidad intente colonizar y/o explotar el planeta Marte, si es que lo conseguimos. ¿De quién será el planeta? ¿Será solo para la ciencia? ¿Quiénes podrán explotarlo? Este tipo de preguntas ya se contestaron para la Antártida, habrá que ver cuáles son las respuestas para la exploración espacial. Personalmente creo que el reciente papel preponderante que están jugando algunas empresas privadas en la llegada y posible colonización de Marte no nos va a salir gratis y querrán su porción de «planeta rojo» en forma de beneficios.

Peo volvamos a Ushuaia. Para llegar hasta este lugar remoto pasamos veinticuatros horas viajando que, con una diferencia horaria de cuatro horas menos respecto a España, nos dejaron el cuerpo con muy poca energía; todo lo contrario que pasaba con nuestra ilusión, la cual crecía por momentos. Y es que, por fin había llegado el momento de comenzar el proyecto PEGASO e investigar cómo algunos gases que produce el fitoplanton marino del océano Antártico participan en procesos atmosféricos y, por lo tanto, influyen en el sistema climático global. Es decir, pretendíamos evaluar la importancia relativa de estos fenómenos en el escenario actual de cambio climático global. Para ello, navegaríamos alrededor de un mes y medio a bordo del BIO Hespérides por Georgia del Sur y el mar de Weddell, en el océano Austral (Antártida), que eran nuestras zonas de estudio. Por supuesto, eso también incluiría alguna parada en las dos bases antárticas españolas: BAE Juan Carlos I y BAE Gabriel de Castilla.

Y, ¿qué mejor lugar para zarpar hacia la Antártida que desde Ushuaia, como han hecho antes otros miles de navegantes? En el puerto, todo se disponía para el inicio de la campaña oceanográfica. Pasamos bastantes días preparando el material y atando (o como decimos nosotros «trincando») la instrumentación a las paredes, mesas o donde se podía. Ya quedaba muy poco para ir al océano helado de la región más austral de América, que los antiguos navegantes españoles bautizaron como la Tierra de fuego, ya que cuando navegaban sus costas veían «fuegos fatuos». Más tarde, se descubrió que dichos fuegos no eran más que hogueras utilizadas por los indígenas de la zona, que bautizaron como «fueguinos».

Y allí estábamos nosotros, listos para zarpar y cruzar el canal Beagle (nombrado así en honor el buque de Charles Darwin que también navegó esas aguas) y posteriormente atravesar el Mar de Hoces (o Paso de Drake), considerada la zona de navegación más peligrosa del planeta; para finalmente llegar a la Antártida. Esta zona se caracteriza por un clima para nada acogedor, ya que las tormentas se suceden una tras otra dando vueltas sobre la Antártida en sentido horario; mientras unas se destruyen y otras se crean sin cesar. Antes de zarpar, el comandante nos explicó a todos el plan para cruzar el Mar de Hoces, que consistía en atravesar el paso entre una borrasca y otra; si no, mal asunto. Casualmente, el tiempo que hay entre una borrasca y otra es aproximadamente el mismo que se tarda en cruzar el Mar de Hoces. Por lo tanto, y como para todo en esta vida, hay que buscar el momento apropiado. Aunque, aun así, lo más seguro es encontrarse episodios tormentosos antes de llegar a la Antártida. En nuestro caso, zarpamos con una previsión de olas de tres metros durante todo el trayecto. Así que tocó atarlo todo a las paredes y otras superficies para evitar que volara por los aires mientras navegábamos, no solo la instrumentación científica sino también las sillas, las mochilas, las maletas, las botas, en fin, todo lo que podáis imaginar.

En este punto, conviene mencionar que el BIO Hespérides cumple numerosas funciones en aguas antárticas. Pese a lo que pueda parecer, no solo se limita a la investigación oceanográfica, sino que también realiza tareas de abastecimiento, transporte y manutención en coordinación con las bases antárticas españolas. La Base Antártica Española (BAE) Gabriel de Castilla y la BAE Juan Carlos I, ubicadas respectivamente en isla Decepción e Isla Livingston, están allí de forma permanente durante todo el año, es decir, que sus estructuras no se desmontan cuando llega el invierno. Esto origina que durante la gran parte del año que están deshabitadas, la nieve se acumule encima de las infraestructuras. Por ello, todos los años ha de ir personal con antelación para, literalmente, quitar a palazos toda la nieve que imposibilita el acceso y correcto funcionamiento de las bases. En ese caso, el BIO Hespérides también aporta su grano de arena al transportar al personal civil y militar que desempeña esas tareas. Y en esta expedición, como en otras ocasiones, también transportaba a científicos españoles, que iban a desarrollar sus investigaciones en las BAE. Así, investigadores de la Universidad Politécnica de Madrid iban a estudiar la dinámica glaciar de los glaciares Johnson y Hurd, en las inmediaciones de la BAE Juan Carlos I. En dicho proyecto también participaban investigadores de instituciones científicas japonesas, así como de otros países tan singulares como Uzbekistán. Estos investigadores tienen instalada una red permanente encargada de medir el balance de masas (pérdidas y ganancias) de ambos glaciares, desde la campaña antártica 2000-2001. Dichos glaciares pertenecen a una red internacional denominada World Glacier Monitoring Service (WGMS). Por tanto, su objetivo no era solo mantener esa red en activo, sino también instalar instrumentación (sensores térmicos y de presión) en el lecho de los glaciares mediante sondeos de agua caliente a unos ciento cincuenta o doscientos metros de profundidad, así como extraer muestras de formas de vida para su estudio biológico y determinar los espesores de hielo mediante el uso de ondas electromagnéticas. Uno de los investigadores que lideraban este proyecto me contó sus peripecias cuando solo tenía veintitrés años en la base de los EE. UU. llamada Amundsen-Scott, en el Polo Sur (no en la costa de la Antártida, sino en el auténtico Polo Sur) donde estuvo un año entero. Allí vivían en una tienda de campaña a -25°C de temperatura, donde cualquier cosa que se quisiera conservar en estado líquido o semisólido (al menos cálido) debía guardarse dentro del saco de dormir por las noches. De esta manera, en numerosas ocasiones durmió amorosamente con tubos de pasta de dientes o toallitas. Muchos ahora mismo os estaréis haciendo la pregunta del millón, ¿cómo iban al baño en aquella época en el Polo Sur? Pues resulta que las letrinas estaban cavadas al aire libre (recordemos: a -25°C o menos) y los excrementos se recogían en bolsas, para posteriormente tratarlas en el barco cuando venían a recogerlos. Periódicamente, un avión volaba desde Nueva Zelanda y dejaba caer paracaídas iluminados (ya que era invierno austral, es decir, oscuridad completa), en los cuales había suministros, comida, etc. Dicho avión tenía que recorrer cuatro mil quinientos kilómetros de ida más cuatro mil quinientos kilómetros de vuelta, acompañado de otro avión nodriza para suministrarle combustible.

En el Hespérides, también viajaban vulcanólogos. Resulta que la isla Decepción, donde se ubica la BAE Gabriel de Castilla, es un volcán activo. Vista desde el espacio, tiene forma de anillo, ya que es un cono volcánico, y se accede a dicho anillo por un paso muy estrecho conocido como los Fuelles de Neptuno frente a playas de arena volcánica negra. Al tratarse de un volcán activo, puede erupcionar en cualquier momento y es necesario realizar una «vigilancia sísmica». Para ello, se utilizan técnicas de sismovolcánica mediante cuatro estaciones sísmicas portátiles que se instalan en dicha isla. Aparte, existen otras tres estaciones permanentes: una en isla Decepción, otra en isla Livingstone y otra en caleta Cierva.

Aunque no todo van a ser vulcanólogos u oceanógrafos. A mucha gente le sorprenderá saber que también hay matemáticos en la Antártida. Concretamente conocimos a un grupo de matemáticos de la Universidad de Extremadura que se dedicaban a la meteorología, y puedo asegurar que su trabajo no es nada fácil, ni mental ni físicamente. Se desplazan de siete a veinte kilómetros diarios, mientras cargan con una maza de cuatro kilos, con la cual clavan piquetas en el permafrost (suelo congelado) para realizar sus investigaciones, sin contar con la instalación de torres meteorológicas. Asimismo, también había investigadores que se dedicaban al estudio de especies invasoras (concretamente Poa pratensis, una gramínea comúnmente conocida como «espiguilla») y otros que investigaban si los contaminantes orgánicos persistentes emitidos desde el resto de los continentes son capaces de llegar a la Antártida tras cruzar el océano Austral.

Como veis por mis compañeros de viaje, aún queda mucho por descubrir en ciencia, como sucede con el proyecto PEGASO. Es realmente interesante ver cómo algunos de los organismos más pequeños y *a priori* insignificantes de nuestro planeta, como el fitoplancton marino, son capaces de regular algunas propiedades de la atmósfera en el ámbito local y eventualmente del clima global si están involucrados en los procesos de formación de nubes, pero mejor vamos por partes.

Siempre nos han contado, desde que éramos muy pequeños, que para que se forme una nube solo necesitamos vapor de agua y que al llegar a una altura determinada de la atmósfera este vapor se condensa y «pluf» se forma una nube, pero ojalá fuera así de simple. Para que se forme una nube se necesitan pequeñas gotas de agua unidas entre sí que formen gotas algo más grandes, lo que eventualmente formaría la nube, eso sí que es cierto. Sin embargo, esas gotas no se forman solamente nutriéndose del vapor de agua que hay en la atmósfera; sino que necesitan de otros agentes llamados «núcleos de condensación» en los que pasar de estado gaseoso a estado líquido. Estos núcleos de condensación son partículas sólidas o semisólidas muy pequeñas a las cuales pueden adherirse las moléculas de agua hasta formar una microgotita. Es un fenómeno parecido a cuando se condensa el vapor de agua en un vaso con agua muy fría en verano. Las gotas de agua que se condensan fuera del vaso no provienen del interior, sino de la humedad ambiental de la habitación. Es decir, para que se formen las gotas se necesita una superficie inicial a la que las moléculas de agua puedan adherirse. Lo sorprendente es que los núcleos de condensación pueden ser muchísimas cosas distintas: virus, bacterias, compuestos orgánicos volátiles, hidrocarburos, partículas sólidas en suspensión, etc. Sí, también virus y bacterias que flotan en la atmósfera, aunque parezca ciencia ficción. Tanto a estos organismos como a partículas, que pueden ser orgánicas, cristales de sal marina, etc.; los conocemos como aerosoles primarios. Es decir, partículas que cuando son emitidas por el océano y pasan a la atmósfera ya podrían actuar como núcleos de condensación de nubes sin reaccionar con ningún otro compuesto químico, pero en nuestro grupo de investigación, y en mi tesis doctoral, nos hemos centrado en el estudio de unos compuestos llamados gases traza. Es decir, gases que se encuentran en una concentración muy pequeña, pero que participan en importantes procesos atmosféricos, ya que en la atmósfera son capaces de reaccionar con una serie de compuestos químicos y se transforman en aerosoles, en este caso aerosoles secundarios, que también pueden actuar como núcleos de condensación. En resumen, el estudio *in situ* de estos compuestos, así como de su interacción con otros compuestos, fenómenos y procesos, era el objetivo del proyecto PEGASO en el océano Antártico. De entre todos los gases traza producidos por el fitoplancton marino, el más famoso es el dimetilsulfuro (DMS). Este compuesto del azufre, aparte de su papel como precursor de aerosoles secundarios, es el compuesto que da el olor al mar, aunque mucha gente piense que el olor del mar es a «sal», lo cierto es que no. De hecho, podéis probar a oler un salero de vuestra casa, a ver a qué huele (*spoiler*: no huele al mar). El olor del DMS es también el del marisco, de hecho, se utiliza para aromatizar los famosos palitos de «cangrejo» que se usan en ensaladas. A su vez, el DMS es un compuesto esencial para algunas aves marinas, concretamente para algunas de las pertenecientes a la familia de las procellariiformes, en la que se incluyen los petreles y las pardelas. Gracias al DMS, estas aves pueden «oler» donde está el fitoplancton y saber dónde es mejor ir a cazar, ya que donde hay mucho fitoplancton, hay mucho zooplancton y donde hay mucho zooplancton también hay peces. De hecho, sus conductos en el pico son tan característicos que antiguamente se les conocía como «tubinares» debido a que actúan como conductos olfativos, pero también sirven para secretar el exceso de sal ingerido al comer o beber agua de mar. Sin embargo, de momento no os voy a hablar más del DMS, sino que os voy a contar la historia del isopreno, el gas traza que investigué en PEGASO y durante mi doctorado. Concretamente la de la molécula de isopreno que se fue de «Erasmus» desde el océano hasta la atmósfera.

El isopreno (C_5H_8) es un hidrocarburo biogénico que se encuentra en el planeta Tierra. ¿Y qué significa esto? Pues, a grandes rasgos, que está formado por hidrógeno y carbono, y que ha sido producido por la actividad de los seres vivos. Lo sorprendente de este compuesto es que participa en multitud de procesos esenciales para los ecosistemas y el clima global, de manera similar al DMS. De esta manera, cuando se encuentra en la troposfera, la capa más baja de la atmósfera afecta al potencial para oxidar otros compuestos químicos, a la formación de aerosoles orgánicos secundarios y al clima. Pero, para realizar todo esto tiene que abandonar su «casa» y volar lejos. El isopreno se genera tanto en tierra como en los océanos, ya que es un subproducto de la actividad fotosintética de los organismos marinos, principalmente del fitoplancton, los cuales, como buenos padres contemporáneos, han vivido por encima de sus posibilidades durante mucho tiempo y el joven isopreno se ve obligado a volar. Él lo tiene fácil, no necesita ni buscar el vuelo más barato de una compañía aérea *low cost*; ya que en la atmósfera siempre se encuentra en una concentración más baja y simplemente se deja llevar hacia la troposfera. Sin embargo, en algunas zonas del planeta sucede lo mismo que en el aeropuerto de Castellón, no vuela nada, ni siquiera el isopreno.

El isopreno no solo se produce en los océanos, sino también en las plantas terrestres. Debido a la actividad fotosintética de los ecosistemas terrestres (bosques, praderas, estepas, etc.) se emite una cantidad global de unos 500 tg C/año (Tg: Teragramo=1.000.000.000.000 gramos), principalmente por parte de los bosques tropicales. Por otro lado, los organismos marinos emiten un total de 0,2 a 11 tg C/año. Es decir, el isopreno es más de monte que de playa. Así que, ya sabemos quién es el isopreno, donde «nace» y quiénes son sus «padres». Y también sabemos qué hace en la atmósfera: su erasmus particular. Al salir del mar por simple difusión y llegar a la troposfera, entra como una treintena de solteros y solteras a una discoteca y lo da todo, ya que es un compuesto biogénico altamente reactivo. Por lo tanto, intenta «reaccionar» con todo lo que pueda durante su vida media de una o dos horas, en la cual le da tiempo a «hacer de las suyas» en la troposfera. De esta manera, las moléculas de isopreno se convierten en aerosoles secundarios, que pueden actuar como núcleos de condensación y facilitar la formación de nubes. Resulta curioso que, al alejarse de su hogar, el joven isopreno, aunque casi invisible e ignorado por mucha gente (como muchos jóvenes de hoy en día que cogen sus maletas para emigrar), es capaz de realizar proezas tan impresionantes como alterar el clima local e incluso global. Quizá, ya vaya siendo hora de ayudar e intentar comprender a todos los «isoprenos» del mundo, ya que no conviene olvidar que son «altamente reactivos».

Todos estos procesos en los que participa el isopreno y otros gases traza que son tan vitales para el clima global, obviamente, se pueden ver afectados por algunos de los agentes del cambio global. Por desgracia, aún no podemos saber con exactitud cómo, cuánto y qué podemos hacer para evitarlo. A veces pienso que el fitoplancton marino, harto por verse impactado por el aumento de la temperatura, la acidificación de los océanos, etc.; nos quiere transmitir un mensaje como el que habéis leído al principio, un manifiesto que nos haga ver, de una vez por todas, el equilibrio perfecto y, a la vez, tan delicado de nuestra huella en el hogar al que llamamos Tierra.

NAVEGANDO ENTRE HIELOS

«La ventaja que tienen las costas bravas es que, al pie de aquellos elevados muros, mejor que en parte alguna, puede apreciarse la marea, la respiración, el pulso (digámoslo así) del mar. Insensible en el Mediterráneo, es notable en el océano. El océano respira al igual que yo, concuerda con mi movimiento interno, con el de arriba, obligándome a contar incesantemente con él, a computar los días, las horas, a mirar al cielo. Me recuerda lo que soy y que vivo rodeado de gentes».

La mer, *Jules Michelet (1861)*

He de reconocer que pocas cosas me han impresionado más en mi vida que ver tan de cerca los icebergs antárticos, es algo en lo que todo el mundo coincide en destacar, ya que es único. En nuestro caso, aún antes de acabar de cruzar el Mar de Hoces, ya nos encontramos con varios de ellos por el camino. Puede ser una obviedad, pero son gigantes, desmesuradamente majestuosos. Son como pequeños montes flotantes, algunos de ellos tienen estructuras verticales afiladas que recuerdan a cristales puntiagudos, mientras que otros son planos y parecen lugares sobre los que incluso podría edificarse. Sin embargo, no son un hogar para nosotros, sino de otras especies de seres vivos como, por ejemplo, los pingüinos. Estas aves marinas tan populares suelen pasar gran parte del tiempo en los icebergs que flotan en el océano Antártico para descansar de su incesante búsqueda de alimento, principalmente krill (*Euphausia superba*), así como para evitar ser depredadas por especies como las orcas o las focas leopardo (*Hydrurga leptony*), esta última es una descomunal foca que alcanza los tres metros de longitud y solo es depredada por las orcas en aguas antárticas. La primera vez que uno ve icebergs o pingüinos entra en un frenesí de emociones que, sin embargo, decae de manera inversamente proporcional al tiempo que pasa en la Antártida y el número de veces que los observa. Es bastante común que al primer pingüino o iceberg que uno ve en su vida les eche unas cien fotos, pero este entusiasmo desaparece progresivamente y, al final los graznidos, saltos y chapuzones de estas aves pasan a ser parte del día a día.

La campaña PEGASO iba a durar alrededor de un mes y medio rodeados de esta fauna y de unos paisajes increíbles, lo cual nos haría rabiar al pensar que debíamos estar muchas horas en el laboratorio en lugar de admirándolos. Pasar más de un mes embarcados, tratándose de aguas antárticas, suponía mucho tiempo de navegación. El comandante del BIO Hespérides nos comunicó que iba a ser la expedición más larga llevada a cabo hasta el momento en dicho buque sin atracar en ningún puerto. Es decir, durante un mes y medio tendríamos que nutrirnos de todo aquello previamente adquirido en Ushuaia. Por lo tanto, era más que posible que algunos alimentos frescos desapareciesen las primeras semanas y no volviéramos a degustarlos hasta pisar tierra.

Durante todas esas semanas nos dedicaríamos a perseguir *blooms* por las aguas del océano antártico, pero ¿qué es un *bloom*?, ¿y cómo se persigue?

El *bloom* de fitoplancton es un fenómeno caracterizado por una gran producción fotosintética del fitoplancton marino que se da en una masa de agua determinada, fruto de la llegada de la primavera (y el consecuente aumento de la temperatura y las horas de luz) y/o de un aporte puntual de nutrientes. Es decir, es una zona del mar donde hay mucha cantidad de fitoplancton, así como de otros seres vivos de las redes tróficas que dependen de ellos. De hecho, *bloom* en inglés significa «floración», porque sí, la primavera también llega a los ecosistemas marinos. Nosotros queríamos estudiar dónde se producen los gases traza que son capaces de participar, entre otros fenómenos, en los procesos de formación de nubes. Ya sabemos que algunos de ellos los produce el fitoplancton, así que qué mejor sitio para lograr dicho fin que en esas aguas. Sin embargo, el océano «se mueve», es decir, los *blooms* de fitoplancton van siguiendo la masa de agua en la que se han formado, por lo que geográficamente cada día pueden estar en un lugar diferente. Así que nuestro objetivo era situarnos en dichas masas de agua y perseguir a los *blooms*. Para ello, en oceanografía se suelen usar unas boyas especiales llamadas lagrangianas que nos ayudan en todo momento a conocer dónde se encuentra nuestra masa de agua de interés y, por lo tanto, el ansiado *bloom* de fitoplancton. Dichas boyas lagrangianas cuentan con una vela pero que, en vez de ir por fuera del agua, tienen una disposición hacia abajo. Es decir, son unas velas que, en vez de utilizar el viento para mover la boya, lo que utilizan es el sentido de la corriente marina. Conviene destacar que muchas veces el viento y la corriente van en direcciones y/o sentidos opuestos. De esta manera, la boya siempre estará en la misma masa de agua, ya que se moverá allá donde ella vaya. Así, el BIO Hespérides solo se tenía que encargar de perseguir estas boyas durante uno de los días en los que necesitásemos trabajar en cada *bloom*, por lo general una semana, para poder coger muestras y hacer experimentos sobre la misma masa de agua.

El primer lugar que visitamos fue Islas Orcadas, donde nos quedamos trabajando algo más de una semana en un *bloom* que encontramos rápidamente, puesto que gracias a las imágenes de satélite nos podíamos dirigir a aquellas zonas que tuvieran una concentración sospechosamente alta de clorofila. Al llegar a él, lanzamos dos boyas lagrangianas y empezamos a trabajar en la zona. Durante esos días el trabajo era frenético, no solamente muestreábamos agua del sistema de continuo o de la roseta-CTD, sino que también realizábamos experimentos en cubierta. Aparte, también realizábamos muestreos desde la zódiac, de los cuales fui responsable junto con mi supervisor al ser el más joven del grupo y tener menos tareas de laboratorio. Los muestreos en zódiac implicaban calzarse el traje de supervivencia y adentrarse en el océano helado durante unas dos horas, a veces un par de veces al día. Y digo helado porque la temperatura del agua a veces es menos de 0°C, concretamente de unos −2°C. Muchos os estaréis preguntando cómo es de fría el agua del océano antártico, mejor dicho, cómo se siente. Para explicarlo, yo siempre suelo decir que es como el agua que se está descongelando y nos da dolor de cabeza si la bebemos deprisa. La diferencia es que todo ese océano está a esa temperatura. Y esto es un hecho que puede parecer obvio y que muchos ya supondríais antes de leerlo, pero lo que es bastante impactante no es la temperatura *per se*, sino aceptar el hecho de que si caes al agua en pocos minutos estarás muerto por hipotermia. Estos son los tipos de pensamientos que, a veces, solían rondarme por la cabeza cuando navegábamos en la zódiac para coger muestras alejados varios kilómetros del BIO Hespérides. Bueno, de ese buque y de prácticamente cualquier otro porque en un mes y medio casi nunca vimos otra embarcación. Otro de los tipos de muestro de agua marina que realizábamos es el de la conocida como «microcapa superficial del océano», que es la película que recubre la superficie del agua. Es algo difícil de explicar, definir y entender, incluso para los expertos en el tema, pero, a grandes rasgos, es como una fina película en la cual se deposita polvo atmosférico y otras partículas, así como donde se encuentran algunas moléculas hidrófobas. Es, a fin de cuentas, como la piel del océano, mejor dicho, como la epidermis. Muestrear esta capa es algo muy, muy complejo. En nuestro caso, utilizábamos una técnica muy curiosa que nos ocasionó múltiples bromas por parte de los militares. Esta microcapa puede obtenerse al introducir un cristal en el agua en sentido perpendicular a la superficie. Al extraerlo, la capa más superficial, la microcapa, se adhiriere a las paredes del cristal. Posteriormente, el cristal se limpia con una pequeña espátula y con ayuda de un embudo se recoge el agua muestreada que no es otra que aquella que forma la microcapa superficial. Como puede suponerse, esto es un proceso que ocupa mucho tiempo, puesto que se recogen unos pocos mililitros en cada «limpiada» de cristal. Tardábamos algo más de una hora en muestrear el equivalente a una lata de refresco de trescientos treinta mililitros. Todo esto a una temperatura del aire que no superaba los 0°C y el agua helada que dolía al resbalar por las manos. De hecho, algún que otro día, mis dedos palidecían y, al llegar al buque de vuelta, los tenía que meter un rato en agua tibia. Me lleve más de una bronca del médico del buque, pero bueno: «todo sea por la ciencia».

En Islas Orcadas tuvimos un tiempo de lo más variado: días soleados, nublados, ventosos, fríos e incluso calor. Esos días disfrutamos de unos paisajes de extraña belleza. Como nos movíamos por una superficie relativamente pequeña persiguiendo nuestro *bloom* de fitoplancton, el paisaje que veíamos era prácticamente el mismo todos los días, pero desde distintas posiciones. En uno de esos atardeceres espectaculares, con las Islas Orcadas totalmente cubiertas por nieve, decidimos acercarnos a visitar los dos imponentes icebergs que veíamos a diario. Ver estos monstruos de cerca es una experiencia sobrecogedora, sobre todo al pensar que la parte sumergida es varias veces más grande que la que asoma en el exterior. Sorprendentemente, nos pasó algo que pocas personas tienen la oportunidad de ver y, según dicen, solo sucede una vez en la vida; aunque a nosotros nos pasó varias veces en un mes y medio. Estuvimos alrededor de media hora al lado de uno de los icebergs y extrajimos pequeños trozos de hielo que se desprendían para realizar algún experimento. Hasta ahí, todo normal: una visión increíble de distintos tonos azules, aves y pequeños icebergs que flotaban alrededor. Sin embargo, al llegar al buque nos informaron de que había un iceberg que se estaba rompiendo y se daba la vuelta, y era el que acabábamos de visitar. Resulta que cuando los icebergs se derriten llega un momento en que se dan la vuelta sobre sí mismos y la parte que se encuentra sumergida sale a la luz. Dicho iceberg, que poco antes estaba entero y tenía un aspecto compacto con una parte superior aplanada; de repente pasó a tambalearse e iba desprendiendo trozos de hielo del tamaño de pequeños edificios. Su parte inferior emergió del océano cual *kraken* y quedaron visibles los tonos azulados y las formas de hielo onduladas de su sección sumergida.

No solo eso, Islas Orcadas nos ofreció la experiencia «faunística» más intensa de la vida de muchos de nosotros. Al trabajar en una zona aislada para muestrear el agua más superficial del océano Antártico con cinco mil metros de profundidad bajo nuestros pies, sucedían cosas increíbles. Los animales del entorno se acercaban a nosotros como si fuésemos un enorme trozo de madera a la deriva, por lo que tuvimos visitas de aves como petreles gigantes (*Macronectes giganteus*), albatros de ceja negra (*Thalassarche melanophrys*), skúas del polo sur (*Stercorarius maccormicki*), etc.; algunas de las cuales, con su envergadura de varios metros, planeaban sobre nosotros o venían nadando como si fuesen patos. Un par de veces se acercaron a la embarcación lobos marinos antárticos (*Arctophoca gazella*) que nos miraban con muchísima condescendencia y nadando a nuestro lado durante unos instantes para después alejarse lentamente. Aunque, sin duda alguna, las grandes estrellas fueron los pingüinos barbijo (*Pygoscelis antarcticus*). Absolutamente todos los días se acercaban a nosotros nadando, saltando y buceando. Les llamaba muchísimo la atención el espejo que introducíamos en el agua y se acercaban en grupillos de cuatro o cinco para verlo. Hasta que un día, un pequeño pingüino bautizado como Mikjail por parte de la tripulación, se nos acercó demasiado. El pequeño Mikjail siempre iba solo hasta que nos encontró y, tras dar varias vueltas alrededor de la zódiac, ¡se atrevió a saltar dentro! No contento con saltar una vez lo intentó en numerosas ocasiones más y al final estuvo con nosotros en unas cuatro ocasiones. En conclusión, podríamos decir que, en Islas Orcadas ni siquiera los pingüinos te tienen miedo. Es lo que sucede en los lugares donde no habita el ser humano o, donde habita, pero no hace ningún tipo de daño a la fauna.

Sin embargo, también fue en estas aguas donde tuvimos un percance que ciertamente entrañó bastante riesgo. Una mañana despertamos con una niebla que impedía ver lo que teníamos a pocos metros de distancia. El océano se había vuelto blanco. Y esa mañana tocaba de nuevo salir a muestrear con la zódiac a un grupo de cuatro personas: dos militares y dos científicos, incluyéndome a mí. Tomamos todas las precauciones necesarias y nos embarcamos. Poco a poco nos fuimos alejando del BIO Hespérides, el cual rápidamente dejó de verse. No había mucho oleaje, pero las olas eran muy amplias y suaves, aunque nunca llegaban a romper, era como un mar de fondo extraño. Mientras muestreábamos, varios animales marinos se acercaron a nosotros, aunque solo nos podíamos percatar de su presencia una vez se encontraban muy cerca, ya que no podíamos verlos venir. Alguna ballena y también lobos marinos antárticos nos sorprendieron a muy poquitos metros. Incluso tuvimos la visita de un ejemplar del ave más famosa del océano antártico, después de los pingüinos, el albatros viajero (*Diomedea exulans*) que puede alcanzar más de tres metros de envergadura, como seguramente era el caso de la que nos visitó a nosotros. Supongo que se extrañó de que estuviéramos en medio de la niebla y empezó a sobrevolarnos, cada vez más cerca. Finalmente, aterrizó en el agua y se acercó hasta nosotros nadando, de una forma muy semejante a un pato, pero uno muy grande. Cuando ya incluso podíamos tocarlo con las manos, aunque no era nuestra intención, se dio cuenta de que no había comida y echó a volar. Tras un par de horas de trabajo, nos dispusimos a volver. Sin embargo, en un lance fortuito, el gps se estropeó y no podíamos geolocalizar el buque. Es decir, nos encontrábamos flotando en el océano antártico, rodeados de niebla y sin saber la distancia exacta a la que se encontraba el BIO Hespérides. Por suerte, llevábamos un par de *walkie-talkies* con los que pudimos llamar al puente de mando del buque, pero claro, no veíamos nada, ni siquiera el sol. Así que iba a ser muy difícil orientarnos. La solución fue ir hablando con ellos sin parar mientras hacían sonar la bocina del BIO Hespérides. Así, tras algo más de media hora, conseguimos llegar orientándonos únicamente por el sonido. Tras el susto, nunca olvidaré la cara que puso el comandante, máxima autoridad en el buque, cuando le dijimos que por la tarde tendríamos que volver a salir a muestrear en la zódiac. Cuando uno vive una experiencia de este tipo no puede evitar preguntarse muchas cosas, entre ellas, las que hemos escuchado la mayoría de quienes nos dedicamos a la investigación: «¿Tú eres científico de bata o de bota?». Esta pregunta hace alusión a si eres más de los que desarrollan su trabajo entre las paredes del laboratorio o si, por el contrario, te gusta más el trabajo de campo. Evidentemente esto es una generalización errónea, de hecho, es muy común que los científicos sean de bota y de bata a la vez. En la investigación hay muchísimas más tipologías de científicos y, por consiguiente, de metodologías de trabajo distintas. Así, puedes perderte en la niebla del océano antártico a temperaturas bajo de cero y media hora después estar preparando muestras de fitoplancton en el laboratorio.

Nuestra travesía acababa de empezar y tras Islas Orcadas nos dirigíamos a uno de los lugares más emblemáticos de la Antártida: el mar de Weddell, al este de la Península Antártica. Nombrado así en honor al marinero británico James Weddell, quien en 1823 llegó a adentrarse en él alcanzando una latitud de 74°S. Aparte de marinero, Weddell también era cazador de focas, que eran muy utilizadas en la industria peletera del momento. De hecho, existe una foca a la que también da nombre: la foca de Weddell (*Leptonychotes weddellii*), que es el mamífero que más al sur habita en el planeta. A mí siempre me ha parecido irónico que una foca tenga el nombre de aquella persona cuyo objetivo era cazarlas en aguas antárticas para vender las pieles al mejor postor. Eran otros tiempos. Y los tiempos de la exploración antártica guardan muchas historias que merecen ser recordadas.

El día 19 de enero de 1915, unos cien años antes y, en esas mismas aguas del helado mar de Weddell, Ernest Shackleton a bordo del Endurance y apoyado por una tripulación de veintisiete hombres escapó por poco de la catástrofe. El Endurance quedó atrapado por el hielo en su expedición hacia la conquista del Polo Sur, poco antes de llegar a la bahía Vahsel. Fue entonces cuando comenzó su aventura contra las condiciones extremas de las largas noches polares, el hielo, el intenso frío y la desesperación por liberar el barco, que fue a la deriva en un bloque de hielo durante el invierno antártico. A nosotros nos hubiera tocado vivir algo parecido si no dispusiésemos de la tecnología necesaria a bordo del buque ni de la información que nos proporcionan los satélites. De esta manera, podemos saber con precisión qué zonas se encuentran cubiertas por hielo y cuáles no. Esto aquí resulta de vital importancia ya que, durante el invierno, el mar de Weddell permanece prácticamente helado alcanzando su banquisa extensiones inmensas. Al llegar la primavera se empieza a derretir lentamente y eso condiciona cuándo se puede navegar. Debido a nuestras previsiones, durante la campaña PEGASO no nos pudimos introducir mucho en el mar de Weddell y nos quedamos en las zonas adyacentes. Durante esos días, realizamos experimentos. Fueron días intensivos de muestreo con dos CTD por jornada y muestreos diarios en zódiac. Eso sí, el barco se tenía que reposicionar sin cesar todos los días, ya que estábamos completamente rodeados de icebergs y de placas de hielo marino que amenazaban con colisionar con el BIO Hespérides, pero no hay mal que por bien no venga y durante esos días pudimos ver hielo de todos los colores, desde azules a marrones. De nuevo, disfrutamos de numerosos avistamientos de aves como los petreles antárticos (*Thalassoica antarctica*), que nos sobrevolaban en bandadas rozándonos la cabeza, o pingüinos de las especies barbijo (*Pygoscelis antarcticus*), papúa (*Pygoscelis papua*) y adelia (*Pygoscelis adeliae*); estos dos últimos hasta ese momento no los habíamos visto de cerca. No como los malditos barbijos, que rodeaban el barco gritando sin cesar desde bien temprano. Aparte del ruido, muy poca gente conoce que los pingüinos, sobre todo sus colonias, huelen fatal. Eso sí, son graciosos, interesantes y nadan a velocidades de vértigo. Por otro lado, también avistamos desde la zódiac al primer ejemplar de la temida foca leopardo (*Hydruga leptonyx*), que contaba con más de dos metros de longitud; y, de nuevo, a numerosos lobos marinos antárticos. Durante nuestra navegación en el mar de Weddell, también pudimos observar ballenas más cerca que nunca, lo malo es que uno nunca tiene la cámara a mano cuando aparecen. Esos días, en general, las salidas en zódiac fueron absolutamente espectaculares, nos pudimos acercar muchísimo a las placas de hielo e incluso navegar entre ellas. Entre el silencio estremecedor de los hielos marinos y los distintos tonos de azul de las aguas solo se escuchaban los sonidos de las golondrinas antárticas y petreles que hacían piruetas y emitían algún graznido. Por cierto, cogimos algunas muestras de esos mismos hielos marinos para realizar experimentos en el laboratorio del BIO Hespérides. Concretamente, teníamos que seleccionar aquellos hielos que tuviesen microorganismos creciendo en su interior de manera abundante. Este tipo de hielos son muy fáciles de reconocer, ya que suelen encontrarse en la parte inferior de las grandes porciones de hielo marino que quedan sueltas. Respecto a la metodología de recolección es bastante básica, principalmente consiste en coger los trozos directamente o romperlos para separarlos de la porción de hielo más grande, ya sea a golpes o incluso hachazos. La elegancia de una técnica no tiene nada que ver con su efectividad. Así, pudimos recoger varias decenas de kilos de este tipo de hielo tan preciado y que se encuentra en muy pocos lugares. Una vez de vuelta al buque, introdujimos dichos hielos en tanques especiales de experimentación para conocer su papel en la formación de aerosoles mientras se derriten. Algo que hasta ahora no se había investigado en esta zona del planeta.

Los días en el mar de Weddell iban llegando a su fin y tocaba trincar de nuevo todos los instrumentos científicos a las paredes y guardarlo todo muy bien en cajas, ya que nos esperaban días movidos, muy movidos navegando rumbo a las Islas South Georgia en plena corriente circumpolar de vientos antártica, dónde las tormentas se sucedían una tras otra. Fue como cruzar de nuevo el estrecho de Drake. El plan inicial era estar en las Islas South Georgia durante unos tres o cuatro días, para posteriormente volver de nuevo al mar de Weddell y a sus zonas adyacentes, donde finalizaría la campaña. Por lo que, contando con volver a Ushuaia al final de la campaña, todos los integrantes de PEGASO cruzaríamos unas cuatro veces el estrecho de Drake.

La llegada a las Islas South Georgia fue bastante movida, como se esperaba. Sin embargo, fue allí, pese al mal tiempo, donde encontramos el *bloom* de fitoplancton más potente. Es decir, donde más microorganismos fitoplanctónicos hallamos e investigamos. Estábamos literalmente bañándonos en diatomeas, sobre todo de la especie *Corethron criophilum*, a las que no parecía importarles el mal tiempo. Las olas de cuatro y cinco metros eran una constante que te mecía mientras trabajabas, no cesaba nunca. Al movimiento incesante hubo que sumar las tormentas de lluvia y nieve que se iban sucediendo, así como la densa niebla que tuvimos durante todos los días, rodeando el BIO Hespérides. Todo ello propició que solo pudiésemos salir en una ocasión a realizar los muestreos rutinarios en zódiac, para colectar muestras de agua superficial. Debido a esto, los avistamientos de fauna fueron mucho más limitados que en las otras localizaciones, restringiéndose a nuestros permanentes acompañantes: albatros, petreles, priones, etc. Aunque esto no es del todo cierto, ya que un día nos llamaron desde la central de máquinas del BIO Hespérides para informarnos de que una de sus conducciones se encontraba llena de krill antártico, por lo que no tardamos en llegar con un recipiente donde introducirlos y poder observarlos. El krill antártico posiblemente sea uno de los seres más emblemáticos de estos ecosistemas. Aparte de su conocido papel como alimento de las grandes ballenas, juega un papel importantísimo en el ecosistema marino antártico. A nivel trófico, las aves también se alimentan de estos pequeños crustáceos, tanto las voladoras, como los pequeños priones antárticos (*Pachyptila desolata*) que gozan de gran maniobrabilidad en el aire; como las nadadoras, como nuestros queridos pingüinos barbijo. Por otro lado, dentro del hielo marino se forman pequeñas oquedades y conducciones que permiten que haya organismos fotosintéticos viviendo en ellos. Cuando los cardúmenes de krill encuentran uno de estos hielos marinos llenos de fitoplancton se acercan desde abajo y raspan su parte inferior alimentándose así de estos organismos. Estos tipos de hielos son los que muestreábamos para nuestros experimentos y esta es la razón principal de que tuvieran tonalidades marrones y verdes. Y así, entre krill y muchas aves dejamos las aguas de las Islas South Georgia y nos dirigimos de nuevo a hacia el continente antártico, concretamente a la Península Antártica donde realizaríamos algunos experimentos más antes de partir de vuelta a Ushuaia. Conforme nos alejábamos de South Georgia, los icebergs cada vez eran más grandes, había menos niebla y la fauna se dejaba ver de nuevo.

Sin embargo, antes de volver a Ushuaia también teníamos que ayudar en las tareas científicas de las BAE, para el transporte de personal y víveres. Así, pudimos visitar las dos españolas, Gabriel de Castilla y Juan Carlos I, y las de otros países que estaban en sus proximidades. Es fascinante ver cómo en la Antártida las distintas bases de investigación colaboran entre sí. Sin embargo, dicha colaboración no solo se queda en el ámbito científico, sino que se traslada a partidos de fútbol, carreras, concursos de fotografía, etc., todo lo necesario para poder pasar el rato durante varios meses a miles de kilómetros de tu hogar. También pudimos visitar algunas de las pingüineras, es decir, las zonas de cría de pingüinos barbijo y papúa, así como realizar varias excursiones por los montes cercanos. Montes que, como era de esperar, estaban cubiertos de nieve desde la base, por lo que subir unos pocos cientos de metros era un verdadero ejercicio de alpinismo. Aparte de las bases españolas, tuvimos la suerte de poder visitar Palmer Station, perteneciente a los Estados Unidos de América. Los estadounidenses nos recibieron con café y galletas, y con una agradable conversación con sus investigadores. Algunos de los integrantes de nuestra expedición, de hecho, ya habían trabajado previamente en algunos proyectos de investigación en esta base, así que se sentían como en casa. Nos contaron que, al acabar un proyecto de investigación, es tradición bañarse en las aguas del pequeño puerto ubicado delante de Palmer Station. Y me consta que es una práctica que se sigue haciendo. Lo que más nos llamó la atención es que Palmer Station tiene una tienda donde se puede adquirir su propio *merchandising* e incluso pagar con tarjeta de crédito. Es más, se vanaglorian de ser la tienda ubicada más al sur del mundo, y tras adquirir un gorro de lana, embarqué de nuevo en el BIO Hespérides para poner rumbo a Ushuaia.

Han transcurrido ya muchas campañas oceanográficas a bordo del BIO Hespérides que se podrían contar por centenas. De hecho, con treinta años de vida, son cientos de personas las que han navegado a bordo. Es muy difícil describir con palabras lo que aquí se siente, pero también resulta difícil explicarlo visualmente ya que, como me comentaba una de las investigadoras que más veces ha estado en la Antártida, da igual la cámara de fotos que tengas, muy barata o cara; es imposible plasmar la belleza de estos lugares en un número finito de píxeles y bytes de información. En ocasiones, las imágenes no son suficientes para capturar esta realidad, ya que no solamente es necesaria la vista, sino también el olfato, el tacto, el oído e, incluso, el gusto. Porque sí, en la Antártida hasta el aire huele diferente. Todo es diferente. Si tuviese que describir qué se siente diría que es una mezcla entre vivir en un documental, la mili y un campamento de verano, o lo que es lo mismo, estar rodeados de icebergs, ballenas, aves, delfines, etc. dentro de un buque con régimen militar mientras convives durante mucho tiempo con personas alejado de tu hogar (y casi sin acceso a Internet). Al principio es demasiado chocante, desde la ventana de tu camarote ves pingüinos saltando, sales al exterior del buque, y ya sea en el puente (arriba) o en la cubierta de popa (abajo), eliges un punto al que mirar, el que quieras, ya sea estribor, babor... donde te dé la gana y el paisaje te deja sin aliento. El viento es increíblemente fuerte y frío, y si nieva, los copos se clavan como cuchillos en la piel. No transcurren ni cinco minutos hasta que observas algún ave, mamífero marino o iceberg. Aquí, la fauna tiene una actitud distinta hacia el ser humano. Parece que se ríen de ti, te miran con el desdén de quién tiene el mejor hogar del mundo. Se acercan, te observan y se van; como si lo hicieran con condescendencia. Las aves vienen a ver si comen algo, a las ballenas les da por jugar con la proa del buque buceando por debajo de un lado a otro, yendo de babor a estribor y mareando a un grupo de científicos armados con cámaras que por mucho que se esfuercen no van a captar ni un 1% de la esencia de ese momento. Se cachondean de nosotros: veinticinco años viniendo los mismos pardillos con chaquetones rojos, verdes o azules por aquí y aún desconocemos muchísimo de su hogar. La ruptura de la rutina, las experiencias nuevas y la belleza que te rodea, hacen que la vida se ralentice al recorrer lentamente espacios inmensos, desconocidos y apasionantes. Aquí los días parece que duran más de veinticuatro horas, es un frenesí sensorial.

Todo principio tiene un final y todo final tiene su principio. Así como el fin del mundo (Ushuaia) da paso al principio del continente antártico, el fin de una gran experiencia solo abre puertas a las que están por venir. Y de esto va un poco la ciencia. Tras varios años investigando, me imagino que estamos rodeados por una gran esfera, como en la película *El show de Truman*, en la que los límites de la esfera los impone el conocimiento del que disponemos. Conforme uno va aprendiendo, se va acercando más a esos límites y empieza a darse cuenta de que posiblemente detrás haya algo. Es decir, aprender es simplemente acercarse progresivamente al límite de lo que se sabe acerca de algo. Sin embargo, de la misma manera, si una persona no se esfuerza en aprender siempre se quedará lejos de los límites, es más, pensará que estos límites no existen y que ya se conoce todo. Y, por supuesto, que él ya conoce todo lo necesario. Así, mientras que la gente sabia duda acerca de los límites del conocimiento, pues se ha esforzado en vislumbrarlos, otros se comportan de manera arrogante mostrando una gran seguridad en sí mismos. A veces, desde la ciencia se observa la llegada al «final» de estos límites de algo con gran impaciencia, porque nunca es el final. De hecho, cuando te vas acercando a uno de los límites de nuestra esfera imaginaria te das cuenta de que nunca se acaba, nunca es el fin. En eso consiste un poco la ciencia, en acercarse a los límites del conocimiento para derribarlos. O al menos intentarlo.

Tras cuarenta y cinco días de navegación y casi dos meses fuera de nuestras casas, navegando por el frío océano Austral y con una multitud de emociones y experiencias en la mochila, la llegada a Ushuaia marcaba el final de nuestro viaje en todos los sentidos. Se apreciaba la confusión en el ambiente, las ganas de volver con la incertidumbre de no saber cuándo podríamos regresar a la Antártida. Por ello, el puerto de la ciudad más austral del mundo se alzaba como un símbolo de esperanza, ilusión, alegría y melancolía a partes iguales. El silencio llenaba los rincones del barco, mientras todos mirábamos por las ventanas, desde el puente de mando o las camaretas, la inexorable llegada a nuestro destino con una media sonrisa.

Todos tenemos nuestros sueños. Suele haber sueños más grandes y otros más pequeños, pero por encima de todo, está «el sueño». Ese sueño al que aspiramos cuando somos pequeños, volar, explorar, ser invisible o capaz de respirar bajo el agua. No lo que se quiere ser cuando los obstáculos de la vida y la pérdida de ilusión hacen mella en los ánimos; lo que hace que la ilusión se retraiga hasta los confines de nuestras más íntimas pasiones, presentándose solo, a veces, en forma de sueños por las noches. Para algunos, ese sueño era ir a la Antártida, a uno de los confines del mundo. Sin embargo, tener la suerte de cumplir «el sueño», tal vez sea una desgracia, ya que por un lado te sientes realizado, mientras, por otro, dejas un hueco muy difícil de llenar. Un hueco que siempre había estado ahí y que ahora habrá que volver a llenar. Bendito problema.

Ojalá que, a alguna persona joven, o no tan joven, este libro le sirva para perseguir sus sueños y darse cuenta de que, aunque en algunos países no se encuentran las mejores condiciones para hacer ciencia siempre hay oportunidades que, como los *blooms* de fitoplancton, hay que ir a buscar. Al fin y al cabo, no conviene olvidar que cuando aprendes algo de historia de la ciencia te das cuenta de que los científicos y las científicas nunca lo han tenido fácil. No es nada nuevo, nunca ha sido cómodo hacer avanzar el conocimiento. En la Edad Media había que luchar contra la inquisición para que no te tachasen de hereje y te quemasen en la hoguera, como a Giordano Bruno por proponer que el sol era simplemente una estrella, otra más como las que se veían en el cielo por las noches, pero que estaba más cerca. En nuestro tiempo, a la hora de iniciar nuestra carrera investigadora, tenemos que luchar contra otros inquisidores tengan el nombre que tengan, ya sea el de crisis económica, brecha generacional, precariedad o lo que sea. Gracias a eso, seguiremos cumpliendo sueños.

LA VUELTA AL MUNDO EN 90 DÍAS

«—¿El señor va a viajar? —preguntó.
—Sí —respondió Phileas Fogg—. Vamos a dar la vuelta al mundo.
Picaporte, con los ojos excesivamente abiertos, los párpados y las cejas en alto, los brazos caídos, el cuerpo abatido, ofrecía entonces todos los síntomas del asombro llevado hasta el estupor.
—¡La vuelta al mundo! —dijo entre dientes.
—En ochenta días —respondió míster Fogg—. No tenemos un momento que perder».

La vuelta al mundo en 80 días. *Julio Verne*

El año 2016 comenzaba con una noticia que era difícil de creer: íbamos a dar la vuelta a la Antártida navegando. Habíamos sido seleccionados para participar en la Expedición de Circunnavegación Antártica (ACE), la primera en la historia de carácter internacional que iba a dar la vuelta completa al gran continente helado. Esta vez el proyecto no tendría lugar a bordo del BIO Hespérides, sino del buque oceanográfico ruso Akademik Tryoshnikov (Akademik, de ahora en adelante) entre diciembre de 2016 y marzo de 2017. Y la financiación y liderazgo del proyecto no sería española, sino del Instituto Polar Suizo (entidad formada por instituciones científicas suizas como la Escuela Politécnica Federal de Zúrich o la Escuela Politécnica Federal de Lausanne), el Ministerio de Asuntos Exteriores de dicho país y también inversores privados. En ACE participamos veintidós proyectos científicos internacionales liderados y formados por investigadores de todos los continentes (menos de la Antártida, claro), concretamente de unos veinte países distintos. De esos veintidós proyectos, solo uno de los seleccionados era español y solo cuatro españoles participaríamos en la expedición: un barcelonés, una valenciana, una mallorquina y un cartagenero. Para que luego algunos digan que a los del Mediterráneo no nos gusta el frío. Reflexionando un poco, uno se da cuenta rápidamente de que darle la vuelta a la Antártida es, al fin y al cabo, darle la vuelta al mundo; puesto que se cruzan todos los meridianos del planeta. Eso sí, es un viaje más corto que darle la vuelta a las regiones tropicales del planeta, como hizo Juan Sebastián Elcano. Si Phileas Fogg tardó ochenta días en dar la vuelta al mundo, nosotros íbamos a tardar noventa. Lo que no está nada mal, puesto que el objetivo de nuestra expedición no era ir del punto A al B, sino el de hacer ciencia. Y la ciencia lleva su tiempo. Durante los aproximadamente tres meses de navegación en el océano Antártico, ACE se dividiría en tres etapas (llamadas «Leg 1», «Leg 2» y «Leg 3») en las que los grupos de investigación irían relevando a los científicos, ya que prácticamente nadie realizó la circumnavegación completa. La «Leg 1» zarparía de Ciudad del Cabo (Sudáfrica) para navegar por el océano Antártico y las islas subantárticas, como las pertenecientes a los archipiélagos de Crozet o Kerguelen, para finalmente llegar a Hobart (Tasmania, Australia). La «Leg 2» empezaría en Hobart y llegaría hasta el glaciar Mertz, en la Antártida, para estudiar cómo el desprendimiento de un iceberg gigante que tuvo lugar allí recientemente podría afectar a la vida marina en dicha zona; finalmente regresaríamos navegando a Punta Arenas (Chile). Por último, la «Leg 3» partiría de Punta Arenas para visitar la Islas South Georgia y regresar de nuevo a Ciudad del Cabo. En cada etapa, embarcarían aproximadamente, unos cincuenta investigadores.

El objetivo de ACE era muy ambicioso: recopilar información para poder comprender cómo el cambio climático está afectando a la Antártida y al océano Antártico desde la óptica de numerosas disciplinas científicas. Allí íbamos embarcados oceanógrafos, pero también meteorólogos, zoólogos, botánicos, farmacólogos, geólogos, microbiólogos, químicos, físicos, matemáticos, etc.; de setenta y tres instituciones científicas, incluyendo a algunas de las más potentes del mundo como, por ejemplo, la Universidad de Cambridge. Era lo más parecido a las antiguas exploraciones científicas en las que se juntaban las disciplinas más singulares para describir territorios que nunca antes habían sido vistos por el ser humano. Sin embargo, ACE no solo englobaría las tres etapas mencionadas anteriormente, sino que se les ocurrió que ya que el Akademik tenía que ir desde Bremerhaven (Alemania) hasta Ciudad del cabo, se podría aprovechar dicho trayecto para hacer ciencia. Y así es cómo nació la idea de la ACE Maritime University (La Universidad Marítima ACE): cincuenta estudiantes de máster y doctorado de más de veinte países distintos realizarían este trayecto acompañados de algunos científicos participantes de ACE que les impartirían clases teóricas y prácticas de cómo hacer ciencia en el mar. Los estudiantes que podían participar debían estar estudiando en universidades de los países colaboradores y promotores de ACE. Y, por desgracia, España no era uno de esos países por la decisión del Gobierno de España de no invertir en ACE, lo cual no es de extrañar conociendo el lugar en el que han dejado a la ciencia española en los últimos años, aunque este es otro tema. Por lo tanto, los estudiantes españoles no podían solicitar una plaza. Para que os hagáis una idea del carácter internacional de ACE, os contaré un poco acerca de nuestro proyecto de investigación: «SORPASSO» («Surveying Organic Reactive gases and Particles Across the Surface Southern Ocean»). Su objetivo era llevar a cabo las primeras observaciones de la distribución circumpolar de trazas de gases y partículas superficiales del océano importantes para la química atmosférica y el clima, y descifrar sus controladores biológicos, químicos, hidrológicos y ópticos. Para cumplir tan ambicioso objetivo, «SORPASSO» contó con la participación tanto de jóvenes investigadores como de científicos expertos del Institut de Ciències del Mar (ICM)-CSIC (Barcelona, Cataluña), Plymouth Marine Laboratory (UK), Plymouth University (UK), University of Warwick (UK), Takuvik UL/CNRS Laboratory (Québec, Canadá), University of Technology Sydney (Australia), INIBIOMA Bariloche (Argentina) y el Instituto Química Física Rocasolano-CSIC (Spain). En mi caso, fui seleccionado para participar en la ACE Maritime University y la Leg 1. Es decir, zarparía de Alemania a principios de noviembre de 2016 y llegaría a Tasmania a finales del enero de 2017, lo que suponía más de dos meses navegando rumbo a mis antípodas. Estos son los ingredientes con los que nació la primera expedición internacional para la circunnavegación completa de la Antártida con fines científicos.

Como para cada expedición oceanográfica, teníamos que preparar el material científico necesario en nuestras instalaciones en Barcelona para enviarlo a Bremerhaven, de donde zarparía ACE. Sin embargo, esta vez no enviamos el material en furgonetas o avión, sino que fuimos nosotros mismos los que transportamos todo el material conduciendo un camión desde Barcelona hasta Bremerhaven. La ciencia, de nuevo, daba muestras de su carácter «eminentemente glamuroso». Sin embargo, fue una experiencia ciertamente interesante para un cartagenero como yo, pues a lo largo del trayecto no dejamos de ver en ningún momento camiones cargados de fruta y verdura procedentes del Campo de Cartagena. Supongo que los europeos abastecidos con todos esos alimentos no eran conscientes de la insostenibilidad de muchos de los sistemas de cultivo empleados para obtenerlos y que solo tres años después originarían la mayor crisis que ha vivido el Mar Menor en las últimas décadas. Cuando uno habla del término «sostenibilidad» con la gente, se da cuenta de los elementos perversos que a veces entraña su mal uso. Por ejemplo, hace unos años cenaba con un amigo inglés en su casa ubicada en el mismo país, allí me comentó que él comía solo fruta y verdura en lugar de carne, sobre todo, evitaba la vaca, para reducir sus emisiones. Esta premisa es, *a priori*, cierta, pero excesivamente simplista por múltiples razones, aquí os muestro la suya. Lo primero que le pregunté es si la verdura y fruta que comía era de temporada, respondió que no lo sabía, así que asumamos que no. Lo siguiente fue si esa fruta y verdura había sido cultivada en Gran Bretaña, la respuesta también fue negativa. Cogí varios de los envases de su frigorífico y cuál fue mi sorpresa cuando le indiqué que esos alimentos habían sido producidos cerca de mi ciudad natal y que el sistema de producción de numerosas plantaciones no es precisamente «sostenible». Su cara fue un poema, aunque no puedo culpar a un británico de saciar sus ansias de jugosos vegetales, ya que su alternativa más sostenible sería pasar los años a base de conservas, patatas, cebollas y algunas fresas. Mientras viajábamos rumbo a Bremerhaven no podía evitar acordarme de mi buen amigo y de los miles o millones de personas de toda

Europa que se alimentan de vegetales del Campo de Cartagena con la misma buena intención, pero con el desconocimiento de la historia completa. ¿De quién es la culpa de que esto suceda? No es de nadie solo, pero tampoco de todos. Seguramente de muchos, sobre todo de aquellos que conociendo esto no actúan en consecuencia para cambiar las cosas. Mientras pensaba en aquello, el Mar Menor seguía eutrofizándose y nadie de los que podía haber cambiado las cosas hizo nada para evitar lo que vendría después.

Llegamos a Bremerhaven tras dos días de viaje. Creo que es la ciudad más gris que he visto en mi vida, aunque bien es cierto que en esa época del año las lluvias y la niebla son una constante. Allí nos esperaba el Akademik, con un 50% más de eslora que el Hespérides. El barco era increíblemente grande y, además, era nuevo: había sido botado en 2012. Sin embargo, este hecho se contradecía un poco con la realidad. El Akademik estaba muy oxidado y la pintura se caía a pedazos, nada que ver con el cuidado al que se veía sometido constantemente el Hespérides por parte de la Armada Española. Sin embargo, la verdadera sorpresa estaba en su interior. El suelo estaba abombado, las paredes (en la jerga marina «mamparas») y el techo eran del mismo color marrón oscuro que las sillas y muebles, y el óxido también reinaba por las partes metálicas del interior del Akademik. El camarote mantenía la misma estética, pero tenía la ventaja respecto al Hespérides de que tenía un sofá. Las camas, eso sí, eran más pequeñas. A nuestra llegada a los laboratorios, nos dimos cuenta de que las mesas, sillas, etc., también eran algo pequeñas. Sin embargo, lo más llamativo era que tanto el mobiliario de las habitaciones como el del comedor y los laboratorios era ciertamente «viejo». No tenía sentido que un barco que había sido botado en 2012 tuviera más pinta de haber pertenecido a los años de la URSS que el Hespérides que, recordemos, fue botado a principios de la década de los noventa. Estuvimos una semana descargando el material y montando el laboratorio, y en esos días resolvimos el misterio. Efectivamente, el Akademik había sido botado en 2012. Sin embargo, desde el Gobierno ruso, digámoslo así, no se consideraba el mantenimiento del buque como algo prioritario. Era más importante que este buque pudiera hacer la competencia en dimensiones y capacidad a los de otros países, sobre todo a EE. UU. Así que esa era la razón del óxido reinante de su exterior y, en menor medida, interior. No obstante, seguíamos sin saber cuál era la razón del mobiliario antiguo, pequeño y claramente «pasado de moda». Muchos pensábamos que simplemente era fruto de la estética rusa y que, al fin y al cabo, no debíamos de infraestimar las diferencias culturales. Sin embargo, la realidad siempre es más cutre de lo que uno puede imaginarse. Un oficial me comentó que lo que había sucedido fue que cuando construyeron el buque se quedaron sin dinero para «amueblarlo». Es decir, tenían un buque que había costado muchos millones de euros, una de las joyas de la corona de la oceanografía rusa, pero por dentro estaba «vacío». Así que, ¿cuál fue la genial idea que tuvieron? Pues utilizar el mobiliario del buque oceanográfico previo para el nuevo. Es decir, no es que la apariencia interior del Akademik tuviera tintes soviéticos, es que literalmente eran de aquella época. Sin duda, aquel mobiliario no era el más idóneo para las nuevas generaciones, que somos un poco más altas y grandes que las anteriores. Nuestras piernas casi no cabían debajo de algunas mesas y en la cama nos dábamos constantemente con el cuadro de madera en la cabeza cuando el barco se movía. Eso sí, no puedo negar que esta no fuera una práctica de lo más sostenible posible. Incómoda y poco práctica, pero sostenible. Por otro lado, absolutamente nada del barco estaba escrito en inglés, no hablemos ya de castellano. Solamente en ruso. La comida, de momento, era normalita. La tripulación era bastante maja y nos ayudó en todo lo que necesitamos, no sin antes pasarte un rato gesticulando; ya que tampoco controlaban mucho el inglés. Los más de dos meses que me esperaban en el buque ruso tenían pinta de ser de lo más entretenidos.

Zarpamos un sábado del mes de noviembre de 2016 desde el puerto de Bremerhaven. Hacía mucho frío, viento y llovía intensamente. Partir siempre es duro y en aquellas condiciones más, si tenemos en cuenta que levamos amarras a las 22:00

de la noche y la oscuridad ya hacía horas que bañaba las calles de Bremerhaven. Cenamos todos juntos antes de embarcar y mientras subíamos al Akademik, un grupo de cantantes alemanes entonaban canciones tradicionales en dicho idioma, como tantas otras veces en el pasado se había hecho cuando las grandes expediciones partían de ese puerto hacia alta mar. Eran un grupo de unos diez cantantes ataviados con prendas tradicionales alemanas y farolillos que daban una tenue luz debido a las velas que tenían en su interior. Antiguamente hubiera sido grasa de ballena, así que por fin veíamos cierto signo de modernidad en las inmediaciones del Akademik. En esos momentos recordaba la partida del Puerto de Cartagena dos años antes, de día, con orquesta, familia y amigos. Reinaban la alegría y las ganas de zarpar con ilusión por las aguas del Mediterráneo. Esta vez, las sensaciones eran algo distintas. El ambiente era intrigante y daba algo de reparo. Parecía que estábamos reviviendo una escena en la que en cualquier momento Jack el Destripador podía salir y llevarse a alguno de nosotros. Para colmo, la previsión meteorológica indicaba que íbamos a tener un tiempo tormentoso durante, al menos, los primeros días de navegación. Aun así, llegó el momento. Zarpamos. Y como siempre íbamos dejando atrás las luces, cada vez más pequeñas. Al día siguiente despertaríamos rumbo a las costas de Inglaterra, donde paramos un par de días en Southampton.

Como esperábamos, los primeros días de navegación hasta Southampton fueron horribles. Una borrasca nos acompañaba con tormentas y olas de hasta seis metros. Desde el primer día que nos despertamos, el barco se movía muchísimo. Muchos investigadores estaban tan mareados que no salieron siquiera de su camarote. El mal tiempo hizo que llegásemos a Southampton un día más tarde de lo previsto. Así que solo pudimos estar un día en la ciudad. Lo suficiente para que algunos pudiéramos visitar a nuestros amigos emigrados a dicha ciudad y gozar la de «grandiosa» gastronomía británica. Sin embargo, había algo prioritario que hacer en Southampton. En el Akademik para desayunar solo nos servían café soluble, y solo tenían de un tipo, aunque teníamos una cafetera de cápsulas que estaba sin usar. Así que el objetivo era adquirir el valioso café nada más llegar (ya os conté lo importante que es el café para no marearse). Entramos al primer supermercado que vimos y adquirí, exactamente, ciento veinte cápsulas de café. Eso serían unos tres cafés por día para el próximo mes, y algunas cápsulas extra para invitar a la gente. En Ciudad del Cabo volveríamos a comprar. Otra cosa que nos empezaba a preocupar era la comida. Digamos que la diversidad brillaba por su ausencia. Las comidas y cenas siempre, y cuando digo siempre es «siempre», eran a base de carne. Carne en sus múltiples formas: filetes, salchichas o albóndigas. A veces acompañada con un poco de arroz o pasta sin ningún tipo de salsa. Sin embargo, las albóndigas eran su plato estrella. Y las llamo albóndigas, pero no eran tales, era carne picada aplastada en forma de bola con las manos, sin sal o ningún tipo de especias. Las recetas que degustamos en el Akademik darían para varios capítulos, pero os ahorraré el sufrimiento. Por otro lado, el desayuno consistía en pan tostado con una especie de salami ruso que siempre era el mismo y, los domingos, en un increíble alarde de *haute cuisine*, también teníamos huevos hervidos. Como este era un tema que nos empezaba a preocupar de verdad, compramos comida que pudiéramos transportar en nuestro camarote, como frutos secos, verdura enlatada, fideos chinos o latas de algún guiso de verduras con guisantes y semejantes.

Cuando zarpamos de Southampton empezó lo fuerte, la expedición se tornó mucho más seria y los muestreos comenzaron. Aun así, teníamos tiempo para relajarnos en el laboratorio, escribir, pensar y, en general, hacer ciencia sin parar. En el Akademik solo teníamos conexión a Internet en un punto de wifi que estaba en la quinta (sí, quinta) planta del buque, a la que se podía subir andando o en el ascensor. Ya que, este buque contaba con un ascensor. No os recomiendo la experiencia de subir en un ascensor mientras el suelo se mueve bajo tus pies, mucha gente nunca cogió el ascensor por esa razón. Aparte, no sabíamos si el ascensor también venía del buque anterior de la URSS, así que no nos fiábamos mucho. Es decir, el Internet era mucho más limitado que en el Hespérides y una de las mejores cosas de no tener prácticamente conexión a la web es que te hace estar mucho más atento a tu trabajo y otras aficiones como la lectura. Es increíble la cantidad de tiempo que perdemos delante de la «pantallica» sin darnos cuenta.

En los laboratorios todo iba sobre ruedas hasta que tuvimos un percance. El sistema de muestreo en continuo del Akademik no funcionaba del todo bien y estuvimos intentando arreglarlo. Para ello, tras limpiar algunas de las canalizaciones y apretarlas correctamente, dejamos que el agua fluyese. Sin embargo, una de las piezas se soltó y el agua empezó a inundar toda la zona de laboratorios coincidiendo con que justo durante unas horas no había allí nadie trabajando. Al llegar por la tarde casi se podía surfear, había dos dedos de agua en uno de los laboratorios recorriendo el suelo de un lado a otro a causa del vaivén del barco. El agua había salido al pasillo y estaba por todos lados. Así que pasamos todo lo que quedaba de día fregando y recogiendo agua. El movimiento del barco era insoportable, por alguna extraña razón se movía muchísimo más que el Hespérides. Mientras que este se movía casi siempre en sentido proa-popa, el Akademik siempre se movía «de lado», es decir, de babor a estribor. Gran parte de los participantes no podían asistir a sus clases o al laboratorio, unos pocos aguantábamos estoicamente gracias al café y a que sabíamos que parte de nuestro doctorado dependía de las muestras obtenidas esos días.

Llegó un punto en el que hacía tan mal tiempo que no estaba permitido siquiera trabajar. Así que solo podíamos comer, escribir y echarnos en la cama o en el pequeño sofá que teníamos en la habitación. Mi compañero de camarote, otro estudiante de doctorado, pero de la Escuela Politécnica Federal de Suiza que investigaba la atmósfera oceánica, tampoco se mareaba. Así que esos días los pasamos inflándonos a chocolate suizo que había traído él, a fuet que traje yo y vaciando nuestras amplias, casi infinitas, reservas de café. Mientras tanto, las olas rompían con fuerza sobre los ojos de buey del camarote y veíamos el color azul oscuro-verdoso que tienen las aguas por algunas zonas del

Atlántico Norte. De hecho, el Akademik se inclinaba tanto que, desde dentro del camarote, sentados en el sofá bebiendo café, podíamos ver la columna de agua a través de los ojos de buey, como si fueran gafas de bucear. Nuestro camarote pasaba la mitad del tiempo bajo el agua y la otra fuera. Es lo que tiene que el buque se balanceara de babor a estribor, como si el mar siempre estuviera de través. Aquellos días pudimos observar muy, muy poca fauna. Únicamente algunas gaviotas que nos acompañaban en nuestro eterno balanceo.

Por fin llegó la calma. Las olas pasaron de los seis metros de altura a uno o dos metros, por lo que podíamos trabajar con normalidad. Vuelta al movimiento y al trabajo, mientras navegábamos al oeste de la costa de Francia. Tras varios días navegando, era la primera vez que veía a algunas personas que aún no había conocido. El mareo que tuvieron fue tal que no salieron en ningún momento de su camarote y tenían que alimentarse gracias a otros compañeros que les llevaban comida de la cocina. Sin embargo, la calma no iba a durar mucho: íbamos a encontrar otra borrasca en los próximos días. Mientras tanto, también esos días, comenzaron las clases de la Maritime University. Así que nos tocaba dar clase a alumnos de nuestra misma edad e incluso más, y prácticamente la misma experiencia laboral que nosotros, lo cual era bastante curioso. Sin embargo, las clases eran bastante interesantes ya que, la mayoría de los científicos no coincidían en el mismo campo de investigación, por lo que siempre tenías la oportunidad de escuchar materias ajenas a la tuya súper interesantes. Por ello, los que éramos «profesores» también asistíamos a las clases. Bueno, por eso y porque, aparte de trabajar, tampoco había nada más interesante que hacer.

Los días trascurrieron con normalidad dejando atrás Francia y posteriormente la Península Ibérica. Tras diez días de navegación por el océano Atlántico desde que zarpamos de Bremerhaven, por fin vislumbramos unas luces: las de Gran Canaria. Y cada vez más y más calor, como en la campaña Trans-PEGASO. Las frías aguas del mar cantábrico y del mar del Norte dieron paso a la costa portuguesa y a la costa de Mauritania. Entrábamos en zona tropical, lo cual era una buena noticia para los que nos gusta el calor. Por fin podíamos tomar el sol en nuestros descansos, mientras nos adentrábamos en el Golfo de África rumbo a Ciudad del Cabo donde sería verano. El tiempo cálido ayudaba a levantar el ánimo y a apreciar la naturaleza que nos rodeaba. Así, avistamos varios grupos de delfines comunes (*Delphinus delphis*), tortugas marinas y algunas ballenas que no nos dio tiempo a identificar. Entre la humedad, el calor y el sol radiante, la mayoría de la tripulación, de piel bastante blanca, ya presentaba el típico color rojizo. Creo que nunca había habido tantas gambas en la superficie del océano Atlántico tropical como aquellos días. Sin embargo, el trabajo en el laboratorio, en estas condiciones, se hacía más duro. La temperatura exterior se notaba mucho más, sobre todo, si le sumas que era un espacio cerrado y con las luces encendidas, por lo que podías ahorrarte el viaje a la sauna. Sí, se me había olvidado contaros que el Akademik también tenía una sauna. Había un día para los chicos, otro para las chicas y otro para la tripulación (a ellos, se ve, no les importaba mezclarse). Seguíamos navegando rumbo sur y la llegada a la zona colindante a la línea del ecuador conllevó el avistamiento de numerosas especies de fauna interesantes. La más característica fue la de peces voladores, y estaba lleno de ellos. Saltaban y planeaban de una ola a otra. Parecía que desde Trans-PEGASO, dos años atrás, estas aguas no habían cambiado. Otro avistamiento de fauna interesante fue el que protagonizó un investigador italiano especializado en plásticos marinos, quien se encargaba de realizar sondeos visuales buscando restos de este material. Fue precisamente durante uno de estos sondeos, cuando avistó varios tiburones martillo de unos tres metros.

Como decíamos antes, había investigadores de muchas temáticas distintas a bordo, lo que hacía de esta expedición un lujo en cuanto al aprendizaje de la metodología de trabajo de diferentes áreas de la ciencia. Por ejemplo, los investigadores de la Escuela Politécnica Federal de Suiza comenzaban esos días con los lanzamientos de radiosondas para trazar perfiles verticales de la troposfera. Y, ¿cómo lo hacían? Básicamente ataban a un globo lleno de helio una serie de instrumentos pequeños, que iban transmitiendo datos al Akademik mientras el globo ascendía. Contemplar uno de estos lanzamientos desde la cubierta es especialmente bonito, merece la pena verlos cada vez hacerse más y más pequeños hasta que no los puedes distinguir. Para nosotros, era como un pequeño lanzamiento espacial que nos aportaría unos datos valiosísimos acerca de la atmósfera que teníamos sobre nosotros mientras navegamos. Estos lanzamientos se realizaban desde la cubierta del Akademik, mientras varias personas descansaban en hamacas y otros hacían equilibrios con varias *slackline* atadas de un sitio a otro. Y es que en una campaña oceanográfica hay tiempo para todo. De hecho, durante esos días por aguas del ecuador tuvimos una grata sorpresa por parte de la tripulación. En su parco inglés, nos intentaban explicar no sé qué de una manguera con agua del mar, no sé cuándo, en no sé dónde. Tras esperar algunas horas, descubrimos que en el nivel inferior de la popa del Akademik habían montado una ducha a presión enorme de agua marina, que consistía en una tubería oxidada llena de agujeros. Un lujo. Y estaba en funcionamiento la mayor parte del día. Así que, aunque no podíamos saltar al agua y bañarnos en aguas abiertas, pudimos pegarnos un buen baño justo al lado de estas aguas de peces voladores, tiburones martillo, ballenas y tortugas marinas. Los días avanzaban a la velocidad dictada por la unánime rutina que regía los días en este suelo, que mecía nuestra jornada laboral. Finalmente, tras veinticinco días de navegación marítima por el océano Atlántico, llegamos a nuestro destino, Ciudad del Cabo (Sudáfrica). Para muchos fue la primera vez que pisamos el continente africano (uno menos en la lista). Una vez llegados a Ciudad del Cabo, estuvimos en puerto entre cinco y seis días preparando la «Leg 1». Esto quiere decir: reuniones, montar instrumentación, revisar equipos, arreglar desperfectos y más reuniones, pero también conocer a los nuevos integrantes de la siguiente etapa y despedir a quienes habían sido compañeros nuestros durante más de un mes.

Zarpar de Ciudad del Cabo fue duro. Solo quedábamos unos siete del total de setenta, entre estudiantes y científicos, que habíamos formado parte de la Maritime University. Ahora empezaba la expedición ACE en serio, la circunnavegación de la Antártida, durante la cual íbamos a tener mucho trabajo que hacer y muchos problemas que solucionar. Zarpamos el 21 de diciembre de 2017 rumbo al océano Antártico y a nuestro primer destino: isla Marión, perteneciente al archipiélago de las islas del Príncipe Eduardo en el océano Índico, una de las paradas previstas en las islas subantárticas y que pertenece a Sudáfrica. Pese a que la Antártida, el continente, no pertenece a ningún país, esto no sucede con las numerosas islas que hay a su alrededor. Hay quien piensa que Cabo Agulhas es el punto más al sur de África, ignorando que, a mil cuatrocientos kilómetros de distancia, a mitad de camino hacia la Antártida, se encuentra el territorio más austral de África: el archipiélago de las islas del Príncipe Eduardo (isla Marión e isla Príncipe Eduardo). Por lo tanto, estamos hablando de un lugar remoto en la transición entre el océano Antártico y el océano Índico, que contiene algunos de los ambientes más únicos del planeta. Las islas del Príncipe Eduardo son volcánicas, de reciente formación, y muestran un paisaje que entremezcla el azabache con los tonos marrones verdosos de la vegetación que ha colonizado la isla tras su formación. Y así las conocimos, tras una semana en ruta. Navegamos durante la noche y con las primeras luces del día pudimos apreciar las sinuosas formas de la costa de la isla Marión. Unos paisajes volcánicos plagados de acantilados y con grandes contrastes de color, nos daban los buenos días. La isla Marión es la de mayor tamaño del archipiélago. También conocida como «la isla que fue invadida por los gatos», ya que, pese a su aislada posición, no se ha librado de la intervención humana. Entre los hechos más famosos aquí acontecidos, resalta la problemática que surgió por la introducción accidental de roedores en la isla y el más que desastroso intento de controlarlos con gatos. Si nos detenemos en la fauna, aquí pueden encontrarse diferentes especies de pingüinos, focas y albatros, al ser una importante zona de cría para numerosas especies. Poco tardamos en percatarnos de la presencia de algunas colonias de pingüino Rey (*Aptenodytes patagonicus*) muy cerca de donde estábamos fondeados. Dichos pingüinos estaban acompañados de algunos lobos marinos antárticos (*Arctocephalus gazella*) y elefantes marinos (*Mirounga leonina*), además de pingüinos Macaroni (*Eudyptes chrysolophus*). Estos, junto con algún que otro lobo marino, se acercaron a curiosear a los alrededores del barco.

Al llegar a la isla Marión muchos investigadores desembarcaron vía helicóptero, mientras que otros nos quedamos navegando en los alrededores de la isla lanzando varias roseta-CTD y muestreando el fondo marino desde el Akademik. Los investigadores que desembarcaban estudiaban materias tan diversas como la composición química de los lagos, la biodiversidad de insectos o la distribución de especies invasoras. Incluso un químico de la Universidad de Florida se había embarcado en ACE con el objetivo de buscar nuevas biomoléculas en las plantas insulares y en los corales de aguas profundas de la Antártida, susceptibles de usarse con fines medicinales. A bordo del Akademik, durante esta etapa, viajaban también ornitólogos y especialistas en biología marina, que todos los días nos informan de la fauna que habían observado. Así, habían visto los primeros albatros viajeros (*Diomedea exulans*) y también varios grupos de rorcuales (*Balaenoptera physalus*). Es increíble poder apreciar el tamaño de los albatros viajeros, ya que es la especie de ave voladora de mayor envergadura y una de las más grandes del mundo. Además, también nos contaban que todos los días, alrededor de las 11:00 de la mañana, un grupo de orcas residentes de la isla solía acercarse a la orilla para alimentarse, pero pese a nuestros esfuerzos y a los numerosos expertos en cetáceos que llevábamos a bordo, no fuimos capaces de verlas. Navegar con expertos en fauna marina y terrestre del océano Austral es una auténtica maravilla. Por ejemplo, con nosotros viajaba un investigador de la Universidad de Ciudad del Cabo que llevaba visitando estas islas desde 1984. Sí, más de treinta años. Mientras navegábamos se pasaba horas y horas clasificando y cuantificando las aves que nos sobrevolaban. Pasamos allí alrededor de tres días, durante los cuales los grupos de investigación de sistemas terrestres insulares tuvieron sus momentos más ajetreados de trabajo. Los compañeros que se encargaban de evaluar y cuantificar el plástico marino nos informaron de que habían visto grandes cantidades durante los primeros días de navegación y una vez llegados al océano Antártico. Y es que, ni siquiera el océano más remoto del planeta, el océano Austral, puede escapar de las actividades humanas. Por otro lado, investigadores de la Universidad de Cambridge recolectaron muestras del suelo de la isla para conocer los procesos de sucesión ecológica y la composición microbiológica. Un dato curioso: tras recoger los testigos de sedimentos, se envasan al vacío de una forma similar a la empleada con el embutido recién cortado. Otros investigadores, del Western Australian Museum, estaban interesados en muestrear los organismos que habitaban en los entresijos del Kelp (*Durvillaea antarctica*), la enorme macroalga parda marina característica de zonas costeras. Algunos nos ofrecimos voluntarios para echarles una mano y pasamos alrededor de una hora navegando en la zódiac del Akademik, intentando «echarle el guante» a estos organismos. Tuvimos encima lluvia y viento, pero disfrutamos de pasar ese buen rato fuera del barco, mientras los albatros sobrevolaban nuestras cabezas. Finalmente, encontramos algunos moluscos y algas epifitas (que viven encima de otras) que pudimos seleccionar, etiquetar y preservar para su posterior análisis. Abandonamos la isla Marión y, a medida que nos adentrábamos en el océano Antártico, fuimos perdiendo la conexión a Internet, que era cada vez peor, y ni siquiera sabíamos si el servicio nos iba a permitir seguir comunicándonos mediante mensajería instantánea durante las próximas semanas. De hecho, nos avisaron de que lo más probable era que ni siquiera pudiéramos llamar a nuestra familia y amigos por Navidad. Pero así es la vida en mitad del océano, así es una expedición científica y el confort al que estamos acostumbrados en nuestra vida cotidiana, en tierra firme, es algo totalmente prescindible. Cuando llegamos a los 40°lu de latitud sur las olas ya hacían tambalear el buque, que no cesaba en su movimiento de un lado a otro. Los mareos volvieron y el trabajo apremiaba más que nunca. Nuestra próxima parada eran las islas Crozet, donde probablemente celebraríamos la entrada del año 2017.

Como os decía, durante esta campaña tuvimos muchos problemas, como en cualquier campaña oceanográfica. Sin embargo, nos pasó una historia que nunca he hecho pública y merece ser contada por primera vez en este libro: *Cómo unos calcetines salvaron una expedición científica*. Cuando abandonábamos la isla Marion, el sistema de muestreo en continuo del Akademik se estropeó. Varios investigadores bajamos corriendo a la zona de máquinas, allí donde estaba la conexión a través de la cual el agua era bombeada hacia nuestro laboratorio. Tras discutir en ruso un buen rato, comprendimos que no tenía solución y que necesitarían «unos días» para arreglarlo, lo cual en ese barco significaba que a lo mejor nunca se arreglaba. Así que lo que hicimos fue hacer uso del ingenio que se agudiza en situaciones de este tipo. Teníamos que hacer algo, o conseguíamos hacer fluir de nuevo agua hacia el laboratorio o muchos días de trabajo, o incluso semanas, se perderían. Antes de embarcar, en Ciudad del Cabo, algunos investigadores compramos una manguera de proporciones bíblicas «por si pasaba algo». Y, bueno, ese «algo» había pasado. Así que cogimos la manguera y el material de fontanería y jardinería que llevábamos para montar y desmontar instalaciones para muestrear en el laboratorio, y trazamos un plan. Resulta que la toma de agua estaba averiada en la canalización que conectaba con el laboratorio, pero eso no impedía quitar esa parte y hacer una «canalización» nueva. Así que quitamos la estructura original y acoplamos la manguera que habíamos comprado que medía la friolera de ciento veinticinco metros de largo. Fuimos desenrollando la manguera y atándola a las paredes de las tripas de la zona de máquinas del Akademik. Tras varias decenas de metros, la sacamos por una trampilla a uno de los pasillos principales del buque y la pegamos a una de las paredes usando cinta adhesiva para recorrer las últimas decenas de metros hasta el laboratorio. Lo conectamos todo, accionamos el mecanismo de bombeo y el agua empezó a fluir de nuevo por los instrumentos del laboratorio. Habíamos conseguido bombear agua, pero no por las cañerías usuales, sino por los propios pasillos del buque. El agua antártica, literalmente, fluía al lado de nuestros pies. Sin embargo, esto tenía un problema: mientras el agua circulaba por los pasillos en dirección al laboratorio se calentaba y cuando llegaba al laboratorio medimos que tenía una temperatura 2 °C superior a la real. Pero no solo era un problema la temperatura, sino también de luz. El alumbrado de los pasillos al incidir en la manguera excitaba los pigmentos fotosintéticos de las comunidades que allí habitaban, por lo que nuestras medidas de clorofila también se podían ver afectadas. Así que teníamos que aislar la manguera para conseguir que el agua no se calentase tanto. Por suerte, teníamos muchos metros de un material aislante que había traído un grupo de investigación, así que fuimos forrando la manguera metro a metro. Desgraciadamente, cuando no llevábamos ni la mitad del recorrido nos quedamos sin material aislante. Y aquí es cuando se nos ocurrió una idea que podría pasar a los «anales cutres de la oceanografía»: pedimos a todos los investigadores y personal técnico que donasen un par de calcetines, a ser posible de montaña, de esos que abrigan bastante. Conseguimos unos cien pares de calcetines que fuimos cortando y usamos para envolver la manguera haciendo uso de cinta adhesiva. Esta idea nos permitió recubrir unos cincuenta metros de la manguera, justo lo que necesitábamos hasta el laboratorio. Tardamos dos días en hacer todo este proceso, pero parecía que el sistema provisional funcionaba. Una serpiente de calcetines de colores adornaba los pasillos del Akademik y, como estábamos en Navidad, también cumplía la función de decoración navideña. Finalmente, el personal del buque consiguió arreglar la canalización original y solo tuvimos que hacer uso de la serpiente un par de días que no pudimos casi trabajar por el mal tiempo. Eso sí, la anaconda de los calcetines siguió en los pasillos del Akademik durante los meses siguientes.

Tras dos días de navegación llegamos a las islas Crozet, un conjunto de islas que son territorio francés y dónde hay varias bases de investigación, así como estaciones meteorológicas. En concreto, estuvimos la mayor parte del tiempo trabajando en la isla de la Posesión, realizando muestreos de agua, aire, sedimento marino, testigos en lagos, etc. Un sinfín de técnicas que sirvieron para comprender mejor los procesos ecológicos, geológicos y climáticos, entre otros, que se dan en las islas subantárticas y el océano Austral. Los que trabajamos con gases y microorganismos estábamos acostumbrados a que nuestro trabajo fuese, *a priori*, poco llamativo. En ocasiones, «envidias» a colegas que trabajan con otras temáticas tan intuitivas y fáciles de apreciar como el estudio de los plásticos o los cetáceos, pero ya estábamos acostumbrados. Así que, como siempre, lo más impresionante fue poder avistar la fauna del lugar. Algunos, entre los que me incluyo, tuvimos la suerte de desembarcar y hacer varias caminatas por la isla. En la playa Des Américains pudimos observar una gran colonia de pingüino Rey (*Aptenodytes patagonicus*) que rondaba los dos mil individuos. No os podéis imaginar lo que son varios miles de pingüinos juntos, sobre todo si tienen el tamaño de los pingüinos Rey. La mayoría estaban liberándose de las plumas viejas y estas volaban por toda la isla como semillas de dientes de león. Observar a tantos juntos recordaba al típico juego de «Buscando a Wally». Podría haberse escondido aquí vestido de amarillo, negro y blanco, y no habría sido posible encontrarlo. El ambiente era increíble. Estos pingüinos son más grandes que los pingüinos Barbijo (*Pygoscelis antarcticus*), Papua (*Pygoscelis papua*) o Adelia (*Pygoscelis adeliae*); que vimos en 2015 en el Proyecto PEGASO. Se mueven con mucha más elegancia y son tremendamente curiosos. Manteniendo siempre la distancia con ellos, llegaba un momento en el que se te acercaban poco a poco haciendo reverencias como queriendo comunicarse contigo. A veces, tras imitarlos una y otra vez éramos capaces de mantener verdaderas conversaciones con ellos basadas en asentir con la cabeza. También habitan en estas islas grandes poblaciones de petreles antárticos (*Thalassoica antarctica*), albatros viajeros (*Diomedea exulans*) y skúas (*Stercorarius maccormicki*). Tras varias horas de caminata, llegamos a una de las playas de la isla de la Posesión donde escuchamos una enorme algarabía de gritos emitidos por las distintas aves que estaban concentradas en un lugar concreto. Al acercarnos, avistamos a un grupo de petreles gigantes (*Macronectes giganteus*) devorando a un pingüino rey, al cual se habían encargado de dar muerte previamente. Lo cual supimos porque, aunque cuando nosotros llegamos ya estaban descuartizándolo, mientras les observábamos tuvieron tiempo de cazar un par más. Parece que todo el mundo se come a los pingüinos, por si no tuvieran bastante con las focas leopardo o las orcas, los petreles también se alimentan de ellos. En dicha zona observamos una gran cantidad de restos de pingüinos devorados, por lo que aquella debía de ser una zona en la que les daban caza, suponemos que debido a que está bastante alejada de la orilla y no deben tener tiempo de escapar. Mientras, los petreles nos observaban con cautela en la distancia luciendo sus picos relucientes llenos de sangre mientras se peleaban por el mejor bocado. Recordaban a las típicas imágenes de aves carroñeras, como los buitres que aparecen en los documentales. Abandonamos esa zona y nos dirigimos de vuelta a la playa para coger la zódiac de regreso al Akademik. En nuestro camino, pudimos observar muchísimos grupos de elefantes marinos (*Mirounga leonina*), desde ejemplares recién nacidos a los enormes adultos, pasando por los juveniles. Es difícil apreciar en las fotos o vídeos el tamaño real de estos animales. No solo sorprende su longitud, sino también su volumen corporal. Son auténticas moles del tamaño de un coche, perfectamente adaptadas a su ambiente. Según los expertos, aún se sabe muy poco de los hábitos alimenticios y la dieta de los individuos de esta especie. Sin embargo, sí se conoce que bajan a grandes profundidades para alimentarse de moluscos y crustáceos. Cuando están fuera del agua suelen estar durmiendo o peleándose entre ellos. Al luchar, inflan su característica «trompa» e intentan clavar los dientes en el cuerpo, y principalmente en el cuello, del adversario. Tuvimos la suerte de presenciar algunas de estas peleas y daba miedo verlas incluso a decenas de metros de distancia. La isla de la Posesión es un lugar que, a quienes tuvimos la oportunidad de visitarla, nunca olvidaremos. Volvimos al Akademik y pusimos rumbo este, dirección a las islas Kerguelen, también francesas.

La llegada a las islas Kerguelen era una de las partes más esperadas de la expedición. Estas eran las últimas islas que teníamos que visitar antes de poner rumbo a Australia. A su vez, era el archipiélago más grande que íbamos a visitar en esta etapa, por lo que los científicos que tenían que trabajar en tierra firme necesitaban pasar allí la mayor cantidad de tiempo posible. Lo cual significaba descanso y aburrimiento para los investigadores marinos, que nos teníamos que quedar a bordo del Akademik esperando varios días a que volvieran de trabajar en tierra firme. En total, estuvimos tres días fondeados delante de las islas Kerguelen, rodeados de enormes ejemplares de kelp. Es un archipiélago muy interesante puesto que también pertenece a Francia y en dichas islas se introdujeron en 1954 una decena de renos de la Laponia sueca con fines cinegéticos, es decir, para la caza. Sin embargo, puesto que allí no había depredadores naturales y tampoco se cazaba tanto, la población aumentó hasta alcanzar varios miles de individuos en la década de 1970. En esta isla también habitan o han habitado otras especies introducidas como muflones, ovejas, conejos, cerdos, gatos y ratas. Es por ello, que las islas Kerguelen son un lugar ideal para el estudio de la introducción de especies exóticas invasoras por acción del ser humano. Durante esos días, numerosas especies de aves nos visitaron y fueron posiblemente los momentos más tranquilos de toda la expedición, no había olas y muchos pudimos aprovechar para leer los pocos libros que aún nos quedaban pendientes. También volvimos a echar una mano a nuestros colegas muestreando kelp desde la zódiac. Una mañana, mientras tomábamos café en cubierta, un compañero pegó un grito al que acudimos corriendo los tres o cuatro que estábamos charlando. Llegamos justo a tiempo para observar como un grupo de lomos negros y blancos se alejaban. Orcas. Por fin, tras casi dos meses navegando por el Atlántico, el Índico y el Antártico, las veíamos. Estuvimos esperando al día siguiente en el mismo sitio y a la misma hora, pero no volvieron. Tocaba zarpar de nuevo y no había tiempo para buscar más orcas.

El viaje hasta Hobart (Tasmania, Australia) duró dos semanas. Durante los primeros días avistamos un numeroso grupo de cetáceos que no pudimos identificar hasta que estuvieron lo suficientemente cerca. Era un grupo de treinta ballenas piloto

(*Globicephala melas*) que se dejó fotografiar e incluso llegaron a pasar por debajo del Akademik para seguir su ruta. Mientras leéis este capítulo, tal vez muchos os estéis preguntando una cosa: si íbamos cruzando meridianos, también debíamos ir cruzando husos horarios, ¿cómo se cambia la hora durante una campaña oceanográfica? Por lo general, cuando se trabaja en el mar existen dos horas: la hora local y la hora UTC (Coordinated Universal Time). Así, mientras que la hora local varía, la hora UTC siempre es la misma independientemente del lugar del mundo en el que estés. Sin embargo, la hora local es la que rige nuestro día a día y esa sí que hay que ir cambiándola conforme se cruzan husos horarios. Para ello, cada buque tiene su estrategia. Por ejemplo, en algunas ocasiones el capitán del buque decide que la hora local es la hora del lugar de partida y que al llegar a puerto se adquiere la hora local del lugar. Es algo parecido a cuando viajas en avión y llegas a un sitio donde, de golpe, son diez horas menos o más. Sufres *jet-lag* los primeros días hasta que te acostumbres y listo. En el Akademik, en cambio, lo que se decidió fue una medida que podría considerarse en cierto modo «tortura». Durante toda la «Leg 1» mantuvimos como hora local la de Ciudad del Cabo y Hobart estaba a nueve horas de diferencia. Así que, en lugar de cambiar la hora al llegar a Hobart o haberla ido cambiando poco a poco durante la campaña, conforme íbamos cruzando los distintos meridianos, el capitán decidió que lo «mejor» era adelantar los relojes una hora cada día durante los últimos nueve días. ¿Habéis tenido sensación de cansancio o malestar cuando en países como España se cambia la hora por el horario de invierno o de verano? Pues imaginad nueve días seguidos de cambios de hora. Los últimos días nadie podía dormir por la noche, trabajábamos como *zombies* y llegamos a Hobart con peor cuerpo que si hubieran cambiado la hora de golpe al llegar. Pero llegamos, que era lo importante. En Tasmania tuvimos la oportunidad de visitar la increíble naturaleza de sus alrededores, como sus bosques llenos de Dicksonia (*Balantium antarcticum*), un helecho gigante que recordaba a las películas de *Parque Jurásico*; o el último lugar donde habitó el tigre de Tasmania

(*Thylacinus cynocephalus*). Después de varios días en tierra, llegó el momento de volver a casa tras casi tres meses en el océano. Nos despedimos de nuestros compañeros que continuaron en la expedición ACE durante las dos últimas etapas y recogimos nuestras cosas. Nuestro grupo de investigación iba a dar la vuelta al mundo alrededor de la Antártida e íbamos a tardar bastante, aunque como contaba Julio Verne en *La vuelta al mundo en 80 días*: «La Tierra es más pequeña, puesto que puede ser recorrida diez veces más rápido que hace cien años». Sin embargo, yo espero que la Tierra no se haga más «pequeña» y que muchos de sus rincones sigan siendo lugares extraños, misteriosos y únicos; esperando a ser descubiertos por la ciencia.

LOS SECRETOS DEL LAGARTO AMARILLO

«Los tahitianos se manejan en el agua como si fuesen anfibios».
Charles Darwin, Tahití, 18 de noviembre de 1835

El océano Pacífico es enorme. Esta frase, pese a reseñar una obviedad, es algo que nunca me cansaré de decir. En numerosas ocasiones, les enseño a nuestros a estudiantes de primaria o secundaria una imagen del océano Pacífico visto desde el espacio. Prácticamente no se puede apreciar ningún punto de superficie terrestre, así la Tierra parece más que nunca «una canica azul», tal y como empezó a conocerse en la década de los setenta gracias a la exploración espacial. Una inmensa bola redonda azul salpicada con nubes flotando aparentemente inerte en el negro espacio abierto. Mientras miran la imagen, suelo preguntar a los alumnos si saben lo que están viendo. Las respuestas suelen ser de lo más variopintas: «Venus», «Naboo» (planeta de Star Wars), «un planeta habitable por ser descubierto», etc. Sorprende que casi nadie suela acertar, más aún si tenemos en cuenta que esta generación tiene a su alcance una gran cantidad de herramientas digitales para explorar su propio planeta. Aunque tampoco creo que haga falta un gran conocimiento informático para clicar sobre la «bola» que es la Tierra en Google Earth y rotar hasta ver la parte del planeta que está detrás de Europa, nuestras antípodas. Cuando les digo que se equivocan y que lo que están viendo es el océano Pacífico muchos todavía no se lo creen, llegando incluso a insinuar que es una imagen manipulada. Y es que es normal que el océano Pacífico nos llame la atención, es tan grande que podríamos poner todos los continentes de la Tierra dentro de él y, aun así, sobraría espacio. Concretamente, el pacífico ocupa aproximadamente un tercio de toda la superficie terrestre o, lo que es lo mismo, unos 180.000.000 km^2. Para que os hagáis una idea, la superficie de la Península Ibérica es de unos 580.000 km^2, por lo tanto, en el océano Pacífico cabrían unas trescientas diez «penínsulas Ibéricas». Y es aquí adónde nos dirigíamos en abril de 2018.

Hasta ahora os he contado cómo se trabaja en ciencia desde buques de investigación o desde laboratorios en tierra firme. Sin embargo, solo hemos comentado de pasada qué son y cómo se trabaja en las estaciones de investigación utilizando los ejemplos de las bases antárticas. No os sorprenderéis si os digo que hay muchas bases de investigación en el mundo y no solo están en las regiones polares. Así, el objetivo de nuestro grupo de investigación era continuar investigando cómo se producen algunos de los procesos de formación de nubes en regiones remotas del planeta. ¿Si tuvierais que ir a un lugar remoto de la Tierra adónde iríais? Pues teniendo en cuenta lo que acabo de explicar acerca del tamaño del océano Pacífico, más de uno estaréis pensando que sería un lugar adecuado; y estáis en lo cierto. Pero, claro, el Pacífico es enorme y queríamos ir a un lugar lo más alejado posible. Hay que pensar que el Pacífico tiene una forma «circular» (pido perdón a los geógrafos por esta burda aproximación), así que por definición un punto lo más alejado de los grandes continentes que lo rodean (Asia, América, Antártida y Oceanía) sería lo ideal. Y uno de estos puntos es la Polinesia francesa, un conjunto de archipiélagos en el océano Pacífico sur que pertenecen a los territorios franceses de ultramar (igual que las islas Crozet y las islas Kerguelen). Si hacéis el ejercicio de buscar en un mapa en vuestro ordenador dónde se encuentran dichos archipiélagos y poco a poco vais alejando la imagen podréis apreciar cómo en todas direcciones hay miles de kilómetros hasta el continente más cercano. Eso sí, hay muchas islas que no están tan lejos, pero lo que a nosotros nos interesaba evitar son los contaminantes procedentes de las actividades humanas que se encuentran en el aire y en el agua. Desgraciadamente, como veremos más adelante, esto es incluso difícil de evitar en un lugar tan remoto; allí donde haya seres humanos, habrá un mayor o menor impacto ambiental.

El núcleo de nuestro proyecto de investigación consistía en investigar la producción, degradación y emisión de gases traza desde los ecosistemas de coral de Mo'orea; de una manera semejante a cómo lo habíamos hecho en el océano Atlántico y Antártico. Ahora bien, ¿qué importancia tienen los corales?,

¿por qué la ciencia les presta tanta atención? Estas pertinentes preguntas deben responderse a partir de una serie de datos muy sencillos. Solo el 0,1% del área mundial de los océanos está ocupado por corales. Sin embargo, se estima que allí se encuentran presentes el 25% de todas las especies marinas que existen. Simple y llanamente podríamos decir que los arrecifes de coral son zonas donde la vida marina «explota» en todas sus formas y colores, en muchas ocasiones en pequeñas y remotas islas, como las de la Polinesia francesa. Este hecho no ha pasado desapercibido para los científicos a lo largo de la historia. Sirva como ejemplo el propio Charles Darwin que llegó a Tahití en 1836 a bordo del Beagle y quedó impresionado por tal cantidad de vida, tras navegar por un océano abierto que muchas veces puede parecer un desierto. Precisamente a la aparente contradicción entre esta explosión de vida rodeada de «desierto» se la ha conocido tradicionalmente como *Paradoja de Darwin*. Cuando observamos un coral, uno podría pensar que se encuentra ante una simple «roca» que tiene colores, en muchas ocasiones, muy vivos. Es decir, que los corales no son seres vivos. Sin embargo, esto se debe a que lo que nosotros vemos normalmente es la estructura calcárea formada por la acción de una gran cantidad de organismos llamados pólipos (del griego «muchos pies», aunque en realidad son tentáculos con los que atrapan plancton marino que les sirve de alimento), que forman su exoesqueleto para protegerse. Los pólipos son animales invertebrados genéticamente idénticos que pertenecen al filo de los Cnidarios (al igual que las medusas), por lo tanto, aunque también existen corales individuales formados por un solo pólipo, el coral es un animal colonial formado por pólipos. Y aquí no acaba la cosa. En el tejido de los pólipos viven otros organismos mucho más interesantes: las zooxantelas, que son algas unicelulares fotosintéticas gracias a las cuales los pólipos adquieren la mayor parte de sus nutrientes. Es decir, la relación interespecífica entre las zooxantelas y los pólipos de los corales es una simbiosis. Las zooxantelas permiten a los corales obtener energía a partir del sol, y por tanto dominar las aguas cristalinas y someras de ambientes tropicales que generalmente son oligotróficos (pobres en nutrientes), y los corales permiten a las zooxantelas vivir protegidas dentro de sus pólipos. Son precisamente las zooxantelas las que suelen dar el color a los corales. Sin embargo, cuando se producen perturbaciones en el medio y cambian las condiciones ambientales, los corales pueden sufrir un proceso muy estudiado durante las últimas décadas: el *bleaching* o blanqueamiento. Este proceso es debido principalmente al impacto que tienen las olas de calor marinas o los contaminantes procedentes de actividades humanas sobre las zooxantelas que, al dejar de poder realizar la fotosíntesis con normalidad ante una situación de estrés, se ven expulsadas de los pólipos. Así, el coral pasa a tener un color blanquecino o directamente blanco y, aunque los pólipos siguen alimentándose del plancton que atrapan, el coral se encuentra en una situación débil. Si esta situación se mantiene en el tiempo, este proceso se torna irreversible y el coral no es capaz de volver a incorporar las zooxantelas, por lo que finalmente muere ante la falta de alimento y solo queda su estructura, inicialmente blanca como la leche y posteriormente recubierta de otros organismos que la irán colonizando hasta su desaparición. A escala global, según los últimos informes del IPCC, un aumento de la temperatura media global de 1,5°C puede acabar con alrededor del 70% de los corales de aguas cálidas; pero, si este aumento es de 2°C casi el 100% de los corales de aguas cálidas podrían desaparecer. Por lo tanto, limitar el aumento de temperatura a 1,5°C puede salvar aproximadamente hasta el 30% de los arrecifes de coral de aguas cálidas en todo el mundo.

De entre las islas de la Polinesia Francesa, nuestro grupo de investigación se decidió por Mo'orea, la «hermana pequeña» de Tahití. Su nombre significa «lagarto amarillo» (*Mo'o* significa lagarto y *Re'a*, amarillo) y proviene de una leyenda que tiene diversas versiones bastante parecidas. La que a mí me contaron es que una pareja que habitaba en la isla de Maiao esperaba un bebé, pero la mujer dio a luz un huevo del que salió un lagarto amarillo, al que llamaron Mo'orea. Y Mo'orea siguió creciendo y creciendo hasta que se hizo demasiado grande y lo abandonaron en el mar en una canoa cerca de Tahití, hasta que murió ahogado por las corrientes. Su cuerpo llegó a la isla de Mo'orea actual, que antes se llamaba Aimeho. Allí, unos pescadores lo encontraron y entre gritos y algarabía decidieron renombrar a la isla como Mo'orea. Allí se encuentra la base de investigación estadounidense Gump Station, que pertenece a la Universidad de California en Berkeley, en la que trece investigadores de instituciones de distintas nacionalidades (España, Estados Unidos de América, Austria y Australia) desarrollaríamos el proyecto BIOGAPS («Biogenic trace gases and their cycling processes in the surface sea»; en castellano: «gases traza biogénicos y sus procesos en el mar superficial»), liderado por nuestro grupo de investigación. Como podréis suponer, esta vez no debíamos enviar todo nuestro material científico en camiones desde Barcelona, pero iba a ser incluso más difícil. Teníamos que preparar todo el material científico necesario para una expedición científica de un mes de duración que sería enviado vía avión hasta Mo'orea. Cuando uno quiere enviar tal cantidad de material por aire, se enfrenta a un gran reto: las compañías aéreas te cobran, sobre todo, por el volumen de las cajas que envías, no tanto por su peso. Es decir, para ahorrar costes uno tiene que convertirse en campeón nacional de «tetris» montando cajas que no superen 1,60 metros de altura. Para que os hagáis una idea, en el proyecto PEGASO enviamos unas cien cajas de Barcelona a Cartagena, para que desde allí llegasen a la Antártida. Para BIOGAPS, teniendo en cuenta que éramos un tercio de los investigadores en comparación con PEGASO, enviamos unas diez. Y «puedo prometer y prometo» que en esas cajas que enviábamos a Mo'orea por aire no cabía ni siquiera un bloc de notas más. Eso sí, lo bueno de enviar las cosas de esta manera es que llegaban directamente a su destino, a Gump Station, varios días antes de que llegásemos nosotros y no nos teníamos que preocupar por su transporte.

Una vez aterrizamos en Tahití, tras más de veinticuatro horas de viaje en avión, nos recibieron varios tahitianos con canciones tradicionales. Parecía que más que a trabajar íbamos de luna de miel. Una vez dejamos el aeropuerto llegó el primer *shock*: el calor y la humedad. La temperatura estaba por encima de los 30°C, lo cual, siendo muchos de nosotros de la cuenca mediterránea, *a priori* no nos debería preocupar mucho. Sin embargo, el problema era la humedad. El calor era asfixiante y prácticamente no podíamos dejar de sudar. Aunque estuvieras quieto, sentado a la sombra, notabas cómo el sudor emanaba de tu cuerpo como si acabaras de salir de una sauna. Si bien es cierto que llega un punto al que uno se acostumbra, durante el mes que allí estuvimos trabajando el sudor no cesaba, simplemente lo tolerabas. Si hay otra cosa por la que se caracteriza el océano Pacífico sur es porque la radiación incidente es mucho más intensa que en otros lugares del planeta, como Europa. Por lo tanto, es mucho más fácil quemarse, incluso para los que no solemos quemarnos nunca. Así que, aparte del calor y la humedad sofocante, nuestro mejor aliado durante nuestra estancia en Mo'orea iba a ser la crema solar factor 50. ¿Habéis probado a echaros crema factor 50, con lo densa que es, en vuestra piel totalmente sudada? Efectivamente, es una guarrería; pero una guarrería vital para nuestra salud. Al calor y la humedad había que sumarle la ingente cantidad de moscas, mosquitos y otros insectos que nos acompañaban incesantemente. La llegada a Mo'orea fue bastante impresionante, ya que había que coger un ferry con el que recorrer diecisiete kilómetros hasta llegar a nuestra ansiada isla. Conforme avanzábamos en nuestro trayecto, se podían apreciar las enormes montañas escarpadas de roca volcánica cubiertas por una frondosa vegetación tropical y, una vez estuvimos más cerca, los majestuosos arrecifes de coral llenos de vida donde tendríamos que trabajar.

La isla de Mo'orea tiene una forma curiosa, si alguien viese una imagen desde el espacio, es algo parecido a un «ángel» con sus dos alas, aunque la realidad es más terrenal, así que, dejémoslo en que tiene forma de mariposa. El Pacífico alberga numerosas islas, como Mo'orea, que se encuentran en el denominado cinturón de fuego del océano Pacífico y son, en su mayoría, volcánicas. En el caso de Mo'orea, tenéis que imaginar un volcán que surgió del fondo marino hace entre 1,5 a 2,5 millones de años, a miles de kilómetros de profundidad, y alcanzó la superficie del océano para sobresalir formando una isla. Así que Mo'orea es, en resumidas cuentas, un antiguo volcán que ya no está activo y las antiguas paredes de este ahora son una cadena montañosa que alcanza su mayor altura en el monte Tohivea (a 1207 metros sobre el nivel del mar). Cuando uno mira Mo'orea desde lejos y ve sus altas montañas, tiene la sensación de que ocupan el centro de la isla, como puede ocurrir con el Teide, en la isla de Tenerife. Sin embargo, el centro de la isla es un enorme cráter desde el cual se pueden apreciar todos estos majestuosos picos a su alrededor. Tiene dos bahías: Bahía de Cook y Bahía de Ōpūnohu. Los nombres ya te dan una pista de la relevancia de las actividades coloniales en esta isla. Toda su geografía está cubierta de vegetación tropical hasta prácticamente todas las cimas de sus montes. Nada más llegar no pudimos evitar pensar que era lo más parecido a las islas «Sorna» o «Nublar» de Parque Jurásico que habíamos visto nunca. Actualmente viven unas dieciséis mil personas de manera permanente en la isla, cuatro mil de las cuales se encuentran en el pueblo Pao Pao-Maharepa, situado en la Bahía Cook. Por su parte, la estación de investigación Gump Station está ubicada al inicio de la Bahía de Cook, cerca del pueblo de Piha'ena y consta de varios laboratorios que literalmente llegan hasta el agua. Agua que, por supuesto, se usa para llevar a cabo numerosos experimentos científicos; la mayoría enfocados al estudio del impacto del cambio climático en los corales marinos. Nada más llegar a los laboratorios iniciamos el montaje de todos nuestros aparatos que habían llegado en perfectas condiciones procedentes de Barcelona. Al menos en el laboratorio había aire acondicionado y se podía trabajar sin sufrir los «sudores polinesios».

Los participantes del proyecto de investigación nos alojábamos en las instalaciones de la propia Gump Station, pero no tan cerca del mar. En las inmediaciones de la estación, tras subir unos cien metros por la ladera del monte, se encuentran una serie de cabañas de madera desde las cuales se ve la desembocadura de la Bahía Cook y los arrecifes de coral que limitan la isla con el océano abierto. En la subida hasta nuestras casas, por una estrecha carretera de cemento para facilitar el acceso, uno ya podía apreciar aspectos curiosos de la vida en la isla. Por un lado, había una ingente cantidad de árboles de mango y papaya, así como plataneros, muchos de los cuales ya tenían frutos maduros y nos informaron de que podíamos comer todos los que quisiéramos. No nos iban a faltar vitaminas para trabajar durante un mes en la isla. Por otro lado, a veces escuchábamos ruidos en la densa vegetación que había a ambos lados. Nos habían informado de que no había problemas con perros salvajes y que la mayoría de fauna eran aves de varias especies bastante pequeñas en tamaño. Sin embargo, los ruidos que escuchábamos eran de algo más grande y se movían muy rápido. Al poco de llegar, me quedé observando desde el balcón de nuestra casa y descubrí que eran pollos. Toda nuestra zona, y parte de la isla, estaba llena de pollos semisalvajes que se alimentaban de los restos de comida de los habitantes de la isla, así como de vegetación. Al igual que los mangos, los pollos también podían cazarse para comer, siempre y cuando uno estuviera seguro de que no tenían dueño. Por si hay alguna duda, diré que no cazamos ninguno. En general, una cosa que llama mucho la atención es que la fauna es muy escasa. Los procesos de colonización de seres vivos entre islas han sido uno de los fenómenos más estudiados por los ecólogos durante los pasados siglos, desde Darwin hasta E.O. Wilson, un entomólogo y biólogo estadounidense conocido por su trabajo en evolución y sociobiología. Intentaré explicarlo de manera breve y simple, aunque es algo muy complejo. Lo que hemos aprendido de todas estas investigaciones es que cuando se crea una isla por acción volcánica los organismos que van llegando, al principio, suelen ser los menos «complejos» y más adaptables a las situaciones extremas. Posteriormente, van llegando otros que conformarán un ecosistema en el cual se irán introduciendo lentamente organismos más complejos, como mamíferos, ya que necesitan otros seres de los que alimentarse y no pueden vivir de la fotosíntesis. Los estudios de la biogeografía insular de las islas en el Pacífico sur han descubierto que el archipiélago de Tahití fue una de las zonas a las que más tarde llegó la colonización de organismos, debido principalmente a su lejanía con respecto a islas más grandes como Nueva Zelanda o Australia, o al continente americano. Esto origina un hecho muy curioso: estamos en una isla con una vegetación propia de la selva tropical; pero no hay animales como monos o jaguares, como pudiera creerse. En tierra firme, aparte de los pollos y perros, solo hay muchos insectos, salamanquesas y algunas especies de lagartijas pequeñas, como *Emoia cyanura* que tiene una preciosa cola azulada. Aunque esas son algunas de las especies que se pueden encontrar en espacios abiertos, no tardamos en darnos cuenta de que había otras que preferían la compañía humana. La primera noche, mientras intentaba dormir, escuchaba pequeños correteos por la habitación, pero mucho más suaves que los de un roedor. Hacía tanto calor que tuve que salir un rato al salón, donde seguí escuchando de vez en cuando el mismo ruido. Volví a mi habitación a coger mi linterna y me puse a investigar nuestra cabaña, cuyo techo tenía unos cinco metros de altura. Al poco me di cuenta de que hacia donde enfocaba el haz de luz unos seres marrones salían corriendo, escondiéndose donde podían, también en los vasos y tazas que habíamos lavado y se estaban secando en la pila. Eran salamanquesas (más conocidas como «geckos») de la especie *Gehyra oceanica* que se encuentran presentes en numerosas islas del Pacífico, no solo en la polinesia, sino también en la Melanesia y Micronesia. Así que, estas salamanquesas, que tienen un tamaño mayor al de las que estamos acostumbrados en la región mediterránea, se contaban por decenas en los techos y paredes de nuestra casa. Allí permanecían escondidas durante el día, y al caer la noche salían a alimentarse de los insectos que inevitablemente entraban en nuestra cabaña, ya que debido al calor teníamos que mantener algunas de las ventanas abiertas. Sin embargo, pronto constatamos que no se comían todos los insectos. Algunas moscas pusieron huevos en nuestro cubo de basura y en un espacio de dos días el suelo de nuestra cocina estaba infectado de larvas de mosca. Corriendo, sacamos las bolsas de basura a la calle para llevarlas al contenedor más próximo. Entramos a casa a lavarnos las manos y cuando salimos dispuestos a acabar la desagradable tarea, vimos como las bolsas estaban rotas y la basura esparcida por todos lados. Los pollos salvajes habían roto las bolsas y estaban dándose un festín con todas las larvas de mosca. Pollos de los que, a fin de cuentas, nosotros nos tendríamos que alimentar. Biogeoquímica pura y dura. Otro de los interesantes encuentros con la fauna del lugar lo tuve en una zona alejada de nuestra estación de investigación. Salí a correr una tarde y, tras pasar el pueblo de Pao Pao, seguí adentrándome en la selva algunos kilómetros. Cuando ya no podía correr más, me paré al borde de un pequeño río que desembocaba en la Bahía de Cook. El agua estaba cristalina y no había absolutamente nadie. Al introducir los pies en el agua algo me rozó y, a simple vista, pensé que era una rama. Para mi sorpresa, se trataba de tres o cuatro anguilas de agua dulce (*Anguilla sp.*) que acudían adónde yo me encontraba. Salí corriendo de un salto pues en ese momento no recordaba si tenían dientes o no. Posteriormente me informaron de que, en algunas islas de la Polinesia Francesa, como Huahine, a estas anguilas se las consideran sagradas y los habitantes las cuidan y alimentan. Seguramente es lo que también sucede con las que yo me encontré en Mo'orea y vinieron hacia mí buscando alimento.

Como sucede con las aguas cristalinas de las Islas Baleares y la relación que tienen con la oligotrofia del medio, en Mo'orea las aguas también tienen esos colores, incluso en más tonalidades distintas. De hecho, suele decirse que algunas zonas del océano tienen todas las tonalidades del color azul, y algo similar sucede en Mo'orea también con el verde, uno puede encontrarse aquí con todos sus tonos con solo sacar la cabeza del agua y admirar, a la vez, las aguas y la vegetación de la isla. Bucear en esas aguas, bajo mi punto de vista, es tan asombroso que resulta ridículo. Es, literalmente, sumergirse en un acuario que no tiene fin. Pequeños peces de colores nadan por todos lados, numerosas rayas (sobre todo, de la especie *Himantura fai*) que parecen no tenerte miedo y un sinfín de corales y esponjas. Por supuesto, también hay muchas anémonas donde habitan distintas especies de los célebres peces payaso (englobadas en la subfamilia *Amphiprioninae*). Más adelante nos adentraremos en los fondos y especies de las aguas de Mo'orea con más detalle. Así que sirva esto como un «aperitivo» y, hablando de aperitivos, la gastronomía de Mo'orea fue una de las cosas que más me llamó la atención. Básicamente, consiste en fruta (mucha de la cual se recoge de los árboles de los alrededores) y pescado o, mejor dicho, mucha fruta y mucho pescado, cocinados de todas las maneras que pueda uno imaginarse. Los primeros días tras nuestra llegada, otro grupo de investigación que había estado trabajando en este paraje se marchaba de la isla, y los encargados de la Gump Station en colaboración con una asociación de promoción de la cultura local, organizaron una cena tradicional de despedida elaborada en hornos tradicionales que consisten, a grandes rasgos, en enormes agujeros en el suelo en los que la comida se cocina lentamente. Así, probamos un nutrido compendio de diferentes vegetales como plátano o mandioca, y carnes de varios pescados; principalmente llampugas o, como ellos lo llaman, *mahi mahi* (*Coryphaena hippurus*). También comimos pollo, seguramente alguno no muy afortunado de los que pululaban por nuestras cabañas, y probamos una especie de alga comestible de la zona con lima que, para nuestra sorpresa, estaba bastante buena.

Los primeros días de la expedición los dedicamos a comprobar que todo el material e instrumentación científica funcionaba correctamente. Los muestreos en las aguas de Mo'orea los realizaríamos a bordo de una lancha de unos ocho metros de eslora. Por suerte, nosotros no éramos los encargados de manejar la embarcación, sino que lo haría un empleado nativo, llamado Tonny, con el que viviríamos grandes momentos. No solamente queríamos recoger agua en determinados puntos de la isla y sus arrecifes, sino que también queríamos conocer las propiedades del agua sobre la que navegábamos. Para ello, instalamos una manguera acoplada a una bomba que succionaría el agua conforme el barco se desplazara. En el otro extremo de la manguera, a bordo de la lancha, se encontraba una serie de sensores que registraban los datos en un ordenador portátil que también llevábamos en la lancha. Es decir, podíamos conocer en tiempo real cuáles eran algunas de las propiedades del agua que teníamos bajo nosotros. Eso sí, con el coste de tener cables y mangueras por el ya de por sí pequeño espacio de nuestra lancha de muestreo.

Los primeros días, la rutina de muestreo consistió en salir con el barco con diversos utensilios como bidones, frascos o botellas, para recolectar agua que posteriormente íbamos a analizar en el laboratorio. Para mí, los primeros días fueron bastante infernales ya que, aparte del calor y los mosquitos fui el primero en pillar una gastroenteritis que me tuvo en cama durante un día entero sufriendo unos dolores insoportables. Incluso llegué a ir a muestrear, en un estúpido alarde de resistencia, en mis precarias condiciones. Así, cuando nos encontrábamos en el punto más alejado posible de la estación de investigación, mi estómago empezó a dolerme como pocas veces recuerdo; sumado al calor insoportable y al sol radiando sobre mi cabeza únicamente cubierta con un sombrero. El resto del muestro me lo pasé hecho una bola, encogido, en la proa de nuestra lancha, donde soplaba algo de aire. Al llegar a tierra firme pasé bastante tiempo en el baño y el resto del día tumbado sobre la cama. Superado lo peor, por la tarde bajé un rato a ayudar en la estación de investigación y tuve la oportunidad de hablar con algunos nativos y me explicaron que, pese a que parecía que había muchos corales, estaban disminuyendo en las zonas cercanas a la Bahía de Cook. Esto se debe a que una industria muy potente en la isla, seguramente la única aparte del turismo, es la de los zumos de frutas. Como comentaba, el clima es ideal para cultivar frutas del estilo piña, mango, plátano, etc. Así que existen varias zonas donde hay grandes plantaciones de estas frutas que luego se usan fundamentalmente para hacer zumos que se venden a un buen precio. El problema es que los fertilizantes que se aportan a estos cultivos cuando llueve, y en Mo'orea llueve bastante, pasan a los pequeños arroyos que desembocan en la Bahía de Cook, la cual recorren entera hasta llegar a la zona de arrecifes de coral. Como consecuencia, no solo producen el blanqueamiento de los corales, sino que también facilitan el crecimiento de otras especies competidoras como el alga *Turbinaria ornata*; de la cual habíamos observado grandes aglomeraciones flotantes durante nuestros muestreos. Como veis, no solo el Mar Menor tiene problemas con algunas prácticas agrícolas.

Al poco de superar mi enfermedad, nos notificaron una oportunidad extraordinaria: íbamos a poder trabajar en el remoto atolón de Teti'aroa, una isla coralina oceánica situada a más de cuarenta kilómetro al norte de Tahití. ¿Qué significa eso de isla coralina? Pues algo fascinante que aprendimos justo antes de llegar allí. Imaginad una isla de origen volcánico a modo de volcán emergiendo de las aguas, aunque esto no siempre sea así. Una vez que el volcán se extingue, sus paredes tienden a deteriorarse por fenómenos físicos, químicos o incluso biológicos como, por ejemplo, por las raíces de la vegetación. Así, el volcán que emerge de las aguas cada vez es menos alto y, parecería, que la isla se va «hundiendo». Llega un punto en el que puede ser que el volcán desaparezca por completo fuera del agua y quede sumergido. Sin embargo, aquí sucede algo muy interesante. Aunque las paredes del volcán sigan deteriorándose, puede darse el caso de que los corales colonicen aquellas partes del volcán sumergidas que estén más cerca de la superficie. Como veíamos antes, los corales son organismos coloniales formados por pólipos y zooxantelas simbiontes. Así, los pólipos son capaces de colonizar las zonas más superficiales de las antiguas paredes del volcán, donde las zooxantelas también pueden hacer la fotosíntesis. De esta manera, se va generando una estructura calcárea que crece más rápido que la velocidad a la que el volcán se «hunde» por lo que el arrecife crece para quedarse siempre cerca de la superficie. Así es como se forman muchos de los atolones que se encuentran en los océanos, sobre los cuales existen numerosos asentamientos humanos, como es el caso de Teti'aroa. Poco a poco la erosión hace que se desgasten también las estructuras calcáreas de los corales, siendo este hecho el que propicia que las playas y, prácticamente toda la isla, sea de color blanco. Desde el espacio, Teti'aroa parece la hermana tropical de la isla Decepción que visitamos en la Antártida: un anillo volcánico, pero de colores blanquecinos, no negros. Sinceramente, no esperaba que mi primera vez en el océano Pacífico fuese a poder visitar un sitio tan espectacular como aquel: el único atolón del grupo de las islas de Barlovento del Archipiélago de la Sociedad, que está formado por trece islotes que apenas llegan a los seis km^2 de superficie entre todos ellos. No es fácil llegar hasta Teti'aroa. En nuestro caso, tuvimos que realizar un viaje de dos horas en nuestra lancha de muestreo bajo un sol abrasador. Como parecía que íbamos a ir muy apretados en la lancha, me ofrecí voluntario para hacer el viaje sentado en la proa de la lancha. Durante gran parte del trayecto, un alcatraz pardo (*Sula leucogaster*) intentó cazar con más o menos éxito los peces voladores que escapaban de la trayectoria de la lancha y pude ser testigo del espectáculo. Mientras tanto, en el horizonte no se veía absolutamente nada, daba la sensación de que nos íbamos adentrando más y más en el océano Pacífico. Poco a poco, un pequeño punto verde con tonos turquesas se fue haciendo más y más grande: Teti'aroa emergía de la nada bajo un sol abrasador. Una vez llegamos a las proximidades de la isla aún nos quedaba un reto por superar. Resulta que, por mar, la única manera de acceder a Teti'aroa es a través de un estrecho paso situado en el suroeste de la isla que da acceso a su laguna interior. Para ello, hay que esperar a que las olas se retiren un poco y acelerar a fondo con la lancha para no darnos con las paredes. Aun así, nos dimos con una de las paredes, pero por suerte no sufrimos ningún daño. Teti'aroa esconde más datos interesantes, aparte de una combinación de inigualable de paisaje, naturaleza y aventura. Sin duda alguna, lo que más llama la atención es el hecho de que este atolón es de propiedad privada. Básicamente, consta de una serie de estaciones con servicios de investigación junto un complejo turístico de lujo fundado por el actor Marlon Brando y llamado, como no, The Brando, pero ¿por qué están ciencia y turismo de alto nivel adquisitivo tan cerca? La respuesta la encontramos en los objetivos de Tetiaroa Society, enfocados en invertir el dinero de este tipo de turismo para hacer ciencia en la zona y promover acciones de conservación de la naturaleza a través de la educación, la investigación científica y el conocimiento tradicional de los nativos. En Teti'aroa, el actor

Leonardo DiCaprio, cuyo activismo ambiental es bastante notable (pese a las mil contradicciones que entraña su caso), ha comprado una pequeña zona de playas a la que han puesto su nombre, DiCaprio's Bay, en honor a una sustanciosa donación. Asimismo, el expresidente Barack Obama estuvo allí mismo un par de meses antes de que nosotros llegásemos.

Nada más llegar a la isla, era la hora de comer. Así que fuimos a uno de los chiringuitos remotos que hay en The Brando. Solo había dos mesas, por lo que parecía que la clientela pese a selecta era escasa. A unos cinco metros de la orilla se podían ver varias aletas de tiburón punta negra (*Carcharhinus melanopterus*), que suelen medir 1,5 m de longitud y aún no habíamos tenido ocasión de ver. Aunque no son tan grandes como los tiburones limón (*Negaprion brevirostris*), que pueden llegar a medir 3,5 m y también pueblan las aguas de Mo'orea y Teti'aroa, su presencia imponía mucho, aunque la nuestra no parecía importarles. Como tampoco la de los comensales que ocuparon la mesa a nuestro lado: el actor Bradley Cooper y la modelo Irina Shayk. Nos habían avisado con anterioridad de que estaba totalmente prohibido sacar el móvil del bolsillo porque muchos de los residentes del complejo se ponían nerviosos y ahora entendíamos la razón. En definitiva, ya os podéis imaginar que llegar a esta isla no es tan fácil, ni barato. Como podéis suponer, el resto de los residentes de The Brando no llegaron navegando en lancha, sino en avión privado aterrizando en una pequeña pista situada entre las palmeras en un extremo del atolón. Sin embargo, nosotros estábamos allí invitados con el objetivo de hacer ciencia y eso tiene menos *glamour*. Los investigadores del proyecto de investigación BIOGAPS pasamos un par de días en Teti'aroa dedicados a dos objetivos principales: por un lado, conocer el atolón y la Teti'aroa Society; y, por otro lado, muestrear en los alrededores. Al respecto de esto último, cogimos muestras en la zona más al noroeste de la isla, en un lago de agua dulce escondido entre cocoteros, en la laguna interior rodeada por todos los islotes y en el arrecife de coral que protege Teti'aroa de las inclemencias del tiempo.

En el centro de Teti'aroa se sitúa la laguna de la que os hablaba antes, la cual tiene unas tonalidades de azul muy distintas si los fondos son arenosos y poco profundos (azul celestre brillante) o si los fondos son algo más profundos y parcheados de corales (azul cian intenso). La laguna, que no tiene ningún paso navegable al océano, salvo el pequeño por el que entramos nosotros, tiene siete kilómetros de largo y treinta metros de profundidad. No pudimos ver casi ninguna especie interesante mientras muestreábamos, salvo algunos ejemplares de águila marina moteada (*Aetobatus narinari*). Tras la intensa jornada, pasamos la noche en una de las casas de los investigadores de la Teti'aroa Society y, a modo de agradecimiento, los investigadores más senior de nuestro equipo se ofrecieron a dar una charla de divulgación científica por la noche para los visitantes. Sin embargo, no pudimos reconocer a ningún famoso entre los asistentes, aunque era gente de lo más peculiar. Al día siguiente, una vez muestreadas todas las zonas de Teti'aroa, emprendimos el camino de vuelta a Mo'orea. De nuevo, otras dos horas de viaje en lancha tras haber estado muestreando toda la mañana. Un total de nueve horas navegando y trabajando, en nuestro último día en el atolón: una paliza. Pero una paliza que había merecido la pena.

Volviendo a nuestro trabajo en la isla de Mo'orea, nuestra rutina de muestreo consistía básicamente en dos clases de muestreos diferente, los cuales no cesaban salvo en los días de descanso (por lo general un día a la semana). Por un lado, teníamos los muestreos diarios en el «lagoon» del arrecife de Piha'hena (donde está la estación de investigación estadounidense GUMP Station), entre la playa y el arrecife, y en el «Back Reef», del arrecife hacia mar abierto. Para ello, todos los días nos levantábamos alrededor de las 5:30 de la mañana, ya que a las 7.00 a. m. debíamos preparar todo el material en el barco para salir a muestrear. Estos muestreos se realizaban una vez al día, variando la zona de muestreo diariamente, para así poder comparar cómo cambiaban los parámetros en función del lugar muestreado. Por otro lado, teníamos los maravillosos y temidos ciclos día-noche. En estos ciclos, estudiábamos durante treinta y seis horas seguidas qué sucede con los parámetros y variables ambientales, biológicas y fisicoquímicas que nos interesaban de estos arrecifes de coral. Para ello, cada seis horas (es decir, un total de seis veces en cada ciclo día-noche), salíamos a muestrear con el barco durante alrededor de dos horas, llenando una serie de frascos, botellas y viales con muestras para posteriormente traerlos al laboratorio. Una vez en el laboratorio todo se analizaba con base en los distintos protocolos, acabando muchos de los análisis, justo antes de que empezase el siguiente muestreo, seis horas después, o incluso después del mismo. Como podéis imaginar es un trabajo muy intenso pues casi no puedes parar para dormir, a no ser que se implante un sistema de turnos. Lo interesante de los ciclos día-noche es que te permiten apreciar cómo cambian los sistemas marinos, y vaya si cambian. Sin embargo, si hay algo que personalmente me resultó impresionante fue muestrear lejos del arrecife de coral, en la piel del océano Pacífico profundo. El océano Pacífico no solo es el océano más grande del planeta, sino también el más profundo en promedio, y en él se encuentra la parte más profunda de los océanos del mundo: la Fosa de las Marianas (11,2 km aprox.). Todo ello conlleva que solo con alejarse un par de kilómetros de la costa de Mo'orea, la profundidad alcance rápidamente varios miles de metros. Es decir, a un par de kilómetros de nuestro laboratorio nos encontrábamos con el Pacífico profundo. Cuando pensamos en el océano global, debemos verlo como lo que es: una vasta extensión de agua que llega a grandes profundidades (la profundidad media del océano es de aproximadamente 3900 metros) y en la que en los primeros cien o doscientos metros se hace la fotosíntesis. A partir de esa profundidad, reina la oscuridad y en ella los organismos habitan mediante diversas adaptaciones fisiológicas sujetos a los ritmos de la evolución por selección natural durante millones de años. Pero, a nosotros solo nos interesaba el agua superficial de ese Pacífico profundo, concretamente íbamos a muestrear a una localización sobre un fondo que se situaba a unos mil trescientos metros. Fue allí donde, pese a que había olas y nos mareábamos bastante, además de trabajar sin parar, pudimos observar algunas de las especies de fauna que no se ven en las proximidades de los arrecifes, como un grupo de varios calderones tropicales (*Globicephala macrorhynchus*) y otro de delfines de hocico estrecho (*Steno bredanensis*), estos últimos llegan a medir más de tres metros de longitud y pesan alrededor de ciento cincuenta kilogramos de media. Es increíble la cantidad de especies marinas que pueden soportar estas pequeñas islas y sus arrecifes de coral, incluso algunas de las más grandes del mundo están presentes en las aguas de Mo'orea, como las yubartas (también conocidas como «ballena jorobada», *Megaptera novaeangliae*). Uno de los días que muestreábamos en aguas abiertas, nuestro patrón decidió que le apetecía intentar pescar algo para llevar a su casa. Así que echó un par de aparejos por la borda y estuvimos dando vueltas un rato. Varios *mahi mahi* pasaban a una velocidad increíble alrededor del barco, pero ninguno «picaba». En mi cabeza no podía dejar de pensar en el que posiblemente ha sido uno de los libros que más me ha marcado, *El viejo y el mar* de Ernest Hemingway; con su eterna lucha con el pez espada (*Xiphias gladius*). Finalmente, consiguió pescar dos ejemplares de varios kilos de atún de aleta amarilla (*Thunnus albacares*), uno de los cuales nos lo cedió para que lo cenáramos esa misma noche estilo *shushi*.

Durante semanas nos dedicamos a muestrear estas aguas con el objetivo de evaluar los impactos del cambio climático sobre el océano. Pero esta es solo una de las técnicas gracias a las cuales podemos comprender y evaluar determinados fenómenos. Otra forma de obtener información sobre el océano, por ejemplo, es utilizar boyas ARGO. Actualmente, existen unas cuatro mil boyas oceanográficas flotando por todos los océanos del planeta, que miden parámetros como temperatura, salinidad o clorofila, y envían esos datos a distintos satélites para que puedan ser consultados en tiempo real por los científicos. Quizás exista la creencia de que estas boyas oceanográficas solo se encuentran en la superficie del océano, ya que la función de una «boya» no es otra que flotar. Sin embargo, a los oceanógrafos también nos interesa conocer qué sucede en las capas más profundas del océano. Así que estas boyas suelen bajarse hasta profundidades de unos dos mil metros y, tras recorrer las profundidades para medir parámetros oceanográficos, vuelven a subir a la superficie. Esto nos permite, por primera vez en la historia, monitorizar la temperatura, salinidad y la velocidad de las corrientes marinas. Y, además, los datos son de acceso libre, por lo que cualquier persona puede consultarlos desde su ordenador. Sin embargo, la tecnología marina no solo se muestra en forma de boyas o instrumentos de laboratorio, sino también en otras formas más complejas, como por ejemplo los satélites. Mucha gente preocupada por el medio ambiente se pregunta, bien intencionadamente, por qué nos gastamos tanto dinero en enviar satélites al espacio cuando hay tanto que investigar que no requiere tanto dinero y son cosas más cercanas a nosotros. Esta es una pregunta, como digo, bastante recurrente en muchos sectores de la sociedad y que muchos estudiantes se plantean al inicio de sus carreras universitarias. La actitud crítica con el gasto de dinero público en investigación es fundamental, pues nos debemos a la sociedad que nos aporta la financiación. Sin embargo, a veces se corre el riesgo de criticar algo cuyas aplicaciones se desconoce. Resulta curioso cómo gente concienciada con los negativos efectos del cambio climático antropogénico, es capaz de estar en contra de los programas espaciales, cuando estos son, y han sido, las herramientas fundamentales para constatar su existencia. Ya que, la lucha contra el cambio climático requiere de evaluación y seguimiento, para lo cual son imprescindibles los satélites. Es decir, necesitamos herramientas para poder medir qué está sucediendo a escala global, por ejemplo, en la superficie del océano en cualquier momento. Pocas herramientas mejores se me ocurren que miles de «ojos» flotando en el espacio que nos permiten ver y estudiar nuestro planeta. Como hemos visto, a través de la superficie del océano se emiten una serie de gases en concentraciones muy bajas, muchos de ellos producidos por el fitoplancton marino, por ejemplo, como subproductos de sus actividades metabólicas. El fitoplancton marino tiene propiedades ópticas que permiten su teledetección, por ello es posible utilizar los satélites para poder detectar las zonas donde hay más o menos fitoplancton, incluso de qué especie es, y estimar la producción y emisión de estos gases. Por ejemplo, desde los satélites, no solo podemos «ver» la temperatura o la concentración de clorofila del océano superficial, sino que también podemos cuantificar otros parámetros biogeoquímicos como la concentración de algunos compuestos del carbono. Por ello, en aquellas zonas donde los satélites detectan grandes concentraciones de partículas de carbono inorgánico (comúnmente conocido como PIC), significa que hay abundancia de cocolitóforos, pues el exoesqueleto de este tipo de fitoplancton está formado de carbonato cálcico. A estas técnicas de investigación marina se les suma otra aún más novedosa: el uso de modelos oceánicos y simulaciones por supercomputación. Actualmente podemos representar el funcionamiento del océano mediante cientos de ecuaciones para simular las corrientes marinas, el intercambio de masas de agua entre el océano profundo y superficial, etc. Además de eso, podemos incluir también el ecosistema plantónico a través de una serie de ecuaciones mediante las que se define quién se come a quién, cuánto pueden crecer los organismos, etc. Así, es posible representar matemáticamente al zooplancton, fitoplancton, bacterioplancton, etc., y podemos simular qué va a suceder en una zona determinada en un momento concreto y hacer proyecciones de futuro. Es decir, podemos acoplar a estos modelos de ecosistema algunos modelos climáticos para tener en cuenta los efectos del cambio climático en treinta, cincuenta o cien años. De esta manera, podemos conocer cómo va a afectar el cambio climático a la vida microscópica marina que tendrá un efecto sobre el resto de las redes trófica marinas, así como otros procesos esenciales para el funcionamiento del sistema terrestre como la producción de gases traza o la fijación de CO_2 atmosférico. Durante mi doctorado he usado algunas de estas herramientas para llevar a cabo varias investigaciones y, con este testimonio, espero contribuir a que cale la idea de que no todos los científicos llevan bata, ni todos están todo el día en el laboratorio ni tampoco están siempre de campaña oceanográfica.

Mitos y leyendas de la Polinesia

No me gustaría acabar de contar nuestra experiencia en la isla de Mo'orea sin contar algo que no he hecho en los otros capítulos de este libro (o, al menos, no de manera tan extensa): la mitología y tradiciones de los nativos de Mo'orea. Así que os contaré algunas de las historias que me contaron durante ese mes algunos de los «mooreanos», algunas incluso tuve la suerte de grabarlas en audio para no olvidarlas. Como podéis suponer, la relación de los habitantes de la isla de Mo'orea con el mar es muy estrecha, pero con la tierra firme también. A sus ojos, el «oasis» es la tierra firme y el «desierto» es el océano, todo lo contrario a ir vagando por el desierto del Sahara. Es por ello que en tierra firme es donde ellos han encontrado a lo largo de los siglos muchos de los recursos necesarios para su vida cotidiana. Es tal su relación con el medio que, tradicionalmente, cuando un bebé nacía enterraban la placenta en tierra firme y tiraban el cordón umbilical al mar, como símbolo de que permanecen unidos a él, siempre. El nativo de Mo'orea, por tanto, se considera a sí mismo como un nexo entre mar y tierra. Al inicio de la década de los 2000, los más ancianos de la isla percibieron que se estaban perdiendo muchas de sus tradiciones y conocimientos acerca de la isla, entre ellos, el de plantas con propiedades medicinales. No solo estaban preocupados porque se perdiera el saber, sino porque se deteriorasen los ecosistemas que mantenían las especies de plantas y animales vitales para su cultura y forma de vida. Por ello, se reunieron con los científicos y científicas que iban a investigar a Mo'orea y crearon una serie de iniciativas a través de las cuales los científicos se comprometieron a estudiar el estado de salud de las lagunas de los distintos arrecifes, así como a investigar la posible desaparición de especies y evaluar problemas como el de las especies invasoras. A cambio, los científicos recibirían asistencia de campo acerca de lugares de interés para realizar sus estudios. Por ejemplo, qué arrecifes son los que tienen más especies de un pez «X» o dónde se suele encontrar en tierra firme la lagartija «Y». Asimismo, continúan fomentando el uso de artes de pesca tradicionales que no dañan tanto al ecosistema, ya que han notado cómo especies que antaño eran mayores en número y/o en tamaño, cada vez son más difíciles de encontrar puesto que determinadas artes de pesca favorecen la sobreexplotación de los recursos y/o dañan los ecosistemas esenciales para que muchas de estas especies se reproduzcan y sus larvas pasen la primera parte de sus vidas, como los arrecifes de coral. Esta colaboración entre científicos y nativos ha ido desarrollándose a lo largo de los años y ambas partes educan a los jóvenes de la isla tanto en conocimientos tradicionales como modernos para lograr una mayor concienciación ambiental. En cuanto a la dieta, ya os he comentado anteriormente en qué consistía la nuestra. Y hay que decir que no parece que haya cambiado mucho, excepto que ahora consumen muchas más bebidas azucaradas. Tradicionalmente su comida ha consistido en pescado, leche de coco, leche fermentada de coco y alguna fruta o verdura que encuentres en la parte de atrás de tu casa, como plátanos. Es decir, con una dependencia nula del exterior de la isla.

Para los nativos de Mo'orea el océano no es una barrera, sino que forma parte de su medio. Allá donde quiera que vayas, de isla en isla o adentrándote en el Pacífico, todo lo que ves es océano. Por lo tanto, es algo tan inevitable que no puede ser una frontera. Los que han viajado a las zonas continentales próximas, principalmente, América u Oceanía, recalcaban con mucho énfasis lo mal que se sentían anímicamente estando lejos del mar cuando visitaban alguna localidad interior. Decían, de forma no tan coloquial como uno esperaría, que el océano forma parte incluso de su «ADN», ya que sus ancestros viajaron por ese océano hace varios miles de años colonizando isla a isla en sus canoas. Dichas canoas son esenciales, o lo eran, en su modo de vida, ya que les ayudaban a transportarse a «aquellos lugares donde el océano les deja vivir». Esto es para ellos muy importante porque significa que el océano «les presta» islas donde poder vivir, por lo tanto, no las poseen, las posee el océano. Es decir, ellos no se consideran en un nivel superior, dueños y señores de las islas, sino que es el océano quién manda en sus tierras y, por lo tanto, en sus vidas. Necesitas al océano para alimentarte, para curarte y para aprender. Así que necesitas de la ayuda del océano y, en el presente, el océano también necesita la tuya. Vivir en una isla con los recursos limitados les ha enseñado desde tiempos inmemoriales a pensar en el medio y largo plazo. En el pasado, era esencial la planificación para poder sobrevivir en un lugar tan aislado. Ello conllevaba un gran racionamiento de comida, así como preservarla en grandes cantidades. Esto era esencial en tierra firme pero también es sus viajes, que eran epopeyas, en canoa a través del Pacífico. Esto se ilustra con una pregunta que me hicieron: ¿Cuánta agua puedes llevar en una canoa para muchos días de navegación por el desierto azul? Se responde solo. Sin embargo, los viajes no eran en solitario, sino en grupos. Por ello, no solo era importante dosificar esfuerzos, sino que la unidad y la toma de decisiones en grupo eran vitales para no morir en el océano. Así, todos tenían que estar de acuerdo de manera unánime en la dirección en la que remar, el ritmo o el racionamiento de la comida. Dicen que esta manera de pensar y actuar ha quedado claramente registrada en su lenguaje y en su cultura, y que ha evolucionado (lingüística y antropológicamente, por decirlo de alguna manera) conforme ellos lo hacían a lo largo de los siglos. El océano no solo es parte de su ecosistema, sino que lo domina todo, incluso lo que hay en tierra firme. Me explicaban que «todo» lo que veíamos en tierra firme tiene que ver con el océano. ¿Cómo llegaron aquí las plantas? ¿Cómo llegaron muchos de los animales? A través del océano: «Están aquí porque el océano se lo ha permitido».

La mitología y legendas de Mo'orea están plagadas de historias cuyos protagonistas son las aves, plantas, montañas, tiburones, etc. Una nativa me contaba que la montaña que tenía a mis espaldas tiene nombre de mujer porque está vigilada por una princesa (cuyo nombre no soy capaz de reproducir) que vive allí. En la cima de la montaña había una charca de peces sagrados que eran con los que jugaba la princesa. Dicen que a veces esa charca vuelve a brotar y los peces de la princesa aparecen, lo que significa que ese año habrá abundancia de peces en el mar. También me hablaron de un árbol especial, escondido en la selva, que cuando florece da una flor con la que la princesa se adorna el pelo, y que tiene un pájaro como mascota, al que dirige mediante silbidos, que solo vuela de noche y que muchas veces se les oye comunicarse. Dicen que a veces se la puede percibir «pero no con la vista», no solo en la vegetación, sino también en el arrecife, que es donde ella va también a pescar y a bucear, sin necesidad de respirar (algo parecido a una «sirena»). La historia dice que un día alguien vendrá de una isla lejana que no posea montañas ni plantas e intentará convencer a la princesa de que se vaya con él, para ayudarle a formar una isla en la que se pueda vivir, en abundancia de alimentos y animales. De momento, ese hombre no ha aparecido y la princesa sigue en Mo'orea. Otra leyenda, que se relaciona con esta, cuenta que tres hermanos, dos chicos y una chica, llegaron en canoa de noche a Mo'orea y, al pisar tierra firme, se pusieron a pelear porque ninguno quería seguir haciéndose cargo de su hermana, pensando incluso en matarla. La chica despertó con los gritos de ambos, que sacudieron toda la isla y despertaron a todos los pájaros, que salieron de su sueño para ir a protegerla. También despertaron a los habitantes que rápidamente fueron en su ayuda. Uno de los jóvenes llegó primero y salió corriendo tras ellos. Uno de los hermanos, furioso, arrojó un arpón contra la montaña, en un intento de dañar a la joven, pero de la vegetación salieron miles de pollos a atacarles. El joven valeroso persiguió a los hermanos y luchó contra ellos hasta el amanecer. Al ver que no podían ganar la batalla, pues tenían a toda la isla en su contra, los hermanos, derrotados, cogieron sus canoas y se fueron remando mar adentro. Y el joven héroe y la chica se unieron al resto de los habitantes de Mo'orea donde, años más tarde, formarían una familia.

Estas son el tipo de historias que los nativos les cuentan a sus hijos, en ellas se enfatiza siempre lo importante que es cuidar de la naturaleza y entender a los animales como parte de sus vidas. Pero, de todos los animales marinos, hay uno que adquiere una especial importancia: el tiburón. Los tiburones son los «guardianes» de las islas del Pacífico. Las diferentes leyendas cuentan que cuando te acercas a una isla navegando con la canoa solo puedes pasar si el tiburón guardián de esa isla te lo permite. Cada tiburón guardián es de una especie distinta y tiene un nombre propio. Y no solo están en las islas, sino que pueden encontrarse en mitad de las corrientes, evitando que las utilices para remar más rápido en caso de que no respetes al océano y a sus criaturas. Por ello, cada persona que quiera llegar en canoa a una isla tiene que agradecer al tiburón que le haya dejado pasar y hacer un ritual. Si no sucede nada, pueden acercarse a la orilla, ya que significa que el tiburón les ha concedido permiso. Cuando los viajeros mueren, tras una vida visitando islas, deben de agradecer uno a uno a todos los tiburones que les hayan dejado pasar a las islas y les hayan protegido cuando ha sido necesario, ya que el vínculo que se establece con los tiburones es para toda la vida. Y es un vínculo que se mantiene incluso en las siguientes generaciones. Así, cuando un navegante muere y su hijo es pequeño y tiene algún problema, solo tiene que llamar a uno de esos tiburones por su nombre y vendrá a ayudarle. De hecho, la persona que me contó esta historia concluyó diciendo: «Estas son nuestras creencias. Nosotros agradecemos a todos los animales lo que hacen por nosotros, ya que desde pequeños nos enseñan que son nuestros protectores, desde el tiburón hasta el gallo. Aprendemos de lo que nos enseñan y compartimos conocimiento. Cuidamos de nuestro mar, cuidamos de nuestras plantas y nuestros animales. Este es el tipo de relación que nosotros tenemos con nuestro entorno. Nos pertenecemos mutuamente».

NADIE ES UNA ISLA

«La vida no es un ensayo, aunque tratemos muchas cosas; no es un cuento; aunque inventemos muchas cosas; no es un poema, aunque soñemos muchas cosas. El ensayo del cuento del poema de la vida es un movimiento perpetuo; eso es, un movimiento perpetuo».
Movimiento perpetuo, *Augusto Monterroso (1972)*

A lo largo de este libro he intentado, esperemos que, con éxito, poner en relieve algunos de los procesos y fenómenos naturales que tienen lugar en los mares y océanos de la Tierra y juegan papeles clave para el funcionamiento de los distintos subsistemas terrestres y las sociedades humanas. De entre todos ellos, el cambio climático ha ocupado un lugar preponderante a lo largo de las páginas. Y es que el cambio climático será, con toda probabilidad, el mayor reto de la humanidad del presente siglo y, si no se producen los cambios necesarios para evitar sus peores consecuencias, también lo será para siglos venideros. Sin embargo, tal y como decía recientemente el secretario general de la ONU, António Guterres: «No es un problema del futuro, sino del presente». La lucha afecta a nuestra forma de relacionarnos con el medio. Sus impactos negativos no solo se quedan en la pérdida de biodiversidad o en la disminución de caladeros pesqueros, sino que impactan al propio sistema socioeconómico de la gran mayoría de países y, por ello, nadie se escapa de ellos. En la lucha contra el cambio climático nadie es una isla. Y es en los mares y océanos donde podemos encontrar muchas de las respuestas para afrontar este gran reto global. Pese a que aquí solo hemos abordado algunas de ellas, los océanos de la Tierra aún esconden numerosos secretos por descubrir y les corresponde a las futuras generaciones de investigadores e investigadoras seguir desentrañándolos porque nos va, literalmente, la vida en ello; estamos en un momento crucial. Como dice el refranero marino: «En mar calmado todos somos capitanes», pero cuando el mar se pone bravío más nos vale tener a capitanes y capitanas de verdad. Aunque nunca hay que confiarse, ya que, como dice otro refrán, «no existe hombre de mar que no se pueda ahogar». Necesitamos que los futuros profesionales en las disciplinas científicas involucradas en el estudio del cambio climático y sus impactos en los océanos sean rigurosos en su trabajo, pero también implacables en la lucha por la aplicación de soluciones. Asimismo, es necesario que esta acción sea trasversal al resto de profesiones. Cada uno de los que estáis leyendo este libro tenéis capacidad de actuar en vuestros respectivos campos profesionales, seáis estudiantes o trabajadores. Por tanto, comprender y aceptar la transversalidad de estos impactos debiera ser el primer paso para tomar medidas. Es decir, la transversalidad inevitable que impone el cambio climático debe ir más allá de la política, llegando a trascender a todos los sectores y agentes de la sociedad.

Aunque en el ámbito político ya se han tomado numerosas medidas para abordar este problema. Un gran ejemplo de calado internacional que refleja la importancia de la transversalidad del cambio climático y sus múltiples conexiones, tanto con los mares y océanos como con otros elementos del planeta y las sociedades humanas que lo habitan, son los Objetivos de Desarrollo Sostenible (ODS) de la Agenda 2030. En septiembre de 2015, la mayoría de líderes mundiales acordaron en el marco de la Organización de las Naciones Unidas los ODS: diecisiete objetivos globales comunes que formarían parte de una nueva agenda de desarrollo sostenible. Dichos objetivos pretenden lograr hazañas aún no alcanzadas por la humanidad, como erradicar la pobreza o proteger el planeta de nosotros mismos. Sin embargo, para que dichos objetivos no quedasen en el fértil campo de la ambigüedad y las buenas intenciones, también se fijaron metas específicas en cada uno de ellos, los cuales deberían alcanzarse en quince años; y así es como nació la Agenda 2030 para el Desarrollo Sostenible. Cuando uno se pasea por los ODS y analiza sus variopintas metas, se da cuenta de varias cosas. Una de ellas es que esta agenda va más allá del desarrollo sostenible y la protección de nuestro planeta, va de qué sociedad global queremos ser y cuándo queremos alcanzarla. Por otro lado, cuando uno llega al cambio climático (el ODS 14 llamado «acción por el clima») se da cuenta de que no es un objetivo aislado, sino que está conectado con todos los demás. No se puede hablar de cambio climático sin hablar de salud y bienestar (ODS 3), producción y consumo responsables (ODS 12), vida submarina (ODS 14), vida de ecosistemas terrestres (ODS 15), etc. Esta es la primera idea que debe quedar muy clara: hablar de cambio climático es hacerlo de océanos, como se refleja en este libro, pero también de salud y de economía. El cambio climático es, por tanto, un fenómeno transversal que atraviesa e impacta en el resto de los elementos de nuestra sociedad.

Pese a que nos encontramos en una situación de extrema urgencia, existen fuertes grupos de presión internacional financiados por sectores contrarios a los ODS que se encargan de fomentar la falsa creencia pseudocientífica de que el cambio climático antropogénico no es tal, sino que es un fenómeno natural en el que no tenemos nada que ver o nuestra contribución es irrelevante. Esto lo hacen de diversas maneras, como por ejemplo difundiendo eficazmente en medios afines y redes sociales noticias falsas o llegando a acuerdos con partidos políticos para que en sus programas introduzcan sus postulados. Respecto a esto último, el negacionismo climático político es más que patente en algunos de los gobiernos más importantes del planeta. Aparte de este negacionismo poderoso y a gran escala, existe otro que se basa en la incultura científica; la cual hace un maridaje perfecto con el ego, la prepotencia y el chafardeo de algunas personas. Muchos científicos incluso hemos tenido profesores universitarios que negaban el cambio climático y que, por cierto, lo siguen haciendo. Lo cual es ciertamente curioso, ya que no olvidemos que negar el cambio climático está al mismo nivel, científicamente hablando, que afirmar que las vacunas provocan algún tipo de autismo o que fumar tabaco no es malo para la salud. Por ello, muchos científicos usamos nuestro tiempo libre en divulgar el cambio climático para concienciar a la ciudadanía y luchar contra el negacionismo. Personalmente, creo que los ciudadanos debemos emular esa actitud que se describe al inicio de la obra Walden, de Henry David Thoreau, cuando dice que: «No pretendo escribir una oda al abatimiento, sino jactarme con tanto brío como el gallo encaramado a su palo por la mañana, aunque solo sea para despertar a mis vecinos». El cambio climático está aquí y es real, no hay ningún debate científico acerca de ello. Recomiendo encarecidamente, por tanto, a todos los lectores de este libro hablar de cambio climático con otras personas, sobre todo si piensan distinto. Muchos podéis ser el gallo que despierte a vuestros vecinos, familiares y amigos.

A lo largo de este libro hemos puesto nuestra atención, sobre todo, en el aspecto científico de la lucha contra el cambio climático y otros problemas ambientales. Sin embargo, la solución no pasa solo por la ciencia, desgraciadamente. Existe una opinión extendida en ciertos sectores de que la solución a los problemas ambientales, en general, y al cambio climático, en particular, es meramente técnica y que, a grandes rasgos, puede ser resuelta por la comunidad científica internacional a través de su seguimiento, diagnóstico y/o descubrimientos. Pese a que el papel de la ciencia en la lucha contra el cambio climático es un hecho incuestionable, no puede obviarse también que está sujeto a la política y, por lo tanto, a la propia sociedad. Esta es, de hecho, una de las críticas que se hace a quienes se toman al pie de la letra el lema «Unite Behind the Science» que suelen usar los jóvenes que se manifiestan por todo el mundo bajo la plataforma «Fridays For Future» y otras afines. De alguna manera, parecería que hay gente que cree firmemente que los investigadores vamos a conseguir generar un «cambio político-social a una velocidad sin precedentes», tal y como establece el IPCC, por el mero hecho de tener «los datos» de su parte. Sobre todo, cuando sabemos que los datos no bastan para convencer de algunas cuestiones científicas. Por no hablar de las condiciones de precariedad y resto de problemas, no solo en España, a los que los profesionales de la investigación científica nos vemos sometidos; y que merman nuestra capacidad de acción social.

Es incuestionable, entonces, que la lucha contra el cambio climático debe ser transversal. Muchos creemos que dicha transversalidad en la búsqueda de soluciones y medidas no se puede realizar únicamente desde un comité de «sabios» seleccionados en una inexistente, o cuanto menos ineficiente, meritocracia. Por otro lado, cabe no olvidar que esto no va solo de ciencia y de política, las empresas y entidades financieras deben formar parte irrenunciable de esto; principalmente debido al poder incluso superior al político del que gozan algunas de ellas. Sin embargo, hay cierta tendencia a cerrar este grupo en estos tres actores, olvidando a colectivos y/o entidades de la sociedad civil como las ONG, movimientos ecologistas o ambientalistas (no olvidemos que ecología y ecologismo no es lo mismo) o incluso sindicatos de trabajadores (la lucha contra el cambio climático, si no es justa, puede tener impactos sobre numerosos puestos de trabajo como los de la minería, etc.). Esta exclusión viene motivada por las tendencias acientíficas de algunos de esos colectivos del pasado, muchas presentes aún hoy en día, como su rechazo por temas de salud a los transgénicos. Sin embargo, esto no debería ser excusa para poner en entredicho su compromiso ambiental y con el cambio climático. Bajo mi punto de vista, la comunicación y divulgación ambiental y del cambio climático ha estado en sus manos durante muchos años por dejadez de los profesionales científicos. Por lo tanto, creo que si hoy parte la sociedad tiene cierta conciencia ambiental es en gran medida gracias a ellos. Un gran ejemplo de esto es la Asociación de Naturalistas del Sureste (ANSE) en la Región de Murcia, que ha estado luchando por el medio ambiente y todas sus formas de vida desde hace décadas, tanto desde la divulgación de sus problemáticas como liderando y participando en proyectos de investigación científica cuyos resultados han sido publicados en revistas científicas. Actualmente, tras la crisis que vive el Mar Menor, ha reforzado muchas de sus iniciativas y lanzado otras nuevas, como la adquisición de una parte de las Salinas de Marchamalo, ubicadas en la zona sur del Mar Menor para recuperar la actividad salinera y conseguir que sea compatible con la conservación y recuperación de la biodiversidad de la zona.

Pese a la creciente concienciación ambiental que parece vivir el mundo y la especial sensibilización con respecto al cambio climático, no todo es color de rosa. Como decíamos, ahora mismo también nos encontramos en un contexto internacional de auge de negacionistas del cambio climático cuyos argumentos van de la mera negación del mismo a transmitir ideas a la sociedad como que las soluciones al cambio climático las van a tomar «las élites» a puerta cerrada y esto perjudicará directamente a las clases trabajadoras. Es decir, suelen hacer de la conspiranoia su mejor arma política. A su vez, intentan que la sociedad no se movilice y actúe contra el cambio climático a través de la ridiculización de figuras y entidades de la lucha ambiental. Este tipo de triquiñuelas tienen, por desgracia, más recorrido de lo que podríamos pensar. Ante esta situación deberíamos tener claro que hay que escuchar qué dice la evidencia científica y actuar en consecuencia. Si lo hacemos, nos daremos cuenta de que los científicos repiten una y otra vez que las voces de la sociedad civil, incluidas las del mundo ecologista o ambientalista, han de ser tenidas en cuenta en la lucha contra el cambio climático. Sirva de ejemplo el propio IPCC que dice que «el fortalecimiento de las competencias para la acción climática de las autoridades nacionales y subnacionales, la sociedad civil, el sector privado, los pueblos indígenas y las comunidades locales puede apoyar la implementación de acciones ambiciosas implicadas al limitar el calentamiento global a 1,5°C». En esta línea, se pueden extraer muchas acciones distintas, aunque implicar a la sociedad en la lucha contra el cambio climático a través de la mejor evidencia aportada por profesionales científicos es todo un reto. En países como Reino Unido, Francia o España se han creado, o se van a crear «asambleas ciudadanas para el cambio climático». Es una propuesta interesante cuyo éxito posiblemente radicará, entre otras cosas, en su capacidad de convencer y hacer partícipe a la sociedad, siempre y cuando se cuente con profesionales expertos en la materia en aras del rigor del debate y las propuestas que de ella emerjan; así como de otros profesionales del ámbito público y privado. Otro aspecto interesante sería determinar el carácter vinculante o no de las decisiones que se tomen en dichas asambleas ya que, si se establecen como una mera entidad de debate o divulgación del conocimiento científico, esto podría acarrear cierta frustración en los participantes pues podrían percibirse como una herramienta ineficiente en cuanto a transformar sus propuestas en cambios políticos reales. En conclusión, podemos afirmar que la evidencia científica nos indica que hemos de escuchar no solo a los profesionales científicos o invertir más en ciencia e innovación, sino también escuchar las demandas de la sociedad civil preocupada, colectivizada y activa en la búsqueda de soluciones. Por otro lado, algunos creemos que también es necesario evitar a *influencers*, opinadores profesionales y oportunistas, totalmente inexpertos en la ciencia del cambio climático, cuyos argumentos suelen estar cargados de proselitismo ideológico y evitan aquellas partes de los informes del IPCC que no les interesan. En conclusión, tenemos que usar la mejor ciencia posible y todas las herramientas democráticas que están en nuestra mano para hacer que la lucha contra el cambio climático sea lo más justa posible. Y, sobre todo, para hacerla cuanto antes.

He hablado varias veces en el libro acerca de que el cambio climático va a impactar principalmente a los más débiles y, también, a aquellos que viven en determinadas regiones costeras, cuya vida depende también de la salud de los ecosistemas marinos. De hecho, según varios estudios científicos, el cambio climático es más importante para las migraciones que otros factores, como económicos o políticos, de algunos de los países de origen. Según ACNUR, la Agencia de la ONU para los refugiados, los riesgos de desplazamiento forzado por desastres naturales se han duplicado desde 1970, gran parte de ellos debido al cambio climático, en países como Somalia, Yemen y Sudán del Sur. Según esta misma entidad, en 2018 hubo un total de 17,2 millones de desplazados o refugiados climáticos. Resulta curioso que este último término no estuviese contemplado hasta hace poco por el derecho internacional, ya que desde ACNUR recomendaban que se usase el término «personas desplazadas en el contexto de desastres y cambio climático». Esto era debido a que dicha figura no existe en la Convención sobre el Estatuto de los Refugiados de 1951. Sin embargo, esta circunstancia ha empezado a cambiar, ya que en diciembre de 2019 el Comité de Derechos Humanos de las Naciones Unidas (CDH) emitió un dictamen por el que establecía que «una persona refugiada o desplazada por causas climáticas o por desastres naturales no puede ser devuelta a su país de origen si con ello se pone en riesgo el ejercicio de algún derecho fundamental, como es el derecho a la vida». Este pronunciamiento se debió a la lucha de una persona, Ioane Teitiota, ciudadano de la República de Kiribati, un conjunto de archipiélagos formado por treinta y tres atolones coralinos y por el volcán Banaba en el Pacífico Tropical. Residía en Nueva Zelanda cuando le informaron de que debía abandonar dicho país y regresar a Kiribati. Él ha estado varios años defendiendo que le estaban haciendo regresar a un lugar del que se vería obligado a volver a emigrar. Parece que, finalmente, podrá quedarse en Nueva Zelanda, pero otros no correrán tanta suerte.

Tampoco podemos olvidar que el cambio climático también es una cuestión de salud. De hecho, la Organización Mundial de la Salud estima que entre 2030 y 2050 se producirán unas 250.000 muertes adicionales cada año asociadas directamente a las consecuencias del cambio climático, principalmente debido a las olas de calor, la diarrea, el paludismo y la desnutrición infantil en aquellas regiones afectadas por la escasez de agua. Un cuarto de millón de muertes al año durante veinte años son cinco millones de muertes asociadas directamente al cambio climático. No solo los médicos salvan vidas, luchar contra el cambio climático también.

Durante las próximas décadas, la crisis climática y ambiental serán los dos mayores retos que debamos afrontar como sociedad global. Si no lo hacemos, podemos tener una cosa clara: las generaciones más jóvenes, quienes ya han llegado o están por venir, serán quienes sufrirán los efectos de nuestra inacción durante más años. A lo largo de estas páginas hemos descubierto por qué nuestro planeta se ha calentado un grado centígrado de temperatura con respecto a valores preindustriales, especialmente en los mares y océanos, y también qué puede pasar si el aumento es de 1,5°C o 2°C. Por todo ello, la transición ecológica a un nuevo sistema socioeconómico es primordial, tanto a escala local como nacional e internacional. Este calentamiento global está afectando no solo a los ecosistemas marinos o terrestres, sino también a la salud y al bienestar de las personas. En algunos lugares, como la región mediterránea, ya se han constatado sus efectos, que irán a peor. Fenómenos meteorológicos extremos como tormentas más intensas y sequías, impactarán en sectores estratégicos para nuestra economía como la agricultura o el turismo. Por desgracia, el cambio climático es un fenómeno global, pero sus impactos son locales. Por lo tanto, no son iguales en todos los lugares del planeta y, por esa misma razón, muchos países no pueden ni deben conformarse con igualar lo que hacen otros países que sufrirán un impacto menor. Muchos creemos que, en un auge global de movimientos nacionalistas, debemos convertir la lucha contra el cambio climático y la transición ecológica en nuestra mejor bandera. Según el IPCC, para frenar el calentamiento global es necesario reducir nuestras emisiones globales de dióxido de carbono en aproximadamente un 45% para el año 2030. Este comité de científicos también nos recuerda que: cada incremento de temperatura, por pequeño que sea, importa; cada año que pasa, importa; y cada decisión que tomemos (o no tomemos), importa. Pero, en esta lucha, no estamos solos. A través de este libro hemos aprendido que la naturaleza posee diversos mecanismos conocidos, y otros aún desconocidos, para poder paliar sus efectos negativos. Sin embargo, para descubrirlos, se requiere de un esfuerzo científico colectivo, que no entiende de fronteras, para poder conseguir aquello que Pío Baroja nos contaba en El Árbol de la ciencia cuando establecía que «el acuerdo de todas las inteligencias en una misma cosa es lo que llamamos verdad».

Por ello, los oceanógrafos y oceanógrafas del mundo dedicamos nuestro tiempo a estudiar el cambio climático en los diferentes océanos del planeta. Lo cual nos lleva a trabajar en lugares tan remotos como la Antártida. Pero no podemos hacerlo en según qué condiciones, ya que, para luchar contra el cambio climático, se necesita de una valiente y decidida inversión en investigación. Así como de una reforma del sistema científico global, que elimine los elementos que deterioran nuestra profesión, como la precariedad laboral, el nepotismo o la endogamia. Sin olvidarnos de la dificultad de muchos científicos de poder desarrollar su carrera científica en su lugar de origen. Por supuesto, también necesitamos el impulso de los avances tecnológicos, cuyo objetivo transversal debe ser la sostenibilidad no solo en sus usos y aplicaciones, sino también en su desarrollo y fabricación. Los retos que supone el cambio climático no se resolverán solo con nosotros, los científicos, pero de ninguna manera se conseguirán si no nos implicamos y trabajamos de manera coordinada con la sociedad civil y sus representantes políticos. Por último, debemos concienciarnos de que esta es una lucha compartida por las distintas generaciones, que han de actuar como una entidad transfronteriza para encontrar soluciones globales. Y eso es precisamente lo que reclaman millones de jóvenes alrededor del mundo: aún no es tarde, pero tenemos que actuar ya. Para mí, como científico, es un movimiento que me llena de esperanza y que confío en que transmita su mensaje a las generaciones más mayores, que son aquellas que tienen el poder y la capacidad para aplicar las medidas que necesitamos para proteger y conservar nuestros océanos, así como para luchar contra el cambio climático.

EPÍLOGO

La tenue luz de la mañana ilumina los árboles delante de mi casa de San Diego, California. Esta noche ha habido mucha niebla en esta zona que es prácticamente semidesértica, así que hay abundante rocío sobre toda la vegetación. Los colibríes (*Calypte anna*) ya empiezan a pulular bebiendo algunas de estas gotas y dándose un festín con sus flores habituales. Ya hace horas que los mapaches (*Procyon lotor*) y coyotes (*Canis latrans*) de la reserva natural próxima a mi urbanización han dejado de buscar comida en los contenedores y en las barbacoas de los parques. Aún no ha llegado el verano, por lo que las serpientes de cascabel (*Crotalus sp.*) no están del todo activas. Escribo las últimas líneas de este libro mientras me preparo para abandonar California y regresar a España tras seis meses de estancia para acabar mi doctorado, cerrando así una etapa de diez años dedicada a investigar los mares y océanos de nuestro planeta, y su relación con el cambio climático. Soy consciente de que lo que hacemos en ciencia es poner un pequeño ladrillo en la pared infinita del conocimiento científico que seguirán construyendo los que vengan después. Y es en esas nuevas generaciones, se dediquen a la ciencia o no, en las que yo tengo esperanza. En los que están por venir. Mucha gente considera que tener esperanza es pecar de iluso. Yo creo, sin embargo, que a veces no sabemos cómo, ni cuándo, ni por qué; pero, como decía Ian Malcolm en *Parque Jurásico*, «la vida se abre camino».

Agradecimientos a los argonautas *olvidados* del libro

A lo largo de este libro, muchos de los lectores y lectoras se habrán dado cuenta de que constantemente se han omitido la práctica totalidad de los nombres de las personas que coprotagonizan todas las peripecias científicas narradas. Esto no se debe a que esta serie de historias constituyan una oda únicamente a la persona que las ha escrito, sino que al hacer este libro en un formato autobiográfico y con un enfoque claramente narrativo, hemos considerado que mencionar a personas que solo iban a aparecer en un capítulo podría confundir al lector. Esta decisión seguramente sea doblemente extraña para los profesionales de la investigación científica, pues estamos acostumbrados a agradecer a prácticamente cualquier persona que haya dedicado algo de su tiempo a contribuir a los artículos científicos que publicamos para difundir nuestros resultados. Pese a que esta norma la hemos mantenido a lo largo de todo el libro, los nombres de todos los hombres y mujeres que han sido bienintencionadamente excluidos de las narraciones no quedarán sin su correspondiente y más que merecido reconocimiento. Y digo más que merecido porque no es que simplemente sean grandes profesionales de la ciencia y el mundo universitario, capaces de realizar esfuerzos físicos e intelectuales sobrehumanos para alumbrar algunas de las mayores incógnitas de nuestro planeta, sino que también han tenido que aguantarme a mí durante muchos días, meses e incluso años de sus vidas. Y yo, sinceramente, no sé qué es más difícil física e intelectualmente. Para averiguarlo, lo mejor es que si tenéis la oportunidad, se lo preguntéis a alguno de ellos. Aquí les tenéis:

El libro empezaba narrando mi participación en la Cumbre del Clima de Naciones Unidas (COP25) que tuvo lugar en Madrid en diciembre de 2019. Mi participación no hubiera sido posible sin el inestimable apoyo financiero y académico de la Comisión Fulbright de España y del Dr. Andrew Barton de la Scripps Institution of Oceanography (University of California, San Diego), los cuales me permitieron interrumpir mi estancia de investigación en California un par de semanas para poder participar en el foro internacional más importante para la toma de decisiones políticas de acción climática. También me gustaría agradecer especialmente a la Dra. Melania Guerra por sus esfuerzos para organizar mi participación en la COP25.

Mis dos años de trabajo en el Mar Menor me llevaron inexorablemente a dedicarme profesionalmente al medio ambiente y las ciencias del mar. Quisiera agradecer en primer lugar al Grupo de Investigación de Ecología Marina y Ecosistemas Marinos Costeros, liderado por el Dr. Ángel Pérez Ruzafa y la Dra. Concepción Marcos, por abrirme sus puertas cuando no tenía ni veinte años. Agradecimiento especial también a Gabriel Hernández, la Dra. Marta García y Antonio López, con los que pasé tantas horas de frío en el Mar Menor en invierno procesando muestras en el laboratorio. Con vosotros empecé en la ciencia y, por lo tanto, se inició este libro.

Las aguas del Estrecho de Gibraltar son bravas, pero no tanto como las doctoras Emma Huertas y Susana Flecha del Instituto de Ciencias del Mar de Andalucía (ICMAN-CSIC), gracias a las cuales participé en mi primera expedición científica. A fecha de hoy, la boya que pinté sigue aún en funcionamiento. Pese a mis descubiertas habilidades artístico-oceanográficas, decidí continuar con la ciencia, lo cual ha sido un acierto, pues mis cualidades artísticas no han sido tan prolíficas.

En las frías aguas del Mar del Norte se encuentra el OceanLab de la University of Aberdeen (Escocia, Reino Unido). Gracias a la Dra. Evina Gontikaki y la Dra. Ursula Witte pude trabajar por primera vez fuera de España y aprender cómo funcionan las comunidades bentónicas marinas en estuarios. Tal vez, dentro de no mucho, alguna de las bacterias del Estuario Ythan a su paso por Newburgh nos revelen cómo poder eliminar los vertidos de petróleo de una manera más efectiva, eficaz y eficiente.

Si tengo una segunda casa, esa es Mallorca. El mundo del plancton dejó de ser un casi completo desconocido para mí gracias a poder realizar mis estudios de Máster en Cambio Global en el Instituto Mediterráneo de Estudios Avanzados-IMEDEA (CSIC-UIB), en el grupo liderado por la Dra. Susana Agustí y el Dr. Carlos Duarte. Gracias especialmente a Bea Carreja y Maribel Cerezo que tanta paciencia tuvieron enseñándome a criar copépodos y a utilizar una cantidad significativa de instrumentos científicos en los laboratorios del Instituto. El mundo de los «errantes» es inmenso, como una sopa de letras gigante cuyos mensajes esperan ser descifrados. Gracias también a la Dra. Iris Hendriks por acogerme varios años después en el mismo grupo de investigación y poder hacer parte de mi tesis rodeado de los montes de la Serra de Tramuntana.

La etapa más recordada por la mayoría de investigadores científicos es la predoctoral, es decir, aquella conducente a obtener el título de Doctor. En mi caso, no iba a ser menos. Gracias al Dr. Rafel Simó y al Dr. Sergio Vallina por tutorizarme con rigor, profesionalidad y empatía durante los años de la elaboración de mi tesis doctoral en el Institut de Ciències del Mar de Barcelona (ICM-CSIC). Sobre todo, por permitirme que ideas a iniciativa propia se transformaran en capítulos de mi tesis doctoral y que las haya podido desarrollar en países como Canadá, Suiza o Estados Unidos. En esa línea, gracias al Dr. Martí Galí, Barcelona Supercomputing Center, y al resto del equipo de TAKUVIK en la Universitè Laval (Quebec, Canadá) por enseñarme todo lo que sé acerca del uso de satélites para comprender qué sucede en el océano. Gracias a la Dra. Cara Nisen, la Dra. Meike Vogt y el Dr. Niki Gruber del Instituto Politécnico Federal de Zúrich (ETH-Zurich) por acogerme, enseñarme y dejarme hacer uso de sus herramientas de supercomputación. Gracias al Dr. Andrew Barton y al resto del «Barton Lab» por seis meses haciendo ciencia en un ambiente inmejorable a orillas del océano Pacífico. Por último, agradecer a mis compañeras de doctorado Pau Cortés, Marina Zamanillo y

Marta Masdeu por todos los momentos compartidos en Barcelona y en lugares remotos del planeta. Gracias también a todo el personal del ICM-CSIC, por más de cinco años de compañerismo y aprendizaje.

No me gustaría olvidarme de toda la tripulación del BIO Hespérides, el BIO Garcí del Cid y el Akademik Treshnikov, así como del personal de la Unidad de Tecnología Marina (UTM-CSIC) y la Armada Española, sin los cuales la investigación oceanográfica no sería posible. Los científicos nos limitamos a hacer nuestro trabajo, pero son el resto de profesionales quienes tripulan y mantienen los buques de investigación.

Otras personas no me han acompañado en las peripecias narradas en este libro, pero sí lo han hecho a lo largo de la escritura del libro colaborando de una manera u otra en el proceso: Llúcia Ribot Lacosta (periodista científica), Dr. Francisco López Castejón (Universidad Politécnica de Cartagena), Miguel Ángel Ruiz (periodista de Medio Ambiente La Verdad), Ad Absurdum (Divulgación histórica y cultural a través del humor), José Manuel Pereñíguez López (Investigador Predoctoral de la Universidad de Murcia), Daniel Gómez Gras (ICM-CSIC), Daniel Torregrosa (divulgador científico), Dr. Marcos Fontela (Instituto de Investigaciones Mariñas-CSIC), Hinano Murphy (Association Te Pu Atitia, Moorea, Polinesia Francesa) y Dr. Sergi González (Agencia Estatal de Meteorología – Antártida).

Por supuesto, no puedo olvidarme de agradecerle a Rocío Sánchez Lajarín y a Juan Rubio, de la Editorial Raspabook, su esfuerzo e infinita paciencia. Gracias por dejarme escribir el libro que a mí me apetecía. Así como a Asun Martín y Raúl Gómez de Dokusou por llevar a buen puerto, nunca mejor dicho, el libro en su etapa final.

Gracias fraternales a Andreu Escrivà. Cuando acabé este libro y tenía que pensar en quién podría hacer el prólogo, pensé «Haré una lista de una persona que tiene que reunir X, Y y Z requisitos». Resultó que en la lista solo salía un nombre, y era el de Andreu. Gracias por mostrar interés desde el primer momento y hacer un análisis conciso de todo aquello que hemos querido transmitir con este libro; por ejemplo, que la mejor manera de explicar cosas complejas es a través de historias reales o que la épica nunca es más importante que el ingenio y la colaboración. Finalmente, perdón por la envidia, creo que sana, que te generó el tener que leer este libro durante el confinamiento debido a la pandemia. Te debo unas marineras y un caldero.

Finalmente me gustaría agradecer a las distintas fundaciones, entidades, etc.; que han esponsorizado mis investigaciones durante estos diez años: El Ministerio de Ciencia e Innovación (Beca JAE de Introducción a la Investigación), el Ministerio de Educación (Beca ERASMUS), la Universitat Politècnica de Catalunya (Beca de Mobilitat Internacional per Investigadors), la Fundación «La Caixa» (Beca de Doctorado en España) y la Comisión Fulbright de España del Ministerio de Asuntos Exteriores, Unión Europea y Cooperación (Beca Fulbright de Ampliación de Estudios-Modalidad Investigación Predoctoral).

Asimismo, a todos los españoles y españolas que gracias a sus impuestos permiten que se haga ciencia de primer nivel brindando la oportunidad de investigar a muchas personas que de otra manera no podrían convertirse en científicos y científicas. Que no se olvide nunca que el talento está distribuido de forma homogénea en el mundo; sin embargo, las oportunidades y los recursos no. Los científicos y científicas necesitan de dichos recursos para seguir descubriendo fenómenos, procesos, etc. para así comprender mejor el mundo que nos rodea. Este libro es también para todos aquellos jóvenes argonautas que aún no lo son, incluso para aquellos que, aún sin pretenderlo, lo acaben siendo. La vida profesional, como la vida misma, es, en estos tiempos, aquello que pasa entre crisis económica mundial y pandemia.

Referencias

Adjeroud, M., Kayal, M., Iborra-Cantonnet, C., Vercelloni, J., Bosserelle, P., Liao, V., ... & Penin, L. (2018). "Recovery of coral assemblages despite acute and recurrent disturbances on a South Central Pacific reef". Scientific reports, 8(1), 1-8.

Ansari, A. A., Singh, G. S., Lanza, G. R., & Rast, W. (Eds.). (2010). *Eutrophication: causes, consequences and control* (Vol. 1). Springer Science & Business Media.

Belando, M. D., Bernardeau-Esteller, J., García-Muñoz, R., Ramos-Segura, A., Santos-Echeandía, J., García-Moreno, P., ... & Ruiz, J. M. (2017). *Evaluación del estado de conservación de las praderas de Cymodocea nodosa en la laguna costera del Mar Menor*. 2014-2016. Murcia: Instituto Español de Oceanografía y Asociación de Naturalistas del Sureste, 157.

Bezemer, K. W. L., & Payarols, F. (1952). *La Lucha por el Polo Sur: el destino de las grandes expediciones sudpolares*. Labor.

Boulton, C. A., Allison, L. C., & Lenton, T. M. (2014). "Early warning signals of Atlantic Meridional Overturning Circulation collapse in a fully coupled climate model". Nature communications, 5(1), 1-9.

Buckley, M. W., & Marshall, J. (2016). "Observations, inferences, and mechanisms of the Atlantic Meridional Overturning Circulation: A review". Reviews of Geophysics, 54(1), 5-63.

C. D. Keeling, S. C. Piper, R. B. Bacastow, M. Wahlen, T. P. Whorf, M. Heimann, and H. A. Meijer. "Exchanges of atmospheric CO_2 and 13 CO_2 with the terrestrial biosphere and oceans from 1978 to 2000". I. Global aspects, SIO Reference Series, No. 01-06, Scripps Institution of Oceanography, San Diego, 88 pages, 2001.

Chown, S., & Froneman, P. W. (Eds.). (2008). *The Prince Edward Islands: land-sea interactions in a changing ecosystem*. African Sun Media.

Clark, P. U., Pisias, N. G., Stocker, T. F., & Weaver, A. J. (2002). *The role of the thermohaline circulation in abrupt climate change*. Nature, 415(6874), 863-869.

Conde, C. (1959). *Los poemas de Mar Menor*. Cervantes Virtual.

David, A., Fernandez-Armesto, F., & Williams, G. (2018). The Malaspina Expedition 1789–1794: *Journal of the Voyage by Alejandro Malaspina*. Volume I: Cádiz to Panamá. Taylor & Francis.

Darwin, C. (1860). *A naturalist's voyage round the world*. Journal of Researches into the Natural History & Geology of the Countries visited during the voyage round the world of HMS "Beagle" under the command of captain Fitz Roy, RN.

Diaz, J. I. (1995, October). "Antarctica and deep oceans: scientific targets for the R/V Hesperides. In 'Challenges of Our Changing Global Environment'". Conference Proceedings. OCEANS'95 MTS/IEEE (Vol. 1, pp. 468-471). IEEE.

Duarte, C. M., Alonso, S., Benito, G., Dachs, J., Montes, C., Pardo Buendía, M., ... & Valladares, F. (2006). Cambio Global. *Impacto de la actividad humana sobre el sistema Tierra*. CSIC. Consejo superior de investigaciones científicas.

Escrivà, A. (2018). *Aún no es tarde: claves para entender y frenar el cambio climático* (Vol. 29). Universitat de València.

Esteban, R., Verborgh, P., Gauffier, P., Giménez, J., Guinet, C., & de Stephanis, R. (2016). "Dynamics of killer whale, bluefin tuna and human fisheries in the Strait of Gibraltar". Biological Conservation, 194, 31-38.

Fernández, J. G. (2006). "Anfibios colectados por la Comisión Científica del Pacífico" (entre 1862 y 1865) conservados en el Museo Nacional de Ciencias Naturales de Madrid. Graellsia, 62(2), 111-158.

Flecha, S., Pérez, F. F., Murata, A., Makaoui, A., & Huertas, I. E. (2019). Decadal acidification in Atlantic and Mediterranean water masses exchanging at the Strait of Gibraltar. Scientific reports, 9(1), 1-11.

Galera, A. (2016). "El Arca de Neé: plantas recolectadas por el botánico Luis Neé durante la Expedición Malaspina". El Arca de Neé, 1-446.

Garcia, E., & Castelló, A. *El vaixell oceanogràfic Garcia del Cid*.

Gasol, J. M., & Kirchman, D. L. (Eds.). (2018). Microbial ecology of the oceans. John Wiley & Sons.

Gonzalez, S., & Vasallo, F. (2019). *Antarctic Climates*.

H.-O. Pörtner, D.C. Roberts, V. Masson-Delmotte, P. Zhai, M. Tignor, E. Poloczanska, K. Mintenbeck, A. Alegría, M. Nicolai, A. Okem, J. Petzold, B. Rama, N.M. Weyer (eds.). (2019). "IPCC, 2019: IPCC Special Report on the Ocean and Cryosphere in a Changing Climate".

IGBP, I. (2013). SCOR. In La acidificación del océano. Resumen para responsables de políticas–Tercer simposio "El océano en un mundo con altos niveles de CO2". Programa Internacional Geosfera-Biosfera, Estocolmo (Suecia).

Lafuente, J. G., & Aldeanueva, F. C. (2001). "La climatología y la topografía del Estrecho de Gibraltar determinantes de las propiedades termohalinas del agua del Mar Mediterráneo". Física de la Tierra, 13, 43-54.

Leichter, J. J., Alldredge, A. L., Bernardi, G., Brooks, A. J., Carlson, C. A., Carpenter, R. C., ... & Holbrook, S. J. (2013). "Biological and physical interactions on a tropical island coral reef: transport and retention processes on Moorea, French Polynesia". Oceanography, 26(3), 52-63.

Leon, V. M., & Bellido, J. M. (2016). *Mar Menor: una laguna singular y sensible. Evaluación científica de su estado.*

Liu, Y. W., Eagle, R. A., Aciego, S. M., Gilmore, R. E., & Ries, J. B. (2018). "A coastal coccolithophore maintains pH homeostasis and switches carbon sources in response to ocean acidification". Nature communications, 9(1), 1-12.

Lloret, J., Marín, A., & Marín-Guirao, L. (2008). "Is coastal lagoon eutrophication likely to be aggravated by global climate change?". Estuarine, Coastal and Shelf Science, 78(2), 403-412.

López-Ocón, L., Ponsati Obiols, A., Molina Nortes, J., Pérez-Montes, C. M., Blanco, P., Izquierdo Moya, I., & Díaz-más, M. (1998). *La comisión científica del Pacífico* (1862-1866).

Lovelock, J. (2000). *The ages of Gaia: A biography of our living earth.* Oxford University Press, USA.

Lovelock, J. E., & Margulis, L. (1974). *Atmospheric homeostasis by and for the biosphere: the Gaia hypothesis*. Tellus, 26(1-2), 2-10.

Marcos, C., Torres, I., López-Capel, A., & Pérez-Ruzafa, A. (2015). "Long term evolution of fisheries in a coastal lagoon related to changes in lagoon ecology and human pressures". Reviews in fish biology and fisheries, 25(4), 689-713.

Margulis, L., & Sagan, D. (2001). "Microcosmos: cuatro mil millones de años de evolución desde nuestros ancestros microbianos" (No. 523.1 M331m). Barcelona, ES: Tusquets Ed.

Marquet, P. A., Valladares, F., Magro Ruiz, S., Gaxiola, A., & Enrich Prast, A. (2018). *Cambio global, una mirada desde Iberoamérica.* Departamento de Publicaciones, Consejo Superior de Investigaciones Científicas (CSIC).

Marshall, J., & Speer, K. (2012). "Closure of the meridional overturning circulation through Southern Ocean upwelling". Nature Geoscience, 5(3), 171-180.

Masson-Delmotte, V., P. Zhai, H.-O. Pörtner, D. Roberts, J. Skea, P.R. Shukla, A. Pirani, W. Moufouma-Okia, C. Péan, R. Pidcock, S. Connors, J.B.R. Matthews, Y. Chen, X. Zhou, M.I. Gomis, E. Lonnoy, T. Maycock, M. Tignor, and T. Waterfield (eds.). (2018). *IPCC, 2018: Global Warming of 1.5°C. An IPCC Special Report on the impacts of global warming of 1.5°C above pre-industrial levels and related global greenhouse gas emission pathways, in the context of strengthening the global response to the threat of climate change, sustainable development, and efforts to eradicate poverty.*

Mazorra, C. M. S. (1994). *Catálogo de los insectos recolectados por la Comisión Científica del Pacífico* (1862-1865) (No. 5). Editorial CSIC-CSIC Press.

Menéndez, A. R. (2007). *Canarias, territorio de exploraciones científicas: Proyecto Humboldt: expediciones científicas a canarias*. Editorial CSIC-CSIC Press.

Moussa, R. M., Fogg, L., Bertucci, F., Calandra, M., Collin, A., Aubanel, A., ... & Planes, S. (2019). "Long-term coastline monitoring on a coral reef island (Moorea, French Polynesia)". Ocean & Coastal Management, 180, 104928.

Pedrós-Alió, C. (2013). La vida al límite. Consejo Superior de Investigaciones Científicas (España).

Pedrós-Alió, Carlos (2018). *Bajo la piel del océano*. Plataforma Editorial.

Pérez-Ruzafa, A., Marcos, C., Pérez-Ruzafa, I. M., & Ros, J. (1987). "Evolución de las características ambientales y de los poblamientos del Mar Menor" (Murcia, SE de España). In Anales de Biología (No. 12, pp. 53-65). Servicio de Publicaciones de la Universidad de Murcia.

Perez, F. F., Fontela, M., García-Ibáñez, M. I., Mercier, H., Velo, A., Lherminier, P., ... & Padin, X. A. (2018). "Meridional overturning circulation conveys fast acidification to the deep Atlantic Ocean. Nature", 554(7693), 515-518.

Puig-Samper, M. Á. (1988). *Crónica de una expedición romántica al Nuevo Mundo: la Comisión Científica del Pacífico* (1862-1866). Centro de Estudios Históricos, Consejo Superior de Investigaciones Científicas, Departamento de Historia de la Ciencia.

Puig-Samper Mulero, M. Á., & Rebok, S. (2012). *España explora: Malaspina 2010*. Fundación BBVA.

Rodríguez Fornes, P., Sorribas, J., & Castellón, A. (2007). *Marine Technology Unit (UTM-CSIC) 2007: an overview of CSIC ocean facilities.*

Sánchez, M., & María, S. (2019). *Turismo sostenible en La Manga del Mar Menor*.

Sardet, C. (2015). *Plankton: wonders of the drifting world.* University of Chicago Press.

Scharfhausen, C. C. (2002).

Scott, M. (2019). *Climate refugees and the 1951 Convention*. In Research Handbook on International Refugee Law. Edward Elgar Publishing.

Simó, R (2018). Mar, gel i cél: Diari antàrtic. Núvol.

Summerhayes, C. (2018). "Around Antarctica: journal of a scientific expedition". V. Yok-Thot Sentilhes Éditions Paulsen, Paris. 2017 ISBN: 978237502-0432, 256 pp. Antarctic Science, 30(4), 265-266.

Tejero, H., & Santiago, E. (2019). *¿Qué hacer en caso de incendio?: Manifiesto por el Green New Deal*. Capitán Swing.

Terauds, A., Cooper, J., Chown, S. L., & Ryan, P. (Eds.). (2010). Marion & Prince Edward: *Africa's Southern Islands.* AFRICAN SUN MeDIA.

Valderrama, J. L. R., Tagarro, S. D., Jiménez, A. H., & Cervantes, J. S. (2019). "Servicio de Datos de la Unidad de Tecnología Marina" (UTM-CSIC). Mapping, (194), 32-42.

Wesselbaum, D., & Aburn, A. (2019). "Gone with the wind: International migration. Global and planetary change", 178, 96-109.

Wilson, E. O. (2017). *Medio planeta: la lucha por las tierras salvajes en la era de la sexta extinción.* Errata Naturae.

Wunsch, C. (2002). "What is the thermohaline circulation?". Science, 298(5596), 1179-1181.

Zavatarielli, M., & Mellor, G. L. (1995). "A numerical study of the Mediterranean Sea circulation", 25(6), 1384-1414.